The Astonishing Mr. Scripps

The
ASTONISHING

The Turbulent Life of

Mr. Scripps

America's Penny Press Lord

VANCE H. TRIMBLE

 Iowa State University Press / Ames

Vance H. Trimble, recipient of a Pulitzer Prize for national reporting in 1960, was city editor and later managing editor of the *Houston Press* (1939–1955), news editor of the Scripps-Howard national bureau in Washington, D.C. (1955–1963), and editor of the *Kentucky Post* (1963–1979). Since his retirement in 1979, he has written four biographies.

Title page: E. W. Scripps. This and all photographs in *The Astonishing Mr. Scripps* are courtesy of the Scripps-Howard newspapers, and family sources.

© 1992 Vance H. Trimble

Manufactured in the United States of America

♾ This book is printed on acid-free paper.

First edition, 1992
Second printing, 1992

Library of Congress Cataloging-in-Publication Data

Trimble, Vance H.
    The astonishing Mr. Scripps : the turbulent life of America's penny press lord / Vance H. Trimble. – 1st ed.
        p.   cm.
    Includes bibliographical references and index.
    ISBN 0-8138-0679-8 (alk. paper)
    1. Scripps, E. W. (Edward Willis), 1854–1926. 2. Newspaper publishing – United States – History – 19th century. 3. Newspaper publishing – United States – History – 20th century. 4. Publishers and publishing – United States – Biography. 5. Journalists – United States – Biography.   I. Title.
Z473.S394T74   1992
070.5′092 – dc20
    [B]   90-22401

For two giant newspapermen from Oklahoma,
Paul Miller and Walker Stone, both now gone,
my lifelong friends and mentors.

CONTENTS

Author's Acknowledgment

My interest in the life of Edward Willis Scripps began in a kind of scary way. On retiring in 1979 as editor of the *Kentucky Post* I was hired by the Scripps-Howard editorial director to update *The Scripps-Howard Handbook,* a compendium of concern principles, policies, and personalities. By far the greatest of the latter is the Old Man. I grew up in the company knowing the legends, but in revising the *Handbook* began to discover I didn't really know the founder, and puzzled over the contradictory nature of the legends—this daily study and work automatically programming my subconscious and causing me in my weary bed to dream of the old days.

Ed Scripps's spirit definitely is not locked on the floor of the Atlantic Ocean. He barged into my dreams and prodded me into tackling the story of his life. It is a fact that he did believe in mysticism and felt he had somewhat demonstrated a personal power of mental telepathy. I did not hear his voice; I didn't see him. But I have always had an active and acute subconscious that gives me nighttime inspiration—and I absolutely and definitely *felt* the presence of Scripps in my bedroom and clearly *understood* the mission he was urging upon me. I felt impelled by EWS to tackle this book.

This was just at the beginning of 1981.

I approached Charles E. Scripps, the concern chairman and a friend of forty years. I said I intended to try to produce a biography that would fully reveal his grandfather's life—the good and the bad, evenhanded but uncensored. I asked not financial support from the concern, only access to the voluminous EWS files in the headquarters in Cincinnati. Charles smiled a little at my account of E. W. invading my dreams, but agreed to make the files available. He agreed the book should be uncensored, but made one request. One of E. W. Scripps's children was then alive—Nackey Scripps Meanley, who had eloped.

Charles asked that I try to not embarrass her, and I agreed to keep that in mind. (Mrs. Meanley has since died.)

I flew at my task, thinking I faced possibly a year and a half's labor, with the perhaps typical majestic visions of best-seller, mini-series, fabulous royalties. Dreams are not reality. My chore proved long, always back-breaking and at times haunted by black dispair. Even so the challenge was a seductive lure that kept me struggling on. I couldn't let myself be a quitter, and so at long last emerged a publishable manuscript that brings the glow of satisfaction and pride — and relief!

By no means did I do it alone. Many helped. I sincerely thank them all.

My debt to the entire Scripps family is incalculable. The grandchildren who were too young at E. W.'s death to remember much of significance were nonetheless able to recall tales of colorful and interesting events that had been handed down by their elders. I spent long hours tape-recording the recollections not only of Charles but of his brothers, Robert P. Scripps, Jr., whom everyone calls Bob, and the late Edward W. "Ted" Scripps II. Robert A. Mathes, secretary-treasurer of the E. W. Scripps Trust, facilitated my burrowing into the 350,000 pages of the Old Man's personal file at corporate headquarters, abetted at time by his aide Melanie Garrard. (These papers have since been placed in an archive at Ohio University.) Dick Scherrer was also of assistance at corporate headquarters.

My wife Elzene and I descended on Denison Library at Scripps College, Claremont, California, to scan 50,000 pages of correspondence between EWS and his sister Ellen, whose legacy is very much alive at that school. Judy Harvey Sahak, the librarian, and her staff opened the files, cleared off private desk space, and in every way tried to make enjoyable a research task that occupied us — and their space and interest — for six weeks. There, too, we met

Nini McCabe, one of EWS's great-grandchildren, who was helping catalogue Ellen's papers, and was able to give considerable help.

Others in California who donated their time, guidance, and recollections were the late Edgar F. Elfstrom of Fullerton, the late Mrs. Harry L. Smithson of San Diego, Miss Josephine Scripps of Hi-Hopes Ranch at Del Ray (a granddaughter), the late John P. Scripps, Jr. (a grandson), and his son Paul K. Scripps, of San Diego, Miss Eloyse Johnson of San Diego, the late James G. Scripps, Jr., of Del Mar (a grandson), and two other grandsons in San Diego, Capt. Tom Meanley and his brother Edward. Also Mrs. Farley O'Brien of La Mesa, and Ernest Jaqua, Jr., and Mrs. Dorothy Drake of Claremont, and William H. Elbert of Big Bear Lake, second engineer on the "Ohio's" final voyage.

Valuable firsthand information came from James R. Young of Anderson, South Carolina, who was Scripps's aide-de-camp throughout the final cruise and who supervised his burial at sea, and from his talented wife Marjorie. As a native of Rushville, Jimmy Young was also an astute guide to research into E. W.'s boyhood.

I owe much to Warren S. Wilkinson of Grosse Pointe, Michigan, a great grandson of James E. Scripps, and a former director of the Detroit Evening News Association. Much before my research began, Warren was devoting countless hours to compiling historical facts and photographs of the Scripps clan. The bulk of the photographs in this volume came from his collection, or from those rescued from early Miramar days albums by Paul K. Scripps, who likewise is an able family historian. Other family members and the corporate archives also supplied photographs.

Oliver Knight of El Paso gave a brief interview but of greatest value was his high calibre volume of the EWS disquisitions, *I Protest,* a handy everyday encyclopedic research tool. Among others to thank are Sherman Dye of Scripps-Howard's Cleveland law firm, the San Diego Historical Society, Mike K. Jordan of Seattle, Washington, Dick Maschi of the Scripps-Howard Newspaper Alliance library in Washington, D.C., Negley W. Cochran of Eastlake, Ohio, Tom Barensfeld, librarian of the defunct

Cleveland Press, Mrs. Albert Britt of Nonquitt, Massachusetts, Hillary Cummings of the University of Oregon, Gerald Warren of the *San Diego Union,* the staff of the Library of Congress for access to the papers of Roy W. Howard, and to Ferdinand C. Tuebner of New York, publisher of *Editor and Publisher* magazine.

Encouragement and information came from several friends who are former editors or news executives in Scripps-Howard including the late Lee B. Wood of New York, Frank R. Ford and Earl R. Richert of Evansville, Indiana, Alfred Hewitt of Fullerton, California, George Carmack of San Antonio, Texas, Boyd Lewis of Vienna, Virginia, and Charles Egger and the late Don Weaver of Columbus, Ohio.

In E. W.'s birthplace I was assisted by Willard Potter, editor of the *Rushville Times,* and by Mesdames Hilma Mermillion and Lavina Walton, and other officers of the Schuyler County Historical Museum.

To write a first-rate biography is much more difficult than I had thought. When I was drowning in a half-million words of copy, a lifeline was occasionally tossed me by two renowned writers who are friends of long standing, W. A. Swanberg of Southbury, Connecticut, and George Scullin of Stony Brook, New York. And for an insightful critique that finally put me on target my enduring thanks to the editorial chiefs at Iowa State University Press, Richard R. Kinney and Bill Silag.

For her careful researching and police-reporter skills, her patience and understanding, and willingness to travel far and wide on this project, I give lasting gratitude — and first dibs on royalties — to Elzene Trimble.

And one final thought: I think this book would definitely please EWS.

▬▬ P.S. What's in a Middle Name?

The spelling of Edward W. Scripps's middle name has been a subject of debate. During his lifetime it appeared in print both as "Wyllis" and as "Willis." His factotum of thirty years, Harry L. Smithton, chastised the Old Man's lawyers in the 1920s for misspelling it "Willis" on a document — but said Scripps would sign it that way just to avoid any delay. EWS himself didn't really give a hoot about the spelling. Usually he just signed "E. W. Scripps" — and in a careless, slanty scrawl that wandered across the page. Smithton was convinced Scripps was named after his maternal grandfather, Wyllis Osborn, whose name was spelled in the British style. Smithton also relied on the family tree published in 1903 by brother James E. Scripps, which identified him as Edward Wyllis Scripps.

Newspapers and magazines of his day generally used "Wyllis" — including several of his own and *Time* magazine when they printed his obituary. The "y" was so persuasive even a 1988 article in *Business Week* called him Edward Wyllis.

However, after Ohio University at Athens in 1983 established a school of journalism bearing Scripps's name, executives of his trust undertook to settle once and for all the lingering controversy over the spelling of his middle name. The corporate researchers found that two family histories published in 1882 and 1891 by brother James E. Scripps both list Ed's middle name as "Willis," indicating the "y" in the later 1903 edition could be an error.

In the E. W. Scripps Company files it was found EWS signed his full name only thirteen times — twice as "Wyllis" and eleven times as "Willis." And in San Diego's Greenwood Memorial Park a "Scripps" monument stands in the family burial plot bearing the names "Edward Willis 1854–1926" [though his body rests on the floor of the Atlantic Ocean] and "Nackie Holtsinger, wife of Edward Willis, 1866–1930." This gravestone should have been accurate because it was erected when his son Robert and his sister Ellen were both alive.

At any rate, "Willis" has been officially adopted by the Trustees of the Edward W. Scripps Trust, and that is good enough for me. In this work I have used the official version, except in instances where it was written otherwise in certain documents, such as the text of the prayer recited by Jimmy Young when the "Ohio" crew cast Scripps's body into the deep. Any student of his life can be sure all the hubbub over his middle name would have merely amused E. W. as a lot of bother over an insignificant trifle.

The Astonishing Mr. Scripps

1

The Bookbinder's Thirteenth Child

The little barque "Minerva" docked in Baltimore in July 1791, bringing William Scripps, forty-one, who had sold his prosperous London shoe factory. He was madly afflicted with the grand seigneur fantasy, dreaming loftily of creating in America a personal barony, with a manor house, parks, crops, retainers, and game.

He met one disaster after another, and his dream drowned in misery. But the son left behind in England, nineteen-year-old William Arminger, rose from clerk at the *London Daily Sun* to publisher and became wealthy.

In 1834 and again in 1844, William Arminger Scripps came to America and looked up his family. All were dead except brothers John, a preacher, and George Henry, a tanner. Both lived in an Illinois frontier town, Rushville. The Londoner was captivated by the raw grandeur of the prairie and impulsively bought 160 acres one mile south of the Rushville courthouse. But he had in mind a specific use for the land.

His forty-one-year-old son, James Mogg, was rated the second or third most artistic bookbinder in London but had gone bankrupt twice. Two wives bore him eight children; both died, as did two offspring. The father handed James Mogg a pouch of sovereigns amounting to $1,000, and sent him, with his six surviving children (the oldest thirteen), to Rushville to make a start as a farmer.

Enroute, James Mogg and children paused in Chagrin Falls, Ohio, to visit family acquaintance Timothy Wyllis Osborn, a grist miller, and met his daughter Julia Adeline, a schoolteacher who was thirty and single. Later that winter James Mogg married Julia, writing his father: "I have at last got a help meet in the person of Miss Osborn (that was).

3

. . . I have much cause to be thankful. . . . The children are much pleased."

Farm life galled James Mogg and ruined his artist's hands. He tried to escape, with ingenious ventures, but always failed and came back to his hated plow. The wilderness farm barely sustained the growing family.

Over the first ten years of marriage, Julia bore the ex-Londoner five more children, two boys and three girls. The last was a sickly, red-haired, "squalling brat" — the bookbinder's thirteenth offspring.

But Edward Willis Scripps was born June 18, 1854, with the heart of a dirt farmer, the soul of a poet, and the flaming brain of a crusading newspaper publisher.

Eddie Scripps's earliest memory was of his mother sitting him in a high-chair at the dining table in a red plaid dress, probably when he was about two. "I can remember the days of my diapers," he recalled in his autobiography, "when I could not master the intricacies of expression necessary to pronounce the names of my brothers and sisters." That was a problem of sheer numbers. The two upstairs "dormitories" in the farmhouse were occupied by the daughter from James Mogg's first marriage, another girl and four boys from his second, as well as Julia's five offspring.

Ten years of toil and worry sapped the better part of Julia Scripps's disposition and depleted her comeliness. By the time Eddie was born, Ma was approaching menopause and looked severe and sour. Her unhappy face was wide and blunt, accented by a broad nose and squaw-like high cheekbones. Her hair was tightly pulled back, and her mouth — in photos of the time — grimly clamped and her gaze stern. Her ears were unattractive, uncommonly large. She had a stocky figure and favored somber attire.

As a young man, James Mogg was handsome as a matinee idol, with large head, wide-spaced direct eyes, a long, straight nose that expanded over the nostrils. His mouth was notable, small, thin-lipped, a trifle effeminate; his chin sharp and slender. In a photo at age thirty his dark hair is fine, silky, and long. He wore sideburns that ended in a wide flare at his upturned collar. His clothes were well-tailored and looked expensive. By his sixties he still had a distinguished mien, with thinning gray hair and a wispy beard. His eyes were then sunken with an expression of much suffering, and the end of his nose had grown fat. He grew more drawn and fragile-looking in his final years.

Maintaining discipline at home fell largely to Julia — and in work-weary exasperation she often enforced it with vengeance. When she laid Eddie across her knees and spanked him, the blows didn't hurt much but filled him with "enormous mortification and humiliation," and he recalled being at times "murderously angered."

There was never real affection between child Number 13 and his mother. Yet Eddie came — many, many years later — to see another side of Julia. "My mother had no time to be just. When she was not overworked and overburdened with anxieties, she was not only cheerful but bubbling with humor and mirth." Those times, however, didn't seem to come often.

From earliest years, Eddie was closer to sister Ellen than to his mother. Eighteen years his senior, short and homely, she was a ubiquitous engine of energy, never in bed before midnight, always up at five or six, bustling in the kitchen in full-length aprons, donning white gloves to sort the laundry, every spare moment avidly reading. She had intense small dark eyes, a not-petite nose, but a small straight mouth, a delicate jaw and chin. Her hair was normally pulled back, the ends coiled in a plait, revealing rather large ears. She was not much over five feet tall; her many layers of floor-sweeping petticoats — the fashion of the day — made her appear stocky, which she was not.

Eddie followed Ellen about the house, recalling her as "finically clean" and soft-spoken. As surrogate mother, she began his education early. By three or four, he knew the ABCs and was beginning to read. The grown-up Scripps remembered: "She was either teaching me spelling, the primer, or reading me stories, or talking to me, explaining things that were read about or things around us." The withdrawn little redhead would lay on the floor or perch on a stool to hear her read. His eyes glowed when she began poetry and the plays of Shakespeare.

Books were plentiful in the Scripps farmhouse. James Mogg had brought several hundred volumes from London. His large library had been acquired under the custom of London bookbinders retaining as sort of a toll one or two volumes from each order produced. Exploring the shelves as a child, Eddie found a wide variety — from Tom Paine's *Age of Reason* and Locke's *Essay On Human Understanding* to Robertson's *My Father Was a Church of England Man,* and other theological works by English clergy. He admired the hand-tooled leather of the Shakespeare set, and could pull off the shelves a large collection of English poets: Campbell, Coleridge, Goldsmith, Cowper, Wordsworth, Hood, Alexander Pope. He noticed MacPherson's *Ossian.* He encountered novels by the Brontë sisters, by Fanny Burney, Thackery, Marryat, Victor Hugo, Turgenev, Goethe. There were books on travel, and a copy of the translation of Ernest Renan's *Life of Jesus.* (Of course, the child could not yet fully comprehend the printed page.)

As he turned four, Eddie was startled, mystified, and saddened by abrupt changes in the household. Brother Tommy, not quite ten, fell ill and died. Half-sister Elizabeth left home, to marry a farmer. Ellen, almost twenty-two, and James, twenty-three, also quit the farm, he permanently to attend commercial school in Chicago, to work as a bookkeeper, to finally break into journalism on his cousin John Locke Scripps's *Chicago Tribune*. Ellen was to be gone only a year. Having received an inheritance (perhaps $3,000) from grandfather William Arminger's estate, she enrolled in Knox College at Galesburg, Illinois—and became one of the first women in America to acquire a college degree.

Ellen's absence disturbed Eddie. Terribly missing being read to, he pestered Annie until she took up the tutor chore. Annie, then ten, sensitive, already slightly crippled by rheumatism, recognized the depth of his loneliness and frustration. She and Ellen were to become Eddie's most trusted and lifelong confidants, privy to his even innermost secrets.

Of the Scripps sisters, Jennie—Eliza Virginia, four years Eddie's senior—was the prettiest. Spirited almost to the point of being flighty, she had rich long curls and dark-rimmed eyes. Curiously, none of these three sisters ever married.

Eddie's first assigned chores were driving cows in from pasture and gathering kindling for the woodbox. At sheep-shearing time he helped pick apart the wool—oily and smelly—to get out burrs and dirt. He helped gather wild grapes for raisins, sliced apples, peaches, and pumpkin, for drying or preserves. The Scrippses made sausage, lard and soap, and cured hams, selling the excess. They also peddled their surplus butter and cheese, molasses, and cider.

At chopping wood, Eddie was a dud. "I would have to strike a hundred or two hundred times with my axe," he remembered, to sever a four-inch limb. Most youngsters stripped a milk cow in ten to fifteen minutes, but it took Eddie an hour—because poetry was singing in his brain. "My favorite diversion while milking was to make up rhymes and then try to scale my verses to the swish of the milk in the pail."

As a field hand, however, Eddie always was as good as any boy his age. He learned to use the hand rake and the horse rake on hay crops, to handle the scythe and cradle, to plow and hoe sugar cane, corn, and potatoes. "I always liked to work in the dirt."

Even as a toddler Eddie heard much and understood little of the explosive controversy that was tearing the nation apart—slavery. Pa hitched up his buggy on October 20, 1858, and drove into Rushville to hear Abe Lincoln speak on the courthouse steps. Eddie, four years and four months old, shyly stood on the seat beside his father. Everyone was interested in what Lincoln might say. He already had attracted attention with his dramatic "house divided" debate against United States Senator Stephen A. Douglas, whom he was trying to unseat.

With the election only days away, practically the whole town turned out, among them young women of Rushville society, as such. When Lincoln laid aside his stovepipe hat and stood up with the tails of his frock coat flapping in the breeze, one of the belles dangled a little Negro doll baby in his face.

Lincoln stared at her from haunted eyes. After a long moment, he spoke quietly. "Madam, are you the mother of that?"

In boyhood Eddie first became aware of the importance of newspapers. At the family hearth he had heard much of William Arminger Scripps's prominence as a publisher in London; but in those years that seemed a remote city he never expected to see, or to have touch his life. He knew that one great uncle and two second cousins were associated with the Rushville weekly newspapers. But these seemed trifling publications; they did not impress him like newspapers from Chicago and other great cities.

This was the period in which he was proud and excited about John Locke Scripps, a son of "Uncle George" who had gone to Chicago in 1848 and helped establish at age thirty the *Chicago Tribune*. He later also founded the *Chicago Democratic Press,* which merged in 1858 with the *Tribune,* John Locke becoming editor and throwing the influential paper's support behind Lincoln for president. He also wrote a biography of Lincoln that was helpful. He was repaid by being appointed postmaster of Chicago.

The Chicago editor, small but with a large head of thick gray and black hair, periodically came to Rushville and often visited the farmhouse because he admired Ma. Little Eddie would sit quietly and listen to the great man whose newspaper was said to be considered in the West what Greeley's *New York Tribune* was to the East. The editor would ease himself into Ma's best rocker and talk of his personal friendship with Emerson, Thoreau, Longfellow, and other literary lights.

In Rushville the *Prairie Telegraph* had been established in 1848 by one of John Locke's brothers, Benjamin Franklin Scripps. He died suddenly at twenty-eight and "Uncle John" pitched in to run the weekly, later changing its name to the *Rushville Times.* Then, the third of these brothers, George Washington Scripps, established the *Schuyler* (County) *Citizen* in 1885 as the outgrowth of local political rivalry. Eventually it merged with the *Rushville Times,* which is a daily still publishing.

Meantime, Eddie's oldest half-brother James was pursuing a promising career in Detroit. After serving an apprenticeship on the *Chicago*

Tribune, he had taken the position as commercial editor on the *Detroit Advertiser.*

The winds of war were about to engulf the Scripps tribe, and initially Eddie was too jejune to be aware of the impending tragedy. Lincoln was elected, the South seceded, and then Confederate cannon boomed across Charleston harbor. The war was on! His older half-brothers George Henry and John Mogg, both working in a timber camp at Saginaw, Michigan, threw down their axes and rushed to enlist as privates in Company B, 27th Michigan Infantry.

In Rushville other Scrippses answered the call to the colors. Elizabeth's husband, Enoch David Thomas Sharp, thirty-three, reported to Company A, 89th Illinois Volunteers. The war stirred the patriotic blood of James. He joined the Detroit Light Guard and handed in his resignation at the *Advertiser.* His bosses would not hear of that. "Plenty of men can join the Army," they protested, "but few can manage a newspaper." On the spot they promoted him to general manager and sold him a three-seventeenth interest for $3,000—most of which he had to borrow. For "essential service," he was exempted from military service. Within the year he won his spurs as a journalistic executive, engineering a profitable merger of the morning *Advertiser* with the evening *Tribune.*

The summer of 1863 when Eddie was nine the war's tragic impact came home. Going south to assault Vicksburg, brothers George and John Mogg endured stifling marches and sometimes rations of "only cornmeal gruel and molasses" and water dipped out of creeks. Matter-of-factly, they wrote home of "bullets whistling by" and told how "occasional grapeshot would cut off trees above our heads."

Heat and miserable food finally did in George. Too ill to walk, he was shoved aboard a regimental sickwagon, transferred at the Yazoo River to the packet *Dacotah* and taken to a Union hospital in Cincinnati. On the brink of death, he lay there a month. Then, crippled for life with synovitis, he was mustered out and sent home to Rushville.

At about that time Private John Mogg Scripps wrote that the 27th Michigan was marching south under General Ambrose Burnside to check Stonewall Jackson. The opposing armies met October 9, 1863, at Blue Springs, Tennessee. John Mogg was a frontline skirmisher, and rebel bullets were whistling their song of death. Ma's trembling hands opened the telegram from the Army. Private Scripps had been shot dead. He was not quite twenty-three.

Eddie didn't know how to console his mother, nor his half-sister Elizabeth when another telegram came. Husband "Tom" was captured and imprisoned at Richmond. Soon he was exchanged, only to be recaptured at Chickamauga and sent to the notorious stockade at Andersonville, Georgia. He died there of dysentery June 13, 1864.

When Eddie started in the village school at seven, older boys jeered him as "Turkey Egg," bullying him, cruelly ignoring him when choosing sides in games. Rheumatic knees left him often unsteady, vulnerable to stumbling or easy knockdown. Even his own brothers would hoot at his unprepossessing mien — weak chin, "dreamy" eyes, freckles and flaming hair, soft and silky, worn long and parted in the middle.

From a book he discovered that many of the great men of history were redheads. Secretly he copied a list, beginning with Caesar and Napoleon, including poets, literary men, scientists, and philosophers. At the end, his childish scrawl added one — Edward W. Scripps.

Being snubbed and made an outsider did not bother him. "I was only happy when I was alone or unnoticed," he would recall. After "suffering from being whipped, scolded, jeered at, teased and bothered," Eddie would sneak up to the garret with a candle stub and a book or escape to a grassy field where he could lay on his back to study the clouds. Running away was to become his lifelong habit.

When the sky darkened and roiled and a fierce storm cracked across the farm, Eddie would rush excitedly to a window, enthralled by the lightning flash and the crash of thunder. From the time Ellen first pulled down Shakespeare at hearthside, books were Eddie's great love. Poetry truly touched chords deep within his soul. Late in life he was to estimate that he had spent half his waking hours with books.

It was, of course, Ellen who created "my particular appetite for poetry — a capacity to quickly grasp and draw from poetry a stanza, a line, a single word perhaps, pictures enormously large and infinitely small; whole songs, in fact, not sung; the comprehension of problems most abstruse, and their solution." The boy grew to consider himself a "born poet." His dreams of destiny first took shape on the farm. He would write poetry, and thus become an important figure in literature.

The Scripps children were regularly escorted to the Methodist church in Rushville, and to frequent outdoor summer camp meetings. Initially, Eddie believed there is a God and that "the Bible is a true story." But he was never satisfied "with what I was told of God's actions." He became "very critical" of the Bible stories read by his Sunday School teachers. "I became convinced," he would observe later, "that no one knew more about God than I did; and I knew nothing."

His juvenile inability to reconcile doubts about the Deity must largely be attributed to his general rebelliousness, and the pseudo-sophistication that derived from constantly having his nose in a book. Surrogate mother Ellen, confidante and intellectual model, obviously was a strong influence. She was, surprisingly, a non-believer, an attitude instilled by childhood punishment from an overzealous aunt. Even in manhood, Scripps would be commonly regarded an atheist.

One afternoon when he was about fourteen Eddie sat down in the upstairs boys' "west room" and pulled one of his favorite volumes from his homemade book case. He was too preoccupied to notice footsteps on the stairs. The jangling of keys on a ring caused him to look up. He knew he would see his half-brother James, down from Detroit on one of his infrequent visits to the homestead.

James stared, not at Eddie, but intently at the book in the boy's hands, still absently rattling his keys.

Eddie felt wary; there had never been a closeness between them. It was different with half-brother George, fifteen years his senior, who was friendly, warmly dubbing him "wonder boy." It was rare that James even spoke to him. Already in his mid-thirties, this big brother was an important figure in Detroit newspaperdom.

Squatting down, James abruptly took the book. *"The Peter Parley Tales!"* he said. "How well I know these books. Pa brought them over on the *Francis Burr.*"

Eddie, as he described this scene in his memoirs, watched James's eyes begin to glitter, his voice rising in excitement, finding some urgent desire to appraise the little book—even if his sounding board was no more than an insignificant country boy. With full beard, heavy-lidded eyes, and a rather large nose, James was a taller, somewhat thinner version of his father. He had a perhaps more intelligent-looking face, tended to cock his head slightly to one side, exuding something of an imperial air.

James sat down and began flipping the pages, starting a lecture to his audience of one. There was a "secret" hidden in these Peter Parley stories, he explained. They were all old, previously-published yarns, mainly of crime, romance, and travel. Peter Parley (the pseudonym of S. G. Goodrich) had drastically condensed them, whittling everything down for easy, fast reading. And in the most simple language. A child could comprehend them.

That formula, James explained, would work wonderfully well in journalism; that is, modern journalism. James was eager to try it. He sketched his plan for his kid brother.

"Now the idea that my brother submitted to me," said Scripps's autobiography, "was the publication of a daily newspaper, very small in size, with large type, and which, by reason of having condensed writing, would contain all the news, all of the miscellaneous matter, and even the love stories that could be found in any of the large—as he termed it—'blanket sheets' that were then being issued as newspapers in this country."

The blanket sheets sold usually for five cents a copy, too expensive for the dollar-a-day working man. James would keep his paper small, four pages, and sell it cheap—one or two cents a copy. Fortune smiled that day on Eddie. The scheme he heard so clearly narrated was to become the key to not only James's success in the newspaper world, but likewise the copy-cat cornerstone of the far greater publishing triumphs of the kid brother.

From about his twelfth year Eddie regularly worked at his father's side. There was little camaraderie between them, separated by fifty-one years, but the bookbinder's son had love and respect for his father. He watched Pa work on a multitude of inventions—a novel corn planter, for instance, that was a great time-saver. Unfortunately someone "stole" the idea before Pa could think of getting a patent. One of his most helpful contraptions was a unique mechanical lift that hoisted crippled Annie easily from porch to buggy.

To augment the farm's meager cash income, James Mogg Scripps operated a circular saw for cutting cordwood that was powered by two horses walking a treadmill. He also, in winter, sawed blocks of ice from the farm ponds and stored them in underground bunkers lined with straw and sawdust for sale in July and August at a penny a pound. For several years he crushed cane in a cast-iron mill and fired up five vat boilers, producing up to 125 gallons of syrup a day.

Pa, in his mid-sixties, began to hobble about. He retreated to his worn parlor chair, propping up red and swollen feet on a cushion.

The farm work fell more and more to Eddie. Finally at age fifteen he had to drop out of school. He grew tall and developed muscles and stamina. He could do as much hard work in the fields as a hired man. While he did sometimes dawdle at routine chores, he actually enjoyed working in the dirt. It was pure pleasure to tackle corn, sugar cane, or potatoes with hoe or plow. He kept his eye on the starting point as he moved along the rows, thrilling to see the cultivated area grow as he worked toward the finish. He realized that he, a kid, was doing much more in a day than the usual hired man. That gave him an idea. He persuaded Pa to let him hire energetic town boys to work for twenty-five cents a day, instead of paying an adult one dollar. The boys came eagerly for a chance to earn spending money.

Eddie was disappointed that the boys tended to cluster in a pack, doing about as much bantering as labor. He fretted about that and hit on brilliant strategy. Field work could be a game, almost as much sport as a tug-of-war. He organized a contest for the boys, to see who could finish his row first. The boys flew to their task. Eddie won. The losers protested in unison; the game was unfair, he had been "practicing" for months. He must be excluded from the races.

Laughing inwardly, Eddie stepped aside. He started them off on a new contest and retired to a corner of the zig-zag rail fence to read his book. Thereafter his hardest labor was acting as referee.

Seeing him perched on the rail fence while the other boys grunted and sweated in the field, Ma sniffed that her youngest was "the laziest boy in Schuyler County. . . . Eddie always seems to be sitting on the fence watching the other fellows work." From his vantage point, Eddie was struck by how much valuable land was wasted in the numerous zig-zag corners. He arranged with his father to lease enough unused ground to constitute an acre, spaded it, and planted his own mini-crops of Irish potatoes, sweet potatoes, and sweet corn. He turned a nice profit.

Next he turned his entrepreneurial eye on Pa's cordwood saw, the only machine of its kind around Rushville. He leased it and contracted outside work. At first he emulated Pa, doing the hardest work himself, lifting a small log from the pile, carrying it to the machine, pushing it through the blade, while his dollar-a-day helper held the tail end and threw aside the surplus butt. It soon dawned on Eddie that the hired man ought to do the heavy lifting instead of the light.

At the end of his first cutting job, it required two or three days to line up another customer and move the machine. Running the saw netted him two or three dollars a day; his "down time" thus was costing him $4 to $9. That wouldn't do. His "lazy boy" mind came up with the answer. On his next job his dollar-a-day man operated the saw, and Eddie hired a boy for twenty-five cents to throw away the ends. He left them and went out to line up more sawing, booking in a few hours enough jobs to keep the machine busy for a span of several days. That left him with plenty of idle personal time—to read.

He had helped Pa strip-mine a vein of soft coal that ran along Willow Creek on the farm, a few inches or a few feet below the surface. Now he dug enough to sell surplus in town. And he continued to store and peddle ice. These deliveries put him regularly inside the Rushville saloons because they were good ice customers. Daily in summer he encountered "the rough brutes who acted as bartenders . . . the maudlin drunk, half-drunk, and partly exhilerated customers . . . hanging around the bar." He developed a "loathing" for both the sellers and buyers of whiskey.

This feeling became so strong he rushed to join an organization called the Good Templars, taking their pledge to remain a teetotaler until age twenty-one. He kept that pledge; but when he did take to the bottle he was to turn into such a hard and steady drinker that his health was all but wrecked.

From his bed of pain, James Mogg Scripps kept close watch on his farmer son, often calling him to his side for long and probing talks, gauging the lad's contentment and loyalty. The old man recognized this was no proper life for an ambitious, poetic, well-read, enterprising, and creative boy. For thirty years the father had been hopelessly trapped in the humiliating ruts of frustration. Eddie must not be!

With Ellen doing the penmanship, Pa began dispatching urgent letters—to Chicago, to Detroit, to London. These missives begged some relative to offer Eddie employment.

2

"Come back, Whittington! Come back!"

With two distant and slender job prospects, Eddie finally escaped his rustic bondage six months after his eighteenth birthday. Rushville, on a southern branch of the Chicago, Burlington, and Quincy Railroad, had only two trains a day. Eddie climbed aboard northbound Passenger No. 2 at 4:17 A.M. on Saturday, November 2, 1872.

In his first suit of store clothes, he felt uncomfortable and conspicuous. He wore his father's fairly new overcoat (which slowly dying James Mogg realized he no longer needed). In sister Ellen's oilcloth travelling bag were packed his few home-sewn shirts, underwear, and sox.

Instead of buying the $8.75 ticket, he presented the conductor his brother James's railroad pass issued to the *Detroit Tribune*. His vested suit cost $14 at the Rushville general store where cousin John Scripps Sweeney clerked. Eddie had ripped loose the lining of the vest and sewed inside a secret money cache. This emergency nest egg totalled $80, the savings from his zig-zag crops, sales of cordwood, coal, and ice.

On the morning of Monday, November 4, he reached Detroit to find snow falling and muddy slush in the streets. With a map drawn by his brother Fred, who had once visited Detroit, he reached the *Tribune* office where he was greeted by his half-brother William, now thirty-four, who had started as a *Tribune* printer and rose to foreman of the newspaper's job-printing shop.

Soon James appeared. He gave Eddie a nod, said "Howdy," shook hands, and passed on. James thought his baby brother a nuisance and a bother; he felt Ellen had spoiled the conceited brat. What good would the boy be? He couldn't write a legible hand; his lines never went straight, slanting so horribly they all but fell off the bottom of the sheet.

14

He could not spell. And, despite all his reading, Eddie had not acquired the habit of speaking correctly.

James thought he saw an "out" to escape the Eddie burden. Pa's nephew, Ernest Saunders, a chemist and pharmacist, had come from London to open a pharmacy in Detroit. On condition that Eddie be taken on as an apprentice, Pa had agreed to invest about three hundred dollars in the Saunders Drug Store. A similar one-third interest had been taken by James.

Taking the newcomer out for breakfast, Will explained that Ernest Saunders did not yet have his drug store open. Meanwhile Eddie would come into the *Tribune* counting room as an office boy. He would report about daylight, sweep out, start the fires, and for the remainder of the day run such errands, Eddie recalled, "as could be trusted to the greenest and gawkiest country boy perhaps that ever went to the city to make his fortune." His pay would be three dollars a week.

In his first trembling day in the counting room, Eddie's inner ear kept tuning in a persistent refrain: "Come back! Come back, Whittington—Lord Mayor of London!" Stunned by his entry into this "practical world," the Rushville boy had tried to recall from the hundreds of books he had read any edifying tales of village lads venturing into big cities. One emerged and haunted his mind—the story of the lad from an English hamlet who had gone to London to make his fortune only to be rebuffed and frightened.

Disgusted with London's turmoil and his life of dirt and poverty, this fictional lad ran away from his harsh master, heading back for the green fields and woodlands of his village. But pausing on a hill outside the gates of London, the boy "heard the bowbells ringing, and listening to them he fancied in their deep tones he heard an appeal for him to conquer his own cowardice, to return to the labor that he had sought, and promising him that he would yet be Lord Mayor of the greatest city in the world. He went back and the promise of the bowbells was kept, and he became the Lord Mayor of the city."

The tale, Scripps would recall years later, was vivid enough to buck up the 1872 version of "Whittington" who was gawking and fumbling through his first day at the *Tribune*.

At Ernest Saunders's pharmacy, carpenters and painters were still at work. That did not at all displease Eddie; he still harbored a keen revulsion for store-keeping. The business side of newspapers held no charm either. There was much—actually everything—for the green farm boy to learn about newspapers. On errands inside the plant, Eddie gawked at the machinery and pestered the men with questions. He sniffed the distinctive aroma of a newspaper—the slightly acrid and musty smell of ink and newsprint. The *Tribune*'s giant cylinder press awed him. It rumbled, clanked and rattled, shaking the building and raising almost as much racket as a steam locomotive. On each revolution it somehow daubed the forms with ink rollers, grabbed a wide sheet of white pulp paper with tiny metal claws that popped up mysteriously, sweeping it down under the cylinder for a lightning impression. The press then spit out the printed sheet—either to be stacked and run through again on the opposite blank side or, after the second run, to be cut and folded and delivered. Most of all he was intrigued by typesetting. He gaped at the speed and dexterity of the compositors. They were in the main a colorful, friendly, and carefree bunch. Many were bohemian nomads, tending to wander from newspaper to newspaper, staying a few months, weeks, or perhaps only days. Eddie observed these men drag up a tall stool, and often a rusty bucket to catch their tobacco squirts, and position themselves in front of the *case.* This was a wide cabinet of shallow drawers, broken into many compartments to hold the type fonts.

With his eye on the hand-written copy, the compositor would dig flying fingers into the drawer and nimbly extract one letter at a time. Capitals were in the *upper case* drawer, a companion to the *lower case* shelf. Each piece of type was inserted singly into a holder that was one-column wide and called a *stick,* line by line. Eddie was baffled that the compositors seemed never to even glance at the type compartments. Then it dawned on him—they had memorized the arrangement of the individual letter compartments.

By feeling for an underside *nick,* the printer also could keep from inserting any of his type upside down. Speed paid off—literally. Compositors proofed up their own galleys and were paid a few cents for each column inch of type shown on these *strings.*

Letters home showed Eddie disgruntled, homesick. Sister Annie chided him: "Mercy! What a mood you must have been in. . . . Would you like us to send you by express one of the molasses coolers for you to hide in when you want to get away from everybody? Or would you rather have a hayloft or a heap of old carpet rags on which to repose your weary bones? Poor fellow."

The *Detroit Tribune* entered 1873 in financial straits. The boom caused by the Civil War was over. The paper now barely made expenses. Although James was the largest individual owner, minority stockholders banded together and deposed him. "James's resignation has been accepted," Eddie wrote his father. The kid brother had largely underrated James, although the older man was a night-and-day work slave, a serious reader of literature, had gone through the Bible twice, and had an unusually keen grasp of the business side of newspapering. For instance, he knew that the *Tribune*'s job shop was prosperous and growing, though advertising and circulation revenues were off badly. This point had escaped the rebel stockholders and their new president. James cannily proposed trading his and Will's *Tribune* stock for all the job business, including type fonts, presses, and so forth. The new *Tribune* bosses accepted immediately. Soon the job shop was paying handsome profits while the newspaper itself sank deeper into the red. Into the job shop went Eddie and a Rushville cousin, George C. Scripps.

"I wanted to learn something about books," he recalled, "and I thought that sticking type out of the case, or running presses might lead to better things. In those days most reporters and editors graduated from the case. Especially do I remember that nearly all the newspaper reporters and other writers in Detroit were ex-printers. I was even allowed to learn how to 'kick' a Gordon press (operated by a treadle and used to print such small items as business cards)." But not for long was he satisfied. In a sour mood, he began abusing his Gordon press, grew increasingly sloppy and careless. As bad as that job was he was about to step into a new one even more distasteful.

Feeling the bite of the early February wind off the Detroit River on his neck, with soapy water dribbling down his shirt sleeves, Eddie stood on a high stool on the sidewalk washing the front windows of the Saunders Drug Store.

The London pharmacist was breaking him in from the bottom up. After cleaning the windows, he spent one day washing hundreds of bottles. Then Saunders sat him at a bench with mortar and pestle, amid boxes of drugs to be ground into powder. Next he was escorted to the basement. Saunders pointed out a cask of alcohol, bottles of coloring and flavors, a barrel of sugar and the water hydrant. He laid out a batch of "recipes" for mixing brandy, whiskey, port, sherry, and various "Bordeaux" wines.

"Some druggists are foolish enough to buy liquors," he confided. "That's a waste of money. I make my own."

Fond of chemical experiments, Eddie began enthusiastically. Within two days he had the shelves lined with bottles of ersatz liquors. But the odor of coal oil and various acid compounds began bothering him. It would take seven years, Saunders explained, for Eddie to serve his apprenticeship. Then he might earn $400 or $500 a year.

"Right now," said Saunders, "you'll be more trouble than you are worth. But I'll start you at a dollar a week."

Eddie was astonished. Two dollars a week less than he was paid in the job shop! And he still had to sweep out! He was winding up his first week. Of a sudden he resolved it was also his last. He did not tell Saunders of his decision. The druggist, leaving, told Eddie to be sure to turn out the lights when he locked up.

The boy nodded, but still said nothing, He didn't even ask for his one-dollar pay. He just didn't show up Monday morning.

Eddie wandered out Jefferson Avenue, and climbed dusty stairs to a gloomy loft, pungent with fresh pine shavings and sawdust. He found an Irish mechanic named Lynch carrying an arm-load of newly cut slats to the loom where he turned them into window blinds. They exchanged warm greetings, and Eddie got right down to business; he wanted to work with Lynch as a "partner."

They had met when Lynch installed some of his blinds at the *Tribune*. Now he bluntly pointed out that this business couldn't grow because Lynch's custom was to make up bundles of normal-sized blinds, then personally go out and peddle them before resuming production. Eddie, thinking of his success in taking advance cordwood orders, proposed to go out and line up customers for specific sizes. Thus they could increase volume and reduce costs by keeping the loom humming.

"We can make barrels of money," Eddie promised. They shook on the deal.

Eddie hit the streets and filled his pockets with orders. The loft was busy twelve hours a day.

In this period he made no attempt to contact his brothers, but he did write home, reporting the ups and downs of the greenhorn "Whittington." Selling blinds meant good money, he wrote, but he was not forgetting his long-term goal of returning to a printing office to serve the apprenticeship that would launch him into a literary life.

On an afternoon in March Eddie was bent over a table stencilling a new blind. A ring of keys jangled in his ear. He glanced up to find brother James standing over him. Paint was flying, and the older brother quickly stepped back out of range. He shook his head in wonder and broke out laughing. He had come to reclaim the prodigal. But his manner and tone infuriated the quick-tempered kid brother and a quarrel erupted.

James handled that by turning on Lynch, warning him that Eddie was still a minor, threatening trouble. Lynch, with a timid man's fear of the law and important people, meekly terminated his partnership with Eddie, who hotly denounced his brother's "meddling."

But tempers cooled and the prodigal returned to the job print shop—on promise of eight dollars a week. Secretly Eddie was happy to be back around ink and paper. They held real significance if he intended to develop his literary talents — and he fretted, unable to decide whether he should be poet or novelist. Learning basic printing would be beneficial in either pursuit. So he attacked his old job with new spirit.

Letters from Rushville usually threw Eddie into one of two moods — homesickness or indignation. Often he stuck an incoming envelope in his pocket and didn't open it for a day or two because "I never feel homesick except when I read or write about home."

Ma wrote that Pa was still bedridden, but hoped to soon get out on crutches. "Your pa says you do not write explicit enough. He wants to know all about what you are doing, whether you are earning your board, and what it is you are doing. . . . Do you ever think you like to be at home? Yes, I suppose if you could have your own way and do just as you had a mind to, you would be here."

Though it took much effort for her crippled hands to scratch out a letter, gentle Annie worried about her brother's soul. "You did keep me waiting a good while for a letter. Sorry to hear you have been sick. My dear child, you must take care of that stomach, or it will make you trouble. . . . I do not object at all to your reading Shakespeare and am glad you do but, oh Ed, it can never do for you what God's word would and could be if you were to take that for your companion, and you can find no nobler life to study than Our Savior."

On Easter morning — April 13, 1873 — Eddie got up at dawn to attend the early service at St. John's Episcopal Church with James, his wife Hattie and children, and other relatives. Ernest Saunders and sister Agnes were in the choir, and the young druggist sang a solo.

As they emerged from the church, a policeman recognized James and rushed over. "Mr. Scripps — haven't you heard! The *Tribune* has burned down!"

James uttered a groan and set off in a rush for Jefferson Avenue. Eddie and the others followed. As they turned into the alley back of the *Tribune* building, they saw smoke still rising. The walls were standing but the interior was a charred ruin, all six floors destroyed.

Firemen were starting to roll up their hoses. Eddie and his brother went to the rear door that led to the engine room in the basement. Gray pools of molten metal congealed in the sooty water on the floor. Tons of type in cases on the upper floors had melted, dripping a molten rain that had hampered and imperiled firemen. The small presses of the job shop lay in a black heap.

The first thought was of insurance. In splitting off the job shop from the newspaper, James now feared he might have overlooked coverage on the equipment he and Will owned, or that the policies had been permitted to lapse.

When the safe was opened and the policies examined, the insurance situation was just the reverse. Everything in the job shop was well- or over-insured, the newspaper itself not. The insurance adjuster, not overly familiar with printing plants, made his tour of the wreckage and declared the loss total. In the prompt settlement, James and Will each received about $15,000.

The fire brought the Scrippses to a crossroad. Will elected to use his insurance money to reopen a job printery. Something different was in James's mind—his old dream of launching a cheap, small, condensed newspaper for the working man of Detroit.

He called Eddie aside and revealed his decision. "Remember that *Peter Parley* idea I explained to you? I'm going to give it a try!"

3

The Two-cent Evening News

One-third of the 20,000 homes in Detroit did not subscribe to any newspaper. There clearly was a reason for that, James told Eddie. The city's current dailies were too big, too dull, too wordy—and too expensive. Blue-collar families couldn't afford a nickel a day for one of the blanket sheets.

Realizing he was going against the tide, James proposed to fill that gap with a little newspaper, selling for two cents a copy on the street or six daily copies home-delivered for ten cents a week. It would be only four pages, each 14 by 20 inches, which would come from folding a single sheet measuring 28 by 20 inches. There would be six columns on each page containing all the local and national news, of course boiled down in the Peter Parley fashion, along with several columns of advertising.

James would be a pioneer not only in size and condensation, but also in the evening field. An afternoon daily had been launched in New York in 1870, but nearly every other American newspaper was published mornings. James believed that most working families would prefer to read the news around supper time. He had already chosen a name: *The Evening News.*

In the spring of 1873, while getting his scheme worked out, James suddenly adopted a new appraisal of the kid brother who had been underfoot for six months. Eddie, despite what Ma said about being lazy, had demonstrated he could take hold of hard work and get it done— faster, better, and of course, easier. James fancied that kind of knack and energy. He undertook serious discussion with Eddie about the nuts and bolts of his *Evening News* project. They made an unlikely pair;

Eddie was two months shy of nineteen, and James, thirty-eight, had been a newspaperman for sixteen years, fourteen in Detroit.

Without capital to buy a press and equipment, James signed a contract with the rival morning paper, the *Detroit Free Press,* to print his little paper in the daylight hours when their two-cylinder press was otherwise idle. He also rented two vacant rooms in the *Free Press* building for his newswriters and typesetters. He subcontracted his composition to a skilled printer, and engaged an outstanding solicitor to sell advertising on 25 percent commission.

While the little paper was being hatched, on May 12 came the dreaded telegram from Rushville. Pa had died, not quite seventy. It was heartwarming to see the respect Rushville had for James Mogg. Half the town, Eddie observed, came out for his funeral. It was decided Ma, Annie, Jennie, and Fred would remain on the farm. George, the crippled old soldier, wanted to sell off his land and cattle and move away, perhaps coming to Detroit. Ellen, exhausted from keeping a string tied to her finger through the long death vigil so the old man's slightest move would awaken her, wanted to join the *Evening News* staff. Her quick pen and encylopedic brain would qualify her for anybody's newspaper, certainly her brother's.

So Ellen, wan and little, looking nearer fifty than her thirty-seven, arrived in Detroit in mid-June. She went into Will's job shop as proofreader. Eddie was there, too, to help her, and to collect bills. Brother George arrived from Rushville, clumping around on his crutch, nervously looking for a place to squirt tobacco juice. He was considering selling his farm and stock to invest his capital in the job shop. He and Will negotiated, but reached no agreement. George went home to convert his property to cash, and to then return for more talk.

The pace James kept up, his long hours, the scurrying to all parts of the city to ready his newspaper for launching reminded others of a wry saying about this family's determination: "If a Scripps drowns, look upstream for his corpse."

Eddie wanted to become a reporter, but James convinced him he should start as a carrier. Buying his papers at a penny a copy, delivering two hundred customers at ten cents a week, he could show a profit of $8 a week.

Eddie began to think creatively. Why should he race through the streets with a bundle of papers under his arm? He could hire some youngster, just as the laziest boy in Schuyler County had done, to do the work. He promptly worked up a thousand subscribers, divided them into routes, and hired ten boys at a dollar a week each. He calculated that would leave him a weekly profit of $30.

James kept a close eye on him, seemingly with approval, writing in his diary for Saturday July 26, 1873: "Warm. Giving Eddie a great deal of my time. Planning editorial organization."

At the lunch hour on Saturday, August 23, 1873, newsboys filled the side street at the *Free Press*—a good-natured mob, curious, impatient, noisy. In the ink-splattered pressroom, James E. Scripps gravely watched the forms of his four-page infant locked in place. With him were Ellen, Eddie, most of the reporters. At 1 o'clock the press began slowly grinding. Newsboy Jack Shepherd sneaked inside, daringly stuck in his hand and snatched the third copy off. He raced to the Russell House bar and shoved the little tabloid into the face of wealthy gambler Jim Scott. "Want to buy the first copy of the *Evening News?*" Scott generously handed the boy a quarter.

In the pressroom, Eddie grabbed a copy, and gulped at its crudity. Most new papers, he was to learn, look bad. But this one! Even a green youngster could see it was a far cry from what he promised subscribers: "The very best newspaper ever published!" Three of the six columns on page one were filled with advertisements. James had written an impressive "sort of salutary" outlining the paper's purpose and promising to be independent in politics. The deficiencies of the first issue were at least partially overcome by one strong characteristic—brevity, and a comparatively large number of news items. The cheap little paper *was* easy to read!

That is if subscribers ever got a chance to see it! The press went slow. James finally blew up and accused the *Free Press* people of deliberately running slow to injure the Scripps venture. His protest availed nothing. It took until 8 o'clock to run the 10,000 copies.

James slunk home. "It's a fiasco!" he told his wife Hattie. His first issue cost a total of $175.73; the day's take was only $126.69. He tossed most of the night, wondering how long he could cope with fifty-dollar-a-day losses. Back at work Monday, James studied the first issue more carefully. True it was not as handsome as he had expected, due mainly to careless press work. But, by golly, it certainly was a *news*paper, brimming with information!

Not only local events, but "the latest by telegraph." Composer Verdi was writing a mass that demanded female voices. . . . John Stuart Mill's will left copyrights and other property to his stepdaughter. . . . Miss Clara Barton was recovering from neuralgia caused by work among soldiers in the Franco-German war. . . . A new volume of poems from Longfellow would be out soon. . . . Mrs. Charles Reade had produced a new story which the *Evening News* suspected "savors her husband's trash."

Under the heading "Detroit Items" were fifty-one paragraphs. The Roman Catholics were to dedicate their church, the recently-purchased former Westminster Presbyterian building, now to be reconsecrated as St. Aloysius. . . . There had been a rash of traffic accidents, involving a buggy wagon and two horses — even one occasioned somehow "by a cow's tail."

Each day Eddie saw the paper get fresher and brighter. In the fourth issue the editor threw out his chest a little: "The *News* this afternoon contains about seventy items of important city news, besides three extended articles on subjects not touched by the morning papers. All the other papers of Detroit have succeeded in gathering about thirty facts."

Favorable reaction came in; at first a trickle, then a small flood of congratulation. The newspaper began to create a stir among the lunch-pail brigade which turned out shoes, pharmaceuticals, railroad cars, wagons, tools, and oddments; and with the sailors, smithies, trainmen, pick-and-shovel laborers — and their wives and children at home. James Scripps had found his "blue collar market" — about 5,000 subscribers.

Eddie worried, along with the others, about the harmful effects of the slow press. In desperation, James acted. From Governor Johnson J. Bagley of Michigan he borrowed $5,500 at 10 percent interest and bought Judge John J. Speed's house at 65 Shelby Street. It became the paper's home. James erected a brick annex in the garden for a press-room, establishing the editorial and composing rooms in the main house. He began looking for a press and found one. From the *Chicago Tribune* he bought for $10,000 an idle four-cylinder press that had been built in 1884 for the *Boston Herald.*

The new venture lost money, and capital dwindled. The one Scripps who did have funds hobbled in again from Rushville. George, rapidly selling his farm holdings, already had $2,000 fattening his wallet. Eddie took him aside for a talk. Instead of investing in Will's job shop, would it not be wiser and safer to put his cash in the *Evening News?* The boy mentioned that Will was hard to get along with, and his business prospects were not bright.

Listening thoughtfully, George rolled his tobacco cud from cheek to cheek. It was still his feeling this kid brother was something of a wunderkind with sound ideas. So he handed over to James his two grand, and later invested $10,000 to $12,000 more as he finished unloading his property back home. That infusion of capital turned out to be precisely what was needed to get the little paper over the hump. It was an investment that would eventually make George a millionaire.

James sought success by the cautious and conservative route. But he had given his dinky, two-center the city's greatest news staff — "a brilliant crew of pirates," said their peers, admiringly. "Had I held everything down to my views," James said later, "I should have produced a good but dull paper."

The two men who topped his news staff, Robert Budds Ross and Michael Dee, could not have been held down. Dee, thirty, was a headstrong crusader, philosopher, iconoclast, brilliant and witty writer. An ex-printer, he was a bohemian and atheist. Ross, thirty-five, was a Canadian Scot, six-two, ex-printer and hobo who fell in at New Orleans with soldier-of-fortune William Walker and helped him invade Honduras to overthrow the government. Walker was captured and shot; Ross escaped, became a Confederate cannoneer, and blockade runner. Later as a reporter in Detroit, Ross caught James's eye by winning a prize given by the *New York Tribune* for the best article on the death of Charles Dickens.

Swallowing his distaste for reckless flamboyance and irreligion, James made Dee city editor. Recalling the free-flowing Peter Parley style, James told him: "Have the boys write the paper as people talk in conversation." Dee and Ross promptly had the *Evening News* shaking up staid Detroit.

Eddie had 2,000 subscribers on twenty routes. That was almost half the paper's circulation. He got behind in collections. He laid his troubles before James, who coldly put him on a cash basis.

Eddie flared up. "Okay, I quit!"

The worried advertising agent interceded to patch up the break. James relented. Eddie promised to work harder and catch up. He did. In a few weeks he was so on track he was making a profit of fifty dollars a week — more money than the city editor, the ad man, or even the editor-publisher! "I was nigger rich," he recalled. "I put on a silk hat and went to a hotel to live."

With free time, Eddie began looking for pretty faces. He bathed more often, carefully groomed his silky red hair, brushed his clothes, put on his topper. He hung around the Opera House, the Theatre Comique, and The Varities hoping to meet actresses, yearning for romantic adventure. Only nineteen, he explored the night life haunts of the city with reporter Bob Ross and his brother George.

He had not lost his desire "to get into journalism . . . real journalism . . . to be a writer, in fact." James got fed up with the boy's persistent yammering, and agreed to give him a test. He put Eddie at a table with a lamp, pencil and paper, and dictated the facts for a short news item. It took Eddie ten minutes to hand in his copy. James read it and guffawed. "You'll never make a writer!"

Eddie jumped up, and angrily threatened to go to the *Free Press*. Suddenly James turned sober, spoke soothingly, and offered a challenge that appealed to Eddie. In the 1870s newspapers could only get copies to customers in outlying towns and villages by mail or through drugstore newsstands. The *News* started off with about a thousand so-called country circulation, but it soon dried up. James wanted to get it back — and more!

The solution, Eddie decided, would be a scheme no newspaper had yet tried — setting up a route in each small town with a carrier who would receive his papers via fast daily steamship or train. The key would be to find a boy who was dependable, keen to get new customers, popular, from a deserving home. "The best type of boy," he noted, "would be the ten- or twelve-year-old son of a widow, who was known to be worthy, a hard-worker; in fact, had the sympathy of the community. More than half of my success depended on getting the right boy to carry the route."

Eddie personally worked as a solicitor in outlying towns, then employed canvassers. James had promised him a handsome bonus, $250 for the first thousand new subscribers, $500 for the second thousand, and $750 for the third. In three months Eddie had 3,000 new circulation in the country.

A keen student of human nature, Eddie had developed the knack of quick canvassing, able to determine in seconds by mannerisms and voice tone, etc., how to concentrate on "live" serious prospects and quickly abandon potential duds and deadbeats. He explained his techniques to James who listened thoughtfully and then told him to "lay off the country" and go back to developing his Detroit routes. Still "feeling nigger rich," Eddie made no objection. However, he was surprised to discover that James promptly assigned a reporter to continue the country work, cutting the $750 bonus to $250.

"My brother made the mistake of greatly underestimating personalities and overestimating methods," Eddie recalled. "He tried to make silk purses out of sow's ears, always trying to build up success with a method rather than a man."

Another of their English cousins, Arthur Deacon, had come to Detroit. Like Ernest Saunders, he tried running a drug store and also failed. To provide him employment, James proposed that Eddie, whose city routes now served 3,000 customers, rent half his setup to Deacon for fifteen dollars a week and the other portion to an *Evening News* agent for a like amount. Eddie agreed.

Thus in the fall of 1874, at not yet twenty-one, he had a weekly income of thirty dollars, not a lick of work to do, and a brain flaming with ambition.

Eddie now was more determined than ever to become a reporter. He badgered City Editor Mike Dee. After repeated rebuffs, Eddie shrugged, winked at Dee, and left the office. An hour later he returned, bringing a cheap pine table and a kitchen chair. He set them in a corner, laid out pencils and paper. He marched back to Dee's desk, and pointed to his table and chair. "There's my station. Anything you need, Mike, I'm ready. Go get news. Be copy boy. Run errands. Shag copy, proofs. Cover fires. Take messages. Anything you want done. Just anything!" The boy smiled broadly. "And all gratis!"

At his table, he serenely took up the morning papers, and began practicing rewriting and condensing stories. Occasionally he caught Mike Dee giving him a quizzical look. As he wrote later: "To have a free messenger boy six feet long, more than half legs, easily able to walk four miles in an hour, and to run twice that far and never tire—was something of an acquisition."

Dee couldn't pass up such an offer. In about an hour he called on Eddie to run an errand. Then another, and another, and another, and another. In a day or two the city desk had him flying all over Detroit, dawn to dusk.

Every day he struggled with pencil and pad, composing imaginary items, rewriting or condensing previously published stories. Soon Dee and the reporters were helpfully coaching him. At his pine table, Eddie closely studied how the newspaper was put together. Of paramount importance for an afternoon paper was an early start. James insisted the *Evening News* mention at least briefly every item printed in the morning papers. Early "rewrite" was thus an essential but tedious chore; the reporter assigned that task must come in about dawn. When Bob Ross took his turn, he'd arrive growling and out of sorts. A confirmed nighthawk, he could not abide early rising.

Eddie took to coming in before anyone else, doing just what the early rewrite man was called on to do—cut up the morning papers, mark clips that deserved a follow-up story, and then brief down all the other local items. Later he would compare his practice effort with what the rewrite man did.

One morning, after a hard night, Ross came in almost half an hour late, sat down and began fumbling with the morning papers. Eddie walked over, carrying a sheaf of copy. "Bob, look! I've been here awhile and I have done most of the rewrites. Might save you time to fix up my copy, at least part of it. Here!"

Ross snatched the sheets out of his hand. He bent over to dress up the copy, and after two or three pages began to grunt with satisfaction. He turned to Eddie's follow-up clips, comparing them with the morning editions. He scratched his head, made an ugly scowl, and finally snorted: "Kid, you can do this stuff about as well as anyone in the shop. It's a damned shame . . . a man of my talent having to turn out this chicken-shit!"

Ross then habitually came in late. Eddie always had the rewrite ready, and he got better at it. Other reporters given the chore caught on and managed to be tardy. Very quickly Eddie became the actual rewrite editor. He began laying the follow clips on Dee's desk, suggesting which reporters should be assigned certain stories. Within a few months City Editor Dee was sending the cub out to do routine reporting at city hall or courthouse. Under Dee's wing and eye, he soon was *de facto* assistant city editor.

Now the city editor himself came in later. Relieved of much of his desk routine, Dee had time to let himself out and spark up the paper with more of his own brilliant writing. Eddie's scheme succeeded so well that "it was not many months before Dee was only titular city editor and I was actual city editor."

As a Scripps, he joined the family councils where the early crises were met — and somehow solved. By the end of the second year, with 8,000 subscribers, the *Evening News* showed a $6,000 annual profit.

George Scripps had been intrenched in the organization since October 1, 1873, with his own roll-top desk and a private cuspidor. He was listed as treasurer and director, and under James's aegis, acted as business manager. Detail work bored the crippled ex-soldier, so he recruited another Rushville cousin as his clerk, John Scripps Sweeney.

Gruff, often unpleasant, and shrewdly simple, George by his penny-pinching frugality contributed significantly to holding down publishing costs. In any business day a dozen times he'd grunt "No!" He clumped out to the composing room and fired on the spot any printer careless enough to drop and "pi" his type.

The *News* was incorporated on its second anniversary with fifty shares at $1,000 par value. James was issued thirty shares, George sixteen, Ellen two, Eddie one, and John Scripps Sweeney one. On listed capital of $28,975.45, Eddie's single share represented in round numbers an investment of $600, paid for in the main by part of the country circulation bonus he had not drawn. Ellen had acquired her $1,200 stake by letting her fifteen-dollar-a-week pay accumulate in James's tin cash box. Cousin John was permitted — as "family" — to scrounge loans and notes to guarantee his $600, this being a practical matter as Michigan law required five stockholders for forming a close corporation.

Eddie kept up a correspondence with the farm, mainly with Annie, but could not find free time to go back for a visit. He got wind of George engaging in unwise amorous adventuring in Detroit, and worried that in indiscriminately sowing wild oats, the lame brother was risking a harvest of unwanted problems. The ex-soldier persisted, recklessly skating on the edge of disaster.

Cub reporter Eddie, still four months shy of his twenty-first birthday, discovered that to earn his spurs covering metropolitan news required spunk. He confessed in a letter home that what he wrote was not "the sharp things . . . but the dryest of dry things." He was reporting "all the police news, recorders, Superior, etc.," and also covering the Canadian town on the opposite shore of the Detroit River, Windsor, Ontario. There he had his first journalistic battle.

On February 11, 1875, he wrote Annie about his run-in with the Windsor chief of police, who ejected Eddie when he tried to cover a trial. "This man has sworn to give me a thrashing. I told him he was a fool. I went home and wrote him up, calling on the people of Windsor to kick such an ass out of office." Next time the police chief collared Eddie, the judge interceded and the reporter came out on top. The indignation of the Windsor chief was vented, fortunately in only verbal abuse.

Eddie, meanwhile, was turning out a torrent of copy. Did James know it? As a conscientious editor, never allowing a line in the *News* until it passed his eye, he had a clear idea of the cub's work. Also every item in the paper was marked for him with the writer's initials.

Eddie kept his own marked copies, and in September 1875 carried them in and piled them on James's desk. He asserted a year had passed and he felt he had finished his apprenticeship, and was now "ready for business." The older brother soberly fingered the stack. Then he smiled, opened his checkbook and wrote a check, and slid it across the desk. Eddie picked it up, stared for a long moment, and broke into a grin; the amount was $520. In his head he made quick calculations. Journeymen reporters were getting $15 a week; as a cub for a year he'd made ten. Fair enough.

"Guess I'll take the boys out tonight and celebrate." He did. It was his first jag on whiskey. Mike Dee and Bob Ross had to carry him to his hotel bed. Next morning his head was the size of a pumpkin. But, treacherously, he had acquired a taste for booze. He discovered there was a universal opinion that a reporter who did not, or could not, drink was deemed incapable of taking important assignments. Crack reporters were always "hail fellows well met," and it was assumed the best place to turn up a hot news story was at the bar, and further that the best time was after the third or fourth drink.

Eddie remembered Mike Dee lecturing him on the subject, "advising me of the necessity of being mildly bibulous and of not being too bibulous. . . . It was my duty to be very crafty in my behavior at the bar. . . . Call for light drinks, or if spirits were insisted upon, to take advantage of my companion by stealthily spilling on the floor the greatest part of my drinks. He even quoted Latin to me, as I remember: *In vino veritas* — get your man drunk and he tells the truth."

Raging sexual desires had long disturbed Eddie. He hoped, he later explained, "to escape this continual self-condemnation and temptation by marrying early. . . . I had a number of experiences with young women who knew how to take care of themselves. As I had considerable to do around the theatres, I had many acquaintances amongst the actresses. For some time I had not been very careful in the matter of showing myself publicly with young women who, though not of the demimonde class, were still not above suspicion."

Eddie tried to "reform" — but in vain. "Conditions being as they were, it was physically impossible for me to practice celibacy for more than a brief period of days, or at most, weeks." He often found "intelligent and effective work" at his profession impossible. "Walking and running, rowing and swimming, the most violent kinds of exercise had to be kept up by me all the time to make existence endurable. I always had of necessity some sort of acquaintanceship with nice young women. Now I set out deliberately to extend so far as possible the number of such acquaintances. . . . I was looking for a wife."

Feeling "clumsy, awkward and loutish," he enrolled in dancing classes. He watched young Detroit men who had a reputation as beaux. He tried to ape their ways and to become a "dandy."

In January 1877, Eddie was sent to Lansing to cover the Michigan Legislature. He did well — with his reporting and in courting society girls there. To his brother Fred he wrote in July 1877: "There is hell to pay out in Lansing. I would not set foot in that little city for a clean thousand. . . . Try engaging yourself to two or three persons at the same time."

On his return to Detroit, he convinced James to promote Mike Dee to managing editor, opening the city desk for the kid brother at fifteen dollars a week. The "boys" went to the saloon to celebrate. Nobody had to put Eddie to bed that night; he had learned how to carry his liquor.

The *News* prospered. By January 1878 James had erected a four-story newspaper building at Shelby and Larned Streets.

City Editor Edward W. Scripps, at not quite twenty-four, discovered cigars, and began smoking a dozen a day.

"I never smoked before breakfast," he wrote in his memoirs, "but from the time I had eaten my morning meal until I lay down at night to sleep, the only time I was not smoking was when I was eating my meals or attending a theatre, church, or some social function. As a journalist I was a privileged man around the theatres, and saw most of the plays from the wings or behind the curtain of a box because I could smoke there. . . . I quit going to church because I could not smoke there."

4

On the Lam from Sex Scandal

Despite his battlefield limp, tobacco cud, and smelly pipe, and solid aversion to soap and scrub-brush, George Scripps was a striking figure, just turning forty. He had thick, wavy black hair long enough to cover his ears, a mustache and full beard, deep-set eyes — dark and soulful. A bachelor with money to spend, he trod a welcome path among creatures of the demimonde. None of these pliant companions should have been foolish enough to expect matrimony.

But when erotic misadventure snared him just at the beginning of 1878, George left town — quickly and quietly. As Ed Scripps put it, "There were both business and personal reasons for the avoidance of publicity." James's diary refers vaguely to "blackmail."

From exile out west, George penned an urgent appeal to Ed to chuck his city editorship and join him in his wanderings. George offered to pay all expenses. Ed wrote Annie: "At last one day, being utterly wretched myself, at James's suggestion I wrote to George plainly stating that I would go with him on one condition — a six-months European tour."

Ed was just then in a funk; James had expressed disappointment about his journalistic progress. In the past year, James groused, Ed had improved "not one jot" as an editor. The brother-publisher tried to soften his censure, however, by asserting it does not require "a brilliant writer to be a good editor."

"Now I know that," Ed wrote Annie, "but I would rather a thousand times be a brilliant writer of no account in a business way than the best editor that ever lived. I like money well enough but it takes a pile of it to make me feel half as well as the consciousness of having written a clever paragraph, or experienced a thought in becoming words."

Ed struck a deal with James to write travel articles from Europe for the *Evening News.* At $15 each, he hoped to send in about two a week and find a nest egg of about $800 on his return.

The brothers sailed from New York on March 15, 1878. Their ship encountered storms and they reached the British Isles in not the best of fettle. At Liverpool the old soldier limped ashore, his mind accustomed to the Detroit frugality of five-cent beer and ten-cent sandwiches, and wandered for an hour to find cheap lodgings.

But in London Ed now insisted on more respectable rooms and they were quartered on South Moulton Street, opposite their grandfather William Arminger Scripps's former house in one of the city's most fashionable sections.

On foot, by hansom cab and public conveyance, and by barge on the Thames, Ed spent days exploring London. He made the obligatory pilgrimage to St. Paul's Cathedral and strolled the Strand and other thoroughfares, sharply struck by weathered, crumbling, and sooty stone facades, the fussy cluster of roof and turret, gable, the quaint shops, dwelling houses and taverns which his guide book lumped together as antiquities. He intensely studied foreign manners and customs. At night he dared walk the cobblestones of White Chapel and other slums, eager to observe the denizens as well as the lords of London. The boy from Rushville searched passing faces, hoping to somehow detect clues in the expressions of these Londoners to answer his own nagging questions. As he would recall, "I was considering deeply my own case — what goal in life I should seek; what attitude I should take toward society and its conventions; by what road I should arrive at that eminence which I had so long dreamed of."

London's spring social season was in full sway. Nearly every night Ed watched gleaming carriages pull up to carpeted doorways and debouch elegantly-attired guests. Curiously, these nobles and their ladies did not impress him. As he put it: "Male and female, old and young, they looked to me a rather measly, scrawny, ornery crowd." In sharp contrast, most drivers and footmen were generally tall, finely-formed, good-looking young Englishmen. Observing them he self-consciously made a comparison. They wore cockades; what about his own attire? He glanced down at his yellow dog-skin gloves. He was gripping an ivory-top cane of switch dimensions, and wore a loud light-colored plaid sack coat with matching trousers, a silk hat, and a diamond stud in his shirt front. Only days earlier a young lady cousin sniffed that his attire made him look "like what the English call a perfect bounder."

He walked until midnight, mentally struggling with his uncertain ideas of destiny. In America he had grown up with a clear feeling about the true equality of man; now in London's night fog he lost faith in his former theory. Sadly he acknowledged that the world actually is occupied by two classes of men — one a very small class and the other very, very large; one slave-drivers and the other slaves. He recalled, "I recognized that I had no choice other than to be a slave driver or a slave."

From boyhood he had counted himself a "radical" or revolutionist, often mouthing, "God damn the rich, God help the poor." As a dirt farmer's son he believed no good citizen deserved income greater than one dollar a day. In Detroit as a newspaperman his eyes were opened; he realized that a buck a day was not adequate. He raised his personal sights, deciding that $3,000 a year was "the utmost income" he would ever permit himself. If great fortune struck, or if he somehow became acquisitive, he hoped to be unselfish with his riches.

In his three or four weeks in London, Ed was unable to shake his feeling of depression. George was always grousing about the expense of their travel. It is not surprising that Ed and George finally quarrelled — over a trifle: a half-penny tip.

Having lived mainly on the farm until he was thirty-five, hoarding 80 percent of his income, and in his three or four years in Detroit boarding at James's, George was largely ignorant of the customs and manners of hotels or restaurants, or trains and ships — where most servants largely subsisted on their tips.

George thought the practice, as did many American tourists, "highway robbery." In London he developed a positive hatred for the tattered street-sweepers who stationed themselves at busy intersections and with course brooms maintained a fairly clean path from one curb to the other. One morning they found Oxford Road covered with mud and slush, but the street-sweeper had cleared a reasonable path. As Ed passed the sweeper he reached for a half-penny to tip him, found none in his pocket, and handed over a penny.

Limping along three paces behind, George observed this, hurried up, and scolded Ed for being extravagant with their common purse, which in reality was the older brother's purse. "Not everybody tips street sweepers," Ed admitted. "But everybody who is somebody does — and I consider myself a somebody." On the street, they had a hot quarrel. Ed threatened to break off the trip and return to Detroit. George gave a sardonic laugh; how could he, with no money?

Ed unbuttoned his jacket and lifted the edge of his vest, revealing a small bulge. Just as he had done on leaving the farm, he had concealed a secret cache in the lining of his vest — small, but enough for passage home from Europe. The older brother blinked, concerned now, but still grumbling.

"Then he took another tack," Ed wrote later. "He told me he never intended to marry, that there were only two members of the family for whom he had any respect or affection, Ellen and myself . . . that Ellen would never need help . . . that he intended to make me his sole heir."

That did not faze Ed. "I told him I was not going to sacrifice my independence in any respect for the purpose of inheriting the biggest fortune he could ever hope to make."

In the end they patched things up. They agreed to halve travel costs up to this juncture, and spend separately during the rest of the tour. George would lend Ed the necessary funds—to be repaid on return to Detroit. Thus Ed was free to spend or tip as he chose. Ed counted on being able to reimburse George from his travel-letter earnings.

Ed began to "fairly loathe" London. "Vice was not only rampant, but public. I had read Dante's *Inferno* and I could recall nothing in Dante's description of Hell that was more loathesome to me than the sights I could see in London." It was almost May. The great Paris Exhibition of 1878 was opening. Eager to press on, Ed took passage alone across the Channel; George would follow a few days later.

On May 1, from 13 Rue Lacharrière, Ed poured out his rapturous impressions in a letter to Annie, back in bucolic Rushville:

> Paris is a gay jolly city and like a bad young man as I am, I am seeing as much of the gaiety and jollity as I can. . . . But besides that, this is a beautiful city and full of beautiful things. Pictures superb by the mile, statues by the thousands, palaces grand and open to the public, churches so exquisitely beautiful as to be indescribable, parks without number filled with fountains and statuary, broad beautiful boulevards forever presenting the same holiday effect, beautiful women in carriages and on the street, theatres grand and concerts delightful. Cafes whose splendor outshines royal palaces.

This was a heady experience for a farm boy not quite six years free of cow manure on his boots. "Oh, it is all pretty, harmonious and enchanting. Paris is an intoxicating drink I love to quaff!"

Yet, characteristically, he had laments, too: He was bogged down in writing private letters. He was finding interesting material for columns for the *Evening News,* but when the time came to write he always ran off to see some new sight. "I am studying up on French, of course. Not to

use here—to get at the inside of some of those wonderful French books.
. . . Six months here I could become proficient. Studied some at home,
but of pronunciation I am entirely ignorant."

George arrived from London. For a change he was cheerful. Ed
wrote home that George had become "a wonderful funster" who could
see the humorous side of things. "Mark Twain in *Innocents Abroad* was
not as funny as George."

But the moonlit vista on the banks of the Seine was not so engrossing that Ed's mind was completely taken off his ambition to become a
literary man. His dreams had finally crystalized. He had set his goal. No
longer would he work for a salary, or at such "little make-shifts of
making money" by controlling circulation routes.

He would be his own boss, start a newspaper of his own—subject to
orders from no one!

Moreover, he would use the Peter Parley principle—a daily of four
pages, rigidly condensed, and costing the reader only one cent!

"As soon as George came [to Paris]," Ed recalled, "I told him of my
project and offered to take him into partnership with me on certain
terms. I proposed that when we got home we should go to Cleveland,
Ohio, and there start a new paper—an undertaking that would be more
venturesome than the founding of the Detroit *Evening News*."

Ed nominated himself editor and George business manager.

"He was to furnish the money and leave me alone, and I was to
furnish the brains and make us both rich. George was in a rather reckless
mind. . . . He would have been just as receptive to a proposition to go
into mining, any sort of manufacturing, or any enterprise whatever. He
agreed to my proposal."

Straightaway Ed fired off a letter to James "telling him of my project." That must have been during the first week of May. "I was surprised
to receive a letter from him by what was practically return mail, approving the suggestion, but demurring, as I remember, to the proposition of
my being editor of the new paper—he considered me as being too raw
and inexperienced yet."

In his diary for May 16, 1878, James wrote: "Cool. Planted mel-
ons. . . . Thinking of a plan of starting a series of cheap papers in various cities as Cleveland, Buffalo with delegates from the *News* office in
charge."

By the time he left Europe, Ed had mentally formulated his "chain"
concept. He swallowed wholesale James's entire pattern for a little newspaper—except he intended to sell it for one cent! His decision to turn his
newspapers into crusaders for the underdog American blue-collar
worker would come later.

Rome beckoned magically to Ed Scripps. He had read the history of the Eternal City in his father's library back on the Rushville farm. Now he began to feast his own eyes on the actual ancient vistas. "Everything in and about Rome came to me with exciting familiarity from my memory of it in books." And in this foreign place he was about to have a singular experience—one that thrilled and fascinated him, and which he would vividly recall his whole life.

It occurred on his twenty-fourth birthday—June 18. He wanted to give his brother the slip, and be by himself. "I did not want George three feet behind me. I did not want to hear his everlastingly cynical and sometimes mirth-provoking humor. . . . I did not want to laugh at Rome; and particularly on this 18th of June, I was in no mood to laugh. I spent the day alone, a good part of it in the old churches."

The memorable hours of that day are recorded in vivid detail in one chapter of the autobiography Scripps wrote thirty-seven years later. From this account it is very clear that a spell haunted him on his birthday, some echo from the past that stealthily followed him into the cool interiors of musty cathedrals, across sun-drenched piazzas, into the magnificent shadows of crumbling arches and stone pillars—everywhere he went this day in Rome.

In his frame of mind, perhaps he fancied he could vaguely hear echos of the thunder of stallion hooves, the squeal of racing chariot wheels, the tumult and cheers in the *Circus Maximus*. Scripps always felt he had some rare potency for mysticism or mental telepathy; it is not unlikely he now began to feel implacably drawn into some phenomenon of ethereal communication—with the ancients, the generals, and the emperors, the great leaders of the empire. From across the dead centuries, were they perhaps trying to guide his destiny?

Deep in his reverie, Scripps stopped to take dinner in a restaurant on Via del Corso, and when he emerged continued to stroll, smoking a cigar. Says his autobiography:

> I do not remember when, in the moonlight, I discovered the pillars of the ruins of the old Forum, and beyond, the dusky outlines of a mammoth building; dusky simply because the street lights here were sufficiently bright to make even the pillars of the Forum appear in the shade. But I walked on down past the Forum where there were no bright lights, and then I discovered what the large building was that I had seen. There was the moon shining, I believe pretty nearly a full moon, lighting up the Colosseum. I walked on and entered the Ampitheatre, and in the middle, or near the middle, of the floor of the great structure— then entirely unexcavated and covered with earth—there lay a huge capitol of one of the columns.
>
> I climbed up and lay prone on this fragment of stone, and there I lay

for hours, smoking innumerable cigars. My mind teemed with the memories of old Rome. I had not long before concluded my reading of Gibbon's *Decline and Fall*. I dreamed of the emperor who built the Colosseum, and many other emperors, Roman generals, and soldier adventurers, and I recalled to my mind the names and deeds of many other great men.

Into his moonlight reverie came marching a parade of olden characters . . . Spartacus . . . Marius . . . Pyrrhus . . . Hannibal . . . Fabius Maximus . . . Julius Caesar . . . Augustus . . . Pompey . . . Marc Antony. Ed Scripps felt he was poised to embark on his own great adventure. Which of these stalwarts of Rome should he choose as his model?

His autobiography gives the answer:

> Perhaps my choice was an odd one, but it fell on Fabius Maximus; he who was patient and knew how to wait. . . . The world belongs to him who waits, if he doesn't wait too long; if he only waits long enough for his opportunity and is then quick to seize it!
>
> A boy . . . hot-blooded, irascible in temper as I was, for me to start out on a career of mutiny by a process of waiting!
>
> But from that day to this I have been ruled very largely by the resolution I made that night in the Colosseum in Rome. Let the other fellow have all the glory; let him occupy the place in the limelight; for me I only care to have the power. I do not care for the use of the power until it is necessary or useful to me to use the power. It was to wait and wait patiently for the opportune moment and then act promptly.
>
> As I dreamed, I poetized . . . my philosophy . . . and deepened and strengthened my resolve to be one of the great men of the world. I proposed no greater career for myself than that of journalist; but as a journalist I saw, or thought I saw, that I could apply and make use of the story of the Roman empire. I decided that I would establish a little kingdom such as Rome was in its prehistoric beginning. I decided that I would extend this kingdom of mine, which would consist of my first newspaper, to another and then another newspaper, and I determined so long as I lived to go on extending my kingdom into perhaps an empire of journalism.

He viewed his fantasy in the Colosseum moonlight realistically, nearly a month later, on July 26, writing sister Annie: "The chances are ten million to one that I will never succeed. . . . My monument, if it ever rears itself above the low level of a dream, shall not stand on the groans of a million fellow human beings. . . . On the contrary I would have it reared aloft not by captive thousands but emancipated generations.

"The day of the sword has passed. The pen is the scepter of this century and will be for ages to come. The press is the engine by which the grand object must be achieved, and the power is now existent, only waiting for the hand of a man wise enough to direct it. In a lifetime I may at least start the ball rolling.

"Well, I am a dreamer, am I not? Burn this letter and say nothing of its contents."

After leaving Rome, the Scripps brothers visited Venice, Florence, and Switzerland. They took in a small part of Germany, stopping at Strasbourg. But Ed was tiring of adventure.

"I wanted to get back to America. I wanted to begin my life's achievements. I had been an apprentice to life too long. . . . It was time for me to begin the real work of life."

5

Brainchild Number One

Eyes blazing, Eddie Scripps cried out in angry protest. At his desk in the *Evening News,* James grimly gave him an icy bookkeeper stare, unflinching and unbending. Eddie was too green and inexperienced to go to Cleveland as editor and start the new paper. That was James's decision, and he didn't intend to budge. George squirmed in his chair, uncomfortable, trying to stay out of the cross fire. James had picked a man off the *News* staff, Burgess, to be the Cleveland editor. Eddie exploded—Burgess was an old stick!

"Besides," Ed cried, "starting a paper in Cleveland was *my* idea!"

That didn't faze James. They were meeting in September 1878 only a few days after the brothers had returned from Europe. Ed had hurriedly taken George to look over Cleveland and they had agreed it presented a good opportunity for a cheap newspaper. However, George had cooled on the idea of going there himself to be business manager.

Now in this confrontation, with George looking at his pipe and avoiding Ed's gaze, the kid brother could see his dreams of empire slipping away. James set his jaw. Ed began to feel panicky. He turned to George, his wounded eyes begging. He was powerless without financial backing from his two half-brothers. To sway James once his mind was locked on negative was virtually impossible. Disappointed and sad, Ed struggled to subdue his hurt and anger. If George suddenly got stiffnecked and sided with the *Evening News* publisher, it would be a disaster. He must move with caution.

He got up and paced the floor. He was trying to think—how to overcome James's lack of confidence and George's indifference. At length he drew up a chair facing James, and started an earnest monologue—talking calmly, intelligently, and persuasively. He ticked off reasons James should reconsider. First, he guaranteed to find a replacement for himself as *News* city editor. Second, now that George had changed his mind and didn't want to be business manager, there was another excellent candidate — John Scripps Sweeney! Their bright and aggressive cousin from the Rushville general store had become a protégé of both James and George. He had graduated to the job of assistant to George, and acted as *News* cashier. Also he was experienced — and clever — in advertising.

Not only that, Ed argued, he and John each held one share of *News* stock. On the actual value of each share, James and George would be justified in lending a total of $2,000. It would require capital of only $10,000 to start the Cleveland daily. Thus the two older brothers would need to invest but $3,000 each. They would own 60 percent, and control, with Ed and John Sweeney each owning 20 percent.

The sincerity and logic of Ed's argument began finally to soften James's stern face. Still, he muttered that Eddie was inexperienced and lacked maturity. The younger brother granted that, but shrewdly and flatteringly asserted he would depend on the patriarch to give guidance and counsel — and would be obedient to James's suggestions and commands.

For an hour Ed pleaded for his dream. James, not too willingly but hopefully, at length gave in. How quickly the project moved thereafter is reflected in James's 1878 diary:

> *Thursday, September 26* — Pleasant day. Meeting of George, Ed, John and self to weigh and decide on purchase of press for Cleveland enterprise.
> *Saturday, September 28* — John at Chicago negotiating for press for Cleveland paper. Bought of Hatchett Supply type at $4.75. . . .
> *Monday, September 30* — Held second meeting at office and decided on name, size, types and so forth and sent Ed and John down by steamer. . . . Suffering from a cold.

Under a balmy Indian summer sky, the ex-Rushville cousins hustled about Cleveland, strangers in boomtown crowds. They went in search of office quarters. The rent, George insisted, must be cheap. They prowled back streets on the downtown fringe. On an alley called Frankfort Street, they found vacant a ramshackle two-story brick building. Near the corner of Seneca Street, it was next to a vile vaudeville theatre, and across the street from the greasy and unremitting odors of a low-class cafe. The rent was cheap. For four rooms on two floors, the agent asked $33.33 a month. They took it.

Already Ed had decided on a name — the *Penny Press.*

Unlike Ed, John Sweeney was dreaming not of underdog uplift, but of running a newspaper to pile up personal wealth. "Just wait," he told Ed confidently, "I'll be driving matched bays with a rig as classy as any in this burg. Besides, I intend to marry some young lady with money."

On the latter score, Ed had no doubt his cousin's prospects were excellent. Just turned twenty-three, Sweeney was handsome and glib, slender and a trifle over six feet, strong-looking. With tall forehead and neatly trimmed dark hair, he wore neither beard nor mustache. Since boyhood he had been an avid outdoorsman. Ed always envied John's skill in bagging mallards with a twelve-gauge and his casual success with fly rod. In Detroit John also became a minor champion in golf and tennis.

Even though his cousin was fourteen months younger, Ed felt he had picked up a great deal of poise since leaving their rustic hometown. Sweeney's direct, friendly gaze, his musical voice, and ready wit were ideal natural tools for a salesman.

Before opening their doors, they found their finances tight. The printing press John had obtained in Chicago for $4,300 required payment of $2,500 in thirty days, the balance in six months. They spent $800 for a dinky Baxter upright steam engine to power the press, and put $1,200 into type and fixtures. They would face a weekly payroll for a staff of two dozen men and boys.

"John, we can't pay ourselves much," Ed said. "Just enough for room, board and laundry. I say fifty a month apiece . . . until we show a profit."

Ed intended to try a new distribution method. Instead of customary routes with carriers, the *Penny Press* would be sold on the streets. This presented a profitable opportunity of two or three hundred newsboys. A young hustler could buy copies wholesale at the pressroom door for half a cent, thus earning fifty cents for each hundred sold.

Ad pickings were expected to be slim. Sweeney likely would not find it easy to lure merchants into buying space in a newspaper of only four pages, each ten inches wide and sixteen long, with no established circulation routes, a complete novelty in size and content, and issued from a disreputable Cleveland alley.

Yet based on the popularity achieved by brother James's *Evening News* among Detroit blue-collar families, Ed calculated his paper would likewise become widely read and appreciated by the Cleveland working man, who up to this point had no organ interesting in fighting his battles for fair treatment. Ed noted Cleveland's steel mills, grain elevators, and hundreds of factories turning out paint and varnish, bicycles, sewing machines, telescope lenses, drugs — even ladies dresses in *standard sizes,* that a stunning innovation! John D. Rockefeller set the town astir, creating his Standard Oil Company monopoly.

Sweeney agreed with Ed that the existing newspapers not only were dull and old-fashioned, but were sharply caste-minded. Any person with social, business, or political "pull" could "kill" an unpleasant story or get a favorable "puff" published prominently. Thus conditions appeared ripe for the new paper. As one keen journalistic observer recalled: "Cleveland at that period consisted of a distinctive social upper class, who feared not publicity of their oppression and iniquities, because they 'influenced' the established newspapers, thus a great mass of iron workers, oil workers, sailors, shipyard workers, and others of the common folk, who really had no exponent of their own interests, and being without organization, had to take anything that capital handed out."

With a month wait for their Frankfort Street plant to be ready, the cousin-partners returned to Detroit. Ed resumed his job as *Evening News* city editor. But not for long. He discovered his successor right in the newsroom — John McVicar, one of those printer-graduates from the *case,* a plodding, uncomplaining Scotsman. Now Ed was free to direct his full thought to the forthcoming birth of his own first child of his brain. It would be helpful, he reasoned, to invade neighboring Ohio with a letter of commendation from Michigan's governor, Charles M. Croswell. He got one, on official stationery, dated October 14, esteeming him as "a gentleman of ability and character. He is an [*sic*] vigorous writer, an active energetic business man of large experience in the newspaper line." He got a similar letter from his congressman, Alex Lewis.

In Cleveland about that time a few billboards blossomed to herald the coming of the *Penny Press,* with its debut set for Saturday, November 2, 1878. That, incidentally, would be precisely six years from the day that Ed Scripps escaped the Rushville farm.

Upstairs and down, Friday the first of November seemed near bedlam in the *Penny Press* building. Everyone rushed around, feeling deadline pressure for tomorrow's start-up. Ed stomped dozens of times up the steep rickety wooden stairs and through the short hall — "dark as pitch and dirty as a gas house" — to the second-floor editorial office. Every few minutes he found himself expected to make a decision — for partner Sweeney, for reporters, the composing room foreman, etc. He was even called on to help move in furniture.

It abruptly struck Ed just how much a derelict the ramshackle building was; he recalled someone giving directions to Frankfort Street: "Go north on Bank Street and turn left at the first street that has an odor you can't stand!"

In the middle of the editorial room sat an ancient pot-bellied stove, rusty red from squirts of tobacco juice. Six "desks" nestled against the walls—actually cheap pine kitchen tables. There were six or seven kitchen chairs, a rough shelf for the file of newspapers, and "an imposing battery of spittoons." At the end was "a sort of cupboard" floored with grimy red carpet; this space the editor-in-chief had commandeered as his "private office." (When the carpet was taken up a year or two later it was found so stiff from dried tobacco squirts that had missed spittoons, it stood upright. Someone suggested using it as an office partition.)

To lend a hand and his experience, brother James came down from Detroit. The patriarch intended to personally adjust the ink fountains and rollers on the "turtle-back" press, a four-cylinder, type-revolving Hoe that previously was used by the *Chicago Tribune*. The handset type was made up between V-shaped column rules in curved cast-iron "turtles" which were fitted onto the press's main cylinder, which was four feet in diameter, and locked into position with keyed wedges called *quoins*.

When a leather belt from the wood-fired Baxter steam engine began turning the main cylinder, four men or boys would leap upon narrow platforms and single-feed sheets of newsprint into the four smaller impression cylinders. The Hoe could handle 4,000 sheets an hour, but one large disadvantage was that the press printed only one side at a time, necessitating each sheet going through the Hoe twice.

A striking figure with boots, red whiskers, and a wide-brimmed gray fedora, Ed tried to work at his desk on copy for the Saturday paper. Interruptions were constant. He scribbled away to compose something for the first issue that would express the rationale for the Scripps clan's entry into Cleveland journalism—just a few short paragraphs to crystallize the ideals of the infant paper.

He recalled how James had presented their concept in the initial *Evening News*. Ed tackled the same points—brevity in reporting the news; universality of appeal, to rich and poor, to business leaders and laborers, to men, women, children of all races and creeds; cheap enough to be afforded by all; and delivery timed for evening hours which were freer for newspaper reading than were mornings.

Finally he sent this copy to the composing room:

> What the business men want is a newspaper which will present before them all the news of the day in as short and concise a form as possible. They

haven't time to spend hours searching thru the length and breadth of a blanket sheet, shifting out of much chaff the few valuable kernels of important news.

What the laborer and mechanic wants is to be able to get all the information of the large daily papers at a price which he can afford to pay.

What the ladies want is to be able to keep as well posted as their husbands without having to wade thru columns to obtain information that might be placed in a paragraph.

What everybody wants is a daily newspaper at a time convenient for reading, containing all the news of the day, containing not one line of uninteresting matter, and cheap enough so no one will miss the price of it. The *Penny Press* will supply those wants.

Never before, of course, had Ed Scripps, aged twenty-four years, four months and fourteen days, had the responsibility for bringing out a complete newspaper, not even such a dinky little tabloid as this.

After everyone else had gone home for the night, Ed sat alone in his cubbyhole office. At his table he had a sheaf of copy paper and his soft lead pencil. Out in the composing room, the page turtles stood with thirteen or fourteen empty columns. These must be filled with news type by press time Saturday.

Ed, furrowing his brow, toyed with his pencil. This November evening was cool and there was no blaze in the old pot-bellied stove — but he began sweating. "I had," he recalled, "a regular case of buck fever or stage fright. . . . I could not think of one word to write."

Gloomily he stared at the blank paper — but not for long. He arose, slapped on his gray fedora, and stumbled down the dark stairway. He decided to go to his hotel and get a good night's sleep — for a fresh early start Saturday.

He was already falling back on one rule he had adopted as his guide for life: "Never do anything today that can be put off until tomorrow."

At dawn Saturday Ed dressed, hurried his breakfast, and by 7 o'clock was back at his desk — before anyone else came in. "I had no time to worry or even to think," he recalled. "The printers were due in a few minutes, and they must have copy. I began to produce it."

The great bulk of news matter in the first issue was "local" since the *Penny Press* was starting with access to only five hundred words of telegraph. To augment that the staff had sifted out-of-town papers for national briefs.

Of thirteen and one-half columns of space in the first issue, Ed estimated he produced about half of it in a furious binge of steady writing, in a few hours grinding out perhaps 3,000 words.

Much of the "news" in the first edition was thin gruel. Even so, the

Penny Press had spark and verve — and a wide variety of "shorts" as well as a few longer interviews that spared no punches on the foibles of Clevelanders.

Two full columns on the front page were occupied by the first ad John Sweeney had sold, an impressive offering of fire and marine insurance by Brooks and Manning Company of Cleveland. On the other three pages were a total of five and one-half columns of ads — from clothiers, an ink-maker, a sewing machine dealer, plumbers, a safe and vault merchant, a cigar store, a business college, a rupture and truss expert, a furniture store — even from a justice of the peace who also was a detective, promising "collections and all legal business attended to." Thus slightly more than a third of the space in the first paper was taken up with ads.

No headlines adorned page one. Prosaic in appearance and content, the *Penny Press* resembled a sort of chatty newsletter, with dashes separating short paragraphs. (The very first item was an "editorial.")

The "lead" column, on the left side of the page, started thus:

The viaduct should never be a toll bridge.

— —

The prospects for war with Mexico are diminishing.

— —

Did you ever see a more beautiful fall than we have had this year?

— —

The circulation of the *Penny Press* will presumably be very large and the advantages its columns will offer to advertisers will be obvious.

— —

The insanity dodge failed McGill, and today Cleveland's bench and jury stand higher for this fact in the minds of all lovers of strict justice.

— —

The yellow fever has about run its course in the south. It has not been so malignant and wide-spread in a quarter of a century as it has been this year.

— —

England had a narrow escape from losing her able prime minister, Lord Beaconsfield, one of the greatest statesmen of the age, he being stricken down by apoplexy. At last accounts he was recovering.

Those seven items filled the top quarter of the first column. Near the bottom of the column the editor asserted that Cleveland has always been noted for its newspapers and opined that the city "will not fail to welcome a good thing that is offered her" — a cheap new daily.

Then he ran his four-paragraph squib explaining "why" the paper was launched. In another paragraph he identified the proprietors, "Scripps and Sweeney," with brief reference to their backgrounds in Detroit newspapering.

In the second column, Ed Scripps clearly outlined his editorial policy:

> "What are your politics?" asked a certain Cleveland gentleman today of the editor of the *Penny Press.*
>
> The gentleman was asked to look for his answer in the paper. Here it is:
>
> We have no politics, that is in the sense of the word as commonly used. We are not Republican nor Democratic, nor Greenback, and not Prohibitionist. We simply intend to support good men and condemn bad ones, support good measures and condemn bad ones, no matter what party they belong to.
>
> We shall tell no lies about persons or policies for love, malice or money. It is no part of a newspaper's business to array itself on the side of this or that party, or fight, lie and wrangle for it. The newspapers should simply present all the facts the editor is capable of obtaining, concerning men and measures before the bar of the public, and then, after having discharged its duty as a witness, be satisfied to leave the jury in the case—the public—to find the verdict.

Nothing like the little penny sheet had ever been seen by Clevelanders. It contained, as Ed Scripps had promised, not a line of uninteresting matter. Most news was told in short, boiled-down paragraphs. But there were a few longer articles—human interest stories.

The longest was an eight-hundred-word account of a squabble between a General Slayton and his French-Spanish wife, involving a punching and shoving encounter in their Cleveland home to which police were called. The space given to a question and answer interview between the reporter and the aggrieved wife seems somewhat at odds with the proclaimed policy of brevity in telling the news—but the story was candid and intimate, and thus quite readable.

Running 1,200 words, the longest piece in the first issue was fiction, the daily short story on the back page. Titled "Charles Colquitt," it was the saga of a rich man's son in "Abbeyton" and his troubles with a beautiful but ungrateful wife. After getting his readers hooked, the *Penny Press* editor abruptly at the height of suspense broke off the tale— and revealed it would be concluded in Monday's edition.

Under the heading "Reporters' Pickings" were such items as:

Twenty-nine marriage licenses have been granted during the week.
. . . Will Payne Avenue ever be graded and paved? It is now in an impass-
able condition. . . . The city treasurer's office was filled this morning with
school marms drawing their pay. . . . St. Peter's Church, corner of Superior
and Dodge, will soon be repainted and two cupolas added to the roof.
. . . Market Master Beck confiscated about 15 carcasses of veal at the Central Market this morning owing to the fact that they were entirely unfit for
food. . . . Fears are entertained that the little steamer Morning Star, which
left this port for Canada a week ago for a load of ice, is lost as she has not
been heard from since leaving. . . . A water pipe burst last night for the
third time at the corner of Eagle and Erie Streets. In repairing it today the
ground caved in, partially burying an Irishman under the wet clay. With his
head just out from under the mud, he shouted, "I'm drowning. Be Jasus,
sind for the Pope!"

Cleveland's established newspapers were intrigued not only by the penny
sheet but also its young fireball editor. From the front window of the
evening *Herald,* office clerk Elbert H. Baker frequently saw Ed Scripps
striding by with his broad-brimmed hat and proud swagger, "attempting
to appear courageous . . . looking as if he had just come in from the
plains of Texas or some other rough state. . . . The only thing lacking
was a six-shooter." (Actually in his hip pocket Ed carried a revolver—
and would find occasion to draw it more than once in Cleveland.)

At the outset most rival editors scoffed at the puny upstart. But not
E. B. Smalley, who had come out from the *New York Tribune* to edit the
Herald. Looking over the first issue of the *Penny Press,* he told Baker:
"Young man, here is a new and far-reaching move in journalism."

To others, it appeared too frail, too simplistic to survive. Publisher
Edwin Cowles made a private game out of predicting the date of its
demise. With the newest, biggest, and fastest press in town (10,000 copies an hour), Cowles owned the five-cent morning *Leader* and the two-
cent afternoon *News.* Every afternoon he bustled to his office to grab the
latest issue of the *Penny Press,* slap it down on his desk and measure the
inches of advertising. With a stub pencil he made rapid calculations and
chortled uproariously. The little paper was losing so much money, he
roared, it would go bankrupt in two months.

For the first month the paper actually would lose about $85 a day.
(Total November revenue from advertising and circulation turned out to
be only $816.66 against the expense of $3,271.51.) That strained their
meager capital, but Scripps and Sweeney and their men battled on, cap-
suling the news in tight paragraphs, taking the side of the blue-collar

worker, spitting in the eye of the capitalist, printing news that previously had been suppressed or ignored.

Circulation of the *Penny Press* grew rapidly and the daily loss in the cash box began to shrink. The amused smiles on the faces of rival newsmen soon turned to anxiety, then amazement, and finally to envy. Cowles, glowering and spluttering, suddenly quit publicly predicting the date the new paper would die, and began violently hating Ed Scripps and his organ because it was now cutting into *News-Leader* profits.

Soon Cowles and Scripps would be sniping at each other in print, opening a turbulent feud that would come close to sending Ed Scripps to prison.

For the first few weeks Ed uncharacteristically was a true workaholic. He arose at 5 A.M. at the American House on Superior Street where he got room and board (not good) for eight dollars, and went straight to the office. By 8 or 9, he had laid out the work for the day, read the papers and done a little writing. He then took off fifteen minutes for breakfast—and his first cigar of the day. Next he pitched in, "reading and revising copy, pushing the foreman up in his work (sometimes with curses) so as to get the first edition started in time." At 2 P.M. another fifteen-minute break for "dinner" and his second cigar.

Ed described this typical day in a letter to his sister Annie, continuing: "Back to the office. Work is now but light. Only a couple of columns of copy to be handed out, unimportant local and telegraph. Men come to see me and bore me. At 3 o'clock our second edition goes to press. From that time until 4 o'clock, the time of going to press with our third edition, I am too weary to do much of anything and the third edition is made up of scraps and ends, a little telegraph, a few local items, etc. I give out 'time' copy for the next day, story selections, etc., mostly reprint. At half-past four, completely fatigued, I do nothing but take a little walk, talk to the men or visitors, or go to my room and take a nap."

At 6 o'clock he ate supper with John Sweeney, talking business, of course. "Then I lay down on the sofa for a rest, my third and last cigar of the day. Then back to the office—letter-writing, revising copy, and preparing for the next day. So to bed at 10 P.M. Such is my life on weekdays."

Ed drove his small staff. He wanted the paper "well-filled and off in good shape." If things "get to hitching, then trouble begins for all who surround me," he wrote sister Ellen. "They are learning that there is no rest for those near me unless they are accomplishing results. . . . I think my chief duty lies in simply seeing that a good paper is made, rather than making it myself."

The editor's cockiness on occasion would show up in an item in the news columns, viz.: "The *Penny Press* is a week old today. Has it not wonderfully improved?"

In late November, Ed observed that while his little paper was not yet in a secure niche, "people are beginning to have confidence in us" and circulation was larger than any other Cleveland newspaper, some days hitting 14,000. He wrote Annie:

> On the whole I have met with better success than I expected. I never thought myself brilliant or capable of doing any brilliant work. I have simply thought I could make a tolerably fair paper. . . . James says he is satisfied. Ellen is delighted and some of the newsmen who never thought much of my ability are a little surprised.
>
> There is mighty little poetry in all this work. I do not feel an inch higher up than when I was working for the old *Tribune* at three dollars a week.

On Sundays Ed would "lay abed late," spend a few hours at the office, "writing letters, talking with John, and smoking." He usually attended church Sunday nights, he wrote his sisters, and seldom went to places of amusement, and "never any social gatherings. . . . Business is enjoyment enough for me right now."

That was not the exact truth. While not sparing himself as a workaholic striving to make the *Penny Press* succeed, Ed was at the same time caught in a contradictory emotional storm—his unsatiated yearnings for "literary fame" and his unremitting ache for the soft touch of a woman.

His vibrant libido kept him restless and tormented. When Annie wrote asking about his romances, he responded: "Oh, yes, I still have girls. But none of them expect anything of me." For a sensitive person steeped in romantic poetry, it seems incongruous that Scripps could be so uncavalier and business-like about love. It is clear that he didn't have the time, or patience, or the inclination for the subtleties of courtship. When he selected a fair lady, he expected to beckon her—to bed or to the altar—with a quick snap of his fingers.

Somehow he retained strong, but loose and one-sided, romantic fixations on girls he had grown up with in Rushville. Especially was this true of two of his cousins, Lida Scripps and Jessie Sweeney, the latter his business partner's tomboy sister, who was just turning twenty.

"Some way or other," he wrote Annie, "I have always looked on this young lady as my property and half-expected to make her my wife someday . . . and could corner her into it if I tried."

A potential love triangle had developed. Brother Fred, the twenty-eight-year-old bachelor living back on the farm with Ma, also had his eye on Jessie. Told of this by Annie, Ed grandly vowed he would step aside. "I never cared enough for any woman to run the risk of hurting anyone's feelings by marrying her. I think it would be impossible for me to ever care enough for Jessie to want to marry her for a moment if I thought by doing so I would rob Fred of the one great desire of his life."

Besides, Ed assured Annie, he had "lots of things" he wanted to do before getting married. "I want to go back for a year's travel in Europe" — this from a greenhorn editor barely three weeks into the journalistic challenge of his life! — "and I want to get immensely wealthy and by that time I may be ready to sacrifice her [Jessie] without any pangs. Nothing would please me better, next to knowing Fred has recovered from his foolish infatuation, than to hear of their marriage. Does all this read contradictory? Well, my life is a contradiction, and always has been. . . . What a conceited puppy I am anyway."

6

The Killing of Henry Chisholm

A bright aggressive staff had come to the *Penny Press* for love of the game, not money. For city editor Ed brought Henry Little out of retirement. A former Detroit *Evening News* reporter, Little had been laid up a year with rheumatism. If Detroit colleagues are to be believed, Little, born a Canadian, already had been "a practical printer, a lawyer, a member of the bar of Michigan, a doctor, an experienced politician, an ex-county clerk, an ex-county superintendent of schools."

Scripps's star reporter was eccentric Maurice Perkins, a former newsman in Detroit and Toledo. Sharp-eyed, foxlike, thin as a rail, Perkins skittered around Cleveland in an overcoat that swept the ground, pockets always overflowing with papers and clippings. His witty, imaginative, pungent writing had long impressed Ed.

Total editorial room payroll ran a little over $150 a week. Little and Perkins each got fifteen. Ed paid his expert on local background, old-time Cleveland reporter John A. Spencer, eighteen. One reporter asked Ed what were the rules for the staff's personal conduct. He said there was only one: "No man shall dress worse or get drunker than I do."

Scripps vowed to print all the news, without fear or favor—*and to go to press on time every day!* He took command of the composing room, knowing that type-setting invariably caused day-to-day conflict between advertising and editorial departments. Chiefly it was a question of whether advertising copy was to be put in type ahead of news stories, with the latter to suffer if time ran out before the press deadline. This formula divided authority between co-equals, instead of one in-total-charge publisher, and it would become perpetual—and controversial—on Scripps newspapers, inspiring decades of bitter "church and state" arguments between editors and business managers, turning them into rivals for dominance.

It became legendary that Editor-in-Chief Scripps's favorite admonition to a reporter was: "Boil that down!" Only the most terse news stories would pass his blue pencil. But there were occasional exceptions — and perhaps that is what made his little paper so successful.

On February 13, 1879, the *Penny Press* account of the public hanging of one McGill for killing his sweetheart Mary Kelly filled two entire pages, ten columns of type recounting tiniest details of the horrific spectacle.

The *Press* got deep into investigative reporting. There were varied crusades: exposés of "tricks" of the funeral trade, vile practices at the Workhouse, miserable living conditions in the city's poor sections, even a look at the mysterious thirty-minute daily delay in opening the public library. (The librarian said his staff was "putting books back in [*sic*] the shelves" but *Press* reporters hid in the bushes and saw the library crew really was playing hookey to do grocery shopping.)

Ed's bare-knuckle approach to news, and his pro-labor sympathies were winning the paper strong favor in blue-collar homes. But the *Penny Press* was developing powerful enemies — the wealthy industrialists and the kowtowing rival newspapers. The *Leader*'s vitriolic Edwin Cowles, who bullied the other blanket-sheet editors, developed an intense hatred of the brash red-headed editor on Frankfort Street.

Sarcastically the *Leader* needled the *Press* in such terms of endearment as "that moronic sheet," "our little cuspidore," "that yellow Frankfort dog." Cowles was engaging in blatant libel and he knew it. Ed could play that game. He retaliated with vigor; his columns bristled with slurs. One *Press* headline (February 26, 1879) bluntly called attention to "The *Leader*'s Latest Lie!" Scripps's references to his feuding rival included "poor old towser," "the late lamented," "Jaundice," "Our Aged Friend," "Pappa Cowles' Pap." Ed was on a precarious collision course. Cowles was a dangerous foe.

From Detroit, James kept an uneasy eye on the fledgling. On occasion he was impelled to rush to Cleveland to put out a fire. He held the heavy hand of authority, as disclosed by these 1879 diary entries:

Thursday, February 13 — Dee still sick. Shocked today by an outrageous article in the *Penny Press* and started to Cleveland at 7 P.M. to take some action in regard to it. Laid over at Toledo in cold and discomfort from 10 till 3 A.M.

Friday, February 14 — Arrived at Cleveland at 7 A.M. Spent forenoon with Ed and John in their room talking over mistake they are making. Wrote

disclaimer of libel published by Ed on Wednesday. Suspended for a time Ed
and [city editor] Little and started home at 3:30.

Such a reprimand did not seem to daunt Ed—and least of all the
Penny Press's outright support of trade unionism. Cleveland's monied
interests thought the red-haired editor a revolutionist. He was not only
for the working classes, he was *against* the capitalists.

Scripps had deep-rooted conviction that the poor were viciously
kept under the heel of the wealthy, and that the nation's press was subservient to the rich. Only the educated plutocrats could afford to read the
blanket-sheets, which kowtowed to political and commercial pressure.

The *Penny Press,* he reasoned, could at least lift "the dense ignorance" that blinded Cleveland's workers to their potential concentrated
political might, to their opportunity to unite for a fairer share of the
profits of the factories. His philosophy was injected into his newspaper
as editorial policy. Thirty-seven years later he recalled: "It has been my
effort to make it harder for the rich to grow richer and easier for the
poor to keep from growing poorer." Headstrong and cocky, hell-bent on
just one thing—success, Ed was wild and callous. He was willing to risk
his life and break all of Ohio's laws that stood between him and his goal.

"When a man is fully prepared to take any risk," he recalled, "or
pay any penalty in order to accomplish some one thing, it rarely ever
occurs that a man has to take any risk or pay any penalty. I heard an old
Texan once say that in his country a man who had a pistol seldom had to
use it, but when he did not happen to have a gun around, he was sure to
need it mighty bad."

Ed was "chock full of opinions and ideas that were more the result
of emotional activity than reasoning," he later conceded, "so having a
barrel of ink and plenty of paper, I just turned myself loose on the
public."

Not only contentious, the young editor was a living contradiction.
While he was packing a gun, demeaning the city's big shots, and printing
all of Cleveland's unpleasant scandal, Ed Scripps was preaching to his
staff that "a reporter must always be a gentleman," and defying anyone
to prove that he lacked personal integrity.

There was a streak of meanness as well as stubbornness in him. He
admitted "an almost instinctive hatred for all men in power." His boyhood reading made him "despise" shopkeepers. Ed never lost a chance to
poke his finger in the eye of an advertiser. His aim was to push revenue
from subscribers alone so high that he'd need only a little income from
ads—so that merchants would never constitute enough of a profit source

to be able to "blackmail" the editor of his independence. Merchants kicked furiously against his attitude and practice; John Sweeney must have spent hours gnashing his teeth in frustration, but Ed could not be swayed.

Ed didn't believe a publisher "with a thousand-dollar-a-day potential" ought to do a three-dollar man's job, as he chidingly told brother James. He began inventing excuses to lay abed and come late to the office, and leave early. Taking books to read, he would go off to some country hotel, or spend time rowing or sailing on Lake Erie. His chief preoccupations were "just resting" or "doing hard thinking." He was saving himself to "do four men's work" in times of emergency. Scripps considered his main role was "to make an important decision about every six months."

The rigors of Cleveland's winter undermined his health. Severe bronchial attacks brought on colds and sieges of coughing that lasted weeks. His extreme irritability after a hacking, sleepless night was another excuse to avoid going to the office. Some of his absences lasted weeks.

Even Ed wondered whether his success was abetted by his indolent ways, or just fool luck. Or a knack of choosing good ambitious men. One of the latter was Robert F. Paine, Jr. Twenty-two, a greenhorn who first tried being a law student, Bob Paine cubbed briefly on the Cleveland *Plain Dealer,* then moved to the struggling labor paper, the *Daily Advance,* where he was jack-of-all-trades. His father was a respected attorney, former Common Pleas Judge Robert F. Paine.

On his daddy's letterhead, Bob had scribbled a plea October 23, 1878, that he was "cussed anxious" to work on the new paper. Ed, busy, brushed him off. Several weeks later he stopped off at the *Daily Advance* to look over the eager applicant. In the dim editorial room he saw but one person, a frowsy fat boy stretched out on a plank table, asleep. Ed punched him awake and asked for Robert F. Paine, Jr. "That's me," said the sleepyhead. Ed started. It was two in the afternoon — what the devil! With a grunt and a sneer, Ed turned on his heel. What he didn't know was that the fat boy since 1 A.M. had been snipping telegraph from the morning papers, scouring the city for "local," writing headlines, and reading proof.

Ed forgot about the sleepyhead until early April 1879, when returning from a trip to Detroit he found Bob Paine in his own office writing waterfront news. City Editor Little had hired the kid. Ed blew up. Little protested that Paine was working free — until Ed got a chance to pass on his stories. Grudgingly, Scripps gave the fat boy $6 a week — and a try-out. Paine had another worrisome and visible handicap. In a teenage hunting accident he had shot off his left hand. That did not seem to slow him down.

Editor-in-Chief Scripps enjoyed camaraderie with his little band of hell-raisers. "He ran with and pokered with us boys," Bob Paine would recall fifty years later, "the darndest, pepperyest, finest companion a fellow could ask." There was plenty of boozing and other high jinks. After one afternoon's fishing, most of the staff was returning in a yawl, with Scripps and Sweeney at the oars. The two began complaining about each other's rowing and leaped up to fight it out. The fracas dumped everybody overboard.

They all bobbed to the surface through the Cuyahoga River's four-inch bosom of Standard Oil mixed with Graselli chemical works residue and waste from an upriver soap factory. "The Old Man," as they called Ed even then, bobbed up beside Bob Paine, "his whiskers bearing all the hues of the rainbow and some things that no self-respecting rainbow would harbor."

One reason "The Old Man" was eager to sail, row, hike, ride horse-back, or roister with "the boys" was that such action helped take the edge off his ever-throbbing carnal appetite.

Sometime during 1879, he acquired a mistress—a second-hand paramour. She was young and pretty Elizabeth Brown. Abandoned by her first lover, who left for adventure out west, she cast about for a new protector. She appears to have been from a family Ed knew in Detroit. In some fashion their relationship was established. She came to Cleveland, where in her own abode, the young editor supported her.

It was in this period that Ed first discovered the power of his mean mien—the devastating stare of his "evil eye." He was awakened in his rooms at the Weddell House by a note from the office warning him to look out for a certain man who had threatened "to get him."

The first thing Ed did was to call the waiter to bring his breakfast. He dressed and started walking up and down his sitting room thinking of how to handle the emergency. By chance he caught a full view of his face in the mirror. Because he had a noticeable cast in one eye, people usually thought of his gaze as "dreamy." That would not apply this morning.

"I will not say that my face was distorted with anger and excitement," he recalled in his memoirs, "but pale as it was there was such an expression on it, especially about the eyes, as to startle me. It seemed to me that my face was the face of a very dangerous man.

"I strove to retain the expression and study my own face for awhile. Then, by an act of will, I smoothed out my features and saw myself normal. Time and again I practiced this change of expression. For the first time then was revealed to me why it not infrequently occurred that men — big, strong fellows — had backed away from me."

This, however, was not false bravado. Ed always carried a pistol. "I knew I would kill somebody if I was touched. . . . During the first ten years of my career as a journalist it was not uncommon for editors to be shot, or for editors to shoot other people. Horse-whipping of editors was sometimes indulged in, and more often threatened."

To start a paper with but $10,000 capital was daring, if not ridiculous. For five straight months, Scripps and Sweeney lost money. To stay afloat, they had to borrow from the *Detroit News* an additional $2,500.

Then in April 1879 they suddenly wanted to shout hooray. What had started out an eighty-five-dollar-a-day loss finally turned into a profit — not much, just $8 a day. In May they lost $26 a day; June showed a profit, $10 a day. But in July they were again losing, $17 a day. The dog days of August started off bad, with a daily deficit of about $40.

James and George Scripps arrived unannounced. The Detroit brothers promptly dropped a bombshell. The *Press* could no longer run in the red. It must be operated on its current income — or closed down!

Ed and John exploded. This ultimatum was ridiculous. It couldn't be done!

James calmly pulled out his bookkeeping ledgers, showing the little paper could count on an average monthly income of about $1,700. That would give Ed about $200 a week to run editorial, and John a like amount for his part of the operation, which included buying newsprint. James conceded this meant cutting expense about 25 percent, and letting some people go.

Ed was stunned. As he would recall: "I protested against any change, almost with tears in my eyes, certainly with a choking voice. Sweeney lost his temper and declared he was going to quit. A stormy interview of two or three hours ended by my brothers going to a hotel and Sweeney and I going off together to discuss matters."

In the end, Ed and John decided it would be better to retrench and make a fight for survival. The cutback was made at once. Old *Penny Press* files reveal some short-term loss of spark and variety in the news. But neither circulation nor advertising fell off; revenues from both showed substantial increases, to the amazement of Scripps and Sweeney. By the end of the year, the *Press* would be making a profit of close to

$100 a week, and in January 1880 would declare its first dividend — $600.
(And it would see profits begin a steady climb: $12,072 for 1880, $16,384
for 1881, $24,732 for 1882, and $32,912 for 1883.)

This experience taught the moody Ed a valuable lesson: "There, in
that case, was demonstrated to me . . . that men make money and
money does not make money. It is the man that makes the newspaper,
not the man's capital." Buckling down and whittling costs, Scripps discovered that neither he nor Sweeney, healthy and in their mid-twenties,
had been exerting themselves to even 50 percent of their capabilities.

"We had to steam up a little," Ed recalled, "to think a little harder,
work a little harder and — poof!!! went all our difficulties and all our
fears."

It began as a routine entry on the Cleveland police blotter. One John
Smith had been arrested for beating up a prostitute in a public brawl.
Maurice Perkins was the *Penny Press* reporter covering police. He either
knew, or was tipped by a friendly cop, that "John Smith" was actually
the son of one of the Chisholms of Cleveland society. Henry Chisholm
was president of the Cleveland Rolling Mills and his brother William was
the other principal owner. Both had sons; Henry's was named Stuart
H. — and the initial is of crucial importance in this episode — and William's son was named Stuart, without a middle name or initial.

In his police court news, Perkins wrote that Stuart H. Chisholm had
been arrested for disorderly conduct. Unfortunately, he had listed the
wrong man; the culprit was the other Chisholm, his cousin Stuart, the
son of William.

The item was printed just as Ed Scripps was leaving for a few days'
visit in Detroit. He returned to Cleveland the morning of Saturday,
August 9, 1879. That was the day the volcano of indignation seething
inside Henry Chisholm over the "damned insult" would erupt.

At the office of the *Press,* Ed was informed of the serious blooper
Perkins had pulled. Technically, the item constituted libel, the reputation
of Stuart H. having been adversely affected by the misconduct of his
cousin. Ed shrugged, and went to have breakfast. "I had become used to
libel suits, and, while I was annoyed by the misadventure, I was not
greatly alarmed," he recalled.

He should have been alarmed. He returned from his hotel to find
the *Press* office in turmoil. Henry Chisholm had sent one of his clerks to
ask Maurice Perkins to come to the steel mill and explain what he knew
of the police case. Perkins innocently walked into a trap. In Chisholm's

private office, the steel tycoon, husky and about sixty, glowered at the frail reporter, a lean, tall, cadaverous young man.

A side door was flung open and a dozen burly steelworkers burst into the room. Seeing danger, Perkins attempted to pull his revolver, but the gun was knocked out of his hand. Perkins was dragged into a back room and stripped of all his clothes. Someone produced a bucket of black paint used in coating iron, and several brushes. His tormentors painted his skinny body from head to toe, and for good measure poured the last of the bucket on his head.

Henry Chisholm stood watching, "laughing gleefully on beholding the suffering of his victim," the *Press* would say later. The paint-coated reporter was thrown naked into the street where someone picked him up and drove him to his home.

All this had occurred while Scripps was leisurely having his bacon and eggs. News of the assault stunned him; he knew about paint and realized "that unless Perkins was immediately cleansed, death would almost certainly result soon."

Ed rushed to Perkins's home, found a doctor had been called, and that the reporter "had been scraped pretty clean" and put to bed. The nervous shock had brought on a siege of violent hiccoughing. Ed would recall: "I told Perkins that Chisholm had made a terrible mistake . . . and that soon his friends and attorneys would tell him this, and there would be a great effort to settle with Perkins and hush the whole matter up. Perkins's face lit up; he saw prospects."

Though a brilliant writer, Perkins was nonetheless so unstable that later he would be identified as "an opium-eater" and eventually, after a stellar career in New York, would jump out a window to his death.

Now Ed was studying the hiccoughing figure in the bed. He realized Perkins would be tempted to settle for a small amount, taking away the paper's opportunity to make a "sensation" out of the incident.

"Listen, Mo," Scripps said, "I'll personally guarantee you a $5,000 settlement. Let me send a lawyer to talk to you. But regardless I'll pay you $5,000, if no one else does."

Perkins continued hiccoughing. Ed told him that in all probability these spasms would stop when the shock wore off. "I advised him, however, not to try to stop it, or not to allow the doctor or his wife to dope him for the purpose of stopping it. He gave me a wink."

In rented carriage, Ed sped to his lawyer and dispatched him to Perkins, and then headed for Frankfort Street. Turning the corner, he found a mob jamming the street in front of the newspaper, apparently on the verge of a riot. The driver was frightened; he told Ed he had heard it "whispered around" that thugs planned to sack the *Press* office. He refused to drive any closer until the editor taunted him for his cowardice.

Ed stood up in the back seat, pulled out his revolver and brandished it above his head. "Now," he commanded his hackman, "drive straight into that mob. You have a right to the street!"

The milling men fell back and let the buggy through. Ed saw no angry faces. He recognized the men as employees of Chisholm's rolling mill "who simply were under orders. . . . I think they would have mobbed and gutted the office had there been no serious obstacle to overcome."

At the locked front door, John Sweeney, brandishing a pistol, let Ed in. The rear door was guarded by the foreman and printers with guns and mauls. The confrontation was touchy. The hesitant mob milled around, making no move to rush the building. Ed suspected police had been given instructions from the political bigwigs to play it cool; but the cops couldn't ignore the threat of riot for too long, either. In about thirty minutes police arrived. The mob dispersed. No one was arrested.

Ed anticipated Chisholm would next utilize ordinary legal routines. There would come, he felt certain, arrest warrants for criminal libel. Several of his employees were property owners. He began arranging with them to put up bail for any *Press* employee who might be arrested.

As expected, a deputy sheriff arrived about 9 A.M. with warrants for Scripps and Sweeney on the charge of criminal libel. Ed hustled the deputy, Sweeney, and his employee-bondsmen into carriages and went immediately to the courthouse to post bonds.

They returned to the office to find all work stopped. A second deputy stood there "attaching" the newspaper under a $50,000 civil damage suit warrant. The deputy ordered "hands off" by the printers until appraisers could make an inventory. Ed must post a double bond— $100,000. That sum was too large for his employees.

Ed argued with the deputy there was a Saturday paper to get out with a big story to splash. He promised none of the equipment would be moved or harmed. The officer shook his head.

The young editor looked frantically at his watch. It was after 10. When were the appraisers coming? The deputy sheriff didn't know. It was clear no official intended to hurry the process. Ed summoned his lawyer, Judge Paine, the father of the fat boy. Paine rode over to the courthouse and demanded some action. That didn't help much. But the two appraisers presently appeared.

Ed paled when he saw Edwin Cowles and William Gleason walk in, smiling wryly. Cowles not only was the *News-Leader* publisher with whom Ed had been trading page one personal insults, he was as well a

Republican kingpin who could make any city or county office-holder dance. Gleason, formerly of the *Plain Dealer* pressroom, was the county's ranking Democratic power.

Ed had Sweeney quickly bring forth all their invoices of purchase, showing exact cost of the whole plant. He offered them to Cowles. "With these you can appraise the whole place in five minutes," Scripps said.

Cowles declined. He announced he was going to personally inspect and appraise each and every item — cellar to roof.

Scripps and Sweeney had a bigger problem, anyhow — getting a $100,000 bond. There were in those days no bonding companies. Ed knew several prominent business men who had gone out of their way to applaud the little paper for honesty and fearlessness. "Naturally I turned to them for help," he recalled. "Naturally enough, they deserted me — every last one of them."

He wired his brothers in Detroit to bring or send a substantial deposit and his Cleveland banker would then provide the $100,000 bond. The day dragged on. Late in the afternoon Judge Paine finally departed, advising Ed to be patient and let the law run its course. He could think of nothing else to do.

Not only did Ed fear the Saturday issue wouldn't come out but also that the delay in posting bond might keep the paper shut down for several days. Thinking hard, he paced restlessly. Of a sudden his face lighted up, and he tore down the stairs. In his buggy he whizzed six blocks to the little cottage where Judge Paine had his law office.

The judge was out front on the sidewalk, tipped back in his cane-bottom chair. Ed leaped from his carriage. "Judge, what rich man do you know in this town who hates Chisholm as bad as Chisholm hates me?"

The lawyer started, and then settled back to think. In a minute or two he slapped his thigh, threw back his head and guffawed loudly. "Come on, Ed. I will go with you and get him."

They drove across town to a shabby cottage. Judge Paine went inside and brought out Samuel G. Baldwin, old, scrawny and unkempt, dressed like a day laborer. Ed's eyes popped. Could this be the rich man who could post a bond for $100,000? Quietly, Paine explained that over the years Baldwin had amassed half a million in real estate in the red-light district where he acted as bondsman for the prostitutes and thieves.

Why did he hate Henry Chisholm? Years ago Baldwin and Chisholm had been involved in a law suit. Something Baldwin said on the witness stand infuriated the steel tycoon, and as the little man stepped down, the brawny Chisholm slapped his face. Baldwin swore a grudge to his dying day. Lawyer Paine, fortunately, had remembered that incident.

In five minutes they had Baldwin at the courthouse. He readily signed Ed's bond, making it unnecessary for the appraisers to finish their slow chore. With fresh court orders turning the plant back to Scripps and Sweeney, and dragging along a deputy sheriff to promptly enforce them, Paine and his client galloped back to the newspaper office.

Dusk was settling. It was close to 8 o'clock. How long would it take to go to press?

During the troublesome day, Ed and Sweeney alertly had hidden aces up their sleeves. Barred from working with their own type, Ed had slipped over to a neighboring job printery and, by paying liberally, made arrangements for his printers to use the job shop type and galleys. This enabled the *Press* crew to make preparations for issuing the Saturday edition.

Henry Little and Bob Paine and others wrote the story of the attack on Perkins, and its aftermath—the mob and the nasty legal moves to close down the newspaper. Between jumps, Ed edited the copy.

Thus when the all-clear came, it didn't take long to make up the forms and slap them on the *Press*'s old turtle-back.

The other Cleveland newspapers had printed not one word of the trouble between the *Press* and Chisholm. Even so, the city was abuzz with rumors of the confrontation. These started when the afternoon *Press* failed to appear on the streets at its regular time. By word of mouth, gossip spread of mysterious goings-on. Citizens were eager to get their hands on a *Penny Press* and learn the facts.

Anticipating heavy demand, Sweeney had assembled several hundred extra newsboys, and hired a small armada of buggies and wagons to gallop these hawkers and their bundles to the outlying sections of Cleveland.

Everyone worked at top speed. Finally about 9 P.M., the turtle-back began spewing out papers.

The story was headlined:

— — — — —

9 O'clock Extra!

— — — — —

ATTACKED!

— — — — —

The Press Office In The Hands
Of The Sheriff

— — — — —

A Part Account Of
The Affair

— — — — —

Then followed an abbreviated story of the assault on Reporter Perkins and the subsequent legal attack on the newspaper. Covering only basic facts, it ran about five hundred words. Obviously Ed was in a hurry to get on the streets.

Everywhere people grabbed the little penny sheet, and gasped in surprise at the vengeful actions of an important citizen. Ed kept the turtle-back grinding until midnight, turning out three or four times the normal run. Even on Sunday, newsboys were still peddling copies.

That was, of course, merely round one. Scripps and Sweeney still faced Chisholm's libel suit — which could send them to prison — as well as the $50,000 civil damage suit which imperiled their entire newspaper operation.

On Monday August 11, the *Penny Press* did not make much of the episode, except to announce Scripps and Sweeney "hold no malice, but are keeping an armed guard day and night" at the newspaper office. On August 12, the *Penny Press* carried this item: "The *Plain Dealer* made a small mistake. Will the Chisholms attack them, too?"

The enormity of his offense began to dawn on Henry Chisholm. One report said members of the Baptist church, where he was a deacon, refused to take communion with him. But he had his attorneys working on Perkins, trying to buy him off. Perkins kept dutifully hiccoughing, but his weakness worried Ed. "[Perkins] was sorely tempted; for to a man who was getting fifteen dollars a week, a roll of bills of about five hundred dollars looked like a fortune. I had great trouble to keep him down."

Suddenly, from a most unexpected source, Scripps got strong support. His bitter rival, Edwin Cowles, published an item in his morning edition asserting the *Leader* could not condone the paint-bucket attack on the reporter.

Against one of the richest men in town, Ed knew he was still at a great disadvantage in carrying on a stand-up fight. So he resorted to his strongest weapon — ink and paper. In the August 18 issue, the *Press* carried this brief at the top of the lead column on page one:

CHISHOLM'S INFAMY
On Saturday, the 9th of August, 1879, Henry Chisholm, president of the Cleveland Rolling Mills Company, enticed Maurice Perkins into his rear office and there committed a brutal outrage upon him. Chisholm laughed gleefully on beholding the suffering of his victim. The *Leader* does not and cannot justify the attack on the reporter.
— The *Cleveland Leader*

This was not to be just a one-time item. Ed's idea was to keep the story alive "to remind the people of Cleveland every day of what Chisholm had done. . . . I did not propose to allow the incident to be forgotten." It was clever on Scripps's part to attribute condemnation of the steel tycoon to the *Press*'s known bitterest newspaper rival. That made it stronger than Ed Scripps's own self-serving complaint.

After the item had appeared at the top of page one for about a week, Ed's friends began to warn him the "Infamy" blurb revealed Scripps's own vindictive character and would hurt his newspaper with the public. He turned a deaf ear. Every day he published the "Infamy" item — in the same spot, but giving it a clever twist. To show it was more than a local issue, that journalists elsewhere deplored the black-painting of a reporter, Ed in several issues attributed the item not to the *Cleveland Leader* but to another daily that had reprinted it, the *Hudson Enterprise.* Then for a longer period he credited the blurb to the *Ann Arbor* (Michigan) *Democrat,* which added its own deadly postscript: "Hanging is too good for the low-lived scoundrels."

Reports came to Ed that Chisholm "was suffering terribly in spirit" because of this daily reflection on him. He ceased to go to his office, said the rumors, kept off the streets, and refused to attend social functions. He was an obstinate Scotsman, refusing pleas from his family that he make peace with the paper. He would not make the first move. Meanwhile, Perkins, reported by the *Press* to be "jerking on the verge of death," sued Henry Chisholm for $25,000 damages.

With the town gossiping about "Chisholm's Infamy," early in September his banker and his doctor came to Frankfort Street and climbed the dingy stairs to the editor's tobacco juice-splattered office.

Chisholm, they asserted gravely, had been driven to bed, seriously ill — wasn't that punishment enough? "All this," said the doctor, "is costing Mr. Chisholm his health — and probably his life." The editor was not moved. "Mr. Chisholm," Ed said bitterly, "showed no mercy to that poor weakling reporter, and is entitled to no mercy from Perkins's employer and friend."

Scripps told the banker his duty was to advise Chisholm to immediately pay Perkins "a handsome indemnity" and withdraw his libel suit against the *Press.* The visitors brightened. They already had Chisholm's pledge he would do that the moment the paper quit publishing the "Infamy" paragraph.

The red-haired editor bristled, and demanded his adversary make a personal surrender. The visitors left, with his message. Ten days later Chisholm's chief lawyer brought direct word to Ed: "That Mr. Chisholm felt he was a dying man, that Chisholm was really a Christian, and that he wished to right the wrong and prepare himself for death." Ed doubted the steel man was even close to dying; he had looked robust.

Still, the "surrender," plus a promise to pay Perkins $5,000 and withdraw the suits against his newspaper satisfied him. And on September 18, 1879, the item headed "Chisholm's Infamy" disappeared forever from the *Penny Press*.

Ed carried news of the settlement to the still-abed reporter. "I told Perkins to quit hiccoughing and get up and dress and go back to work or go off on a frolic."

The tragedy did at least hasten Henry Chisholm's death. Perkins did not receive his money until January 7, 1881; Chisholm died a few weeks later. Ed was shocked. In his autobiographical "History of The Scripps Concern," he wrote:

> I may be mistaken, but I have never believed that remorse killed Henry Chisholm. But neither have I ever had any doubt but that Chisholm's death was caused by me. Had I taken a pistol and shot him to death, I would have felt no more and no less responsibility for that death than I have ever felt since.
>
> It is true that I did not know I was killing Chisholm when I was killing him; but I believe that had I known I was killing Chisholm at the time, I would have pursued identically the same course, and I would have felt no more remorse—no more guiltiness—under those circumstances, and I have felt none. Then I believed I was not only doing what was right, but that I was actually performing a public duty.

By the end of 1879 Ed Scripps was already beginning to get restless and dissatisfied, though the little paper was then turning a one-hundred-dollar-a-week profit. Life was becoming humdrum and he dreaded what he called "the bitter ennui of slow-going success." He wrote Annie:

> I still feel constantly impelled to reckless deeds of folly—to kill time. . . . I have grown to have a positive hatred of the city. I despise my paper. The former is peopled with the most vile, dishonest, impure hypocrites and flunkeys that ever breathed. The latter is such a little thing and cost such an unconscionable effort that it sickens me. True I might build it up to be a great paper, but that is not what James wants. He wants it to make money.

If James and George would only give him a chance, he could make them millionaires, pushing their interests "the length and breadth of the country." In the same breath, he told his sister that "I am owing money right and left and altogether I fancy I am the most indebted man in the city."

Being financially hard-up didn't scotch Ed's dreams of owning a bigger paper—perhaps all by himself. He was offered half-interest in the *Chicago Telegraph*. "I know it could be made profitable," he wrote Annie. "I want to go to Chicago. I am tired of living in country towns." He took the train to Chicago and examined the *Telegraph*—but didn't like what he saw.

If he was not to move on to Chicago, then why not to the Windy City's ambitious rival, that burgeoning Missouri metropolis on the west bank of the Mississippi?

At the end of February 1880, Ed had done his hard thinking and was all set to strike out again to pioneer more cheap journalism. He turned over the running of the *Penny Press* to John Sweeney and City Editor Henry Little, and climbed aboard the southbound train.

7

Those St. Louis "Mudhole" Blues

On the verandah of the Planters House, Scripps settled into a rocker, lighted his after-dinner Santa Fe, watched April dusk settle over the impressive skyline, and tried to size up St. Louis. The depth of "southern" overtones in this gas-lit, horse-drawn metropolis surprised him. He was struck by the city's marked gentility and casual pace, the drawling patois, the white-jacketed black waiters, the Negro hordes along the levees and on the streets, the abundance of "old Confederates." The ethnic mix included early-day French, zesty, brawling Irish, scrupulously clean Germans, the latter making up a third of the 350,000 population.

He observed that conservative St. Louis—some rivals dubbed her "stodgy"—took her newspapers seriously. Was it ready for another daily—the *Evening Chronicle?*

When Ed strolled to the corner of Third and Chestnut to look at the leading newspaper he was taken aback by the size and magnificence of the *St. Louis Republican*'s five-story brick building impressively capped by artistic gables and mansard lines. It was a morning paper of 20,000 circulation, with Sunday and weekly editions that gave it influence throughout rural Missouri. Its arch rival, the morning *Globe-Democrat,* had an imposing plant at Fourth and Pine. Both newspapers were violently into politics.

In the afternoon field his *Evening Chronicle* would have to butt heads with Joseph Pulitzer's money-making *Post-Dispatch* which had fast presses and a modern plant at 321 Pine Street. The city's three or four German-language newspapers did not concern Scripps.

His first impressions were good. St. Louis had an encouragingly large blue-collar market—and a boom was on. Just six years earlier completion of the Eads bridge, of three steel-arched spans—an engineering marvel that took seven years to erect—had eliminated the difficulty of bringing by ferry all railroad freight and passengers into the city from East St. Louis. Long the nation's leading flour miller, St. Louis now was growing in shoe manufacturing and brewing. Packetboats still lined the river but their era was ending as railroads expanded. St. Louis was truly a working man's town.

The morning papers were old-fashioned blanket-sheets, selling for five cents a copy. As in Detroit and Cleveland, they wouldn't necessarily impede a new daily. The scrappy *Post-Dispatch,* however, was a different story! Though he had written Annie he was now "trembling with ambition," the invader unaccountably began to get cold feet. He felt certain St. Louis would readily accept the Scripps brand of cheap journalism. But he cringed at the prospect of family infighting about a new startup. Certainly no venture could be launched here on a measly $10,000 capital.

The lone St. Louisian who knew Ed Scripps's secret mission was the city editor of the *Republican,* thirty-four-year-old Stanley Waterloo. They conferred privately half a dozen times at the Planters House. With his own ambition to launch a new St. Louis afternoon daily, Waterloo had contacted the Scrippses several weeks earlier. He was a seasoned man, an 1869 graduate of the University of Michigan, with experience as a reporter on several Chicago newspapers. His bold ideas and quick mind impressed Ed; he agreed Waterloo could buy one-fifth interest in the new *Evening Chronicle* and be its editor.

Waterloo, too, developed some misgivings. He feared the *Post-Dispatch* had seized the blue-collar market. He was in awe of its forceful proprietor, a Hungarian refugee who served as a paid conscript in Lincoln's cavalry. The skinny and sickly Pulitzer had come west in 1866 to scramble for a toehold in St. Louis's strong Teutonic atmosphere. The boy tended mules, worked as a waiter, hackdriver, even helped bury victims of a staggering cholera outbreak. All the while he was learning English and making powerful friends who appreciated his sharp mind and knowledge of chess and the classics. They helped the beak-nosed, near-sighted émigré parlay his wit and energy into a varied career—political handyman, legislator, lawyer, and newspaper reporter.

When the *Dispatch* went bankrupt in 1878, Pulitzer bought it for $2,500 at the sheriff's sale. Smartly and promptly he engineered a merger with the tottering *Post,* and now the combined *P-D* zipped along with 8,000 circulation. Pulitzer, now sole owner, was clearing $40,000 annually. He was in 1880 only thirty-three and still a human dynamo. On a shoestring he had out-Scrippsed the Scrippses!

In launching his *Post-Dispatch,* Pulitzer had promised that his newspaper "will serve no party but the people . . . will oppose all frauds and shams whatever and wherever they are; will advocate principles and ideas rather than prejudices and partisanship." Thus he had pretty much thrown his arm around the same credo the Scrippses had enunciated in launching the *Detroit News* and Cleveland's *Penny Press.* Pulitzer and Scripps also were alike in espousing the blue-collar cause, and sensational and crusading reporting.

After quietly looking over the scene for about three weeks, Ed concluded they should invade St. Louis at once. But his brothers had reservations. James, in particular, was not sure it was a good venture. Ed took the train for Detroit. James noted in his diary April 30, 1880: "Ed arrived this morning . . . reports favorably on St. Louis project." Still the brothers could not reach a decision. James dispatched George to St. Louis to talk secretly with Waterloo, look around, and give his opinion. May dragged on. Still no decision. Ed, glum, returned to Cleveland.

"On return have been idling," he wrote Annie May 11. "I am afraid my St. Louis project is going up in smoke. If it does I will probably go to Cincinnati or Pittsburgh. . . . I am getting greatly bored here. Wish I could run away and hide someplace. I don't fancy the bother of another paper a cent's worth, but I suppose I should soon be just as tired of doing nothing."

Abruptly, on May 19, James decided the *Evening Chronicle* was a "go." Ed returned to St. Louis. Now it was his turn to have second thoughts — becoming victimized by his own contradictory nature. In deep depression, feeling he had "become a fool," he poured out his heart in a letter to Ellen:

> Why had I not clung to the old life on the farm? Why had I abandoned the life of books? It would have been tiresome but had I not tasted the excitement of the town I never would have known how dull it was. It is quite possible that I should have much sooner become reconciled to it than I will ever be to this feverish discontent that now possesses me at all times. . . .
>
> Why was it necessary to lay myself on a rack of mental torture in order to forget how slow the hands moved on a dial, how many hours it took to make a waiting day, how many days make a year, and how many years it took to make a life? Then I thought of Florence, of Rome, Paris and of the many things of beauty I had seen and wanted to see again. . . . I am growing old. My freshness is fading, my capacity for enjoyment is dying so terribly fast. Then, too, I feel my life is to be a short one. But that has never caused me regret.
>
> Today I almost resolved on one thing . . . after I have got one more

paper either here or elsewhere on its feet I would lay down my work and go ahead for one long year and forget myself if possible among the strange and beautiful sights of the old world.

Ed certainly was in a rebellious mood for one scheduled to start a daily newspaper from scratch in just three weeks. "You may wonder why I do not say more about the proposed new paper," he informed Ellen. "The reason is that I do not feel the slightest interest in it tonight. . . . It will be a success and I am going to work hard to make it so. But enthusiasm I have none left. I am too lazy just now to work up even a tolerable affection of such a feeling."

The *Evening Chronicle,* the only paper in town to be priced under a nickel, would start up about June 12. Ed had the romantic notion that it ought to debut on his birthday—June 18; but that would be a Friday, not considered suitable for a first issue. The elder brothers dictated a modest start. Only $130 a week was budgeted for the entire editorial expense, with Ed and Waterloo each drawing thirty. Ed wanted each to get fifty. James proposed sending George to be business manager and Ed preferred John Sweeney. "George has ten times the mental and moral calibre that John has," he wrote Ellen. "But calibre is not what I want. I want work. Mean, nasty, disagreeable work. . . . George's health will not permit him to do too hard work." Ed suggested George take over the Cleveland paper while Sweeney came to St. Louis. When George rejected that, Ed snapped at him: "If you think I am big-headed and riding a high horse, why crack me on the head and knock me off the horse, and come here yourself, or send anyone else you want. I am willing to clear out. . . . There is too damned much mulishness in this firm." Ed sent James a nasty letter, accusing him of "absolute niggardliness" in starting the *Chronicle.* Overnight Ed cooled off. He wrote James and George he had "acted somewhat hastily."

But a veritable explosion took place in Detroit. James fired back a stinging letter accusing Ed of "arrogance, visionary bombast, and drunkenness," and overstepping his authority. He ordered an immediate halt to the St. Louis project. Adding insult, James sneered that Ed's judgment was "only mediocre." This letter hit Ed "like a clap of thunder" that left him "panic-stricken." He was opening his mail at dinner at the Planters House. "For the first five minutes . . . I felt like running, some wild thoughts of the far west, the gold fields and so forth flashed through my mind. . . . By the time I finished my ice tea I was thinking of other matters."

Determined to "save" the St. Louis venture, Ed promptly went to his room and scratched out an apology. "I was impatient of delay," he wrote James. "I was desperate and wrote a foolish letter. . . . You should remember that I am only twenty-six years old and have had a very loose moral and mental training." Before he could post this letter, a second from James arrived with harsher criticism. It jarred Ed. He tore up his first letter, and sent a groveling telegram. Then in a new letter he denied the "false" charges, admitting it had been "inexcusable" for him "to get angry and write a peevish and silly letter. . . . I am ashamed of myself."

Hastily, Ed petitioned Ellen to intervene in the family quarrel. He felt surprised that his brothers "find out for the first time that I am an arrogant, assuming, bombastic, champagne-drinking knave, and yet with all an amusing cuss. . . . I know I am conceited but I never hesitate to obey orders when I understand them."

Having enlisted Ellen as peacemaker, Ed took the May 29 night train to Detroit. Ellen met him at the depot with word that James had cooled off. Ed's own wrath had abated. "So we all met and had it out pleasantly enough," he informed Annie. But nothing changed. It was still to be a shoestring start-up. Waterloo was to be editor, George business manager, and Ed "superintendent." Ed predicted that within two years each would be making $10,000 annually. James and George would advance all capital, taking 6 percent notes for Waterloo's and Ed's stock, 20 percent each. "If the paper fails, we would lose nothing," Ed told Waterloo. "That's why they ask us to work for small salaries."

As summer came on, Ed was finding his vibrant libido steamy — and active. His mistress Elizabeth Brown spent several weeks in St. Louis. And, casually and carnally, Ed squired local girls. His random womanizing was not secret from his Cleveland colleagues. In a gossipy letter from the *Press,* Bob Paine remarked: "How's 'tail' in St. Louis? The girls here . . . have become so cussed high-toned that they've raised the price way above the reach of a man of moderate income."

Ed's sexual adventuring, his whiskey drinking, steady smoking, and his periodic bursts of frenzied work in starting the *Evening Chronicle* — all took their toll. Losing weight, he was headed for severe bouts of illness. His indulgences seemed more a mysterious psychological need than pleasure. He could not easily fall in love; but he truly yearned to marry and settle down and raise sons. An unmarried man, he wrote Annie from the Planters House, is always "more or less of a bummer and a rascal." For the sake of business, "if nothing else" he ought to think of settling down to a decent, respectable life.

When letters revealed that Ed was considering offering Jessie Sweeney or Fanny Bagby a job on the St. Louis staff, Annie expressed concern. Obviously she had qualms about either being under Ed's dominion. After all, he had thought of Jessie as a possible bride, though she was his cousin, and Cousin Fanny was also young, lively, and fetching. Ed took pains to reassure Annie. "No, I advise you to keep perfectly easy on account of the girls coming here. You may get mixed up in one of those uncomfortable family rows. . . . It is a matter of pure business. You need not fear for anything else. Besides, I shall at most not remain here over six months . . . and no woman is connected with my plans."

On July 2 the carefully guarded secret was out. St. Louis learned it was getting a cheap new paper. Ed made the announcement in the Sunday papers. He listed the partners as Waterloo, "late of the *Republican*," George, and himself. The "capital, experience, and skill" concentrated on the *Evening Chronicle,* said the announcement, should make it "as grand a success" as the *Press* with 16,000 permanent circulation in Cleveland, and the *Evening News* with 27,000 in Detroit, and similar cheap papers in Chicago, New York, Boston, and Philadelphia.

The price of two cents, or ten cents a week, "doubtless will secure it immediately a circulation far in excess of any that has before been attained. . . . While cheap, it is proposed to maintain a standard of excellence not a whit below those of the other St. Louis papers. . . . First issue will be 20,000 copies. . . . Advertising rates at the outset will be comparatively low." The first issue was to come out July 24. But the press arrived late from New York — and a part had to be rushed back for repairs. Finally, the *Evening Chronicle* made its debut Saturday, July 31, 1880, with a sale, James's diary noted, of 16,000 copies. St. Louisians had never seen a newspaper so compact. In size, appearance, tone, content, and slant, it was virtually a carbon copy of the four-page Scripps papers in Detroit and Cleveland.

Heavy or serious news in the first issue was at a minimum. There was a five-hundred-word account of musicians setting new rates: $7 for Sunday steamboat excursions, $10 for balls that last until 5 A.M., $16 a week for theatre productions. Another long article explored the rise in railway mail thefts, and the slim chance of catching the crooks. Many news items were small-town gossip. Examples:

PURSUED BY PHANTOMS
About 7 o'clock this morning a man rushed wildly down Chestnut Street crying for help. He was taken to the Chestnut Street station by Officer Fenlon. He said he was pursued by two enemies. He was suffering terribly from delirium tremens, and was sent to the hospital by Sergeant Watkins.

A BATHER DROWNED
August Moeller, thirteen years old, was drowned in the river near Pittsburgh Dyke, East St. Louis, yesterday afternoon while bathing. The body

was recovered shortly afterwards and conveyed to the residence of his parents at 1222 North Ninth Street, this city.

EDDIE SNOOKS' LESSON
Eddie Snooks, thirteen years old, living in the rear of No. 1320 North Seventh Street, was squirting a hose at short range at the rear end of a frisk mule belonging to his father, when the animal reached Eddie with his off hoof, and caught him on the scalp, raising a slight abrasion.

As in its sister papers, the *Chronicle* printed a long piece of fiction, "Lord Wilbury's Ruin" — in Ed's style. Doubtless because of St. Louis's heavy Negro population, there was a dialect piece in which an old plantation mammy recounted the exploits of her master's three daughters under the heading, "Yallabama's Cinderella." Half of page one and about a quarter of the others contained ads — offering for sale tents, hats, stationery, silverware, oysters at Tony Faust's, shoes, trusses, family medicines, barber services, dry goods, groceries.

When the *Chronicle* was barely a week old a new quarrel exploded between Ed and James — over starting a new paper elsewhere, in Buffalo, New York. The idea originated with Mike Dee of the *Detroit News* and Henry Little and John Sweeney of the *Cleveland Press*. Each had been expected to be cut in for part of the St. Louis paper. Only Sweeney got a piece, 10 percent. Dee and Little were about to quit and try to launch the Buffalo venture. Ed blamed James's selfishness. Hotly, the Detroit patriarch accused Ed of meddling and intransigence. Finally James quelled the revolt by awarding equal quarters of the stock to himself, Dee, Little, and Sweeney.

Not only frustrated and unhappy, Ed was actually ill. He had the worst cough of his life. He had to leave his office and go home, almost fainting. Part of his health problem had to be worry over the *Chronicle*'s dismal start. It lost money heavily and was "going down, down, down," Ed wrote Ellen. George wrote for advice on enlarging the paper. James, assuming the idea was Ed's, replied "the damned fool" who advised it should be fired. George blew up, again threatening to resign. Ed jollied him out of it. They cut their pay to $10 a week, "the wherewithal to pay our cigar and lemonade bills."

Ed was busy fending off all-out war from Pulitzer's *Post-Dispatch*. Never had Ed been up against such an aggressive, mean rival who tried dirty tricks. Shocked, he reported to James the *P-D* was bribing *Chronicle* carriers to transfer their route customers to the Pulitzer paper.

Though the Hungarian was much more mature because of his seven-year age seniority, there were striking similarities between Pulitzer and Ed Scripps—right down to their red whiskers. They shared a number of traits in common: intellect, imagination, daring, personal courage, the keen nose-for-news instinct, belief in the common man's right for a good life. They were both pistol-packers, though only Pulitzer had drawn blood with his weapon.

The *Post-Dispatch* shop "was a paternalistic chaos presided over by a Pulitzer who could be enthusiastic, eloquent, indignant, or profane but never quiescent. He had the rare ability to communicate his fervor and sense of mission . . . drove his staff hard . . . and himself harder . . . and mingled with them in shirt-sleeves." As a young legislator in 1870 Pulitzer had fired his four-barrel Sharp's pistol at a burly lobbyist who had called him "a puppy and a liar." The lobbyist was only wounded in the knee, but the episode dampened the Hungarian's ardor for gunfire.

Though the *P-D* publisher was known to go armed, that did not spare him other encounters. While carrying home a sack of tomatoes, he saw a thug start across the street toward him. Pulitzer "flung a tomato at the man" and fled into his house. But in March 1880 when Editor William Hyde of the *Republican* knocked Pulitzer down in the street in a political argument, the near-sighted publisher, his glasses broken, managed with difficulty to draw his revolver from under his heavy overcoat. Bystanders wrested the weapon from him, and no shots were fired.

There is no indication that Joseph Pulitzer and Ed Scripps ever had a face-to-face encounter in St. Louis. Where the philosophies of the two became poles apart was on unionism, in which Ed fervently believed. Not so Joe. Pulitzer paid well, $35 a week to top reporters, with two-week paid vacations, paid sick leave, gold watches and other prizes, and a Christmas feast for the newsboys. He believed in treating printers fairly but when they tried to organize his backshop, he threw out the leaders and fired union sympathizers. He assailed their bargaining effort as "simply one form of mob law" that would force a newspaper "to take out a license . . . from irresponsible . . . unknown men who assume no risks and share no losses." In the same period, Ed was writing sister Annie: "Tomorrow I have to meet a committee of printers who want their wages raised . . . whom we can neither afford to pay more or offend by a gruff refusal."

Fearing the *Chronicle* was going to sink, a frightened George dispatched an SOS by telegraph August 25 to James, who grabbed his hat and reached the scene at 5 o'clock the next afternoon. Ed again threatened to quit. He wanted $50,000 new capital. James offered $15,000. Also cheap shots from the *P-D* disturbed Ed. "I understand the ordinary business of obtaining circulation," he observed, "but I am not accustomed to underhand work. . . . The peculiar circumstances of the case perplex me greatly." James studied the situation, realized he'd have to re-think his down-hold, and authorized Ed to spend $250 a week to build circulation. That should have satisfied Ed. It didn't. He wrote Ellen: "I am to stay here six months. I am not glad of it. I do not feel confident of my health holding out so long. . . . I am really doubtful of my ability. . . . They are expecting too much of me."

Even so, Ed plunged in and quickly had "the office considerably improved" and found his work "more interesting and engrossing." The paper gained 200 subscribers a day. He got James's permission to go into the editorial department "and breathe a little fire into it." He explained to his brother:

> I want characteristic men writing for the *Chronicle*—men who when they write dip their pens into their gall or their heart's blood and not into the colorless saliva that drivels from their mouth. . . . Waterloo is making the same mistake I first made in Cleveland. He is making a complete newspaper. I learned that success did not so much lay in having everything in the paper as in having *everything* that was in the paper *good*.

By the first of October the *Chronicle* still lost $100 a day. Even so, Ed went to Detroit, demanding "full control." James gave him total sway editorially, but not in the business office. The perked-up Ed crowed to Ellen:

> All my victories have been won by reckless ouslaught. A successful charge is always better than a siege. By vehement self-confidence and egotism and arrogance, if you will, I have won more in days than patient merit would have gained in years. . . . Should I know that three months hence I would be a corpse, I would not change my present plans one iota.

On October 28 Ed wrote Annie, "I am feeling pretty well just now, as we are getting off an excellent paper."

Two days later, James made a historic entry in his diary: "The *Telegraph*, our new Buffalo paper, made its appearance today."

The *Chronicle* circulation jumped to 13,000 on strength of the Presidential election, and then fell back to 10,000. In the day-to-day fight, Ed frequently found himself in "a very disagreeable wrangle, and brute force and pure impudence are about the only way I have of obtaining my way."

Somehow Ed seemed to feel he was winning the battle of St. Louis. He took time to socialize more. "Out to a card party with three pretty ladies and three gawky men. Bad whist players. Had bad cards. Great bore." Discontented, he again felt itchy feet. On December 21 he disclosed to Annie that he was going to Chicago to make a new attempt to buy the *Telegraph.* "The *Chronicle* is now safely on its legs"—an astounding statement, of course!—"and I am getting impatient to get away from this horrible mudhole city. J. E. will object to my going into Chicago but George backs up the idea strongly . . . I think I shall be quite as well off at hard work as loafing around drinking and smoking as I have been doing a good deal of during the past few days."

As customary, Ed and George spent Christmas with James. Seeking a way of bringing the family interests into some order, James told his diary December 28: "Settled upon organizing the Scripps Publishing Company in which consolidate our various newspaper interests." Adapting to journalism the holding company structure then coming into vogue, James made the initial move that was to eventuate as America's first newspaper chain. The Scripps Publishing Company would hold the family's stock in Cleveland, St. Louis, and Buffalo—but not Detroit. James intended to keep his flagship *Evening News* a safe harbor against any calamity that might befall the expansionist publications. Ed went on to Chicago—to encounter more discomfort and disappointment. He reported to Annie: "I met McIntyre in Chicago. He was drunk. I got very drunk myself, but kept very close to my room in the hotel and suffered nothing worse than a headache."

His bland assessment that the St. Louis paper, five months old, was safely on its feet seemed to have come out of Ed's bottle. In some fashion James felt Ed had assured him the *Chronicle* would "make the riffle" with the advent of 1881. It came nowhere near it, of course—and it seems extremely incongruous that the penny-counting, fiscally sharp Detroit brother could have accepted any such rosy forecast. In mid-January, James blew up and angrily descended on St. Louis. He demanded Ed step aside, but the kid brother jumped to his feet, blamed "circulation and advertising blunders" by others and brazenly demanded total control—and got it!

"The terror of my life," he wrote Annie, "has been a fear . . . I might fall [off his career ladder] and break my neck. . . . I tremble now lest I have taken one step too many. . . . I am standing now at the top of a pile of very loose stones and if one of them slips, I'll come to the bottom a mighty bitter fellow." Ed staved off disaster only long enough for James to send brother Will to replace George. On January 28 James again stormed into the *Chronicle* to have an "overhauling" of Ed and "bring him down seven pegs."

Until midnight and late into the next afternoon, the brothers squabbled. James proposed giving Will and Waterloo control, leaving Ed "barely managing editor." Furious, the kid brother argued against that for three or four hours, and then threw up his hands. "James, I told you when I lost control of myself, I would leave the paper. That has happened. Hold as security for my debt all my stock in the three papers, but allow me twenty dollars a week for the next year, and I'll leave you to run things as you see fit." It was something to consider but James, possibly at George's urging, began to soften. They talked further and finally James backed down enough to leave Ed in charge "for the time being."

That was just delaying the inevitable. Even Ed had lost all hope of eventual harmony. He wrote Ellen: "I'll never have another business engagement with him until he has apologized for calling me a muddler and a liar. P.S. This letter had better go into the fire." A greater concern gnawed at Ed. Was he perhaps losing his mind? "The worry . . . has unsettled my mind somewhat," he told Ellen, " . . . and I sometimes fancy that maybe my words and actions indicate even a degree of insanity. It must be that this is the case for I have never before experienced such difficulty as I am having in holding my own with my associates."

In the sleet, mud, and fog of the "mudhole city" that he now hated, Ed came down with the worst cold of his life. "For twenty of the twenty-four hours I am either asleep or in too much pain to think of anything. The doctor is robbing me. My landlady is ill and I have a little newsboy sleep on my sofa and take care of me. He is good little fellow, but I am afraid he will get tired and run away. What will we do?" That question, in a letter to Ellen, may had been only rhetorical. But she gave him a jolting answer—stern advice that seemed too harsh to issue from the pen of his surrogate mother, indicating Ellen obviously was gravely concerned for his physical and mental health. On February 17, 1881, she wrote him:

> It seems to me that the time has come for you to stop work for a time. In the first place your health evidently demands a rest from the embarrassments and you would probably find yourself after a few months of perfect freedom from care, annoyance and labor in a condition to resume business under far more favorable conditions. . . . There is no reason, no necessity, pecuniary or otherwise, for your sticking to business when it's to your detriment otherwise. You have enough to live on, and live luxuriously, if you did not another stroke of work.
>
> Throw up your active connection with the *Chronicle;* go abroad, throw off dull care and give yourself up to the *dolce far niente* until nature, the great healer, shall have restored you to a fit condition to cope with the difficulties and complications.

Two days later Ellen offered to come to St. Louis and nurse him, as she had Pa. But by then he was better.

The sage counsel from Ellen had started a decision forming in his mind, or rather, perhaps, hastened it. In St. Louis Ed Scripps could not hack it — not now. The bustling city, still a strange environment, the *Post-Dispatch,* and all its dirty tricks, his colleagues, some tending to be false friends, the family bickering to which no end seemed in sight, his own quirky mental state, with wild highs and bluests of lows.

Something, probably a combination of these pressures, was doing him in!

Even the weather was his enemy. March 4 brought St. Louis the most miserable day he had ever encountered — "rain, mud and dust, all mixed together." It was the day President Garfield was being inaugurated in Washington. "But we cannot get a word from our special correspondent sent on for reporting the big show. Hence we are writing the thing up from home, dating it from Washington and putting big headlines over it. Of course it is a fraud, but there is no greater fraud than the whole presidential business. I am in doubt whether the country ever had a president with a title honestly acquired."

On March 12 wearily Ed made his decision. He took the photo of Lida Scripps off his mantle and stowed it safely in his valise. He gazed out on the dreary winter landscape; he knew there would be no bowbells sounding out along the muddy banks of the Mississippi to call back this Whittington to be the Lord Mayor of St. Louis.

"My health is broken," he wrote Annie. "My spirits are depressed. My weakness is confessed. . . . I have lost a great deal of money here. . . . I fear for my sanity. Aye, I am plunged into the deepest of the fearful abyss, the blues!"

With his tail between his legs, the beaten man slunk off to the depot. He was abandoning Waterloo and his brother Will and the sick, sick, sick *Chronicle* to the not so tender mercies of the voracious Joseph Pulitzer and the vagaries of the "mudhole city."

8

The Pain of Libel and Love

A m I a clap-trap humbug, or a genius?"
Ed Scripps studied the question he had
just scribbled. Night was falling over Cleveland, still caught in winter's icy vise. In the
tobacco-splattered editor-in-chief's sanctum of the *Press,* he was trying
to report to Annie on his fate since slinking away from the ignominious
debacle in St. Louis.

"I have not," his letter continued, "made up my mind. I rather
suspect the former. If that be so, I have done well. If the latter, there are
other avenues for quick flying ambition, if I do not choose the slower
and surer path that now lies before me."

From St. Louis he had gone directly to Detroit and completed the
scheme "which in my anger I had abandoned" — formation of the Scripps
Publishing Company. Stockholders were James, George, Ellen, John
Sweeney, and Ed. The S.P.C. would have full control of all business
interests outside of Detroit. This network of newspapers had just grown
by one. James had invested $10,000 in the scuffy little afternoon *Penny
Paper* that the young Wellman brothers had a year earlier launched in
Cincinnati, taking control and sending C. A. Worthington, the *News*'s
first circulation manager from Detroit to direct its affairs. The other
S.P.C. papers were, of course, Cleveland, St. Louis, and Buffalo.

Cleveland's keenest and meanest journalistic rivalry raged between
Edwin Cowles's once-dominant *Leader* and *News* versus the blossoming
evening *Press.* Largely because it was cheaper, and scrappier, the one-
cent *Press* in its first twenty-eight months leaped to an average daily
circulation of 17,716. The combined *News-Leader* sold only 7,000 copies
a day; the other Cleveland dailies, the *Herald* and the *Plain-Dealer,*
distributed 7,500 and 1,500, respectively.

In March, the *Press* on page one accused the *Leader* of a "bare-faced lie" in daily publishing a claim that it had more circulation "than all the Cleveland newspapers combined," and Ed offered to give $500 to the Newsboys' and Bootblacks' Home if the claim could be proved. The Cowles organization made no response to the dare. More than a newspaper war, the rivalry was a bitter personal feud between Cowles and Ed Scripps—as clearly demonstrated by the Chisholm episode, and other confrontations, and in-print insults hurled between them.

Ed had blood in his eye. He yearned for fresh harpoons to jab into his hated competitor. So his face lit up in mid-April when he heard that the *Leader* was losing so heavily that Cowles had to place a mortgage on his own home to raise needed operating funds. Straightway he sent a *Press* reporter, M. J. Haley, to interview Cowles and ascertain the facts. When Haley started asking questions, Cowles exploded, and some sort of clash occurred between the two.

The *Leader* got first crack at the story. In its April 13 edition it reported Haley had come to Cowles saying he was "a reporter on that blackmailing penny sheet, and wanted to show him a scurrilous article." Cowles was quoted as saying he "attacked Haley with a pencil, and kicked him down stairs into Superior Street."

The same day the *Press* struck back furiously: "The *Leader* today adds some of the blackest, foulest lies to a list already too long for publication." The Scripps paper explained it "honestly desired" to give Cowles a chance to comment on the report that the *Leader* "was on its last legs and Cowles had to mortgage his home." The *Press* continued: "Cowles has in the last two years never missed an opportunity to malign and insult the editor of the *Press,* who is sensitive because he is young and a stranger to the city. Three times Cowles has denounced Ed Scripps as a blackmailer. Can anyone believe that a wealthy and thoroughly sound corporation which has gained a reputation for honesty would try to squeeze money out of poverty-stricken Cowles? Age, great financial difficulties, political mortification, and family trials and ill health have rendered Edwin Cowles well-nigh imbecile."

The *Press* quoted Cowles as lisping to Haley: "Peck a little loudah, I am tomewath hard of hearing."

Haley was not kicked down stairs, corrected the *Press,* asserting: "It is quite credible to fight a live lion, but to maltreat an almost dead jackass is quite beneath the dignity of a *Press* reporter."

The two papers kept lobbing insults at each other until on Friday April 15 Ed published this page one editorial that proved a blockbuster he would come to rue:

A PRECIOUS CREW

The people have witnessed the old style of Cleveland journalism.

To start with, the old man who lost the roof of his mouth by youthful indescretions and who now edits the *Leader,* uttered a witless, thoroughly transparent falsehood.

All the papers are a sorry lot and the *Press* takes no pride in their company.

That constituted a terrible costly blunder — slander of the most vicious type that on its face appeared very likely false but even if true hardly possible to prove in court. Ed had published sheer, indefensible libel!

Heaping on coals, the *Press* reported without substantiation also that Cowles "lost his horse and his watch at lewd and disreputable places." These libels were, of course, more than any public figure would suffer without retaliating.

Cowles did the expected — and Ed and the *Press* went through somewhat of a replay of the Chisholm embarrassments of 1879. Filing libel charges, Cowles went straight to the heart of the insult, saying the *Press* allegation that he lost the roof of his mouth "meant by venereal disease."

Ed's last edition on Saturday April 16 was rolling merrily off the turtle-back at 4 o'clock when Deputy Sheriff Freeman strode in and shut down the newspaper. Brandishing a warrant, he attached the property, pending appraisal, for damages. On his heels came a constable arresting Ed on a charge of criminal libel. James DeVeny, a printer, went with Ed to post $500 bail on the criminal charge. Again arose the threat of the plant being tied up for appraisal. Ed sent an SOS for Judge Paine to again come to the rescue with Sam Baldwin, the red-light district bondsman.

Thus it was not until 7 P.M. that the *Press* was able to flood the city with an "extra" detailing its latest woes. In the flush of excitement, Ed mistakenly looked on the affair as something of a stunt that would bring favorable notice to his little paper. That evening he wrote Ellen:

I am convinced that for business reasons we should congratulate ourselves. . . . The last thing that any Clevelander would think of is that the *Press* would be blackmailed. . . . Every time I have shown any anger in the case everybody laughs at me for fearing the effects. . . . I have consulted Judge Paine about the case and he only laughed at it.

It certainly was no laughing matter. Henry Little and John Sweeney and others pointed out the grave danger. Little couldn't see how Ed "will avoid paying a big sum and being convicted. Unless he can prove how Cowles mouth was diseased and that he did perform certain indiscretions, I fear he will be in a bad boat." Promptly Ed changed his tune, showing great fear. He wrote Ellen: "I am in for it again. . . . I am as blue as ever a man was. . . . Though I laugh, swagger and boast, I feel tears starting . . . [but] I must stand up to the rack, bear the torture. . . . I am going to prepare for the battle . . . the biggest job of my life." His first move was to counterattack, having Cowles arrested for criminal libel on the "blackmail" allegation. Then Haley sued Cowles for $30,000 damages.

In mournful, soul-searching letters Ed blamed his misfortune on his wretched health and his desperate unhappiness, the latter stemming from his ill-fated romance with his cousin Lida Scripps. To Ellen he confessed: "I cannot plead as an excuse of all my misdoings . . . a broken heart. At a certain time a certain party was in my plans of life. The failure of this has thrown me a little off track . . . a little more adrift than I was before. . . . I know that I should not be trusted with a pencil and paper. I am simply off my mental balance."

With startling candor, Ed disclosed that for some time he had occasionally used an opiate, the inference being it was morphine. "During the trying days of the *Chronicle*'s early history I seldom resorted to this remedy except when necessary to sleep or go crazy, or when in great physical pain. I have taken it by injection under the skin. I have as great a horror of such a remedy as you have. . . . I am simply discontented, restless and unhappy. Yes, I am certainly going to Europe this fall if I can possibly get away. . . . The chances are now three to one not only of my being convicted but of me being sentenced to imprisonment. . . . Would it not be a novel experience if I should spend one of my birthdays in prison?"

In Ed's latest feud the key element seems to have been virtually overlooked or ignored—the simple question of the veracity of the allegations about Cowles. There is no correspondence in Scripps's files which makes any claim that he actually had the goods on his arch rival. Surely he would have found occasion to comment on such proof, most likely to have boasted, because truth of the damaging allegation would have been surefire defense in his upcoming libel trial.

Ed's repeated threats to give up and run away and hide clearly indicated he again was in the evil clutches of his contradictory nature. "The thing idleness is doing for me," he wrote Ellen, "is giving me lots of time to think. The result is I am thinking myself into a state of self-contempt and self-meanness never before experienced in my darkest

days of morbidness. . . . I feel that I had rather be half-crazy with foolish thoughts than half-idiotic with liquor. . . . My mental strength is just
like a woman's smile. For the greater part of the time it is weak and
flabby, but at rare intervals I feel like a giant."

Ed's mental stability perhaps was at low ebb on July 2 when the
telegraph flashed word that an assassin had gravely wounded President
James A. Garfield in Washington. Garfield was shot as he walked into
the capital's railway station. Carried to the White House, he hovered
between life and death. The *Press* put out its first "extra" at 11:30 A.M.
and by 4 o'clock 30,000 copies had been printed. About dark Ed asked
the telegraph editor for the latest bulletin. "Sinking fast, doctors hopeless; he's evidently dying," said the wire editor. "Gee!" exclaimed
Scripps. "We've got white paper for only 2,000 copies, but it would
hardly be safe, would it, to announce his death?" And Scripps went
home.

The telegraph editor assumed he had been told what to do. He
fabricated a story saying Garfield had died and rushed out another "extra." That night 2,000 *Press* readers stood on the corners, their arms
around one another's shoulders, shedding tears of bitter, personal grief.
Garfield did not die until the following September 19. The fake "extra"
didn't seem to faze Scripps. In his Monday July 4 paper only this faint
apology:

> The President, dead or dying, is creating a tremendous impact on the
> political scene.
> The Associated Press report of the President's death at 7:10 P.M.
> Saturday was so much in accordance with the probabilities that it found
> universal credibility all over the country.
> How the mistake came to be made can easily be imagined.

In the summer of 1881, Ed's ten-year obsession with his pretty
cousin Lida Scripps suddenly flared into a crisis. He was beside himself
to marry her. Lida, a year or two younger than Ed, lived with her parents
at Astoria, Illinois, a small town fifteen miles northeast of Rushville.
Her father was a well-to-do banker. The parents were horrified at the
thought of marriage between first cousins. Lida, who had hardly seen Ed
since village school days, was not impressed with his haphazard, off-and-
on, long-distance courtship, largely by letters.

She was stunning. Her honey-blonde hair, silky and glinting in the
sun, usually was piled atop her head, pinned neatly. His mind's eye
tormented him by catching, very often, the pulse throb beneath the

milky satin of her swan-like neck, the sparkle of her even teeth, her full pouty lips. He dreamed again of the soft timbre of her voice, her light gentle fingertips, the smell of her—blossoming pink roses.

Despite his other crises with business, the family, his own health, he devoted hours and hours in contemplation, intrigue, and action to try to win her. Finally, the first of May, he mailed her a marriage proposal. "It was very brief," he told Annie. "It had no nonsense. It was simply a direct statement of my affairs in a business, health, and social way, all of which were marked down to be on the safe side. Then I made the proposition and asked for an answer. I have not yet had time to receive a reply. You may think I was foolish to do this. I do. . . . Whatever the answer will be, it will settle the question forever, and that was necessary for my peace of mind."

Lida left Ed dangling; he must have construed her weeks of silence as another rejection—but still didn't accept it. And on his twenty-seventh birthday—June 18—was still struggling to keep himself "pure" and worthy of Lida's love, but at the same time ready to run away from everything. He wrote Ellen that he'd never be able to settle down. "I would like to tear myself out by the roots . . . and make a bold plunge into some newer life. I can't help getting in some kind of a scrape. . . . I feel like defying something or somebody all the time. I read novels and play whist to keep my mind out of more dangerous occupations." He urged Ellen, as soon as James returned, to go with him for a year's tour of Europe.

Then a few days later came Lida's answer—negative. Ed seized her response and tore into the task of analyzing all nuances of the letter. Lida seems to have pleaded a superior filial "duty" to parents. "I would like to think I had lost her through such heroism of the heart," he confided June 24 to Annie. "However, I do not believe a word of it." He wondered if her father thought him a fortune hunter, or if Rushvilleites had maliciously "magnified" his vices to her. He said forlornly that "probably Lida and I will be old folks before we see each other again." He asked Annie to "by any means" discover the true reason for his rejection. "Probably the real reason is that she does not like me well enough to accept me under any condition."

Ed later went to Rushville, and spent several days. It is presumed he met Lida face to face, at least once. Whatever transpired, he came away gloomy. Writing Ellen August 24 about this trip, he complained that Fred seemed not inclined to talk to him and "Annie and the women folks in Rushville are talking and stirring up trouble." He did not mention Lida.

Although the Cowles libel case exploded in April it lay dormant through the summer, scheduled for trial October 12. In August Ed secretly tried to reach an out-of-court settlement. He felt that "would be cheapest and easiest way out" and he should pull it off because it had been his "ridiculous blunder." He also was "pulling strings" in Columbus and Washington, and proposed to "support the Republican" in the fall elections in exchange for getting out of his jam.

On September 17 James returned from Europe. He was not unhappy about the state of business in the main, but made clear that it was up to Ed to get out of the Cowles scrape as best he could. Real fear welled up in Ed's heart. He wished "a hundred times a day I was out of it." He imagined himself behind prison bars. But he didn't give up; he began fighting dirty, trying to unearth scandal on Cowles.

Ed's libel trial began Thursday morning October 13 before Judge Tilden and a packed courtroom. Judge Paine was assisted in the defense by noted Cleveland lawyer Martin A. Foran. They entered a not guilty plea for their client who sat beside them while jurors were selected. This slow process was done with great care on both sides. Bias ran deep in the city; both defense and prosecution wanted favorable, or at least impartial, men in the jury box.

A certain line of defense testimony was proposed by Paine and Foran. Judge Tilden rejected that as inadmissible. The defense lawyers turned to Ed, questioningly. He appeared, for a moment, in shock. He slumped in his chair. Looking crushed, he sat silent a minute or two. Then he pushed back from the table, sat upright, his shoulders squared and his red-bearded face tight. He gave the bench the full glare of his "evil eye." Then he leaned over to Paine and Foran and whispered a few words.

Judge Paine blinked and laboriously got to his feet. "If it pleases the court," he rumbled, "in view of the adverse ruling just now rendered, our client chooses to offer no defense of any nature to these charges—and will let the verdict of guilt or innocence rest with this fine jury." The old lawyer paused, and then placed his hand on Ed's shoulder. "Mr. Scripps has no fear now of the felon's cell since, under the circumstances, no dishonor can come from his incarceration." Judge Paine sat down.

Before the case could go to the jury, there were closing arguments to be made. In the main these were plain-spoken orations dealing not so much with the alleged libel, but rather out and out appeals to poor-versus-rich bias. Bluntly Foran told the men in the jury box it was "not a case of libel . . . and besides Cowles started it. The *Press* is the poor man's friend and the aristocrats are trying to crush it."

Judge Paine, a commanding presence and a strong orator, called the criminal charges merely a newspaper fight. "Only the enemies of Ed Scripps are testifying," he asserted. "They are trying to hurt his business and help theirs. The *Press* is the only paper in Cleveland that *dares* to speak its opinion concerning men in public life. It is always on the side of the people and justice. It is no wonder that the great hate it, and the humble love it."

The old attorney tugged at his coat collar and then expressively spread wide his arms. No one, he said, believed Cowles had a vile disease. He ambled to the rail of the jury box, and then turned and faced the spectators. He stared at them for a long moment, giving his head a faint waggle. There was a look of mischief in his eyes. Slowly he turned back to the men on the jury and studied their faces.

Judge Paine cleared his throat. "If it was said of Mr. Foran," he began, jerking his thumb at his cocounsel, "that he had been discovered in a flagrant attitude in the Water Cure Woods, and that he had been discovered in a peculiar position in a church, or that he had taken a woman to Buffalo and spent the night with her in a room there after which she returned to Cleveland no worse than when she went away because she had not been well served, then it might be believed of him that he could have contracted a loathsome disease, but no one would believe that of Cowles, of me, of the court — "

A burst of laughter interrupted him — joined in by spectators, jurors, and some of the attorneys.

The prosecutor in final summation called the *Press* article "an infamous libel" and made a ringing demand for a guilty verdict and severe punishment of Ed Scripps. On Thursday October 20 Judge Tilden completed his instructions and at 10:30 A.M. the jury retired. Ed watched them file out, realizing the enormity of his reckless gamble. He had offered not one word of testimony in his own defense. For a time Ed remained around the courthouse. Outwardly he looked calm; inside he trembled with fear. Perhaps deciding on no-defense was a terrible blunder. If that backfired, he'd surely wind up in prison.

Two or three hours passed. Behind locked doors, the jurors obviously were having a struggle. Restless and worried, Ed left the courthouse and went back to his office. The afternoon dragged on. There was no sign a verdict was near. The jurors emerged to eat supper, and again retired behind locked doors. No word came from the jury room until the following morning. The foreman, a man named MacIntosh, brought them back into the courtroom to ask Judge Tilden to clarify one item in his charge. "I didn't close my eyes until 5:30 this morning," MacIntosh said. "We argued and balloted all night long."

Ed was at the courthouse early that morning. Cowles, looking care-worn and anxious, arrived late. The first edition of the *Press* carried a headline: "27 Hours." The jury had been trying that long to resolve the case. The *Press* story said "jurors could be heard through the thick doors after supper debating and arguing." A courthouse rumor began to circu-late that they stood eight to four for acquittal, "but with no chance of reaching agreement."

After lunch Ed and his lawyers returned to the courtroom to await word. One o'clock passed. Then two. At two-thirty, the jurors began their twenty-ninth hour of deliberation. At five minutes until three the jury bell rang, calling the bailiff.

There was a scramble in the courtroom. Judge Tilden came from chambers and mounted the bench. Assistant Prosecutor Loren Prentiss came in. Ed and his lawyers stood up as the jurors filed in a little after three.

They had reached a verdict — Not Guilty!

For a moment Ed stood frozen, stunned by disbelief. Then he gave a heavy sigh and broke into a huge grin, and leaped across the room and grabbed jurors by the hand, smiling and pumping their arms.

So it was all over. The most dangerous crisis in his young life had passed. He had gambled, and won. On page one of his next issue, Ed attempted a magnanimous gesture. An article headed simply "The Libel Suit" said: "The *Press* wishes its thousands of readers to believe in its sincere regret for having been surprised into a vulgar expression of tem-per on its part." But Scripps could not resist the temptation to both pat Ed Cowles on the head, and then kick him in the pants, adding: "The *Press* has nothing but sympathy for its opponent who is old, decrepit, and unfortunate, with property heavily encumbered and cursed by an unhappy temper which obscures his native intelligence and business abil-ity." Now, finally free of the Cowles trial pressure cooker, Ed had reached another crossroad.

He yearned for escape — to run away. He had reasons aplenty. The "vile people" of Cleveland. Boredom of the daily humdrum of newspa-pering. New strife was on the horizon with James, and possibly even with John Sweeney. He fancied himself a heartbroken lover, now that Lida had finally "given him the mitten." His health was wretched, maybe dangerously so. He could not shake his cough; occasionally he spit up blood. Fearing tuberculosis, he consulted Dr. J. E. Jones. The physician was unable to confirm that he had consumption, but gravely recom-mended Scripps seek a milder climate and rest if he wanted to prolong his life.

"What about North Africa — Algiers?" Ed asked. He recalled the doctor's reply: "He said something to the effect that Africa might be just as good a place as any other for an unmarried man to die in, provided he had means to secure the ordinary comforts of an invalid or a moribund." At that time Ed estimated his annual income from $8,000 to $10,000, though he never saw much of it which went to repay stock-purchase loans.

Dr. Jones's opinion was merely a reinforcement, or a convenient excuse, for the decision Ed already had made. For weeks he had been arranging to put into effect his scheme of going abroad with Ellen for a year of travel and study. So, as the doctor had said, what matter whether he died in America or in Algiers?

But first he faced a wrangle about stock in the *Cleveland Press* he must settle with James. They met in Detroit and James's diary for Monday October 24, 1881, tells the result:

> John Sweeney arrived yesterday afternoon and spent the day at the house and holding meeting of SPC. Ed obstreperous and quarrelsome and day ended by my selling out to him all my SPC stock, 23 shares for $23,000, he paying 1 share *Evening News* stock at $5,000, paying $350 per month till $18,000 with interest at 8 per cent to be paid.

His business affairs now in tidy shape, Ed spent a few days packing his trunk and valise. At the Detroit depot on November 1, he and Ellen boarded the train for New York. They were booked to sail November 3 on Guion Lines' *Nevada* for Scotland — and a long vacation from the cares and troubles at home.

9

Blackmail from the Boudoir

His twenty months overseas materially changed Ed Scripps. He came home on the eve of his twenty-ninth birthday considering himself not only mature but in fine physical and mental trim, as fit as anyone he might go up against. He and Ellen had meandered lazily about Europe and North Africa. The "fleas . . . bedbugs . . . general filth" of Algiers disgusted him, but he lost his cough in the sunny clime and gained thirty pounds. In his Italian hotel room, Ed swung from the door frame and "developed big muscles" and practiced "turning handsprings over the bed." In the snowy mountains of the Holy Land, Ed and his sister raced their Arabian stallions down the treacherous trail to Damascus. He wore his pistol because their tourist caravan was robbed three times.

When they came ashore in New York June 1, 1883, Ed believed he had abandoned much of his youthful vanity and conceit, no longer was he ambitious to become great. His goal was to be "more human" and cast off some of his "pecularities and eccentricities."

"I was weary of all my philosophy and all my thinking," he recalled in his memoirs. "I did not care to learn anything more about anything." He had firmly resolved to be independent. He would not re-enter the newspaper business unless he could control the property he would manage.

Ed had to hurry on to Cleveland. There was a new mess in his private life he must attend to—which he described to Annie as "a little scandal . . . I thought it best to come face on the spot."

What he had to confront was a stir created by his former mistress Elizabeth Brown. She had been angrily complaining to the Cleveland newspapers that he had run away, leaving her penniless, inferring that

89

she had expected marriage, not desertion. Now she wanted revenge by public exposure of their former sexual alliance.

To his old newspaper colleagues, Ed offered a confidential but candid explanation. It was true Elizabeth Brown had lived more than a year at his expense, but he thought he had managed to "shake" her months before leaving Cleveland. Coming from a good family, had she been sensible, he calculated she might have become a Detroit socialite.

The concubine's wail that her ex-lover was a heartless wretch failed to produce any lasting uproar in Cleveland. But Elizabeth Brown still harbored a burning passion for vengeance.

Ed's most imminent threat was an upheaval brewing within the Scripps Publishing Company. All the papers except Cleveland were awash in red ink. James already had run up the storm flags, and was pressing for prompt realignment of the individual family holdings in the four papers. Ed, rankled that "you all think I'm such a blacksmith," begged time to examine conditions in Buffalo, Cincinnati, and St. Louis before being forced into any decision affecting his holdings.

John Sweeney wanted to break up their partnership. Showing excellent profits while Ed was abroad, he felt his solo direction of both editorial and business affairs of the *Press* would be superior. He pressed Ed to either sell his shares, or buy the Sweeney interest. James wanted Ed to consolidate all his holdings into one paper—the *Evening Chronicle*—and go to St. Louis and take command. The heavy debt the teetering paper had acquired frightened Ed. As for the *Telegraph* in Buffalo, it was virtually bankrupt, and James intended to unload it—for whatever token price the Buffalo *News* would pay to eliminate competition.

The property that most interested Ed was the puny little Cincinnati *Penny Paper,* now renamed the *Post.* In debt $10,000, it was a scrawny four-pager that had never made ends meet. What mainly attracted Scripps was the city, a thriving business port on the Ohio River with almost a quarter million population—plus the fact that it was the town's only one-cent daily. Besides, he was certain he could greatly smarten up the *Post.*

While looking over Cleveland, Ed let his heart dictate a detour. He took the train to Bloomington, Illinois, with a ring in his vest pocket. He was headed for Wesleyan University to propose to Jessie Sweeney. His cousin, not yet twenty-five, coyly encouraged him, then stunned him with a "no." At the moment Ed didn't resent the rebuff—but the turndown would savagely haunt him for months.

Jumping back into business, Ed plunged into a tug-of-war with James over the S.P.C. In Cincinnati, *Post* business manager Worthington was blue and desperate. Fearful the paper was about to collapse, he agreed to surrender his stock in the *Post* to Ed for $1 so he could in no way be held liable for the paper's $10,000 debt.

For three weeks the S.P.C. partners negotiated. Finally emerged a compromise! Ed felt gloriously triumphant. At last he had acquired controlling interest in at least one newspaper, the independence he had promised himself. His paper was to be the sinking Cincinnati *Post*. He was superbly confident he could end mismanagement and make it pay — handsomely.

At the end of the stock shuffle, Ed controlled six-tenths of the *Post*, eleven shares valued at a total of $15,000, and three-tenths of the *Evening Chronicle*, twenty-eight shares worth $22,400. To acquire this position, he had traded one of his Cleveland shares to John Sweeney and borrowed from James $35,000. Still owning fourteen Cleveland *Press* shares worth a total of $25,000 and one share of the Detroit *News* valued at $10,000, Ed thus had a total holding of stock valued at $72,400, encumbered by the $35,000 loan.

It was agreed that Ed not only would run the Cincinnati paper but also would be editorial director of the *Chronicle*, where James would control the business side. The Detroit patriarch was, of course, in the saddle at the *Evening News*, and planned to dump the Buffalo wreck as soon as he could. John Sweeney was left in sole command in Cleveland.

"We are all so far apart now and possess such exclusive interests," Ed informed Ellen July 6, "that I think we ought to get on without quarrelling further."

From the starchy white dining room of the St. Nicholas Hotel, Ed Scripps emerged into the morning bustle of downtown Cincinnati. A murky canopy hung low in the July sky, stretching from the tumult of the waterfront to quiet green summits of the seven hills. This smog, he mused ruefully, was a price paid daily for the throbbing industrial boom. All day long smoke would belch from trains and steamboats, soap factories and slaughter houses, iron works and machine shops.

Striding toward his squalid office in a twenty-foot alley called Home Street, he contemplated his newest newspaper battleground. Certainly this one did not scare him. He already sensed an advantage for his *Post* in the juxtaposition of the city's commercial, political, and social structures.

He looked up Vine Street toward the shady mansions in which brewery barons and millionaire merchants sought to surround their families with Old World culture, music, art. Over wine and after-dinner cigars their concerns were miles distant from the fretful and despairing thousands of blue-collar toilers whose sweaty aspirations rarely rose above their dollar-a-day pay, this evening's bumper of bug juice, and perhaps, for those with hot blood, an occasional sneak visit to a lupanar.

Between these high and low societies, political bosses had the city by the throat, mulcting the rich and crushing the poor under a cruel heel. Blatantly strings were pulled in city hall and statehouse by the Tom Campbell-Boss Cox machine. The powerful, of course, got the plums. To win clear sailing, gas company and traction monopolists and other boodlers readily divvied up. The courts were mainly corrupt tools of a band of crooked lawyers. Elections, the necessary key to power, were rigged and swung by sizeable armies of patronage dupes.

The working man was vulnerable. Uninformed, unorganized, and leaderless, he was easy prey. Gambling racketeers and unscrupulous saloon-keepers could skin him and chop him up just as deftly as any pig dispatched through the city's packing houses.

With a wry snort, Ed entered his "office." It was a single small room in which was clustered the entire force — editorial men, printers, advertising salesmen, the office boy, and business manager Worthington. Cheap pine railings separated the departments. In the basement was the rattletrap Hoe press. The whole layout was hardly worth $5,000. Somehow that didn't faze Scripps.

Expenses were running about $2,500 a month, with barely $1,000 coming in. Mentally, Ed toyed with schemes for converting this $18,000 deficit into a $10,000 profit. With scrappy crusades against "Policy Bill" Smith and similar miscreants, the penny paper was developing a strong following.

Circulation stood at 13,000. But 6,000 of this went at heavy expense into the suburbs and rural areas. Ed ordered outlying deliveries lopped off. From now on, the *Post* would concentrate on strictly city news coverage. In flair, condensation, and courage in printing Cincinnati news, Ed reckoned his little sheet could outdistance the opposition newspapers. As he sized them up, each had peculiarities that kept it from being a first-rate operation. Each of the rivals had business or political axes to grind. Ed, of course, had none. And he had the advantage of selling for a penny against higher priced competitors.

The *Post*'s afternoon rival was the fat and prosperous *Times-Star,* which rough-cut millionaire David Sinton had purchased to create a job for his son-in-law, Charles P. Taft, socialite half-brother of the future President William Howard Taft. Charles Taft had no talent for, nor real interest in, journalism. While he fandangoed in society, the *Times-Star* was actually run by general manager Louis R. Leonard. The *Times-Star* sold for three cents; the morning papers for a nickel. Ed had Leonard pegged as a "weakling," and characterized the nominally Republican *Times-Star* as a "trimmer in politics," devoting its main thrust to boosting Sinton's gas and streetcar franchise interests.

He watched his editorial staff checking the two morning papers. The strongest and most influential was the *Cincinnati Enquirer,* owned and edited by John R. McLean, who had inherited a considerable fortune from his father, a one-time blacksmith who rose to be a boon companion of President Grant and acquired his wealth dabbling in politics and real estate. With a reputation for being "dissolute, immoral and thoroughly unscrupulous," McLean attempted to imitate the style of the elder James Gordon Bennett's *New York Herald* and the notorious *Chicago Times* edited by Wilbur F. Storey. The *Enquirer* was the principal organ of Ohio Democrats.

"While it was reckoned a great newspaper," Scripps would observe in his memoirs, "it was universally regarded as being unreliable in its news columns; while it did not suppress much news, it distorted and discolored all news where such distortion and discoloring would serve the business interests or political ambitions of its editor."

The other morning sheet, the *Cincinnati Commercial Gazette,* Ed regarded as "extremely high class" in some ways. It was edited by Murat Halstead, ranked as "one of the three or four great editors of his day." It was "an out and out political organ of the Republican Party. Its editorials were fine. As a newspaper, it was not even third class."

Almost at once Ed fired up a public feud with the *Enquirer*'s "Johnny" McLean, hurling an assortment of slurs.

By a few odd turns of Fortune's wheel, Ed found himself both lucky and unlucky in his array of troops. The *Post* editor, the old Confederate cannoneer Robert Budds Ross, was out of action—grievously ill from a disease picked up from loose living. For weeks he had been confined to his room and colleagues considered the case hopeless. Sitting in as his substitute was a neophyte reporter, thirty-year-old John H. Ridenour. A curious character, he had vacillated between a career in medicine or the ministry after graduation from a small Ohio college. He had quit as a male hospital nurse to become a *Post* reporter.

Ed was satisfied with Ridenour's work but flabbergasted by what he learned of cub reporter Lemuel T. Atwood. Thirty-one, married with two children, Atwood was making but $7 a week, though he held a law degree from Michigan University and had been for seven years a practicing attorney.

"You ought to quit," Ed counseled. "I can't pay you more—you're still in your ABCs in journalism. You can make more money as a day laborer!"

Atwood shook his head. "No. God gave me a mind and a capacity to do my Maker a greater service than manual labor." A poor writer, Atwood's copy was as dull as a law brief. But he was accurate. And so loyal, Ed felt certain Atwood "would burn down my plant if I asked him to." He had no meat on his bones, his color was off, and Ed noticed him constantly chewing tobacco — apparently to ease his own hunger so his measly pay could feed his family.

Not long after Ed took over a "wild and insane-looking" stranger applied for a reporter's job, introducing himself as Delos R. Baker. A former thirty-dollar-a-week special writer on the *Enquirer,* he was married with several children. Ed wanted no *Enquirer* men, and certainly couldn't pay thirty a week.

"Give me fifteen dollars," said Baker. "The Lord will provide the other half. I know — I've prayed about this."

Ed wanted no fools. Baker persisted. Quizzing him, Scripps discovered the man had had a brilliant career in the pulpit until his church excommunicated him for heresy. "I want no unfrocked priests," said Ed. Baker remonstrated that his excommunication was no reflection on his character since he had only lost caste and his license to preach for rejecting a church dogma.

In finally taking him on, Ed wound up by fortunate happenstance with three religious zealots on his staff. Ridenour was a practicing Presbyterian, Atwood a confirmed Swedenborgian.

Precisely that combination triggered a tremendous circulation boom for the *Post* in the summer of 1883. It stemmed from the arrival of a young evangelist known as the Reverend "Boy Preacher" Harrison. He pitched his tent on the city's outskirts and started holding meetings. "Boy Preacher" intrigued Baker.

Buttonholing Ed, Baker said: "Now if this were a Democratic or a Republican rally, and we were partisans, we would be giving this detailed coverage, using lots of space. Well, we belong to the Lord's party, and partisans of the Lord are having a great rally here in Cincinnati, so why not deal with it the same way?"

Ed considered that thoughtfully. Ridenour and Atwood immediately jumped behind Baker's scheme. Realizing their dedication and enthusiasm would produce a superior job on an idea they had originated, Ed gave the green light. They wrote column after column on "Boy Preacher" Harrison. He became an overnight celebrity. Crowds flocked to his tent. He had to buy a bigger one, and move it nearer downtown. The *Post* took on a religious fervor, editorials frequently being prayers or sermons. The penny paper went so far overboard that Murat Halstead stopped Scripps on the street to chide him. "You've turned your paper into a regular Sunday School Advocate," he quipped. "Boy Preacher" took Cincinnati by storm. In three months he converted 3,000 lost souls.

The effect on *Post* circulation was staggering. In a just a few months it quadrupled. Once finding a good thing, the *Post* would ride this circulation-building wave by clinging for a long time to a policy of extensive religious and church news coverage, Protestant and Catholic.

Worthington, who had been sent by James to Cincinnati in 1881, was in Ed's eyes an incompetent blockhead. But before Scripps had to swing his ax on the business manager, Fate intervened. A rich uncle in Detroit left Worthington $100,000. He took the next train out of Cincinnati.

Logical choice for new business manager was the advertising solicitor, Milton A. McRae, twenty-five, a robust six-footer of Scotch-Canadian stock, assertive, aggressive and vain, an untiring human steam engine. A Detroit native whose father had failed in business, McRae had worked a short time as ad solicitor for the *Evening News* before James transferred him in 1881 to assist Worthington.

Ed really didn't like McRae. For one thing his pay was $25 a week, highest on the *Post* except for the editor. Too, McRae had an obnoxious habit of bluntly criticizing Ed's ideas for running the paper. He detested the "Boy Preacher" stunt until the beneficial results opened his dollar-conscious eyes. Having heard in Detroit of Ed's reputation as a womanizer and boozer, McRae, with raised eyebrows, was disinclined to accept Scripps's avowal he would wipe the slate and lead a clean life in Cincinnati.

Still McRae attached himself like a leech to Ed, running to and from the depot to carry his valise. He virtually monopolized Scripps's evenings and Sundays in incessant conversation about advertising and business— and himself. "He never lost an opportunity to blow his horn and to impress me with his great capacity," Ed recalled. Neglecting his wife and son, McRae literally tried to take over his boss, regarding him as a sort of "impractical genius" who needed a mentor and guardian although the ad man was four years Ed's junior. Even so, Ed elevated him to business manager, a step that was to lead to a forty-year association in which Mac would become his twenty-four-hour-a-day generalissimo, and eventually partner.

On Thursday August 2 a pretty woman in her early thirties, with radiant hair and a glint in her eyes, stepped off the train from Detroit. She asked someone to direct her to the office of the *Post*. Looking up, Ed saw Elizabeth Brown appproaching his desk. It was a moment he had long dreaded. For two years he had not laid eyes on her. But her showing up was not a surprise. She took a chair, and got right down to business. Ed must not cast her off; he must take her back.

"I love you," she said, "and will unto death."

Nervously, Ed stared across the desk. She looked fresh and radiant, supple, beautiful; her eyes were cold. Her scent wafted into his nostrils and sent his pulse pounding. Her nearness itself was a threat. He knew it was not romance — only blackmail!

He had discreetly kept tabs on his former mistress; he was aware that even now she had a new lover in Detroit, a businessman who wanted to marry her.

Ed steeled his heart and his nerve. He rejected her demand. Immediately she countered with threats. She vowed to follow him to his hotel and make a scene and disgrace him. She also would go to Rushville and reveal all his heartless perfidy to his mother and sisters, and to the village. Now only money could buy her silence.

In blackmail, Ed well knew, there is only one way out. He took it.

Scripps beckoned the acting editor, Ridenour. "This woman has a story to tell about me. Get reporters from the other papers over here — and summon a policeman."

Surprise flashed across her face. Then she smiled. It struck Ed that she liked the prospect of impending publicity, linking her to him.

Three opposition reporters arrived. McRae rushed in, wringing his hands. He begged Ed to not continue the confrontation, fearful the scandal would stigmatize the *Post* and wreck its business. The policeman appeared. Ed calmly related the story of their relationship, though the telling pained him.

"I think I lost nothing of her respect — a certain sort of devotion that such women have for their lovers — by the course I had taken," Scripps noted in his memoirs.

He asked but one favor of the reporters — that they mention he had come to Cincinnati with every intention of leading a clean, moral life.

Elizabeth Brown was arrested on a charge of disturbing the peace and obediently accompanied the policeman to the station. McRae tagged along to post $25 bond so she would not be locked up.

Immediately she returned to Ed's office. She begged him to not prosecute her. Her temper suddenly exploded and she shouted that such cruelty would make her want to kill him. Ed laughed off that threat. But later he wrote Ellen: "I will take ordinary precautions. . . . Of course I can't run away and it would be cowardly to prosecute a woman through fear of bodily injury."

Reverend John Scripps with wife Agnes
Corrie. (*Warren Wilkinson*)

George Henry Scripps (1790–1859) of
Rushville, Illinois, son of William the
Emigrator, and brother of Reverend John
Scripps, with wife Mary Hiler. (*Warren
Wilkinson*)

William A. Scripps, older half-brother of
Edward Willis Scripps. (*Warren Wilkinson*)

James Mogg Scripps, father of EWS, during his days in Rushville. (*Warren Wilkinson*)

Julia Adeline Osborn Scripps (1814–93), third wife of James Mogg Scripps and mother of EWS, her fifth and last offspring, and his father's thirteenth child. (*Warren Wilkinson*)

James Mogg Scripps farmhouse at Rushville, in which EWS was born. (*The Cincinnati* Post)

Rushville, Illinois, EWS's birth-place, about 1885, looking north on Congress Street. (*Warren Wilkinson*)

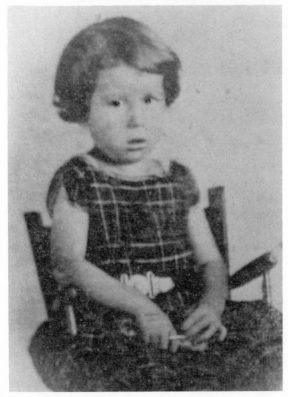

Earliest photo of Edward Willis Scripps at about three. In his unpublished autobiography EWS remembered sitting in his highchair in a little red-checked dress. (*Warren Wilkinson*)

Edward Willis Scripps, apparently in the
early 1880s when he was a busy publisher
and editor riding herd on newspapers in
Cleveland, Cincinnati, and St. Louis.
(*Scripps-Howard files*)

Edward Willis Scripps in a serious pose that
was published on the cover of *The Fourth
Estate,* a weekly trade magazine, dated New
York, Saturday, May 11, 1912, reporting he
was about to launch a new daily paper in
Philadelpia. (*Scripps-Howard files*)

James E. Scripps seated with wife Harriet in the garden of their
Detroit home in 1898 with son Willie, far left, and daughter
Grace. (*Warren Wilkinson*)

The James E. Scripps mansion at 598 Trumbell Avenue in Detroit.
(*Warren Wilkinson*)

Sketch of telegraph newsroom at Detroit *Evening News* in the
1880s. (*Warren Wilkinson*)

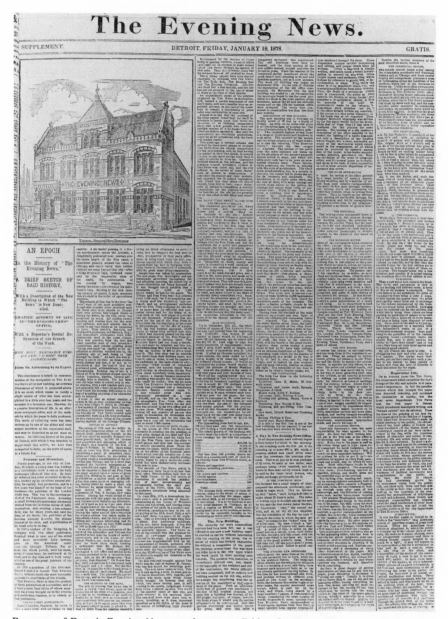

Page one of Detroit *Evening News* supplement on Friday, January 18, 1878, announcing that although only a little over four years old, the newspaper had erected a new building (shown in sketch) and reciting the history of the Scrippses from the time of William Arminger at the *London Sun*. (*Warren Wilkinson*)

Replica of page one of Cincinnati's *The Penny Press* of Thursday,
July 13, 1882. (*The Cincinnati* Post)

104

Inside page of *Detroit News* dated May 29, 1906, giving details of the life and career of James E. Scripps, brother of EWS. (*Warren Wilkinson*)

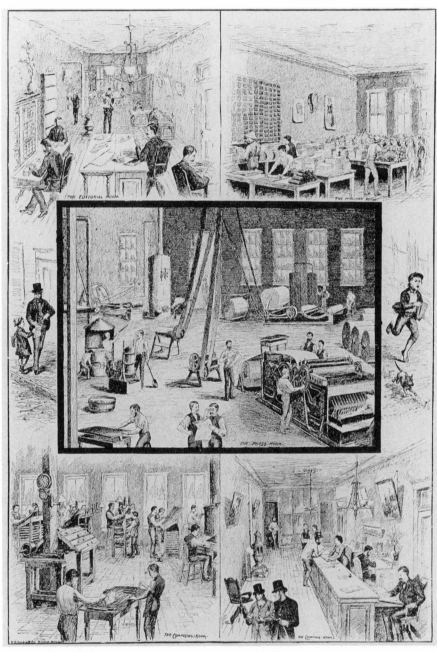

Sketch of the Cincinnati *Post* drawn by Peter J. Schaefer, and
appearing on September 26, 1885, in *The Graphic,* page 291. (*The
Cincinnati* Post)

106

Robert F. Paine, EWS's first editor in
Cleveland, and later his main editorial
chieftain of newspapers, wire service, and
syndicates, with pet bulldog, probably at
Miramar in 1890s. (*Paul K. Scripps*)

First home of the *Cleveland Press* on squalid Frankfort Street.
(*Scripps-Howard files*)

Scene from the secretaries' workroom at Miramar around 1910. This unidentified secretary is using an early "invisible" typewriter, probably a Remington. Note the many carbon copies being produced—the chronic mode for EWS's correspondence. Typebars struck from the basket beneath the platen which had to be lifted to observe what had been written. Also note the telephone for which EWS built his own line to San Diego. (*Paul K. Scripps*)

City copy desk of the Cincinnati *Post* in 1910. (*The Cincinnati* Post)

McRae escorted her to the depot, bought a ticket back to Detroit, handed her a small sum for travel needs—all at Ed's direction—and rushed back to the newspaper. He at once confronted Ed, demanding that Scripps get the story killed. Ed shook his head; he would not ask the other papers to suppress a legitimate story. That didn't stop McRae. He immediately braced Halstead and McLean, and at the *Times-Star,* Leonard. Halstead agreed to kill the story if Scripps personally made the request. McLean was willing to suppress the blackmail attempt if no other Cincinnati newspaper published it.

McRae dragged the *Commercial Gazette* reporter back to the *Post* to see if Ed would personally ask the article not be printed. Again Ed shook his head. That was strictly something for Halstead himself to decide. As a matter of fact, Scripps volunteered, if he had such an item involving Murat Halstead, the *Post* would print it. McRae turned pale.

And next morning he went stark white when he opened the *Commercial Gazette* and found on page four this headline:

SCANDALIZED SCRIPPS
**Peculiarly Perplexing Predicament
for Penny Post Proprietor**

— — — —

And All About a Woman

— — — —

Mr. E. W. Scripps' Indiscretions Get Him
Into Trouble—His Ex-Mistress Follows
Him About, And Is Arrested

Murat Halstead's paper left out no detail. The story ran half a column, asserting she was "hounding him for money . . . she became abusive and threatened to shoot him . . . [her] lips were white with passion, she could not speak coherently . . . while Scripps was in Europe she circulated all kinds of tales about him. . . . For a time it was the talk of Cleveland." The story said Scripps came to Cincinnati "five weeks ago and dreaded this meeting. He paid her bail and hired her lawyer."

Similar stories were published in the *Enquirer* and the *Times-Star.*

The day the scandal became public, Milton McRae dreaded calling on merchants who were buying ad space in the *Post,* expecting to be tossed out in disgust. He got no bad reaction. As Scripps later recalled: "As he went down the line . . . some of his customers joked with him about the incident and laughed; others spoke with some admiration; and even very real or affectedly pious men expressed their satisfaction with the man whose deeds coincided with the principles enunciated by his papers."

Journalistic legend credits Scripps with "splashing the whole story on his own front page." Far from the truth. Despite his bravado, when it came to having to hang out his own dirty linen, Scripps executed a shameful but masterful job of weasling in the *Post.* The only mention of the episode in his own newspaper was this tiny item at the bottom of page one:

Almost a Sensation.

Yesterday afternoon a woman entered the office of the *Post,* and attempted to make a scene at the expense of one of the managers. She was invited to leave at once, but refused to do so. A officer was called, who escorted her to the Ninth-St. station. The woman labored under the idea that she knew something which was valuable to her, but seemed to discover her mistake in short order. This morning she failed to appear at the police court, but the complainant was there ready to go on with the case. It is stated on good authority that she left the city late last night for a more congenial clime, and thus ended abruptly what might have been a sensation.

The *Commercial Gazette,* however, followed the episode to its conclusion, incidentally disputing the *Post*'s assertion that Scripps was in police court ready to prosecute. On Saturday August 4 Halstead's paper carried this eighteen-line item:

Mrs. Brown's Bond Forfeited

Elizabeth Brown, the female who has caused Mr. E. W. Scripps so much trouble, was called in police court yesterday morning to answer to the charge of disorderly conduct. After calling her name three different times without any response being made, the bail, $25, put up by Scripps himself, was forfeited. There was quite a crowd of spectators in the court-room, attracted by the sensational character of the revelations of the parties, expecting to hear startling developments. In this they were, however, disappointed as neither the prosecuting witness nor the defendant was in the court-room. Mr. Scripps' motives were questioned on all sides when it became known that he had procured the arrest of the woman, then bailed her out of the station house, and afterwards failed to appear against her in police court.

The event was not a nine days' wonder; but it did hit the press in other cities. Ed saw a long account of the editorial page of a large daily, headed: "Divorce Without Marriage." Two years later a Cincinnati paper would try to rehash the scandal "and that paper was universally condemned."

Ed explained and apologized to Ellen and Annie, saying he was "surprised and shocked at the way the whole affair has been treated by the public here. My morals are not condemned. I am applauded for not approving blackmail. It has done the paper no harm. It has done a little good in the way of advertising. . . . I am credited with good judgment in handling an embarrassing personal matter in such a cool business-like way. . . . I am now publicly on record as a certain type of man . . . branded for life."

By the third week in August Ed had climbed out of the dumps. He took the train to Detroit to confer with his brothers. Circulation of the *Post* was up by 4,000 a day. Receipts from advertising had doubled. These gains clearly impressed James and George.

"I've got to get the *Post* out of that miserable hole-in-the-wall," said Ed. "We need to put up our own building." They nodded assent. He sketched a rosy future. If progress was not interrupted, the first year's profit would be $100,000! John Sweeney, in Detroit to help celebrate the tenth anniversary of the *Evening News,* perked up at this astonishing statement. Ed thought he could detect wheels begin to turn in his cousin's head. Was he perhaps considering trying to revive the old team of Scripps and Sweeney?

Ed acted chipper. At the anniversary banquet he made half a dozen speeches. He drank a champagne toast to every lady present. Some old acquaintances in Detroit looked at him quizzically; he had just had his beard shaved, leaving mustache and goatee.

Then came an urgent telegram from McRae. Ed must return at once. Police were trying to arrest Editor Robert Budds Ross and a young reporter, F. B. Gessner, on a nasty charge of libel. McRae was hiding Ross in his house and had sent Gessner scurrying across the Ohio River to be out of jurisdiction in Kentucky. Ed jammed the wire in his coat pocket, clamped down on his cigar with a scowl, and hurried to the depot.

The *Post* had pointed the finger of corruption at Dr. John C. Beck, the city health commissioner. The druggist at Fifth and Elm, Eugene Spangenberg, complained that he had offered $50 to a saloon-keeper he understood to be the agent for Dr. Beck for the right to furnish medicine to poor people in Wards 18 and 19. Spangenberg told reporter Gessner that Dr. Beck gave the franchise to another druggist who paid $60. The *Post* on Friday August 24 published this exposé at the top of page one.

Dr. Beck exploded. He was in the clique of lawyer Thomas C. Campbell and "Boss" George B. Cox which controlled the city—usually supported by Johnny McLean and his *Enquirer.* The health commissioner marched into Spangenberg's pharmacy, hotly upbraided him, voiced strong threats, and repaired to the courthouse to swear out libel warrants. The newspaper's only evidence was tenuous—Spangenberg's oral statement.

Initially the paper sought to brush off the importance of the libel suit. On Saturday August 25 it published a squib captioned, "Dr. Beck On His Ear," saying the physician was "rash enough" to sue the paper, again repeating the gist of the accusation. On Monday August 27 the *Post* got a little tougher:

> The *Post* knows well enough it does no good to boast and brag. It has no intention of doing so. Its strength and pluck will be judged of better after it has got a little further advanced in a contest with a gang of political tricksters, unprincipled lawyers, and proprietors of gambling houses. . . .

Ed Scripps was now at the helm of the newspaper's defense. Tempers were rising, the Campbell-Cox gang beginning to sense a serious threat. The quarrel built up a terrible head of steam. The explosion came Friday August 31 when Scripps led Ross and Gessner, and McRae, and the *Post*'s two lawyers, Warner Bateman and Major Blackburn, before Police Judge Von Martels to enter pleas of not guilty, and to demand a jury trial. The judge was a servile tool of the ring.

As the hearing broke up, a gang of hoodlums led by George Campbell, Tom's brother, rushed the *Post* people. George Campbell sneaked up behind McRae and struck him in the head. The muscular McRae was staggered but threw a wild punch that floored his assailant.

The thugs seized the ailing Ross, dragged him into a side room, slammed the door shut, and beat his face bloody. McRae smashed the door with a chair and rescued the editor.

George Campbell, back in the fray, then led a dozen cronies rushing in a semicircle at Scripps. Ed stood his ground, fixing the hoodlums with his evil eye. Momentarily, they hesitated. When they came on and were about two yards away, he instinctively stretched his right hand toward his hip pocket. The half-circle froze, faces blanching.

"He's going to shoot!" someone screamed. The men turned and ran.

Ed withdrew his hand from his pistol pocket. He knew he would have shot to death the first man to touch him.

Back at the *Post,* Scripps went to his desk, got a pile of copy paper, and began writing "Scripps' Card"—his declaration of war on the Campbell-Cox gang. The article would fill two columns on page one the next day.

Dr. Beck, he wrote, was a miserable quack who had advertised his ability "to restore the seal of chastity of erring or unfortunate women."

The *Post* men, Ross and Gessner, were in dire need of a friend. "And, by the Almighty, I propose they shall find one in me at whatever cost." He deplored George Campbell's cowardly attack on McRae.

Then he fired a stunning broadside against Cincinnati corruption, signaling the start of an uphill crusade that would occupy the *Post* for three decades—until the Boss Cox yoke was finally lifted in 1925. His "card"—customarily considered a challenge to a duel—concluded:

> My attorneys caution me against making any indiscreet remarks about the case. I have told them I will make no remarks on which I cannot trust my reputation as a gentleman and a journalist, but I have no intention of showing the white feather.
>
> I shall do my duty in this matter as every citizen should. I shall demand a fair trial and make a fair fight, and if, for penning this article, which I consider perfectly blameless, I am imprisoned in person, pounded to death by thugs, or ruined in my fortune, I will not be so much the sufferer as the tens of thousands of other citizens of Cincinnati.
>
> If any friends of justice come to my assistance in this contest I shall advise them to leave me, on peril of their lives and their fortunes. But something ought to be done by the city at large, not to protect me and my friends, but to save themselves from public shame and disgrace.

The melee at police court was so crude that for once the other Cincinnati newspapers came to the defense of their little penny competitor.

On September 29 the libel case came to trial. Some of the jurors had been fixed. But the gang didn't reach enough; the jury hung—six for acquittal, six for conviction.

Through the trial Ed haunted the courtroom, fearing skulduggery. He sat all night outside the door of the jury room. Elated with the outcome, he sat down September 30, and wrote Annie: "I have not left the courtroom save for a half hour or so for the whole time until about an hour ago. The jury went out at midnight and I sat up watching and waiting for a verdict. I knew shortly after the jury went out it was disagreeing and I dared not leave the court for long for fear of a job being put up to 'work the jury' for conviction. The jury came in at half-past seven this morning reporting 'no agreement.' I consider this under the circumstances quite a record. You see, I have kept a clear record and never lost a case. I wish I were down in the woods picking up nuts or laying on the ground instead of being buried in this great smoky city fighting for life and money."

Fought to a standstill, the Campbell-Cox clique finally ended the episode with a *nolle pros* of the libel charges.

Apart from the fuss with Commissioner Beck, Ed encountered other flurries of turmoil. Two new libel suits popped up in St. Louis, for $20,000 and $60,000. In Rushville Ma somehow carelessly burned up a $100 bank draft he had sent. He promptly replaced it and urged her to spend more money to "gratify" him. He pushed ahead with building a new plant for his *Post,* plagued by his own underestimates of the cost. Politics intrigued him. He "took a little dip" and was "fairly successful" in a lively tussle with Cincinnati politicians, his "little paper scoring the first knockdown—only there are too many people who won't do just as I want them to."

His interest was, naturally, a peoples' party for the blue-collar class, imagining himself the potential leader. "Oh, I assure you that should I live here five years longer, I could get into Congress—whether I wanted to or not," he boasted to Annie. But Senator George Pendleton of Ohio came along, and, as he sadly told Ellen, "took possession of my party and kicked me out in the cold." That didn't kill the political bug that had bitten him sharply, but did shelve it for several years.

Suffering a cold, he lay abed one morning for a full hour thinking of changes. He decided to cut down on whiskey and work, to go along with Senator Pendleton in politics for the good of the common man, and resigned himself to freely spending money to build up his business.

In October came a message from Stanley Waterloo in St. Louis—he wanted to buy control of the *Chronicle* or sell his stock. "I one day may be a competitor in the same field," Waterloo wrote. The point could not be missed; his letter was on stationery of the rival St. Louis *Globe-Democrat.* Ed started thinking hard about the St. Louis situation.

He had taken the sickly *Post* and converted it into a glorious money-maker. Scripps's goal was to earn a half million dollars for himself in three years!

Borrowing a page from James's techniques for precise penny-pinching, Ed realized any paper must operate on its current income from advertising and circulation. That was the first lesson that James had taught him and Sweeney in Cleveland. It was Ed's idea to carry it even further—mandating a 15 percent built-in daily profit. Each dollar that came in was precisely carved up. Fifty cents belonged to the business manager—to be spent for newsprint, ink, pressmen, delivery men, clerks, ad salesmen, quarters, and equipment. The editor got thirty-five cents. That was to pay for getting the news and setting it in type—hiring reporters, paying telegraph tolls, etc., as well as meeting the composing room payroll. Ed, of course, wanted the printers under total control of the editor, which effectively gave him an okay over anything that appeared in the newspaper.

And Ed mandated that none of that eighty-five cents was to be squirreled away; every penny must be spent to assure the best product they could bring out. That left fifteen cents profit—untouchable dividends for the stockholders from each dollar of revenue. What could be simpler? Scripps laughed, remembering how James, George, and even John Sweeney had been fond of showing him figures to prove that all his brilliant editorial record was but a slave to their business genius. But in Cincinnati he calculated he had beaten the financial record of any of the three by ten lengths.

"It requires a great deal of good sense to keep a fortune," he exulted, "but to make money—bah! Any baby who has got pluck and knows how to manage can do that."

Ed was looking sharply at St. Louis, where he was the nominal overseer of the editorial end of the *Chronicle*. Perhaps the lure was the idea of trying to get personal revenge on the "mudhole city" that had once whipped him. Also, now that the Cincinnati *Post* was on its feet, his appetite demanded a new challenge.

He invited George to take the train and meet him in St. Louis where together they could reappraise the opportunities. Ed wanted control of the *Chronicle*, but to obtain that he'd have to invest $40,000. He blithely intended to borrow that from George. He was staggered when George confided that his whole income was not running over $50,000 a year.

On November 12, 1883, from his room at the Southern Hotel in St. Louis, Ed wrote Annie:

> I have bought controlling stock of the *Chronicle*, and in one fell swoop have plunged into a personal debt of $40,000! Of course, I intend to make $100,000 at least, but what if I don't! I have shut my eyes and jumped in. . . . This dirty town beat me once. I expect to win, of course. I am playing a game of whist where every card lost represents a $1,000 bill. I've got to win, or lose big money!

The atmosphere at the *Chronicle* was not what Scripps had anticipated, nor to his liking. The new boss felt his reception was cool, perhaps even hostile. That worried Ed. The closest approach he found to friendship at the *Chronicle* was flunkeyism and fulsome flattery. He told Annie: "Suspicion, slander and treachery turn up everywhere. . . . I find myself so often in the same day feared, hated, or held in contempt—and loved, respected, and admired. . . . I certainly have the gift for waking other people's passions in the most astounding way."

One of Annie's letters broached the idea that a trip to California might help her crippling rheumatism. Ed immediately offered to pay for it — a thousand or two thousand dollars. "Go. Take Corrine with you. I can't go with you, but plan to visit California in six months. Ellen can go with you. Good idea for Ma to go, too."

Suddenly, the climate in St. Louis somehow improved. His *Chronicle* men started warming to him; and the public developed an apparent new respect for the paper. "There has been a change in the *Chronicle*. . . . That dull deadness in the office has begun to give way to light-hearted industry. . . . I have just begun. Wait a month and you'll agree there is not a better paper!" he wrote Ellen on December 5. "By hook or crook, I will succeed. I can't go slow. You know I always wanted my horse to go on the dead run."

10

Wooing the Parson's Daughter

On New Year's Day 1884 Scripps was caught up in an uncertain romance with the daughter of his St. Louis landlady. "Miss Minnie" was a doll—slightly over four feet, weighing eighty pounds, stylish, musical, a sharp cardplayer, bright-eyed, and vivacious. Her mother, once wealthy, had turned her mansion into a lodging place to afford pushing her daughter in society. The publisher of the *Chronicle* made a likely quarry.

Miss Minnie tolerated Ed's cigars and whiskey, but she made him sit on a parlor stool extending his arms to hold a skein of yarn while she knitted. He complained to Ellen on March 12: "There I sat, a great fool sweating and swearing inside of me . . . as if I was a small boy expecting to be spanked if I made a tangle of the threads."

He wanted to marry her, he told Ellen and Annie, but couldn't quite bring himself to propose. Finally he did November 6, and quoted to Ellen the text of his proposal: "What I says, says I to her, If you love me marry me, and if you don't love me don't marry me. And I don't give a continental what you do, only don't be so infernally skittish about it."

A ton of bricks fell on Ed. Miss Minnie gave him the mitten!

Ed was caught up in the heaviest kind of day-to-day business pressure. Under his personal command were two hard-to-manage newspapers, a day's train ride apart. Critical problems seemed to arise with each new dawn. Almost invariably when he felt comfortable in St. Louis some urgent problem called him back to Cincinnati to make a decision on the scene. And vice versa. To save working time, usually he took the night train.

In March Cincinnati suffered a calamity—the "courthouse riot" over a miscarriage of justice, and the Scripps paper was deeply involved

in it. Fifty were killed, three hundred wounded. It stemmed from the
fatal beating of a robbery victim. A few dollars were taken and the body
hidden in the suburbs. Two laborers, William Berner and Joseph Palmer,
a Negro, were arrested, and confessed March 1. The *Post* called them
"murderous fiends."

Tom Campbell, the jury-fixing lawyer, got Berner off with twenty
years in prison. Even the trial judge couldn't stomach such a light
penalty, excoriating the jurors as unworthy and a disgrace. The *Post* on
March 24 called the verdict "the most outrageous ever rendered," and
went on to quote the ex-sheriff: "The public can't stand this sort of thing.
I would not be surprised if a mob goes to the jail tonight. . . . I will be
with the mob."

Fearing violence, authorities secretly spirited the two killers out of
the city. Four nights later 7,000 citizens jammed Music Hall in protest,
got fired up, and marched on the courthouse-jail a few squares away —
where twenty men accused of murder were behind bars. The mob
torched the building, and fought off firemen. Then the rioters smashed
open a gun store — and bullets began whistling. It took thirty-six hours
for National Guard troops to restore order.

The *Post* called the burning of the courthouse "the first blood in the
people's war on legal corruption." In an extra on Sunday March 30, the
Post asserted: "Mob rule cannot be justified. . . . The people have been
driven to self-defense . . . through the chicanery of lawyers." Two days
later: "Do not blame the people. Blame the corrupt courts." Apparently
Cincinnatians were of a mind to do that; the riot precipitated the decline
of Thomas Campbell as a fixer and graft boss.

Milton McRae, with his advertising hard-sell, plus his eagle-eyed
cost control, was getting the Cincinnati *Post* on a solid profit footing.
But the St. Louis paper's finances were mean and fickle.

"Here I am dragging along a miserable poverty-stricken hand-to-
mouth life," Ed complained to Ellen, "with fifty or sixty dollars a week
to spend and no money to hand the poor devil who is hard up, and no
money to send home, no money to buy a riding horse, and not even
enough to keep myself fashionably clothed. The last case of wine sent up
to my room is not paid for. I bought McRae's new baby a forty-dollar
present on tick, and so it goes."

George sent Ed $200.

By his thirtieth birthday — June 18, 1884 — Ed already had braced
James and George in Detroit for a showdown on finances. Ed recalled it
as "quite a session" — but he managed to get all his stock in his own
hands, secured by notes. His total debt staggered him — $48,000. "Rather

peculiarly," James observed that Ed was perhaps the only Scripps to ever get so much credit and owe so much money.

His interest alone amounted to three thousand a year — $60 a week! But Ed footed up his prospective income, and was satisfied he could meet his obligations. Annually he counted on $1,500 from the Detroit *News,* $5,000 from the *Cleveland Press,* $5,000 from the Cincinnati *Post,* and nothing at all from the *Evening Chronicle* — a total of $11,500. Besides interest he would be out $3,000 a year for living expenses, $1,000 for incidentals, leaving $4,500 for a "sinking fund."

The "mudhole city" was about to bid a long goodbye to Ed Scripps. This time he didn't have his tail between his legs. He had brought the *Chronicle* to the point of making progress, if not yet profits. But he was transferring his personal headquarters from the banks of the Mississippi back to the Cincinnati shore of the Ohio River.

Before settling down again to business at the *Post,* however, he intended to take a long trip through the South, with a side jaunt to Cuba. He felt woefully ignorant of the increasingly important Negro problem, of Dixie's economics and politics. Now was a convenient time to investigate.

Ellen, a sensitive and careful observer and skilled reporter, had agreed to accompany him. Both were encouraging James's and Hattie's eldest daughter, Anna, eighteen, to make it a threesome.

James and Hattie were dubious about a girl as young as Anna making such a journey. Finally they gave in, and the three travellers, in bouyant spirits, boarded the southbound train in Cincinnati December 16.

By carriage, street car, and weary foot the trio explored New Orleans — the French Market, cathedrals, cemeteries, shops on broad esplanades, the bustling river wharves, and especially the Exposition that marked the one-hundredth anniversary of the first cotton export to England. To young Anna this was high adventure. She stirred to the city's quaint foreign flavor, its cobbled avenues, the romantic somnolent gait, ancient mossy brick buildings, iron-grilled mansions whose half-open gates revealed embowered gardens in drowzy decay. Dark-skinned Creole women sauntered to market in bright turbans and wide fluffy petticoats. The moist air was fragrant with the scent of exotic flowers. The street patois seemed a strange, lazy music of French-Spanish tones. Ellen was

loading her diary with color and facts—about cottonseed mills, the
Mint, sawmills, shipping, labor, the Expo exhibits, as well as personali-
ties, customs, travel details.
Christmas and New Year passed. Not unexpectedly, Ed caught cold.
Ellen gave him quinine. He got worse. Ellen wrote in her diary for
January 4, 1885:

> At home all day. Raining & gloomy. E. proposed to go & drown him-
> self, but found river too dirty. So returning went into a drugstore and asked
> for morphine. The druggist on learning his intentions refused to sell it to
> him. So he bought a cigar and came back to nurse his disgust with the
> world.

That was a characteristic charade, of course. One who knows E. W.
Scripps's eventual fame as a journalistic giant, on par with Pulitzer and
Hearst, might wonder at his pathetic and tempestuous behavior at this
juncture in his career. Wildly seesawing between castles in the air and
deep funk, he could not go long without recklessly risking his future and
fortune on a single day's rash capriciousness. He was often an enigma to
himself—impulsive, aleatory, minatory, at the same time daring, courageous, and steel-willed. His constant reading—far-ranging research—
built in the older and mature Scripps an astonishing intellect, which was
to shape him into a closet philosopher of later discovery and an amateur
but authentic human behavioral scientist.
    Admittedly lazy, always yearning to "run away," he was as bachelor
a fickle womanizer whose exploits in both scented society boudoirs and
steamy mean street dives might have cost his life for a greasy dollar or a
jealous kiss. Only in his last days did he truly overcome slavery to the
bottle. Whiskey, too, might—and almost did—wreck his life and greatness. One of his secrets of success was in knowing how to expertly pick
strong men as subalterns to do his work and push his dreams. His
brain—when he really worked it on journalism, and that was not very
frequently—gobbled up new ideas, trends, inventions such as the automobile, telephone, duplex telegraph, type-setting machines, wireless,
and the like he could adapt to keep his organization in the fore of
newspapering. He would be the first to make feature syndication nationally successful.
    After touring historic old St. Augustine, Florida, on January 28
they boarded a launch that bobbed out to sea to intercept the steamer
Niagara, bound from New York to Havana. In Cuba they skittered
about by train, ship, carriage, on horseback, aboard the giant-wheeled
volante, on foot—seeing Marianoa, Matanzas, the caves of Bellamer,

plantations, beaches, bazaars, factories, concert halls, and personages. From time to time Anna and Ed squabbled, but within an hour would be laughing and teaming up in escapades that left out Ellen. They waltzed wildly at a great carnival, attracting admiring glances. At 5 A.M. they sallied out to greet an incoming passenger liner.

Mail from home arrived—with upsetting news. Rheumatic Annie had put herself in the hands of what Ed called religious quacks. She was now in Milwaukee and needed money. Furiously, Ed wrote:

> You can have the money, but it makes me swearing mad you are giving it to a pack of swindlers. If I were in Milwaukee, I would put the law and the newspapers rooting out this pack of false pretenders as I did a set professing the same creed in Cincinnati a few months ago. We landed one of those rascals in prison. . . .
>
> It was such a plain worn-out old swindle, that of offering you medical attendance for a dollar a mile and then roping you into a $200 lecture course. . . . If your friends are not murderers . . . instead of paying them $200 for their hoodoo business, offer them $1,000 for the slightest benefit— or nothing for no service rendered.

The charlatans had Annie solidly hooked. She doggedly clung to the faith healers. They were to milk Annie of cash—from Ed's purse—for several years. They lured her into a sort of commune Scripps sneeringly dubbed "a Jesus Christ factory."

It was a different Ed Scripps who returned from the four months' ramble. To a marked degree he was more mature, less frenetic, more business-like, less libido-driven. Instead of a dreamy builder of air castles, he now appeared a hard-core realist.

McRae discovered that right off. With glum face, he handed Ed a bad-news ledger. The *Post* again was losing money. Ed studied the red ink figures, snatched up a pen and whipped out a succinct memo. Mac was running the paper too loosely. Get *something* for every paper printed: absolutely no wasted newsprint. Quit hustling circulation; go after more advertising. That would solve the problem.

Ed had not changed his two main goals—to succeed grandly as a newspaper publisher, and to lead a quiet moral life. The tick of the clock was beginning to disturb him. He redesigned his lifestyle. Everyone always thought he had to have the gaiety and excitement of the city. They said he was an abject slave to the wine cup, cigars, and a woman's bed. Scripps began hunting a quiet home in the country. He wanted tranquility, green grass and fragrant flowers, blue skies, and the quiet evening

breeze. He had no love affairs "legitimate or otherwise," he informed
Annie. The yen for drink didn't die, but he totally cut out wine, and
"became almost a teetotaler." He cut his smoking in half. Feeling a
strong urge to write, he sharpened a handful of pencils.

Scripps discovered an ideal rural retreat. His classified ad seeking
"rustic room and board" was answered in mid-May by Colonel Charles
A. Gano, sixtyish, well-educated, once rich, and married to a second
wife half his age. Ed inspected the Gano residence on a small farm and
found it "quite grand" and even more isolated than the old homestead at
Rushville. He could look out and see nary a sign of village life, and only
occasionally a barn or farm house. The Gano place was sixteen miles
north of downtown Cincinnati, and only a fifty-minute ride on the Cincinnati, Hamilton, and Dayton Railway, "with trains going and coming
all day."

Ed moved in, looking forward to exploring the countryside with
long walks, and doing some heavy reading. He also bought a fine Kentucky saddle horse. He could keep his own hours and breakfast was
always ready when he called for it. The Colonel and his wife went out of
their way to be friendly.

Ten days or so after he became their country boarder, Mrs. Gano
induced Ed to accompany her to a social in nearby Sharon at the Cum-
berland Presbyterian Church. The first person they met was a smiling,
fresh-faced brunet in white frock so short and simple Scripps mistook
her for a preteen schoolgirl. Mrs. Gano introduced her as "Miss Nackie"
and moved on.

For a few moments Ed regarded the girl. He concluded that though
she was only a child, "she was a very beautiful child. She was rather
diffident and reticent, but still she had a certain poise that attracted me."
Instead of mingling, Ed concentrated his charm and conversation —
dropping for effect a few French phrases — on the dark-eyed girl and
monopolized her evening. On the way home, he questioned Mrs. Gano
about the girl. "Oh, she's Nackie Holtsinger — the parson's daughter."
The Reverend Samuel K. Holtsinger, explained Mrs. Gano, also pastored
the Presbyterian church at West Chester, a mile and a half up the road
from the Gano farm. Nackie played the organ there and sang in the
choir. "She's not a child," said Mrs. Gano. "She has just graduated from
Hughes High School in Cincinnati. Eighteen, maybe nineteen. She plans
to teach music out here."

Lately Scripps had been an infrequent church-goer, but the following Sunday he took his evening stroll up West Chester way and went into
Reverend Holtsinger's church. "Seeing my little girl dressed up in sober,

or tolerably sober, church clothes, with a long dress on, it dawned on me she was not such a child after all," he recalled.

Next day Ed called on Nackie Holtsinger at the parsonage near the West Chester church and properly met her parents. The next evening he was again knocking on the door of the parsonage. Virtually every free evening Ed called on the girl. Once again Cupid's arrow had pierced the fickle heart of the gangling red-head. He alerted sister Annie in a letter written June 15 from St. Louis:

> By the way, another Eve has entered my garden of paradise over there in Ohio. This one is in the shape of a pleasant little girl of seventeen or eighteen, just out of school and the daughter of a country parson. . . . Now don't think I am on the rocks again. I am only qualifying my previous description of my Eden where there were supposed to be no disturbing influences. I hope and expect you will hear no more of this dangerous foe to the calm and contentment of your long-afflicted brother.

Considering himself an "old, old man" at age thirty-one, Scripps was disturbed that he would be courting a girl twelve years his junior. "I abused myself roundly for my infatuation," he recalled. "I reminded myself of my resolution to marry someone nearly my own age. I recognized the absolute impossibility of telling this young girl just what sort of a man I had been and was, for that matter, and I recognized that if some brute should tell her, she would be utterly unable to understand."

Scripps saw only one possible escape from this romantic snare—to move away. He determined to give up his rooms at the Gano place, but procrastinated about leaving. Cute little Nackie, innocent and demure, had the wayward bachelor solidly on her hook. Running away from her was out of the question. "I only found myself more tempted than before," Ed recalled. "I could not keep away from that parsonage."

The romantic quest gave him a dangerous physical jolt. One evening as he rode away from Nackie's home, a sudden storm crashed out of the night sky. Ed, in pelting rain, undertook to leap his mount over the tollgate on the road. At that moment lightning flashed; his steed faltered, and stumbled, throwing Ed into a pile of rocks. Limping, he sought help at the toll-keeper's house. An unsympathetic woman thrust her hand into the rainy night for his two cents toll and slammed the door. She was, ironically, the grandmother of Roy W. Howard, then a two-year-old tyke destined to grow up as a boy reporter in Indianapolis and later rise to chief generalissimo of the Scripps newspaper empire.

As usual, romance had Ed in a contradictory swivet. The day after his horse fell, he wrote Annie:

I wrote you about the little Presbyterian church girl I met here. Well, we have been having a perfect little summer idyll, she and I. What will come of it, I don't know. I suppose it will go the way of all my romances — aglimmering.

I spend nearly every evening with her. She sings and plays, we walk and talk — moonlight and all that. But every now and then I make a bad break. I do something shocking. I have got that old daredevil spirit in me. She don't know anything. A country parson's daughter and so young and inexperienced.

I don't understand but she looks on a glass of beer as something wicked. Perhaps her friends tell her that "That city chap ain't to be relied on no how."

Either Ed was unsure of Nackie's affection or fearful of again getting the same mitten, or simply could not make up his own mind to plunge into matrimony. His heavy wooing made his pulses throb — and conversely his next breath plotted to run away. On September 6, he wrote Ellen that he was "entitled to a vacation" and asked her to join him on a three months' trip to Mexico. They could ask George to go along. Perhaps they might go to California. "We ought to cross the continent some time." If Ellen was not interested, he might go off alone — to China or Japan.

Despite idyllic evenings at the Holtsinger parsonage, Scripps daily hopped on the C. H. & D. train at the nearby West Chester station and rode into town, furiously involved in business. The *Post* already was hard pressed to compete with its established rivals for readers and advertisers. Now a cheap new afternoon daily, the *Telegram,* started up in Cincinnati. Behind it was Ed's arch enemy, Tom Campbell, the jury-fixing lawyer who had started losing his political clout in the wake of the courthouse riot. Campbell's sole purpose appeared to be to wreck the Scripps's paper.

That likewise was the chief aim of the hated Johnny McLean of the *Enquirer* who secretly helped Cincinnati Republican leaders launch a new cheap morning daily, the *Sun.* For two years the *Sun* would train a heavy bombardment on the *Post,* though in the end the morning paper would be done in by its own internal intrigue.

This was a newspaper war more vicious than Ed had ever before experienced. Now he was better prepared for battle. He felt sanguine about his little penny sheet. McRae kept the *Post* loaded with ads, partly because its rates were the lowest in town. Bravely, Ed ordered a new and faster press.

The *Post* marched its 1,500 newsboys through the downtown streets with banners and a brass band, and took the whole lot to the theatre.

Watching the parade from the St. Nicholas Hotel, Ed was delighted when the band struck up "Yankee Doodle Dandy" and the whole line, four blocks long, burst into song. Instead of being hurt by advent of the *Telegram,* the *Post* circulation shot up 2,000 — reaching 32,280, a gain of almost 20,000 in two years. Scripps beamed, too, when the office ledger showed August 1885 receipts were $7,500 as against but $2,600 in the same month of 1883.

It was clear that Ed considered the prettiest sight anywhere in the whole beautiful Mill Creek Valley the sweet and smiling, bright-eyed lass in the white frock at the West Chester parsonage.

After sundown in late September Ed set out on his nightly hike from the Gano farm to the parsonage. He glanced up at the harvest moon, and set his jaw. This might be a foolish night, he warned himself. He vowed silently to do nothing that would indicate to Nackie his true desire. It would be an ordeal, being in her alluring presence, susceptible to the perfume of her beauty and unsullied maidenhood. He must steel himself.

"Before I entered the house," he recalled in his memoirs, "I feel sure that I was steeled. Two or three hours later when I left the parsonage, I was engaged to marry, and even the date had been fixed, subject to the father's and mother's consent, for only a few weeks in the future."

The actuality of the betrothal left Scripps either dazzled or perverse, or both. He did not shout the news from any rooftop. He kept his engagement secret from his closest men at the *Post.* He told no one in St. Louis, no one in his family, not even compassionate sister Annie, long the intimate confidante and counselor in his many amours.

On Sunday October 7, not quite four months after they first met, Ed and Nackie were married. The ceremony was performed in the parsonage parlor, the only witnesses being Colonel and Mrs. Gano and the bride's father and mother. The Reverend Mr. Holtsinger read the service.

The excited newlyweds rushed to the train for a honeymoon trip to the seashore at Old Point Comfort, Virginia, scheduling first a mountain stopover at White Sulphur Springs, West Virginia. Ed doubtless arranged to travel on railroad passes, one of his whims. He would be introducing his unsophisticated bride to both romance and adventure. Also to luxury. He recalled: "I remember that my wife's trousseau consisted of one little brown dress — so short that the bottom of it came well above her shoe tops — and a little turban hat to match it."

From their bridal suite in the rambling resort hotel, Nackie gazed wide-eyed at the vast reaches of Chesapeake Bay, Hampton Roads, and the Atlantic. She drank in the invigorating sea breeze, doubtless pinching herself that such a romantic episode was not a fleeting dream.

After a week or two, Ed rustled up some hotel stationery and got around to telling the news to his family. The bride and groom spent a month in bliss, returning via Washington, D.C., to see the sights. By the time they were back in Cincinnati, Mrs. Edward Willis Scripps was carrying her first child—a son to be born on her twentieth birthday.

Scripps was kind and attentive; his bride was radiant. They found it amusing later when a letter of congratulations came from one of Ed's distant cousins in London, passing on advice he'd received as a newlywed from an old gentleman: "When one is in the fire, let the other be in the water."

On Christmas Day 1885, Ed stood with Nackie and Ellen on the balcony of the Menger Hotel in San Antonio looking down on the sunny plaza and the bullet-pocked, crumbling walls of the Alamo. They found the Texas weather as warm as June at home. But Scripps was beginning to wonder whether it was not a mistake to drag a bride a couple of months pregnant off on a long, rugged tour of Mexico. Having arrived only two days earlier, they were waiting to be joined from Detroit by James and Hattie, who were bringing along their seven-year-old Grace.

The three from Detroit arrived and the party headed for the border. On January 30, 1886, their train chugged into the mountain foothills at Saltillo. Ellen's diary criticizes their hotel: "Beds with no sheets, no blankets, tortillas to eat, and an abundance of fleas."

At the door of the hotel saloon they were startled by a booming voice. "Hey, Ed! . . . James! . . . Why, Miss Ellen!" They were being hailed by the barkeep. They recognized him as Charlie Bean, who had grown up with them in Rushville. They exchanged their home-town gossip for tales of Bean's many adventures south of the border, capped by going broke as a sheep rancher. He offered sage counsel: "If you can eat tortillas, you can eat anything, and you'll get along." Nackie had an upset stomach and nobody got much sleep that night.

At daybreak they piled into the stagecoach. Ahead lay a dangerous trail—380 kilometers of steep, rocky trails crossing narrow, high mountain passes to Zacatecas. The Scripps women were doubly nervous. Bandits lurked in the hills, Charlie Bean had told them. The robbers ruthlessly knifed their victims because "dead men tell no tales." Charlie comforted them by revealing 150 highwaymen had been caught and executed at Saltillo.

The stage's six-mule team rarely paused. The wheels groaned over stones and through dry gullies, the jolts jarring passengers' teeth. Sweat-stained and caked with dust, they pulled up finally at Zacatecas. In a few days they caught a southbound stage to Augascalientes, and there rejoined the railroad to reach Mexico City on February 4. Ed found fine hotel rooms on the third floor of the Iturbide, which Ellen's diary describes as "a hotel of proportions and accommodations. The price, $2 a day, a la carte."

Sights and sounds in the mile-high capital captivated them for several days. James suffered an unfortunate gallstone attack and abandoned the vacation, starting back to the United States, leaving Hattie and Grace. The other Scripps tourists made train excursions to Puebla and Vera Cruz. On March 4, beginning to weary, they returned to Mexico City and the Hotel Iturbide.

Washing travel grime off his face, Scripps snatched a towel awkwardly off the hotel rack. One corner of the rough cloth poked into his left eye. The sting made him cry out. Quickly he splashed his eye with water, but the pain persisted. Through the night the eye throbbed. Next morning it was badly inflamed, swollen almost shut. Ellen took a look and decided it was a medical emergency. She found a young American physician named Parsons had been living a year in Mexico City, and summoned him.

His examination disclosed marked laceration of Ed's conjunctiva, already ulcerous. Dr. Parsons promptly disinfected Ed's eye with bichloride of mercury, cauterized the wounds, dilated the pupil with atropia. Scripps broke out in a hard chill and began thrashing about on his bed. The physician calmed him with an injection of morphine. Ellen, veteran nurse of the family, gently edged the distraught and inexperienced Nackie out of the way, and took command of the sickroom.

Dr. Parsons next day found the eye worse. Again he cauterized and put Ed out with a hypo. Ellen could see the physician was greatly concerned. "There's a sympathetic reaction in the optic nerves," he explained, hesitantly. "The sight of the injured eye is, frankly, in danger. We must protect the other!"

He washed out the right eye and closed and sealed it with collodion. The effect was that Ed now lay on his bed "blind." There was another young American physician in Mexico City, a Dr. Gustine, whose father was a famous oculist in New Orleans. Dr. Parsons called him in. The two physicians were in and out of the hotel room every few hours. Often they came at night. They continued their treatment and kept Ed sedated with morphine. This concerned Ellen. Dr. Parsons agreed there was a chance Ed might become addicted to the drug. It was a gamble they'd have to take.

The crisis deepened. Nothing halted the raging ulceration. The wounded left eye, the doctors muttered, could fail any moment, and trigger blindness in the other. They learned a Philadelphia oculist, a Dr.

Gross, had arrived on vacation. They rushed to consult him, but he could offer nothing new. Dr. Parsons was forced to consider what he called "la dernier resort"—to puncture the cornea and withdraw the aqueous humor. That to a degree would "flatten" the eyeball and reduce friction and pressure on the inflamed tissue.

Should he risk this drastic surgery? Already, perhaps, sight was gone in this left eye. At least the operation might prevent sympathetic blindness in the other. The three doctors reviewed their options. Time was running out. Action was demanded—even a hundred to one gamble!

Dr. Parsons took sterile syringes and a scalpel out of his bag. With Ed already unconscious from morphine, the surgery took only minutes. Drs. Parsons and Gustine hovered over the patient. In a few hours they noted a change—certain favorable signs. They unsealed the "good" eye and made a quick check for damage. They sighed audibly. So far there was none. Even 2,000 miles from home, and knocked out with drugs, Scripps was a target for business problems. At this moment arrived from St. Louis a blistering six-hundred-word complaint from Henry Little. The *Chronicle* managing director was furious about what he considered mixed signals from the absent boss. He wrote:

> God, man, what do you mean? In one letter you criticize my pace, and in the next you shout "to boom is not our policy!" The hell of it is you have no policy that can be relied on over a change in your diet. . . . I don't think your effort to run your papers from the long range of Mexico is a blooming success. . . .
>
> James writes to cut everything down. Don't boom! Don't brag! Oh, hell! Die in the trenches, as I did in Buffalo? Not if I know myself. I was promised better treatment. . . . You can never again put me in the boat I am in now. I wouldn't go through the last three months for every bit of newspaper property on God's green earth.
>
> Your cold-blooded decapitations have done enough harm. I haven't any money, debts are accumulating. George refuses to whack up.

Ellen, of course, did not plague Ed with this letter; he was much too ill to try to handle any newspaper crisis.

Within forty-eight hours the ulceration definitely was subsiding. "La dernier resort" had turned the tide. Slowly, but steadily, the bad eye returned to normal. That battle had been won. But now Ed faced a second battle—equally dangerous. Clearly, he had become a morphine addict!

In a blunt discussion, Dr. Parsons told Scripps there was but one way out—to quit "cold turkey." The cure meant Ed must find courage to resist for seven straight days his craving for a shot of morphine. At the end of a full week, he should no longer be a slave to the narcotic. But withdrawal could prove a terrible, terrible ordeal.

Restless, weary, thrashing about his bed in the Iturbide, Scripps decided to begin the cure. He awakened the first morning thinking himself in great pain. But he clenched his teeth and vowed he would take no hypo. In memoirs written forty years later, he vividly relived that ordeal:

> Two or three hours had elapsed since I had been dosed. I determined to resist my craving for as much longer a time. Noon came. A full quarter of a day had passed — one-twenty-eighth of the suggested seven days.
>
> I had suffered extremely. But I had been able to endure the pain. I determined to make the six hours twelve. This was one-fourteenth of the whole time allotted for the most serious part of the fight.
>
> To myself I said, "It is a pity that all of this day of suffering should be wasted." If I took another dose I would get immediate relief . . . [then later] I would have to begin another seven days' course.
>
> I would fight it a full twenty-four hours, and I did. One-seventh of the whole time had passed. I was lying on an iron bedstead. I got some relief from my suffering by bending all the strength I had by pushing at the bottom of the bed and pulling at the iron rods at top. . . . It had been hell every minute. . . . But if I took another dose, I would have to begin the fight all over. . . .
>
> I spent another terrible day and another terrible night, and the iron bedstead suffered too. But two-sevenths of the time had passed. . . . The next day and the next night there was no surcease of pain. . . . Another day and another night. . . . and another day and night. . . . The pain was bad enough but I was within two days of the end. The doctors praised me and tried to furnish relief by giving me whiskey that burned my mouth like pure lye. . . . Another day, and another day, the last. I was still wretchedly nervous but no longer did I feel the pain like a red-hot poker pressing under my eyeballs.
>
> More trials of whiskey. It wouldn't do. But I got out of bed, dressed and walked about. I still craved the drug. Several more weeks were required before I felt perfectly normal.

By April 14, Ed was able to take the train and start home, through El Paso. Two weeks later, he and Nackie were safely in Cincinnati, and the other travellers in Detroit.

11

First Son—and Then a Tragedy

The Edward W. Scrippses returned to a room at Cincinnati's St. Nicholas Hotel. But since they were expecting their first child in about two months that was no appropriate home. Besides both missed country living—open fields, fresh air, quietude, saddle horses to ride mornings, and rustic lanes for moonlight hikes. Boarding at Colonel Gano's was not, of course, permanently suitable.

So Ed searched for a farm to rent or buy. In the general vicinity of the Holtsinger parsonage and the Glendale railroad station, a few miles further north but still an easy train commute to Cincinnati, he discovered the place they wanted. On thirty-four acres at West Chester, just over the Butler County line, stood a pretty old white farmhouse that had been solidly built with two-foot by two-foot oak beams, offered at $5,000. Ed considered it a bargain and promptly wrote Ellen asking loan of the purchase price. Even before she could reply, he bought it. He had to pay one-third down, the balance in two years.

These terms were so convenient he would not need to touch Ellen until the last payment came due in 1888. He wrote her: "I knew you would help me. . . . The place is large enough to furnish Annie a home if she wants it . . . and Jennie a place to visit. Would not be a disagreeable place for you to loaf."

Seeking furnishings for this new home, Ed ambled into one of Cincinnati's largest stores, the John A. Shillito Company. Totally heedless of his country attire, he had a bedraggled slouch hat atop his red hair, and wore a weathered work shirt and beat-up khaki pants, stuffed in scruffy boots. Clerks looked, and sniffed. This bearded rube couldn't buy anything that cost over a dime. They bustled away.

Scripps, puffing his cigar, wandered about alone, inspecting tables, beds, rugs, etc. Finally a shy girl clerk approached. "Sir, may I help you?" Ed grinned. "I think," he replied, "I'll just buy one of everything in the store." He carefully gave her an order that startled the manager; it was Shillito's biggest sale in a year!

With his income from his stocks now $20,000 a year, Ed was in no rush to resume routine newspaper management. He had the *Post* booming; the papers in Detroit and Cleveland were prospering. Only the St. Louis *Chronicle* was struggling to survive.

One executive role did, however, appeal to him—boss of all four papers! Currently Ed was doing some of his celebrated hard thinking about his own future. He had a knack of prescience and it alerted him that the gallstone attack which forced James to abort his vacation in Mexico was a significant omen. That was but one of several crippling seizures that had hit him. As Ed saw it, James, though only fifty-one, was doomed to not live long.

Who then would become king of this four-city publishing empire? Who in the ranks stood higher in successful experience and proven ability than Ed? No one. That was Ed's sincere appraisal. He didn't hide his ambition, writing Ellen: "I should be entitled to be general director of the whole league . . . while I am still young and anxious for it. . . . I can't afford to wait many years longer. I must be in Congress before I am forty as I shall need ten years to get into the Senate."

But the political bug was not foremost in his mind, John Scripps Sweeney was. To Ed, this shrewd, energetic cousin was his closest and most-feared rival. John held a certain edge—James considered him a personal protégé. The grapevine out of Cleveland reported Sweeney growing restless. Married to Elizabeth Stanley, daughter of a Cleveland railroad magnate, John was now a father, his son having been born in April. He was a hard-driving athlete and outdoorsman. His post as managing director of the growing Cleveland paper was not a big enough challenge now. Sweeney confided to James: "It is not money I want, but control."

Ed endeavored to keep on amiable terms with James. He decided to flatter him by naming him godfather of his coming first child.

On the morning of her twentieth birthday, July 19, 1886, Nackie awoke early with a start and shouted for Ed to fetch the doctor. Her labor was hard, and painful. Angry and impatient, she cried loudly. The infant's large head was causing a tear that would require two stitches to repair. Finally, in her arms nestled a healthy, robust boy.

Ed examined the little creature with utter fascination. The infant seemed unusually well developed. His bones were large and strong. He had long legs and arms, with large feet and long, untapered fingers. His eyes and hair were dark (the eyes to become dark blue and the hair brown instead of red). In the contours of the head, Ed saw resemblances partially to his own, to Nackie's, and to Nackie's father. He sensed the child inherited his own fire and spirit, leavened by Nackie's Teutonic disposition.

For fully two weeks he pondered a name. A girl he would have called after Nackie or her mother. For a son he was torn between Blair Osborn or George James, preferring the latter "for nickname purposes. . . . But on counting up I find fully one-third of all males in the Scripps family are Georges." Finally, he named his first-born James George Scripps.

Nackie was uncomfortable, impatient, and demanding while she healed. Between answering her whims and directing a squad of workmen fixing up the farm, Ed did not get into Cincinnati for six weeks. Visitors trooped in. Ma came from Rushville. James journeyed by train September 2 to pay "a social call" on his godson. Ellen accepted an invitation to come later and stay a few weeks.

To rheumatic Annie, in a sanitarium at Quincy, Illinois, Nackie penned this report: "Ed measured our boy last evening and looked all around the house for something you know the length of, and finally thought of the *Evening Post* and found the boy was just its length— twenty-four inches. We think that is tall for a baby of four weeks."

If not from a squalling baby, Ed's rustic calm was nevertheless disturbed by distress cries—from the outside. They emanated from the newspapers at Cleveland and St. Louis. In both cities trouble was brewing that the country squire could not long ignore. James, surprisingly vigorous for a "doomed" man, was squarely, as usual, in the middle of these problems. In Cleveland arose the threat of rebellion, or possibly a decamping, by fidgety John Sweeney. In the "mudhole city," the *Chronicle* suffered from the same old cancer, red ink, losing $500 a month.

For his part, Ed had about given up on Henry Little, was in fact trying to steel himself for totally writing off the *Chronicle*. James asked Ed to try to again infuse new life in the paper, urging him to spend a week in St. Louis. The country squire resisted. He felt he must stay free and be ready to leap into the breach in the crucial Cleveland crisis. John Sweeney made dire noises, saying unless he could acquire more stock in the *Press*—a concession Ed strongly opposed—he would resign.

That might merely be bluff. Ed couldn't tell. All he knew was that his own income was heavily dependent upon continued prosperity of the *Cleveland Press*. If Sweeney decamped, Ed would move there and take over, even if neglect of the *Chronicle* cost all he had invested in it. After all, thousands of future dollars were at stake in Cleveland to mere pennies in St. Louis.

But James insisted Ed spend one week at the *Chronicle*. "Find the weak spots and remedy them. . . . If you can give the *Chronicle* a little personal attention a rapid decline may be checked. Otherwise I see no hope." Ed took the night train to St. Louis. James joined him there. They tinkered with personnel, made cuts in editorial and circulation, and the paper began to improve—the most impressive plus being that it got back to living within its income.

The crisis in Cleveland, rushing pell-mell toward an explosion, fell under a pall in late November when tragedy hit the Sweeney household. John's son Stanley died suddenly at age seven months.

Late in December Ed joined the other directors in Detroit to come to grips with Sweeney's ultimatum. "There was considerable antagonism between us," Ed would recall of his cousin rival. "It was quite evident to me that a big fight was on and James was inclined to give way to John, that George and the other directors were firm in their opposition, I passed over matters lightly and got out of town so John and James could settle things between themselves."

The start of the new year—1887—brought heavier business pressure on Ed. John Sweeney notified James he was resigning his managing directorship of the Cleveland paper effective March 1. He had under consideration launching a newspaper of his own—in Minneapolis or in Pittsburgh. Further, he claimed two *Press* executives would go with him, advertising manager Charles Seabrook, who was Sweeney's brother-in-law, and editor Bob Paine.

So now the Scripps directors faced an actual challenge. It still might be a bluff. Ed knew for certain Sweeney was telling a stupid lie about Paine. Bob was too loyal to desert; Seabrook might. There was no change in Ed's resolve—if asked, he would abandon the pretty farm and take over in Cleveland.

For the first time, tension began in his marriage. Nackie was, after all, twelve years his junior, a naive choir girl who had not yet really grown up. His loving kindness had given way more frequently to autocratic commands, his caresses to abrupt and harsh reprimands. That was his way. He was caught up in intense hard thinking about serious affairs of business—not to be harangued with something as picayune as whether or not Jim had wet his diaper. Ed went around with a scowl. As he saw it, John Sweeney was intriguing to actually harm the *Press,* and perhaps the other papers as well. Ed realized fully he was locked in a lethal duel with his cousin. And it was a contest he dare not lose!

At this juncture, in the middle of January 1887, Ed was summoned to a lengthy war council with James and George, including meetings in both Detroit and Cleveland. Nackie, still girlish enough to think he belonged exclusively to her, was miffed to find him called away. The moment he climbed aboard the train at Glendale with his valise, she felt lonesome. In an hour or two her mood darkened — she was unloved.

She peppered him with daily letters, venting her unhappiness, whining, feeling "quite miserable," and accusing him of writing her "so cruelly." She was angry that he wrote only three times. "I am too unhappy. Please come home." She needled, too. "I thought sure you must be near home last night for there was a demijohn of whiskey came from the city. I thought sure you would follow it."

Nackie got contrite. "I received your poor little letter saying that I had forgotten you, my darling! You know I hadn't forgotten you, didn't you?" Later: "It makes me so miserable to read how well contented you are away from me when I am so lonely here. Can you really love me, darling? . . . You used to like to be with me. Can't you come to me and comfort me?" He couldn't run home; he was fighting doggedly for their present and future fortune.

Smoke curled up from grumpy George H. Scripps's pipe in the directors' room at the Detroit *Evening News*. It mingled above the table with puffs Ed exhaled from his Sante Fe. Wearing a weary, pained expression, James E. Scripps fiddled absently with sheets of paper before him.

It was now late in the day Monday January 24. These daily hours-long sessions were draining James, now suffering chronic abdominal pain. He must take a long vacation from business. He already had decided that. He was taking his family abroad for perhaps a year, intending to sail from New York by midsummer and visit the Carlsbad spa.

The board had finally reconciled itself to losing Sweeney. Ed suggested hiring as his successor a bright neophyte, E. Willis Osborn, treasurer of a Cleveland iron company. Ed knew Willis well; he was his cousin on his mother's side. He would learn fast. After some give and take, Ed was authorized to hire Osborn at $2,600 annually. Willis could, if profits didn't drop too much, earn $5,200 next year. Further if Sweeney decided to sell his sixteen shares of *Press* stock, valued at about $19,000, Osborn could buy it with a loan from the Scrippses.

Ed went to Cleveland to install the new boss. But Sweeney did a flip-flop and rushed to Detroit to tell James he had decided to stay on the job. The flabbergasted senior brother told him to go see Ed and try to unscramble the mess. Sweeney took the train to Glendale. Ed, who had just returned home, sent his carriage to the depot to bring him to the farm. They met in a cordial and friendly atmosphere.

To make amends both for their quarrels by correspondence, and because he sincerely desired his wife—now again pregnant—to learn details of the publishing business, especially its financial nuances so that she could protect her interests should tragedy overtake him, Ed brought Nackie into these sessions. She served as secretary of the conference, preparing in her beautiful script several documents that detail their discussions and agreements.

Ed now felt certain James did not have long to live. That belief was the cornerstone of his maneuvers with Sweeney. He did not want his cousin out of the concern, feeling John was too valuable to lose. The country squire just wanted Sweeney pushed far enough aside that Ed would get his long-yearned-for chance to control the whole business.

The "grand design" that Ed had first dreamed up back in 1880 must be carried out. Basically that called for formation of a group, a syndicate, a "league" of all the Scripps papers, to be operated by a central authority. That could yield great benefits. For instance, newsprint and ink and other supplies could be purchased for all as a single order, insuring lower unit prices because of volume. Men could be transferred from one paper to another, wherever they were most needed. It would be feasible and economic to employ high-priced star reporters and special writers because their copy would be published in four papers, instead of just one.

Another goal was to a coordinate a bureau in New York to secure a greater volume of "foreign" advertising for the "League" papers from national accounts. Likewise, Ed envisioned opening a Scripps news bureau in New York. It would supervise a Washington correspondent reporting government affairs, and appoint "agents" in key big cities to supply special dispatches and facilitate the exchange of news between League dailies. The bureau would place a few good men in Europe to cull papers abroad for the best condensations and translations. His travels had convinced Ed most European reporting was sloppily done. The League papers also could use assistance in securing suitable fiction for their daily "story" column. The New York bureau could easily develop contacts with authors, agents, and magazines.

As to Ed becoming the outfit's chief executive officer, James had no objection. He did caution Ed to not tamper with James's holdings in the *Evening News,* by far the most valuable in the League. Both George and James were anxious, however, to step back and let Ed take over active management.

So Ed faced Sweeney beside the fireplace in his farm study, with his own strategy all worked out. Painstakingly he had written a list showing every point of disagreement—perhaps a dozen—between them, and noted each solution. Thus he was able to rapidly reel off a series of moves that reconciled the disgrunted cousin and buried their old rivalry, leaving James pleased and feeling free to go abroad for his health.

First, the Osborn deal would stand. Second Sweeney would move to Detroit to become general manager of the *News* at $10,000 a year. He would remain nominal managing director of the Cleveland paper at fifty a week. This arrangement suited Sweeney. Informed by telegram, James immediately approved, asserting that "George and myself are losing our grip and new blood is essential for further growth."

To prevent any more squabbles over the stock, Ed drew up a document he termed a Quadripartite—agreement of four parties—to be signed by himself, Sweeney, James, and George. Though a stockholder, Ellen chose not to participate. Terms of the Quadripartite bound all four not to sell any of their stock to outsiders; also each agreed that upon the death of any signer one-half of his stock could be purchased by the surviving signers. James noted in his diary on February 11, 1887, that the pact "will assure good management of the companies after our deaths."

When they gathered in Detroit on February 10 and 11 and formally signed their agreement, James viewed the Quadripartite as a stunning peace treaty. Yet in the next room, secretly Sweeney pressed Ed for a side agreement under which, if James died and Osborn failed, John would be entitled to buy twenty unissued shares of *Cleveland Press* stock for $24,000, which would give him control of that newspaper. Even at that moment Sweeney was plotting double treachery. By using kinsman Seabrook as a willing "inside" henchman, he intended to cause enough sabotage at the *Press* to make Osborn fail.

But at first there was no hint of this coming discord. Sweeney stepped into his post at the *News* and Osborn took the helm at the *Press*. John and his wife moved into James's house, urged by the host "on Lizzie's account, fearing that until she feels at home in Detroit, if left without company, she might get homesick and interfere with John's usefulness here."

Nackie behaved better while Ed was away to finalize the Quadripartite, and then had to go on to St. Louis. "It is so terribly lonesome when you are away," she wrote February 22. She confided she had thought about buying a blue-ribbon horse she had run across for $225, adding, "I'm just writing this to make you laugh."

Her conscience hurt February 24 because she had written but once a day. But she jested that spared him from "your naughty little wife who knows so well how to trouble you. . . . Darling, I don't think it right for husband and wife to be away from each other so much." She mentioned the horse again. It was a beauty; she was afraid somebody else might snatch him up. "I don't want to interfere with your business. Do write me every day."

Her next letter commiserated with Ed over the fact that James had just a few months to live. "I'm taking good care of myself," she noted, "so that I can be nice and well and be able to take care of you nicely when you come home." And again she brought up the horse. She had gone ahead and bought it, borrowing $75 from her father. "Now if I just had enough money to buy a pretty little phaeton, I would be fixed."

Ed must have been more alert now on how to avoid matrimonial strain. He sent her a breastpin, and she wrote February 26 thanking him for a "perfectly lovely" gift. She hated for him to be all alone in that "dreary, dismal St. Louis and feel real bad that I am not along to comfort you a little bit at nights anyway. . . . Well, perhaps it is foolish that I am awfully much in love with you."

In St. Louis, it was just short of chaos. Henry Little had gone, physically exhausted, to Hot Springs, Arkansas, to soak his rheumatic joints in the baths. James, frightened, was pressuring Ed to devote one-half his time to running the St. Louis paper. Ed did not care to provoke a new rupture with his elder brother, but he had no intention of saddling himself with personal management of the *Chronicle*.

Ed reached into his bag of tricks. He summoned Milton McRae to St. Louis and informed him the *Chronicle* was now his baby. To spur him on, Ed arranged for James and George to lend McRae $2,500 with which to purchase one-fifth interest in the tottering paper. Circulation had sunk to a miserable 7,500. Mac's first move was to cut the street sales price in half, to one cent. Sales leaped. But St. Louis was not a "penny town." The little urchins selling the *Chronicle* had trouble making change. McRae, innovative as well as energetic, pulled a rabbit out of his own hat. He induced merchants to feature sales items at prices ending in forty-nine cents, ninety-eight and ninety-nine cents. To further increase the supply of coppers, he badgered Washington officials to send $10,000 in pennies to the "mudhole city."

In a few weeks *Chronicle* circulation shot up to 25,000. Advertising contracts for March increased $5,000, and old and large merchants began coming back. "McRae is booming the paper. His head is too big for a bushel basket," Ed informed Ellen on April 25.

Now again more or less a man of leisure, Ed spent his time at West

Chester. One night, he wrote Ellen, "Nackie got mad and went into another room and the wind rattled her shutters and she came back to abuse me for not getting up to drive the burglars out. She waked me to remind me that if I loved her I would not go to sleep while she was talking." As her time approached, Nackie began to grumble about being pregnant. As Ed reported May 17 to Ellen: "She says if I were in her place I would not be anxious for a large family. I am anxious though."

George came for a visit. He warned Ed that Sweeney had started plotting anew for a duel to the death. "Watch out," admonished George, "for a stab in the back!" In the joust with his jealous cousin, Ed clearly had come out on top. To assure uninterrupted continuity of affairs in his absence, James had relinquished to Ed his presidencies of the *News,* the *Press,* and the *Chronicle.* Already president of the *Post,* Ed Scripps had now achieved the supreme leadership position he had so long yearned for. Now he was the concern's Number One boss, a virtual dictator. It was this development, George was warning, that had again ignited Sweeney's envy.

Ed and Nackie were invited to the June 1 wedding of the James Scripps's eldest daughter, Ellen W., twenty-four, to young Detroit businessman George Gough Booth. They sent a fifty-dollar nut dish. Rather than buy a whole new maternity wardrobe, the heavily-pregnant Nackie remained at home; Ed went alone. Her first letter cautioned him to closely observe the nuptials and report every detail. She added: "And have you changed your shirt yet? Well, you must change it when it gets dirty. You remember I told you that before you left, don't you?"

Ed's attention was not on his soiled linen, but on dirty tricks pulled by John Sweeney in his new rebellion. The treacherous cousin was conniving through Seabrook to embarrass the tyro Osborn. Seabrook snidely reported Osborn cleaned out valuable old files and sold the contents as waste paper. Sweeney went to Cleveland and got in a shouting match in the *Press* office with Osborn. On June 20 he complained to the directors that Osborn was disobedient and incompetent, and demanded his ouster. Ed wouldn't hear of it.

Sweeney then promptly tried to compromise Ed's integrity in James's eyes by confronting the patriarch with the memo regarding the twenty shares of *Press* stock. John cried that Ed was reneging on a private understanding. James reacted mildly; he suggested John and Ed settle the matter themselves.

James intended nothing should interfere with his trip abroad. He thought he could rely on the inflexibility of the Quadripartite to prevent or minimize damage that might stem from any clash between the rival cousins. He sailed from New York as planned July 20 on the *City of*

Rome with Hattie, daughters Anna, now twenty, and Gracie, nine, and son William, four. They were accompanied by Ellen.

The voyagers had hardly cleared port before Sweeney exploded. He fired off a bitter letter of complaint to James, to catch up with him in London. John threatened to repudiate the Quadripartite agreement. Not possible, Ed countered. Not unless all four signers were in full agreement. And Ed vowed that he intended to fight to see its terms were literally carried out. Ed asserted James was too far away to arbitrate, ought to be left out of the quarrel, and afforded freedom from worry and the chance to regain his health.

Ed was sticking close to the farm, an attentive husband, reporting to Annie that Nackie "needs the same attention as a little girl, which she still is. No one would think that she is the mother of that boy I hear booming in the drawing room. That boy is a wonder of good health, good spirits, bad manners and impertinent remarks. But I am so proud of him."

For her twenty-first birthday, Nackie's "surprises were just what she demanded on penalty of never speaking to us again," Ed wrote Ellen, "a ten-dollar gold chain for her one-dollar watch from me, and a mirror from her mother and father."

Sixteen days later came cruel tragedy. On the evening of Thursday August 4, Nackie went into labor. At midnight she bore a son, fine-looking, thoroughly developed, large. But he never breathed.

Ed stared in disbelief as the doctor finally suspended his frantic effort to fan the tiny spark of life. Ed's face went black with grief and anger. He stalked out into the night.

A terrible wrong had been done him. He clenched his fists, feeling a maniacial urge for vengeance. The physician called it an "unavoidable accident." But thoughts of Nackie's "uncourageous whims" wandered into Ed's mind. He must not blame her, yet he felt this tragedy would inevitably affect their relationship. He swore he wanted no more children; he was not cut out for domestic life. He would try now to lose himself in business. Everyone must be aware to not try to condole with him. He wanted all this forgotten—and very quickly.

Shortly before the sun came up, a lone mourner with a shovel was on his knees in the little cemetery—Ed Scripps burying a nameless son.

12

Lessons from Frederick the Great

On the sandy shore at Old Point Comfort, Virginia, they strolled as the September sun went down. Nackie, smiling, walked with her mother and Katy the nurse. Ed, carrying fourteen-month-old Jim, followed, probably only listening absently to the surf's rumble, deep in thought about business.

Returning to their honeymoon scene had definitely aided Nackie's recovery. Ed congratulated himself for coming back to the rambling old Hygeia Hotel. Loss of the baby was more difficult for him to rationalize than her. Seeming somehow to blame Nackie, Ed brooded throughout August, ignoring her, creating a gulf between them. But Nackie got him to "return" with a kiss and her promise "to be good, oh, for ever and ever. . . . After that," he wrote Ellen, "what father could be hardhearted enough to continue the bread and water and the dark room. . . . The sensation is delightful when Jim is laughing and crawling to me and Nackie is not in rebellion. . . . She declares she's a woman. Poor infant! She needs a guardian . . . and I have someone to guard."

If his personal world was again sunny, the reverse climate haunted his business affairs. In every office there was trouble. John Sweeney's spies were creating turmoil at the *Press*. Their latest intrigue was to accuse Willis Osborn of a mysterious disappearance. When Ed got to the bottom of that, it developed the tyro business manager had been off looking into something known as "the widow sewing machine scheme" which his associates knew about.

Circulation took a frightful tumble at the Cincinnati *Post*. Ed laid out a plan in June to get it back. But editor John H. Ridenour was bullheaded and in a rut. He did nothing. Ed told him he must obey orders. "You're too autocratic," fumed Ridenour. "I quit!" Temporarily Ed made

the religion writer, Delos Baker, editor and talked Ridenour into going to
Washington to report government news for all the Scripps papers.

Even McRae flared up in St. Louis. Ed thought Mac meant to have
his own way or strike. That was only a jest. "When I am dissatisfied,"
McRae wrote October 3, "you'll hear from me candidly and earnestly."
Of much concern, too, was long-time associate Henry Little. Ed fired
him after his St. Louis failure, but commissioned Little, a brilliant
author, to write the popular daily "story" for all four papers. That didn't
work. Little turned out, in installments, five long serials. One, "The
Ward Striker," was rejected by the *News* and the *Post*. Little was outraged, protesting to Scripps, "That was written entirely on your suggestion." Little was dissatisfied with his pay. Ed felt cheated. Finally, the
two old friends parted company.

In early November first word from James since his departure three
months earlier reached West Chester. The letter stated Osborn "was not
learning much" and should to transferred to Cincinnati to work directly
under Ed's "eye" and be trained for some future job. Actually Osborn
was making substantial gains at the *Press,* yet Sweeney's sly tricks
poisoned the mind of the absent kingpin. Adding further insult, James
suggested Ed not "annoy" Sweeney. "To get good results from John, he
must be kept happy and not in a state of nervous disappointment."

Ed could only shake his head. "It was the same old trouble," he
wrote later. "James recognized in John his pupil and imitator of business
methods and in me his antipode. He was therefore striving for John's
predominance over mine, and always failing."

Rival cousin strife continued. Ed wanted to open a news bureau in
New York; Sweeney would not let the *News* go along. He also sabotaged
Ed's effort to get fairer representation for the two "southern" papers
from the Scripps ad agent in New York. With a magnifying glass,
Sweeney examined Osborn's books. He discovered a $2,600 entry had
been erased. He screamed about "forgery." Ed suspected Osborn was
being set up, but couldn't be certain.

When Sweeney raised an issue, George, representing the swing vote
on the current three-director board, elected to play it safe. "His whole
policy," Ed wrote Ellen, who was abroad with James and family, "is to
let well enough alone as long as present profits continue and to not
bother about the future."

Ed conceded the *News* was doing "startling things" in advertising.
Receipts for November alone were $12,000. But circulation was stag-
nant. Sweeney badgered the *News* editors to pounce on any "sensation."
Under his chiding, managing editor McVicar leaped hard when a Dr. J.
B. Book's wife was granted a divorce in Detroit only twenty-four hours

after filing suit. The *News* headline read: "Whoop La! The Book
Divorce Case Railroaded Through!" The scandalized physician and his
wife both sued for libel.

All four Scripps papers came daily in the mail and Ed read them,
complaining the small print blinded him. In his library Ed found
Thomas Carlyle's *Frederick The Great*. Reading the book, he was struck
by marked similarities between his life and that of the hot-headed com-
bative Prussian king.

"I have been trying to extract from this book some lessons myself,"
he wrote Ellen. "You will have to laugh when I tell you what lesson I
think I have taken to heart, and I think I did not need a Carlyle or
Federick the Great to teach it to me. It is to stick by my own opinions
and by force or strategy if possible maintain them, but failing that, by
sheer endurance wear out all opposition."

Just before Christmas the country squire's peace and quiet was
rudely shattered. A "disgraceful scene" had just occurred in the office in
Cleveland. Letters and telegrams advised Ed that everyone was threatening to quit, even Osborn! George wrote indignantly that Osborn was
"making a damned ass out of himself." John Sweeney demanded immediate action—a board meeting to fire Osborn. Groaning, Ed packed his
valise and took the train to Cleveland.

On Friday December 24, 1887, the three-man board converted a
parlor at Cleveland's Weddell House into a pseudo courtroom. Sweeney
proposed to act as "prosecutor" of the case against Osborn. Ed sat as
"judge" at the head of the table. George was "jury." Ed brought in a
shorthand reporter to make a verbatim record.

First witness was Will Speed, the *Press* circulation manager. He
luridly described the "disgraceful" clash in which Osborn blew up and
fired him. Charles Seabrook, the ad manager, and Fred Purdy, assistant
editor, supported Speed's recitation, adding harmful licks of their own.
Editor Bob Paine, however, testified Osborn was shamefully treated
from the first, that he didn't resign but had written John unless harmony
could prevail the paper would go to the devil, and he didn't want to go
along. That was Paine's own feeling. "Put somebody in charge. I don't
care who you make boss. But if you can't end this continual mess, I'm
quitting!"

Sweeney insisted he had proved his case. He suggested Osborn quit
and take a cash settlement. Ed and George found the charges unfounded
or trivial. Nor was it lost on them that Sweeney was maneuvering to
"collect" on the disputed "promise" that if Osborn failed John could buy
enough stock to control the *Press*. George and Ed found Osborn "not
guilty," and then in effect fired Sweeney from the *Press* by abolishing the

office of managing director. Sweeney rushed out to cable a protest to James in Rome, who sent back no reply but subsequently wrote Ed and George to use restraint and to not prevent John from *booming* the business.

From Cleveland Ed sent home a wire that the crisis was over, and Nackie wrote back:

> I am glad you have beaten John. How I would like to see you tonight. I would not be cross at all but just love you.
>
> I think I will have a delightful piece of news to tell you when you come home. I will not tell you now. I want to wait until you are here and see how happy it makes you. I am happy on account of it.

It was easy to guess Nackie's good news. She was again with child. "You will congratulate me on this," Ed wrote Ellen, "but there is no good thing to be acquired in this world without its counter Poiseuille. The trials I must undergo are certain, while the reward is only doubtful."

The drubbing he took in Cleveland did not dissuade Sweeney from pursuing sly intrigue inside the *Detroit News*. His record of advertising lineage gains was truly outstanding; now if he could bring in a peppier managing editor and trigger a spurt in the stagnant circulation he could enhance James's estimation that he was vastly superior to Ed.

Though in rustic seclusion, Ed had his own effective espionage apparatus inside the Detroit and Cleveland papers. Thus he was not unprepared in mid-January 1888, when Sweeney made his move, which was to direct editor Mike Dee — whom he had won over — to fire managing editor McVicar so he could bring in Fred Purdy from the *Press*. They expected McVicar to blow up. He took the news with a smile, pulling out a letter signed formally by Edward W. Scripps, president of the *Evening News*. It stated that if any effort was made to discharge him, McVicar immediately was commissioned "general manager" over the entire editorial department.

"Mr. Dee was thunderstuck and humiliated and mad," Ed would recall. "He asked McVicar to discharge him. McVicar had his orders from me to the contrary and would not do it." The thwarted hatchetmen fired a protest to Europe, telling James the whole news staff was "demoralized." James responded mildly. From Rome he wrote, "In the settlement of the Osborn matter you were probably right. . . . Try to heal the wounds of John's pride. . . . Why not withdraw all interference. . . . Find out what John wants . . . humor him."

Ed gave that a try. But John insisted nothing would suffice except James come back. By writing Ellen regularly, Scripps kept his older brother apprised of his low opinion of Sweeney, such as: "He is one of those vulgar villians of the French novel, a financial scoundrel, a sort of Balzac's Dr. Tilley."

On business trips to Detroit, Ed had paid social calls at James's Trumbull Avenue mansion. The patriarch's daughter Ellen W., called Nellie, and his son-in-law George G. Booth were "house-sitting" while the family was abroad. Living with them were George and half-sister Jennie.

Ed observed Booth at close range and was impressed. So was George. Young Booth was a successful architect and salesman of iron work. They talked him into coming into the *News* business office to learn newspaper publishing. James approved the scheme. Ed made Sweeney think it was George's idea so that James's son-in-law could checkmate Ed. Sweeney swallowed that.

In Cleveland, the *Press,* unshackled from sabotage and squabbles, zoomed in ad profits as circulation topped 40,000. Ed sent the staff congratulations and five hundred cigars. He authorized an additional press and a $5,000 annex for it. He credited the gains to Osborn:

> Willis is working 16 hours a day and Sunday. . . . Osborn is either a conceited ass or else his nerve and ability are of the first order. I know he had rather work for $10 a week and succeed, than $200 and not. John's actions have at least procured us this much, that Willis had rather kill himself with work than allow John to have the least reason for saying, I-told-you-so.

It was at this point that word leaked out that John Sweeney was starting a newspaper of his own—the *Indianapolis Sun,* hiring his editor and business manager—Fred Purdy and Charles Seabrook—from the *Cleveland Press* and raiding the *Detroit News* for his circulation manager. Although "stealing" Scripps men, Sweeney did not plan to resign from the *News;* instead he would supervise his new venture from a distance. The first issue of the Sweeney paper appeared May 12, 1888. It was four pages, one cent, a copycat in nearly every respect of the Scripps cheap journal. George was furious about John's double-dealing.

From Venice, James voiced surprise and distrust. He wondered if Sweeney's starting his own paper might not violate the Quadripartite. He considered writing John a "plain letter" challenging whether his action was "square and loyal."

In the spring and summer of 1888, West Chester family life commanded more of Scripps's time than business affairs. He was patterning his management style on his boyhood propensity to sit on the rail fence to watch others work for him. He refused to stand over his newspaper managers. Only every week or so did he journey into Cincinnati; rarely did he visit St. Louis, Cleveland, or Detroit. Sweeney was pretty much left on his own.

The country squire's time was divided between "bringing up" Nackie and little Jim and fixing up the farm. He enlarged the house, had it painted brilliant white, built paths, bridges, a "smokehouse conservatory," and supervised planting of shrubs and trees.

From three windows were vistas he called "my great paintings." To the east: "the shady orchard with two cows, young calf, horses, and view I call *Rosa Chef d'Oeuvre*." To the north: "the sloping green meadow, a clump of maples, elm and willows, the steeple of the little Catholic church and the whole village and many of the villagers to be seen. This I call *Murillo* from one painting of his I remember." Prettiest of all was the western view: "Distant hills and all the fairest landscape and beautiful sunset. I call this one *Clouds*."

On long country walks where he could muse undistracted, Ed was rethinking his moral and ethical values and responsibilities as a newspaper publisher. Changes in his ideas and ideals were also triggered by extensive reading. He devoured Tolstoy, discovering the books meaningful. Often he read until two or three in the morning.

His revision of insight was greatly sparked by the surprise settlement of a dangerous three-year-old libel case filed by the former Kentucky lieutenant governor. The plaintiff, tired of the squabble, volunteered to drop his suit — provided the *Post* openly confessed its wrong, and paid his two-hundred-fifty-dollar lawyer bill, plus $32 court costs.

In this settlement Ed saw a much bigger lesson, one that caused him to do a 180° turn in policy for his newspapers. The moral demonstrated was clear and simple. It was wrong for a newspaper to be perceived as the town bully. From a matter of principle, and also from the standpoint of profit. Ed felt deeply about his discovery, and made an immediate change at the *Post,* explaining to Ellen:

> Another thing to be considered is the difference between my old methods — which unfortunately are still those of the *News* — and where the former was to win by fear, while the latter is by favor.
> By my (new) methods of conducting the *Post* I have gained for the newspaper and myself general goodwill and kind feeling. This makes the

business more comfortable and I believe more solid. I have been steadily at work pulling the *Press* around into the same line, healing up old sores, making more warm friends for it and its proprietors.

My idea is to make a good interesting paper that will sell as a foundation. Then for influence, obtain it by solid, sound argument and kindly persuasion instead of by the usual method—old fashioned fierce attacks and exposures.

The reputation of a bully and a cynic or a sharper is unprofitable in journalism as in private life. The reputation for bravery, kind-heartedness, and honest dealing is just as profitable in journalism as in private life.

Ed pushed his League concept. Finally he had his New York news bureau, headed by Ridenour. It would feed the four papers digests of matter from eastern newspapers, magazines, and books. Scripps contracted with Postal Telegraph Company for a two-thousand-word early morning wire report at a bargain 1.4 cents per word. Privately, he wished James was holding his hand. This wire news was going to cost at least $15,000 a year!

Ed began to feel that the "wild steam engine" of his youth finally was hitched to a giant force for good or evil, with responsibility squarely on him. "Where before I thought of business as a pastime, an employment, an amusement, an exhilirating exercise of the facilities," he confessed to Annie, "it has now become purely and simply a great duty. . . . To family, offspring, a thousand others, employees and friends . . . dependents for my judgment whether they live well or ill. . . . Whole millions whose daily life may depend on how well I do my work. I am no longer a boy. It is not a time to waste in dreaming or rest, but a place for work—work with my own hands and brain."

Scripps convened his four editors in Cincinnati to devise mutual goals and methods—initiating an annual editorial conference that would outlive him, and continue to the present. He carefully noted a question from James: "Speaking of themes for sensation, what kind of idea would it be for the papers to write up Alaska exhaustively?" The boundary dispute with Canada was focusing American attention on the territory. Within a short time Ed would be sending his own reporter-explorer to the distant land of "icebergs and polar bears."

Late-term pregnancy problems afflicted Nackie in July. She awoke with swollen feet. The skin on her legs stretched almost to breaking, alarming Ed. She suffered neuralgia and acute gastroenteritis. Ed sat up with her several nights in a row; then he began to break down, with a fever and delirium coming on. Nackie was alarmed, forgot her own ills, and tried to nurse him. "Nackie felt she had to take care of me," Ed wrote Ellen. "She almost ruined me by sending for doctors all times of the day and night. They broke the fever by giving me quinine and anti-pyrine and morphine in gradual doses."

On Wednesday August 8 Ed got out of bed and declared himself well. That afternoon Nackie keeled over with cholera morbus. She vomited and wretched so badly Ed felt sure her unborn child would be killed. "I took more morphine to hold myself up," he wrote Ellen, "and kept on until midnight when anxiety, previous medicine, weakness, and morphine broke me down into hysteria."

In his delirium, Ed threw a tantrum. While Nackie stood clear, wringing her hands, he "kicked around the table and chairs" and staggered outside and wallowed in the dirt. With some struggle, the doctor and nurse managed to wrestle him into bed and knock him out with a double morphine injection and a large dose of chloral.

Nackie lay awake, wan and worrying. At four in the morning— August 9—she went into labor. Fearful the sound would disturb Ed, she bit her lip and refused to cry out. Fortunately the birth was quick and easy. Otherwise it would have been another tragedy. Her cholera morbus contortions and convulsions had wrapped the umbilical cord around the infant's neck almost strangling it.

Once again she bore a baby that wasn't breathing. Frantically the doctor and the nurse resorted to heroic resuscitation efforts. They began kneading the tiny chest, forcing air in and out of the lungs. They kept going for twenty minutes. Finally there was a gasp, and the cry of new life. It was another boy, large-framed, with a long body and limbs, very dark hair, well-formed, and unmarked.

Nackie's recovery was rapid and complete, but Ed continued "weak and limp" well into the middle of August. His trouble was more mental than physical—a severe case of the blues, his worst in three years. It had been coming on for weeks, inspired by his dread of James's return to mediate the John-Ed war. There really was nothing to fear on that score. James was in Ed's corner. That was clearly expressed in a letter from Milton McRae who had just talked to James in London. Mac, depressed by the death of his own brother and weeks of eighteen-hour days, was relaxing on his first real vacation—six weeks in Europe.

Yet Ed somehow expected "a drubbing and a humiliation." Business had turned bad. It seemed "all my fancy grand accomplishments were melting away to zero" which he feared would reactivate his "reputation of being a crazy drunk, a conceited fool, a rascally adventurer, etc. . . . dashing headlong into something I was not fit for."

He confessed to Ellen he was having doubts of his sanity. "I hardly dare write a letter for fear that its recipient will discover the sign of an unbalanced mind. Occasionally I seem to come to myself and feel certain that I have been insane the moment before. . . . I know that better men than me are often stricken with feelings of their own unutterable little-ness and meanness. . . . But I have gone down when I have least cause to complain."

In late August Ed began to feel stronger, restless for the showdown in Detroit. On long evening walks, he tried to think ahead. He weighed 180, and as "brown and red as any farmer," his health again tiptop. Any domestic disturbances continued to center on Jim. The new baby was well, growing fat and strong at his mother's breast. His hair was turning red, but at age two weeks he still had no name. Ed couldn't decide on one. He rejected Sam, after Nackie's father, and wrote Ellen: "I've thought of John Locke, also my own name but I may live so long as to make it unpleasant for him to be junior, especially if Pa amounts to anything. If anybody has a choice for a name I would like to have it. I think I will put several such names on slips of paper and put them in a hat and let him grab one for himself. Then he will be halfway responsi-ble at least for his own name, and can't kick about it later on."

No hat was used. But it was six weeks before the parents finally selected a name — John Paul Holtsinger Scripps.

On September 1 James returned. Ed hung back, giving him time to listen privately to any tales *News* people wanted to spill. Then on the fourth he went to Detroit. James greeted him warmly. The four directors got right down to the business at hand. For the next five days they would debate their problems. Ed made clear he wanted Sweeney discharged as manager of the *News*. James snorted in mild contempt, refusing to be-lieve the ambitious cousin was not a man of common sense and expe-rience.

After long haggling, James finally wrote what he considered fair terms for settlement, and had George hand-carry it to Sweeney, request-ing the immediate return of the letter after John wrote "yes" or "no" on the back. Instead John stuck the paper in his pocket — for what other reason than possible ammunition against James in a future lawsuit? On another sheet, Sweeney wrote "no" and gave it to George. This insolence and suspicion was the final straw for James. Fuming, he denounced his protégé as "no better than a common pilferer." Ed later wrote Ellen: "It was painful to see the changes through which James passed — magnanim-ity, kindly consideration, embarrassed awareness, indignation, and finally disgust."

One question troubled Ed: Did James want to pursue the "League" idea? He did, "satisfied with what had been done by me, and that the general-in-chief idea was the correct one," Scripps noted. While James delved deeper into affairs at his newspaper, Ed took the train back to West Chester to await a summons for a final session.

At the farm a pleasant surprise awaited. He had been complaining about two-year-old Jim still being attired in dresses. Nackie met him leading a boy wearing knit woolen pants and jacket and cap atop his "lazy like curls . . . like a regular little lord," as he told Ellen, adding:

> I am thirty-four years old and the father of a family. There are times when I feel happier and more in love than ever a bridegroom could be. This beautiful day in the last part of September is one of the times when life is worth a good deal more than living to me.

On Monday September 17, 1888, came the climax in the Detroit boardroom. James relinquished his office of general superintendent, in effect making Ed the supreme executive as president of the *News*. Sweeney was badly rattled. His old mentor had given up on him. The board directed him to resign as managing director and business manager. Almost in tears, he complied. The patriarch meantime had discovered how outstandingly his son-in-law had taken hold. So George Booth was installed as the new business manager under Ed's wing.

For the first time Ed actually pitied John Sweeney. Perhaps this misadventure was not his fault; the directors had put a man of captain's ability into a general's uniform. He simply could not succeed beyond his own depth. Now, at the table, Ed leaned forward and made another of his sudden and astute personnel moves. He proposed to rehire his cousin as advertising manager of the *News!* There was no better man available, and John would easily be worth $1,000 a month to the paper. Sweeney accepted with no hesitation.

With all strife neatly subdued, Ed Scripps once again had total control—all four newspapers safely in his realm. And he had a proud wife. On September 18, Nackie wrote: "Your two letters came. . . . What a time you have had of it! I am awfully proud of you. How is it that you always come out so victorious? I am so glad of it. How must John feel after boasting so, to beg on his knees to you? I want to take long walks with you, and have long talks. . . . I'm trying to be brave but am awfully lonesome for you."

Now that Ed was undisputed king of the mountain, old self doubts came back. He told Ellen: "Now is my crucial test. Flunkeyism, flattery and all do their utmost to make a fool of me, and if they do not succeed I will indeed have cause for pride. My real anxiety is to find out just what my stuff is. I have always been a student and a thinker and a self-styled philosopher. My anxiety is to find out whether I am not also a captain man with a general's uniform on."

13

Reckless King of the Hill

Ed Scripps stepped out of a tailor shop onto Manhattan's Fifth Avenue wearing a stylish new suit, and a wide grin. Often the prosperous country squire had stalked into the Cincinnati *Post* in a farmhand's battered hat, faded khakis, sweaty work shirt, and scuffed boots. Fastidious McRae, chagrined, would hastily summon a bootblack and Scripps sheepishly would submit to a shine. Most of his life Scripps would favor casual—and comfortable—togs, usually tailored khaki twills, and loose jackets. When he became a millionaire, his valets would try to dress him up—sometimes as garishly as a fop or racetrack dude. Whatever he wore, he would messily dribble his tie and vest with soup or egg. He was never a fastidious diner.

Now visiting New York to jog his League idea, Scripps's habitual careless dress had caused him to be embarrassingly mistaken for a foreigner just off the boat. When he wrote Nackie, who was visiting Ma in Rushville, about deciding to get new attire, she responded gleefully. "I am so sorry you were taken for an immigrant, but I am glad you are going to get some new clothes. For you are so pretty that you ought to have pretty clothes. Now isn't that taffy for you?"

This significant transformation in the visible character of the easygoing squire—known a mere seventeen years earlier as Schuyler County's laziest boy—was occurring in early October 1888. It was a deep, through-and-through change. This was a dynamic and totally *new* Ed Scripps—as the *Evening News* crowd in Detroit found out at once!

He had come to a decision—to take over, with absolute, one-man control! Since specific duties had never been legislated for president of the Scripps Publishing Company, he could make all decisions on his own, unless stopped by the board. It was time to quit piling up immediate profit, and invest capital to push all four papers. Now thirty-five, at his creative peak, he must hurry, as he intended to retire at forty and let younger men lead. From New York he sent a flurry of telegrams. Nackie was to bring her babies and nurse and meet him in Detroit. His cook and maid were summoned from West Chester. He wired his brother Will's wife Ambrosia that he would pay all bills if his family could occupy guest rooms in their Detroit home. Everything clicked. In forty-eight hours, the S.P.C.'s new dictator had moved in only a buggy ride away from the *News* plant.

Three quiet years of exile as a country squire had strengthened him for being "in business again . . . hitched to a heavy load." He wrote Ellen: "I feel so strong and controlling among these poor nervous mortals of the city that I cannot at all times resist the natural spirit of a bully. . . . I have got things by the nape of the neck and the seat of the pants and on the rush. . . . I've done a lot of thinking. . . . I am able to decide quickly."

His decisions spurted out in a torrent. Stunning innovations, a wide-ranging shake-up of men and machines. "I have taken everything in my own hands in all affairs, business and editorial," he crowed, "and reorganized." Ed announced he was launching a *Sunday News,* invading the *Free Press*'s exclusive field, a totally new paper with its own staff and printed on better grade newsprint. His next decision was to order the *Evening News* changed to seven columns and increased to eight pages every day so it could accommodate the spurt of advertising flowing into metropolitan dailies. He told Booth to open his money bags and get 50,000 circulation. Then Ed placed orders for three new presses and started putting up a brick annex to house them.

Ed was hell-bent on forging the four papers into a League. By the end of October, Ed felt "the machine is running smoother than ever. Nackie does not like my way of doing, of course. She is a little dazed about it. She thought I belonged to her and resents the shape things are taking and she finds she is only mine."

The new dictator was keenly worried about reaction from the absent patriarch, who was back touring Europe. "I hope James will just keep quiet," he told Ellen, "and not get scared as I do things he never drempt [*sic*] of. . . . I put the lines in my hands. You know how I drive. It is a little reckless, but because one or two straps may break is no reason for him to get scared." He offered a rationale for assuming the dictatorship. "Dismissed from my thoughts all attention to my own peculiar personal interest, financial or otherwise. I disregard any individual paper and have determined to look on the Scripps League as one concern. I shall work and spend and make money for the concern as a whole and trust I myself as well as all the papers will be gainers in the end."

His life in Detroit became a sort of madhouse. "I have quit reading, quit dreaming, philosophizing, entirely broken off my old pastoral life and habits. I am wearing the most fashionable clothes. I am walking briskly along pavements or dashing through crowded streets or over the county by carriage and cars. I've spent my days in company with hundreds of men, talking and arguing." His whirlwind of activity, however, was starting to build a small mountain of jealousy, distrust, and business conflicts that hid a coming volcano of brotherly warfare.

Detroit staffers found Ed's pace dizzying. He offered editorship of the new Sunday paper to Charley Thompson, the Washington correspondent. "I'd like to think it over," said Thompson. "Sure," replied Scripps. "Just let me know in one hour!" To revitalize the news staff— known a decade earlier as "a brilliant crew of pirates"—Ed fired editor John McVicar, who had turned wishy-washy. McVicar blew up but later conceded the paper improved after he departed. Now Ed shifted his command post back to the West Chester farm. But not as a lally-gagging country squire.

The League chieftain drove himself relentlessly, advising Ellen, "I don't believe you have any idea of my present capacity." On another trip to New York in January 1889, Scripps did not sleep for three nights, having one appointment after another. "I kept up my strength with whiskey cocktails and reduced my circulation and nervous excitement with antipyrine, a splendid remedy by the way for all sorts of fevers, headaches, weak and nervous affectations. I enjoy the hard work, but I know it has got to be stopped or it will kill me."

On closer look, Scripps realized his Cincinnati paper urgently needed attention. Milton McRae had developed into "a big-headed blowhard" who was acting "like if he didn't own the *Post,* he ought to." The business manager's unpardonable sin was trying to boss the boss. Ed one morning descended on the *Post,* harshly revamped the whole operation, and handed it back to McRae. The latter wailed like "a busted bladder" and made noises about quitting. But in the end McRae rolled up his sleeves and worked harder.

Ed's wild spending spree at the *Evening News* savagely cut profits. From Bristol, England, James complained that the reports "horrified" him. "What in the world can you be doing to cause a drop in average [monthly] earnings of $8,500 to fall to $1,200 in the face of our largest advertising increase?" Ed thought he was wisely investing capital in the newspaper's growth.

John Sweeney approved all this, but George Scripps and George Booth were disturbed. Finally came a blowup between Ed and brother

George. The country squire ordered dividends cut to $7,000, and George raised the amount to $10,000. "That's two sets of orders," Ed screamed in a letter. "I must resign; let someone else serve as president!" Angrily, he likewise sent the same ultimatum to James. The younger brother was spoiling for direct confrontation on who was to be king of the hill. "I wrote all I possibly could to James and George," Ed explained to Ellen, "to awaken anger and resentment against me, to stimulate their belief in my big head and cause them to teach me a lesson." Ed vowed he would welcome a stronger leader to displace him.

No immediate response came from James; but George surrendered at once — and so abjectly it hurt the squire. George receded purely "out of personal consideration" for his younger brother. "George's short letter to me closing the fracas," Scripps reported to Ellen, "does not even mention the business aspect of the case but so completely surrendered to me and assured me of his support with few and simple words, rough and uncouth as his style of epistilation always is, made me ashamed of myself, and made me feel like crying."

For his part, James, traipsing around Europe trying to spend $50,000 for Ruebens and other old masters to donate to a Detroit art museum, decided just to give Ed more rope. To Ellen, he made this assessment: "I was a few months ago very hopeful that Ed would at last turn out a successful manager but my faith is weakening. I fear he is a mere adventurer making a big dash on the chance of success with equal chance of failure. But I shall not interfere. He will have till July next either to vindicate his ability or acknowledge his incapacity."

From his command post at the West Chester farm, the chief thought his League was "paying out just so-so" in the spring of 1889. Financial records for the whole concern show that for 1888, James earned dividends of $80,000, George $51,000, Ed $28,000, and Ellen $8,000. "I guess business is all right," he informed Ellen, still abroad with James and his family, "but I am heartily sick of it again. There is no one to fight me — that is anyone worth getting mad at."

To fight the new siege of blues that had overtaken him, Ed dug in his garden, advised Nackie on raising chicks, rediscovered his children and Jim's discipline problem, sought mental stimulation in his library, and dispatched McRae over to Kentucky to bring back two blooded saddle horses on which he and Nackie could get stringent exercise.

"I am morbid, self-weary," he moaned to Ellen, "and yet this infernal ego comes up and torments me as badly as it ever did in my most indolent days."

On their new steeds, a mahogany bay and a silver gray, Ed and Nackie raced over the countryside. The six-hundred-dollar thoroughbreds were "broke to rack, trot, lope, etc." in splendid shape, but were a little younger than the squire had expected.

Even the bucolic idyll gave Ed some unexpected jolts. "Nackie and I were out riding our horses the other day. My horse stumbled when we were running and I had a slack rein fell and he threw me off. I jumped out of his way and besides skinning one side of my face and blackening one eye, I had no great damage done me. Nackie jumped off her horse to help me and did a great deal of good, of course. It imposed upon me the duties of hoisting her 155 pounds of body back onto her saddle when I was all shaken up and mad and swearing streaks a mile long under my breath. Oh yes, horseback riding is healthy exercise."

Tough-minded little Jim, now nearly three, was spoiled rotten, Ed was convinced, by Nackie, Mrs. Holtsinger, and the servants. "I've had to lay violent hands on Jim, and in fact spanked him so hard that my hands tingled for half an hour afterwards. Jim became an angel." After another spanking episode, Ed jumped around pretending he'd hurt his hand. That didn't impress Jim; Ed had the feeling he was losing the boy's respect and love. But it had the effect of making the child "more manly. . . . He'll take a tumble and never whimper. He has an idea I consider all squalling alike, whether for a cut finger or the moon, and naturally he argues there is nothing to be gained by showing the pain in his finger."

The father admired the way "naughty and obstinate" Jim tried to be "inventive" to have his way. "We had been in the woods gathering wild flowers down by the old Pisgah church. We had gathered all we wanted. Nackie was tired and it was time to go home. Jim had been having a good time throwing stones I had gathered for him into the stream to see them hit and splash. Mama: Come, Jim, we want to go home. Jim: No. No go home. Jim don't want go home. Mama: Yes, yes, come on home. Jim: Boohoo, boohoo. Ergo: Jim, shut up, quit your squalling or Papa will spank you. Jim, drying his eyes and trying to look good-natured: Oh, Mama, see the water running. Mama: Yes, is it not a pretty brook? Jim, turning to Papa: Yes. Jim will go home when the water runs away, Papa. Only wait till the water runs away. Oh my, it is running so fast. It will all be gone soon. And the boy, having the cheek to suppose his father could not understand his pawn, sat down to watch the water run away."

The idea for the first newspaper exploration of Alaska was hatched in the office of the Cincinnati *Post* in the spring of 1889. Sometime earlier James Scripps had expressed an interest in looking into the border dispute between Canada and Alaska. But the expedition was triggered when a young reporter, E. H. Wells, looked at an atlas to check the spelling of a Yukon river. Seeing vast unexplored tracts, he virtually grabbed Ed Scripps by the lapels and loudly volunteered to go to Alaska and write up the unknown wilds. Ed admired go-getters, men of action. Within days, Wells had his rail and boat tickets. McRae bought him a thirty-five dollar camera outfit "and got somebody to teach him how to use it."

The intrepid Wells did a rattling good job, sent back reams of keen copy and outstanding pictures. His success on this venture led to other explorations for the League — on one of which he would become a hero courier out of the frozen North. Later he would become a Scripps "pioneer" in starting papers in the Pacific Northwest.

What proved the League's most sensational and successful venture had a prosaic birth. George Booth idly noticed a two-paragraph news story that England was sending an official delegation of workers to the Paris Exposition of 1889. Booth yearned to come up with a bright idea of his own. Why not send from the heart of America a delegation of the blue-collar workers all Scripps papers championed? Perhaps as many as ten craftsmen from each of their four cities. Booth fired off a brief proposal to West Chester.

A few days later Ed sat in Booth's office to discuss the stunt. Scripps was studying the memo. "Not a whole lot of money, fifteen hundred dollars."

Booth practically jumped out of his chair. "You're wrong," he gasped. "My cost estimate is fifteen *thousand* dollars!"

Ed didn't even blink. "Okay. . . . Get started."

The Paris highlight was to be completion of the Eiffel Tower, at 984 feet the world's then tallest structure, made of 7,000 tons of iron, 18,038 plates and girders, and 1,050,846 rivets, with three hydraulic elevators.

Launched as the "Scripps League American Workingmen's Expedition to the Paris Exposition," the scheme caught fire immediately and explosively. Carroll D. Wright, United States Commissioner of Labor, drew up a portfolio of ideas. Secretary of State James G. Blaine directed all diplomatic doors opened to the expedition. Letters to senators and congressmen boomed the trip. From readers in the seven hundred towns within the Cincinnati *Post* circulation territory alone came three hundred nominations of workers to be considered. It was a prize to be sought — an expense-paid, ten-week, first-class tour of England, Germany, and France.

Delegates selected included locomotive engineer, mower and reaper machinist, watchmaker, farmer, blacksmith, carpenter, paint and paper makers, wagon and carriage mechanic, shoemaker, tobacconist, pork-packer, baker, locksmith, foundry worker, miner, architect, stovemaker, electrician, ship carpenter, streetcar builder, and civil engineer.

Julian Hawthorne, son of poet Nathaniel, was hired as expedition historian. The League's Charley Thompson, Lemuel T. Atwood, and a few other reporters and editors went along to assist the workmen in writing up their observations and experiences for publication back home. The expedition sailed July 24 from New York aboard one of the finest ocean liners of the day, *City of Rome.*

The expedition was greeted by the Mayor of Liverpool, in broadcloth, with gold bullion aglet. The Midland Railway provided a train for use in England. In London, Robert Lincoln, United States minister to the Court of St. James, threw a banquet attended by members of parliament and other dignitaries. Paris, of course, opened its doors wide. A gala dinner took place in a vast dining room on the first platform of the Eiffel Tower. Whitelaw Reid, United States minister to France, presided. Guests included Chauncey M. Depew, Frederic Auguste Bartholdi, telling of fifteen years' work on the Statue of Liberty, and Buffalo Bill Cody, who gave the Americans box seats to his Wild West show then playing Paris.

The social side was augmented by pilgrimages to Brussels, Cologne, Crefeld, Glasgow, Leeds, Manchester, Lyons, and other industrial centers. In dispatches for the League papers, the delegates concluded that the American workman was "better housed, better fed, better paid, better clothed and generally better off than his European fellow."

From the outset tight-fisted George Scripps frowned on the costly stunt. James, observing from Europe, at first "heartily approved" and glowed at the national press attention paid the venture on the delegates' return September 31. But he howled when the cost soared to $25,000.

Scores of lesser schemes were carried out the spring and summer of 1889. They ranged from dispatching League reporters to cover the rush of "Sooners" into Indian Territory to claim tribal lands being opened to white homesteaders, to raising relief funds in League cities when the May 31 Johnstown Flood swept to death more than 2,000 Pennsylvanians. (Henry Little wanted to turn the disaster into a fiction serial; but Scripps said readers were already gagged on Johnstown's awfulness.)

Ed became so busy in so many League activities his correspondence began to inundate his library desk at West Chester. He sent for a typewriter, and hired a full-time stenographer. For the rest of his days he was never again to be without either.

The steadily simmering challenge between James and Ed over "one-man" rule finally exploded in mid-May. The trigger was a cryptic cable the patriarch sent from Carlsbad, Czechoslovakia, where he was taking the baths. Addressed only, "Scripps, Detroit," it said: "Do not close any contracts. Have written."

There was no doubting what the cable meant. James was saying "No!" to buying new presses and doubling the *Evening News* to eight pages. Ed, who had notified James of this intention, blew up, of course. In a flurry of stinging letters, Ed berated the absent brother for his interference and demanded a clear path for his "one-man" regime until James could return and resume command. "I am still astonished . . . that you have forgotten . . . that I was no one's figurehead or puppet, but an officer acting according to *my own judgment*." Ed volunteered to step aside the moment James could again take control.

In a May 14, 1889, letter James asserted: "I am indignant about the quarto [eight-page] presses and I thought I was supreme in the concern. You have been too hasty. The *News,* as long as I live, will be the paper of my ideas. . . . I am afraid you are taxing your strength and would caution you to be careful." He offered practical tips: Get a good night's sleep, list pressing duties, and handle them in rotation. "This," Ed noted, "is not the first or the hundredth intimation of this writer to me that I might be getting off balance, he so often being startled by the novelty or force of some of my expressions."

But things rocked along, day to day, unstable and uncertain. James was not yet ready to come home. Of course, nothing could really be settled until the majority stockholder returned to Detroit. The troubled Ed was testy with McRae who was having problems with his editor in St. Louis and the ad manager in Cincinnati. "I am willing to do what I can," McRae retorted when he was jumped on, "but Great God! I am getting tired of this everlasting strain of trying to please you. . . . No wonder I get blue."

Filling the summer gap, Scripps took his family to St. Clair, Michigan, to vacation on the lake. He needled Ellen: she was "shirking" her family duty, and ought to quit traipsing around Europe. Likewise, he wrote James he "should come home immediately. What good is this attack on the fort when you have my standing offer of surrender?" On August 19, James returned to Detroit—and the stage was set for the showdown.

On arrival the older brother was "clearly annoyed." Every day his ire mounted. Ed did not show up right away, and that was taken as a snub. James found his coffers almost bare; the *News,* he thought, was being "milked" to help its sister papers, especially on the Paris expedition. The monthly profit of $8,000 seemed to have trickled down to a mere three hundred. He conceded Ed had about doubled revenue, but expense was much too heavy. The current "prosperity" might easily collapse. James also detected a "plot" in the modernization splurge—to make *News* stock more valuable to Ed and the Quadripartite survivors in the event James died.

Ed, who had been attending a Butler County political convention in hopes of exerting some influence in the Ohio gubernatorial contest, came three days later to Detroit. He was good-natured, cocky, and ready for a fight. James sized him up as wanting "whole hog or none." Ed was adamant that the League be maintained. To satisfy everyone, he would step out as president and turn day-to-day management over to McRae and other executives. James grumbled that would give leadership to "second-raters." Ed insisted the *News* remain part of the League. "It is out of the question while I live," James noted in his diary.

James was cautious about forcing an actual showdown. He could see his actions already had made John Sweeney an ally of Ed's. It was imperative for James to have brother George's vote on the board of directors. He thought he had it. Still their directors' meetings were at first largely debates. But John Sweeney felt he was catching the most heat in the duel of brothers. After a board meeting, he walked Ed to his train, shaking his head. "Say, Ed, where am I? Whose turn is it to knock me down next time? When I was with James you said I must stand with you or get knocked out. I took my medicine. . . . Then along comes James and knocks me out, and where am I? Say, won't you kick me?"

By that time they had reached Woodward Avenue. "I was laughing so," Ed said in recounting the episode for Ellen, "that I rolled over on the pavement."

A newsboy was standing nearby. John went up to him. "Say, boy, here is a nickel. I'll give it to you if you will kick me."

"Naw," said the boy. "I won't neither. You'll kick me if I try. I ain't no fool."

"Come on, I won't hurt you. Here, I'll give you a quarter to kick me—just once."

"What's eating you?"

John flung the quarter at the newsboy. "Dammit take the money anyhow. I'm a damned fool anyway."

"Right you are, boss."

James viewed the fight more soberly. On August 23, he told his diary: "Ed leaves this evening for West Chester, disconcerted and mortified. He is an unscrupulous schemer, using one person against another to carry his own ends and throwing them away when no longer servicable [*sic*]."

Ellen came back from Europe in mid-October, but perhaps to escape the din and embarrassment of the brothers' squabble, planned to take the train to California to see sister Annie. The forty-two-year-old rheumatic cripple had been for nearly two years at Dr. Horace Bowen's Remedial Institute, West End, Alameda, California. Ed branded the institute staff as bunco artists running a "Jesus Christ factory." Even so, he contributed about half of the $3,000 a year it cost to keep Annie there.

The timing of Ellen's return proved opportune for Ed. In one angry clash in Detroit, James turned on Ed and abruptly demanded immediate payment of all Ed's notes, which were past due but drawing 6 percent interest and were secured. Ed owed James $14,000.

"And," James snapped, "now — all cash!"

At that moment Ed could lay hands at most on perhaps $3,000 — from the *Post,* not a cent from the *Chronicle.* He glared back at James, mortally certain the older brother intended to foreclose, taking all Ed's newspaper stocks, leaving him out of the business.

Ed begged for a little time — "until tomorrow." He tried to think of an escape. He knew no banker — he hated them — who would rescue him. He came up with an idea, and rushed to the depot. He grabbed the night train to Rushville, and laid his plight before Ellen who was visiting the old homestead. He already owed her $19,000, but knew she had $3,000 in the bank and a like amount on deposit with James. If she would advance these funds to lift his indebtedness to James, Ed would secure his new consolidated debt of $33,000 to Ellen with all his newspaper stock. He calculated his *Press* shares were worth $90,000 and his part of the *News* at least twenty. He promised to try to pay her back fast. He knew Ellen would never threaten him with foreclosure.

In his unpublished autobiography Scripps dramatically pictures this midnight ride to get Ellen's help as a totally surprising coup that turned the tables on a greedy brother. On seeing his defeat, James "proved he was a 'good sport' by spreading a broad and genuine grin across his countenance. . . . He truly was a man who admired resourcefulness."

That did not stave off Ed's ouster as king of the hill. James wooed George, and even Sweeney. They joined forces and ousted Ed not only from his directorship at the *News,* but also from the board of the Cleveland paper. Ed immediately exploded.

On the earliest train, the toppled ex-king of the hill rushed back to West Chester, so furious with himself and angry at the world that he directed his stenographer to impound all incoming mail — and not disturb him with any of it.

The first of February 1890, the country squire began keeping a horse saddled and tied to the front gate and another hitched to the buggy in the barn. The servants and hired hands were not allowed beyond hollering distance of the house. Ed himself kept close, often blowing soap bubbles to amuse Jim, going on four, and John Paul, almost two.

Neighbors were amused. Everyone knew Nackie was expecting — just any day now. Few, if any, appreciated the depth of Ed's fear that any ill-timing might kill both Nackie and her new baby. Snow had fallen, leaving muddy roads. The buggy was to rush the operator to the telegraph office to wire the doctor to come. The saddle horse was to hurry the physician out to the farm.

Ed had calmed down, had pushed his business affairs off on McRae, spent nights reading histories of nations with Nackie. Except for dreading the delivery, Ed was at peace. "Those two boys of mine — do you think I can long keep ill-humored when they are frolicking around me?" he asked Ellen. "I confess to no feeling of disappointment that the colts have more mettle than I contracted for."

At 8 o'clock on Monday morning February 24, Nackie gave birth to a six or seven pound girl. It was fairly easy. Ed had counted on another boy, of course. "Having a daughter on my hands, too, is just a little embarrassing at first and dazes me a little." He wired news of Dorothy Blair's arrival to sister Annie at the "Jesus Christ factory" to pass on to Ellen who was visiting her there. He even forgot his anger enough to send a telegram to Detroit.

The country squire professed a "feeling of horror" at returning to business, but secretly he yearned to rev up the throttle on a newspaper. He had no money worries. Ed's annual income was now running $54,000 and Ellen could count on $15,500. John Sweeney was still advertising manager of the *News,* but quarrelling with James over his share of the profits. They were rapidly heading toward a break. "John is a rascal and James is a blind man," Ed observed to Ellen. Ironically, the boom started under Ed's dictatorship was paying off handsomely all around the old League. For the first half of 1890 the *News* had a profit of $75,000, the *Press* $39,000, the *Post* $22,000, and even the weak *Chronicle* $3,500.

Sweeney threatened to sue James. He was promptly fired. John pirated some more Scripps staffers and started a cheap daily in Baltimore. James was asked to take over the failing Kansas City *World* but turned it down. McRae tried to interest Ed in grabbing the *New York Graphic* for $10,000 but was unsuccessful. Ed agreed to work with James as codirector of the New York advertising office but the League news bureau there was dismantled.

The squire couldn't keep his hands off his Cincinnati paper. He sent McRae off on vacation to Yellowstone and moved in again, ousting some old men, getting newer stronger ones, winding up "with a model staff of sixteen." He told Ellen his new focus: "Cincinnati is the gateway between the North and the South and its journals should be the leaders in the movement of peace and better treatment and good will between the two sections."

McRae tried to trick Scripps into signing over to him voting rights on the *Chronicle* stock he was buying on time. Ed caught that and accused McRae of trying to get in cahoots with James Scripps to vote Ed out of any say-so in St. Louis. McRae, red-faced, pleaded guilty. Under ordinary circumstances Scripps might have fired him outright for being underhanded. But Ed must have been doing some thinking about how poorly McRae was being rewarded as his right-hand man — competent, always available, untiring, and a proven money-maker, despite his swelled head.

Generously, Ed forgave the one stumble. But he wisely went even further and offered Mac a partnership, to receive one-third of all profits from Ed's holdings he managed. Ed back-dated it to the first of 1890. McRae immediately accepted, observing, "While I do not think it will make me work any harder than I have ever done, it will naturally keep my mind on my business." Mac vowed to accept the partnership as "a life one."

The first of November came a distressing letter from the "Jesus Christ factory." Dr. Bowen reported that Annie had been "seized by a violent attack of biliously dysentery . . . and . . . is in a critical condition caused by retrocession of her rheumatistic troubles to stomach, liver, pancreas and bowels."

Ed got the word in New York where he was checking up on the advertising sales. Ellen wired from Rushville she was getting a train ticket to California at once. Ed telegraphed he'd go with her. In a scramble, because banks were closed, Ed borrowed $100 from his ad agent and got a wire sent to Chicago to okay cashing his check for $400. Ellen got $100 from Nackie, and $300 and two Pullman tickets from McRae.

In Chicago on Wednesday, November 5, 1890, they met and boarded the 11 P.M. westbound Santa Fe, praying they would reach Alameda before their stricken sister died.

14

In Love with a Rattlesnake Mesa

As the coastal steamer rounded Point Loma, Ed Scripps got his first view of San Diego harbor and the sprawling "boomed-and-busted" town of 10,000 Ellen insisted he ought to see. She was right; the sunny climate reminded him of Algiers. This was the first week of December 1890, and the temperature was 57°. He rented a horse and buggy and roved the rugged stony hills and deep valleys looking for acreage to buy.

Ellen remained with Annie at the Alameda institute. It had been a close call for their sick sister. By the time their train from Chicago arrived November 9, she miraculously had passed her crisis, and in a week or two was much better. As long as he was on the West Coast, Ellen urged, Ed should look at San Diego.

His cousin Fanny Bagby, who had been working on San Diego newspapers, introduced Ed to two men who knew the local real estate market, Paul H. Blades, managing editor of the *San Diego Union* with whom she was carrying on a romance, and salesman E. C. Hickman. In his buggy, Scripps and Hickman ventured into the treeless wilds north of the city, up steep canyon trails, across dry creek beds, scraping through sage brush and wild lilac to explore tablelands.

Sixteen miles north of San Diego they drove one day atop a mesa beyond Murphy Canyon and west of El Cajon Canyon, reachable by no road, not even a trail. Ed stood up in the buggy and looked around. Far to the west he could see the sparkling indigo expanse that was the Pacific Ocean; the shore was a dozen miles away. Nowhere was visible another human, or a house; they had stirred up only coyotes and rattlesnakes in their trek up to this high plateau. There was no creek or lake; no water visible at all.

This barren spot was land to hate. Scripps loved it. He told Hickman: "Get me about four hundred acres—this mesa, that valley Fred wants—for under $5,000, young man, and you'll make a nice commission."

Hickman moved fast. He got options to buy the mesa and about 400 surrounding acres for $2,160. San Diegans who heard of the transaction laughed at a "durn fool" who would pay even $5.45 an acre for untamed, waterless, treeless land "a jillion miles from nowheres."

They didn't know that's exactly why Scripps wanted it; nor were they privy to his vision of turning it into an oasis and building a castle on the highest rise of the mesa. Not even Nackie then shared this dream. Back home, she pouted over his absence, whining that she felt unloved and neglected. Ed, too, felt pangs of separation. En route he had filled the backs of eight Western Union blanks and mailed them from Council Bluffs, Iowa, describing the dash in Chicago to the wrong depot, and barely making the train.

On his mid-December return home, her eyes widened in delight when he painted for her his California dream. He promised to take her to San Diego right away. But first he had to cope with business problems. He was spending $50,000 for new presses at the *Post* and *Chronicle,* causing the Cincinnati profit for 1890 to shrink to $32,000 and just break-even in St. Louis. Thus he elected to defer dividends from his papers.

James angrily retaliated, and although his *News* had a $134,000 profit for 1890, stopped dividends, too. The *Cleveland Press* put $120,000 in real estate for expansion, cutting 1890 earnings to $77,000. If James stopped *Press* dividends as well, Ed would be badly crippled for operating funds and note payments. He complained to Ellen his older brother was trying "to starve me into submission . . . and get my stock in the *News* and *Press* by fair means or foul."

It was a bad time to be feuding with James and George. Ed needed money. He and his partner had hoisted a banner—"The Scripps-McRae League." Under it, they had launched a third newspaper, the *Kentucky Post,* a cheap, four-page sister of the Cincinnati *Post,* which began publishing September 15, 1890, just across the Ohio river in Covington, Kentucky. Ed knew James wanted a complete business break, but George was again becoming friendly. At a February 4, 1891, meeting Ed managed to get back on the *Press* board. But John Sweeney threw in a monkey wrench, demanding James buy his *Press* and *News* stock for $150,000. James wouldn't. Sweeney promptly filed a lawsuit trying to dissolve the Quadripartite.

Anxious to return to San Diego, Scripps boarded the train in mid-

February with Nackie—both on passes—and took also his mother, now seventy-six but active, on a $72.50 ticket. Fred was already there, getting a team and wagon and supplies. Ellen and Mrs. Holtsinger stayed at the West Chester farm to care for Jim, John, and the baby girl.

Scripps knew precisely the kind of "castle" he wanted to build— three one-story wings with "towers" at each corner, ringing a large court-yard about one hundred by one hundred feet square, the double-thick walls to be built of brick and adobe about ten feet tall. The roof would be flat to serve as a "promenade" from which to look at the distant Pacific Ocean. He was his own architect, drawing crude facade details he remembered from a Moorish-style castle he and Ellen had seen on the northern shore of the Adriatic Sea. It was the castle at Trieste in which Austrian duke Maximilian—later to be executed in Mexico—honey-mooned in 1857 with his Belgian princess Carlotta. From San Diego's dominant Mexican and Spanish influence, Ed chose a name for his castle and ranch—"Miramar," which he translated as "view of the sea."

Ed was determined to make this barren land a garden spot and a retreat for the whole family. Nackie was not so sanguine about Miramar. Her face was "a foot long at first sight of the desert" and she grunted she "would not let her children live so far from a doctor and so near a rattlesnake." She was pregnant again which Ed told Ellen "changes her and makes life unsatisfactory for her and a little trying for those around her." He was certain time would banish her "whim" of disliking the parched mesa.

California already was a magnet for others of the Scripps clan, influenced by the presence of Annie on San Francisco Bay and Fanny Bagby and Ed in San Diego. From Detroit to San Diego came brother Will, bringing his ailing wife Ambrosia in belief the climate would re-store her health.

After a month of preliminary work, Ed took Nackie and his mother—all on Northern Pacific Railroad passes McRae had wrangled—home. Fred remained at their tent camp on the mesa to plant his own one-hundred-acre orchard of lemon, orange, and olive trees, and to begin construction of the Miramar ranch castle.

One of the first messages Ed received on his return to Ohio was that Fanny Bagby had married her newspaper friend, Paul Blades. She was thirty-nine and a half, her husband ten years younger. A letter from Fanny Blades on May 2, 1891, gave Ed a double jolt. Fanny reported Fred was not making payments on notes Hickman felt responsible for and was overdrawn at the bank. "That's a bad way," she wrote, "for a stranger to get started in a new town."

Swaggering, his jaw set for fight, Scripps became a familiar sight on the streets of St. Louis the summer of 1891. Once again he was out to seize the goal that had eluded the *Chronicle* throughout its eleven years — the circulation lead in the "mudhole city."

Just turned thirty-seven, Ed was fit, with agile, creative mind and steely nerve. He put himself on the *Chronicle* payroll — $250 monthly sent direct to his bank in San Diego to help finance construction at Miramar. He rolled up his sleeves and mapped strategy with McRae. They put in a new editor and business manager and boldly sent them out, with extra money, to hoist the paper's 27,000 circulation to 100,000! Sneered rival St. Louis publishers: "Impossible!"

To celebrate the newest addition to his family, on September 25, 1891, Ed ordered four hundred good cigars distributed to *Post* and *Chronicle* employees. He had a new son, born uneventfully at West Chester. For a few days Ed considered naming him Edward Roberts McLean Scripps, so he would be called "Robin" instead of "little Ed" which Scripps abhorred. They finally settled on Edward Willis (from Ma's family) McLean (from Nackie's). Just as soon as Nackie weaned the new arrival, they would be off again to California. This time he wanted to go in style — by private railway car. McRae haggled for a cheap rate. Finally he got a private car from the Santa Fe for $1,500 — half cash and half in advertising space in the *Post* and *Chronicle*.

In late summer the guru of the "Jesus Christ factory" at Alameda, Dr. Bowen, died. Ed saw an opportunity to get his sister Annie out of the institute's clutches. He offered to donate one hundred acres of his land in San Diego county "on which your order can build a residence for service to mankind. . . . The fact that I don't like any of them except you should not be a factor." Annie agreed to consider the offer.

The building of Miramar had started ragged and slow. Fred lost track of the design and had to write Ed for details. While carpenters and masons began the castle's first wing, a crew of laborers hacked a winding road up the rocky slope and cleared mesa underbrush. These were drifters, living in a bunkhouse, happy to get $25 a month and meals.

When Scripps arrived in mid-November 1891, he stepped up the tempo. On the private car with him came Nackie, their new baby and — with nurse — the three other children, Ed's mother, Ellen, James's daughter Anna, and her husband Edgar Whitcomb. The twelfth member of the party was grumpy George, daily warming up again to the grownup wunderkind.

The master of Miramar was hard hit by an almost personal tragedy back in Cleveland. The young wife of Bob Paine, editor of the *Press* and

Ed's closest male confidant, got hooked on morphine and died of an overdose. Paine went berserk, throwing himself on Eve's grave, and making a shrine of "her little shoes." He drowned himself in booze, walked off his job, and wandered to Washington, D.C., where he slashed the wrist of his handless stub, only to be saved by a congressman friend. Fortunately, Eve "visited me in a dream," Paine said, and urged him to hang on for twenty years. He began singing and whistling as of yore, and asked Scripps to tell him what to do. The result was Paine resumed his editorship, leaping back into the Cleveland journalistic fray as hard as before.

As little contact as possible with the people of San Diego was Scripps's earnest desire. Especially their newspapers. His aim was to live privately at Miramar, virtually as a hermit. But he was in daily contact with Blades and Hickman, trying to acquire adjoining land. They changed the subject and implored him to join them in buying a failing newspaper, the *San Diegan.* He wanted no part of it but finally agreed to back them with a $2,500 loan. His confidence in cousin Fanny Bagby Blades doubtless made him weaken, knowing she would influence the venture.

Blades and Hickman failed to buy the *San Diegan,* but another paper, the *Sun,* established in 1881 but never a success and now about to be foreclosed, came on the market at $5,200. They took out a $2,700 mortgage at the bank, and Scripps supplied the other $2,500 in cash. He had no feeling about the *Sun,* for all he cared it could be publishing on the moon.

Talk surfaced about mid-January 1892 linking bachelor Fred Scripps to a young girl in the Benoit family at Linda Vista, the railroad flag-stop nearest the Scripps ranch. Ed questioned Fred who swore he had not been intimate with the girl, but she complained to a constable named Tom Weller, who tried to take it to the grand jury. Ed mentioned the gossip to Nackie. "I tell her all I can in order that the mother of my children may be as wise as possible. Yes, family secrets, good and evil, all alike. There is nothing the mother of a boy should not know about men."

On April 11, 1892, Ed loaded his party aboard the private car "Crockett" to return to West Chester for the summer. With the Benoit case hanging fire, Fred went along to attend farm business at Rushville. One month later Fred was back in San Diego. Cousin Fanny Blades wrote Scripps: "Fred has come back and registered at the Horton House. So did Miss Emma Jessop. This has caused gossip at the hotel. . . . A grand jury has been called. In the B— — case, I am informed the younger boy and girl have testified Fred was often at the house and whenever their father was absent Fred sent the pair off for a drive in his buggy while he stayed with the elder girl. On one of these times they returned sooner than the hour they were expected to remain away and what they saw is in direct contradiction of Fred's statement to you. Paul feels certain the matter will go to the grand jury."

Fred was not worried. He told Annie, "Ed has an interest in one of the San Diego newspapers and would never allow anything to be printed." E. C. Hickman passed that on to Ed, and then apparently decided to "fix" the case on his own. He wrote Ed June 20, 1892: "Regarding the grand jury, I have used money and influence to stop the other [Fred's case] business. . . . If I have failed I will never mention the cost. If I have won the case will give you detailed report of the expenses and means used. . . . I shall be East the last of September as Miss Lida Scripps and I are to be married the second of October at Astoria."

[Hickman had met and wooed Lida when he came to San Diego to visit Fanny Bagby Blades. Lida returned home, became for weeks strangely silent, and abruptly sent back his ring, crushing Hickman.]

Both those items of news doubtless startled Ed, but he could dwell on neither. Once again he was trying to end the squabble with James and deal with Sweeney's lawsuit that could cause much trouble. John finally cut the price and offered to sell his stock for $140,000 and end the quarrel. James still wouldn't deal. George, with Ed acting as middleman, stepped in and bought the stock for $120,000. The brotherly feud was not over, but certainly less dangerous.

Then came startling developments in San Diego. E. C. Hickman had intrigued successfully to get Fred off the hook in his sex case, writing Ed July 2, 1892:

> With regard to the case Weller tried to make against Fred, I can only say that the papers introduced by Weller were lost by a committee of the G.J. who were looking up the case and the loss was caused by an officer from Los Angeles who did it at the request of a friend of mine in San Bernardino. It cost me $584.

That left Hickman short of cash. His note was due at the bank and he urged Scripps to pay him back right away. On July 11, Ed borrowed $584 from the *Post* and sent Hickman a check. He pretended not to know it was for an underhanded act, writing Ellen: "I don't know who gets the money . . . and take it for granted the expenses were all legitimate. Of course nothing must be said about this costing me any money, especially to Fred. He is just foolish enough to speak of it in a way to cause me to be suspected of using illegitimate means in his behalf."

Ed Scripps paid a price for not being able to be in two places at the same time. When he was about to cross the threshold of forty, he inaugurated the practice of spending the winter at Miramar and the spring and summer at West Chester. When he was not out west, Miramar usually got in a mess; when he was on the ranch, his newspapers were apt to get messed up.

Despite expense and foul-ups, Miramar house took shape, imposing, stalwart, and beautiful—just as Ed had envisioned. When Nackie first saw the wing after the masons and plasterers finished, she began to admire the castle. The ranch was turning out, as Ed had hoped, a haven for the Scripps clan, indigent as well as rich, the healthy, and the sick. His mother, losing her hearing, sense of taste and smell, had her own quarters, as did Annie and her nurse, Will and his sick wife, and Fred, who had married Emma Jessop, pretty and twenty-one, half his age. George, too, spent winter months at Miramar.

In the summer of 1893 when Ed was forced to rush from Ohio back to the ranch because his mother was dying, he described for Nackie how his dream castle had blossomed, promising: "This I know will be your favorite and future home. . . . By sheer luck I believe that we have found here the most charming spot for a home in the most favored locality in the best part of the whole country."

At Ma's bedside on June 18, 1893, Ellen tried to call the dying woman's attention to the fact that it was her last child's thirty-ninth birthday. "Whether she understood or not, I do not know. . . . Hers has been a laborious exciting life—full of unexpected events." In the late afternoon she quietly died. They buried her in Rushville.

That boyhood penchant for sitting on the fence and watching others do his work for pay and glory never died in Scripps. It became his creed as a publisher, stronger as years passed, reinforced by experience—and eminently successful as he explained:

> Remember the story of the old Greek Lycurgus, who giving his people a code of laws, made them mean to keep them till his return and then went off never returning.
>
> Something on the same principle I have given my men tasks hard to perform, hastening away before circumstances may occur which may cause me to consent to less performance, leaving them bound by honor and self-pride to meet me on my return with accomplished results and no excuses.
>
> I have all my life had my own plan of administration. It has several features. It proscribes doing anything that another can do. It is to develop men rather by imposing on them responsibilities and by a twice-long and

intricate course of instruction. Its aim is to limit the scope of action of a chief to a constantly decreasing set of subjects, each piece of detail being turned over to some other who has developed a capacity for it.

Each year the chief should become less important to the maintenance of what he has established with more liberty and greater capacity to enlarge the business. In twenty years I have done probably not more than ten essential things and twenty other important things. I might have done more of both had I not wasted so much time and effort on doing things that I could have let others do.

The absentee dictator's iron hand occasionally prompted local revolts. While Scripps got down on his knees and dug with his hands in the parched Miramar soil in 1892 through 1895, enjoying not only the sweaty toil but also the challenge to bend Nature to his will, his men in St. Louis snarled and clawed, sometimes at each other, irritated and over-burdened by the lofty goals he had set before them.

Word of strife between his business managers and editors reached Miramar. Scripps sent an agent to investigate and tell him what to do — Lemuel T. Atwood, who now at forty-two had risen to editor of the *Post,* getting $60 a week. The *Press* was abuzz with discord. So Atwood was dispatched to Cleveland. Business Manager Osborn, Ed's cousin, had let advertising and circulation slump. When Atwood gently prodded him, Osborn fired a hot protest to Miramar: "I see it don't make a d— — bit of difference how many hours I put in or how hard I work, I get little or no credit. I am doing the best I can and I suppose it is your privilege to bounce me."

There was also something wrong with Bob Paine; he had quit grieving over the tragic death of Eve, and talk was he was carousing and drinking. Scripps wouldn't accept office gossip and found it too embarrassing to confront his editor friend. So he had him tailed by a Cincinnati private detective. The private eye found Paine "is now married to a young lady from Michigan, a Miss Merrick, the sister of the *Press* proofreader. The wedding took place about a month ago. He seems to be perfectly happy and is not drinking." Paine discovered he was being investigated and wrote Miramar: "Of course I know you have nothing to do with it. . . . I hate to suspect Atwood, but I do." Scripps candidly confessed that he had hired the sleuth, and the editor wrote back that "I bear no hard feelings and am okay and doing the best work of my life."

A few months later Paine did fall off the wagon. This time Scripps was not coy. He sobered up the editor and forced him to sign that he would relinquish his option to buy $100,000 in *Press* stock if he again drank. With so much at risk, Paine quit booze — permanently. Scripps himself understood that resolve, writing Ellen: "I found Paine drinking like a fool. . . . Abstention from liquor does not affect my desire for it. It requires a steady effort to be temperate."

The *Chronicle* continued an amazing climb. The proud and once-invincible *Post-Dispatch* was forced to cut to one cent. Still Pulitzer's paper slipped, dropping to around 30,000, while the Scripps-McRae paper finally crossed the seemingly unattainable goal Ed had set — 100,000 circulation!

"The St. Louis *Post-Dispatch* is thoroughly rattled," Ed advised Ellen August 23, 1894. "The *Chronicle* has done this. Pulitzer is wild at discovery of having been so far distanced without being warned. He is discharging his men right and left. McRae, Young and Osborn have been each offered good salary and stock, and turned him down. Pulitzer is preparing to give us a battle royal in an effort to regain the prestige of his paper."

In Detroit, James Scripps fumed, still trying to extricate himself from the family partnership. While Ed placated George, James foolishly aggravated him. George, returning from a trip out west, found his desk and safe had been moved from the *News* down the street to an office building. George exploded. He was given the lame excuse his office was needed for other staffers. George was not mollified and blew up again when he went back to occupy his old bedroom at James's house only to find he had been put in a small one. Angrily he grabbed his valise and clumped out, going to Will's house.

While squabbling with James and beset by aggravations at his newspapers and the ranch, Ed fell ill. He had chest pains which a San Diego physician diagnosed as a form of heart trouble. "Regret to hear you have angina pectoris," McRae wrote. "There is a thing called tobacco heart. . . . I hope you are thoroughly scared and your excesses in smoking and drinking will be, as a result, greatly reduced. . . . Do not be fool enough to jeopardize the future for sake of a few cigars and an occasional drink of the old stuff."

Scripps was at West Chester in the summer of 1894 when Annie provoked an uproar at Miramar by calling brother George "bad and nasty," accusing him of attempting liberties with the young female servants. She ordered him out. Ed sat down hard on his sister. "Let us stop all this. . . . Female gossip and feminine folly have made Miramar house fairly reek with filth."

Nackie Scripps grew genuinely fond of life on the ranch. Two of her blooded Kentucky saddle horses and a fast team had been brought out from West Chester. She enjoyed riding almost daily, often with Ed, down to the seashore. She was not without congenial companions; many of the Scripps clan were semipermanent residents, and others visited. Her mother and father came out occasionally from Cincinnati. There was room enough—as construction of the ranch house proceeded to forty rooms—for everyone to have a private bedroom plus sitting room. Ed had a third room to serve as an office, complete with typewriter and stenographer.

The isolation had drawbacks. When Nackie thought of any emergency that would require a physician coming out from San Diego—a two hours' hard ride—she frowned and was perturbed. In the fall of 1895 she showed that concern about need for a doctor—for she again was pregnant. Her time would come in late October or November. Ed was sympathetic to her fears, suggesting they should have a second residence in the city.

They found a prize—the twenty-room Judge Britt place, half-brick, with a spectacular rose garden, located on a small residential hill near the business district. The price, including all funishings, "even china and bed clothes," was $9,500. Ed arranged for Nackie to buy it on easy terms from her $6,000 annual allowance. A few weeks before her accouchement she would move to the town house, with her mother and servants.

It dawned gradually that their little girl was afflicted. At first Nackie thought Dolla just "slow." The child never spoke and exhibited an odd stare. One physician "clipped her tongue" but that didn't help much. When three, she spoke with the vocabulary of a one-year-old. Doctors who examined her in Cincinnati and San Diego were agreed—she had "suffered a prenatal catastrophe." Ed was directed to a Mrs. Westendorf who had trained under physicians and ran a special kindergarten in Cincinnati. She impressed the Scrippses as "kindly, and with magnetism." They sent Dolla to her, paying $280 a month to board the child and stable her pony. Dolla after several months got over her shyness, improved in dexterity and speech, but still was unable to properly care for herself. Nackie quarrelled with the teacher, dooming this special care arrangement.

In early 1895 Ed Scripps directed his vaunted hard thinking toward consolidating and expanding his newspaper league. Within his grasp were the essentials: men and money. With brother George's respect and admiration now warmly rekindled, the old soldier's purse could furnish financing. The untiring human dynamo Milton McRae would supply the executive muscle. Ed always seemed a little uneasy about the gamble he was taking on McRae, explaining to Ellen: "Though not ideal, Mac is the best material at hand. . . . You can make a rogue honest by trusting him, and a fool wise by depending on his judgment."

George was invited to become a partner in the Scripps-McRae League by adding his controlling interest in the *Press* to the current League members, the Cincinnati *Post,* the *Kentucky Post,* and the St. Louis *Chronicle.* Ed proposed pooling all their dividends and salaries from the League and sharing this revenue. George and Ed would each take two-fifths and give McRae one-fifth for serving as general manager of the four newspapers.

On June 15, 1895 — just three days before Ed's forty-first birthday — the partnership deal was struck. (McRae was then thirty-seven and George two months shy of fifty-six.) In reaching this "tripartite" compact, Ed told Ellen he "made more concessions than I once would have contemplated. But I have secured one-man power. I am trustee of all George's and Mac's holdings; . . . [the partnership] is perpetual and can't be broken except by unanimous consent. It in no way affects or governs our various corporations. It is not likely there will be any divisions between George and me. We will enlarge dividends and have more time to make business."

Scripps was acutely aware of the prowess of Joseph Pulitzer, if only from their head-to-head slugfest in St. Louis; but he scarcely had noticed thirty-year-old William Randolph Hearst, then cutting giant journalistic teeth on his *San Francisco Examiner,* and with millions inherited from his father soon to rocket to coast-to-coast newspaper stardom.

Union printers in Cincinnati, alarmed because typesetting machines were displacing hand compositors, proposed starting their own evening paper, the *News.* Scripps warned they would fail. They admitted he "was recognised as one of the best and fairest" publishers in the country, but George "told me that if a revolution came I would have to suffer with the rich, and I admitted it. . . . Mine will be the first throat to be cut." Ed foresaw the future correctly; the printers' paper lasted only thirty-three days.

In San Diego, Paul Blades had become the dominant partner in the *Sun,* had secured a successful niche in the city, and wanted a larger field. Scripps viewed him with admiration and a little envy. Blades cast his eye on the nearest big town — Los Angeles. The *Los Angeles Record* was for sale. He tried to get Scripps interested — just as Ed's expansion fever was getting high. They went to Los Angeles and sized up the property. Ed proposed the Scripps-McRae League acquire the *Record,* but cautious McRae vetoed the suggestion, and George ignored it. Scripps fooled around a couple of months and then decided to go it alone, in a slim partnership with Blades. On September 15, 1895, Scripps bought the *Record,* three-tenths for Blades and seven-tenths for himself. "I believe," he told Ellen, "the *Record* will tempt me further afield." He was 100 percent right about that.

15

"Some Ass of a Doctor Is Scaring You"

On the night of Saturday, October 26, 1895, Dr. Edwards was hastily summoned to the Scripps town house in San Diego. Scripps, distraught from worry and wild-eyed from whiskey, met him at the door. In her upstairs bedroom, Nackie was going into labor. "If you bring them both through," Scripps growled, "I'll pay you five hundred dollars. . . . If only one lives — nothing! . . . If you let both die, I'll shoot you!"

To Dr. Edwards this was no idle jest. He repeatedly had warned that Nackie's Bright's disease could make this birth dangerous. Scripps expected the worst. The physician hurried up the stairs, mindful that Scripps habitually carried a hip pocket revolver.

Going into the parlor, Scripps hunched down in a chair and wrapped his head in a blanket to drown out his wife's screams — or so she said thirty years later in one of their quarrels. On Sunday afternoon Scripps drove out to Miramar and wrote Ellen:

> About 3 o'clock this morning Nackie gave birth to a living child — a boy. The birth was premature by a month. The child is very small, not over five or six pounds, but seems vigorous and the doctor thinks he will live.
> Nackie suffered very much, more than she has ever suffered before. . . . If Nackie lives it probably will be because he was premature. . . . The danger is great now and I am not reassured. I came out here feeling it better for me to be away from Nackie for a time and with a phone in the house can get there in an hour's time.

Choosing a name for the new son posed the usual dilemma. They agreed to call him "Robert" but there was some confusion on his middle

173

name. E. W. wanted that to be "Plowright," an English ancestral name. James E. Scripps's 1903 family genealogic history lists the child as "Robert Nackie." Yet he grew up as Robert Paine Scripps, presumably the namesake of the editor of the *Cleveland Press.*

Having found an excuse to go off the wagon, Scripps apparently kept up his heavy boozing. "I am very sorry to hear," McRae wrote November 15, 1895, "that you have been drinking and smoking again so much. Of course you have been under great nervous strain. The League work, the *Chronicle*'s losses, and the Los Angeles paper, your wife's dangerous illness, etc. is enough to break you up and it is pardonable if you get cranky and jump the traces."

No small part of Ed's fretting seemed to center on the dismal prospect that his wife, barely thirty, had developed medical problems that could interrupt or hamper their connubial relations. Writing Ellen about an unrelated matter, Scripps broke in to observe, "Nackie seems more beautiful and more powerful over me than ever before in her life, and I am glad of it. I had rather be an animal man than an intellectual giant."

Subsequently, Nackie went to Cincinnati for a physical by her trusted old family physician, Dr. W. H. Taylor, while Ed stopped off in Cleveland for business. That night she wrote him: "I am frightfully alone. . . . I think I will go out and buy a dog for company. . . . Please don't send me any more typewritten letters. They make me cold." Two days later she sent cheerful news; Dr. Taylor found her well, urine perfect, and heart okay. "He also sees no reason why I should fear having another child."

The physician's report elated Scripps, stirring him to hastily arrange a romantic odyssey—taking Nackie for a month's trip to Europe. The overseas excursion apparently did not enthrall Nackie. "I regret," McRae wrote Ed in London, "Mrs. Scripps was cold and didn't enjoy. I am amazed you played poker and won. Friends in San Diego tell me you are a shining mark for your friends, but a good loser."

In the fall of 1897 Nackie again suffered morning sickness and went to see Dr. Edwards. The physician was at once alarmed. On October 22, Scripps wrote Ellen: "Dr. Edwards says another child will kill Nackie—but . . . " For the seventh time in twelve years, she was pregnant.

With his $50,000-a-year income heavily committed, Scripps could not alone finance his entry into Los Angeles journalism. Both brother George and McRae had turned thumbs down on buying the *Record.* So the chagrined master of Miramar had to forget that he hated bankers worse than rattlesnakes. He called on his poker club cronies at San Diego's Bank of Commerce and came out with a $10,000 line of credit to get Paul Blades started.

The *Record* was a scraggly underdog. Its ancient press frequently broke down. Advertising revenue was slim. It definitely was the weakest of the Los Angeles dailies. Scripps watched this struggle from a distance. "Blades gladly accepts all my advice and assistance . . . and shields me from all care and worry instead of running to me for help in every little trouble." That left him free to enjoy life at Miramar. "In digging, plowing, ditching, building and planting — engaged in these pursuits I am always happy. . . . The cure of worn out affections and interest is in wallowing in soil and rolling over rocky roads. Don't you see in my letters, Mac, that I am becoming more humane, more respectable, and more likeable. If you don't see it, I know it."

His Miramar idyll suffered unexpected jolts. He was saddened by the tragic death of brilliant but erratic Maurice Perkins, his reporter who had been painted black in that celebrated Cleveland episode. Long ill, Perkins, forty-five, on October 16, 1895, dived out a third-floor window of a hospital in Indianapolis where he was on the staff of the *Sun,* and writing a nationally syndicated humor column.

A financial shock came from St. Louis. The *Chronicle* had whipped Pulitzer in circulation, but was now awash in red ink, creating for 1895 a loss of $65,325. That earned McRae sharp reprimands.

George Scripps was pushing the husband of their niece, Will Scripps's daughter "Floy" — Will Kellogg, the ambitious but sly ad man who had come from the *Detroit News.* George wanted to stake Kellogg to an interest in the *Los Angeles Record,* but E. W. vetoed that. Kellogg, he said, could never succeed as long as he would willingly accept such a gift. But to satisfy George, Kellogg was installed as general advertising manager of the League at $10,000 a year.

The *Chronicle* kept losing heavily while the rival *Post-Dispatch* bragged it was making $100,000 a year. The *Chronicle*'s profit tailspin shocked, mystified, and rattled McRae. He decided to experiment with musical chairs. Willis Osborn was brought down from Cleveland as the new business manager and Herbert Young sent to fill his job at the *Press.* The switch pleased neither. Osborn discovered the St. Louis paper's finances "a stinking, rotten mess" and at once lopped $1,000 a month off expenditures.

Out in Los Angeles, Paul Blades's valiant — but so far losing — fight stirred Scripps's confidence. Just when Blades was exhausting the last of his taw, Scripps obtained an additional $25,000 from a Cincinnati bank and authorized the *Record* to put up a new building and buy a new faster press.

The fever to add still more papers broke out in the Scripps-McRae League late in 1896. In Kansas City, the bankrupt *World* was to go on the sheriff's block December 22. McRae sent Kellogg to look it over; and Kellogg "went simply insane" over buying the paper, reporting back it had lost only $4,000 since August and owned its linotypes. McRae hurried to Kansas City and found Kellogg grossly inaccurate; the *World* had lost $20,000, and only rented its typesetting machines. McRae, uncertain, went on to Cleveland to consult George Scripps. Staying in Kansas City, Kellogg kept dickering to make a deal but Mac decided "no." Still Kellogg could not be stopped. On December 30, 1896, McRae again wrote Miramar:

> A new deal came up today with regard to the Kansas City *World*. They made us another proposition through Kellogg and we accepted. We get three-fourths at the same price they asked for two-thirds. . . . Kellogg will purchase one-fifth. George agrees to furnish loans of $3,000 a month for one year. . . . Don't think I am mercurial in changing my mind. . . . It will pan out all right in the end.

The newest League paper was up against singularly fierce competition—Colonel William Rockhill Nelson's *Kansas City Star,* which McRae described to Ed as "one of the best in western America. . . . Nelson, sixty-two, crusty, three hundred pounds, 'owns' Kansas City, is rich and lives in a palatial house. He went to St. Louis intending to start a paper and found the *Chronicle* already there and went on to Kansas City to start the *Star.*"

George Shives and Kellogg were assigned to oversee *World* business and advertising matters, respectively, to divide their time between St. Louis and Kansas City. At once they began quarrelling.

In St. Louis, the big problem was Willis Osborn. McRae thought Osborn, just engaged to a farmer's daughter, was dissipating too much at night and didn't know what was going on at the *Chronicle*. More surprising—and dangerous—he was in touch with Joseph Pulitzer. Melville Stone of the Associated Press alerted McRae as a close friend that Osborn was wangling for a job at the rival St. Louis *Post-Dispatch*.

Scripps was shocked by this apparent disloyalty of his cousin. Likewise he was angered by hearing that Will Kellogg freely gossiped about Scripps family finances, details of which he picked up from wife Floy, forecasting a mighty estate squabble if either George or Ed should die.

"If you don't either discharge Kellogg or shut him up," E. W. wrote McRae, "I will come home and do it myself. Sometimes I feel that you yourself dislike to admit to your subordinates that I (and not the League) am supreme. . . . Obey my orders as you expect your orders to be obeyed."

McRae shut up Kellogg. Then he went to St. Louis to straighten out the Osborn conflict. On October 3, 1987, McRae discharged Osborn, who immediately protested by wire to Scripps that he was surprised and knocked off his feet.

> I am cut to the quick. I am unable to get a reason except that you have instructed McRae in your own handwriting to dispense with my services or you would act yourself. It is like a thunderbolt out of a clear sky. No complaints — business second to none in the League. The Pulitzer position was unsolicited but if accused of seeking it, why wasn't I let go when I could have had it in a minute instead of waiting until it was filled by another? . . . I'm discharged, humiliated and embarrassed beyond degree after eleven years of successful management. You sought my services and took me from a lucrative business. . . . For God's sake, don't treat me as though I was a yellow dog until I warrant it.
> Yrs, Willis

Ten days later Osborn sent another message: "I haven't heard from my telegram. It is strange what a difference a little money and power makes. Sometimes after a man reaches the topmost rung in the ladder he turns his back on those that helped him ascend. . . . Your treatment of me has been unmanly, cowardly, and outrageous. . . . I leave for home tonight." His letter crossed one in the mails in which Scripps explained:

> Last May I met you feeling more hopeful for your future than for two years past. You wished to remain in St. Louis. I promised nothing, but decided that you should remain.
> In July you told me you were considering Pulitzer's offer. I told you that you could not honorably do so. You differed with me. . . . You felt you had a right to leave my concern at any time and carry with you for use of my competition that knowledge which your high and responsible position entitled you to receive in confidence from me. . . .
> I am not coward enough to let you believe that any but I am responsible. . . . When you told me that you had a right to use such confidence for the benefit of a competitor who would pay your price, my mouth was closed. After that I could tell you none of my plans.

Growing even angrier, Osborn then contended he had been employed on a year-to-year basis, and demanded a year's dismissal pay, threatening to sue. He said McRae was a false friend, "and so are others. . . . I nailed one of your sweet-scented gen'l managers in a damned lie that he'd taken to headquarters and made him sit down and write an apology and acknowledge himself a shitass and a scoundrel."

Scripps advised McRae that Osborn was writing abusive letters. "I suspect he was full most of the time." Scripps conceded that on the *Press* Osborn did have an unbreakable contract, but gave it up when he went to the *Chronicle.* This might strike unbiased observers as somewhat devious handling of Osborn's vested rights, inasmuch as he was in effect "transferred" from one paper in the League to another. Two months after his discharge from the *Chronicle,* Osborn went to work at the rival *Post-Dispatch.*

In Chicago's Auditorium Hotel on Saturday morning, June 22, 1897, Ed Scripps sat in his room with brother George and Bob Paine and watched a flustered Milton McRae grab his hat and dash out the door. Heading downstairs to a directors meeting of the Associated Press, McRae carried a last-minute request by the League papers to join the reorganized wire service. McRae, visibly rattled, was afraid Ed had waited too long making up his mind.

In recording the scene later, Scripps said he looked at George and thought his brother was beginning to suspect what was up. But Paine, in the dark, was boiling mad. Only Scripps knew of the secret stack of telegrams his secretary had ready to send out. Scripps felt smug. Oh, what a clever trick he was about to spring!

For thirty years rival wire services had been battling haphazardly to supply America's growing newspaper field with telegraph reports. James E. Scripps had always sided with the AP crowd, but Ed kept his papers aligned with its chief rival, known as the United Press.

The idea of an association for collecting news from distant points got its biggest impetus at the outbreak of the Civil War when the telegraph was new and expensive. Even the big New York papers found tolls so high they shared the same dispatches and prorated expense. Out of this practice grew the first formal Associated Press, dominated initially by the "big four" New York dailies. This main AP was a mutual company but for a fee it fed regional Associated Press affiliates in the Midwest, South, and West. After a few years some Chicago newspapers grew disenchanted with their treatment by the New York clique, and pulled out and started their rival United Press. The two competitors battled inconclusively for several years for news, and clients to print it. Internal rot set in. Crooked directors began to milk both outfits. Some AP executives secretly bought UP stock, and began swapping news and pulling other dirty tricks.

When this was revealed, the remaining Chicago members of the regional Associated Press rebelled, seized power, and effectively took over as *the* Associated Press for the whole country. The AP papers in New York immediately decamped, going over to the United Press. The battle between AP and UP raged on. Finally the United Press started slipping — badly. Now on this momentus Saturday in Chicago the UP was finally bankrupt; the Associated Press was sweeping everything before it — and feeling pretty smug.

One reason Ed Scripps had linked his papers over the years to the UP was friendship he had developed with Walter Phillips, the brilliant United Press manager. Through Phillips, Ed got special privileges that sharply cut the cost of obtaining telegraph dispatches for his papers. On the other hand, brother James, with whom Ed was still on the outs, was a director and important figure in the new Associated Press, to whose executive meeting McRae was now hurrying.

Months earlier the Associated Press had offered Ed Scripps 25 percent of the stock in the reorganized wire service plus voting rights if he would bring into membership his League papers. This Saturday was the deadline. McRae was furious that Scripps had dilly-dallied to practically the last minute. But Ed had done that with deliberate intent.

Scripps had two main objections to the new AP setup. First, it would mainly serve morning papers. The Associated Press in the past often held back important news from the "day" report, thus favoring AMs over PMs. Also Associated Press franchises were exclusive, meaning no new competitor could invade a member's territory and obtain AP service. Thus if Scripps planned to start more newspapers — which he did — he might have trouble finding for them a source of adequate telegraph news. Further, the AP was trying to set up an impossible barrier for the start-up of any new rival by enacting legislation which prohibited any member from buying any service other than the AP. That might easily lead, Scripps feared, to the creation of a national news monopoly — the AP's. Scripps, on principle, was dead set against any kind of a monopoly, especially on news.

That being the case, why had he let McRae scamper down to the AP meeting to ask for membership? The secret lay in Scripps's own experience in operating a small-scale wire service over the years to augment the inadequate "day" report provided by the old United Press. He started this auxiliary service with his League news bureau in New York in 1888, bolstered by a one-man office in Washington. His papers exchanged important news and received dispatches from a few other strategically-located afternoon newspapers on a swap basis. Cleverly he had wangled from Walter Phillips free use of the vast telegraph circuits of old United Press when they were otherwise idle. This had permitted him to move thousands of words daily at an average cost to his papers of $20 a week.

But now with the old UP bankrupt, unless the League joined the new AP, Scripps-McRae papers would receive no telegraph news except that supplied by its own in-house network, which was called Scripps-McRae Telegrams. Scripps had Bob Paine running both the *Cleveland Press* and this wire service. Paine, whimsically but appropriately dubbed the SMT the "Adscititious Report." It was bob-tailed and inadequate, but Scripps knew that with more men and money it could be expanded to effectively cover the whole country for afternoon newspapers, perhaps doing a better job than the morning-oriented AP service. Besides, it would make telegraph news available in any city—even those served by the AP—where he might want to establish a new paper.

This was the trump card Scripps yearned to play in this showdown now taking place a few floors below his room in the Auditorium Hotel. He wanted the Associated Press directors to give the Scripps-McRae League's application the hardest kind of turn-down!

He hoped it would be insulting enough to stir the pugnacity of brother George and also the fighting Scotch blood of McRae. Otherwise neither of his partners would give him their whole-hearted, firm, and aggressive support needed for the new venture he ached to launch.

In less than an hour McRae came storming back to Scripps's room, his eyes blazing. The AP directors had let him present the League petition for membership and voting rights. Then the AP men laughed at him. It was too late now to come in as Class A members; the Scripps-McRae papers would have to sign up as mere clients, with no say-so.

McRae had exploded, and so did George when he was told of this demeaning rebuff. Then Ed unveiled his secret plan—to at once expand the Scripps-McRae Adscititious Report, and sign up as clients all the afternoon papers that were being left high and dry by the collapse of the United Press.

He brought out his sheaf of telegrams. One was addressed to every afternoon daily in the country that was outside the AP. His stunned partners at once brightened, and endorsed the scheme enthusiastically. The secretary rushed to the telegraph office and filed the messages.

This, Scripps decided, would be organized as a profit-making company, which meant the Scripps-McRae League would bear the total expense of collecting and transmitting the dispatches over the wires. They would charge customers weekly fees on a sliding scale, determined by the circulation size of the paper served and the number of words it wanted. The concern's cost would, of course, be very heavy in the beginning, but Ed anticipated substantial profits within a few years.

It was chiefly this shoot-out with the Associated Press that had brought Scripps east from his ranch. Years later he wrote in his autobiography that his challenge to the AP in Chicago was basically his "greatest service" to journalism because it prevented the AP from seizing a monopolistic stranglehold on telegraph news. Yet, he had other reasons, too. For one, he was still smarting from put-downs by brother James, an AP stalwart. And, of course, in any game Ed Scripps had to have one-man power!

But replies to his flood of telegrams gave Ed a rude jolt. Someone had beat him to the punch! J. B. Shales, publisher of a small daily in Pennsylvania, had also come up with the idea of launching a new wire service to compete with the AP. And he had acted more quickly! Shales already had called personally on papers in the East and signed up clients. He got about half the dailies that Scripps had counted on. That would mean a hard blow to Ed's pocketbook; his cost of gathering and sending out the news would be just as large, and his revenue only about half what he had anticipated.

But Ed was undaunted. He grabbed the train for New York where Shales was setting up headquarters. Even though Shales had wealthy backers, the Pennsylvanian immediately recognized that if two new telegraph news agencies opened up they would cripple each other, perhaps mortally.

So Scripps and Shales decided to divide the territory. Shales's organization, to be known as Publishers Press Association, would gather and deliver news only to its clients in the Atlantic states, and be also responsible for getting foreign cables. Scripps would cover the rest of the country. Fortunately, he already had an outpost on the West Coast, a little wire operating out of the office of the *Los Angeles Record* called the Scripps-Blades Report.

Ed lumped everything together, and rechristened his network the SMPA—Scripps-McRae Press Association.

The Publishers Press Association and SMPA would exchange their dispatches, thus providing clients of either wire access to a full national and overseas report. A leased trunk wire capable of moving 14,000 words a day was opened between SMPA's headquarters located in the *Cleveland Press* building and Shales's offices in New York. Scurrying about, Bob Paine got SMPA in business practically overnight.

For the salaries of newsmen and telegraph tolls, the Scripps-McRae Press Association would have to spend about $10,000 a month. Getting anywhere near that much revenue from clients at the outset was impossible. Small papers usually were satisfied with a cheap "pony" report of five hundred words a day. That cost the *Benton Harbor News,* for instance, only $10 a month. For a fuller report the *Memphis Herald* paid $246.50 monthly, the *Dayton Herald* $180, the *Denver Post* $100, the *Indianapolis Sun* $60, the *Fort Smith Record* $45.

Within a few weeks SMPA was serving eighty-six clients, bringing in about $5,662 a month. To make up SMPA's big operating deficit, Scripps decided to temporarily sock it to his own papers. The Cincinnati *Post,* which had been paying less than $100 a month for its telegraph news under the old United Press, was immediately assessed $1,648.71 a month. The Kansas City *World* had to pay $1,141.02 monthly, the Cleveland *Press* $979.33, and the St. Louis *Chronicle* $725.86, a total of $4,494.92.

Ed Scripps had come up with an expensive dream. Now it would be up to Paine's men in the trenches to turn it into a paying proposition.

On the day after Christmas 1896 Scripps called sons Jim, ten, and John Paul, eight, into his office at Miramar to get their signatures on a "contract"—typewritten, in legal phraseology, bound in a blue manuscript cover—that would regulate their dollar-a-day allowances.

The formal-looking document required that the sons "shall pay for all their clothing, toys, and all other personal expenses, and accept no presents from anyone (not even a piece of cake or candy) without the knowledge and consent" of their mother or father. They must tell their father of all destruction or injury to property, "and pay for same." Lastly, that "James George Scripps and John Paul Holtsinger Scripps agree never to deceive E. W. Scripps or let him remain in ignorance of their doings of what they know he thinks to be wrong."

It was his sincere and firm intention that his children, especially his sons, "lead natural lives . . . to grow and develop as nature would have them develop, untrammeled, unbent, undwarfed by any other agency than a purely natural one." He believed his boys were better off growing up out in the country, even though Miramar was remote and isolated. Likewise, he feared formal schooling would "stunt" their minds.

Until the previous September he had enrolled Jim and John Paul in the nearby Linda Vista elementary school. Now he had brought them home and hired a tutor, a well-read young man from San Diego named A. C. Kinyon. The father arranged the curriculum; the tutor was to see they did their lessons.

"My idea of education," Scripps explained to McRae, "is signified by the original Latin of which it is a derivation—which indicates a drawing out—that means the development of what is original. My quarrel with the school and college is that both more or less suppress what is original, attempt to build up that which does not exist in the child's mind and in fact by training try to produce a mind and a character similar to that of the teacher or professor." Scripps had strongly resented any female interference in bringing up the children — even from Nackie.

Scripps readily indulged his wife as when Nackie asked him to go to the rescue of her cousin, Mrs. James Anderson of Richmond, Indiana. Mrs. Anderson's husband, a ne'er-do-well lawyer and secretary of the Odd Fellows Lodge, had been suspected of embezzling $1,800 from the lodge. The district attorney, loathe to prosecute a fellow member of the bar, was nevertheless about to take the matter to the grand jury. Scripps directed McRae to see what could be done.

The Cincinnati *Post* lawyer was sent to Richmond, about fifty miles away. Things looked bad, but the newspaper lawyer was hit by sudden inspiration. He pulled off a clever coup, simply by arranging to purchase its account ledgers from the lodge. The price was $1,800, coincidentally the precise amount missing. The lawyer burned the books.

This left the D.A. with no "evidence" of a crime. Thus Lawyer Anderson was off the hook. McRae went further and gave him a fresh start, a job in the *Post* circulation department. (Later McRae recouped part of the newspaper's outlay by taking title to Anderson's Richmond house and selling it for $700.)

On March 19, 1898, Nackie suffered a "false start" in the seventh month of her pregnancy. Scripps got the buggy and immediately took off with her for the San Diego town house and Dr. Edwards. "Before I knew it, the children, nurses, and servants were there, too. I spent one day and night. The racket was too much for me. I came back to the ranch."

Her time was supposed to come in May. As usual, Scripps expected tragedy. "It is possible the child may not be born alive," he told McRae. "However, Nackie and I have agreed to name him Milton A. McRae Scripps . . . to impress on the boy . . . that consideration which is due from loyal friend to loyal friend."

The baby, however, was a girl, born at the town house Monday, May 16, 1898. Once again selection of a name — obviously not Milton — seems to have caused a dilemma. In the 1903 James E. Scripps genealogy she is listed as Julia Margaret Scripps; but she grew up as Nackey Elizabeth Scripps — the difference in spelling perhaps chosen to differentiate her name from her mother's.

At this juncture Scripps was in a disagreeable mood. He quarrelled with Nackie about financial help she proposed to offer her parents, and ordered them off the West Chester farm. McRae in his correspondence with Miramar easily detected just how disturbed Scripps's mind had become. He tried to pinpoint the cause. "I am sure you are rattled about something and believe you are scared about yourself. You think you are not going to live long. I know from the way you have acted lately some ass of a doctor is scaring you. . . . Don't smoke and drink too much, and you will live to be head of everything with which the Scripps name is connected."

To sister Ellen he did not attempt to minimize the towering obstacles he encountered in his battle with the bottle. "My health is better," he told her August 27, 1898. "I have made a hard fight against alcohol and nicotine. Wrote today and smoked and drank. The result will be a setback. I am between the devil and the deep sea. *If I have nothing to do, I stimulate; if I have much to do, I stimulate.*"

16

Despite God, Man, or the Devil!

I n August 1898, Paul Blades scouted San Francisco as a possible new territory for the Scripps banner. McRae, having heard something was afoot, threw cold water: "It would be folly."

While Blades now rode the train north to San Francisco, the "explorer" from the Cincinnati *Post* who had made a splash with three excursions into Alaska — E. H. Wells — was walking the streets of another important West Coast city — Seattle — sizing it up as an ideal city in which to launch a cheap Scripps paper. He mailed a proposition to McRae, who passed it on to Miramar — not unexpectedly thumbs down.

Blades's objective was to buy the San Francisco *Report*, weakest of the three afternoon dailies. It had 7,000 circulation versus the 85,000 of William Randolph Hearst's flamboyant *Examiner.* Blades assured Scripps he was not afraid to go up against the thirty-five-year-old sociable, witty, and wealthy Hearst, a slender, tall blond with golden mustache, who wore racy attire, swung an expensive gold-headed walking stick, and for ten years had rocked the city by the bay with sensational newspaper high jinks. It was a town of five-cent, not penny, papers.

Control of the *Report,* grossing about $100,000 a year, could be bought for $20,000 from the aging editor who wanted to retire. Slightly in the red, the newspaper owned $27,000 worth of equipment, five linotypes and three rotary presses, encumbered only by a debt of $2,300. It was a dull, uninspired paper.

Perhaps the most astounding aspect of the *Report* episode is that even before the deal was finalized Scripps was angling to pluck out of Cincinnati a most unlikely journalist to be his San Francisco editor.

Ten years earlier Scripps had spotted possibilities in the young sporting editor of the Cincinnati *Post,* a rambunctious redhead named George A. Gohen. Ed had tried to get him "jumped" to an editorship, but Atwood and McRae resisted. They felt Gohen was perhaps too feisty, especially after he unexpectedly returned from a fishing trip, found his wife with a race track jockey, and threw her out the window. In time Gohen advanced to city editor, then managing editor, but deserted the *Post* to go to the rival afternoon *Times-Star.* Gohen, now thirty-one, had a typical handicap — a drinking problem.

Still Scripps wanted him — so badly that he wired Gohen an offer of $75 a week to edit a paper the League did not yet own.

On November 17,1898, Blades wrote a check for $32,000 and the League took full ownership of the *Report.* The pressmen were upset, and pulled a short wildcat strike. Blades was nettled to belatedly discover that carriers owned their routes and could interfere with operations. Scripps had advised him to go slow on changes, and to continue the five-cent street price.

If George Gohen was an implausible choice for editor in San Francisco, what could be said of Ed Scripps agreeing to be majority stockholder in a new Seattle daily with E. H. Wells as his operating partner?

Philosophically Scripps had pristine guidelines to govern selection of an editor. This was the all-important "genius" who must virtually carry the project to triumph on his own shoulders. The editor was invested with total responsibility for news, local editorial policy, censorship of questionable advertising, and full say-so over all type-setting. A new editor should be young and unmarried. No previous training and not too much formal education were desirable characteristics. He must not have been editor of a lesser paper nor held any similar position.

In short Scripps was looking for "someone just-like-me." His pattern was clearly a reflection of himself twenty years earlier when he brazenly flung his inexperience on Cleveland journalism and bulled the *Press* to magnificent success. Wells did not, of course, meet even one of these criteria. He was not young (thirty-eight), nor single, nor devoid of previous experience as editor (having flopped in a tryout at the *Kentucky Post*), and he had a wife and small daughter. Even so, he was Scripps's kind of man. Ed would never forget how he explored the Alaskan wilds.

Wells's adventures fit the temper of the journalistic times. It was the era of newspaper stunts — such as *New York World* reporter Nellie Bly reducing Jules Verne's fictional *Around the World in Eighty Days* to an actual seventy-two days, six hours, eleven minutes and fourteen seconds. Wells had been unable to keep Alaska off his mind. The Klondike Gold

Rush in 1897 lured him back to try his luck as prospector and part-time reporter. He found no gold, and finally wandered down into Seattle in 1898. He encountered not a sleepy lumber port, but a bustling and growing city alive with thousands of newcomers. There were only two daily newspapers, the dominant morning *Post-Intelligencer* and the *Seattle Evening Times*. Why not go up against them with a four-page paper? It could be done!

Not only impetuous, Wells likewise was dogged. He kept after Ed. It took three months to get an okay from Miramar. On November 28, Scripps agreed to team up with Wells—but with several surprising stipulations. First, Scripps was to be a secret partner. He would hold majority stock, Wells 15 percent. The publisher would be known as Wells & Company. If the cat was let out of the bag, the deal was off—at Wells's expense. "I want blind obedience to my orders, and unquestioned compliance to my wishes," Scripps wrote. He agreed to send a rotary press and one linotype from his San Francisco plant. Wells was to draw $20 a week as salary from capital, and—because of his family responsibilities—an additional five a week as a loan, to be repaid.

For the first time, too, Scripps gave a sort of "working interest" in a paper to one of his secretaries. He was impressed by Hamilton B. Clark, who had been his Miramar shorthand stenographer for a year. Intelligent, well read, he was gentlemanly, and ambitious. Clark deserved something better than his $60 a month, with board. Ed gave him 5 percent of the stock and ordered him to Seattle to send totally candid reports back to the ranch. Clark would prove one of Scripps's "happy choices" of executive talent. And his achievements would prompt Scripps in succeeding years to undertake similar experiments with other of his secretaries.

From his rattlesnake mesa, Scripps kept close tabs on the *Report,* fully determined to call the shots. Keeping up a steady correspondence with Gohen, Ed warned him to be prepared "to see me take almost any extraordinary and remarkable course. . . . I count altogether on your personal force, your loyalty and intelligence in obeying my orders in the beginning and not upon your business judgment or even your journalistic judgment in business."

Warming to his theme, the boss reminded Gohen that the foundation on which Scripps newspapers were successfully built

was not low price, not high literary skill, not artistic typography, not fine paper, not a large amount of reading matter . . . but that nearly everybody was a lover of gossip—and that they wanted to learn things with as little labor as possible . . . a four-line paragraph, no matter how badly worded, would sell newspapers better than the most elegant article that could be produced by the brightest minds.

Scripps had second thoughts about risking the Seattle project to old-timer Wells and greenhorn Clark. An impressive and successful — and younger — newspaper chief was close at hand, Edwin F. Chase, who for two years had "cleverly managed" the *San Diego Sun*. On January 25, 1899, Scripps informed Wells he was sending Chase to take over as business manager, with one-fifth interest, adding "Somebody has to get this thing open, and he is a young man with action, I think."

In Seattle, Chase and Wells had trouble getting the webbing strung on their reassembled press. "Looks like there are miles and miles of it — no diagram." At last they were ready to launch the *Seattle Star* on Friday, February 24, 1899, but —

> Ole Hoe press refused to go today. It was hitched up and ready to go with Vol. 1 No. 1, but it bucked, grumbled, and thundered. Then it whistled. You may believe it or not, but that press was afraid of the Friday hoodoo. . . . Try again tonight.

Next day they crawled over the press and made adjustments, held their breath, and started it up again. Everything went smoothly. The first copies of the *Seattle Star* emerged from the folder, and E. W. Scripps had staked a publishing outpost in the Pacific Northwest — but, of course, with his ownership a deep, dark secret.

The legend that E. W. Scripps was "a damned old crank" would follow him to his grave. He never disputed it.

His reputation for having a peculiar personality took its quantum jump at the beginning of 1899 just before he turned forty-five.

Until then the singularly strange Scripps was tough-minded, but fair and in the main gentle and considerate. Then he changed. He turned miserly and despotic in business.

It never bothered Scripps that he wore the badge of crankiness. He realized people tended to characterize him thus because he stuffed his pant legs in high boots, and "I wear a full beard when nearly everybody else shaves clean; to that extent I am willing to appear like a man and do not, like my fellows, make myself look like a girl."

As to the boots, they were easy to pull on and off. He spent much time in the country tramping over rough ground and through brush and high grass. "I am entirely free of the pest of fleas . . . [and] saved the annoyance of getting my shoes full of loose dirt, pebbles and sticky things in the grass and brush."

The "damned old crank" also was too busy to be like an ordinary man, as he explained to Milton McRae: "When I have been accused of slovenly habits, almost unintelligible chirography and uncouth and often disagreeable mannerisms, I have had only one self-satisfying consciousness; this is that it takes more time to keep one's self elegantly attired than any man of affairs can afford; that it takes more effort to write a copper-plate hand than it does to produce an able essay; and that politeness to all the world is a business absurdity and a physical as well as a mental impossibility."

He had few intimate friends; but was attentive to his wife and children. But even they were regimented and pigeon-holed. He was self-centered; also selfish — not with his purse — but with his minutes. And he felt he had every right to be. He started sleeping until noontime — because he made it a habit to stay up till two or three o'clock, working and reading.

Avidly he read — or had someone read to him — books, old and new, magazines, touching myriad subjects: science, economics, religion, philosophy, social change, history, government — anything. He was a freak on education. He had rather send his sons to the pesthouse than the schoolhouse. He mandated that they breathe country air, develop their brains and their brawn away from the pettiness — and the temptations — of the city.

His midlife abberation did not so much direct hostility at his family circle as it did at his business. Scripps snarled and stormed around, venting astounding fury on his most trusted lieutenants.

With one hand in this period he would launch new projects to enlarge and extend his empire, and with the other resolutely hammer the soul and spirit of his established papers in such brutal and erratic fashion that thousands of dollars were lost, and some properties were mauled to death's door; indeed a couple would die.

His talk now became not so much reiteration of his cardinal principle of being champion of the underdog as it was of making money. Even his business methods tabbed him, as he wrote later, as a crank. "I am one of the few newspaper men who happen to know that this country is populated by 95 percent of plain . . . and poor . . . people and that [their] patronage is worth more to a newspaper owner than the patronage of the wealthy 5 percent. So I have always run my business along the line of least resistance and for the greatest profit, and . . . I have made money easier than any other newspaper publisher did make it."

Scripps's main interest in wealth was to be able to scatter "the children of my brain"—the little penny papers—across the face of the nation and enlighten the millions of 95 percenters. He desired enough of a fortune to protect his family from adversity—not as millionaires but as substantial middle-classers, with their handsome ranch in California, the picture-book farm in Ohio, and a string of healthy newspapers.

Only a psychological evaluation at that time could have revealed precisely what brought about this deep-seated personality shift. Several factors that influenced his behavior in that winter of 1898–99 are clearly in evidence. Not only had he finished construction of the forty-room ranch house and outbuildings, but his orchards, dams, and roads were largely in place. He had reached a sort of emotional plateau where he could pause and consider his next course of action.

His addiction to liquor cannot be overlooked as a causative factor, or even the main trigger, for his behavorial transformation. By his own admission he was at this point an absolute slave to the bottle.

> During these busy years . . . one thing distressed me more than anything else—my fixed habit of drinking. . . . While I was never really intoxicated more than half a dozen times in my life, perhaps, and while I was not many more times even in the least befuddled or over-exhilerated, I consumed enormous quantities of alcohol. I could drink enough whiskey in one day—without having my brain clouded in the least—to keep four or five ordinary men drunk for a week.
>
> I have never known, or known of, another man who could drink a gallon of whiskey a day—as was my custom for a long time—and at the same time do business or carry on any professional work, and whose life was not quickly extinguished. . . . Later I did reduce my tippling from four quarts a day to two quarts.

No medical authority would accept Scripps's claim that he consumed for a long time a gallon of booze a day. Even a quart or two a day would pulverize an ordinary man's liver in short order and pickle his kidneys. But of course the master of Miramar was no ordinary man. There is ample testimony in his letters that he did drink steadily—and often heavily—from his mid-twenties into his mid-forties, and beyond.

Likewise he experimented—in those less medically strict times—with a variety of uppers and downers: opium, morphine, antipyrine, etc. He craved stimulants when he was busy and harried—but wanted a shot just as much when he was idle and bored. And usually he was in one state or the other.

Perhaps one element that seriously wounded his psyche and triggered this personality change was the ten-year deterioration of his close relationship with his sister Annie, who slowly declined and died September 11, 1898, in California. She was only fifty-one.

Scripps's concern about his own health was not an idle phobia. He had evidence of deterioration. His eyesight was failing—and rapidly. He fully expected to go blind. His body was weak and flabby. There was a perceptible tremble in his hands. When he put on a bathing suit or gym shorts he looked "ridiculous, like those little figures artists paint as brownies." His skin from feet to waist and on his hands had lost nearly all sensitiveness. "When I touch my bare legs it is like touching my feet with my shoes on."

Tearing open the envelope from Cincinnati, Scripps eagerly looked for the bottom line. With a groan, he angrily slammed down on his desk the financial summary for 1898. It was another big disappointment, more of the same bad news that had come month after month to Miramar— declining profits.

This dismal financial picture concerned him deeply. Scripps thought himself wealthy, with a personal income that had in the last seven years fluctuated between $50,000 and $70,000 annually. Yet he was constantly short of cash; and was in fact now several thousand overdrawn at the company treasurer's office. He must—absolutely—have more money.

Even a schoolboy, he fumed, could see what was wrong. Too many unnecessary people on the payrolls—typists, clerks, bookkeepers, messengers. Too many eight-page issues. Money wasted on "beautifying, re-papering, etc." The owners must cease paying for lunches, ice, towels, toilet paper. Too much money spent on telegraph other than news. Not enough advertising space sold. Too many free papers given away.

Scripps took his pen and began making notes of these thoughts. "An employee is no more entitled to a copy of the paper than a baker getting a free loaf," he wrote. It did no good to idly sit out on the ranch and fume and brood. He must initiate direct action.

A few days later, January 16, 1899, he fired off his first memo ordering a drastic "downhold" on all business expense. It signaled the start of a violent economy crusade that would continue steadily for two years and reach the uttermost limits of penny-pinching.

Not only were free papers—including those mailed to Scripps him-self—outlawed but the boss tightened up even on minor traditional office perks and practices. Everyone was prohibited from personal use of passes at theatres, on street cars, on trains, or steamships. Reporters were ordered to pay their own carfare on assignment—and buy their own pencils! Ad solicitors would no longer be provided business cards. No one could get an advance on his pay, even for vacation. No reimbursement would be made for cost of moving household goods of transferred employees. No more money could be put up as prizes. The papers were prohibited from trading advertising for any commodity—be it grand piano or railway ticket. New employees would have to furnish their own bonds.

A stream of such new rules began flowing steadily from the ranch. All important matters would henceforth require a written order bearing Scripps's signature. Nobody could be hired, fired, or promoted without such written approval. All pay raises—even fifty cents a week for the office boy at the *Kentucky Post*—must come to his desk at the ranch. He sometimes took two weeks to act.

He ordained that everyone—including editors and business managers—must be at his desk regularly at 7 in the morning. No exceptions—except by the old man's signed dispensation. Virtually paranoid about waste of space, Scripps outlawed all customary free plugs. Traditionally his papers had carried squibs about merchants' spring openings, etc. No more, said Scripps. McRae protested that in Cincinnati Shillito's department store, spending $25,000 a year on advertising in the *Post,* would be denied "a little twenty- or thirty-line reading notice." But the president wouldn't bend.

Holed up at the ranch, Scripps needed a pair of sharp eyes near the heart of the business to monitor his reforms. He tapped Lemuel T. Atwood, his "Editorial Superintendent," to function as a sort of inspector-general to check on everything and everybody. Scripps wrote him on February 2, 1899: "You may even be suspected of being a sort of detective, a spy of that sort. I explicitly order you to conduct your investigations and inquiries in such an open and straightforward manner as to make suspicion of you and my intention impossible."

Not even the most picayune infraction of the "downhold" escaped Atwood's eagle eye. The Kansas City *World* was called down for putting up $15 for the nomination of leading citizens. And the St. Louis *Chronicle* got in a jam for splurging $200 in prizes for a schoolgirl writing contest. The *Kentucky Post* was upbraided for spending 75¢ for towels, and the editor's knuckles rapped for paying his wife $1.50 "for typing a report."

Spending $1 for toilet paper at the *Cleveland Press* was disallowed. The business manager warned: "I think toilet paper saves us money in the long run; plumbers' bills are liable to occur without it." Indeed, in every Scripps-McRae plant using newsprint scraps as a substitute was clogging sewer pipes.

In Kansas City, Scripps laid it on the line to *World* business manager Larry V. Ashbaugh: break even in thirty days, or resign! Coincidentally,

Ed bet Ashbaugh a straw hat the *World* would lose $2,000 in May. The first of June he got a letter: "We earned $2,000. I bought a straw hat and billed it to you. Signed, Ashbaugh."

The flurry of rules from Miramar that blatantly bypassed his office left McRae embarrassed and hot. He strove to hold his temper. "I am not going to have any controversy," he told Scripps, "over any plan to change any order of yours except so far as reasonable arguments can convince you, if I think you are wrong. If I see a law being violated, I shall consider it my duty to tell you. . . . You told me in Cleveland I must speak plainly. . . . You know you wrote me some months ago that you were going to carry our your plans, and would carry them out, despite God, man or the Devil! After such an assertion coming from you, it seems to me that it would be ridiculous for me to indorse any other plans than those inaugurated by you — or even to mention any."

The early months of 1899 found the three newest Scripps papers in desperate circumstances. The *Seattle Star* was baby-crawling up a slippery unknown mountain. The San Francisco *Report* did dangerous contortions on a lunatic course that even a newspaper novice could see was a certain ticket to disaster. The Kansas City *World,* strangling in a deadly feud between editorial and business chiefs, gasped for life.

It may not have made much difference that Scripps had ordained his ownership of the fledgling Seattle paper to be a secret, his downhold rules were enough to badly cripple it at birth. It took two weeks for the *Star* to sell 368 papers a day — laughable circulation, considering the costs.

The ban preventing a brand-new newspaper giving away free samples was a calamity. The *Star*'s own pressman "nearly fell dead" when told he had to pay a penny for a copy to mail to his mother. One merchant blew up when denied a gratis copy to see his own ad. *Star* reporters were thrown out of police headquarters because they brought no free copies. Newsboys, unable to return unsold *Stars* as they did other Seattle papers, refused to hawk the new daily. A disconsolate Ed Chase lamented to Miramar he "had quit swearing — until I reached this town!"

On April 3 circulation of the San Francisco *Report,* which was 7,000 when Blades took it over just four months earlier, had tumbled to a mere 900! The master of Miramar and Blades had their wires hopelessly crossed. Their notions of how to run the paper were tangled and confused. They were both blundering badly — actually murdering the little paper!

In Kansas City the Scripps paper, sweating for ads and more circulation, got hit by a big surprise. The Kansas City reporters began trying to organize a union to give themselves a twenty-dollar-a-week minimum. The organized printers got thirty. The *World* editor threatened to fire any reporter who joined a union. His boss in Cincinnati backed him up, but the issue was bucked to Miramar.

The *Kansas City Star* ignored the matter, but the *Kansas City Journal,* under pressure from union printers, caved in and let their reporters organize.

To their surprise, the editorial chiefs in Kansas City and Cincinnati learned their antagonism toward a reporter union was not Scripps-McRae policy. The concern was definitely pro-union. Scripps had, after all, founded his newspapers to promote fair treatment for the working man; still it was his contention he had the right to pay off on Saturday night any employee he elected to let go, for whatever reason. He did not feel obligated to pay pensions or for vacations, though in some instances, he did the latter. But Scripps accepted unions, as Milton McRae made clear in a communiqué he sent to Kansas City on August 14, 1899:

> While it is presumed that all our business managers are familiar with the policy of this concern with regard to the employment of union labor, etc., in order that you may clearly understand policy on this question . . . would state that it is a fundamental principle of the concern to have no difference with union labor. That is, to permit strikes.
>
> Our plan is only to employ labor when it is profitable. It is unprofitable to permit labor disturbances. Our idea is to let every man have his own way, pay the union scale in every case, but all the time we will do business at a profit, employing such men and doing such business as is profitable, entering no combination for or against anybody.

In his room at Cincinnati's Grand Hotel, Ed Scripps walked to the window and held his opened copy of *Puck* in the strong light and stared hard at a cartoon. His eyesight was failing. It was difficult to make out even the illustrations in *Puck* or *Judge.*

Describing the incident to Ellen, he added: "My blindness makes it a torture to go out on the street. I suppose you have heard that I have engaged a physician to travel with me this summer. I have turned myself over to him in most respects. He is watching me rather carefully as to diet. He also has got me keeping better hours. As for my nervous condition, I feel much improved. . . . I can go all day in a stormy meeting without fatigue."

This was Wednesday, May 17, 1899. He had been back east for thirty days, personally checking on the effectiveness of his downhold and other reforms. Despite actual infirmities, near-blindness, raw nerves, hard boozing, aggravated by a streak of miserliness, Scripps was nevertheless emulating the two-fisted tycoon. He minutely inspected all his eastern establishments. Ever expansion-minded, he even hatched another League newspaper—Number Ten.

This he decreed on June 6 by electing to replace the special edition the *Cleveland Press* for ten years had been printing in its plant and dispatching by rail to Akron, about forty miles to the southeast. The new paper would be called the Akron *Press*. The change-over would not take place until September 21, to allow time to find a building and send in a rotary press and one linotype.

For this venture and other expansion ideas, the boss decided to canvass some of his lieutenants to become investors. He didn't have a great deal of success. Atwood looked glum and told Scripps he could barely save $50 a year, and had only $1,500 to his name, and that was tied up in a savings account. Scripps was so impressed with what Bob Paine had accomplished with SMPA he handed him a fifty-dollar-a-week raise. "Bob is turning out a good businessman," he reported to Ellen. "He owes nothing and is worth $50,000." Nonetheless, Paine declined to become an investor.

Scripps was perhaps even more niggardly and tough when on the scene than in mailing strict economy edicts from the ranch. "I had to use the club freely on [Will] Kellogg to run Kansas City my way," he informed Ellen.

The *World* lost $60,000 "by Mac letting Kellogg run the paper," Scripps confided. Still he felt it "a good property worth more than it cost." He backed up his confidence by authorizing erection of an $8,000 plant and purchase of a $25,000 battery of new linotypes.

But for some reason the close look disenchanted Scripps with the *World* business manager, Larry Ashbaugh. On June 23 Ashbaugh was startled to open a letter from Scripps asking for a plan "by which separation of our interests can be effected with least possible injury to [Ashbaugh] and fellow stockholders." Ashbaugh did not want to quit, asserting he was "loyal and thoroughly competent," and believed the *World,* which he called "my baby, my life," was destined to be a great newspaper.

His plea fell on deaf ears. Scripps intended to dismiss him. But, ironically, Ashbaugh immediately fell seriously ill with malaria and a 105° fever. McRae sent him a wire: "Mr. Scripps orders and directs you to obey your physician absolutely and positively demands that you shall not worry about business until your physician permits you to do so."

In a few weeks, Ashbaugh, well again, returned to his desk. But within months he would leave Kansas City to start a newspaper of his own.

A few days before Scripps's forty-fifth birthday came troubling news from Miramar. Jim, back from a sail, had broken out with measles, the other children were exposed, and now all were quarantined under doctor's care. The tutor, George H. Hazzard, advised Scripps: "Ted is the only one I am worried about. Any kind of sickness may go hard with him."

The father knew that. Ted, now almost eight, had been sickly since age six, with fever, spells of rheumatism, kidney and gastric pain. In the past spring Ellen had sent Hazzard to closely question Dr. Edwards about the boy's health. The physician stated the lad was more of an invalid than his parents realized, probably to be a lifelong victim of Bright's disease. Foolishly, Ted was permitted to gormandize himself on such indigestibles as raw turnips, carrots, cherries, and guavas. "I have myself seen him vomit guava seeds by the pint," Dr. Edwards told the tutor. "These cases, mind you, extend back over the months; the poor little fellow is simply paying off a debt to nature."

The measles telegram on June 9 sent Scripps racing home on the next train. He found on arrival the children rapidly recovering — except Ted who still was under the weather.

Ted's condition was such a worry that Scripps wrote about it to Paine, who replied, July 18: "I had already heard of Ted's low condition before receiving your letter of the 13th. . . . I love him, for he's all boy. I am anxious with you."

Travail at the family hearth did not, of course, obliterate in the least contentious disturbances in Scripps's business life. Now his trusted generalissimo was making serious noises that indicated he might be on the verge of decamping.

Mac wrote ostensibly to advise that Blades "is up against it in San Francisco. . . . In my opinion, you have not comprehended the real situation. Your chances are ten times better in Los Angeles and Seattle." Then McRae got directly down to his unhappy relationship with the boss:

> I have just one complaint to make and that is that you have not treated me justly of late. If I ever had a right to complain of your treatment it is now. "Might never made right." For years past you have had your rackets with James, George, Sweeney, et al. I believe I was your confidant throughout all your troubles and my constant advice to you was to be square and fair and never fight. I am now acting as I advised you to act.

For sixteen years they had labored side by side — mainly with mutual respect and admiration. Now they were rapidly drawing apart, driven by opposing temperament, and in dispute over business methods. The thread of their partnership had become taut — stretched almost to breaking.

But Scripps was tormented these dusty summer days at Miramar not so much by business worries as by the desperate plight of his son Ted. During July the boy's condition steadily worsened. A nurse attended him around the clock. Dr. Edwards came out every day from San Diego.

On August 2, 1899, just four weeks before his eighth birthday, Ted reached a crisis and sank into a coma. Dr. Edwards and the anxious parents hovered over the sickbed. Finally, in late afternoon, the physician rose from his chair, removing his stethoscope, and grimly faced the Scrippses. "I'm sorry. . . .Ted is dead."

17

Oh, but I Do Love You

George Scripps fell seriously ill the summer of 1899. Three physicians diagnosed his trouble as stomach catarrh. It was actually cancer, and he sank fast. Ed interrupted a tour of League papers and took him by train to Asheville, North Carolina, to see if mountain air would revive his brother's spirit and appetite.

Business troubles abounded. Milton McRae, in angry revolt, resented Ed's "humilitating" orders and wrote the chief: "You are clear off your trolley. . . . If I am such an ass as you think I am, the best interest of the company demands that you part company with me."

Just at that point another son fell ill. Ed left George to rush to Cincinnati where John Paul, eleven, just arrived from the East with his mother, had come down with "a leaky heart." Ed and Nackie, still grieving over Ted's death barely three months earlier, were frightened. The doctor diagnosed this as endocarditis, put John Paul in the hospital four days, and said the boy should, if carefully watched, fully recover.

Ed hurried away to Kansas City. The *World* was tottering. Both Will Kellogg and Larry Ashbaugh had decamped. With backing from George Scripps, his "uncle-in-law," Kellogg had in October launched his own Scripps-style penny paper in Omaha, Nebraska.

Of a sudden, in December, George rallied and decided to continue his convalescence at Miramar. Nackie, meantime, had taken the boys back to her San Diego town house. She wrote on December 15, 1899, that she was lonesome to see her husband, and would not go out to the ranch "until you can go with me. It is going to be very hard to go back there and I feel like I am going to need you to help me through it. . . . The ordeal of coming here was harder than I thought."

On January 12, 1900, the private car "Oceanic" was shunted onto the siding at Linda Vista. George had stood the five-day train ride "very well," but his condition was still perilous.

Just then — in late January 1900 — Bob Paine proposed that George back him in starting a new paper in Chicago! It was something they had hashed over months earlier in Cleveland. Now the idea was red hot.

Though dead serious, Paine flippantly couched his proposition in language intended to amuse George and lift his spirits. "You are not yet an old man. . . . I sincerely believe you'll be on your feet and snorting for new grass like a young colt in four months. . . . We'll win money and glory in Chicago sure, George, then we'll laugh at E. W. Scripps who thinks he's a big man and yet who permits his brain and body to be eaten by worry."

Ed did not resent Paine's scheme. He encouraged it, offering to back a Chicago paper with League money — $12,500 at once for a printing plant and $1,500 a month for operating expense. Paine said he would invest $2,500 of his savings plus $70 a week from his Cleveland salary.

Scripps's singular purpose in starting a Chicago newspaper was to bolster the weak links his SMPA wire service had in the Windy City.

On April 4 Paine was in Chicago closing a deal with a commercial printer who agreed to turn out the *Chicago Press,* described in the masthead as "an evening newspaper published for the people by R. F. Paine, one of them," at a cost of $1,458 a month. Bob was in a hurry to start; later he would set up his own plant. But overnight the commercial printer concluded Paine was an "anarchist" and rudely ordered him off the premises. Bob went to one of the struggling dailies, the *Chicago Inter-Ocean.* Yes, they would set the type and print 10,000 copies of the *Chicago Press* in the hours when their plant was otherwise idle. It would cost Bob $100 a day.

Paine described himself as "happy as a clam." He leaped out of bed at 4, worked furiously far into the night, writing thousands of words of news copy and editorials, doing all the headlines and layout — paying the start-up bills with his own money.

On Wednesday, April 11, 1900, the first issue of the *Chicago Press* hit the streets. By then Paine's exhausting one-man show had taken a disastrous toll; he was bleary-eyed, twitching nervously, virtually a basket case.

Two days later, Friday the 13th, at 11:30 A.M. at Miramar, George H. Scripps died. He was eight months past his sixtieth birthday.

The following day, April 14, a disastrous fire heavily damaged the *St. Louis Chronicle.* McRae rushed to the scene and wired Scripps: "The plant looks as if hell had broken loose." The *Globe-Democrat* and the

Westliche Post fraternally got out the *Chronicle* for a few days until spare equipment could be shipped in from Cincinnati.

The Reverend Henry Bond Restarick was summoned from San Diego to conduct George's funeral on the Saturday before Easter. E. W., whom the preacher knew only as "that peculiar Miramar fellow," met him at the ranch house door, wearing khakis, his pants stuffed in boots, chewing gum. "Will you have a piece of gum?" Scripps asked. The preacher was led into a large room where the family sat around in chairs "as they might for a conversational evening." Scripps, who had written a eulogy, handed Restarick a typed copy. It stated George had lived a quiet life, died bravely, and in his last weeks enjoyed "the roses and other flowers from our garden" and had reverted to a boyhood hobby—starting his own cacti collection.

In part, the script read: "George became wealthy not because he wanted to be rich but because while he had opportunities and ability to make money, he had no faculty for spending it. It will be strange indeed if those of us who are to inherit this fortune make better use of it than its founder."

In his memoirs, Restarik recalls that Scripps handed him $100 and presented a like fee to the musicians, a pianist and quartet, the minister had been requested to bring.

George left an estate of $2,000,000—his newspaper stocks, mining property, and real estate. Ed, designated by the will as executor, was also chief beneficiary. Others sharing the fortune were brothers Will and Fred, sisters Ellen and Jennie and the eldest, sixty-nine-year-old Elizabeth Sharp.

The body was cremated in Los Angeles, and once again a private railroad car was brought out to transport the family and George's ashes back to the cemetery at Rushville. The men, enroute, played poker. The urn of ashes sat on the corner of their table. Scripps was so strapped for cash he had McRae send a $25,000 advance from George's bank account to defray expense of the funeral and estate settlement.

Trouble erupted at once. James demanded Ed agree to surrender the 32 percent of Detroit *Evening News* stock George owned. James would swap for it all his personal holdings in various League papers. Also, James wanted the will probated in Detroit where the *News* had influence. Ed insisted the estate go through the court in Cleveland, where his *Press* was a power. The family split on the matter, with most relatives backing James; only Ellen sided with Ed.

As bad blood boiled over George's money, catastrophe overtook

Bob Paine's gruelling one-man show in Chicago. "I cannot eat, sleep or write," Paine lamented on April 25. "I am at present threatened with complete collapse. I think E. W. would lay me off if he realized my condition. I have been under heavy pressure for the last three years, and the mental and physical machinery refuses to work as it did. I am going home tonight."

It had taken only three weeks for Paine to fall apart. Realizing he was "pretty nearly knocked out," Paine summoned Ed Mosher from Cincinnati to take his place as editor. As the whipped man retreated to Cleveland, McRae rushed to the scene. For sale in Chicago at $2,500 was the modest plant of a defunct newspaper. McRae grabbed it. In a matter of days he had it set up and running in a building Paine had leased at 140 East Monroe Street. Thus the *Chicago Press* no longer issued forth from the *Inter-Ocean* plant, but off its own rotary press.

From internment rites at Rushville, Scripps came directly to Chicago to inspect the newest "child of my brain"—somehow believing his ownership was a secret. "Do not talk to anyone about the *Chicago Press*," he advised Ellen. "I am commonly considered insane by my friends, a fool by my employees, and a rascal by all others." Yet he was decidedly optimistic about the *Chicago Press*.

It had a circulation of only 931, Scripps discovered, but the new paper was "sticking" with subscribers—a very important factor. Scribbling on the back of an envelope, Ed calculated the weight of one hundred copies of the ordinary twelve-page Chicago newspaper. That came to eighteen pounds, about the maximum a route man could regularly carry. That load would earn the carrier at most fifty cents a day. In contrast, a little newsboy lugging the same eighteen pounds, could deliver three hundred copies of the four-page *Press,* and thus make a dollar and a half a day.

But that was to be of no consequence. Rumors flooded Chicago that the mighty William Randolph Hearst was ready to invade the city with a new afternoon newspaper. Everyone knew the field was lucrative; the leading paper, Victor Lawson's *Evening News* was clearing $750,000 a year. Then billboards sprouted—the new *Chicago American* would debut July 4. Hearst bought a seven-story building and installed three octuple presses that could spew out 225,000 copies an hour.

"Hearst's plant cost a cool $250,000," Scripps informed Ellen. "He has one thousand men in his office, four or five of his top generals here. My hopes? Oh, I don't know. We will be up against show, splurge, and bigness. He will fight the *Journal* . . . cripple and embarrass James E. . . . It will be five years before Hearst even learns the *Chicago Press* exists."

In truth, Hearst probably never heard anything at all about the *Chicago Press*. His *American* sprang forth a giant with circulation of 112,000 daily and 200,000 Sunday. McRae, shaken and stunned, suggested they quickly just shut down the *Press*.

Scripps resisted. He conceded Hearst was "filling every crack and cranny of my proposed field" in Chicago — except one. "It is barely possible that the merit of being little, lightweight, easily carried, and quickly read will be a sufficient foundation on which to build a paper capable of competing with such a people's paper as Hearst appears to be making. It is worth one hundred dollars a day for a short time to continue the experiment."

But a few days later Scripps surrendered. He consented to "without saying a word to anyone, quietly close" the *Chicago Press* on the afternoon of July 28, 1900 — a Saturday when by-the-week union employment obligations were fulfilled. Trying to salvage something from the misadventure, Scripps sent a request for Hearst to permit the SMPA wire to operate out of the *American* shop.

If "it takes a thief to catch a thief," why not one alcoholic reform another drunkard? That idea popped into E. W. Scripps's mind and he decided to give it a try — by betting $200 that George Gohen could not stay sober for five months. Gohen had grown to hate San Francisco. He made no progress at all with the *Report,* and Ed had talked to Blades about firing him. Gohen was disgusted with life. So he took Scripps's bet.

He stayed sober, but his triumph, temporarily, over booze didn't save him from defeat as an editor. Gohen was fired March 19, 1900.

The $66,000 in red ink on the *Report* ledgers had Paul Blades himself in the hot seat. Scripps began to seriously consider killing the paper, and finally did. At its demise, Scripps had owned the San Franciscoo daily exactly ninety-seven weeks at an outlay of $114,000.

The family squabble over the will hit the papers in Detroit and Cleveland in mid-1900. Lawyers were trying to nail down in which city George had *actually* maintained his legal residence. "Ellen asked me to destroy certain portions of letters referring to the family," Scripps wrote his attorney. "I told her I would not do so. . . . It is not my habit to destroy letters. . . . Every letter received by me in the last twenty years is in existence, mainly at Miramar."

Scripps should not get too cocky, his lawyer cautioned; the courts might freeze assets of the estate and prohibit strong League papers lending funds to the weak, a cornerstone of E. W.'s method of financing expansionist ventures. As a conciliatory gesture, E. W. accepted appointment of brother Will as co-executor. At once the latter crankily demanded the right to sign all disbursements, even as small as $1. Ed cussed him for "an imbecile . . . the brain of a six-year-old."

James, in turn, was furious at Ed, telling McRae in Detroit that Ed was a terrible crook who "uses and then throws away his men." Mac reported that James "got pretty hot . . . used a lot of epithets . . . walked around like a crazy man." The Detroit patriarch vowed to break George's will at any cost. McRae was worried. But suddenly no longer about his own standing in the Scripps-McRae League.

The boss had hammered the doughty Scot until he really was on the verge of resigning. Then Scripps pulled a spectacular reverse play. Assembling the board, E. W. had McRae elected president of every separate League corporation—in effect making him chief executive officer. Scripps moved himself up to chairman of the board. Still majority stockholder, he had surrendered his cherished one-man power only in principle, not in fact. Everyone knew that. But McRae's vanity was mightily pleased by his ascension.

In another abrupt personnel shift, Scripps wrote out a $2,500 check for his loyal "spy" Atwood and sent him off on a long vacation. Into his place as the concern's top editorial man he moved Bob Paine. Straightway Paine took the first train to his new quarters in Cincinnati, brushed aside aides who wanted to show him great bales of statistics— and began trying to repeal some of the old man's hated downhold orders. He first tackled lifting the edict which prohibited relatives and friends using the papers' railroad passes.

In the fall of 1900, McRae alerted Scripps that he was personally overdrawn $7,000 at the League treasurer's office and had other substantial and pressing debts. Any League overdraft was illegal, Mac warned, and as president he would prohibit them in the future. "No joking, Ed, this is serious." He instructed Scripps to borrow $15,000 at 4 percent from the First National Bank in Cleveland and square his accounts.

Bob Paine, who now had access to the company books, in October 1900, sharply warned the boss, "You are *personally* on the brink of bankruptcy." E. W. had bragged he had the earning power of $10,000 a month. Paine ridiculed that. "For the last year your average monthly income was precisely $6,055.55, for God's sake! You are gambling with other people's money . . . and the future of Jim, John, Bob and Nackie, and the fortunes of a hundred good true men who work for your papers."

Even when in the depths of blues over his money woes, Scripps got to see the lighter side of his predicament—thanks to Nackie. It happened when he was summoned to Cincinnati for a crisis conference. As he told Ellen: "At the hotel I met Nackie. I had a long face and felt like crying. Nackie reflected in looks the same condition. She agreed to help me in my struggle. . . . After a long night's sleep, I sent for the business people. Nackie went out and after a while I began to be disturbed by bellboys running in with packages. They came by the dozen and filled the room with packages. Later when Nackie came in, I reproached her for the expenditures. How did she defend herself? 'Why, Ed, you are poor and we have to begin economizing so I wanted to get everything we needed before. Now don't you think your wife has got some foresight?' "

The boy who thrilled on the Rushville farm to the sensual feel of fresh-dug loam, who was transfixed by the splendor of a sunrise, and enticed and awed by stormy thunder and lightning, remained at age forty-seven passionately in love with Nature.

Miramar had become to Scripps "my own dear mistress" and "only solace." Not only did he find ranching his "most enjoyable and pleasing diversion," it also transported him into a pleasant fantasy factory. As he told Bob Paine:

> As for myself I can say I have no tree so graceful, no cluster of bloom so beautiful as that which has formed my ideal while planting—that image I have painted on dream canvas.
>
> I line hours together, wandering over the ranch, staring at tree, bush, and humble vegetable, enjoying every view, but still more the images I call up to observe what will be here . . . next week, next year . . . and ten years after I am gone.

As 1901 began, the master of Miramar was not quite as busy with his dream canvas as with immediate cruel realities. He must get his life in order. So he decided to simply take himself in hand.

He stopped drinking. He quit smoking. He cut his personal and ranch expenses by clamping on a savage downhold. He turned loose his mighty "financiering" brain on business woes—and they began melting away. By swapping off-setting notes with Ellen, McRae, and the various companies, Scripps got solvent—at least to the degree that would forestall any attempt by enemies to force him into receivership. His old standbys helped materially, by turning on their profit spigots. The *Cleveland Press* at year-end had earnings of $90,000 and the Cincinnati paper made $50,000.

The accountants put on their green eyeshades and set about making an inventory and appraisal of George's estate. Then they sharpened pencils and looked ahead and estimated League earnings. Then they added it all up. Suddenly, Ed Scripps no longer was headed for the poorhouse. He could expect to receive, the accountants announced, an annual income of $134,000. McRae's would be $59,880, and Ellen's $56,664. Scripps decided he could limit his expense to $34,000, and squirrel away a hundred grand a year.

The old man wore out secretaries with long hours and continuous hard work. Many of the bright young men whose flying shorthand pens took down his wide-ranging dictation and then typed a stream of scintillating letters naturally became imbued with the heady mystique of newspapering. Some of the more ambitious he "promoted."

E. W. took a strong liking to industrious George Putnam, somewhat of an ugly duckling. Putnam got his chance—in an impossible situation. The heavily losing Sunday edition of the Kansas City *World* was leased to Ellen and turned over to the greenhorn Putnam to manage. Another young man formerly at Miramar, ex-tutor George Hazzard, also got a try-out as a cub in Seattle. He was lured to the *Sunday World* as friend Putnam's editorial handyman.

Of the changes now taking place in Scripps's outlook on life, one was singularly startling. He abandoned his 100 percent aversion to the schoolhouse. He began looking over nearby military academies. He settled on the Harvard School at Los Angeles and enrolled Jim, almost fifteen, and John Paul, nearly thirteen. The boys did well, the headmaster assured their father.

To tie his sons closer to the land, he hit on the scheme of delegating each in turn, on reaching age fifteen, to be actual ranch manager—to hire and fire men, handle money, make all decisions. "The main idea," Ed explained to his foreman, "is not to make money but to have a pleasant place to live. . . . I am trying to accustom Jim to being self-reliant but it is a little too early to start a boy out. . . . I want him to feel he is my representative . . . and taught to treat everybody properly. . . . The boys can do pretty much as they please. . . . I would rather have one acre of beauty than fifty acres of yielding orchards."

Out in his newspaper empire, things were by no means calm. When the *Chicago Press* folded, Hearst had acceded to SMPA's request to move its bureau into the *Chicago American* building—but not for long. Bob Paine, incidentally, had picked an in-house cognomen, calling the SMPA "Smite"—an obvious reference to how he thought his little David (the Scripps wire) was "smiting" big Goliath (the rich and powerful Associated Press). In the fall the *American* disagreed with "some political news that appeared on the 'Smite' circuit." Preemptorially, the Hearstians ordered the SMPA out of its building, the second time Scripps wire reporters had been booted out of a Chicago newspaper.

"I admit that Kellogg can razzle-dazzle me as no other man can. One day I feel he is a 'bust' and the next day I feel he is worth a million. . . . Sometime when you find me too cocksure about things remind me. It may make me swear, but it will do me good."

Like a moth drawn to a flame, E. W. Scripps was attracted to newspapermen who had the roguish glint of adventure and daring in their eyes.

In the above letter to his attorney, J. C. Harper, Scripps was expressing extreme ambivalence about the man who had married brother Will's daughter Floy. Half a dozen times E. W. had knocked the props out of sly Kellogg schemes, backed him into a corner, and seen him burst out bawling like a five-year-old.

When the Kansas City *World* exhausted its credit, Kellogg proposed to take it over himself, issuing $50,000 in gold bonds to liquidate its $64,000 indebtedness to the League. Once again E. W. was seduced by entrepreneurial bombast—and went along. Now Kellogg lumped the *World* and his *Omaha Daily News* in with Larry Ashbaugh's *St. Paul News*—and they had the beginning of their own chain, eventually to be known as the Clover Leaf League.

But Scripps no longer felt admiration for his longtime West Coast protégé Paul Blades, who wrote the boss that "tales that I want to leave the *Los Angeles Record*" were untrue.

A few weeks later Scripps eased a nasty situation by making one of his tawdry end runs. He ordered Blades to take a month's vacation; while Paul was in the East Scripps fired him. On his return, Blades angrily protested "this injustice . . . to be cut off from position and salary in my *absence*—treated not like one who had a close, familiar and friendly relationship for ten years, but as a mere journeyman reporter or typesetter—that is what surprised, hurt and angered me."

Now that he had been punished, Blades begged for another year to make good on running the Los Angeles paper. But E. W.'s mind was not to be changed.

What happened then was pure melodrama.

Edwin "Hans" Bagby, Fanny Blades's brother, had taken over as *Record* business manager. He fell ill and a doctor diagnosed incipient tuberculosis and ordered him away immediately to the mountains. E. W., then in the East, got this word by letter from Blades, who added, "With Hans's concurrence, I have assumed full charge of the *Record* for the time being." Scripps's short fuse went off like dynamite. In charge — not on your life!

The old man fired off a flurry of telegrams. The first directed Blades to get out! The *Record*'s bank was instructed to no longer honor Blades's signature. A telegram went to John C. Lee asking him to assume control of the newspaper.

Curiously, Lee was merely a "promising chap" Scripps barely knew. Once a street newsboy, his hustle had lifted him to circulation manager of the *Record*. E. W. had seen Lee only a time or two on infrequent visits to the Los Angeles paper. Scripps knew he was taking a risk, since he suggested in the wire to the bank: "Advise Lee, as he is young and inexperienced."

Blades's bold action in taking charge gave Scripps "a giant swearing spell," he wrote Ellen. "Of all the examples of gall, and impudence and imbecility I ever had experience with, this was a masterpiece." In turn, Blades appealed to Ellen. Pointing out that he had been off the payroll six weeks, Blades moaned that he couldn't pay interest on his stock loans and desperately needed to sell his *Record* holdings. "Mr. Scripps is so fixed in his hostility to me for reasons that I do not know."

Scripps knew. At least, he thought he knew. The story was that when Paul Blades went east he had deserted wife Fanny. Ellen checked and found that the gossipers had their facts twisted. The truth was that at the last minute Cousin Fanny surprised her husband by refusing to go with him.

In May 1902, Scripps thundered east on the Santa Fe Limited to attend annual meetings of the League papers. Bold ideas for fresh adventures in journalism churned in his mind. But in his drawing room he lazily relaxed by endlessly playing dominoes with his secretary. Both tried to cheat. If he won, E. W. always put on a bright face.

Back at the ranch, Nackie welcomed her parents for a visit timed to coincide with her husband's absence. She expressed hope E. W. was "getting along nicely . . . and that you can smooth things out easily and not have too much to worry you."

The continuing feud between E. W. and brother James was a cancer that upset business associates of both. In Cleveland at the *Press* board meeting, Milton McRae secretly intrigued with the Detroit patriarch's son-in-law George Booth. They decided to try to bring the warring brothers into a face-to-face peace conference. James was not attending the League meetings; instead his lawyer represented him.

It would be up to E. W. to request the pow-wow. Would he? That was the first stumbling block. Secondly, would the proud and austere James agree?

E. W. had arrived with every intention of pushing for speedy conclusion of George's will, even if that meant washing the family's dirty linen in a public courtroom. Yet, to the surprise of McRae and Booth, he seemed equally eager to try to patch up the quarrel. On May 27, he made the overture:

> Dear James:
> I am willing to meet you in Toledo or Detroit within two weeks from date for the purpose of considering our differences, with hope that a satisfactory solution may be reached whereby our newspaper and personal interests may profit accordingly.
> Awaiting your reply, I am yours affectionately,
> E. W. SCRIPPS
> (It would be agreeable to meet you with Ellen.)

The elder brother did not immediately accept. Two days later he answered that he was sending his lawyer to Cleveland to discuss the proposal, adding,

> My wishes have always been identical with those you express though I had long ago given up expectations of their realization. It ought to be possible that something should be proposed that would meet the requirements of the situation.
> Affectionately, yours,
> James E. Scripps

Their summit meeting took place in Chicago at the Great Northern Hotel over a three-day period, June 2–4. Four colleagues also were present, and the brothers conferred privately in another room twice, emerging from a final two-hour huddle with their arms around each other. The two men with James were his attorney and George Booth. Scripps had brought along his lawyer, J. C. Harper, and McRae.

It was proposed that both E. W. and James retire from active direction of the newspapers, and give McRae and Booth control of the business. "E. W. indicated he was not averse to the scheme," Harper noted. "James thinks better of [genuine business co-operation] than he did. Whether anything results from the Chicago conference will depend on the prudence and self-restraint of the various parties. . . . E. W. is going to think the matter over carefully in the summer and return East in the fall."

In the midst of these peace maneuvers, E. W. again let Will Kellogg razzle-dazzle him. This time Scripps was handed a proposal to take over majority interest from Kellogg and Larry Ashbaugh in the new *Des Moines Daily News*. With his wheeler-dealer knack, Kellogg offered to sell 280/380 of the stock for $116,666. It was a neat little paper, and for some reason Scripps badly wanted it. He did not even bother to consult McRae, but strode into Cleveland's First National Bank and borrowed $35,000 for the down-payment.

This bolstered Kellogg's financial structure, which was usually thin, and left him an important role in Des Moines management decisions. Not only did he gloat over this coup, he also was happy to be brought in for a key role in the truly giant new scheme E. W. launched on this trip — a national newspaper feature syndicate. Scripps called it the N.E.A. — Newspaper Enterprise Association.

Other publishers — such as Hearst — syndicated copy of broad appeal to members of their own chain and some outside clients. But until now there had been no features supplier offering its copy and illustrations to any and all newspapers across the country. The price, of course, would be based on the circulation size of the buyer, thus making the service within the reach of small dailies and weeklies.

The announcement brochure said the N.E.A. package, mailed from Cleveland, would be produced by a staff of high-priced special writers, "news-hunters," and artists. Included would be a daily half-column of serious editorials, half a column of "human interest" editorials, feature write-ups of world celebrities in the current news, accompanied by half-tone photos. N.E.A. staff writers would be ready "at important news centers . . . to jump out at a moment's notice on hot current news such as the Martinique horror, the big strikes, etc."

In addition, said this sales pitch, there would be "good features such as daily [fiction] stories, a little poetry, special articles by special writers on live topics, and special matter for holiday editions." This matter, six to eight columns daily, would be augmented by three first-class cartoons on general events a week, plus small engravings to illustrate humorous telegraph items, and assorted spot news pictures.

To launch the Newspaper Enterprise Association, Scripps called again on his standby and jack-of-all-trades, Bob Paine. This was to be another overnight start-up, financed by a total of $400 a week assessed proportionately against League papers and those of Kellogg and Ashbaugh. These dailies had the advantage of being charter N.E.A. members and would share with those in the Scripps-McRae League the expected profits. Also Kellogg was seated as a director of N.E.A.

Paine jumped right in. He thought it a glorious scheme. He had grand ideas. At once he hit up Scripps to raise the weekly budget to

$2,000 so he could try to hire cartoonists like Homer Davenport and other newspaper stars. "You can see it will be big work," Paine advised League editors, "and that hiring of capable artists, editors and producers must be proceeded with slowly. However, the aim will be to finally get a staff superior to any other in the country."

This was a punishing assignment—stacked atop his other duties as League editorial superintendent and boss of the "Smite" wire service—but Paine undertook it with good humor, reporting to Miramar:

> This N.E.A. you fired at me without sweating a hair is making Robbie sweat blood. Haven't quarters, staff, cash or much else that is distinctively N.E.A. yet we are producing four or five columns daily and I'm firing in assessments to beat the band.
>
> At the same time I'm trying to grab details of Atwood's editorial job and they're thicker than sand fleas at Long Beach. While I'm trying to run N.E.A., SMPA, and the League editorial department, my near relatives and friends insist I'm a long-eared ass for trying to do so much at my age.
>
> My only defense is that Ed Scripps says I can do it, so I can do it.
>
> My office produced, in original letters and copies, yesterday over 240 pieces of mail.

But N.E.A. had a bumpy start in even the supposedly friendly precincts of the League. The *Los Angeles Record* "dumped the whole thing in the wastebasket. . . . Wouldn't give one dollar a month for it." When the *Seattle Star* also complained, Paine fired back:

> The latter part of your letter is mostly bile and would be pretty insulting to a fellow who could be insulted. From my rather brief acquaintance with Pacific Coast editors, I am disposed to take refuge from my old father's advice: "A black-leg can't insult you; if a fool insults you what difference does it make; but if a gentleman insults you, run like hell!" He always got along pretty well on this plan.

Any knocking of the infant syndicate infuriated Scripps. He excoriated editors who did not promptly pay their assessments. He was appalled that so few instantly saw the merit of his long-time hobby of cooperatively acquiring thousand-dollar articles that none of the papers could singly afford. Further, N.E.A. editorials offered an opportunity for the "soul" of the concern to be expressed in a unified way to a national audience of millions of readers.

E. W. took these gripes as a personal affront, as he explained in a letter straightening out the thinking of the editor of the *Seattle Star:* "I want to tell you, you made an awful bad break on that N.E.A. matter.

What you said about N.E.A. you said about E. W. Scripps, for N.E.A. is E. W. Scripps, and was created for just the opposite purpose you supposed it was. Whatever you do, I expect you to hereafter be loyal to this enterprise."

From his mesa, E. W. kept a longing eye on the Pacific Northwest. Still sitting idle was the plant of the defunct *Chicago Press*. Why not ship it to Portland, Oregon, and launch a new penny paper? But before he could act, another publisher started a cheap daily in Portland. From his travels, E. W. also was impressed with Spokane, Washington. A good man to start a penny paper there would be his former secretary, unprepossessing George Putnam. Ellen too admired Putnam and wanted to join in the Spokane project. They sat down with him at Miramar on August 17, 1902, and agreed to put up $12,240, with each of the three taking one-quarter interest. The other fourth was reserved for a future partner.

The inexperienced Putnam proceeded to Portland, foolishly squandered much of his start-up capital on equipment, but finally on November 7, 1902, brought out the *Spokane Press,* a shaky, raw product.

Periodic fits of the blues plagued Scripps most of the year 1902. The *St. Louis Chronicle* was sinking in red ink. E. W. swung the axe on the general manager, George Shives. This brought back certain pangs of regret. He had booted cousin Willis Osborn out of the same job—and a year and a half later Osborn had died in New York. He had slipped, McRae heard, to merely an ad salesman on Pulitzer's *World* and was pretty much of a drunkard. He remembered getting word from Bob Paine: "I am going out this afternoon [April 19, 1899] to help bury Willis Osborn. His mother blames me for the fact that he and I failed to get that *Press* stock. I suppose she blames you for much more."

Scripps discovered—rather belatedly—another talented newspaper-man who would rise to become a major lieutenant. Ironically, the man had been underfoot in San Diego eleven years before the boss took serious notice of him—William H. Porterfield, born in 1872 in Iowa, grandson of a missionary who had come from Scotland to convert Plains Indians. With his widowed mother, Porterfield had come to San Diego in 1891, landing a circulation job on the *Sun,* later becoming a reporter.

Over the years E. W. had slowly come to realize that Porterfield had a knack of soaking up facts, could write in trenchant and readable style, had instinctive sympathy for the poor and inarticulate, plus skill in seeing through "false fronts" and deception.

Overlooking the fact that Porterfield was by this time thirty years old, Scripps offered him on easy terms control of the faltering *San Diego Sun*. Porterfield grinned, and grabbed. E. W. took his note for $6,000 and loaned him $2,000 cash to operate on. It was agreed Scripps would assume 51 percent of the stock at cost if Porterfield made a success. In short order, Porterfield was to become one of the old man's fair-haired boys, a powerful executive in developing the Scripps journalistic empire in the West.

Seven-year-old Bobby and sister Nackey, four and one-half, knew the doctor was coming down to the ranch from Los Angeles, bringing his nurse to administer chloroform. Their mother had explained they would have to be put to sleep so bad teeth could be pulled. That was a ruse to spare them the agony of knowing they would undergo tonsilectomies.

Dr. C. F. Taggart, chief surgeon of the San Pedro, Los Angeles, and Salt Lake Railroad, arrived at Miramar on Saturday night, October 11, 1902, accompanied by a Miss Green in white uniform. At 9 o'clock Sunday morning, the surgery was finished.

Anxiety, fear, the sight of blood, the children's pain – all had Nackie terribly distraught. Indignantly, she wrote her husband:

> This last operation has settled things in my mind. I do not intend to take any further risks about bringing more children into the world to endure such things as these children of ours have had to endure. I simply cannot bear witness to these things. . . . You always manage in some way to escape.

Scripps was then in Cincinnati, wrestling with business as well as preparing for the lawsuit over George's will. Nackie's letter stunned him. Apparently he interpreted his thirty-six-year-old wife's vow to never again run the risk of bringing more children into the world as her declaration of some kind of sex strike.

E. W. fired back a mean response. Its fierceness caused Nackie to grovel in a pitiful avowal of unbounded affection, protesting "I am so terribly lonely without you." Her letter made indelibly clear she had no desire to bar him from her bed.

> As far as living apart from you, I do not intend to unless I should contract some incurable disease such as consumption. . . . As to what I said about taking risks, etc., I repeat that I love you and whatever is necessary to prove it, I can do. . . . Wire me to come. . . . You will not be sorry to have me with you.

At this time, Scripps — under siege from several quarters — imagined himself reeling on the verge of a physical breakdown. "I informed Mr. Atwood that I would have to turn over to him all my business, with full power of attorney to do as he pleased . . . with any part of my property during a period of several months." But E. W. did not crack up, nor abdicate; he slowed down and grimly held on to one-man power.

In the will fight, brother James granted no quarter. Dead set on defeating E. W. in the courtroom, James wrote Will: "Your quandry about getting anything from the estate leads me to explain . . . all I want is a settlement . . . on the basis of what is right, irrespective of money. . . . Ed is not looking for what is right, but what will put the greatest power in his hands."

By the end of November, Nackie had come from California to their country home at West Chester. Scripps was busy and away — in Cleveland, in Detroit, in Chicago. The strain between them continued with the wife desperately pleading by mail for better relations. She wrote a dozen letters while he was in Detroit awaiting the start of the will trial, one ending, "I love you just the same though, and shall be awfully glad to see you again, however mad you may be at me."

Whether caused by her letters, acute loneliness, rising libido, or other reasons, Scripps's heart abruptly softened. He summoned Nackie to Detroit.

Their reunion may have been akin to a second honeymoon, from the tone of subsequent correspondence. Nackie returned to West Chester on Christmas Eve "very tired" but feeling euphoric. "Well," she wrote December 25, "I had such a lovely time in Detroit with you that I expect I will want to go again before I leave. . . . There is a little sprinkling of snow on the ground this morning and it is cold — 16 above zero — but the sun is shining and it is a very pretty Christmas Day."

Next morning she awoke in her upstairs bedroom, leaped up and rushed to the window and looked out, hoping to see enough snow for a sleigh ride. Suddenly as giddy as a new bride, Nackie threw open the window, grabbed handsful of snow off the verandah roof, and gleefully washed her face in it. All of this she related to Ed, adding,

I received your letter last evening and enjoyed it very much. I am afraid you will have a lonely time in Detroit. If you wished, you might come down to the Grand to see me before I go. If you don't, I suspect I will come to Detroit to see you on my way home. Well, I will close for today.
Much love to you, Nackie

The flame of passion had been rekindled in Ed's heart. He promptly urged her to come see him again.

"I will come up Friday night, I think," she responded on December 29. "I will telegraph you when I will come. You should see what a beautiful snow we have this morning. It looks like fairy land. Will you take me for a sleigh ride when I come to Detroit, if there is any snow?"

18

Gambling on What a Boy Can Do

Trailed by a whirling dust plume, the red motorcycle would thunder up the canyon road, careen into the ranch courtyard, halt with a scary jerk. Off would leap a carefree Jim Scripps and hurry off to one of his multiple duties—jacking up his pipeline or orchard work gangs, ascertaining that at least one of his father's Rambler automobiles was ready to roll, tackling the Miramar ledgers, or cracking a thick book for his tutor.

In these early months of 1903, Jim, approaching seventeen, was a muscular one hundred eighty–plus pounds, loyally trying to meet the stern demands of his watchful father—who himself was actively thinking ahead to the day when this eldest son would take the helm of his newspaper empire.

E. W. dreamed of making Jim his "chief aide for all properties west of Denver" at $100 a month and expenses, plus 25 percent of all profits or value increases. "Your book education must continue by reading purely instructive books, devoting two hours daily, or in emergencies average fourteen hours weekly," the father wrote in a memo to be handed to the boy on his next birthday. "Until you are twenty-one, you are not to use liquor or tobacco, or have carnal intercourse with women."

> I don't intend to force you into my business. You may take up as much or as little of it as you choose. While it is extremely desirable that you should have personal experience on the little and young newspapers, it is not absolutely necessary. . . . From being my personal agent in the small affairs you can perhaps more readily acquire a knowledge and faculty for handling large business than you can in any other way.

Then, too, the more you study me and learn my individual characteristics and peculiarities, the better you will be able to understand the nature of all my business and eventually to successfully handle more or less of it.

But Jim would not be permitted to abandon the ranch ledgers. John Paul, fourteen, was yet "too young" to be ranch manager, though E. W. didn't mind the younger son playing mechanic on the two motorcars that cost $3,000 each "to advance his education" even if the machines lasted only six months.

In Detroit, Scripps had been calmer on the witness stand that he anticipated—and quite effective. Brother George, he testified, was perfectly sane and hand-wrote his will—six years before death, and under no outside pressure. Ed's spirits were bolstered, in the opinion of Bob Paine, by Nackie's affectionate visits. "She is a good, true, noble woman with lots of youth in her which you don't appreciate. . . . Mrs. Scripps has, I think, been more or less shut up at Miramar. . . . Ed, it is impossible to understand a woman. . . . The wise man, when he marries, puts two things in his boudoir—a barrel of sugar and an anvil. His success as a married man will depend upon his judicious use of both."

Daytime in Detroit opposing lawyers savagely aggravated the feud between E. W. and James. In the evenings, outside the courtroom, they scrambled to reach a settlement. If the Detroit patriarch mainly wanted a clear separation of their business affairs, what if Ed traded his legacy of George's 32 percent of the *Evening News* stock for the total holdings of James and his family in the other League papers? Bah, that would cheat James! Then suppose Ed paid "boot"—perhaps $200,000?

Everyone chewed on that new proposition. It looked like an acceptable basis for terminating the litigation. Finally James said yes. He and Ed shook hands, leaving details to their legal counsel. The trial judge, apprised, removed one juror, and threw the lawsuit into abeyance to be formally dismissed later. Ed at once took the train back to California. His legacy would still net him $1,000,000.

James, however, immediately had second thoughts, and decided— without telling anyone—to leave the proposed settlement hanging.

Back at the ranch, a veritable forest had sprung up from seeds his men had planted four years ago on the once-barren mesa. Torrey and Monterrey pines and graceful eucalyptus—in twenty-seven varieties— stood twenty feet tall.

But now was the time to plant more little penny papers. Scripps decided to once more tackle his nemesis, San Francisco. This time he would start from scratch: his traditional four-page one-cent people's daily, with back-alley shop and cheap staff.

On March 21, 1903, the first issue of the *San Francisco News* rolled off the press. Business manager, eager for the challenge, was his former secretary Ham Clark. Editor was William D. Wasson, a bright and ambitious reporter from the West Coast wire service known as Scripps News Association. At the end of the second week circulation was a mere 208. Scripps intended the *News* to be the working man's friend — "the mouthpiece for those who have no other mouthpiece." He wished union organizers and capitalists well, but stood ready for battle if either impinged on the welfare of "those plainer, humbler, less fortunate" common laborers.

"Hook yourself tight to the heart of the common people," he admonished Wasson. "Be always with and of them." That meant, of course, jamming into the *News* hundreds of brief items their families would read, including the daily short fiction the women loved.

Scripps had to jump to avert trouble at his Pacific Northwest flagship, the *Seattle Star.* The population of Seattle had grown to 150,000 but *Star* circulation dawdled at 25,000. Business Manager Ed Chase blamed Editor E. H. Wells and got Scripps to oust him. Wells alerted Scripps that in the past prominent lawyers, rich utility and traction executives had tried to bribe him — unsuccessfully — because the *Star* was the only Seattle paper fighting these interests. "This is a grafting town. It is full of grafters. So many new enterprises are under way, so much development work that conditions are abnormal. . . . Any new editor is going to be subject to just that kind of influence."

From the *Cleveland Press,* reporter William P. Strandborg, young and hard-working, was sent out to be the new editor. "Be yourself," Scripps advised Strandborg, "hard, and definitive, and persuasive."

> Make a paper that everybody will read and at the same time will be a certificate of your character as a gentleman. . . . Do what [the other papers] are not doing . . . so that all people will take the *Star* to know all that is going on. Don't be too correct. Don't be afraid of making mistakes. . . . Don't be afraid of trying experiments. Whatever you feel right hard about, that do. . . . Better an enthusiastic damn fool than perfectly correct and prosy.
>
> Don't be afraid to act promptly in dealing with your staff. . . . If you have a bad man, let him go. If you don't trust a man, let him go. . . . Don't permit anyone — myself or the president of your company — to persuade you to employ a man you don't want, or discharge a man you think you can make good use of.

Chase retained Scripps's confidence as top-flight in business. The boss urged Chase to "work yourself out of a job" by delegating more to lieutenants—so Chase would become available to start other papers. There was no let-up in Wells's yammering to start a Tacoma paper. A Northern Pacific railway repair center, Tacoma had 50,000 population and strong morning and evening newspapers.

Milton McRae took a swing through the Pacific Northwest. Surprisingly, he pronounced Wells, now forty-two after sweating out four *Star* years, stronger, more business-like, a good candidate to launch the Tacoma venture. Finally E. W. gave the go-ahead, putting up $20,000 (including investments by ranch employees), keeping 51 percent control, letting Wells take 25 percent of the stock.

In a remodeled stable, Wells installed the old *Chicago Press* equipment. With a daily outlay of $50.59, he launched on Monday, December 21, 1903, the *Tacoma Times*. First day's press run was 753 copies. Scripps mandated a slow, cautious, and economical start; no elaborate books, just a daily listing of receipts and expense, no push for advertising or circulation until the *Times* emerged from babyhood. "Give nobody a title. At first the Tacoma paper has only one officer, a corporal, and all the rest are privates, pure and simple."

In the East, League growth was coming not from birth of new papers but acquisition of old. McRae persisted in Toledo in trying to engineer a merger of the *News* and *Times* with the *Bee*. "It was the hardest work I have ever done," he reported to Miramar. Of the three, only the *News* was profitable, earning $20,000 a year. Mac sent a wire that he could combine the three by laying out $55,000 cash. "Go ahead," Scripps responded, "as long as we get control." The combined *Toledo News-Bee* became League property June 6, 1903.

In the fall of 1903 E. W. began to fear a new "money panic" might sweep the country. He had a personal overdraft at the League treasury of $18,492. His gloomy preoccupation triggered a fit of pique by Nackie. She was then in West Chester for a visit with her parents. On October 3, 1903, she wrote:

> The children are all well, and the weather is all one could wish. It is nice to hear from you even though it is only an answer to a wire.
> If you love me, you are treating me wretchedly by not writing me, and if you do not, it is your duty to tell me so. At any rate you are succeeding in making me very unhappy.
> Nackie

It was another occasion for the master of Miramar to lay aside his boudoir anvil and dip into his barrel of sugar.

E. W. was spending sleepless nights because of the unsettled status of the lawsuit over George's will. The trial was scheduled to resume in January 1904, in Detroit. E. W. decided that the old proposed "settlement" should be physically destroyed. George Booth held both typed copies. Scripps wired McRae, then in New York, to take care of the matter.

McRae met Booth at the Cadillac Hotel in Detroit. For four hours they hashed over broad ramifications of the brothers' feud. Except for a dispute over who should pay $25,000 to sister Elizabeth Sharp, all litigation might have been washed out.

Finally McRae had Booth produce the two copies. James's son-in-law tore them to shreds, and dumped the paper scraps into McRae's hat. "Then we took the hat to the bowl in the bathroom, started the water going and put them in one handful at a time until they all disappeared in the sewer. I could see from Booth's demeanor that he felt . . . a great opportunity had been lost."

But Scripps would not abandon an effort to end the feud with James. He thought hard on strategy and then wrote his brother a personal letter that resulted in an end to their battle. Legal formalities took place March 29, 1904. By agreement, George's will was probated—as written—in Cleveland. The Detroit lawsuit was dismissed. James and E. W. went their separate ways.

In August 1904, Sacramento, California, in the foothills of the Sierra Nevadas, sweltered in the nineties. The thick-set young man making the rounds of the newspaper offices with questions was sweating a lot, not from heat but nervousness. He said he represented a New York City patent medicine company and wanted to know advertising rates and circulation.

He looked so young and green some newspapers thought he was a bunco artist or a business spy. In the *Wednesday Press* office, the visitor got rattled, introducing himself as Mr. Smith, and ten minutes later calling himself Mr. Brown.

By day's end, however, Jim Scripps had a fairly good rundown on Sacramento's five newspapers. Ads cost about a dollar a column inch. Biggest papers were the *Bee* with 10,176 circulation and the *Union* with 5,619.

"Anyway, I done pretty well . . . as I am naturally a pretty good liar," Jim boasted to his father.

The son got back not praise for his undercover work but gentle
scorn.

> While I can only applaud the interest you showed . . . I wish right here
> to plainly and emphatically condemn your method of procedure. I mean
> that I never want you to make false pretenses of any kind. I don't want you
> to lie for any business purposes.
>
> In my young manhood I was poor and often tempted and even submit-
> ted to temptation. . . . Perhaps I am not now entirely free from reproach.
> But your own life and the advantages that you enjoy on my account are
> such as to enable you to afford the luxury of always being fair, open, and
> honest in your dealings.

Sacramento had been targeted for a new Scripps penny paper. The
scheme was hatched by W. H. Porterfield, who had given up active
management of the *San Diego Sun,* while retaining his stock. Porterfield
volunteered to cut Jim in for a 25 percent share of the new paper. That's
why the boy went to Sacramento to check out the competition.

Scripps finally gave Porterfield the go-ahead. He took his usual 51
percent control, pledged $13,500 for the first year's operation, and
agreed Jim could join the staff for experience, but own no stock.

The *Sacramento Star* was born Monday, November 21, 1904. Jim
Scripps lived in the home of a police sergeant, half a mile from the
office. He arrived at 8 o'clock, rewrote *Union* sports, made a list for the
telegraph editor, and covered police court until 10. Then he helped out in
the press room.

"I have a great deal of trouble writing what I want to say," he
confessed to his father, "and in cutting down and lengthening out articles. . . . But I will do it until I can find out something about reporters'
work. . . . Won't draw any pay—thought I wasn't worth it to him at
present."

Jim quickly came of age in Sacramento. Just before Christmas, the
fledgling announced he was ready to try his wings.

> Now, Dad, when I came up here I didn't feel able to try and start a
> paper off. But feel that I would be able to do it pretty well now. . . . I have
> watched the way Porter has started and think I can do as well as he did, the
> conditions being the same.
>
> I am not crazy to start up a paper and if I was a ritch [*sic*] man allready
> [*sic*] I would not do any kind of work. . . . I can do newspaper work as well
> as any other kind. . . . I believe I have as much brains now as I will ever
> have and the only question is how long I had better work for somebody else
> before becoming my own boss.

E. W. must have found heavy irony in the fact that *his* Sacramento paper had to hoist a banner proclaiming it was "sold out" of advertising space. He furiously hated the idea of "counter-jumpers" (merchants) hounding any newspaper to pollute its columns with noxious hucksterism. America's press would never be truly free and honest until newspapers flatly refused to print any advertising matter at all. The famous Charles A. Dana of the *New York Sun* wrote or said something that put Scripps in that notion thirty years before.

Now, in 1904, he was a man with a lofty goal and mission—to establish America's first "ad-less" newspaper, if only to prove it could be done. In the abortive *Chicago Press,* he first saw a glimmer that it might be possible. And in holding down advertising space in his *San Francisco News* to a mere ten columns a day, he continued the experiment. His chief aim was to deny the wealthy merchants any leverage that could help them blackmail a newspaper to derail crusades against oppression of the working man.

He was determined now to go whole hog—to publish a penny tabloid that would live exclusively off circulation revenue. All he needed was to select the right test city, and discover the right "genius" editor. To underwrite the ad-less experiment, E. W. intended to dip into his inheritance from brother George, who had also shared a distaste for advertising. The best city for the venture would be Chicago. And in John Vandercook he thought he had the right man. Scripps bundled up a nineteen-page confidential outline of his scheme and dispatched it to London where Vandercook had been stationed as European manager for Scripps-McRae Press Association.

Though a native of New Jersey, Vandercook broke in at eighteen as a *Cleveland Press* cub in 1891. He had been promoted first to the wire service in New York, and then sent abroad. He was a Bob Paine protégé. Now thirty-one, married, with a small son, he had precisely the family responsibilities Scripps considered major drawbacks for an editor founding a new paper. But the bright and ambitious Vandercook had two qualities E. W. greatly admired and demanded—news savvy and fresh ideas.

His letter to London explained that the ad-less daily would be smaller than even a standard tabloid—sixteen pages each measuring six by nine inches, about the size of a small magazine or book. But the paper would contain the same volume of news as could be found in the ordinary Scripps four-pager—about thirty-two standard columns. The text would be set in easy-to-read long primer with small magazine type headlines—"no scareheads." Half the reading matter would be N.E.A. features, one-quarter telegraph, and the rest a boiled-down summary of local news, all rewritten from competing morning and afternoon news-papers. The staff would be five newsmen, two printers, one circulator, a minimum press crew; of course, no advertising solicitors.

Scripps wanted an easy-to-read paper—"light, humorous, and flip-pant in vein." He was willing to spend $500 a week—of George's legacy. It really didn't matter, he explained to Bob Paine, "if the whole thing should be a complete financial failure. Well, what if it should be? It will only be no man's money that will be lost. George is no more, and the money is hanging up in the air without a possessor who is willing to possess it."

Vandercook was returning to America. He would go first to Louis-ville, Kentucky, to visit his wife's parents. Scripps commissioned him—as he had done with others—to look over Louisville as a target for a cheap penny paper. Then Vandercook took the train to Miramar and they met face-to-face. Vandercook took a negative view of starting a one-center in Louisville. So Scripps leaned back in his rocking chair in his sunny ranch office and spent a couple of days going into the ad-less pros and cons.

No deal was struck at Miramar. Vandercook wanted time to think. On the Santa Fe returning east, he developed a strong negative reaction. From Las Vegas, Nevada, on December 21, 1904, Vandercook posted a long, pencil-written letter. Bluntly he asserted Scripps was not the publisher to make the ad-less experiment. "Your other papers are hostage to the advertisers. Through them you are vulnerable probably more than any other man in the United States." Someone other than Scripps—a newcomer with no other newspapers to be held hostage—should under-take the venture. Vandercook volunteered himself. He offered to put in $1,000 and work at no salary (making his living through outside writ-ing), if Scripps would invest $2,500 a month for three years, and grant Vandercook majority stock control. He also decided New York would be a better test city.

Scripps didn't agree, and at this crossroads, they separated. Scripps turned aside to tackle a multitude of more immediate problems. Vander-cook got an offer to join Publishers Press wire service as New York news director at $75 a week, and accepted.

But Scripps by no means was giving up on his ad-less dream. Nor, for that matter, on achieving big things through John Vandercook.

"Dear Ed: We are just getting into Kansas City so I will write you a line or two." For Nackie it was a struggle to prevent the sway of the speeding Santa Fe Pullman from marring her usual exquisite chirography. It was

Tuesday, January 3, 1905. She was making another trip east to visit her parents at West Chester.

"I am well, have no cold, slept well last night and have been thinking lots of nice things about you. I am the only woman in our car and there are four or five very mangy-looking men. The one ahead of me has consumption and is lame besides." She moved her pen to the top of the next page.

"The one opposite me is an uninteresting old man with a scraggly beard that reaches almost to his waist. The others look as though they were going to a warmer climate for their health. So you need not fear I will have any flirtations on this trip. Hope you are perfectly well, and lonesome because I have gone. I am yours lovingly, Nackie."

Reading this back at the ranch, E. W. knew when his leg was being pulled. His thirty-eight-year-old wife was too much a straight arrow to think of glancing at another man, handsome or mangy. And in truth, he had no time to feel lonesome. He was getting ready for a series of critical business conferences.

McRae arrived to talk about expansion. Now the League numbered seventeen newspapers. The two newest, incidentally, were in state capitals — the *Sacramento Star* and the *Columbus Citizen*. McRae had finally purchased half-interest in the *Citizen* for $75,000 on July 2, 1904. That gave Scripps-McRae five newspapers in Ohio — Cleveland, Akron, Toledo, Columbus, Cincinnati, plus the *Kentucky Post* across the Ohio River in Covington: two in Missouri — St. Louis and Kansas City; four in California — San Diego, Los Angeles, San Francisco, and Sacramento; three in Washington — Seattle, Spokane, and Tacoma; as well as Omaha, Nebraska, and Des Moines, Iowa.

Scripps was eager to expand even more. For six and a half days he and McRae pored over every aspect of their business — especially the future. Often when they took a break, Scripps seated his partner beside him in his Rambler Roadster and whizzed over the dusty ranch roads. On the narrow steep canyon road to La Jolla, E. W. pointed out a dangerous turn as "the spot where I had my first tumble with the machine."

It had happened only three weeks earlier. Scripps was driving alone when his lap robe slipped and caught in a wheel. Leaning out to yank back the blanket, he veered the automobile too far to one side, sending it into a precarious skid up the hillside. "So as soon as I saw what was up, I slid out very easily, but had the machine gone clear over it might have hit me."

Foremost on Scripps's mind in the spring of 1905 was the "changing of the guard" in the League, scheduled to occur in May. E. W. would

retire as chairman of the board to be succeeded for the next five years by
Milton McRae. Members of the League "cabinet" — McRae, Bob Paine,
J. C. Harper, and Lemuel T. Atwood — were summoned to the ranch in
February to consult on the transition. Regardless of any shift in titles,
Scripps in no way would give up his one-man power as majority stock-
holder.

"Dad is going to run Scripps-McRae business in his own way,"
Scripps told Paine, "while he (Dad) is on earth." E. W. limited sharply
the cabinet's function. "The kind of advice I want from my cabinet and
others is how to do what I want to do. I don't ask anybody to tell me
what I should do. I have decided what to do. All I want to know is the
best way to do it."

In vacating the chairmanship and promoting McRae, Scripps was in
effect firing him. Mac still was entitled under his contract to one-fifth of
concern profits, but was stripped of actual power.

Paine felt the two partners were on a collision course. He wrote
Scripps April 17, 1905: "Mac can't reconcile himself to the fact that you
are the biggest toad in the biggest puddle."

To the ranch now were summoned the two top men at the *Cleveland
Press,* Business Manager Willis W. Thornton and Editor Harry N.
Rickey. Each, thirty-two, had risen from the ranks. Thornton would
become the new League president. Rickey, son of Bob Paine's sister,
would replace his uncle as editor-in-chief, Paine moving over to president of SMPA. Thornton and Rickey would be paid $100 a week;
Scripps urged them to save some of it.

The keen interest Scripps developed in scientific inquiry largely dates
from a phone call made by Dr. Fred Baker, one of his poker cronies at
the Cuyamaca Club. The physician, interested in mollusca research,
rang up the ranch to invite E. W. to come in to San Diego and see what
two University of California marine biologists were up to.

Scripps grumbled. His deep-rooted aversion to academia stood in
the way. He told Dr. Baker he didn't care a dime about talking to any
highbrow professors. Yet he was avidly curious about the sea. So he
changed his mind and went down to the waterfront — a reluctant trip that
led to perhaps the strongest personal friendship of his life.

E. W. stepped aboard a research trawler that had been harvesting
live specimens from the ocean depths to meet a Professor Kofold and a
tall, straight, large-boned man with twinkling blue eyes named William
Emerson Ritter. Something about Dr. Ritter — in fact, several things — at
once appealed to Scripps. Though obviously a man of high intellect, he

surprisingly was warm, poised, and friendly. When Scripps talked, Dr. Ritter leaned forward with total concentration. Despite the contrast between the rough-hewn man of the world from Miramar and the scientist from the academic cloister at Berkeley, there was significant similarity in one respect. Ritter, too, was a farm boy, having grown up in rural Wisconsin. They were about the same age, the professor being two years younger.

Later Scripps invited the researchers to Miramar. He sent Jim and John Paul to drive them out from the Coronado docks in his automobile. The open car whizzed the fifteen miles over primitive mesa roads and arrived at the ranch house in a cloud of dust. Ritter stepped out, dirty and shook-up. "Well, boys, that was a great ride you gave us across the mesa. I never knew there were so many rocks near the road, or that the chaparral was so tough." The boys grinned and winked at each other.

Scripps strode out to welcome his guests. Kofold got "the impression that his poise was a studied one and that he was purposefully showing us a rough and uncultured — but artificial — exterior. Why he did it I could not fathom unless he was really a bit fearful of our highbrow possibilities." The rough ride seemed purposeful hazing of the intellectuals. "I think he put the boys up to it," Kofold told Ritter.

Even so, once they got into deep discussions in the ranch office-study, both visitors were genuinely impressed. "Scripps is certainly an interesting man," Ritter noted in his diary. "A man of force which quality he has used well to his own advantage. He doesn't seem to think much of colleges, but the point he makes against them is not very clear."

Scripps found himself intrigued by the challenge of Ritter's ocean inquiries — but even more so in wanting to find out what the man could do. He promptly joined other San Diegans in getting a permanent marine biological research station established at La Jolla. Sister Ellen also was interested. The two contributed $5,000. E. W. also provided a search vessel, the schooner *Loma*. Scripps also agreed to help upgrade the sailing ship with engines and winches. The *Loma* was on the ways for six months at a San Francisco boat yard. Ham Clark inspected the renovation and reported the schooner now so crammed with machinery "the only room aboard is on the masts." When the bill came, Ritter was "chagrined and disturbed," having only $200 in his research account. So was Scripps, but he paid the total cost — $3,556.

Often Scripps would drive down from the ranch to drop in at the laboratory which he called "Bugville." In frequent talks, his friendship with Ritter ripened. Scripps regularly peppered his friend with one question, "Ritter, you are a zoologist. Why can't you tell us what kind of a thing this damned human animal is?"

For his part, Ritter regarded Scripps as a "scientific humanist." They were to be closely associated both as friends and professional colleagues in several major scientifc experiments. Ritter considered Scripps's unorthodox way of thinking unique and advanced.

> Nothing stands out more sharply . . . than his concern with the moral problem and with evidence that the moral problem is really part of the greater problem of the nature of man himself. In this he allied himself with those few of the greatest thinkers from Aristotle and Confucius to Shaftesbury, Voltaire, Dewey, and Santayana, who recognize the problem of morals as an aspect of human nature and hence of all Nature.
>
> His curiosity touching everything and everybody around him was insatiable. His native ability for assimilating facts and principles was astonishing, and the objectiveness of his thinking was naive almost to childishness. . . . By natural bent he was humanistic to the core. . . . So far as concerns humans as objects of knowledge, it always seemed to me that for Scripps human beings were no more separate from the rest of nature than are stars, mountains, and horses.

The intimacy Scripps was to develop with elitist Ritter, who had his Ph.D. from Harvard and who had been a University of California professor since 1891, was paradoxical. Except for Bob Paine, he had no other such male confidant. He had, of course, shared with the Cleveland editor the grittiest of his bachelor-day womanizing, drinking, and roistering, as well as his greenhorn struggles in journalism. Even now he candidly consulted with Paine, and held back from him few secrets of his professional or personal life.

Ritter in some fashion got under the guard by which E. W. held nearly everybody at arm's length—even at times his wife and children. He didn't want even Ritter as a steady companion. "I don't know whether I would not suffer more than I find pleasure in the constant companionship of men of high intellect. . . . There is a certain relief in getting away from men who make me talk and think. . . . The ordinary damn fool human being at worst only bores me but men who are not damn fools and who do not bore me have another way of tiring me out."

In Ritter's case, Scripps started investing time, influence, and money not so much to push forward the frontiers of marine biology, but mainly to see if Ritter could come up with anything worthwhile—"betting on a man," as E. W. put it.

For much the same reason, he sponsored a young self-taught sculptor living with his widowed mother on a small fruit farm on the mesa. Just turning thirty, Arthur Putnam told Scripps he ached to tackle some heroic statues. He had dreamed of doing big bronzes since working at nineteen in a New Orleans foundry. Scripps was not too interested in art. But he liked the "lad" — and decided to invest in his dream. They agreed to try four figures reflecting the history of California, starting with the Indian, the Padre, and the Plowman. (The fourth was a Puma.) Putnam's eyes lighted up when Scripps volunteered to pay him a dollar a day and provide materials for creating the statues. The sculptor found a small studio in San Francisco and set to work. From June 1904 to January 22, 1905, Scripps advanced him $1,748 through the *San Francisco News*.

"The Indian is finished," Putnam wrote Scripps on March 27, 1905. "I didn't exhibit it because of the fire hazard, and will send it down. I think it is a pretty good first effort." The master of Miramar agreed. "I like the Indian, and will put him on a pedestal." Putnam got a chance to study abroad. Scripps was glad.

In both cases, Scripps bet on the right man. Dr. Ritter became a world authority, and Putnam — despite a tragic paralytic stroke — would go on to renown as a sculptor.

Scripps was, of course, eager to gamble heavily on one particular young man — son Jim. That time was fast coming. After eight months on the *Sacramento Star,* Jim made his move. On May 3, 1905, he asked for $8,000 to start a penny paper at Fresno, California.

Jim proposed to launch the *Fresno Tribune* in the fall with a reporter from the *Los Angeles Record* as editor at $20 a week and a linotype whiz he'd met at Sacramento, Bob Merigold, as printer-foreman at $27. Jim would be general manager at $10 a week, holding 15 percent of the stock, his father the usual 51 percent control.

Heading east again on business, E. W. took Jim along so they could talk. In Cincinnati on May 29 Jim decided to go to Dr. Sattler's Hospital and have his enlarged tonsils removed. When Scripps went an hour or so later to visit his son, he found excited nurses rushing about. Dr. Sattler appeared rattled. He grabbed Scripps and blurted there had been an unexpected post-operative "accident." Jim, hemorrhaging violently, had already lost a quart of blood.

"Is there any danger?" Scripps asked.

"I hope not," the surgeon replied. "I've sent for Dr. Thresher, the local expert in such matters."

Scripps went into hysterics. Fortunately, late in the night, the bleeding stopped.

"I don't suppose I was ever more scared than I was for ten or twelve hours after the operation," E. W. wrote Ellen.

By July 26 Jim was in Fresno, with his sleeves rolled up. "He is fully recovered in health," Scripps advised McRae, "and determined to start his paper."

Renting half a blacksmith shop, Jim brought in a $1,000 press and a $2,800 linotype. "I believe you have got . . . the office you need . . . and have begun right," his father advised. "Get your press up . . . begin printing . . . before you even solicit subscribers. . . . Start modestly. . . . Keep every agreement you make with everybody."

Being son of the chief would get Jim no favors in the concern. E. W. wrote "banker" Atwood at headquarters to treat Jim "as though he were a perfect stranger. [His best way] is to submit right at the start to the harshest business and banking rules." He sent Jim a copy, adding, "I want you to learn all about business, general and practical, but also to face the same hardships other young men meet entering business . . . will be of more value to you."

First issue of the *Fresno Tribune* came out Thursday, August 31, 1905. The old man was proud. He wrote Bob Paine: "Keep your eye on Jim's paper at Fresno. Jim is a smart boy and he has got a crackerjack of an editor, I believe. I'm greatly interested in their winning out."

Nackie sent Jim congratulations from Cincinnati, where she was visiting her parents. "It certainly is the finest-looking new paper that has yet been started out."

19

War on Cincinnati's Boss

Late into the night Scripps hunched forward in his hotel chair and talked like a Dutch uncle to his new Cincinnati editor. The *Post* had gone soft; worse, it was a coward. Money talked. The advertising dollar and social prestige held sway. The silk stocking crowd had become everything. Bah! The righteous voice of the underdog had gone silent — or at least shriveled to a weak whine. Who really gave a damn any more about the Cincinnati blue-collar working man?

"Nobody!" Scripps told John Vandercook. "I'm ashamed of the *Post*. We've got to fight!"

At this conference in the Burnet House in Cincinnati on Monday, June 19, 1905, Scripps was declaring war on the city's political boss, the talented and unscrupulous George Barnsdale Cox.

Scripps felt guilty. From his pretty, sun-drenched, far-away mesa he had lazily watched Milton McRae gradually let "the best people" muzzle the *Post*. E. W., spending only a week or two a year in Cincinnati, had voiced objection but far too mildly. McRae was "straddling" — letting the newspaper crusade just enough to convince the public it was honest, but not so vigorously as to run off the big advertisers.

The Cox gang still clutched prosperous and growing Cincinnati by the throat. From his office above the Mecca Saloon at "Dead Man's Corner," Central and Longworth Avenues, the fifty-two-year-old Cox as chairman controlled the city and county Republican Party. His bloc of 25,000 votes could swing practically any election. If more were needed, he bought them at fifty cents or a dollar a head in the flop houses.

Cox kept his political machine oiled with 5 percent kickbacks from 2,000 patronage jobs. But the gruff ex-bartender garnered his million dollar fortune and mansion in the aristocratic part of town from shady deals with "leading" citizens. Even the Democrats were willing to co-operate—for a price. Reformers were ineffective. Honest businessmen were apathetic. Bossism was an accepted fact of political life in most of the big cities across the country. To get things done even in the Ohio statehouse, Boss Cox need only pick up his phone. "When Cox takes snuff," said the wags, "the governor sneezes."

What Scripps commissioned Editor Vandercook to undertake was the defeat of Boss Cox's ticket in the upcoming fall municipal elections.

"What you told me last night was mighty inspiring," the editor wrote his chief next day, "but has some points which cause me a little worry. . . . I believe the *Post* can work up a ground swell of popular indignation. . . . I am afraid . . . the average business man in politics is, so far as my experience goes, a child in the hands of real politicians. . . . I do not know that a newspaperman would be a better politician, but I doubt if he could be much worse."

Vandercook, Scripps's great hope for the "genius" to launch his future ad-less daily, had been editor of the *Post* only since May, $85 a week having lured him back to League ranks from *Publishers Press.*

For daring to war on bossism, the *Post* might have to pay dearly. Some advertisers, thinking any scandal hurt the city's image and thus their own pocketbooks, might boycott the paper. Rival publishers would side with Cox, or keep silent. The *Post* already had been weakened by losing its circulation lead to the wealthy *Times-Star.* And the anti–Boss Cox crusade could further wound the paper financially. Even so, Scripps gave orders to wade right in.

No longer could the *Post* be blind or wishy-washy on graft and corruption. Scripps had always considered the *Post* his favorite in the League. Now it must again stand tall and fearless. "I am not a damn bit holy or good," he admitted, "and I don't pretend to be, but once in awhile I indulge myself in a decent action."

With Milton McRae currently residing in St. Louis to captain the fight for survival there, Scripps looked to Vandercook as the general for the Cox war. For assistance, he was expected to call on Harry Rickey, League editor-in-chief, and Bob Paine, who wore his own scars of experience from similar good government crusades in Cleveland.

The most active corruption warrior in Cincinnati was aristocratic hometown lawyer Elliott H. Pendleton. So disgusted was Pendleton with the spineless reform efforts of the Cincinnati dailies that he had launched in 1903 his own *Citizens' Bulletin,* a weekly tabloid bent on exposing Cox crookedness. Scripps brought Pendleton and Vandercook together to talk strategy. It was about as bad as introducing two game cocks.

Pendleton did not fully trust the *Post*. And the daily's new editor thought the lawyer much too patrician and austere.

One powerful ally from out of town was Lincoln Steffens. The muckraking author was fascinated by the contrast between two cities in Ohio—Cleveland, which he called the best-governed in America under reform Mayor Tom Johnson, and Cincinnati, the worst in the country under the iron heel of Boss Cox.

During 1904 Steffens had started investigating both cities for *McClure's Magazine*. Most of his facts on Cincinnati came from back files of the *Post* and interviews with its reporters. But Steffens went also directly to the Number One source. In his memoirs Steffens says he mounted the steps to the office over the Mecca Saloon, found Cox, and asked point-blank if he was the boss of Cincinnati.

"I am," said Cox.

"Of course," said Steffens, "you have a mayor, a council, and judges?"

Cox regarded the writer with dark, protruding eyes. "I have, but I have a telephone, too."

There was no doubt, Steffens concluded, that Cox had the support of most citizens. But the boss's ward heelers were living on their past reputations, not keeping up their homework.

"He's vulnerable," Steffens told a small group of reformers. "I think he can be beaten."

The big question was how to do it. No attack seemed to permanently wound the gang. In past campaigns the machine occasionally had been crippled, but Cox always managed to repair the damage.

Scripps counseled that the *Post*'s best course would be a sledgehammer series of exposés, reporters digging up every item of graft and corruption they could.

But the first salvo came from the outsider—Lincoln Steffens. His "Ohio: A Tale of Two Cities" was published in the July issue of *McClure's,* calling Cincinnati "corrupt" and its residents "craven cowards."

Vandercook splashed Steffens's piece across page one on June 23— just four days after getting his battle orders from Scripps.

The editor tried a bit of reverse-English to stir up the fighting mood of his city. The *Post* took vigorous exception to the harsh accusations made in *McClure's*. An editorial in the same issue said: "We have the absolute conviction that the people of Cincinnati are as patriotic and liberty-loving as other Americans. We resent with indignation the charge that the people of this city are cowards."

Vandercook had still another ploy up his sleeve. He sent a wire daring Steffens "in manly spirit" to publicly take back his slurs "when the people of Cincinnati within a reasonable time prove to the world they are neither craven nor corrupt."

Steffens telegraphed back: "If Cincinnati will, with votes, prove me wrong, I will admit the injustice."

Scripps beamed when Vandercook published both telegrams on page one.

Now with his *Post* beginning the climb to regain its honor as a fighter for the people, Scripps boarded the train for California, leaving instructions to keep him closely posted on developments.

From opening gun, the Boss Cox war was furious and exciting. The rival *Times-Star* and "the gang" were reported to be "worked up to a frenzy as never before, and both are undoubtedly very desperate."

In his cups, the *Times-Star* city editor let slip that four other big Ohio dailies were joining with the *Times-Star* in an alliance "to drive Scripps-McRae out of existence" by blackmailing its advertisers, and would "spend millions, if necessary." And drunkenly he boasted he intended "to go into the private lives of Messrs. Scripps and McRae and drag a few skeletons out of the closet."

News of these private threats caught up with the westbound Scripps at Omaha. He pooh-poohed any danger. "I am delighted with the situation as it is in Cincinnati. It makes me feel good to see that the *Post* has gone back into the old lines. Every day Vandercook has grown in my estimation."

But Vandercook was having trouble keeping Pendleton as an ally. The reform lawyer blasted the *Post* editor in the *Citizens' Bulletin,* virtually calling him a liar. Vandercook held his temper. Scripps defended Pendleton.

> I can't forget and you must not overlook the fact that while the *Post* was . . . trimming its sails . . . Pendleton was talking right out in meetings and it really was Pendleton's *Bulletin* that shamed the *Post* into doing the very little it did in combatting the gang.
>
> Pendleton is a snob, but he is a sincere snob. He is offensive because he doesn't know how to be otherwise. When he accused the *Post* of lying . . . the man actually believed he was telling the truth.

Finally Vandercook and Pendleton resumed the fight side by side. *Post* Business Manager William Day was not sanguine. He lamented that in the past the paper started fights it couldn't win. "I hope the editor will not make the same mistake."

In the enemy camp, incidentally, and doubtlessly gloating, was a former Scripps protégé — George A. Gohen, who had been the hard-drinking, seventy-five-dollar-a-week editor of the ill-starred San Francisco *Report*. Boss Cox in 1904 had slipped Gohen into a cushy niche as clerk of the election board.

Sharp thrusts by the *Post* began to wound the Cox gang. It retaliated with dirty tactics, sending detectives to hound Bob Paine's estranged wife Rose, seeking scandal. They could have found it — but didn't. Paine had going a new secret romance. On June 28, 1905, he had put a hefty wad of his stocks in trust for Wanda Pole, whom he would later take as his third wife. "Perhaps the gang is going to retaliate by exposing in the gang organs such miserable sinners as myself and others connected with our papers," Paine advised the *Post,* warning that "no personal consideration" for him should deter the fight.

Paine wrote Vandercook: "My personal and private sins are numerous and lurid. . . . I have a record that would drive an old goat out of the tannery; but I had rather have it appear for all time in the common school histories of the United States than that it stand in the way of your uttering one word that you ought to against Coxism."

Cox henchmen in the police department went after *Post* reporters. One making his courthouse rounds was slugged. Two young staffers unfortunately were spotted emerging from a whorehouse. Police collared them, dragging them to court, where they were humiliated and fined. Should the *Post* publish such an embarrassment of its staff? For hours Vandercook anguished about that — and then printed the story. The old man at Miramar was all for that, "not only because it is news, but because it is apropos to the *Post*'s fight for better government."

Scripps cautioned Vandercook he must fight as well as "show fight." He suggested suing the police or the city for damages. E. W. was outraged that the police judge, after "ruling contrary to the evidence," smirked at the newspaper's lawyer, suggesting he "better drop the matter." Scripps told his editor: "We want no coward lawyers either, any more than we do reporters."

No lasting harm would result, Scripps believed, but "these incidents will serve as a warning to all of you and result, I hope, in the greatest caution. . . . And also weed out from the staff the over-timid and the fool-hardy and really base members."

From Miramar the boss advised Paine he would rush to Cincinnati "as fast as the train will carry me" if personally needed. "I don't know what the fight is going to cost . . . or how long it will last . . . but it will win out as sure as the sun rises tomorrow."

Every day during the long hot summer black *Post* headlines battered Cox. Corruption was found in many places. By mid-October the paper could boast it had uncovered $1,178,000 in graft in road construction, schools, banks, the offices of sheriff, county clerk, and recorder.

Across the state the furor started by the *Post,* and picked up even by the unfriendly Cleveland *Plain-Dealer,* threatened to defeat the re-election bid of Cox tool Governor Myron T. Herrick, and generally damage the Ohio Republican Party.

With the election but two weeks off came two significant happenings that would have tremendous impact on the *Post*'s crusade—one the paper deliberately planned, the other totally out of the blue.

Homer Davenport, the celebrated cartoonist of the *New York Evening Mail,* should come to Cincinnati and inject powerful new zing and sting into the Cox war. That was an idea hatched by Paine and Vandercook. They wired for Scripps's permission to try to hire the cartoonist for the campaign's closing fortnight.

Scripps knew how Davenport had blossomed as the Number One political cartoonist in America by such razor-sharp work as his lampooning of President McKinley being dominated by Senator Mark Hanna, and other zingers. The reply from Miramar: "Good idea. Try."

Next day Paine again telegraphed the ranch: "Davenport will come one thousand a week."

"Okay," Scripps responded.

Davenport jammed into his valise drawing paper, ink bottles, and his sharpest pens, and hopped the next train for Cincinnati.

The unexpected event centered around the corpulent figure of William Howard Taft.

It is an episode replete with amazing incongruities. Taft, a native Cincinnatian, was then Secretary of War under Theodore Roosevelt. Not only a staunch, life-long Republican, he was half-brother of Charles P. Taft, owner of the Cincinnati *Times-Star,* which slavishly supported the reign of Boss Cox.

Another bit of irony was that after a chat at the White House with President Roosevelt, Milton McRae had come home and splashed a laudatory editorial on page one of the *Post* on November 11, 1904, firing the first gun in a national Taft-for-President-in-1908 boom—despite the bitter Scripps-McRae rivalry with Charlie Taft's sheet.

Now, in October 1905, G.O.P. leaders in Ohio were alerting President Roosevelt to the fact that Boss George B. Cox, under siege, had suddenly become a hot potato. The Republican Party must cut him down to size. In Washington, President Roosevelt summoned Secretary Taft to the oval office for a private meeting.

"It has been said," Scripps relates in his memoirs, "that Roosevelt advised him that neither the Republican Party nor Taft himself could afford to have a Republican victory in Ohio which would be considered as only a Boss Cox victory. It is said that Roosevelt advised or instructed Taft to go into Ohio and make a speech that would make this clear."

Thus it was that about the time Davenport was hurrying on one train to Cincinnati, another was carrying Secretary Taft to Akron where he made his speech on Saturday, October 21, 1905.

Taft thrust the knife into Cox, swiftly and deeply, asserting: "If I were able, as I fear I shall not be, because public duty calls me elsewhere, to cast my vote in Cincinnati in the coming election, I should vote against the municipal ticket nominated by the Republican organization, and for the state ticket."

The *Post* headline screamed: "Secretary W. H. Taft Denounces Cox; Blow Makes System Falter." The paper praised Taft for his statement, but called on him to open his other eye and also denounce Governor Herrick.

On October 25 Davenport's cartoons began blossoming on page one, and the *Post* would run thirteen before the voters went to the polls. Yet it fell to the *Post*'s own A. E. Bushnell to come up with one of the most biting anti-Cox sketches. It showed Boss Cox, holding a whip and leaning over a billboard containing William Howard Taft's speech, forcing a reluctant billy goat labeled "Chas. P. Taft" to "Eat them words!" off the signboard. Neither the *Times-Star* nor the *Commercial-Tribune* had printed Secretary Taft's statement. Cox was credited with imposing silence on them.

Despite Secretary Taft's indirect but valuable assist in the war on Cox, the *Post* cartoonists treated him savagely. One sketch depicted Boss Cox pompously seated on a bootblack's stand with Secretary Taft and Governor Herrick bending over, polishing his shoes. It was a war with bullets flying in all directions.

The *Post,* of course, was more *against* Boss Cox than *for* the Democratic candidates, Judge Edward M. Dempsey for mayor, and John M. Pattison for governor. Getting a fair election worried Scripps. He urged Lawyer Harper's good-government claque to concentrate its efforts "to assure a fair and honest vote and a fair count." Otherwise Cox could "steal ten or fifteen thousand votes."

E. W. volunteered to donate, if needed, $10,000 to the honest election committee — but he insisted on good men. "I am not willing to give a bunch of old 'foo-foos' or young 'foo-foos' a lot of money to throw away." He donated twice — $2,500 and $2,000.

A blue-ribbon panel of election-watchers was created, headed by Ivory soap tycoon James Gamble. Other members were five important industrialists, eight lawyers, including Harper, four clergymen, led by Catholic Archbishop Henry Moeller, and the secretary of the Anti-Saloon League. Gamble gave $500, McRae $500, and Harper $100.

"Stir up Pendleton to work among the snobs who have money in his social set, and who do not like Cox," the man at Miramar urged.

Scripps hated Herrick for his "supineness to Cox" and told Vandercook that for the governor's defeat "I would willingly forfeit several tens of thousands of dollars from my own fortune."

In the same breath, Scripps — always the down-to-earth realist — reminded his Cincinnati editor that the *Post* had succeeded in "making Cox your greatest asset" — as a punching bag. "If you beat Cox you will learn this — you will learn what a valuable asset you have lost. I am not joking either, Van. I have been a long time learning my trade and there's a lot of it I do not know yet, but some parts of it I do."

In the early evening hours of Tuesday, November 7, the election news came to Miramar over 3,000 miles of telegraph wire.

"Cox concedes. Dempsey has swept Cincinnati. State is for Pattison 75,000. Signed Vandercook."

Minutes later: "Cox entire city and county defeated by fifteen thousand. *Post* made greatest political fight ever made by any newspaper. Signed McRae."

Those preliminary returns were somewhat inflated. Cox was beaten in the city by 7,000 and in the state by 40,000.

Admittedly, Scripps was "startled" by the outcome. He wired congratulations to Vandercook, Harper, Rickey, and others. "I was tempted to add a few words . . . advising modesty on the part of the editors and papers, but I feared this might be misconstrued to mean that I did not give full credit for the work they have done."

He expressed his "great gratification" to the *Post* editor. "I have done some big things myself in the past but nothing to compare with what you and your staff have done."

Nor did he overlook the valiant role of the *Citizens' Bulletin*. Scripps considered the whole state owed Pendleton a great debt. "He kept going through all the downpour of discouragement his little fire at which all of us lighted our torches in the end."

With the fury of the battle over, Scripps could now see its comic overtones. "That whole Cincinnati situation was absurd. It makes me laugh now to think of it." Even so, E. W. admitted he felt "something like a prizefighter who has just won a championship belt. . . . [The League] is a tremendous power when it is rightly directed."

What would now happen, he wondered, to "all those thieves and rascals" who had plundered the city and the citizens for a dozen years? Much of their plunder obviously had been squandered, but "a very large quantity remains in their hands" and Scripps urged the reformers to go after it.

That was partially done. Local and state investigations were launched to try to send the Cox gang to prison. One henchman gave back $214,000 to escape prosecution. Cox himself managed to wiggle out of the net.

From Miramar, Scripps cautioned his men to be alert for a certain Cox comeback, with a spate of homespun advice.

> One of our Californians was out shooting quail. He found a rattlesnake and smashed him in the middle with a stone and then forgot all about the "varmint" until happening to step too close to it, the snake bit him and killed him.
>
> Whenever I kill a rattlesnake, I never leave off the job until I have smashed his head to a pulp and until I have removed the dead body from any place where it would be possible for an unwary man to put his foot on a sharp fang.
>
> You people in Cincinnati have only crippled the gang. If you do not utterly annihilate it and put all its fangs in State's prison or hang them to lamp-posts, you will get bitten again sure.

Unfortunately, Cincinnati was not to heed Scripps's rattler warning. In a few years Boss George Cox again would get another deathlock on the city, and nobody would be able to break it for twenty years.

Merchants whose own toes, or those of friends, were stepped on in the Cox war soon retaliated—by yanking advertising out of the Scripps paper. The first was the Mabley and Carew Department Store. Partner J. T. Carew was a large stockholder in the gas company exposed for its franchise "steal." The John A. Shillito Company also found it convenient to cut down its lineage, as did other merchants.

Thinking far ahead of his time, Scripps had a more exalted concept of his Newspaper Enterprise Association than comprehended even by his own editors. N.E.A.'s daily output of high-priced special articles, editorials, cartoons, mats of photo engravings, and short fiction stories, in his view, constituted the essentials for a national newspaper.

For manager of such an important syndicate, Scripps wanted no less than a superman, writing Paine: "We ought to have a bigger man that you or me, and a half-dozen like us rolled into one. . . . We want a man who won't have to be told what I am thinking about, but will be thinking better and faster than I can—a man whose power of imagination is more penetrating than my own."

More importantly, Scripps decided that N. E. A. would become his voice. On national and state policy questions, he would designate certain "must" editorials and articles to be issued through N.E.A. "and SHALL be printed." Paine was instructed to get this "must" system rolling. He apparently carried out his orders with a sledgehammer. Wryly, Scripps observed: "In some of your letters . . . to our Coast editors . . . you are attempting to feed beefsteaks and raw turnips to suckling babes. . . . Use the club with vigor, but never forget you are a sergeant drilling an awkward squad."

Trouble of another sort erupted at the *Toledo News-Bee*. Business Manager Hiram Crouse and his secretary caused gossip. They left for a trip to Europe, accompanied by her brother. They returned amid new rumors. At his *News-Bee* desk, Crouse was audaciously plotting to launch a rival newspaper. League President W. W. Thornton proposed to descend on Toledo and fire him, but Scripps held Thornton back. "I would no more think of setting you to such a task as I would think of teaching my son to pick pockets and prey in a criminal manner on my neighbors."

On the other hand, McRae was all for discharging Crouse. "When a man enters my house to rob me, I will be unChristian enough to give him a bullet instead of a glad hand."

Crouse finally resigned and started his opposition paper, which he called the *Toledo Press*. Initially, he hurt the *News-Bee* with an inventive contest giving away a house and lot to lure subscribers and advertisers.

Scripps kept close watch on son Jim's infant *Fresno Tribune*. Before the paper was two months old, he saw the glimmer of trouble. By the end of 1905, Jim had developed a self-admitted "streak of sorehead" and was "pretty mad at myself. . . . When I came up here . . . I thought it would be plain sailing but it ain't."

Jim ran out of money and wrote Miramar secretary J. P. Hamilton: "Take this letter in to Pa and explain . . . I am in a bad way and for Christ's sake do something."

Scripps did something. Gently, he called it a day for Jim's first managership, and sent a replacement to Fresno, keeping the wobbly *Tribune* alive for six years. E. W. advised Atwood on January 15, 1906:

> Jim has failed completely and utterly in this respect. . . . My object in starting Fresno . . . is to teach my son some practical lessons in business and to learn myself enough about him . . . to make calculations for his

future. . . . There will be some compensations for both him and myself to be derived from failure, partial or complete. He will be more modest and will in future years, remembering his own shortcomings, be more kind, charitable, and considerate toward his fellows in humbler positions.

I might not be, myself, so arrogant, so harsh and severe toward others had I not had the good fortune of early meeting with successes that were perhaps as much due to favoring opportunities as my own innate abilities.

20

How to Make Dull Editors Bright

On November 14, 1905, Scripps sternly regarded his nervous Miramar visitor, Larry V. Ashbaugh. Two thousand miles away the Kansas City *World* would live or die on the words passing between them.

Scripps had turned over control to Will Kellogg and Ashbaugh and their Clover Leaf associates. But the *World* still kept sliding downhill. Kellogg had tried and failed to wheedle another $45,000 loan out of Scripps.

That led to violent quarrels in the Clover Leaf board meetings. Kellogg threw himself on the floor in a tantrum, crying, kicking, and screaming. Now at Miramar Ashbaugh was giving further details of that stormy scene. Kellogg made then threats to "kill Uncle Ed and then myself." His wife became frightened and hid all the sharp knives in their Kansas City home.

Kellogg was talked into committing himself to Dr. King's Sanitarium at Watkins, New York. Ashbaugh now grimly told Scripps he had been informed that insanity ran in Kellogg's family. "I believe he is insane," Ashbaugh said.

After hours they came to an impasse, and the conference broke up on an angry note. "Hell," snarled Ashbaugh, "I'll go back and throw the whole thing into receivership!" Wisely, however, he went home and adopted the plan Scripps had proposed — cutting expense to the bone, eliminating all unpaid circulation, and running the *World* with two twenty-five-dollar-a-week men, an editor and business manager. "I'll run the *World* with one linotype, if necessary," Ashbaugh wrote Scripps on November 22.

But the situation did not improve in Kansas City. The poor *World*

240

suffered another staggering jolt. A new paper, the *Kansas City Post,* was started; its first blow against the *World* was a hiring raid that took the last few good reporters.

Then Scripps received a startling message from Kansas City, relayed through Atwood on January 9, 1906. Will Kellogg had "escaped" from the Sanitarium and shown up in Kansas City—distraught because he feared his wife was getting ready to divorce him.

"The doctors at the Watkins Sanitarium say that cases like Kellogg usually wind up in homicide or suicide. Please be on guard. Ashbaugh says that Kellogg has left for California."

Not much that happened in the lusty Pacific Northwest shocked the master of Miramar. But he began to fret over disturbing reports about the bohemian life of the editor of the *Seattle Star,* Will Strandborg.

Scripps complained to Bob Paine in a letter August 28, 1905. "He's a little too interested in red wine and pretty girls. Give him a fatherly talk."

But without waiting, E. W. summoned his Northwest chiefs, Chase and Wells, to the ranch. Wells was willing to leave the *Tacoma Times* and return to Seattle to serve as interim editor of the *Star.* Luckily a replacement was available in Tacoma. Wells recently had caught Leroy Sanders "adrift from Salt Lake City. . . . He is hovering around twenty-six, is beardless, blue-eyed, has a proper dome overhead and knows a vast lot. Has remarkable good judgment on news, fine manager of payrolls, sour of disposition, inclined to be grumpy."

Strandborg, Chase reported, was actually on the verge of brain fever. "He has been drinking hard at night, taking chloral and coffee to steady his nerves." Strandborg put himself under the care of a doctor and mailed his resignation to Miramar.

When Wells took over in December he began hearing that the *Star* had become "a blackmailing sheet." For a price, some reporters would kill offensive stories. Ten days after he took over as editor, a real estate dealer came in to complain. He had been asked $75 to kill a police court story.

Flabbergasted, Wells and Chase went with the real estate man and hid in an adjoining office with the door cracked. The *Star* police reporter, named Stratton, breezed in to pick up his money. The real estate man haggled him down to $50. Stratton took a check made out to "cash." Wells and Chase then burst in. They threatened Stratton with prison. The police reporter went white and begged for mercy. Finally he confessed and implicated as his accomplice the city editor, Victor H.

Smalley, who worked under the pseudonym "Dan Dean."

The city editor tried to brazen it out. Then he, too, confessed. He implicated four other reporters, on the *Times* and the *Post-Intelligencer.* Dan Dean said the grafting had been going on for several years, but Strandborg was too naive to detect it. Wells immediately fired his two blackmailers. Every Seattle newspaper carried the story. "Our position before the public," Wells wrote E. W., "is 1000 percent better than it was twenty-four hours ago. Everybody is commending the paper for the exposé of its own men."

The scandal left Scripps "greatly shocked." He blamed Strandborg, suspecting City Editor Dan Dean was holding something over the editor's head. The episode disclosed a danger Scripps now feared he had failed to recognize. "We must take steps," he advised Paine, "to protect our papers and our young men from temptation. . . . I am willing to risk the actual theft of money from various treasuries; but a few more instances such as Seattle might prove that I have no right to own and conduct a number of newspapers . . . [until he could prevent] such a dangerous condition of affairs. I believe Mr. Hearst and Mr. Pulitzer have both suffered greatly by reason of what their agents have done in distant cities without [their] knowledge."

Sweaty men in overalls, shouting "Gee . . . haw!" to their straining teams, guided two-handled earth scoops into the slopes of a Miramar canyon. The horses circled around, the teamsters dumped and leveled, and the roadbed began to take shape. It would be about the one-hundredth mile that Scripps had constructed at his own expense up into the early part of 1906.

Scripps's interest in roads went, of course, hand-in-hand with his discovery of the convenience and pleasure of motorcars. They were far from perfect, giving frequent mechanical trouble; but he kept a fleet of three or four at the ranch.

Perhaps his innate "feel" for the earth helped make him an expert in road design and construction. Those he put down tended to last. He experimented with clay and gravel mixtures to create surfaces that hardened and withstood the onslaught of traffic and the elements.

He personally kept a sharp look-out for trouble spots on his roads. But someone else saw to repairs. That chore he delegated to John Paul, now almost eighteen, and serving his stint as ranch manager.

"Send the Rambler and a crew to fill two little washouts about a mile from the grade near Penasquitas corner," Scripps directed March 19, 1906 — typical of his surveillance and repair technique.

Looking into the future, Scripps already saw John Paul as the editorial chieftain of all his newspapers, Jim running the business end.

The concern's financial report showed the papers in 1905 earned $350,000, their biggest profit ever. The only established papers losing money were the *Spokane Press* and the *St. Louis Star-Chronicle*. For the year Tacoma was only $500 behind "and the losses at Sacramento and Fresno are only an investment."

For five years Scripps admiringly observed the frail figure of John P. Hamilton hunched over the Underwood, typing letters with the necessary four or five blue carbon copies, often until late into the night. He had come to Miramar as a twenty-two-year-old secretary, loyal, self-sacrificing, and above all intelligent.

"But he is not the most robust fellow," Scripps told Bob Paine. "If I send him to start the Denver paper, he will need a strong man to go with him, but not a Strandborg." Scripps yearned to start a penny paper in Denver, the mile-high gateway for east-west telegraph news circuits, and a busy mining capital with a booming future. Hamilton wanted a shot at the venture. Scripps gave the young secretary, now twenty-seven, careful study. One thing was certain; Hamilton knew Scrippsian principles and policies. Considering those thousands and thousands of words he had taken down in shorthand and hammered out on the typewriter, he had a view of the inside of the old man's head equalled by few.

The Denver fever had a solid lock on Scripps. He shot a letter to Atwood to assemble a little plant—a press and one linotype—and have it ready to ship to the Colorado capital. Finally he gave the nod to Hamilton. The secretary calculated it would cost $1,000 a month to publish the new paper—which he named the *Denver Express*.

Just then—February 1906—two members of a citizens' better government organization in Denver—impressed by kudos Scripps-McRae received in the wake of the Boss Cox overthrow—"invited" Scripps to come to Denver with a "reform" newspaper. The two, James F. Causey, a stock and bond broker, and E. P. Costigan, a lawyer, promised moral and financial help.

"I have never yet started a newspaper the avowed object of which was to reform a community," Scripps replied to Causey, "and I am modest enough to recognize that there is not a city in the United States, the majority of whose citizens are not my equal in intelligence and civic virtue."

His practice was to conduct newspapers, not *organs*. "I would not suppress an item of news even if [it] would redound to the advantage of the damndest scoundrel in the community. Nor would I suppress an item of legitimate news [that would] seriously injure the credit and standing of the best citizen in town, and the most liberal patron of the paper."

No financial assistance was needed for the *Denver Express*. But so long as he retained "one-man power," Scripps offered to invest $51,000 and let the Denver group take $49,000 in stock, inviting the Colorado men to come to the ranch and discuss it.

While that scheme was hatching, the idea of going into Evansville, Indiana came up. Father of this unborn penny paper was to be J. C. Harper, now serving as "personal" attorney to Scripps instead of League counsel. On January 25, 1906, at Miramar, E. W. signed "in an off-hand way" authorization for the lawyer to command the Indiana project. "I have no interest in Evansville especially. Getting the right men will be the most important item. You [Atwood] are authorized to consider any kind of a proposal."

The Denver reformers, Causey and Costigan, arrived at Miramar on March 30. The talk was friendly. But no deal was made. They departed, pledging moral rather than financial assistance.

By the first week in April, Hamilton had assembled his staff. There was a surprise addition to the start-up team that climbed aboard the Denver-bound train—Jim Scripps. After all, the old man's son was a "veteran" of two recent start-ups from scratch—Sacramento and Fresno. He might be helpful to this crew of greenhorns.

On his littered desk at Miramar, Scripps picked up the latest issue of the *San Francisco News*. For months he had been cajoling and criticizing Business Manager Ham Clark and Editor William D. Wasson. But with meager success.

Scripps had expected the *News* to have a free hand and be fearless. "I have been greatly surprised and disappointed. . . . Every day of the year is campaign day—a day when a campaign should be waged for some great public interest—far more often than not unrelated to politics. . . . We should be fighting continually for better sanitation, for better education, for better and healthier and more moral amusements, for better homes, for better wages, for better sermons in our churches, for better accommodations on the street cars. I believe that the newspaper editors of this country can do more good than all the other classes of people together . . . by open, candid expressions of opinion, fearless as to mistakes as long as they are fearless in their sincerity."

Instead of firing the editor, Scripps kept trying to reform him. He thought Wasson was aping the fable's fly on the grindstone which became so swell-headed he thought he was making everything turn. The editor was "either pig-headed, or so mentally constituted he cannot understand what I want."

For a week while Wasson was ill, Max Balthaser, manager of the Scripps West Coast wire, temporarily took his place. Suddenly circulation spurted five hundred. Clark attributed the gain to Balthaser's lively editing and murderous condensation. He wrote the ranch: "That gives the *News* the balls you so often mention."

Scripps hated to give up on Wasson, who begged for more money and wanted Scripps to tell him precisely what to do. The boss, of course, didn't have the time. Especially when his suggestions — and direct orders — were so roundly ignored. It was not money spent on a newspaper, E. W. admonished, "that makes it sell. It is the way one spends the money. Just as a good cook will take a few poor vegetables and scraps and leavings of the butcher-shop and give you a feast while a poor cook with all there is in the market will disgust you, so will a good editor (I mean an editor who 'knows news') with his own pen and a few cubs 'rush' a town while the protégé of a millionaire will sink his hundreds of thousands of dollars on a staff as large as an army corps, only to get a 'corporal's guard' of readers."

From his hermit's nest on the mesa, he diligently kept trying to impart lessons in newspapering.

> I have learned that men and women like to laugh better than they do to cry . . . and that in a newspaper, humor is far more acceptable than heroics.
>
> I have learned that even a jolly rascal is a more acceptable companion to the average human being than the long-faced, stupidly-honest man.
>
> I have learned that all animals are naturally indolent and lazy and detest unnecessary labor, and will always take the shortcut to their goal. This means that men like small papers and large type even more than they like completeness and beauty of style.
>
> Better than a long roundabout road which affords the traveler beautiful scenery, the traveler likes the short-cut but . . . he also likes beautiful scenery. Thus the reader who wants a brief item of news prefers to have such an item in an interesting and attractive form rather than in a dull and stupid form.

Even Bob Paine's shattered love life was to become involved in the destiny of the *San Francisco News*.

Facing a messy divorce suit with Rose, Paine felt he must get away from Ohio. Scripps permitted him to chuck his business responsibilities in the East and head for California. For "about a year," Paine would ostensibly try to perk up the West Coast bureau at San Francisco of the Newspaper Enterprise Association.

A few weeks after Paine arrived in the West, accompanied by Wanda Pole who was soon to become his third wife, E. W. had him lending his powerful experience and considerable verve to the faltering San Francisco daily. Scripps instructed Paine on February 20, 1906, to get together with Wasson and try to steer the *News* on the right course.

"Every line of space is worth a gold dollar. The editor would be just as much justified in throwing a handful of gold into San Francisco Bay as he would to use a thousand words of space in one day's issue that could have been saved by a blue pencil."

Finally Scripps began to see signs of success at the *News* which enhanced his conviction that "there is not only a new and profitable field of journalism, but a chance of becoming a great public benefactor by founding and building up a new generation of independent newspapers." Scripps yearned to "send out missionaries" who would "preach the gospel" of this new journalism. He told "banker" Atwood he was considering assembling capital of $200,000 to $300,000, and "found in rapid succession" a series of such new papers.

But just as the little *San Francisco News* seemed finally getting on track, Fate cruelly intervened.

At 5:11 A.M. on April 18, 1906, the hills of San Francisco began to groan and twist and tremble. Buildings swayed, tottered, and crashed. Streets buckled. Water, gas, and power lines flew apart. In panic, 300,000 citizens fled into the streets. Four hundred soon lay dead or dying amid the wreckage. It was one of history's worst earthquake disasters.

Fire erupted, compounding the holocaust. Giant flames crackled and raced down Telegraph Hill to the Bay, leaving a trail of smoke and ashes. Then the scarlet tongues licked paths of ruin in every direction.

The office of the *News* at 340 Ninth Street suffered but minor damage from the quake. Editor Wasson scrambled from home through the city's wreckage to his office. He assembled the facts for an "extra." There was no power to run the press. He "captured" a hand-and-foot press in Jack Smith's nearby job shop and ran off 1,500 dodgers with his story, which included a partial list of the dead. Newsboys appeared, grabbed copies, and rushed off to sell them for twenty-five cents to $1. They easily could have peddled 15,000.

Wasson looked around then at the awful destruction, sank to his knees in tears, and went to pieces.

The *News*'s small wooden building, two miles south of the Ferry

Terminal, sat directly in the path of the most vicious firestorm, which already had obliterated the city's other daily newspapers.

Was there time to save the *News*'s equipment? Certainly not the printing press, a giant too large and heavy to be quickly disassembled and moved. The two linotypes, however, were skidded out of the building into a vacant lot, wrapped in blankets, and buried. The type matrix magazines and other critical parts, typewriters, and books were hustled into the fireproof vault in the basement.

Heroic efforts were underway to curtail the firestorms. Dynamiters rushed ahead of the flames, blowing up buildings to create "gaps" the flames might not leap. Ham Clark stood beside the "graves" of the linotypes, looking helplessly from the newspaper building toward the roar and crackle of the approaching inferno. The dynamiters were now busy less than two blocks away.

Finally, at 4 in the afternoon, Clark and his helpers, with smoke stinging their nostrils, fled for their lives. The fire and the dynamiters came on. It was only a question of which would reach the *News* building first.

21

Wasn't That an Asshole Winder?

First word of the disaster came over the ranch phone from the *Los Angeles Record* about six hours after the quake hit. Fate of the *San Francisco News* and its men at that time was unknown. At once Scripps tried to send a telegram to Ham Clark. He couldn't because official traffic clogged the telegraph and telephone lines into San Francisco.

It was not until 8 o'clock the morning of the second day, April 19, that a telegram came from Clark. It bore dire news—the *San Francisco News* building had burned to the ground. Its press was ruined, but, fortunately all hands were safe. Urgently Clark needed funds—real money, since all but one or two of the banks had burned and no check or draft could be processed.

Scripps immediately opened spigots of the League treasury. He wired Atwood in Cincinnati to dispatch a courier with $10,000 cash to the scene, and to locate replacement equipment that could be quickly shipped—presses, linotypes, stereotyping machines. Scripps ordered Hans Bagby to institute relief action. Bagby dressed a *Record* reporter in khaki, pinned a linen envelope holding $2,000 in his pants pocket, and, through a friendly captain, got him aboard the first troop train pulling out for guard duty in the stricken city. "Find Ham Clark," Bagby instructed, "and give him that envelope." In Cincinnati, Charles Mosher was hurrying to the depot with a ticket to California via the Union Pacific Overland Limited, clutching a satchel filled with $10,000.

On that same day from the scene of the tragedy, Clark wrote to "Dear Boss":

> Hell's been to pay and I think I see my way out. Military law has been our big trouble but with passes we got today we will start operating. . . . We

will take a tent from Oakland (25 × 40 tent) and set up again on our own lots — begin anew where we left off.

The man that built our old shack met me on the grounds yesterday and told me he would rebuild us and help out in every way and I saved plans of the old building. . . . Prices have jumped to mining camp figures when it comes to horses and work.

Of course we will be some distance, nearly a mile, from nearest houses standing, still the quicker we get located on our own grounds the better, even if we only put up a flag. . . .

Cheer up, boss — we have lost a big bunch of money, but we will get it all back.

Bob Paine and Clark went across the bay and set up an "office" in a livery stable. They arranged for the *Oakland Inquirer* to temporarily print their paper. Within three days they were back in business, shuttling the copies by launch across the bay, managing to locate about 7,500 of their 30,000 old subscribers. At the Scripps paper in Fresno, an extra press was dismantled and shipped to San Francisco. Money arrived.

Things were in such good shape by Monday, April 23, that Scripps went ahead with a vacation he had been planning — a six-day automobile trip into the mountains with Nackie and several children.

One signal event that occurred in his absence was the birth on Thursday, April 26, of the twentieth child of his brain — the *Denver Express*. More of such ink and paper progeny were foremost on Scripps's 1906 agenda. By year's end he was determined to have eight more running. They would be, of course, all on the same cheap pattern. Locations already were targeted: Evansville and Terre Haute, Indiana; Pueblo, Colorado; Dallas, Texas; Portland, Oregon; Oklahoma City, Oklahoma; and Memphis and Nashville, Tennessee.

With amazing rapidity, San Francisco started rebuilding. Clark took a notion they ought to abandon the *San Francisco News* and start an entirely new paper in Oakland. Scripps wouldn't hear of that. He counted heavily on Bob Paine "to help clothe with bones and flesh the naked spirit that survives. You have the right to establish yourself as one of the few great spirits of this time in rebuilding the *News*."

It was no surprise when word came to Miramar that the Detroit patriarch had turned dangerously ill. For years James had intermittently suffered vicious gall bladder attacks. Now his illness was more serious — rapid deterioration of the central nervous system.

About then, while Scripps was getting ready to take his family along when he went east on business, his two youngest came down with measles. The same day word came from Detroit that physicians pronounced James's illness terminal. The end could come any day. Ellen at once took the train for Detroit, arriving May 24. E. W. confessed he was "mean and selfish" to send her off alone, but felt he was needed at home.

On May 29, a wire came from James's twenty-four-year-old son William E.: "Father died last night. End peaceful. Funeral Thursday afternoon." Scripps telegraphed back: "I sympathize with yourself, mother and sisters. Should have come east with Ellen except for serious illness in my own family." Scripps made no effort to reach Detroit for the funeral.

Within six weeks of being demolished, the rebuilt *San Francisco News* again flourished. Circulation recovered amazingly, hitting 18,955 by the first of June. Bob Paine still struggled to help re-establish the paper. He had soured on California, telling Scripps candidly he had "a perfect right to belly-ache about San Francisco's chill and fleas."

About ready to leave the ranch on his postponed trip to Cincinnati, Scripps got a frightening jolt. On the morning of June 5, his secretary rushed in breathlessly to tell him that Will Kellogg had just driven up in a buggy, loudly demanding to see Scripps "on business." The Clover Leaf partners, Kellogg shouted, were going into Oklahoma and must have help from Scripps.

"Order him off the place!" said E. W. "I have no intention of talking to him — about anything."

The foreman escorted the excited intruder off the ranch.

This unannounced appearance of a mentally unstable "escapee" from a sanitarium — who had openly voiced threats to kill E. W. and then himself — gravely disturbed Scripps. "I suspect he meant personal mischief," Scripps asserted in a telegram asking Atwood to check into Kellogg's claim about changes in the Clover Leaf. Scripps also notified John Sweeney of the intrusion by E. W.'s one-time "razzle-dazzler" protégé. "He was very excited when he came," said the telegram. "You know what he has threatened."

Scripps was so shaken he immediately hired a private detective to shadow Kellogg and keep E. W. informed of his movements. In a memo reciting "facts of the case" for the detective, Scripps described Kellogg's collapse from "nervous prostration" two years earlier. "He was always erratic, cheeky, and a good deal of a liar. After his breakdown, his characteristics simply became exaggerated."

Kellogg, forty, was reasonably well off with an income of about $20,000 a year, apparently now living with his wife Floy and father-in-law W. A. Scripps at the latter's home in Altadena, California. Scripps wanted to know quickly of Kellogg's travels.

"I expect to leave on the Santa Fe Limited for Cincinnati via Chicago on June 13. It is possible that Kellogg knows of my intention, and it is desirable for me to know whether he will attempt to accompany me on this train. In case he should do so, a detective should plan to be on the train, and alert, to prevent any disagreeable incident."

The other Clover Leaf partners, Ashbaugh and Mel Uhl, wired to not take Kellogg's Oklahoma plan seriously. Uhl explained: "He talked about this before going West and I only gave my consent to pacify him." Uhl also wired Atwood: "Have no more idea of leaving Des Moines than of going to the North Pole."

The situation worried Atwood. He telegraphed Scripps to stay on the alert: "I consider Kellogg dangerous and just now unsettled."

To end the back-stabbing that began to cripple both SMPA and Publishers Press, Scripps proposed in mid-1906 to try to buy out the eastern partner. He delegated John Vandercook to negotiate the purchase. Observed Scripps: "It is owned by wealthy men who have got enough anyhow . . . run by old men, comparatively, who lack initiative, ambition, force, and the spirit of adventure."

Vandercook agreed. He depicted Publishers Press chief J. B. Shale, a former country publisher in Pennsylvania, as a "provincial hypnotized by New Yorkitis." Now owner of a gold mine, Shale had lost his zest for the news business. Bob Paine lamented that the eastern wire had turned slow and dull, sadly neglected by Shale, whom he characterized as a "braying . . . thistle-fed ass."

Nevertheless Publishers Press was the larger with 113 leased wire clients plus 150 papers buying the brief pony report, to Smite's forty-five leased wires and one hundred ponies.

Shale was willing to deliver control of Publishers Press for $160,000. "That price is too high," said Scripps. He sent back Milton McRae to offer $75,000. The Publishers Press chief was outraged. He puffed up and threatened to break off the partnership. McRae leaped to his feet and thrust a paper in Shale's face. "Suits us—sign this!" It was a document Mac had prepared in advance terminating the news combine in thirty days. "It's peace or war!"

Shale drew back in surprise. He had expected no such ultimatum. Vandercook, sitting beside McRae, saw instantly this was the turning point. He understood what was going on in Shale's mind. With no partnership, Publishers Press could not alone cover the whole country, and probably would go bankrupt.

With a loud sigh, Shale accepted the offer.

Thus for $75,000, Scripps on July 19, 1906, acquired the 337 controlling shares of Publishers Press — as well as a bevy of unexpected problems. The wire service was taking in $1,000 a day, but losing $250 a week, and had a floating debt of $100,000. Scripps agreed to assume only $40,000 of the debt.

Initially Scripps intended to merge only management of the three telegraph services, SNA on the West Coast, SMPA in the Midwest, and Publishers Press in the East. McRae was designated president, Vandercook general news manager, and Ham Clark business manager.

Scripps made clear he was in telegraph news for profit — as well as providing antimonopoly public service. He opposed cutting rates to newly-started papers, even his own. "I always resolutely combatted this idea . . . and young newspapers should stand on their own bottom and accept no favors. Perhaps it is because of this Spartan-father treatment of the Western boys that a number of them have developed into strong men and not nincompoops."

Owning Publishers Press put Scripps in a stronger position to launch his ad-less newspaper, especially if in New York but the wire service deal gobbled up the two men he wanted to run it. He still counted on Vandercook to be editor and Ham Clark business manager. But in merging the wire service management, Vandercook left the editorship of the Cincinnati *Post* to become wire service news manager with offices in New York City, where Clark joined him to head up business affairs. They would be thus occupied for months, perhaps years.

When Vandercook took over he found Publishers Press had fifty cents in the bank, a three-thousand-dollar-a-month payroll, and only enough expense money to last last twenty-four hours. Scripps had spent $400,000 in nine years to subsidize his own wire; now he'd be tapped for more coin to get the eastern end on its feet.

Vandercook started cleaning out deadwood. He replaced Shale's incompetent day news manager with the little fireball from the Scripps ranks, Roy W. Howard — a choice the concern would never regret.

E. W. had a strong feeling the telegraph report should wake up the average newspaper editor, who had a tendency to follow the herd. He wrote Bob Paine: "Give an editor a whole lot of good copy, or worse still, copy that a thousand other newspapers use and brag about, and he feels no one has a right to complain if he fills his paper up with this stuff . . . and that the reader who does complain is an ass. . . . Bob, scoops don't pay their cost. What we want . . . is good, easy reading matter — enough of it and not too much, and a paper that keeps its readers pretty well informed."

On the train speeding south to Dallas, Alfred O. Andersson, SMPA's bureau chief at Kansas City, glanced up at his fat suitcase in the luggage rack, with a smug grin. On this Sunday, September 16, 1906, a race was on to start a new paper in Dallas. It was the Scripps-McRae League versus the Clover Leaf League.

The contest really wasn't meant to be; it had started by mistake, by accident, by pure pique, or buttinsky bull-headedness on E. W. Scripps's part. But regardless, the race was on at top speed, and the first team to bring out a new Dallas paper would win rights to the town.

Larry Ashbaugh of the Clover Leaf had been in Cincinnati September 12, trying to borrow $100,000 from the Scripps Central Office to launch new papers in Duluth, Minnesota, and Fargo, North Dakota. In offhand talk, L. T. Atwood mentioned that Milton McRae was sending two men to Dallas to launch the *Dallas Dispatch*.

Ashbaugh hit the ceiling. "You can't! Mel Uhl told Mr. Scripps last July that we were going into Dallas. I'll put a stop to this right now!" He rushed out to send a telegram to Miramar.

Scripps wired back he hadn't promised to stay out of any city. He didn't recall Uhl telling him of their plans for Dallas. But regardless Clover Leaf had never put its intentions in writing—and everyone knew that was the only way E. W. Scripps did business.

Ashbaugh then sent a second telegram claiming exclusive rights to the N.E.A. copy in Dallas. This struck Scripps as an "impudent, sassy ultimatum." E. W. replied that he was willing for Clover Leaf to buy SMPA telegraph service any place in the nation, but N.E.A. would go only to the first paper to start in Dallas.

McRae had already chosen Andersson and Harry J. Richmond to undertake the Dallas venture, to get $25 each weekly, with 20 percent working interest in the penny paper to be built from scratch on the cheap. Each was thirty-two, married, well-experienced. When Andersson heard in Kansas City that it was to be a race, his mind and his feet moved at high speed.

At 8 P.M. Sunday the 16th, he and Richmond reached Dallas—with the fat suitcase. At their hotel they conferred with a lawyer. Their question was whether a newspaper was legally required to publish its office location. The answer was no. That was a relief, because of course they had yet no office. They next routed from bed the president of the Dallas printers union and got him to come to their room. He readily agreed to help find a temporary printing plant. By now it was 12:01 A.M., Monday, September 17.

Andersson stepped over to his fat suitcase. He unbuckled the straps and flung it open. Inside lay a stack of about one hundred copies of a newspaper. The flag read: *"The Dallas Dispatch.* Monday, September 17, 1906. Volume One, Number One." It was a slapped-together four-page edition, filled with a hodge-podge of rather dated wire dispatches, features, old photos and cartoons, with hardly anything about Texas. But it was a Dallas newspaper—and it was legitimate.

Andersson handed a copy to the union official and had him sign an affidavit that it existed. Richmond grabbed an armful, went down to the lobby and passed them out to loungers. Then he stepped out on the street and handed copies to surprised passersby.

At daybreak, they wired Atwood, claiming victory. About noon they met Mel Uhl of the Clover Leaf on the street. They asked if he had yet started a Dallas paper. "No," said Uhl. Andersson handed him a copy of the *Dallas Dispatch.*

Uhl was staggered. He stuttered that he had been informed the race was off, that Scripps had agreed to hold up everything until Ashbaugh could confer in Chicago with McRae. It was Andersson's turn to be shocked. But he was not about to surrender without official word. He and Richmond located a job shop and printed their second issue. They kept going all week, hiring one reporter and digging up local items. Richmond found getting subscribers as easy "as picking leaves off trees."

Then McRae yanked the rug out from under the *Dispatch* duo. In Chicago he let Ashbaugh talk him into reneging. Mac sent Scripps a wire that he had agreed to give Clover Leaf sovereign rights "to Dallas and any part of the Oklahoma Indian nation," adding, "will consider silence your approval."

That last was a big mistake.

The telegraph operator at San Diego phoned the message out to Miramar. By some fluke, Scripps never saw it. He only learned of the Dallas back-down by letter two or three days later—and became furious. He wrote McRae: "Every time I touch this Clover Leaf crowd . . . they nettle me, and make me want to have nothing more to do with them. . . . They have got in the habit of lying to me, or telling half-truths. . . . Ashbaugh was trying to rush you to a conclusion before you could hear the whole story."

Perhaps what most upset Scripps was to discover "that Will Kellogg is back and active in that Clover Leaf bunch." That meant the kiss of death; the old man had vowed to never again get into any deal with that psychotic razzle-dazzler.

Scripps warned McRae also against dealing "in bad faith" with Andersson and Richmond. He demanded to see their written consent before any change was made. To reinforce that, he telegraphed Andersson: "I can better afford to lose many thousands of dollars than disappoint any man who has put faith in me. I have never yet broken a contract. If you leave Dallas and drop from the enterprise, it will be because you want to, and not because I ask you. I advise you to work harder than ever. Answer. Acknowledge receipt of this."

The chastised McRae got busy and instructed his team to keep publishing the *Dallas Dispatch*.

But Ashbaugh would not surrender. He and Uhl took the train to Miramar, arriving October 8. They couldn't budge Scripps. He wired McRae: "Ashbaugh and Uhl left yesterday. Matters were left where they were when they came. They must settle with Andersson and Richmond satisfactorily or there will be nothing doing. I do not think they can."

While Ashbaugh and Uhl were visiting Scripps, none of the three was aware that McRae had sent two men to Oklahoma City to start the *Oklahoma News,* the League's Number 26, which began publishing October 1. Being kept in the dark about that left Scripps "feeling like a chump tonight. I do not know what to write Uhl and Ashbaugh. I do not care so much about Ashbaugh, but it seems to me that Uhl is by nature a square man, and I hate to think that his associates will make use of this to convince him that I am a trickster."

The finale of the spirited Dallas race was played out on October 17 in the *Dispatch*'s temporary office. A dapper stranger came in and introduced himself to Andersson and Richmond as Will Kellogg. With a crooked smile, he came straight to the point: How about quitting Scripps-McRae and bringing their paper into the Clover Leaf League? No thanks, responded the *Dispatch* partners. Kellogg gave them a sly, knowing look. "Your refusal," he said, "will cost Mr. Scripps a quarter million—elsewhere." What he meant was clear to no one, unless himself.

Scripps seemed to be developing his own fondness for enigmas and secrecy. In launching the *Denver Express,* he had enjoined Hamilton to tell no one it was a Scripps-McRae paper. To knowledgeable Denverites, the ownership veil was rather transparent. But when he decided to go into Portland, Oregon, Scripps's behavior was close to paranoid. He kept the venture secret even from his own otherwise trusted secretaries, and insisted it be referred to only by the code name "Columbia." He never fully explained his motives. Nobody in Portland was to know it was his paper; it would publish only its office address, list the name of no employee or agent. It must resemble no other Scripps paper in size, format, or typeface. It would carry no telegraph except that clipped and rewritten from exchanges. To be called the *Eastside News,* it would print only items affecting people living in the half of Portland located east of the Willamet River. It would not circulate on the west bank, nor cover that area.

It would be a typical penny-pinching cheapie. No employee got a free paper — and only five copies were allowed for office use. Editor and business manager would each get $15, plus 10 percent of the stock. Scripps carried secrecy to such extreme that he made the "Columbia" business manager, Melvin Harold Voorhees, ex ad salesman from his Seattle paper, call himself "M. Harold."

On September 29, 1906, the mysterious "Columbia" came forth — the dinky little *Eastside News*. The town didn't know that it was E. W. Scripps's paper Number 25. No one at the paper broke the secrecy. When the *Eastside News* had been in operation about five weeks, Jim Scripps showed up and presented his card. He later sent Dad a memo describing his reception:

> At first Dillon [the editor] was very suspicious and I told him I would stick around until Voorhees came in. . . . He told me not to speak to the men as everything was on the Q.T. . . . "You know when you handed me your card it staggered me, but I noticed your umbrella and your ring have initials J. G. S. on them, and I felt certain your name was Scripps, as per your card. You understand that we are just a couple of damn fools starting a paper here and several people have been trying to pry into our business." . . . Voorhees came in and we talked half an hour. I did not think much of Dillon, but was struck with Voorhees. . . . Both men are feeling very good.

At fifty miles an hour, the new 1906 Packard touring car whizzed along the mountain road "not a foot away" from a cliff with a thousand-foot drop to the Pacific Ocean. Jim Scripps was at the wheel. Buffeted by the wind, his half-frightened Dad frantically held tight, as exhilarated as a schoolboy. On their tail, also daring and reckless, came John Paul in a second Packard, bringing the white-faced secretary.

Adventure by automobile beckoned Scripps often. This exciting twenty-one-day California tour took them 2,000 miles, from 50° and fog on the coast to 110° in the dusty interior valleys, climbing mountain grades of 25°, and virtually sliding down the other side.

"I slept in all sorts of beds," Scripps wrote Atwood. "I ate most anything. The sandwiches in our lunch basket were sprinkled with dust, but I ate them, grit and all."

His motoring hobby was expensive and trouble-plagued. The 1906 Packards cost $3,000 each. He also bought a $5,580 Pierce Great Arrow with a khaki top. He kept five or six machines at the ranch.

Breakdowns were common and frequent, and sometimes dangerous. Driving one car back from Oceanside, John Paul tried to examine the gears while the vehicle was in motion. He fell under, and was run over. Cuts and bruises kept him in the hospital for a week, and limping for another month.

On an October 1907 excursion to the Grand Canyon, both Packards broke down near Williams, Arizona. Scripps wired the Los Angeles garage to send spare drive shafts, universal pins, and rollers. Then, impatiently, he decided he temporarily had his fill of pioneering by motorcar. He grabbed a train back to the ranch, leaving a chauffeur named Atillo to load the broken machines on a freight train and accompany them back to San Diego for repair.

Even Nackie was bit by the auto craze. Scripps bought her a $3,000 Cadillac runabout to use at the West Chester farm on her annual summer visits to her parents. She wrote him:

> I really could not get on without something of this kind. It has been a great pleasure. . . . I have learned a great deal about autoing for there is no one on the place that can move it but I.
>
> So that necessitates my taking it out of the barn and putting it back in and doing all sorts of backing and twisting around with it. I will be quite an expert chauffeuress by the time I reach home.

Nackie regularly visited West Chester because her father's health was failing. On October 10, 1907, Reverend Holtsinger went to Dayton, Ohio, to preach the funeral of an old friend. At the deceased's residence, pain and nausea seized him. He was put to bed and a physician summoned. A woman asked if she could do anything for him. "My dear child," said the preacher, "I don't hear you." Then he died—aged almost sixty-nine.

Fortunately, Nackie was then visiting West Chester. "It all happened in a few minutes," she wrote, "and he did not suffer long, for which I am thankful." She wired Scripps at Grand Canyon where he and the two older boys were on an automobile adventure. Scripps telegraphed back that he was ill and couldn't come to the funeral, but would send Jim.

Milton McRae tossed in his bed. Every night he was a bundle of nerves. He couldn't sleep. Unmercifully, Scripps was ragging him. Everything Mac did—or didn't do, it seemed—triggered stinging criticism from Miramar. McRae was only forty-eight, but he felt old and used up. The pressure had to let up—otherwise he could be pushed over the edge. But

Scripps was not about to relent. It was clear to both men that their long partnership was in danger of rupture.

Incessantly they had quarrelled over the St. Louis quagmire. Onto the back of McRae, Scripps was shoving the entire blame. Now, in November 1906, E. W. angrily accused his partner of again meddling in Cincinnati editorial affairs.

"You do not see the difference between making money in order to run good newspapers, and running good newspapers to make money," Scripps complained. "I have been trying for twenty-four years to satisfy you," responded the jittery McRae, "and have about reached the conclusion I will never be able to."

The boss, too, had reached that conclusion. He made up his mind to fire McRae. Sometime in the spring Atwood would replace Mac as chairman of the League board of directors. McRae would be left with one task, and one only—to straighten out St. Louis.

In a confidential letter, Scripps so informed Atwood on December 7, 1905. "It took me a long time to realize, but I finally did, that Mr. McRae considers himself to really be my guardian and me as a rather brilliant, erratic, changeable person whom he has . . . not allowed to injure himself and yet to be allowed to feel he was . . . having his own way and doing things."

Scripps's own quixotic vanity was now emerging from its hermit shell to take a death-grip on McRae's towering egotism. That was but one factor inspiring the coming rupture. Perhaps the strongest was Scripps's intention to clear a path for his sons to take over the empire. That day he wanted to come soon—as quickly as he could inculcate in them loyalty to his own rigid policies and principles.

Jim, muscular, energetic, and playful, but acquiring an excellent grasp of the twists and turns of the penny paper world, during the summer of 1906 turned twenty. John Paul was eighteen—and getting ready to plunge into practical journalism.

On January 20, 1907, Scripps directed McRae to "abstain from all other business that will take one moment of energy" from making a success in St. Louis. In June 1905 Scripps had agreed to a merger with Nathan Frank's *St. Louis Star.* Now, though he held control, he bitterly regretted the deal.

Like a good soldier, McRae took the dirty duty. On receipts of $319,157 in 1906, the *St. Louis Star-Chronicle* had shown $26,025 profit—only about half the 15 percent Scripps demanded. "I offer no excuses or apologies," said McRae. "I believe I am criticized unjustly. I have worried and fretted so much I find myself a victim of nerves. . . . I object to your telling me I have not tried."

Into the taut scenario of this crumbling partnership now stepped another principal character — John S. Sweeney, cast as a curious Jekyll-Hyde. In Detroit Circuit Court, Sweeney was trying to collect a quarter million or more under the twenty-two-year-old Quadripartite. His chief target was the Detroit *Evening News.* James E. Scripps's heirs resisted even giving Sweeney a dime, terming the old agreement illegal. So as the lawyers wrangled, E. W. was little more than a bystander. Even if Sweeney won, Ed would lose little, perhaps around $30,000, which he considered fair and just.

So Sweeney maintained friendly relations, and brought his wife and son to Miramar for a lengthy visit during a lull in the Detroit trial. Riding the mesa, the cousins discussed the idea of getting back together in the newspaper business — as soon as the Detroit trial ended. Scripps offered Sweeney $1,000 a month to act as sort of corporate efficiency expert to ferret out wasteful practices in the League. Scripps showed Sweeney the books on all his newspapers. With a rueful head shake, Sweeney swore he could easily save $25,000 a month in expense. E. W. believed him.

Then cousin John was off by train to Detroit to resume the trial. E. W. was conspicuously absent from the courtroom. Ironically, Milton McRae was a principal witness, having to undergo rough pounding on the stand in defense of his partner. Will Kellogg testified, too, trying to bolster father-in-law W. A. Scripps's claim to four and one-third shares in the *Cleveland Press,* one issue in the several-sided litigation.

The sly Kellogg took pleasure in cornering McRae outside the courtroom and spilling the news that Sweeney was coming back into the League and Mac was to be dumped. That was another trauma for the embattled McRae. On April 15 he got the official word from Scripps.

The cruel blow fell heavily, Harper reported to Miramar. "Mac feels humiliation more than anything I have ever known . . . says he has tried for months to conceal his nervousness, inability to sleep. But he is not rebellious, will carry out your plans. . . . He wants to be out of the country before he is deposed."

Scripps gave the impression of almost gloating over ousting his partner, asserting he had resented Mac's "looking out for Number One," and considering himself a rival to E. W. "I struck him in his most vital part, the humbling of his egotism. . . . Mr. McRae for some time has been almost valueless to the concern." That was far from an accurate statement; E. W. seemed to be overlooking the difficult purchase of Publishers Press, success in the race for Dallas, and other feats.

Crestfallen, McRae asked to be allowed to immediately go on a six months leave of absence "to quiet my nerves. I was not unprepared for your action. . . . But being sent to St. Louis would be so humiliating I would be of no value to the concern. . . . If I do not get away, I will break down completely. . . . You have repeatedly warned me that I would break down or kill myself with overwork."

Scripps cut off McRae's $24,000-a-year management salary, decreeing half to be given Sweeney when he assumed his job as "corporate economist." The other $12,000 would go as a raise to Atwood. Just then E. W. considered setting up a $10,000 annual retirement stipend for Atwood, even though he did not believe the concern could afford to grant pensions. He also had in mind an identical pension for Paine.

McRae packed hurriedly and fled Cincinnati. He sailed April 30 from New York, writing Scripps: "I don't know where I'm going. I made an effort to please you, picking men, starting papers, keeping hands off. I failed utterly. It was always 'Damned if I do and damned if I don't.' "

When the Quadripartite trial came to an end, Sweeney was on the stand reading letters from James E. Scripps. He choked up, came near tears, and handed the letters to his lawyer to finish reciting. Sweeney lost. In April 1907, Judge Flavius Brooke ruled in favor of the *Detroit News*, deciding the Quadripartite was never a legal contract. Sweeney promptly appealed. The litigation was fated to drag on four more years, making two trips to the Michigan Supreme Court. In the end, Sweeney would gain nothing — except a fat bill from his lawyers.

That he might not live long enough to carry into reality his grandest ideas began to worry Scripps. He summoned to California John Vandercook and Ham Clark on April 27, 1907, for one of his most momentus business conferences. Two stunning decisions were reached: to combine all three Scripps telegraph wires into a single strong service to be called United Press Associations, and to quit dillydallying and actually start as soon as practical the ad-less daily in New York City. If the non-advertising paper got off to a robust start, Scripps would launch others — in Philadelphia, Boston, Baltimore, Chicago, St. Louis, and Pittsburgh.

In combining the West Coast's Scripps News Association with the Midwest's Scripps-McRae Press Association and the eastern Publishers Press to form one telegraph news service, Scripps created a $300,000 corporation. E. W. held 60 percent of the stock, Clark 20 percent, and Vandercook and Max Balthaser each 10 percent. This dealt out Bob Paine, who would have no duties in the United Press except as E. W.'s watchdog. Scripps proposed to hand Paine $20,000 and absorb his SMPA stock.

Clark and Vandercook settled on a name — the *Bear* — and planned to launch the New York paper in November 1907. Nobody seemed to worry that these men were at one and the same time astride two untamed mustangs—the freaky ad-less, and the unproved United Press. Unworried, Scripps seemed to anticipate this conflict eventually would work itself out.

Vandercook's research showed the previous ill-fated United Press company officially went out of business October 5, 1905, and nobody else had adopted the name, so Scripps could rightfully use it. He was sadly in error. Two other minor outfits were calling themselves United Press. Scripps lawyers would be forced to wrestle the sticky problem through the courts for a couple of years before getting clear title to "United Press Associations."

The two oldest Scripps boys were unsettled. Jim still talked vaguely of starting a penny paper in Philadelphia. John Paul got a try-out of sorts when his father took control August 1, 1907, of the *Berkeley* (California) *Independent,* which was on the rocks. John Paul took a 25 percent interest in the Berkeley daily, Number 29 in the Scripps empire, and went there.

In snooping around the papers, John Sweeney stirred up the resentment of Editor-in-Chief Harry Rickey and League President Willis Thornton. "He's the fifth wheel on our wagon," they complained to Scripps. "The same man hired him who hired you," E. W. retaliated, pointedly. "Get all out of him you can."

On September 19, 1907, McRae returned from seventy-seven days at sea, and four months in South America. His nerves still were shot. He could not yet sleep at night. No way was he fit to do business. Scripps still took a hard line toward him. He told Bob Paine: "Mac decided I was a hypocrite for business purposes . . . that he was the great man and I was the hanger-on. I am the concern. If I am false or unjust, the concern has these faults and is not fit to live."

Abruptly Scripps ordered Atwood away on a long vacation and sent Jim, now twenty-one, to Cincinnati to fill in for him. He wanted to see how his oldest boy could handle power. He handed his son a blue-backed document granting a year-to-year power of attorney that made the boy's word law in the concern. Jim would be wise enough, the father reasoned, to seek counsel from J. C. Harper, Bob Paine, and other seasoned executives before deciding tricky problems.

Sitting in as acting chairman, the boy-heir had a few encounters with John Sweeney. Jim agreed with Rickey and Thornton that the old man's cousin's work was of little value. In commenting on that, he also reported that "McRae has the shakes." Finally Scripps himself conceded: "I have my own doubts as to Sweeney's usefulness. . . . Maybe he is too old . . . and rusty."

McRae wanted to come to Miramar and settle up. Scripps felt uneasy about the meeting. So did his partner. Mac was willing to sever the partnership if all surplus funds in Cincinnati and Cleveland and the *Kentucky Post* were declared as dividends and he got his portion, plus a $40,000 pay-back from the "boot" given to settle the George H. Scripps will contest. Also he wanted details of their settlement kept private.

In mid-November they got together at the ranch and after three days McRae left "completely satisfied" with their settlement. "My partner of twenty-five years considered me entitled to a square deal, and gave it to me," McRae wrote Scripps on return to his new home in Detroit.

> The talk we had in your office at Miramar the morning of my departure will forever be one of the green spots in my memory. . . . Forget for a moment my frailties, my vanity, my egotism, and ask yourself if any man you know, outside yourself, would risk or dare more for the concern as a whole than I have done.
>
> Within a few weeks I hope to straighten out, as best I can, the St. Louis situation, and thereafter to think only of the recovery of my health.

In this period, Scripps was plagued not only with philosophical and cultural conflict but physical and personnel problems as well. Fires damaged the *Seattle Star* and the *Tacoma Times*.

Temptations of the flesh and the bottle were the undoing of the editor of the *Spokane Press,* Verne Joselyn. It proved quite unfortunate that the paper's office was located on the ground floor of a house of ill-repute. Joselyn was arrested "drunk with a notorious woman and signed her bond as editor of the *Press,*" Bob Paine noted in his diary of October 24, 1906. Joselyn was fired.

So was the founding manager of the *Denver Express,* John P. Hamilton, the frail former Miramar secretary. It did not happen overnight, and unfolded slowly as almost a comic opera. When the *Express* boss first neglected to conduct business through League channels, Scripps chided: "Look out, Hamilton, or you will acquire Porterfield's habit of looking down with contempt on a man who is only possessed of a gray beard, experience, capital, and other trifles."

In January 1907, E. W. heard Hamilton had his books askew and was boozing. Jim Scripps came in on the train February 23, 1907, and went straightway to the *Express.* He suspended Hamilton, took temporary charge, and ordered an audit. A $900 shortage was found. The auditor was convinced Hamilton had no idea where it went because the books were so poorly kept. Scripps called Hamilton to the ranch, unmercifully dressed him down, and then gave him a new chance. He was instructed to send Scripps a daily report. But Hamilton neglected to do that, and on October 24, 1907, was fired; Boyd Gurley, the editor, was put in charge.

In Nashville, the League paper flubbed everything, and Scripps was forced to surrender. The first editor failed and was let go. His successor did no better. Scripps blamed the men and their methods, not the town. The second editor, Leonidas Polk from Toledo, did not seem to appreciate the mores of the South. Seemingly he insulted Dixie chivalry and womanhood by recounting in print the after-hours visits of a pretty client to the office of a prominent aged lawyer, who discreetly drew the blinds. The *Times*'s story outraged Nashville's antebellum society.

It had cost $23,000 to keep the paper going its first year. A total investment of $45,000 was the estimate to reach the break-even point. Scripps felt the *Times* would never be a "sticking paper," pointing out that of the first 5,000 subscribers signed up, only 1,000 remained. Scripps authorized offering the paper for sale. Nobody was interested. The rival *Nashville Tennessean* did offer to buy its circulation list—for $32.50.

On Saturday night, December 28, 1907, the *Nashville Times* closed its doors.

When Scripps called for his "rules" file, his secretary brought out a batch of manila folders six or seven inches thick. These hundreds of pages began finally to disgust their autocratic author. Many were redundant, some contradictory, the entire mass often confusing—not only to his newspaper managers but also to the monarch of Miramar.

When Bob Paine had escaped marital discord, he had whiled away his interlude in Mexico trying to boil down the seventeen-hundred-odd rules to a more workable size. Scripps even had Atwood take a stab at it. The latter's official revision resulted in a fat document of thirty-seven pages of single-spaced typing. Atwood's lists went as high as "old" rule Number 539. At length Scripps just threw up his hands. On January 7, 1908, he proposed "to make a clean sweep of all my old written rules."

> There are too many of these that are absolutely obselete. . . .
>
> I propose . . . to wipe the slate clean of them and in the place of all the orders governing editorial departments to pass one rule, namely that the editor shall so conduct his paper to cause its sales to increase, and at the same time take care of the working man.
>
> In place of all the rules governing the action of the business department, I would adopt the rule that the business manager must obey the Ten Commandments and make not less than 15 percent cash divisible profits.

Scripps was kidding no one. In no way was he giving up one iota of his one-man power. A lull of a few weeks followed his so-called "clean sweep." Then new "orders" began pouring out of Miramar. No editor, he suddenly decreed, could be changed without his personal approval— reinstitution, of course, of one of the old rules. Then he issued ultimatums. The *Cleveland Press* must make for 1908 a profit of $200,000, the Cincinnati *Post* $100,000, Toledo *Times* $80,000, the *Seattle Star* $30,000, the *Los Angeles Record* $25,000, and so on.

E. W. detected signs that another money panic might sweep the nation. He was very much concerned about money. He needed lots of it. As early as September 6, 1906, his net worth had been calculated for Cleveland's First National Bank as $5,653,000. And on November 13, 1907, his auditors projected that 1908 profits of his combined journalistic enterprises would amount to $529,000. That, however, was not all gravy. He was supporting a raft of losers—Pueblo, Dallas, Spokane, Fresno, Denver, and others. He would have to pay $109,000 to cover their expected deficits in 1908. If Scripps planned to expand further— which he did, new ventures would dip into his earnings for start-up capital and running expense.

It was the eternal fight to squeeze out the mandated 15 percent profit that sent Scripps back to the old rigamarole of rule-writing and sounding stern alarms.

Son Jim was cautioned in his new seat of power in the Cincinnati Central Office to make certain that deadlines on expenses out in the field were rigidly adhered to. "It's a case of no meat on the table," father wrote son on January 16, 1908. "We've got to get the wood chuck."

Snow and ice glazed downtown Cincinnati as Jim Scripps picked his way on the morning of January 5, 1908, toward the Central Office. Of a sudden his feet flew up, and Jim sat down hard. It stung, but Jim smiled recalling a similar tumble on roller skates that had stunned John Paul in the gym at Miramar. That flashback inspired him on reaching his desk to type out a long, warm letter to his brother. It was chatty stuff, with some advice on career, and an invitation to visit Cincinnati.

"I will be glad to see your smiling face, and will take you out and get you cross-circuited . . . like that time in Fresno when we got spiflocated in the Sequoia and I introduced you to Sandy. Remember? Wasn't that an asshole winder?"

Jim closed with, "I'm having a fierce time here."

That the twenty-one-year-old greenhorn was sweating and wrestling with crucial and tricky business decisions would surprise no one, least of all his father. Deliberately, E. W. had thrown him in to sink or swim. Jim grew a beard to mask his youth. He screwed up his courage; and he augmented his guts with long hours of work and study.

Graybeards in the Central Office and around the League, of course, had initial strong doubts. For several anxious weeks they watched this untried boy wield his father's mighty scepter. His performance was surprising. In some ways he was both quicker and tougher than the old man. It was equally clear he had no deep liking for being in charge, but he faced up to the mean duty. The old-timers began to relax. Milton McRae was impressed, telling the father that Jim acted as "mature as a man of twenty-eight or thirty . . . and will surprise you." Ham Clark dropped by the Central Office and reported to Miramar he was amazed how well Jim had "caught on." Incidentally, Clark rued the stop; Jim took the occasion to saddle him with supervising the jinxed Kansas City *World*.

From the ranch, Scripps kept sharp watch. By letters and a few telegrams, he offered advice and counsel. But he issued no orders to his son. Jim was truly on his own, with absolute power to make decisions as if actually the controlling stockholder — such as killing the Nashville paper.

"If I can stand that," Scripps wrote, "I can stand anything you do."

At the end of January 1908, the old man gave the boy a bit of taffy. "I cannot tell you, Jim, how much satisfaction I have taken in watching . . . your work — none of which has been wholly bad and much of which has been wholly good."

Folding the *Nashville Times* was but one surprise. Jim stunned — and pleased — his father with other tough decisions. One gave the old man a kick in the shins. It involved unloading the morning paper in Toledo, the *Times,* an unwanted part of the *News-Bee* acquisition. In a conference at Miramar, Scripps agreed to sell 51 percent to his partner in the *Columbus Citizen,* George W. Dun. When Dun showed up at the Central Office to sign the papers, Jim rejected his father's terms. Dun could not merely buy control, the boy decreed, but must purchase all of the *Toledo Times* stock. Further, the Central Office would make no loan to finance the deal. Dun was miffed, but cooled down and finally made the purchase on Jim's terms.

John Sweeney also ruffled Jim's feathers. Unannounced, Sweeney barged into Jim's hotel room at midnight accompanied by an Indianapolis newspaper associate. Purpose of the intrusion stumped Jim; he reported to Dad that Sweeney just hemmed and hawed. "If I didn't believe

he was square, I would hurry up and pay him off and get him out quick.
. . . He won't put up a cent . . . and if he won't risk his money, I will be
damned if I will take his judgment."

That prompted Scripps to notify Sweeney at the end of January that
their "efficiency expert" deal "has proved impractical" and Sweeney
should quit at once instead of waiting until the end of the year. That
caused hard feelings between the one-time buddies from the *Cleveland
Press*. Sweeney demanded money and stock options. Scripps stonewalled
his business demands, but invited the Sweeney family back to the ranch
for another vacation. Later in the year, Sweeney finally quit, feeling he
had not been fully paid for what he considered "very effective" work
done.

Jim, husky and handsome and lively, was not ignoring his personal
life. He got reacquainted with one of the Cincinnati hospital nurses who
had tended him when he nearly bled to death from the 1905 tonsil operation. She was Josephine Louise Stedem, an attractive athletic brunet, a
good deal older—possibly as much as ten years—than Jim. They started
dating regularly.

He said nothing in letters home of this romance. He did confide to
his father's lawyer at the Central Office that he might marry and wanted
papers drawn to give him a piece of Cincinnati property he was supposed
to inherit, so as to assure him a modest income. The lawyer didn't think
there was any urgency about the request. But there was.

On Thursday, February 13, 1908, Jim and Josephine took out a
license and were married by the Rev. Francis Martin, minister of a Cincinnati Presbyterian church. Jim did not notify his parents. Most likely,
knowing his father's rabid feeling that a young man just starting his
career was usually hobbled and diverted by matrimony, he would expect
the old man to be less than pleased. Likewise, the fact that his bride was
so much older might also upset E. W.

The nuptials astonished the family, as John Paul wrote a friend
March 22: "Yes, Jim got hooked on the 13th of last month. It was a
rather sudden affair. The first we knew of it was from a letter to mama
from my grandmother saying she had seen an account of the marriage in
one of the Cincinnati papers. I kind of had a hunch it was going to
happen, but when it came it took me by surprise. I thought Jim would,
at least, let us know that he was going to do the stunt."

On a visit to Cincinnati, John Paul was struck by his new sister-in-
law, and praised her in a letter to his parents, getting this reply from
Nackie: "You are the first one in the family to see Josephine and it was so
good to hear from you about her. I am so glad that you like her and

know that we all will. I do hope they will come home this month before I go East."

Scripps's correspondence seems to have ignored the marriage. But writing to propose Jim come to the ranch in April for a financial discussion, he added: "Bring your wife, of course."

Aware of Jim's vocal distaste for the harsh Ohio winter and his minimal enthusiasm for the rigors of newspaper publishing, Scripps warned him to beware of failure,

> I have said to you and John that if you desire to be the possessor of any property and hold it in safety and security, you yourself must stand by it, stand over it, watch it, guard it, control it yourself, and be prepared to make any and every sacrifice in the interest of that property.
>
> If you run away from your business and go and take up your residence in some other place, and think first and foremost of your physical and other comforts, it will be only a question of time, and a marvelously short time, when either the business will be ruined or become the property of some other man or men.

Jim was maintaining just such an eagle-eye on the Central Office, and fully controlling its affairs. He was tough enough to bite the bullet. He demonstrated that twice within thirty days by shutting off the League's dismal losses in albatross properties.

In St. Louis, where the *Chronicle* was bravely launched six years before Jim was born, a dangerous new crisis developed. The merged *Star-Chronicle* was in straits, and seemed on the brink of going bankrupt. Nathan Frank, the 49 percent partner, spent "seven or eight sleepless nights" trying to come up with an answer. He believed the paper could survive. Finally Frank made an offer to buy the Scripps controlling interest, under a sixty-day option.

"I took him into Jim's office," McRae reported, "and we talked it over. Jim gave him a genuine Scripps talk and told him no option would be given, neither would his note be accepted . . . without other collateral." This performance also impressed J. C. Harper. He scribbled this note to E. W.: "Jim has fairly won his spurs. The way he handled Nathan Frank would have pleased you. . . . You should be proud."

The boy's tough talk did not deter Nathan Frank. He agreed to pay $100,000, mostly in notes, and so after hundreds of thousands had been poured into a sinkhole, E. W. Scripps's bold venture into the old hated "mudhole city" came to a dismal end after twenty-seven futile years.

"The *St. Louis Star-Chronicle* was sold yesterday," Jim wrote his father on March 26, 1908. "On account of my inexperience and ignorance I would have preferred someone else handle this. This is part of my job and I had to do it. You and Aunt Ellen have made a big bet on my judgment and ability. . . . In starting into business I would have preferred to have gone a little bit slow and cautiously. . . . Handling such big things as this rather takes my breath away. . . . I suppose I am going to make or lose my reputation as a business man in a pretty short time. I prefer this . . . as I believe it is best for the Scripps concern to find out just as quickly as possible what there is in me."

In an equally desperate plight was the Kansas City *World.* For all the eleven years the Scrippses had owned it, the *World* was a loser. A series of editors and business managers had been sent in to try to turn it around. The old man stubbornly refused to surrender, demanding barebones tactics and operation, but still pumping in thousands of lost dollars.

Only three days after sale of the *Star-Chronicle,* Jim conferred with the other Central Office executives about Kansas City. He decided on imediate action, to either sell or close down the *World,* and telegraphed Miramar for approval.

His father wired back: "You must sell or close Kansas City. Consult with Harper, Atwood, Clark. Ellen and I will approve of anything you do. Better keep the plant for use elsewhere."

In a follow-up letter, Scripps said he felt more "relief than regret" over the "outcome in the two Missouri cities." But he mildly rebuked Jim for involving him. "I will expect you in the future . . . to act in a matter of no graver importance . . . without passing it up to me for action." Both defeats, Scripps told his heir, were due to failure of the concern to produce enough good men to take over expansionist management, and confessed, "My own failures have been due to spreading myself over too large a field. . . . We should have learned by this time that the only possible excuse for starting a new newspaper is that we have on hand more good men than we have places for."

No one was foolish enough, of course, to offer to buy the Kansas City wreck. So the *World* was led to the gallows. Charitably, the *Kansas City Star* agreed to take custody of the circulation galleys and fill out paid-in-advance subscriptions. Jim sold off two linotypes for $1,650 each, paid a discharged circulation man's claim for $500, decided to hold onto the *World*'s $50,000 building and plant, and on April 11, 1908, suspended publication.

About then Atwood was winding up a long vacation at Key West, Florida. He notified Scripps he was well-rested and ready to return to his desk. E. W., however, wanted a longer test for his son, and wrote the vacationer: "Jim really doesn't know whether he wants to stay in the business. I am surprised how he has grabbed hold, and now that he has tasted power, he may want to stay." Atwood should return to Cincinnati, take a careful look-see, but not intervene. If he found "things are going well," Atwood must resume his vacation "and give Jim more time to be top man in the Central Office."

A shock was building up in the wings for the old man's dream of finally launching his ad-less newspaper. His hopes for that experiment were tightly bound to John Vandercook, currently his hard-driving general manager of United Press. "Van" was all over the place—doing big and little chores. On a fast voyage to Europe, he found the U.P. London bureau in a rut. To fix that, he brought in the man from Berlin, and sailed right back to New York.

At the Metropolitan Opera he bought a three-dollar "peanut gallery" ticket to hear the great Luisa Tetrazzini. Van wanted to write an article for N.E.A. on how "a voice can get a hold on people who know nothing of music." Next he hopped the train to Chicago and shook up that United Press bureau. He returned to New York and told his right-hand man, the ambitious Roy W. Howard, to go to San Francisco and inject some life into the West Coast report.

Van's ego and impulsiveness began to nettle Scripps, who wrote him a ten-page letter, then thought better of its harsh tone and did not mail it—a procedure often adopted to get sour feelings off his chest.

> My own impression of you, Vandercook, is that you are only beginning to suffer from the sort of conceit which usually attacks a man between the first and fifth year after he has made, or is supposed to have made, a business success.
>
> I had the conceit myself. All the young men who have joined me have suffered from the same malady. . . . It is not only possible but quite likely you will suffer great disappointment and mortification because you are just human enough to think you are bigger than you really are.

Despite pique over the man's vanity, Scripps still counted on Vandercook as his best bet to be the "genius" editor of the ad-less. Vandercook, anxious to get going on it, wanted to call the paper the *Bull,* though Clark still pushed for the *Bear.* The Hoe Company now had the special press ready. All Scripps was waiting for now was the end of the current business panic. Then it would be, Hello, New York! Meet the *Bull* (or the *Bear*)!

The blow fell during the week the Kansas City *World* was being shut down. Scripps's first disturbing word was an April 2 telegram from Ham

Clark: "Vandercook operated on last night. Found appendix ruptured with localized gangrene."

Vandercook had been suddenly stricken while on another excursion to jack up the Chicago bureau. Physicians at Chicago initially were baffled by his abdominal pain. When they did operate, it was too late. Vandercook writhed in agony for a week, his wife Margaret and six-year-old son John Junior at his bedside. On April 11, 1908, he died, only thirty-four.

22

"The Cave of Abdullam"

Could Scripps successfully give up command of his newspaper empire and go into actual retirement by shifting the executive load he had carried thirty-five years onto the shoulders of son Jim, still largely untried and only twenty-two?

In the eyes of his close associates, the more important question was should he dare risk handing the all-powerful scepter to a greenhorn? Not only did many lieutenants shudder at this, some deeply resented it. Still the minions correctly perceived that his Miramar eagle eye would haunt the lad, and if he did fail, Scripps would again assume the throne.

Jim, a fun-loving addict of fast cars, motorcycles, and rod and gun, had no real desire to buckle down to a desk for the ten-hours-a-day grind of learning the intricacies of a complicated, changing, and ever-growing business. But his years of close palship with E. W. had instilled in him a burning pride of family, a keen sense of personal responsibility, and desire to be a winner.

Such faith would be his principal strength in this trial by fire. As he later confessed:

> Sometimes I feel like throwing up my hands myself and quitting the job. But you can bet your hat I will not do this, because to quit myself would be evidence of the fact that I am a quitter and afraid to work. I made up my mind to stick to this job . . . unless I was fired out, and I am going to stick. I might, if I quit, live a life of comparative ease and spend or get rid of whatever my share is of property that my father accumulated. . . . You have no idea what a tremendous strain I'm under all the time. Now, I tell you what, my job is no joke.

271

Jim had been thrown in to sink or swim at a time of harsh national financial panic. But the father refused to wait for better conditions before taking this desperate gamble — fully believing he could guide the boy to maturity and business triumph within two or three years.

"I am not going to bother much about business," he told Jim, "for quite a while. I may never bother myself much about it at all again. I don't see why I should. The future belongs to you and my other children, not to me. For most of my years it was more like fun than hard work. Now it has got to be hard work. . . . I think I have earned the right to sit in the sun."

Father confidently understood how to tutor son to kingship. He would employ the same techniques by which for three decades he had created editors and business managers from "absolutely unknown and undervalued human material." In the main Jim had only to observe the Ten Commandments and "be a gentleman." Scripps determined not to be "too exacting" with the boy and to overlook "juvenile" errors. He truly meant his pledge to allow Jim a free hand to make decisions — and mistakes. He wasn't worried too much about the cost of the latter. As a millionaire, he easily could afford to lose thousands to make this experiment succeed.

When Jim brought his bride of three months for her first visit to the ranch in May 1908, Dad was captivated by the charming Josephine — and dreaming ahead to becoming a grandfather.

Being stuck full time in the Central Office at Cincinnati was a vision that made Jim snort. His father offered a solution. A second or auxiliary Central Office could be established at the *San Diego Sun* building, permitting Jim to spend about half the year — including the severe Ohio winter months — in sunny southern California.

It did not take the boy-king long to earn the respect of his nobles. The editors and business managers of the papers considered him not such a "tightwad" as his father. When they could justify need for more or new presses or linotypes, Jim promptly approved such purchases.

Personnel changes were needed for a variety of reasons — and Jim made them. First he consulted with Dad, and then acted vigorously. He lowered the boom on E. H. Wells who had become mired in dangerous personal debt at Seattle. He even fired his father's cousin, the out-of-favor Hans Bagby at the *Los Angeles Record*. When Bagby protested, Jim suggested E. W. might give him a job as ranch manager.

After sitting uneasily on the throne for nearly a year, the young king decided it wasn't such a bad job after all. On October 2, 1908, he signed an "employment" contract to remain with his father for at least five years, at $1,000 a month. E. W. now was satisfied Jim could hack it. "You are fully capable of discharging all of the duties of the executive head of the concern," the "retired" Scripps announced.

However, Scripps did in the fall of 1909 spend ten days with Jim and John Paul reviewing concern affairs and concluded "there are enough hard, knotty problems on hand to thoroughly exercise the minds and ingenuity of our youngsters." Still, on the whole, he considered the business was "very satisfactory"—more so than if he had continued in personal charge! He further observed to J. C. Harper: "I have also discovered that there has been considerable development in mind-broadening on the part of my sons; they have lost considerable of their boyish timidity, or conservation, and gained in self-confidence and grasp."

Jim was maturing, too, in other ways. Two months before his twenty-third birthday, he became a father; on May 21, 1909, Josephine gave birth to a son, E. W.'s first grandchild. The baby was named after his grandfather.

That Scripps decided quite early to test Jim as a substitute for the nominal head of the Central Office, Lemuel T. Atwood, proved highly fortuitous. For suddenly in the summer of 1909 Atwood was laid low by a dangerous kidney disease. His face took on a doughy look, his legs and feet swelled so he couldn't put on shoes. "I can't go to the office barefoot," said Atwood, and promptly suspended his own thousand-dollar-a-month salary. He wrote Scripps to send instructions for winding up all financial affairs in his hands, and took to his sickbed to await death.

Scripps suggested Atwood come to Miramar and get out in the sun by personally rebuilding a ranch cabin where he could live in retirement on $3,000 annual "deferred compensation."

But Atwood was too ill. In his blunt way, Scripps wrote that neither of them would care "to drag out a life of suffering beyond the period of usefulness. I, too, have seen the hand that is beckoning and heard the voice that is calling, and I would not, if I could, linger on the threshold one day longer than is needful."

Finally Atwood's physician advised Scripps that "the waters are going deep for him. . . . The end can't be long held off." The deeply religious Atwood clutched wife Kate's hand, fondly recalling their courtship and life together, and begging her to read him a daily chapter from the Bible. Frequently he asked visitors to join him in reciting the Lord's Prayer.

On December 7, 1909, he died quietly. Atwood was fifty-seven. Everyone knew he had literally worked himself to death. Even John Sweeney was indignant. "I advised him to get out in the fresh air half of every day. The great mistake was he was doing the work a ten- or twenty-dollar clerk could have done. . . . He had a big strong mind, capable of grasping and analyzing all situations."

Atwood's estate was modest, amounting to $55,000. Scripps decreed his three-thousand-dollar-a-year pension would go to his widow as long as she lived.

After years of hiding in sideline shadows, Scripps suddenly leaped out and tried to personally rally America's flagging political reform. As he put it, he was "doing my level best and blowing hard to keep the spark of revolt alive." Above Miramar's roof he hoisted the rebel flag and diligently strove to convene at his remote castle a small elite band of rich or talented Democrat and Republican insurgents. Once formed, this "syndicate" was expected to rechart and push the common man's "war" on plutocratic oligarchy — all the way from city hall to the White House.

Working with Lincoln Steffens, he put his scheme in writing on July 14, 1908: "It is proposed to form a combination of patriotic citizens of national repute — men who in one form or another proved their willingness to devote a great part of their time and energy, and some part of their fortune, to the futherance of the cause of good government, either of municipalities, states or of the nation — no regard being paid to the matter of past or present party affiliations."

This concept of a "good government trust" was imaginative and courageous, but also so audacious as to harbor certain Don Quixote overtones. Scripps and Steffens wanted to bring to the ranch from all across the country "fighting" politicians, professors, philanthropists, graft-busters, reformers, and muckrakers. This would be an off-the-record "Cave of Abdullam" not to try to impose Scripps's pet ideas on anyone, but to concoct new and more powerful schemes that he could spearhead by means of truth-telling in his newspapers, and through United Press and the N.E.A.

The proposed guest list included Senator Robert M. LaFollette, Rudolph Spreckels, W. S. U'Ren, Tom L. Johnson, E. A. Filene, Louis Brandeis, Walter L. Fisher, Judge Ben B. Lindsey, George L. Record, Professor J. H. Wigmore, George Foster Peabody, Gilbert E. Roe, Joseph W. Folk, Professor Thorstein Veblen, Joseph Fels, Gifford Pinchot, Francis Heney, as well as the editors of *American Magazine* and *Everybody's Magazine,* plus a few others including Arthur Brisbane of the Hearst organization.

Hardly any of these personally knew the reclusive publisher, but most wanted to come to the pow-wow. Scripps volunteered to pay all transportation and other expenses, and to put up everyone in ranch guest rooms. There was one big difficulty—finding a conveniuent date when all these busy people could drop everything and come to California to devote three or four days to "blowing on the spark of revolt."

Scripps was saddling his white charger in the nick of time. Teddy Roosevelt was leaving the White House and as E. W. saw it "the whole country is going hell-bent in the opposite direction of what should be taken by progressive democracy." There was no time to lose. The William Howard Taft administration was turning out more reactionary than Scripps had feared—far more.

When President Taft sabotaged United States Forester Gifford Pinchot's efforts to thwart the flagrant "steal" of public timber preserves and river sites by power and lumber buccaneers, Scripps exploded. At Miramar he talked "like a brother" to Pinchot, trying to egg him on and to expose and pubicly fight the scandal. Pinchot waffled. So Scripps sent a top N.E.A. reporter to Africa to intercept Roosevelt as he emerged from a year-long big game hunt. If Roosevelt felt Taft was betraying him and was as mad as a wet hen, the reporter was to cable a single code word. The reporter, Gilson Gardner, found Roosevelt angry and cabled the lone word—"hen." But Roosevelt wasn't mad enough to fight. Further, he delayed his return to America, causing Scripps to growl in frustration.

"I am still hoping," Scripps told one of his California editors, "that Roosevelt will come home anxious and eager to take up the sword again. I want him to find some of his old followers still unsubdued either by their opponents or their secret inward fears."

It was a slender hope. "Reactionaryism has taken the country and the peoples' leaders are developing discretion—I mean those people whom we fondly hoped were the peoples' leaders, have turned cowards."

When Roosevelt came home, he still did not speak out against President Taft. Despite his own disappointment that T. R. seemed to have lost his fighting spirit, Scripps saw him as still the best leader around which the reformers could rally in the coming 1912 Presidential campaign.

Scripps and Steffens kept trying to fix a date for the "Cave of Abdullam" satisfactory to the majority of the invited participants. Scripps was quite stirred up. "I am more profoundly interested today than I have ever been in my life in the politico-economic situation in the country."

Time was running out. He suggested Steffens try harder to round up the reformers. "I must drop out altogether in a few years," he reminded Steffens, "and I must leave in the hands of others the power for good or evil that I have created. My successors must inherit the brute force inherent in my institution but they can no more inherit the spirit that gave it existence than can the tall ship's mast inherit the life-giving sap of the fir tree in the forest."

Perhaps because he had so many diverse irons in the fire, Scripps was never consistently successful in the game of politics. In point of fact, he was never able to gather at Miramar any elite band of reformers to enter their "Cave of Abdullam" and emerge with a new charter for political insurgents. (He eventually did see a number of them on a one-to-one basis at the ranch.) But Scripps's personal effort of "blowing hard to keep the spark of revolt alive" did have a significant effect on the 1912 Presidential campaign. His may have been the single most powerful influence in bringing forth the Progressive Party, with its ill-fated candidacy of Teddy Roosevelt.

In January 1909, Milton McRae arrived in San Diego with his family to spend the winter. For the first time John Paul, nineteen, met McRae's oldest daughter Edith, a pretty brunet, lively but serious, and just his age.

At the ranch the young couple was frequently thrown together and engaged in serious talk. Not at all a "society girl," Edith confided she was "crazy about California and western life." She was engaged to a Mr. Richardson from Saginaw, Michigan, who planned to take her on an around-the-world honeymoon. Her fiance and his mother had followed the McRaes to California to remain most of the winter.

In March John Paul was again sent east. His father had in mind eventually installing him as editor-in-chief; this journey was to further his son's education, by visiting papers, getting acquainted with key men, studying problems and their solutions. He travelled with the McRaes who were returning to their Detroit home—with stops at Scripps papers in Oklahoma City, Dallas, Memphis, and Cincinnati. There he said goodbye to Mr. and Mrs. McRae who went on to Detroit, leaving Edith and her sister Helen, eighteen, to visit Cincinnati friends. John Paul also stopped over several days in Cincinnati, before going on to Cleveland and New York. Later, en route home, he digressed to spend a few days with the McRaes in Detroit.

John Paul was back in California in time to begin his career as a cub reporter when the *Oakland Mail* was launched Monday, May 3, 1909. After two weeks he wrote his father about his duties, adding:

> I think that I like it up here alright, but so far it's been too damn lonesome. Some way or other I don't seem able to meet up with a bunch that

appeals to me. . . . Everyone around the shop is either married, or goes home early at night, or else they're bum company, so outside of hours about all I can do is wander around or go to my room and read. . . . I've got a motorcycle now, and I guess that I'll be able to put my unemployed time on that. However, I know that I have got to stand the gaff, and will get used to it in time.

There was a more specific cause for the cub's lonesomeness. He was trying to ease the ache by writing three long letters a week and mailing them to a girl in Detroit. To his own folks he made no mention of this correspondence.

Scripps felt called on to offer his son advice — "that's what fathers are for."

All the advice I have to offer as to your job is if you are a cub reporter to be a cub reporter clear through in business hours. All the great men in our concern started in life as cubs, and real cubs not artificial cubs like you. You may not be much of a cub reporter . . . but you can be one man in ten million in living up to a job or down to a job.

When I was younger and more sentimental, I had foolish conceits and dreamed about how I was going to give you boys all the advantages that poor boys would have, as well as your being a rich man's sons. . . . However, the misfortune of my failing health and my peculiar disposition to always get somebody else to do my work has caused you boys to commence your work at the top.

Perhaps you could not do better than to, as far as possible, forget everything else but your present job on your little paper. . . . It means more to me that you should develop power to do something, no matter how big or how little it is, which will be of your own doing — a thing done with your own hands not through some underling.

It was welcome counsel. "I got more satisfaction out of your last letter," the son responded, "than any other I've ever received from you before. You said just the things I hoped you would, and said them in a way that I could fully comprehend."

The cub also assured his father, "Lonesomeness has all worn off now." That was a little white lie; the boy was still pining for his secret sweetheart, Edith McRae. His heart was too full of love to keep quiet. He went home a week later and confessed the romance to his father. The old man took it calmly, but without enthusiasm. John Paul should not contemplate matrimony for about a year and a half — until he was more mature and settled in his career. Scripps suspected Milton McRae was the secret intriguer behind the start of the romance, seeing a chance to tie his humble family to the Scripps fame and fortune.

E. W. fired a critical private letter to McRae. His former partner was shocked; it was his first inkling of the love affair. Mac grabbed the first train to Miramar. For a week he conferred with E. W. behind closed doors.

Returning home, McRae attempted to discourage any marriage plans. Edith, he discovered, already had broken off with her Saginaw suitor. John Paul had proposed "several weeks ago" they get married secretly, but the girl demurred until he could obtain his father's approval. McRae added:

> Confidentially, Jim after my business talk with him in San Diego last Monday took me out to his house and showed me his boy and later admitted that he guessed what I was at Miramar for. He said that fifteen minutes after he first saw me he had written John a "personal lead pencil" letter telling him to stand pat and get married as soon as he could, that he had tried it and knew just what it was from experience and consequently urged him to do likewise.

Surprisingly, John Paul was willing — but reluctant — to put off getting married. "Your word has always been law," he wrote Dad from Oakland July 3. "I've done some things you didn't approve of, but your advice about business and matters that pertain to the lives of men has always been swallowed by me as Gospel. It is yet."

John Paul felt he was learning the reporter trade but admitted he was still quite lonesome. "Ever since about two years ago I have been sort of restless. I didn't seem to be exactly content at home. . . . When I was away, it was either work, or have a hell of a time. . . . Now I'm not going to be home a great deal any more, and what I want is a home of my own. That makes me more anxious than ever to get down to it and get married."

That appeal melted the old man's opposition. He gave the lovers his blessing. On September 8, 1909, John Paul was married — one month after his twenty-first birthday — to Edith in the McRae home in Detroit. The rites were read by the Reverend John H. Boyd of the First Christian Church, which the McRaes attended. Maid of honor was sister Helen.

Scripps, who did not attend the wedding, must have ground his teeth when the *Detroit Times* happily characterized the nuptials as "the launching of another Scripps-McRae League."

But brother Jim, under his authority as reigning king, warmly welcomed the bridegroom home from a Grand Canyon honeymoon, by installing him as manager of the San Diego branch "Central Office" at $500 a month.

Nackie Benson Holtsinger as a young girl. Choir singer and daughter of a preacher, she married EWS when just out of high school and bore her first child on her twentieth birthday. (*Warren Wilkinson*)

Nackie Scripps as a young woman. (*Paul K. Scripps*)

In 1896 photo, Nackie Scripps poses with five of her children. Standing on the left is James George, ten, and right, John Paul, eight. Seated on the left is Edward Willis McLean, five, who died three summers later. Seated right is Dorothy Blair "Dolla," six, mentally crippled by a birth injury. In mother's lap is Robert Paine, about six months old. Their sixth child, Nackey Elizabeth, was not born until May 16, 1898. (*Warren Wilkinson*)

Robert Paine Scripps, March 1901,
aged three years and five months.
(*Paul K. Scripps*)

Nackey Scripps as a young girl.
(*Paul K. Scripps*)

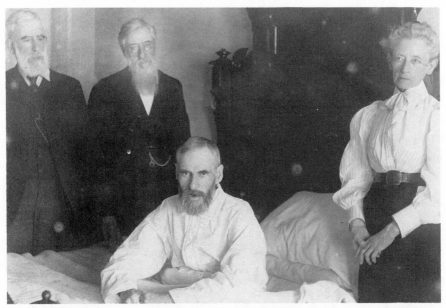

George H. Scripps on his deathbed at Miramar in 1900, flanked by sister Ellen and brothers William A. (far left) and James E. (*Warren Wilkinson*)

Family reunion at Miramar, 1900, occasioned by the death of George. From the left: Eliza Virginia (seated); Ellen B.; Frederick T. (above); EWS with son Robert Paine; unidentified boy, possibly son of Frederick; Nackie; Mrs. William A. Scripps (standing), with her husband and James E. Also seated is Harriet, wife of James E., and Elizabeth Scripps Sharp (in rocker on end). (*Warren Wilkinson*)

A view around 1910 showing Miramar ranch house entrance with
mesa's hillocks in the distance. (*Paul K. Scripps*)

Aerial view of main ranch house, with more lush growth. (*Paul
K. Scripps*)

282

EWS's office at Miramar, with table where he wrote or dictated.
(*Paul K. Scripps*)

Miramar ranch garage/carriage house, in the period from 1907 to
1910. It was, says Paul K. Scripps, "really huge, and had a machine shop, etc., adequate for any conceivable repair job." (*Paul
K. Scripps*)

Edward Willis Scripps in this famous photograph that best shows his force. This was taken in the courtyard of Miramar, his ranch home in California, probably between 1914 and 1916. (*Scripps-Howard files*)

284

E. W. Scripps and wife Nackie, with
dog and bicycle, in courtyard at
Miramar. (*Paul K. Scripps*)

On the roof of Miramar ranch house between 1907 and 1910.
EWS stands at the far right, presumably with his aide Harry
Smithton at the left. Paul K. Scripps suggests the man in the
middle might be Newton D. Baker, who became Scripps's attorney. However, EWS was still somewhat unacquainted with Baker
at the time of World War I. (*Paul K. Scripps*)

Unusual pose by E. W. Scripps in
Miramar courtyard. (*Paul K.
Scripps*)

View of the main courtyard at Miramar from the roof of one
wing. Hillocks of the mesa are in the distance. (*Paul K. Scripps*)

286

In the fall of 1907, EWS undertook a rugged adventure—an automobile trip from Miramar across the California desertlands to the Grand Canyon intending to motor on to Denver. He departed on September 26, 1907, with his companions, sons Jim and John, his secretary Harry Smithton, his cousin E. H. "Hans" Bagby, and a ranch chauffeur-mechanic "Tillie" Sartori. Here John is loading up at Miramar. They reached the Grand Canyon on October 7, 1907, when trouble with the car and news of the death of Reverend Holtsinger, EWS's father-in-law, caused the trip to be abandoned. The cars were sent back to a Miramar on a railroad flatcar. (*Paul K. Scripps*)

On the road to the Grand Canyon, September–October 1907. (*Paul K. Scripps*)

EWS takes time out for lunch on the Grand Canyon trip. (*Paul K. Scripps*)

EWS (left front, in Pierce Arrow) arrives at the Grand Canyon on
October 7, 1907. (*Paul K. Scripps*)

The advent of the motorcar did not come gracefully. The unaccustomed clatter and racket of the machines frequently startled horses into runaways and wrecks. Near the ranch some teams literally kicked their buggies to pieces when a motorist chugged past. In San Diego a ranch team, frightened by the start-up of a car, plunged onto a sidewalk, bowling over pedestrians. E. W.'s brother Fred was hit, suffering serious head and shoulder cuts and a broken arm.

Breakdowns dogged the Miramar auto fleet. At one juncture only two of the ranch's seven motorcars would run. Yet there was no misfortune that seemed to seriously curtail Scripps's ardor for automobiling. As he drove home from an afternoon at the Cuyamaca Club, the universal joint fractured on his new 1908 Packard. He got it repaired and then took off with two Packards into the 110° Imperial Valley—and felt like an adventurer. He wrote a friend June 18, 1908:

> I have just come back from a week's tour of the desert. I had my son John and two automobiles. I have climbed mountains, rolled and tumbled down some rocky canyons, dragged through sand knee-deep, forded rivers, stuck in mud ditches, slept with bed bugs (slept a little between bites), ate what I could, drank warm water, skirted the Salton Sea, staked out two desert land claims, went through sand storms where pebbles as big as hail pelted us, buried the roads out of sight, got lost a dozen times, broke down my machines and repaired them, and am home again today, having entirely forgotten that I had any nerves.

One Cadillac runabout dubbed "the Battle Axe" got heavy use. One secretary, learning to drive it, had a flat. He got out the tire pump. It wouldn't work; some jokester had deliberately slipped a defective one into the tool box. Next day the same secretary spent half an hour trying to crank the car. He complained to Scripps that the Cadillac wouldn't start.

The old man gave him a pained look. "Try turning on the batteries!"

Dolla, the defective daughter, was much in Scripps's thoughts as she reached womanhood, turning eighteen in 1908. He insured her safe future with a $200,000 trust fund, and planned to build a house at La Jolla for her and her nurse-companion. Frequently Scripps went to extremes in investigating medical techniques that might lift her mental fog. The girl had the mind of a ten- or twelve-year-old. She had outgrown a nasty temper, and seemed happy or content in Miss Bancroft's school, The Lindens, at Haddonsfield, New Jersey.

"Three years is a long time for a father and daughter to be separated, as we have been," he wrote her at Miss Bancroft's summer camp, Owl's Head, at Rockland, Maine. "I had hoped to come East to see you this summer, but have not felt well enough."

In truth being around Dolla gave him the horrors. He wrote her from time to time and sent presents, a record cabinet for her nineteenth birthday, a clock for the next — "It's on my desk and it keeps very good time. Thank you." For Christmas he sent books.

Physicians had warned that it was "unthinkable" for Dolla to marry and bear children. Half her offspring might be normal; half would be imbeciles. That was the sobering warning from his trusted family physician in Cincinnati, Dr. F. W. Langdon. Scripps came to the opposite conclusion. Forcing her to become a mother could be the very thing to make her a normal person!

Part of Dolla's problem, Scripps argued, was that she grew up denied association with other children — which compelled her to "live abnormally."

> For a long time I have treaded the idea that when the time came — that is to say, when she becomes physically a woman — I would thrust her into the most complete condition of normality by requiring her to marry and bear children. I am so situated and have the disposition which would make it not only possible but easy for me to do things which another man could not do, or would not care to do.
>
> All of my daughter's instincts are as normal as those of any girl of her age. She loves children, she craves the opportunity for mothering little ones. Her affections for her parents are normal. Her affections for her brothers and sister are normal.
>
> I have the conviction that my daughter lacks so little spiritually of being a normal woman, that the peculiar obligations and sentiments of motherhood, if they had an opportunity of full development, will completely overcome all those defects of character, lack of self-restraint being the only very marked one she suffers from.

Obviously this was a sincere stance by Scripps, but he may have not actually broached the forced motherhood scheme, and instead merely engaged in some of his "thinking out loud" on paper. The carbon copy of this seven-page letter to Dr. Langdon is one of those in the Scripps file marked "Not Sent."

It was a Baltimore specialist, Dr. Henry J. Berkley, to whom Scripps looked for ultimate medical expertise in Dolla's case. The extent of the father's frustration was dramatically revealed when he wrote: "You might better understand my attitude when I tell you that before now I have regretted that civilization has not sufficiently advanced to permit the use of the only practical method of giving relief to unfortunate individuals who are incapable of enjoying life, and are only capable of causing suffering to others—the use of the lethal chamber."

On the train going east with her mother for the summer, pig-tailed, ten-year-old Nackey carried her favorite pet, a horned toad. She caught twenty flies for him, she proudly wrote her father from Albuquerque. Then—disaster! She accidentally dropped him down the Pullman toilet. Chuckling, E. W. dispatched a ranch hand out on the mesa to capture "two more friends" and sent the replacement toads by parcel post to West Chester.

Little Nackey soon switched her affection to a five-dollar bull pup she named "Buster." Dad wrote: "I don't think much of girl bull pups, but I won't kick." Nackey raised chickens, gathered eggs, and planted a vegetable garden with assistance from a Japanese houseboy. The ranch kitchen was her best—and only—customer. She flitted all over the ranch. In July 1909, she came upon two Mexican teamsters whipping a tired team that couldn't pull a heavy load of stone up a steep bank. She forthwith protested in a three-page pencil note to "Dear Dad":

> I spoke to Mr. Trapp, and asked him if he could not lessen the load or put on more horses. He said, "They are not much good if they can't pull that load. Old Frany could out-pull them both." But he must be mistaken as they were both on the grocery wagon and have always done good work, and the grocery wagon horses look as if they were over-worked, too.
>
> The barn is in bad shape, also, as Prince is almost blind and Chief has been run nearly to death. This is not Augustine's fault but because Mr. Clingan will not bring any more horses from Fanita.
>
> The grocery wagon should have four (4) horses as they always have a heavy load and the rock wagon should either have more horses or carry lighter loads. I wish you would speak to Mr. Clingan or Mr. Trapp about this, as I am sure you would not have the horses ill-treated.
>
> With love, Nackey.

Indeed, the master of Miramar would abide no mistreatment of horses. Ranch Foreman R. L. Clingan got his ears burned off. By letter the boss ordered Prince, Chief, and the grocery- and rock-wagon teams sent to pasture for a month's rest, replaced by fresh Fanita horses. Any teamster who henceforth overloaded a team "should be immediately discharged."

Father now faced a trying duty—guiding son Robert out of boyhood into the realm of teenager, where he must seriously train for his dukeship. Scripps had been over this ground before. He altered his technique little, if at all.

At thirteen Bob was drilled by a tutor in books and healthful exercise. He took three cold baths daily. Overhearing someone in the family crack that he was "getting fat," Bob sent photos to his father "to prove I'm only muscular."

Bob still lacked four months of being fourteen when father raised his allowance to $100 a month.

"I regard every boy who has passed the age of fourteen as really a man . . . and has a man's duties to perform. . . . I don't want you to be too serious. . . . I want you to be just as much of a boy as any of them and have all the fun there is coming. . . . I am paying you this $100 a month as sort of an advance wage . . . to relieve me of all responsibility and care for certain things which fathers usually give to their sons."

That September Bob enrolled in Pomona College at Claremont, California, near Los Angeles. "Bob has taken to Claremont like a duck to water, seemingly very contented, very busy, very successful." That news came from Professor Charles C. Stearns, with whom the boy was rooming. "I am sorry he has not written, for he could not fail to let you see his manifest interest in his new surroundings."

Bob did write his mother and managed on October 7 to get off a letter to Dad: "I am having a good time. . . . I am studying History, Biology, Latin and English. I did not try for the Prep. Football, as there is no chance for us little fellows on the team as the senior preps are seventeen and eighteen years old. I think I may make the track team in the Spring, but it isn't going to be easy."

For months after John Vandercook's death no decision was made on his successor as president of United Press. Roy W. Howard had been Van's own back-up choice. His name was discussed. Scripps admitted Howard was "perhaps the most desirable candidate. . . . His extreme youth [he was then twenty-five], the fact that we caught him so soon, and that he feels himself naturally a press association man . . . are all very strong arguments in his favor. He may be only bright and clever. A few months or a year longer of service will let us know more about him."

But the ambitious Howard was not one to wait. He sat down at his typewriter and hammered out a "personal" letter asking for the job. Confessing a "certain audacity," he cited to Scripps the old copybook maxim of making your own opportunity. "If I'm any judge, audacity is not a misdemeanor in your code."

Howard vowed that he "was not afraid" and was willing to keep "plugging and grinding" toward success, just as Vandercook "grew and was cultivated under Scripps methods."

United Press Chairman Clark felt Howard should have the job. But the old man was not so sure. Scripps replied to Howard that he didn't intend to make any recommendation. "You are a young man, which is no crime. . . . You will have a considerable career in our concern. . . . If you don't get one chance, you'll get others. . . . My personal advice is: continue as you have begun; fight your way upward, and win by convincing others of your merit, and refuse, even when opportunity affords itself, to gain anything by personal favor."

Actually Scripps held age and size against the boyish, diminutive Howard. He confessed as much in rejecting "Ham" Clark's suggestion he invite Howard to a Miramar editorial conference in November 1908. "Howard should," Scripps responded, "and must if he is going to succeed, fight his way up rather than be hoisted into position. Not the least part of my bias toward Howard is based on this fact of extreme, comparative youthfulness. . . . If Howard had twice his present vigor it would be better for all concerned."

Bob Paine likewise was not initially enthusiastic, telling the boss he would be inclined to favor Howard if he had more experience and was "not so rattle-headed in handling men."

But Lady Luck smiled on the little gamecock.

Just six months later, in the midst of serious United Press "difficulties," Scripps detected signs that Clark was "going to pieces" and feared "the evils that follow a break-down in nerve and courage."

Scripps fired off a confidential letter to Jim and a few other key men warning that the wire service must have "a firm and reliant hand." He didn't believe in "patching up" United Press by bringing in outsiders. "That young boy, Howard," he advised, "is very young, but that is nothing against him. He has a frail constitution; that is the one blemish. But if Clark is rattled, then as between Clark and Howard, there can be no question about the latter being the best man."

That was sufficient to elevate Roy W. Howard into the presidency of United Press Associations — and from then on there would be no stopping his meteoric rise.

Scripps tried seriously and valiantly to keep hands totally off business in the first year or two of retirement. "Don't expect me to make any decisions. I may offer advice. Remember — you don't have to follow it." Week after week he reiterated those words to his sons and the "young men" he counted on to run his empire.

But these were hectic days. On a dozen fronts the concern was rocked by external explosions, internal quarrels, and business setbacks. Editors and business managers had to be fired. Serious advertising boycotts erupted. Cleanup crusades and political fights stirred up a flurry of mean libel suits. One fightened editor was jailed for contempt of court. Two of Scripps's little papers came to the end of the line.

From his desk at Miramar Scripps knew of all this trouble, but he tried to keep active in other affairs. He didn't want to get involved. "I do not believe in the rule of the dead hand or the palsied hand," he asserted more than once. But to a mere figure of speech there had to be exceptions. The old man's hands were still vigorous, and steady. He could not resist reaching out and taking hold of some matters.

Jim suggested Editor Byron H. Canfield of the *Los Angeles Record* to be editor-in-chief for the West Coast. But it was Scripps who summoned Canfield to the ranch. "I want you to come prepared not to listen, but to talk. . . . You can at least say that you can't . . . or won't take the job." Canfield jumped at the opportunity, promptly established headquarters in Seattle, and began injecting new life into the western dailies.

An aggressive editor took over the *Portland News*—Dana Sleeth, twenty-eight, an experienced "digger" willing to work for $15 a week. Sleeth preferred to be out tracking down scandal rather than sit behind his desk. He soon found plenty. In page-one headlines he exposed "the most daring gang of crooks that ever robbed a government and terrorized a district." Boldly the *News* printed names—rancher "Bully" Hanley, a banker named Ladd, and a Judge Webster. With strong-arm tactics and bribes, said the *News,* they had connived to "steal" 60,000 acres of government range land.

The subservient Multnomah County district attorney had Sleeth indicted December 15, 1908, for criminal libel. That didn't stop the gutsy editor. He came out with another page-one story. He was indicted again. The people of Portland suddenly woke up to what was going on. The *News's* circulation soared.

"Sleeth is a genius, and a very hard man to handle," Scripps wrote Canfield. "However . . . the *Portland Daily News* was hard and fast on the rocks when Sleeth took over, and he has accomplished a great deal since he went on the job. We have in Sleeth an exceptional man . . . probably of greater potential value to your group than any man in it. I know he drinks, and I know about him increasing his salary, buying an automobile, etc. Sleeth is the kind of man that needs close attention about these little things."

Once again rumors flew that *Seattle Star* editorial men were taking graft. Canfield waded right in to get the truth. If he found evidence, heads would roll. "This town is the rottenest damn place on the Pacific Coast," he reported to Miramar. "It is full of graft, corruption, indecency, crooks, pimps, prostitutes, and politicians. The present administration is walking off with enough swag to make a dozen millionaires. The gang is in control all the way along the line. They are after the *Star* hot and heavy."

Kenny Beaton, the *Star* editor, was the center of gossip. "The joints" allegedly were kicking in to the police with "pay-offs" supposed to go to him, among others. Ironically, Beaton has been brought in by Wells as the "white knight" after the previous "Dan Dean" graft scandal. When confronted by Canfield, Beaton admitted he had accepted loans from a political fixer. Canfield fired him.

Surprisingly, Canfield had "plenty of reasons to distrust" E. H. Wells, no longer an executive but still a large *Star* stockholder. "I wouldn't trust his motives in this thing as far as I could throw a bull by the tail. I don't say he's crooked . . . but he's in with the gang."

Perhaps even more shocking was Canfield's barefaced report "that the games of all these grafters and crooks dovetail in together and eventually the trail leads" into the office of Colonel Alden J. Blethen, publisher of the powerful *Seattle Times.*

"He's the big grafter and the big boss and the big influence. He holds mortgage on the property of the men who run the tenderloin. He is fighting hard for a grafting chief of police and mayor. . . . He's got everyone in this town scared, bluffed, and bulldozed. They don't dare to clean up the town if they want to.

"The *Star* is the only independent and free influence in this community. It is the only one that can or dare do anything worth a damn. . . . The only way we do it is to fight. . . . If we don't lick this outfit, they'll lick us, and if they do they'll put the *Star* practically out of business and continue to rob Seattle blind."

In Canfield's eyes it was a dirty war. "This is a pretty rotten bunch up here. . . . They can get a French macque down in the restricted district to cut a man's throat or blow up his building for a few dollars and police protection."

Scripps sent instructions for Canfield to wage all-out war.

> There is nothing for you to do but grit your teeth; demand that your editor be more courageous and aggressive than he ever was before, and fight it out. Don't you know that the other fellow is the damndest coward that ever was? No Blethen . . . no great combination of any sort of business interests can hope to stand up against a fearless, fighting newspaper. These fellows know this a great deal better than you do, and when they know you

can't be bluffed out, they will cower and cringe and "kow-tow" to you until you are sick at your stomach.

You have got your back to the wall, and as long as you keep the other fellow in front of you, you can lick him, but if you turn to run away, or even make any sort of terms with the rascals, they will eat you alive.

Thus spurred on, the *Star* unleashed a stinging exposé of notorious millionaire real estate swindler C. D. Hillman, who promptly sued for libel. The *Star* came right back with revelation of more crooked deals. Hillman's wife and children then sued, raising the damage claims to $250,000. The *Star* again retaliated. A blistering editorial castigating the man filled the top quarter of page one.

"It is up to the *Star* right now to prove to the people of Seattle that it is a real Scripps newspaper," Canfield notified Miramar. "We have got to lick Hillman first and a whole lot of others in rapid succession. . . . I have several men and institutions in this community marked for slaughter. Jake Furth is one of them."

But Furth, Seattle's traction mogul, was a fighter, too. The *Star* took after Furth on November 22, 1910, with an editorial and a cartoon that showed a judge and the "traction trust" sitting on the neck of a "Duwamish Valley resident" who dared ask for lower streetcar fares. The editorial said: "Whenever men clash with dollars, presto! Courts and their accommodating injunctions rush to the defense of dollars!" Furth struck back, using a friendly judge.

The judge issued contempt of court citations against the *Star* and Editor LeRoy Sanders and City Editor Hugh Allen. The newspaper could be fined $300, the men sent to jail for six months. Cleverly, Furth had made use of the judge before whom the Hillman libel cases were pending. He hoped to intimidate the newspaper, which would need guts to rile a judge already hearing a $250,000 damage suit against it.

The *Star* bared its fangs. Across page one it splashed the story of the judge's harsh attempt to muzzle the paper, and defiantly reprinted the offending editorial. Canfield and the *Star*'s lawyer were fully confident the First Amendment protected the paper's right to criticize the courts.

Fear of jail made Editor Sanders nervous. City Editor Allen turned white, and in a few minutes walked in with his resignation in hand. A "business opportunity" had suddenly opened up back in Michigan. Canfield managed to stiffen their spines, and kept Allen from quitting.

The judge slammed down hard. Finding all guilty, he fined the newspaper $300, and ordered Allen behind bars for one month, and Sanders four months. Then ensured a regular melodrama. The judge had two deputy sheriffs standing by to seize the defendants.

Canfield had neglected to pre-arrange appeal bonds. Being led off, Allen let out a howl about his wife being ill. The judge let him go, granting twenty-four hours to post bail. But he said Sanders might skip his jurisdiction by being assigned to another Scripps paper and immediately slammed him in jail.

Under heavy strain and tension, Sanders, according to the Associated Press, "collapsed" while being booked. The *Seattle Times* got in a few mean licks with a headline: "LeRoy Sanders, Jailed by Gilliam, Pitiful Spectacle." Their story asserted "the editor of a scurrilous evening sheet broke down and cried" . . . "played the arrant coward . . ." Canfield informed Scripps: "The *Times* story is the fiercest attack on an editor and a newspaper I have read in a long while. I have seen some pretty fine examples of dirty newspaper work, but this *Times* article puts it over any of them."

Sanders "recovered in good shape" from the "sudden change to jail life." By noon next day, he was free on $2,000 bail and back at his desk leading the *Star* crusade to clean up Seattle.

Nor was Scripps able to stay aloof from a mixed bag of dangerous trouble that assailed his *Los Angeles Record,* just four hours by auto from the ranch. The worst threat to the *Record* came backhandedly because of a terrible tragedy—the October 1, 1910, bombing of the *Los Angeles Times* building, killing twenty men. Authorities arrested James McNamara, twenty-eight, and his brother John, twenty-seven, accusing them of planting the bomb to silence the long and vicious opposition of Publisher Harrison Gray Otis to organized labor. Because the *Record* had always proclaimed itself the staunch defender of the working man, the Scripps paper was stung by wild thrusts of public outrage. Big merchants organized a tacit boycott of the *Record* advertising columns.

The reaction at Miramar was rather sanguine. In fact, the crisis was looked on there as "one of the most fortunate things for the *Record* that could come along"—because it put the staff on its mettle as fighters. Jim Scripps sent a message: "Dad has often said that way down in his heart the average merchant is a coward, and that all his bluffs are indications of his bullying methods and that when a fight is close at hand he is ready to run. . . . Once you get the fear of your paper's power in their hearts they won't bother you further."

The *Record* survived the boycott without serious injury. But the bombing of the *Times* would later rise like a ghost to haunt Scripps—in the wake of getting himself personally involved backstage in the McNamara brothers' trial.

In spite of everything that went wrong, Scripps was getting richer and richer by the year. His net worth was now estimated at about $5,500,000. In 1900 net profits of his empire were $196,845. At the close of 1908, his books showed gross profits of $453,889, with gross losses of $111,849 on his new little papers, leaving a net profit of $342,040.

Several of his little fledglings were very anemic. Scripps hated the thought of having to give up on a single one of them. Jim was more hard-boiled. On Saturday, August 13, 1910, Jim folded the *Oakland Mail*. It had lived only fifteen months, and was Number Four of the children of Scripps's brain to die.

A few months later Number Five turned up its toes—the *Pueblo Sun,* wracked by a terrible succession of inept combinations of editors and business managers, born September 1, 1906, died December 5, 1910.

23

The "Right to Kill" in L.A.

When the Santa Fe from Los Angeles made a flag stop at Linda Vista on Saturday morning, November 18, 1911, Scripps was waiting with his big Packard. Off the train stepped Clarence Darrow and Lincoln Steffens. They were coming to Miramar for a weekend respite from the tense courtroom where Darrow was defending the McNamara brothers accused of dynamiting the anti-union *Los Angeles Times,* killing twenty men. Steffens was covering the trial for the *New York Globe* and a string of other newspapers.

Darrow was beaten down. The muckraker got the idea that a visit to the ranch might be the pick-up tonic that his lawyer-friend needed. Conversation with Scripps almost always proved provocative, original, stimulating. None of these three friends had any inkling, however, that a few words E. W. was to drop in their talks at the ranch would trigger another explosion in L.A. — an unexpected, shocking blow-up in the dynamiters' trial.

On the ride up to the ranch house, Steffens gave Scripps the hint to lay off discussing the murder trial which had Darrow depressed. So E. W. plunged into a variety of current topics — prospects for the 1912 Presidential campaign, political insurgents, progressives, socialism, and the Los Angeles mayoralty race whose Socialist candidate Job Harriman had often come to the ranch for Scripps's counsel.

Scripps noted the sharp contrast between his two visitors — "the big, hulky lawyer and the dapper little literateur." They were indeed an odd couple. "Steffens can't help but be finicky; alike in his ideas and in his person. The only source from which a man like me can take inspiration is his earnestness," Scripps later wrote one of his editors. Steffens took himself too seriously, and was often somewhat a pessimist. "His education . . . and personal experiences fill his mind so full of facts it seems none of them are fully digested."

Darrow had "read all around" Scripps, and was even more eager to discover a book with new ideas. "Everything about Darrow suggests a cynic—everything but one thing and that is an entire lack of real cynicism. He is a great big brute of a man, with every fiber course, but sturdy. Even his sentiment is elephantine."

The three were contemporaries in socioeconomic philosophy, all avowed and active champions of the under-dog working man. They were about the same age, Scripps fifty-seven, Darrow three years younger, and Steffens forty-five. Steffens viewed Scripps as singular. Describing events of that weekend in his autobiography, Steffens wrote:

> Big, bulky, but not fat, his hulking body, in big boots and rough clothes, carried a large gray head with a wide gray face which did not always express, like Darrow's, the constant activity of the man's brain. He was a hard student, whether he was working on newspaper make-up or some inquiry in biology. That mind was not to be satisfied. It read books and fed on conversations of scientists, not to quench an inquiry with the latest information, but to excite and make intelligent the question implied. . . . [Newspapering] was his fun; his business, his chief occupation was to study life in all forms: human, animal, astronomical. Always alone. He did his own thinking, and he had some thoughts: independent, bold, his.

It was a mistake to ignore the trial. Scripps and Steffens saw that as they settled into chairs in the study. The McNamara case was what Darrow wanted to talk over. He was cock-sure one minute, in a funk the next, and seemingly badly frightened. "I can't stand to have a man I am defending hanged," he had told Steffens with ashen face. "I can't stand it."

"Darrow wanted to talk about the case and its meaning to him, and he did," Steffens recalls. "He was monologuing about violence in the labor conflict."

That was precisely the opening Scripps yearned for. He had his own ideas on that subject. Opening a desk drawer, he pulled out an eleven-page typewritten manuscript, a disquisition written six months earlier. He thrust the three-thousand-six-hundred-word document—"Belligerent Rights In Class Warfare"—into Darrow's hands. "Read this aloud."

Darrow began reading, and his expression changed—from curiosity, to surprise, and then to something akin to alarm. Steffens, too, was astonished. Scripps was offering the candid thesis that in class warfare even dynamiters taking lives of capitalists or their hirelings had the same rights as did revolutionaries moving to overthrow an oppressive government — as long as they were acting unselfishly for the common good, and were successful. Darrow read on.

The difference between the act of a man bearing arms taking life and destroying property for selfish personal reasons, self-aggrandizement, or in the spirit of personal spite, and that of another man taking up arms and killing men and destroying property for the purpose of serving others or saving the whole nation or a great section of the nation is extremely great.

In one case the man is an enemy of society and seeks the good of no other person than himself. In the other case the man undertakes great labor and risk for no selfish gain and offers himself as a possible and even probable martyr for the benefit of his kind or his country, or his section or class.

. . . .

Today in nearly all civilized countries there is going on to a greater or lesser extent a revolutionary warfare between the two classes. . . . The warfare is between the employees of capitalistic institutions and the capitalists and their institutions. . . . In the army of labor, and especially of union labor, the leaders and the privates are only restrained from visiting retribution upon their enemies by their fear of the law.

For the purpose of this disquisition let us admit that McNamara is guilty — that he did plan the explosion and directed it, and paid for it. This explosion caused the death of twenty or more innocent men. These men that were killed should be considered what they really were — soldiers enlisted under a capitalistic employer whose main purpose in life was warfare against the unions.

If belligerent rights were accorded to the two parties in this war, then McNamara was guilty of no greater offense than would be the officer of any band, large or small, of soldiers who ordered his men to fire on the enemy and killed a great number of the same.

. . . .

Instead of our government recognizing any such belligerent rights, it will for a long time at least persevere in recognizing the common law rights of only one of the parties in this war. It has formed an alliance, and will continue the alliance, with capital. I think the inevitable result of this course will be the causing of the working classes of this country — who form the vast majority of its people — to recognize as its chief enemy the government itself — through its agents, the courts and various executive and administrative offices, the government taking the side of the capitalist employers as against the great majority of the whole people.

. . . .

> The conditions as to the two parties are so unequal as to property and
> so unequal numerically that it is absurd for any of us to imagine that peace
> and harmony can possibly exist and that warfare of some sort is not only
> inevitable and necessary but right.

How serious was Scripps? Was this another provocative essay intended to stir up the other fellow and trigger an interesting debate?

While Darrow read, he certainly was not bored. His facial expressions jumped around, his voice rose excitedly, and he looked up a few
times to shoot sharp glances at Scripps. Steffens, too, was agitated.

To E. W. such reaction already was familiar. He had proudly submitted this "bit of radicalism" written on May 1 to half a dozen of his
top editorial men, "wondering how far it would be expedient for us to go
with the ideas." He got soundly rebuffed by everyone but Northwest
Editor-in-Chief Canfield. Even accepting murder by McNamara, Canfield waved the bloody shirt, predicting "the common people" would
turn to violence to end their "almost unendurable oppression" unless
relieved by reform.

Bob Paine thought Scripps had gone much too far. Class warfare
should be settled at the ballot box. "We must condemn as murderous
such things as torture at the stake, rape of women, massacre of children,
use of dum-dum bullets, poisoning of wells, and dynamiting of the un-
armed." If the time ever came when the common people can't win with
their ballots, Paine promised "you'll find me, if alive, heading a proces-
sion of dynamitards, or petroleuse. Meanwhile, I cannot indorse bloody
murder as an excuse for stupidity, jealousy and general impotency."
Paine would not follow organized labor "when they go dynamiting, or
poisoning, or torturing, abandoning the peaceful, Christian, moral
powers won for them at Yorktown and established for them at Appomat-
tox."

But now on this November weekend at Miramar Darrow finished
reading—with a deep sigh. This theory wouldn't help him defend two
brothers accused of murder. Bitterly, he described the lay of evidence for
and against him.

"I wish we could get a settlement out of court," Darrow said.

"Oh, it can't be as bad as that," Scripps protested, glancing at Steffens. A few minutes later Darrow left the room.

"Darrow is in no state of mind to try that case," Scripps told Steffens. "He is beaten by it. Why don't you take him up on the settlement
and see what you can do?"

"That wish," said Steffens, "was only the expression of one mood.
He'll have another when he comes back."

That was true. When Darrow rejoined them he laid out his case as a sure winner. For an hour he proved his case, Steffens recalls, "cynically but boldly, even humorously." But by bedtime Darrow was again in the dumps. "I wish we could settle it somehow," he repeated.

Next day, Sunday, Scripps made busy with drives and walks, a two-hour four-cornered "debate" with Professor Ritter at the Marine Biological Station, and another later over the merits of socialism. "We took a vote and it carried unanimously . . . that we were not Socialists. And then we continued to talk all day, just as would pure and unadulterated Socialists."

Scripps was concerned for Darrow, and for the prisoners, and for labor. On Sunday evening he again took Steffens aside and urged him to try for a settlement.

"Have you any hunch as to how to go about it?" Scripps asked.

"Yes," Steffens said. "I have." Steffens described a scheme that had been lingering in the back of his mind.

"Fine," said Scripps. "It — might — work. And Darrow's line of defense won't. You tackle it, and if I or my papers can help, give me a ring."

"I can't act like that," Steffens said, "not on what Darrow says in a mood. I'll tackle him when he is normal, some morning; men's minds are clear and responsible in the morning. I'll sound him after breakfast some day."

"Right, and a morning after a railroad trip is a good morning," Scripps urged, with a little chuckle.

That night in the sleeper riding back to Los Angeles, Steffens lay awake, worrying. The next morning he got Darrow to agree to let him try to settle the case. Steffens next went into the jail and won over the McNamaras. Then he set out to plea-bargain with the court and the community, "in the name of Christianity." Steffens went to the ten "most powerful men" in the business community. He proposed this: No hanging. One McNamara would plead guilty and take a life sentence, the other to get a "light" prison term. Then the Los Angeles "interests" and union organizers must sit down and work terms for permanent labor peace. Ironically, the big men waffled until the *Times*'s General Otis himself agreed it was the best way out.

Despite a few hitches — including Darrow's arrest on a charge of trying to bribe a juror, the plea-bargain went through. In exclusive dispatches to his newspaper clients, Steffens revealed how the whole scheme had sprung from the meeting with Scripps at Miramar.

This revelation surprised and stunned every editor in the Scripps organization. Harry Rickey on Saturday, December 2, 1911, sent E. W. a split message saying in part: "Earnestly urging you to put the clamps on Steffens at once." It was "a great mistake" for Scripps to be involved in any move "to defeat justice" — a posture which would put his men and newspapers "at great disadvantage" even though they know "the purity of your motives." Steffens's stunning dispatch had practically stalled United Press and N.E.A. in their tracks in dealing with the McNamara trial.

The next day Scripps wired back: "Your split message of Saturday received. There will be no improper disclosure. There is no occasion to worry about what has happened or will happen."

E. W. was as surprised as anyone else by the McNamara confessions and the trial's sudden turn, he assured Rickey in a letter December 5. He had shown "Belligerent Rights" to Steffens in confidence and had no doubt but that he would act the part of a gentleman.

"However, I was not only astonished, but had my vanity tickled by the fact that Steffens took up the idea and was able to make so much of it as he did in a short time. I shall be even more amused and flattered if the idea continues to live, and increases its effect in influencing popular opinion.

"The fact that my personality became for a time public matter, was, as you may well imagine, the cause of much chagrin to me. I had no idea that he [Steffens] would ever use my name under any circumstances."

Though Scripps felt no shame, his editorial writers at N.E.A. leaped to their typewriters to try to put the greatest possible distance between what Steffens had revealed of E. W.'s private views on "Belligerent Rights" to kill, and the more calm and righteous public posture of his newspapers.

The Scripps dailies on succeeding days — December 5 and 6 — printed law-and-order editorials that disassociated organized labor from the crimes of the dynamiters. The second editorial did, however, manage to get in a broad swipe at greedy capitalists. The first was titled "The McNamara Confessions and Organized Labor." It predicted

> there will follow a great clamor from the usual labor-baiting sources in an attempt to fix the responsibility for these murderous outrages upon organized labor.
>
> So far as facts appear up to now, and, as we sincerely believe, so far as they will ever show, organized labor has no more responsibility for the crimes of the McNamara brothers than has organized Christian religion for the crimes of some of its ministers, or honest business for the crimes of frenzied financiers who wreck banks and violate the laws of God and man by monopolizing the necessities of life.

Was Steffens's disclosure that Scripps's "Belligerent Rights" philosophy was the centerpiece for the secret strategy to end the trial destined to cause a giant uproar and bring down public condemnation on the Scripps newspapers? The answer is no; the incident was merely a tempest in a teapot. Even in Cincinnati — where Scripps had rabid newspaper enemies — no public mention was made of Scripps in connection with the McNamara case, certainly not by his *Post,* and curiously not by the *Times-Star,* nor the *Enquirer.*

On Chicago's west side in a barny basement a dozen men worked at fever pitch around a Hoe newspaper press equipped with a strangely geared folder. There was little else in the fifty-by-sixty-foot room — one cheap pine desk, one typewriter, a telephone, two linotypes, a hot metal pot and casting box, and a composing stone.

Everybody seemed to be fumbling, testy, and nervous. Neg Cochran, E. W.'s Toledo editor, was cussing a blue streak. It was late afternoon, Thursday, September 28, 1911. They were trying to bring forth Scripps's greatest brainchild, the ad-less newspaper. Nothing was going right.

The big web press was supposed to take the single sheet for an ordinary four-page newspaper, print it, fold it three times, paste together the spline, and produce a dinky little "book" of thirty-two pages, each measuring eight and seven-eighths inches deep by six and one-eighth wide. Its size — not quite as large as a modern comic book — was one novelty; but its chief uniqueness was, of course, that it contained only reading matter — not an inch of advertising, not one line.

Something was badly out of whack with Hoe's design of the forms. The pages emerged out of sequence, some even upside down. Cochran stormed around, trying to correct the screw-up, smearing ink on his shirt, blistering his hands handling the hot plates. In the end they made flat casts, sawed them apart, rearranged the pages and recast all four plates. It was a jury-rigged botch. They wasted four or five hours. But finally at about 5:30 the *Chicago Day Book,* Volume 1, Number 1, limped off the press.

That first issue reaching Miramar by mail startled Scripps. It was much smaller, more insignificant that he had expected. It didn't look at all like a newspaper, and not much like a magazine. It was a regular "What-Is-It?" Page one was filled by a short story — fiction. The local and telegraph briefs were inside. The other contents were a mish-mash: feature stories, editorials, small pictures and cartoons, jokes, sports. The pages were not numbered.

"I don't like the name *Day Book*," Scripps wrote Cochran. They had intended calling it the *Chicago Story Book*, but found there already existed a little magazine called *Ten Story Book*. "Of course, if the flower is sweet and pretty," E. W. conceded, "it does not matter whether it is called a rose or something else."

Having two eight-inch-long columns on each of thirty-two pages, Scripps could see the *Day Book* contained 512 column inches of reading matter. How did that compare with one of his ordinary newspapers cluttered with all those big, ugly advertisements? He picked up that day's sixteen-page *San Diego Sun*. He was pleased to find the *Sun,* though four times as large, had only forty-one more inches of news matter than did the little Chicago brainchild. Not bad.

Scripps sent Cochran a ten-page critique, asked to get three copies every day by mail, and told Neg to decide everything his own way. That free hand didn't last long. In a matter of days Scripps was throwing a tantrum, kicking things around by telegraph, threatening to shut down the infant paper. He was furious that Cochran hadn't yet got the press screw-up corrected. Neg was flubbing around, playing four-dollar-a-day press mechanic, instead of "genius" editor. Hoe got busy and in a week eliminated the mechanical bugs, but there were even more glaring faults in the ad-less operation. It wasn't financial. Scripps was gambling $125,000, at $2,500 a month, aiming for 30,000 daily circulation at which point the *Day Book* should break even.

Cochran couldn't make up his mind whether he was publishing a newspaper or a magazine. Scripps's scheme was to deliver only to subscribers in the immediate area of the printing plant — which was at 500 South Peoria Street at the corner of West Congress — before branching further afield. The little "book" seemed somehow mysterious. Residents were suspicious. Even at a penny, few wanted it. The first issue sold only thirty-two copies. At the end of three weeks, it had only ninety-two subscribers.

In retrospect, Scripps should have quickly discovered Neg was not the right man for the experiment. He was practically zany, certainly wishy-washy, unprepared. The basic Scripps plan for building circulation he foolishly sabotaged. He didn't even do a first-class editing job. He had an alibi for every failure. Scripps's own incredible mistake was to only kick and scream, and let Cochran go right on making goof-up after goof-up after goof-up.

Cochran was a pretty good elbow-bender. His erratic performance strongly indicates the wastebasket at the *Day Book* must have contained a lot of empty bottles.

At times Neg was right on target. He discovered Chicago's big dailies were ignoring a stunning report by a blue-ribbon vice commission. Cochran published it in daily installments that gave lurid details of "gambling, prostitution, white slavery, pimping and all that." He also considered running the Declaration of Independence and the Ten Commandments as feature stories. His was the only paper that wrote up department store elevator accidents, big-wig scandal, and the like. Nothing was censored. He told Scripps he would reprint some of the classics if copyrights had expired—especially Balzac.

Scripps knew that just two things, hand in hand, would make the ad-less a success. First, a truly *interesting* paper. Second, block-by-block canvassing of homes surrounding the printing plant, being ready to make prompt and dependable delivery. He got neither.

The economics of this publishing venture at this juncture are staggering, or laughable, or both. Consider: Carriers bought the penny *Day Book* for half-cent a copy. It required one pound of newsprint costing two and one-half cents to produce fifteen copies. That meant a profit on newsprint of five cents a pound. Thus the first day's sale of thirty-two copies brought in slightly more than a dime! Of course, that does not figure in what Cochran had to pay printers, pressmen, reporters, the circulators, rent, heat, power, etc.

By Scripps's careful calculations it would require a circulation of 30,000 using 2,000 pounds of newsprint to generate income of $100 a day—just about what the old man was then shelling out on the experiment.

Cochran estimated it would take only a year to get 30,000 readers. Scripps kept looking for some "punch" in the *Day Book*. He saw none. In a string of sarcastic letters, Scripps upbraided Cochran. Neg was pretty rattled. For example, he overreacted when one woman stopped the paper because of murder stories. "It set me thinking," he wrote Scripps. "I told the staff to soft-pedal murders, horrible accidents, crime and morbid stuff generally."

In mid-December, Scripps sent an angry telegram: "Your plans are all wrong. Even if they were right I would shut down sooner than go on with them." In a follow-up letter, E. W. demanded: "Why can't you try MY plan? You will have to try it sooner or later; or else before I shut down the paper, I will get somebody else to try it. . . . I am waiting impatiently for you to get down to business. . . . I am ready to bet a thousand dollars to one that you haven't adopted my idea, and don't know what it is."

On January 4, 1912, Scripps summoned Neg to Miramar—at once! He was thinking about shutting down the *Day Book* in March. He had been employing his old trick of mental telepathy to try to get Cochran on target. But that didn't work. Now was the time to look him straight in the eye.

Cochran was on the carpet at the ranch for almost a week. When he departed, Scripps confided to Jim that he might have to give up the Chicago paper as a bad venture. On the son's face came a look of resignation, coupled with some disgust.

"Dad, if the *Day Book* blows up, it is only because you haven't got on the job and stayed on it like you used to do when you was building up your other papers."

"I supposed I was getting too old."

"No, you are not too old. You just don't want to get on the job; that's all there is to it."

Relating this conversation to Cochran, Scripps observed: "So it seems according to Jim's opinion, something could happen, or if you could make me stay on the job, some pretty large things might yet be done."

The conference at Miramar did some good. In a fury Scripps would dictate a harsh Cochran roast, and then lay the letter aside. But he told Cochran on February 12, 1912, he would be writing more disagreeable letters. "I never could accomplish much of anything until I got to swearing and even fighting mad about it. I believe I have cursed and abused and villified every man that I have had any luck with. . . . Attempting to convince him by logic was a waste of time."

In the two weeks after Cochran's return to Chicago, the *Day Book* picked up seven hundred new subscribers. Smugly, Scripps knew that his eyeball-to-eyeball confrontation with Neg was responsible.

"The sudden and marked effect of your being convinced that I really knew what I was talking about in canvassing for a newspaper—the effect it had upon your circulation department was a sort of belated example of experiences of which my mind is well stored. In the old days I used to feel and tell others that I had a hypnotic power and that by sheer force of will I could compel a man to double, quadruple or even increase ten-fold his productivity. It appears that I have passed through you a current of magnetism that increased the average product of your canvassers fully three-fold."

Scripps was disappointed—almost disgusted—with Cochran as an editor. E. W. wanted "new journalism." On February 1, he wrote: "Tonight I have looked over a number of *Day Book*s. They are full of appeals to working men's minds—to their sense of justice or injustice. There are to be found no things that will cause a man to forget that he has to work—that he suffers. There is nothing to make him laugh for the pure joy of being able to laugh, or to appeal to the commonplace interests. It is all uplift, argument and scold, and no fun or frolic and no common everyday plain workingman's gossip and 'chow rag.' "

The man at Miramar offered his own formula for giving "readers a comfortable, interesting half-hour's occupation reading your sheet."

> What we want in at least thirty-one out of thirty-two pages is the kind of thing that any human being, whether in the professor's chair, the salon of the merchant prince, behind the counter, in the blacksmith's shop, in the kitchen, on the streetcar platform, or on the curb would be interested in, that is to say, would thoroughly enjoy. The thirty-second page is enough to furnish all the uplift and intellectual pablum that our duty could possibly call for.
>
> Try to give your readers something in your thirty-one pages that won't cause them to think, that won't even invite them to think. Let them spend the time they devote to reading these pages in entire forgetfulness of rights and wrongs, of ambitions and disappointments. Laughable trivialities that can catch and hold the eye, and lead it on from paragraph to paragraph, are good enough stuff.
>
> You see, Cochran, the world of journalism, unlike that of fiction, is today almost wholly composed of matter that makes men and women think, or think they think, or think they ought to think. . . . What kind of stuff would I advise you to put into your paper—jokes that will make very common people and especially young boys and girls laugh—love stories that are pleasant, that have something of a thrill of sentiment that any woman can feel, and if possible, love stories that will make even a hard-working, tired old working-man father grin as he reads it of an evening—cook receipts— and perhaps some information as to how a poor girl can renovate a hat ribbon, or a poor boy can cheaply clean up last year's hat to make it look decent this year—how to clean an old pipe or mend a piece of furniture.

On April 6, 1912, *Day Book* circulation finally reached 1,400. But Cochran was a bundle of nerves. He admitted to E. W. that he "got the shakes every time a stop comes in." So Cochran summoned his young son Harold to take over editing the ad-less and returned for a while to Toledo where he was still on the payroll of the *News-Bee* as editor.

At twenty-three John Paul was running scared. He was in Cleveland in the spring of 1912, secretly getting ready to take over as head of the Ohio papers, rushing about the state to get acquainted with his editors and reporters, hunting a house to rent, tending a clinging pregnant wife, worrying desperately that he might be too green to handle his big job— and avidly seeking his father's help.

"The closer I get to this work I have ahead of me, the bigger it grows," he wrote March 11. "It looks scarry [*sic*] to a kid like me. . . . I'm not losing my nerve though, but I'll probably make you and Jim think I'm scared by hanging onto old men and methods."

Scripps tried to buck him up, warning that worrying wouldn't help. "Whether you asked for the job or whether it was thrust on you, makes no difference," the father replied March 21. "You are on the job and you have got to do it. Your worrying will neither increase capacity nor enlarge character. You have got to think and you have got to act. Your success will depend on your ability to think right."

John Paul should imagine himself adrift in an open boat at sea. "There is no one to direct you; there is no one to advise you. Your life is in your hands. You will be alone, terribly alone, in coming to a decision." Running the whole Ohio League of newspapers, Scripps advised, "is not nearly so critical a job as that of running one little baby newspaper. In fact, the big newspapers will run themselves, and unless you are a more remarkable man than your father was before you, they will for the most part run you, too. You are not a big enough nor a smart enough man to ruin the papers even if you wanted to."

When it finally emerged that E. W.'s inexperienced boy was waltzing in to take over as editorial chief of eight newspapers, considerable resentment could be anticipated, and did flare up. The current editor-in-chief, Harry Rickey, willingly stepped aside to make an opening for John Paul. Rickey was promoted to president and general manager of N.E.A. at $15,000 a year. The man he replaced, "Billy" Colver, was disgruntled. John Paul wanted to appoint Colver his "assistant" at $12,500. Colver turned it down, and went with the Clover Leaf newspapers as Larry Ashbaugh's chief editor. That angered John Paul. But Scripps cooled the boy down smartly.

"As a matter of policy," the father wrote April 12, "it don't pay to hate anybody. I should consider you entirely unqualified . . . if you should develop a spirit of petty meanness or pique, of spitefulness against those whose course has disappointed you or injured you. . . . I warn you, John, against having the big head. Don't think for a moment that I advise you to be overtrustful and foolishly charitable. Trust no man unless you have to (and incidentally when you are in the trusting business, do it for all it's worth). Remember the friend of today will be the enemy of tomorrow, but at the same time never forget that the enemy of today may be the most valuable friend of tomorrow."

The prospect of becoming a first-time father the middle of September had John Paul enthralled. "I wrote mother and told her about the first little kicks of the baby. They are something different than anything

I've felt before. They pop into my mind at all times of the day; I spend my evenings now feeling for them."

They were already calling the unborn baby "Jack"—anticipating a boy who would be named after his father. This would be Scripps's third grandchild. Jim already had his second son, James George Scripps Junior, born November 24, 1911, eight pounds or ten—depending on who sent the telegram—and described as "a chip off the old block."

Scripps was not niggardly in compensating his sons. On February 4, 1911, he raised Jim's monthly salary from $1,000 to $1,500 and John's from $500 to $1,000. Likewise he gave them generously of the stock in his newspapers, based on their growth in value under the sons' reign. Early in 1911 he handed Jim $90,000 in stock and John $60,000 worth. A year and a half later he gave them other batches of stock, Jim $270,000 and John Paul $180,000. Dad suggested they might want to share some of it with their younger brother Bob.

Jim had a completely free hand. Scripps was well satisfied with his brand of "kingship."

Early in 1911 it was decided to launch a second Texas paper—at Houston, sleepy metropolis of 80,000 on a bayou fifty miles inland from Galveston Island. Chosen to be editor was Paul C. Edwards, for three years managing editor of the *Dallas Dispatch*. He had begun as a 1908 cub on the *San Francisco News*.

Edwards, twenty-nine, was dispatched to Miramar to get his marching orders. Strangely, he was permitted to take along his young wife. Scripps received them graciously but in what struck Edwards as a rather off-hand way. At dinner that mood abruptly changed. The old man, obviously having boned up on Edwards, began firing sharp questions, dissecting his mind to see what made him tick, whether there were flaws in his journalistic principles, and what he knew about Houston.

Scripps ordered him to report to his study at 9 the next morning. For three hours E. W. carried on a wide-ranging non-stop monologue, about his newspapers, about his men, his ideals. In the afternoon Edwards got a ranch tour by auto. Next morning at 9 came candid lecture Number Two. On the third day Scripps sat with Edwards ninety minutes, dictating an eleven-page letter, explaining how to make the *Houston Press* a success.

"Edwards, that's all," Scripps said. "My secretary will give you a copy of this letter before you leave. You have exhausted me. I haven't worked so hard in years as I have worked these last three days with you.

I don't want to see you again. You are welcome to stay here as long as you wish, but don't come near me or try to talk to me. I am through with you. Goodbye."

Edwards shook a limp hand. He thought he detected among the gray-red whiskers the hint of a friendly smile. At any rate he was off to Houston "with a song in my heart" and a valued letter in his pocket.

Even though Scripps was now a millionaire, the *Houston Press* was designed as the typical shoestring operation. Edwards rented a vacant twenty-five by eighty-foot auto repair shop at 709 Louisiana Street. From the Dallas sister paper he bought a castoff Potter press. He acquired also four turtles and chases, one linotype, and "type that would scarcely fill a shirt-tail." He bought a $75 used typewriter and hired two reporters. Edwards was to draw $25 a week, with a chance to own 10 percent of the stock if the *Press* succeeded.

On Monday, September 25, 1911, the first issue of the *Houston Press* was supposed to roll at 3 o'clock. The pressman had no starting transformer. He filled a barrel with water, dangled into it two bare wires. With ropes and pulleys he hoped to move the naked wire up and down to control the electric current and thus gradually start the press.

By 5 o'clock the last plate was slapped on the old Potter. The pressman grabbed his pulley ropes and threw the switch. Sparks flew. Edwards held his breath. The press cylinder groaned and began turning, picking up running speed as the ropes were adjusted. Everybody cheered. They ran 250 copies. No announcement had been made. So when the newsboys raced out to cover the neighborhood they were surprising Houston with its first penny paper. It was the thirty-first Scripps newspaper, springing to life just three days ahead of Number Thirty-Two, the *Chicago Day Book*. In a year's time the Houston paper's circulation was 11,000 and prospects were rosy.

Then came launching of the concern's thirty-third newspaper—amid much turmoil. The *Philadelphia News-Post* brought out its first issue Saturday, May 11, 1912—a regular four-page penny paper—issued from a $7,450 second-hand plant, with a payroll of $2,400 a month. It virtually was a United Press "baby." Ham Clark was publisher. Editor was Marlen Pew, the former N.E.A. chief, once editor of a Boston daily, and lately day editor in the New York United Press bureau. Even Roy W. Howard was allotted a 5 percent stock interest. Jim held for his father 51 percent control.

Except for one compelling reason, Scripps may not have paid close attention to Philadelphia—his "baby" boy was going there to break in as a cub reporter. Teenage Bob was quite a puzzle to his father. They talked little. The boy confided more in his mother. Nackie explained to E. W.

that Bob was interested in art and pure literature, and found newspapering "repugnant." Bob was a dreamer and wrote little poems. Scripps could empathize; he, too, had been a farm boy enamoured of poets, and a yearner for a literary life. Scripps did not intend to force his own profession on Bob, but was mightily pleased when Bob came in and requested permission to take a job as police reporter on the Philadelphia paper. The boy was then sixteen and a half. Father took the occasion to write a ten-page letter of advice and instruction.

"In wiring Jim my consent to your going to Philadelphia," Scripps wrote May 8, 1912, "I stipulated two things: one that you should work; the other was that you should keep up your reading. . . . You should devote a good part of almost every day to reading such literature as will help to develop you intellectually.

"My stipulation that you should work was not to make money but so you can understand and sympathize with your fellows. I do not want you to be a simple onlooker and student and critic of life. . . . Write me just as freely and openly about what you are doing and thinking as I write you. . . . By writing me all that's in you, I will be better able to help you."

Before long vivid letters began arriving from Bob—and executives of the little paper—that literally popped the old man's eyes. Right off the bat, his son and the feisty *News-Post* plunged into rapid-fire, hair-raising, and dangerous exploits.

In the Pacific Northwest, Scripps had on the job as vigorous a crusader as he ever wanted in Byron Canfield—perhaps more so. W. H. Porterfield wrote from Los Angeles in August 1911, urging Miramar to tone down the *Seattle Star*'s furious war on graft and corruption. Jim, responding, declined. "The little Scripps kid" was just going to "sit still and keep from getting nervous."

Canfield was experienced, had always been a scrapper, and didn't seem to be acting rashly. Jim added: "We may get nervous when he turns the corner on two wheels. . . . But he believes in belligerent rights, as does my father. He is sincerely, conscientiously, and confidently fighting for the 95 percent, according to the rules of the game as set forth by E. W. Scripps. I am not going to warn Canfield or give him any signal to slow down. The future will tell. . . . Circulation will go up if his ideas are in keeping with . . . the thought of the under-dog."

The *Seattle Star* exploded a bombshell August 23, 1911, with a four-inch deep editorial stripped across the top of page one asserting Federal Judge C. H. Hanford "must go." The editorial said: "He stands discredited and despised, a disgrace to the courts, a danger to the people, a menace to a free government."

What upset the newspaper was a Hanford injunction forcing street-car riders to pay double tolls to Seattle Electric, whose president was Jacob Furth, a political power who had most judges and the federal district attorney under his thumb. The *Star* urged riders to defy the injunction. It organized a mass meeting for the signing of petitions for Hanford's impeachment.

Seven thousand citizens jammed the Dreamland Rink which the *Star* had rented for the night of August 26. A dozen "responsible, middle-class" businessmen denounced Hanford as a villain, a tool of the hated Stone-Webster street railway monopoly, and also as a drunkard. Outside the rink the judge was hanged in effigy. Canfield was startled to hear thunderous cheers for the *Star*. People began putting 50,000 names on an impeachment petition.

Judge Hanford and the D. A. immediately struck back with charges of "conspiracy to obstruct justice," believed drawn up by Furth's lawyer. Deputy federal marshals arrested Canfield, LeRoy Sanders, the *Star* editor, and their attorney John H. Perry. Also arrested were three speakers—a city councilman, a deputy sheriff, and a labor leader.

"Sanders and I were willing to go to jail for a couple of days," Canfield reported to Scripps, "but decided this would be a bad move." Canfield wanted to show the issue in its true light, a revolt by the people—not just by a newspaper—against a venal court.

So the three citizen speakers volunteered to let themselves be locked up for a day or two to dramatize the conflict. The arrests were timed for a Saturday afternoon when banks were closed. This time Canfield was not caught short or unprepared. He reached in his pocket, pulled out a $10,000 certified check, handed it to the magistrate, and walked free with his editor and his lawyer.

"The fight has just now started," Canfield wrote Scripps. "It should go a long ways toward making the *Star* the biggest newspaper property in Seattle, even if Jake Furth's outfit blows up the building or Hanford and [President] Taft get out the troops and put us all in the bull-pen."

"You and Sanders," Scripps responded, "are making some chapters in the to-be-history of the to-be-famous warfare of the people against their usurping judges. There is no doubt there is at present existing a warfare of the masses against the classes."

Canfield appealed to other Scripps papers to help stir up public wrath. "I'd a lot rather be stood up in front of a wall and shot full of holes than be put in McNeill Island pen, still I can stand it if necessary.

Incidentally, I am going to try to make a trip over there soon to see what kind of a place it is."

Actually there was nothing to worry about. Canfield and his men were vindicated. The federal grand jury met, listened to the claim of conspiracy, and refused to return any indictments.

When that news reached Miramar by telegraph September 28, 1911 — coupled with word that Canfield now intended to step up his crusade — Scripps decided it was time to douse a little water on his Northwest firebrand.

Scripps suggested Canfield should for one year "rest with this last battle won" and turn to "increasing the size of your weapons and looking well after your commissariat." E. W. spelled out plainly what he meant: "You should devote nearly the whole of your energies to making your papers the most amusing, the most generally circulated possible, and give time to your counting rooms to increase money both from circulation and advertising. Be purely pleasing and jolly for a while."

The *Star* did not forget Judge Hanford. Some reporters obviously kept spying on him. Canfield mailed on October 27, 1911, a flashlight photo for amusement to John Paul "showing Hanford leaving the house of a 'lady friend' about midnight October 17. You will note it shows the woman's face quite clearly. Hanford visits this woman four or five nights a week."

The picture was not published, and there was no need; Hanford's goose already was cooked. Criticism of the judge had already reached Washington. To Seattle in June 1912 came a House Judiciary subcommittee to investigate the judge's misconduct. There was too much to white-wash. On July 22, 1912, Hanford quietly resigned.

Judge Hanford was not the only "wicked giant" to lose his scalp to the *Star.* Canfield's relentless recall crusade finally in March 1912 drove out of office Seattle Mayor "Hi" Gill. His Honor had the audacity to sponsor a 250-room bordello two miles south of the city center. The crib house was found to encroach eight feet onto a public street. To rectify this slight error, city council had obligingly awarded the bordello partners a fifteen-year lease on the street.

The newspaper also nailed Gill's police chief, Charles Wappenstein. In May 1912, he was convicted of collecting bribes in the red-light district, and sentenced to three to ten years in prison.

Should the little United Press grab a chance to displace the mighty Associated Press as the American partner of the "big three" press agencies of

Europe—Reuters in England, Wolff in Germany, and Havas in France?
That question jumped up at the June 1912 conference of Scripps
editorial brass in Chicago. Baron Reuter had talked to Roy Howard in
London and secretly offered the deal. The Baron was dissatisfied with
his arrangement with the Associated Press. He proposed the "big three"
sign a ten-year contract to exchange news with the United Press Associations.

Howard was pushing for it. "It would give us a foreign service
which would be unequaled." He almost accepted the Baron Reuter deal
on his own authority, but prudently waited to get other views within the
concern.

United Press then operated with its own men in London, Paris, and
Berlin. These correspondents did have the advantage of an American
point of view, having been trained in the United States. But a large
handicap was inability to get access to official government information
in foreign capitals until Reuters, Wolff, and Havas had it. In Germany it
was a penal offense to release a story before Wolff did. Even if a United
Press man did luck onto something first, the government-controlled telegraph wires would delay his dispatch until the "official" agency copy had
moved.

Not only would agreeing to this exchange give United Press "prestige," it meant faster and more direct access to the news of Europe.
There was one catch. It would cost United Press more—about $35,000 a
year more than what was currently spent on manpower and cable tolls.
Since the United Press's annual profit was now in the $25,000 to $35,000
range, the wire service might go into the red, or at best break even.

The Chicago meeting grew so enthusiastic over the prospect, however, that the editors-in-chief volunteered to chip in a total of $20,000 a
year above what they were currently assessed to support United Press.

E. W. Scripps was not present. He was in peaceful "retirement" on
his California mesa. His son, John Paul, was sitting in. Everybody in the
room was, of course, well schooled in E. W.'s principles.

J. C. Harper suddenly wondered aloud what Scripps would think of
teaming up with "government" news agencies abroad. Wasn't that the
danger he feared in this country—a monopoly or government control of
the free flow of news? Could the United Press be true to the "95 percent"
if it relayed "censored" news from the capitals of Europe?

"Would news of the 95 percent put on the wire by Reuter be stopped
by the government?" asked Harper.

"As to censorship," replied Howard, "I cannot say."

There were a dozen executives in the room at the LaSalle Hotel. It was clear they were on the verge of accepting the Reuter offer. But they needed to act on other pressing matters so a decision was deferred until the following day.

Next morning it was brought before directors of the United Press for a vote. But John Paul posed a question. "Is this to be taken up with Jim?"

U.P. Chairman Ham Clark responded: "I don't think it's necessary."

"Well, it's a ten-year contract," observed the boy, thoughtfully, "and therefore involves a large sum of money. I think Jim should be consulted."

That triggered another caution from Harper. E. W. had a well-known objection to long-term contracts, and insisted they be thoroughly examined before signing.

Clark said: "This motion only authorizes action. It does not direct that action be taken at once."

"Okay, then," said John Paul. "I'll vote yes, with the understanding, Ham, that you and I take this matter up personally."

Later in the day they discussed the proposition, and John Paul won his point. Clark agreed to go to San Diego and present the Reuter deal personally to Jim.

In the official history of the United Press, the rejection of this tie-in with Reuter and the other foreign "government" news agencies is characterized as a singular triumph for the true principles of Scripps journalism. Minutes of the meetings in Chicago's LaSalle Hotel, however, reveal that such a partnership was escaped by only a hair's breadth.

When Clark reached San Diego and outlined the proposition to Jim, the son, of course, would not act on something which so violently flew in the face of E. W.'s basic beliefs without consulting his father.

The wrathful answer from Scripps must have boomed from one end of the ranch to the other: "No!"

Not only did the Chicago meeting challenge E. W.'s stand against monopoly and possible government news censorship, it almost trashed another belief just as basic. The brass took up and seriously considered changing the United Press into a mutual or cooperatively-owned organization, controlled by its 418 clients.

The argument advanced was that this would lower costs and/or provide more news to subscribers. Only 20 percent of the total U.P. revenue came from Scripps papers.

It seemed to have been overlooked that the wire had been established for two reasons, first to see that anyone who wanted a telegraph news service could buy it, and second to show a profit.

Perhaps one reason the Reuter co-op scheme was pushed so hard by certain executives was that if revenues increased, so would the value of stock held by Clark, Howard, and C. D. Lee.

Untimately, the proposal was totally rejected.

From its inception in 1905, The Industrial Workers of the World (I.W.W.) colored America's labor scene with socialistic and anarachistic overtones. I.W.W. agitation, followed by harsh vigilante retribution, erupted all along the Pacific Coast early in 1912 and affected, one way or another, the Scripps newspapers in Washington, Oregon, and California; but the real danger of violence did not spill over on Scripps personally until late that May.

This militant labor uprising confronted E. W. and his lieutenants with a stunning paradox—more so for him than his subalterns. Curiously, although these papers were founded to champion the under-dog blue-collar worker, most Scripps coast editors seemed to consider it "dangerous" to carry news of the I.W.W. demonstrations.

When a contingent of "Wobblies" descended on San Diego, the town went almost berserk with fear. Hastily an ordinance was voted to ban assemblage and free speech on the streets. The I.W.W.'s immediately violated the new law. While police waffled, vigilantes mobbed the intruders, inflicting "torture," and ran them out of San Diego.

In this confrontation, the eyes of San Diegans turned to Miramar, seventeen miles out on the mesa. A visible stream of Socialist Party leaders and union labor officials from Los Angeles flowed to the ranch to consult Scripps. This caused a lot of talk.

The editor of his *Sun* felt caught in the middle. As Bob Paine put it, the editor "steered between Scylla and Charybdis. He didn't roast the I.W.W and he didn't roast the vigilantes. He did give the news. . . . But his giving the facts brought upon him the hostility of the vigilantes and their backers, who included pretty near everybody."

The I.W.W. clash revived tycoon John D. Spreckels's hatred of Scripps, stemming chiefly from the *Sun*'s unsuccessful opposition a year earlier to his fifty-year streetcar franchise. Spreckels turned loose his *Union* to assail the *Sun*'s handling of the "Wobblie" contagion. Bob Paine, whose office was in San Diego, observed that the *Union* "suggested" that the *Sun* be mobbed.

Unrest over the I.W.W. threat abated slowly. Angry talk continued on the streets. People were shaking fists at the *Sun*—though, curiously, neither its circulation nor advertising diminished. Jim, whose office was on the second floor of the newspaper building, heard the muttered hatred, and a repeated threat: *"We ought to go out and get old Scripps!"*

This situation was too volatile for taking any chances. Jim drove out to Miramar and gravely warned his father to be on guard for trouble. E. W. was taken aback. "For a time it made me quite nervous." His emotions were in a whirl. Then his pride emerged and his courage began rising. "There is one thing that I have always been determined on and that was that no man should with either his tongue or by laying on of hands humiliate me. I have never been a brave man, but I have felt that life itself was of small account as compared with personal indignity."

Jim considered the mob threat real. He brought his father a pump shotgun and a box of shells. "You have your revolver," he pointed out.

Scripps and his son stewed over the situation for about an hour. E. W. suddenly got out of his rocker, seized the shotgun and his revolver, and led Jim outside. Twenty yards from one of the telephone poles that marched across the ranch house courtyard, he stopped. For a moment he examined the pump shotgun; then he loaded it and in quick succession he fired off a dozen rounds. Then he took a number of practice shots with his pistol.

"I found my nerves were steady," he later wrote to John Paul, "and felt pretty sure that I couldn't miss a man with either weapon except by accident. . . . I felt at the time a rough and tumble duel would not only be a fitting, but to me the most fitting, way of 'closing up my accounts,' in 'cashing in.' Down at the bottom of my heart I have never felt any extreme aversion to killing or being killed."

For days Scripps kept his shotgun and pistol in ready reach. Jim posted a twenty-four-hour guard at the ranch gate.

One evening a crowd of men came out from town. When they reached the ranch gate, the guard stepped out, with a menacing look and a cocked rifle, barring the way. The men halted and began milling around. They muttered indecisively for several minutes, and then turned back toward San Diego.

Such a lame ending to the crisis disappointed Scripps. The guard was overzealous, E. W. months later told a friend. "I will confess frankly even now that I regret the loss of an opportunity to defend my castle with arms."

Despite his itchy trigger-finger, the mob never came back.

24

In the Shadow of the Dark Angel

On his fifty-eighth birthday Scripps was holed up on his California mesa wishing he "could forget I was ever a newspaperman," struggling to keep his back turned on his business empire, even shunning nearby San Diego, and having "real fun" being a farmer again. "I am having the most enjoyable time," he informed Milton McRae in a chatty birthday letter on June 18, 1912, "working on, or you might say playing with, Fanita ranch."

Scripps had bragged that he could clear $30,000 a year on Fanita. He let his foreman go, and started personally hiring, firing, bossing, and checking up. He remodeled the fifteen-room ranch house, adding three bathrooms, built a giant barn with fifty fancy horse stalls, erected a thirty-two-room bunkhouse "hotel" with four baths and surrounded by a dozen family "villas." He increased the ranch-hands to one hundred. He tripled his alfalfa acreage, bought sixty big brood mares and a Percheron stallion, planted more oat fields and lemon trees, and brought in a drilling rig to sink extra water wells.

He had no idea how much money he was flinging around. He just sent the bills to Jim's office. (He would be flabbergasted a year later to discover that his total investment in Fanita had ballooned in the few years he'd owned the ranch to $272,312! His expenditures: alfalfa, $56,099, fencing, $8,485, buildings, $18,464, running expense, $107,720, and 6 percent interest, $44,738.)

Scripps truly had given up control of the business. Jim, just turning twenty-six, was now an experienced boy-king, ruling with a strong—and perhaps a trifle severe—hand. Under Jim's direction total annual revenues increased from $3,270,360 to $4,505,950, 38 percent, with profits leaping 81 percent, $250,257 to $453,867. In the 1907–1912 span the total average daily circulation jumped from 648,962 to 879,549, up 35 percent.

Though no editor or business manager dared challenge cocksure Jim's authority, it proved a different and sad story with John Paul's overnight ascendancy to Ohio editorial nabob. The lad was unsure, and his troops could sense it. A lot of jealousy and contempt began to surface. John Paul recognized he was having trouble "waking up." He even had nightmares about his plight.

His father warned that John Paul would allow others to pass him by if he didn't awaken. The son responded: "I have an oft-recurring nightmare in which I feel that I am awake but unable to open my eyes or properly move my body, and in order to gain full consciousness I have to double up my fists and pound on the bedstead." Though married, expecting a child, and filling enormous professional shoes, the boy was a terribly green and immature twenty-four.

Still somewhat lost in his own pleasant dream world was the third son. Bob was fiddling with his job on the *Philadelphia News-Post,* dabbling in poetry, running off on side trips to visit John Paul in Cleveland and attend political conventions, keeping up his reading, but smoking too much and letting his physical fitness slide. His letters home revealed he often pined for life on the ranch. His father, however, thought Bob was better off in the East "than playing with business" in California. "Back here," he wrote, "your mind is principally given over to the subject of girls."

The subject in the forefront of the old man's mind—when he was not wrestling with Fanita—was politics. He was an avid buff, but played a cerebral game rather than actively mixing in the front-line battles, or at war councils. He put his sword in by long distance, usually very long distance. Scripps yearned for the progressive wing to capture the Republican Party. Their best hope for President, as he saw it, was Senator Robert M. LaFollette. Scripps became furious when the progressives lost faith in "Senator Bob," ganged up and dumped him, switching allegiance to Teddy Roosevelt.

What upset Scripps most was that the longest knife was stuck in LaFollette by California Governor Hiram W. Johnson—and Johnson hadn't even the decency to consult Scripps about what course his gang intended to follow. That was a mean slap in the face for the publisher whose string of California newspapers everyone felt—especially Scripps—had largely elected Johnson to his office. Scripps and the governor traded a few subsequent insults by mail—and were at outs for a long period.

Scripps invited William Jennings Bryan, still a progressive dark-

horse, to visit him. Bryan couldn't make it. Teddy Roosevelt was coming
to Los Angeles; Scripps got hotel reservations so he could "chew the rag"
for an hour with T. R. But Roosevelt did not promptly set aside time for
Scripps, and E. W. huffily canceled his proposed trip to L.A. "I won't
run after anybody," Scripps snapped to his Los Angeles editor.

Scripps did not trouble himself to go to the Republican convention
in Chicago. But that bunting-draped hall held Scrippses aplenty—John
Paul and Bob, as reporters, and as spectators his two spinster sisters,
Ellen, seventy-five, and the red-headed, bombastic Miss Virginia, sixty.

Staying on the sidelines, Scripps let "the younger men" determine
which nominee would get the support of the Scripps papers. The editors
voted to back the Democrat candidate, Woodrow Wilson, but with small
enthusiam at some papers. Most editors came to realize the Progressive
platform embodied most of the Scripps under-dog aims. Should they
then renege on Wilson? A poll was taken. But the majority of editors
held fast, and would not abandon their endorsement of Wilson.

In his own mind, Scripps was quite ambivalent about Teddy
Roosevelt. He toyed with prompting some kind of a half-way switch
when late in the campaign a would-be assassin wounded Roosevelt in
Milwaukee. The candidate staggered into the hall and delivered his
speech before going to the hospital. That kind of grit greatly impressed
E. W. He called in Jim, they talked, and the son came out amd immediately dispatched to all Scripps editors this wire:

> On hearing of Roosevelt's attempted assassination, E. W. Scripps
> stated that Roosevelt's speech after he was shot proved not only his courage
> and his sincerity but his trustworthiness. That a man cannot lie facing
> death. That we know now he is right. And since our last doubt has been
> removed a much more friendly attitude towards Roosevelt is advised.

It was too late, however, to sway voters. Seven weeks later Wilson
was elected with 42 percent of the popular vote. Taft and Roosevelt
killed each other off, getting, respectively, 23 and 28 percent. It was the
first Democratic triumph since Grover Cleveland left the White House in
1897. Later Scripps, conveniently ignoring the existence of Jim's telegram, would take personal pride in the election outcome. He was firmly
convinced that Wilson could not have won the Presidency except for the
support of his newspapers.

Scripps was unhappy in the late summer of 1912 with the skimpy letters

Bob sent about being a cub reporter in Philadelphia. Bob wrote that his work was "varigated and I am doing everything from short storys to murders. I am getting the hang of how to go after the stuff and how to write it and I really enjoy the game now."

The father dictated a six-page reply, chastising the son. "For thousands and thousands of years boys like yourself have been going away from home and writing back . . . just such puerile, indefinite and altogether absurd letters as you have been writing me. . . . You haven't told me a single thing about your work. . . . If you cannot write more than a short page of matter that you think would be interesting to the one man in the world who is more interested in you than anybody else, how the devil are you going to write things that will interest thousands of people unknown to yourself?"

Bob was jolted. "I suppose I deserve the blowing up all right," he replied. He went into 1,000 words of detail about his experiences. In one chatty letter, Bob told of playing detective — literally — in digging up facts on a woman thought to have poisoned several of her children. "The family moved around a good deal. I worked like a detective for a whole day, and got the stuff, too. I needed to see a baker, but he was asleep. His wife said she had already turned away two or three reporters. I told her I wasn't a reporter but worked for the City Hall detective bureau, and if she didn't call her husband I'd get a cop. She called him, and he told me all he knew."

In Cleveland, John Paul was still feeling the occasional sting of fatherly criticism. Scripps wanted him to read more. "I'm going to order that five-foot shelf of knowledge of Prof. Elliott's and try a whirl at it," John Paul wrote.

John Paul's first baby was a week or more late. That was a big worry. He developed a severe earache. A physician examined him, rammed cotton dipped in cocaine up his nose to his eustachian tube, inflated the canal, and then lanced his ear drum. "I've never been put through such a case of sprouts by anyone."

Days passed. John Paul could only fret and wait for the overdue baby. Finally, on October 6, 1912, grandfather received this wire from Cleveland:

Baby weighs nine pounds, fourteen oz., has brown hair and looks like Edith. I think he is quite long and fat. Edith had nineteen hours siege and was pretty well used up last night at 3. This afternoon Edith is feeling quite comfortable and is doing as well as could be expected and the boy is fine. The baby is to be named after his dad and will be called Jack.

Like an awkward colt, the experimental *Chicago Day Book* staggered on wobbly legs. Its erratic course for almost a year startled and disgusted Scripps. Neg Cochran kept trying one fool scheme after another, especially in delivery methods. Throwing aside Scripps's wise counsel, Cochran now was selling on newsstands and splashing big headlines—the exact opposite of the planned slow, block-by-block insinuation of the ad-less on Chicago. Circulation was about 8,000 a day.

The *Day Book* was being "misled into ruin," Scripps bluntly told Cochran June 15, 1912. In a six-page letter, he pointed out the numerous mistakes. He was feeling "sad and unhappy"—not for himself but for the *Day Book* staff. "You are all trying to discover that very something that is as non-existent as perpetual motion or the elixir of life."

The violent backwash of the circulation wars between the Chicago newspaper giants slopped over on the tiny *Day Book*. Chicago police suddenly prohibited its sale at newsstands; the freaky little book, they decided, was not a newspaper. J. C. Harper happened to be in Chicago. He stormed the city attorney's office, threatening federal court action. Overnight the mayor ruled that the *Day Book* was indeed a newspaper, and it went back on the stands.

Then a startling innovation sparked up the little paper's readability. Neg Cochran began publishing some of his own brilliant "Personal Notes." Scripps blinked, and then let out a joyful shout. This was exactly the kind of down-to-earth copy the *Day Book* needed! "Neg, this flabby old heart of mine just swelled and swelled with pride," he wrote Cochran. "I even felt a suspicion of moisture in my eyes. To be the father of such a publication, I feel to be the greatest honor that I have ever experienced."

Not unexpectedly, Larry Ashbaugh notified Scripps he was invading the Chicago field. He and his Clover Leaf cohorts had been miffed by getting beat out, first in Dallas and later in Philadelphia, by the Scripps crowd. In retaliation, they had pulled out as partners in N.E.A. But Ashbaugh's decision to start a one-cent, four-page Scripps-style daily in Chicago was neither for spite nor revenge. He merely saw the Windy City as a prime market begging for another cheap newspaper. Ashbaugh did not even intend to buck the *Day Book*. He located his new paper in the triangular "Northwest wedge"—which did not overlap the sector of Chicago that Neg Cochran had staked out.

What helped lure Ashbaugh was that he discovered an "angel"—Charles R. Crane—who had inherited control of his family's brass and plumbing manufacturing empire grossing $50,000,000 a year, and was burning to do good with his wealth. The aristocratic Crane was willing to put up $10,000 a month to guarantee publication of a liberal, anti-establishment newspaper in his home town.

The Ashbaugh-Crane venture came to life in August 1912, called the *Chicago Daily Press*. That was the same name, ironically, Bob Paine had used in 1900 for his abortive attempt to launch a Scripps paper in Chicago, only to collapse from drink and overwork, and have to knock his puny defective infant in the head after barely three weeks.

Scripps was not disturbed by the advent of the Ashbaugh-Crane paper. From what he saw and heard, it struck him the *Press* was being poorly run, mainly as a rich man's plaything. Within a year the paper was on the rocks. Ashbaugh wanted out. He turned the paper back to his angel. Crane tried to sell it to Scripps, who had no need for the wreck. Then Crane proposed a merger with the *Day Book,* which he admired. Scripps did not need any help from Crane. But he admired him as a reformer, and decided to go along, taking the *Chicago Daily Press*'s goodwill—not the press and linotypes—giving in exchange a 10 percent interest in the *Day Book*. Crane fully understood that all he was getting was a chance to help foster an experimental paper, and be responsible for one-tenth of the running expense.

Frontier ferment still ruled in the Pacific Northwest. Graft and corruption did not die easily; the Scripps papers kept on the attack. In Portland, Oregon, the little *News* and its courageous editor, Dana Sleeth, continued to expose officialdom's wrong-doing. The politicos retaliated with vicious libel suits. In mid-May 1913, Dana Sleeth and his newspaper were brought to trial. Young John H. Perry, who had successfully defended the *Seattle Star* and earned a concern-wide reputation as "the Northwest Whirlwind," described the Portland trial as the "bitterest" ever held in Multonomah County. But Perry did his job. On May 29, he was able to telegraph Miramar: "The jury acquits Dana Sleeth and the *Portland News,* notwithstanding the rotten instructions of the judge and the jobbery of the county officials."

Next day Scripps wired: "Dear Dana: You're a wonder. I congratulate you. I am proud of you." The Portland editor felt sanguine, too, but recognized that Fate had played a singular role in his triumph. As he wrote Scripps: " 'We' won and of course are strong this P.M. for the jury system. I think the chief elements of the victory were John Perry, Frank Collier, the reputation of the paper and the fact that I came from Nebraska and had socialistic leanings. College chum for juror, socialist for foreman, nuff sed. However, we didn't discover the aforesaid until after the trial was over."

Scripps wrote several more complimentary letters, one saying the concern had only three "really Scripps papers"—edited as he would edit them. One was Sleeth's. The others were the *Day Book* and the *Philadelphia News-Post.* But he sounded a note of caution:

> There is one thing that you and Cochran have in common. You both indulge in booze. . . . I do not want to preach to you. . . . For perhaps twenty years I was a from twenty to forty drinks-a-day-man—perhaps more often forty. Still with all that I am afraid of a drinking man because I know that a quitting time has got to come either by a premature death or a physical breakdown, and neither dead men or physical wrecks are of any use.

Philadelphia was just then seeing plenty of reckless derring-do from the little *News-Post,* still not a year old. Editor Pew had launched an attack on "a thug magistrate" named Carey. The *News-Post* hammered away, daily exposing more Carey dirty work. Other Philadelphia newspapers ignored the scandal, but the political powers grew fretful; an election was coming up. Behind closed doors at City Hall, a secret scheme was hatched to muzzle Pew and his paper.

At midnight police with a criminal libel indictment took Pew from bed and put him behind bars. Next day he got free on bond. Scripps sent a wire to buck him up: "Your courage is good; you will also be patient. Your wisdom and your resourcefulness are yet to be proved. . . . Going to jail under the circumstances is no disgrace. Many of the best men that ever lived have suffered that much and worse. I'm too old to fight now, but my fortune is at the disposal of you and such as you. So long as you are not afraid, it is hardly possible that your enemies can hurt you."

But Pew, thirty-four, with a wife and small child, felt insecure. He was no journalistic greenhorn. At sixteen he had broken in on the *Cleveland Press,* advanced through the ranks into N.E.A., and into United Press, and put in a short stint outside the concern as editor of the *Boston Traveler.* Yet never before had he stirred up such a nest of vicious enemies as now in the city of brotherly love. Carey's gang brandished ten additional indictments, and planned to humiliate the editor with separate midnight arrests on each. Rattled, Pew escaped Pennsylvania jurisdiction by going to nearby Atlantic City, New Jersey, to rest up and think.

Pew returned to his desk and renewed his crusade against the "thug magistrate." But the Philly powers-that-be again retaliated fiercely. New indictments were handed down—even naming as a defendant Charles F. Mosher, the Scripps treasurer, back in Cincinnati.

Scripps summoned Pew and his family to Miramar in July 1913, for two weeks of rest and relaxation—and direct counsel from the boss. Their private talks disturbed Scripps. It seemed to him that Pew's courage was seriously undermined by understandable concern for his wife and child.

In the office of a noted Los Angeles internist, John Paul sat bare-chested on a white enameled table while the physician thumped his ribcage, looked down his throat and into his ears, and listened with his stethoscope.

For four months John Paul had been mysteriously ill. He had come home to the ranch sick in February 1913. His father suspected a case of the grippe, ptomaine poisoning from the train table, even shaky nerves because of worry back in Cleveland over his baby coming late. Scripps summoned the family physician, Dr. J. Perry Lewis. The lad soon recovered, then suffered a relapse, and lately had been up and down. Dr. Lewis consulted other doctors and now had brought his patient to the West Coast's top specialist in stomach disorders.

"We consulted with Dr. Millspaugh for some two and a half hours, and also with his associate, Dr. Colliver," Dr. Lewis wrote the parents on May 30, 1913. "We were unable to learn anything especially new." Dr. Lewis posted the letter from California's famous Paso Robles Hot Springs, where he had decided to submit John Paul to a course of baths. The sick man felt well enough to play golf with his physician, and croquet with his wife.

"After careful study," Dr. Lewis added, "I am forced to agree with his illustrious dad that any special strain in assuming business responsibilities would be unwise for some time to come."

Scripps had decreed that John Paul must at least temporarily "live outside the roar and rattle and stupid struggle of active business life." That left brother Jim in a bind. An active editorial chief was needed back in Ohio. Jim reinstated Harry Rickey. Trouble followed. Vainly, Rickey officiously ordered establishment of a ten-dollar-a-week minimum wage for women employees, without consulting John Paul. Jim thought that was all right. But Bob Paine, Rickey's uncle, detected a plot. "Back East," he wrote Scripps, "there is a disposition to consider John as an interloper and to welcome things that signify his lack of authority. Had I been in Jim's place, a year ago, the battlefield would have been strewn with the corpses of the rebels. Failure to massacre the rebels simply meant stronger disregard and defiance of your plans for your sons."

In Detroit Milton McRae pored over his medical books and quizzed specialists about his son-in-law's symptoms. He suggested John Paul should visit the McRaes and see Detroit physicians. Scripps responded: "I expect John to recover but I do not believe he will ever be able to endure the strain of holding the position of editor-in-chief. . . . John can live a long and happy life if he will be wise enough to refrain from undertaking more than he is physically able to do."

Jim began to see he could get little brotherly help at his empire command post. The previous fall he'd praised John Paul for having the "guts" to sit steady and stick to Scripps policies. "But I am getting more onery [sic] and bull-headed," he explained. "Of the three brothers, one will have to be boss — and that will be me!"

Now with John Paul a virtual invalid, Jim took unilateral action to reinforce his one-man rule. He wrote Roy Howard on April 9, 1913, that he had decided to become chairman of the board of United Press, "as in all other Scripps companies. That means everybody steps down a notch." Howard became U.P. president.

Jim readily accepted the perks of kingship. The previous winter he had built a $5,000 house at Miramar, bought a new $5,000 auto, and had taken an $8,000 stock dividend. By the end of 1913 he would raise his monthly salary from $1,500 to $2,500. He did everything he could to avoid travel, running affairs mainly from two convenient offices, one in San Diego, the other in his residence at the ranch.

Bob, seventeen, had been attempting to understudy John Paul in Cleveland when the mystery illness sent them all back to the ranch. He at last had decided on journalism as his "life business." "I have been told," he explained to his father, "that the only way to learn to write is to write. I want to know how to write as well as possible — perhaps books, perhaps newspaper copy . . . to express my ideas fluently." He did not want to return to the *Philadelphia News-Post*.

During the early part of John Paul's crisis, Bob mainly loafed around Miramar, composing poetry and thinking up plots for short stories, and considering tackling the writing of a novel.

In September, John Paul took a grave turn. Scripps telegraphed Milton McRae that his condition had become "serious, perhaps desperate." He lay, thin as a skeleton, in the ranch house at Fanita, feverish and vomiting, his wife, mother, and nurses hovering at bedside. Five physicians had come to consult with Dr. Lewis. Finally, they agreed on a diagnosis — endocarditis, inflammation of the heart valves that stemmed from childhood rheumatic fever. Only Dr. Lewis held out any hope. The other physicians said the case was terminal. Still Scripps summoned another Los Angeles specialist. "All he did was to increase our panic," Scripps wrote J. C. Harper.

Relations between John Paul and his pretty young wife were being shattered by the months of strain. He imagined he was losing his mind, and power of speech. Nurses tattled that he was often in tears after Edith's visits. She was torn between going to Detroit for sister Marie's marriage to the son of Senator William Alden Smith and loyalty to a sick husband. She did not go. (It was a big event. McRae later disclosed, "being a fool once in my life," he spent $11,000 to stage the wedding.)

Scripps's sympathies were with Edith. "I really wanted Edith to go East if John would have given his consent," Scripps wrote her father. "I'm sure Edith has shed many tears. . . . What's going to happen, Mac, if John turns out to be a chronic invalid? You and I know what a miserable life for Edith would result. Edith is so strong physically, so full of vitality and so thoroughly equipped to live in the world of activities and social occupations. . . . Something very like tragedy is imminent." Tragedy was just then hovering over Fanita — but not yet in this sickroom.

A fierce desert wind began raking the Scripps mesa in September, sending the thermometer at Miramar to 112° in the shade. "Since white men have lived in this country," E. W. wrote Dolla, "there has never been such heat. Tremendous brush fires all around. . . . From the housetop we see every night fires climbing in the mountains."

About 8:15 in the evening of October 19, 1913, smoke began rising from the new Fanita barn. Inside were twenty-five saddle horses. Suddenly, flames burst through the roof. Ranch-hands rushed to the rescue as the terrified animals began screaming and kicking in their stalls. Fed by fifty tons of hay and alfalfa stored in the loft, the fire literally exploded the new barn. Twenty horses, including Nackie's thousand-dollar Kentuckians Barbarosa and Julian, were trapped and perished. Only five could be led to safety. The fire raged until 10:30.

Nackie and E. W. rushed to the scene. They could only watch helplessly, grieving over their horses. "Next day, even to think of it gave me the horrors," he later told Dolla. Origin of the fire was uncertain. Scripps hired a detective to check for arson, but no clues were found.

The tragedy soured Scripps on farming. He halted all new work at both ranches. "I issued orders," he told Dolla, "that no one should even speak to me about Fanita Ranch, or anything on it."

At the far-flung outposts of the Scripps publishing empire, everyday life had of necessity to go on as usual, sympathetic but heedless of tragedies on a remote California ranch involving one young man and twenty valuable horses.

At the center of the command post stood Jim, virtually alone. Of every one hundred decisions, perhaps ninety-nine fell to him. Especially the hard and dangerous. He didn't blink. At only twenty-seven, he was now a resolute, if not ruthless, no-nonsense business czar. He dethroned lieutenants when they failed, with little mercy. If a paper struggled too long, he could either build or bury it.

His own "baby," the *Fresno Tribune,* was on the rocks. For seven years it had been a miserable money-loser. Jim looked at the books and saw only bleak prospects. He promised the editor and business manager jobs elsewhere, gave each a week's salary, and on Saturday afternoon, September 29, 1912, killed the *Tribune.* It was the sixth Scripps paper to die; E. W. had killed one, the *San Francisco Report.* Jim had presided at all the other executions.

The struggle that had begun when Jim was in diapers to hoist the Scripps banner on the West Coast had finally after two decades begun to grind up or beat down a number of editors and business managers. Jim didn't want to be heartless, but his knife was quick and sharp. When a man was used up, Jim cut the string. Some failed lieutenants he moved elsewhere; the others he discarded.

Booze and other mischief brought down some Scripps stalwarts. Ham Clark, who had started as a Miramar secretary, and climbed to the top as the cofounder of the Seattle and San Francisco papers, to chairman of United Press, and most recently to general manager of the *Philadelphia News-Post,* pulled a serious gaffe.

E. W. stepped in and showed extraordinary compassion. He excused the misdeed, and permitted the posting of a "bond" with Jim under which Clark guaranteed to stay straight. Editor Marlen Pew's feathers were ruffled, but Scripps tried to smooth them, writing:

> I have always acted on the principle that men who had great faults had also great virtues. This has made me patient with men and caused me to help them try and try again. . . . The only difference between Clark, yourself, and myself is that Clark has one set of weak points and each of us has another. . . . Now don't go to pouting. If I were not capable of having very strong personal affections I would not have had the grit and stamina which has been required so often of me.

At the *Los Angeles Record,* Jim's dissatisfaction forced out both editor and business manager. To fill the void, Jim drafted his own aggressive, intelligent, ambitious executive assistant, Harry L. Schmetzstorff. Ironically, "Smitty" had started as a Miramar secretary but was fired when he took a couple of hours to conduct a Sunday School class for ranch children while a furious Scripps waited to dictate letters.

Schmetzstorff did not lose a single day's pay; Jim, knowing his high calibre, grabbed him to be his own secretary in the town office. In his new lieutenancy at Los Angeles, however, he began his "boss" role awkwardly—throwing his weight around and picking quarrels. He managed to survive only by the skin of his teeth, and then straightened up.

Like his father, Jim wanted a house full of children. In September 1913, Josephine bore his fourth child, Ellen Browning, named for E. W.'s seventy-seven-year-old sister. Jim now had two sons and two daughters, giving the old man five grandchildren. Scripps wrote Dolla about the newest baby. "She has the thickest head of hair I've seen on a child—three times as thick as baby Jack's [one year old]—but instead of red, his hair is almost white."

In Philadelphia the Scripps paper was taking a mean drubbing. Pew could not see even a glimmer of victory. The black hats had the upper hand, having local judges in their clique. "Thug Magistrate" Jimmy Carey threatened that every time his name was printed the editor would be arrested and jailed.

The situation was so desperate that Scripps sent "Northwest Whirlwind" lawyer John Perry to Philadelphia to try to make a compromise. Pew was indignant, and developed an immediate dislike for his lawyer.

Scripps cautioned Pew that Philadelphia offered "a golden reef of opportunities" for newspaper crusades and that he should take care to not "hunt for trouble, or pick quarrels" at random, but "always choose those opportunities that are fitted to your size and strength and not those that will strain your resources, nervous, mental and financial."

But the Scripps paper's worst handicap in the fight against the libel arrests proved to be Pew himself. Suddenly, the moody editor weakened and decided to try to settle the case himself. Pew began to suspect "secret plots" against him. He ranted against his Scripps associates and fired angry telegrams to Miramar. They arrived at the height of John Paul's crisis in October 1913. Even while fearful that his son was dying—or perhaps because of that—Scripps could be forgiving and compassionate in response to abuse from his editor in Philadelphia. He wrote Perry:

I do not care what he says concerning me, my son, and my friends. . . . Whatever wrong he may do . . . will be solely because of a mistaken judgment, not because of any malice. . . . Pew is just one of those men so finely strung that we practical fellows built of common clay are not able to understand.

Pew finally, in December 1913, threw a tantrum that wrecked a compromise settlement the lawyers were working out, handed in his resignation, and left Philadelphia. No one tried to stop him. Even Scripps had to concede Pew "acted a fool."

Tempers flared in the sickroom at the ranch. John Paul lay in his bed, cringing and resentful, under a blast of stern criticism from his father. Edith stood by, glaring at E. W. Nackie was there, too, and violently angry at her husband.

The episode had its start a few weeks after Christmas. Unaccountably, John Paul had brightened and grown stronger, strong enough to get back on his feet. Both he and Edith saw a chance for an outing from ranch confinement. It was January 1914. They drove into San Diego to stay overnight with Edith's parents and sister Helen who had rented the town house for the winter. A severe storm broke, bringing a deluge that washed out roads, trapping the young couple for eight days in San Diego. John Paul came back to the ranch almost helpless.

That led to Scripps's tirade. E. W. made clear he felt Edith's whims were retarding her husband's recovery. He chastised John Paul for making the foolish journey. Nackie listened, white-faced; and later in private, in turn, roundly scolded her husband for unkind behavior.

Scripps mulled it over, and then called for his secretary. Perhaps he could write out his views, and John Paul would better understand. "Your mother says when I talk to you I speak too loud and harshly, and that I argue too much." That was the start of a four-page letter which went on to explain that the father thought John Paul actually was suffering from neurasthenia, and would eventually recover. But Scripps was convinced that his son had been poisoned against Dr. Lewis—a transparent slap at the McRae family—and "for a long time past you have been acting as your own physician, taking or rejecting medicine offered and advice given." Such decisions surely were beyond the scope of John Paul's limited medical expertise. Scripps wanted him and Edith to follow the father's counsel.

"Only do one thing or the other. Let me attend to the case altogether, or let someone else take the case, engage another doctor, and become wholly responsible. I assure you that I shall be glad to place at the disposal of this person my home, my fortune, and the personal services of myself and your mother."

The sickroom ordeal was fraying the old man's nerves. A few days later he blew up again—not at John Paul but at Jim. It had suddenly come to light in the Cincinnati Central Office that Scripps had overdrawn his 1913 profits by $120,000. It was suggested he cut his Miramar drafts to $10,000 a month.

E. W. reacted angrily, dictating a stern letter accusing Jim of being the real family spendthrift—by withdrawing for himself a $300,000 increment based on the year's profits. "Perhaps you should have taken out only $100,000. With that and your $30,000, you are well paid to handle everything in sight. If you don't want to do it, I will accept your resignation, and get somebody at half the price." He conceded Jim did a good job, but said he would have been satisfied with 75 percent less profit. "The whole family should operate on $60,000 a year. I don't want to be nagged at, or put under a family guardianship. The less I hear of this, the better."

Wisely, Scripps held back that letter. Then he sat up from midnight to dawn talking to Nackie about their family troubles. Next morning he toned down the letter. Jim, however, received both the "unofficial" version and the revise. He made no move to quit but handled the clash adroitly, soothing his father's injured pride.

Jim promised "a more strenuous effort" to adapt himself to E. W.'s ideas. He mentioned that the papers currently were coping with a business depression. "This is a very poor time for anybody to be wandering around loose, without being well supplied with a cool head, lots of guts, and confidence." Jim said he had all that, and felt he could make decisions as well as anybody in the concern, and would take a backseat to none of his men.

He agreed to limit the increment to $100,000, and asked permission to give $25,000 of it to Bob. "I want to force Bob to learn what the business is, and then to apply himself to it. A piece of the pie may have this effect on Bob. . . . He doesn't want to specialize as either a business man or an editor, but wants to become a 'publisher' or a 'general.' "

Once again came a crisis in the sickroom. John Paul was sinking. It was decided to take him to a specialist in San Francisco. Scripps ordered a private railroad car. Just then thunderstorms swept the coast, washing out miles of railroad tracks. It was expected to take at least two weeks to repair the line to San Francisco. All they could do was wait—and pray.

Then out of the blue the harried and distraught father got another jolt. Bob was responsible.

By happenstance Scripps came across a torrid love poem Bob had written. The old man concluded the boy, now eighteen and a half, could only have meant it for Helen McRae. Edith's sister was pretty, about twenty-three, and had recently broken her engagement to a wealthy young man in Cleveland because she found him a dullard. Scripps sized her up as a brazen flirt.

By subtle means, E. W. tried to ascertain whether there were romantic ties between her and Bob. He sent Helen a note requesting a copy of the poem on the pretext of keeping a collection of Bob's work. Helen side-stepped, suggesting father obtain a copy from son. That convinced Scripps the more experienced Helen was using her wiles as an adventuress to lure his son into sexual trysts. But he was too involved in John Paul's desperate fight to live to do little more at the moment than fret about the romance.

The private car was able on March 2, to roll north with John Paul, virtually skin and bones. A week later the car brought him back from the Adler Sanitarium. Roy Howard, at Miramar for a business conference, summed up the situation in a succinct telegram to a colleague back east: "John back. It's hopeless."

Then the case took another bizarre turn. Scripps had always ridiculed his wife's enthrallment with the "miracle cures" of Christian Science. Now he suggested Nackie and Edith call in a Christian Science practitioner. They did. Scripps wrote a Denver friend, Judge Ben B. Lindsey:

> I am enough of a psychologist, or even what professionals call psychic, to fully comprehend and make use of what the medical profession call mental therapy.
>
> I have not to be a Christian Scientist to fully appreciate the value to John of the fact that three large forceful women who are his constant attendants are imbued with a conviction that their patient not only can get well but will get well. The mental and spiritual atmosphere of John's surroundings are ideally wholesome. There is real cheerfulness—not make-believe or forced.
>
> On the other hand, the doctor and I stand by watching conditions and making the best possible use of them. Without remonstrance, the ladies permit the doctor to administer anodynes and stimulants in cases of necessity, and on the other hand, the doctor is willing that the ladies should recognize in him a friend, though a blind and mistaken one, and that they should attribute rather to the powers of their own cult than to his medicines any fortunate developments.

The dark angel was even then hovering over the ranch. However, his inexorable shadow fell not then on the sickroom, but on the ranch road just outside. On March 17, a four-horse hitch was bringing in a load of cordwood. A ranch motorcycle whizzed by, spraying dust and frightening the team. The horses ran away, stopping only in a tangle of harness when they smashed the wagon up against Jim's garage. Rushing out, Jim discovered the teamster, W. I. Mossholder, sprawled in the road, unconscious. Jim tried to give first aid, but the man died in fifteen minutes, stunning the ranch.

John Paul continued to waste away. For hours at a time he clutched his mother's hand, and turned wounded eyes on his young wife. Scripps frequently sat at his bedside, anguished that this son was not yet even twenty-six. Little Jack, eighteen months old, was brought in from time to time.

On the evening of April 22, 1914, Scripps went into the sickroom. John Paul lay in a coma, barely breathing. Scripps sat down beside Nackie and Edith and the nurse. Dr. Lewis came in and out. They kept their vigil through the long night. At daybreak Jim came in and sat with them. The sad hours dragged on.

Shortly after 9 A.M. Jim emerged from John Paul's room, and beckoned his secretary. "Send this telegram to all the relatives and our editors and business managers: 'My brother died at nine o'clock this morning.' "

25

A Sort of Barbarian from the West

Fierce summer thunderstorms were tormenting Washington, D.C. Outside his hotel window the damp pavement glistened when Scripps stirred on the morning of Wednesday, July 1, 1914. The old man sat on the edge of the bed growling instructions to his secretary while pulling on a pair of boots. The gloomy, still-threatening sky depressed him. Tuesday's downpour had caught and drenched him. He already was in a state of anxiety over personal troubles. His head ached and his stomach was queasy. After being gone nine weeks from his California ranch, he was as grouchy as an old grizzly, and homesick.

The phone rang. Handing it to him, the secretary said it was the White House.

"Sir," said the caller, "this is Joseph Tumulty, private secretary to President Wilson. The President would like you to have lunch with him today."

"No," Scripps snapped in a gravelly voice. "I wouldn't take lunch with anybody!"

Abruptly he hung up. Slapping on his dark velvet beret, he lighted up a Santa Fe and began puffing vigorously, glaring angrily at the world in general.

Gradually the enormity of his gaffe dawned on him. Harried and restless, he went to the window and stared out on the misty street. Scripps appeared unusually hulking and bear-like, with his wide sloping shoulders, bull neck, and massive head with wispy graying hair. The impression of giant size was bolstered by the loose fit of his tailored but baggy suit. Showing marked disdain for the niceties of fashion, he still was wont to sprinkle ashes on his vest and stain his ties with dribbled eggs or gravy. On this trip, his first east of the Rockies in ten years, he was discovering that strangers regarded him as "a sort of barbarian — respectable as such, but nevertheless troublesomely uncouth and abnormal."

His dark, wide-set eyes doubtless flashed as he turned to his secretary and his whisker-flanked mouth looked savage as he demanded to know what was delaying his breakfast.

Reporting the episode later to sister Ellen, Scripps wrote: "As I hadn't had my breakfast, I was in no amiable mood. . . . After I had concluded my breakfast . . . I wondered if I hadn't committed some terrible breach of etiquette. I was a little disturbed and felt like damning [Secretary of State William Jennings] Bryan and [Secretary of the Interior Franklin K.] Lane for asking the President to see me."

The death of John Paul had largely triggered Scripps's decision to come east, to escape the sad memories and scene of the tragedy. He brought anger with him. He was still furious over Bob's affair with Helen McRae, outraged especially that it flamed while the rest of the family grieved at John Paul's deathbed. That girl was nothing but a sex-pot adventuress taking advantage of an inexperienced boy! Scripps had ordered Bob to break off the romance and wait until twenty-one to consider marriage. Bob, desperately infatuated, was also defiant. He exploded in anger, and refused to quit seeing the girl. They were, however, separated. Her father banished Helen to the East, in the "custody" of relatives.

But the unrequited Bob, a "prisoner" on the ranch, angrily feuded with his father — and their quarrel continued by mail as Scripps travelled across country to Chicago, New York, Baltimore, and now Washington. Moreover, Bob was balking at an order from Jim to at once begin learning the ropes to succeed the dead brother. All this trouble kept the old man in turmoil.

With frequent and deep changes of mood, Scripps suffered spells of neurasthenia, described medically as nervous exhaustion. He regarded the affliction a deserved and malignant legacy from his libido-driven escapades of bachelor days, and possibly aggravated by hard drinking. He also was a heavy cigar smoker — up to thirty a day; but they were such mild Santa Fes that he tried to rationalize that they soothed rather than assaulted his nerves.

Scripps was worried, too, that his marriage of three decades was souring. His wife was decidedly — and vocally — unhappy. Scripps complained in May to Ellen that Nackie "is absolutely incapable of feeling sympathy, or interest in, my work." [That had not always been true.] Often they were now at odds over how to deal with the children, including Bob. To cheer up Nackie, E. W. suggested they sail to Europe for a six-weeks vacation. She was not interested. He lamented to Ellen that they were "drifting apart." He wrote in June to his lawyer: "Mrs. Scripps and I had a serious talk last night and arrived at no conclusion."

Travelling with them was Nackey, sixteen and sprightly. She had a health problem of no small dimension. She suffered a heredity blight, a slightly crooked eye, and poor vision. On this trip east the father intended to have corrective surgery performed. But a Chicago ophthalmologist kept the Scrippses sitting an hour in the waiting room, and the old man finally got up and stalked out. Other surgeons in Baltimore subsequently decided any operation on Nackey's eye should wait a year or two.

Two men high on Scripps's list of people to see in the East were Charles R. Crane, the millionaire Chicago brass and plumbing manufacturer, and Norman Hapgood, editor of the historic *Harper's Weekly*. Scripps had been corresponding for about a year with Crane about freedom of the press and expression, the rights of workers, social and political reform. He had joined Crane and a few other tycoons who were subsidizing *Harper's Weekly* to assure Hapgood an open forum for his liberal views. From California Scripps had sent two of his publishing experts to New York where they promptly whittled the weekly magazine's annual deficit from $185,000 to $60,000. Crane eagerly joined Scripps in pushing the Chicago ad-less experiment which he saw as the newspaper wave of the future, imploring E. W. to immediately start another such in Washington where he felt a truly free newspaper was urgently needed.

That was something for Scripps to think over—later. He had been pleased to find the *Chicago Day Book* now almost breaking even, and felt that within eighteen months it might be out of the red. He boasted to Lincoln Steffens: "It should be comparatively easy for other men, younger and hence more vigorous, to establish other such papers. . . . I would feel then that despite all my shortcomings I shall have done a big man's big life work, when, if ever, I shall have demonstrated that the people can have a free press, not only without having it subsidized or endowed, but a free press that will not only support but magnificently reward those who conduct its various units."

Although the ad-less venture currently was Scripps's Topic A, he had other eccentric irons in the fire, or ready to pop in. One idea broached to Crane was to establish a correspondence society composed of intellectuals or "anonymous altruists" who would communicate with each other on a confidential basis. He wanted Jane Addams to be a member and went to Hull House to talk to her about it. Scripps desired as members men and women "who have distinguished themselves in some branch of altruistic work," or those of considerable learning who were willing to make themselves publicly useful, or unselfish rich or experienced leaders, those progressives eager to devote their energies "to society as a whole" to improve or substitute "new customs for old."

His candidates for this undertaking, besides himself, Crane, and Jane Addams were Ida Tarbell, Judge Ben Lindsey, Gifford Pinchot, Rudolph Spreckels, Colonel William Nelson, Lincoln Steffens, Professor Charles E. Merriam, Professor Thorstein Veblen, William Jennings Bryan, Francis J. Heney, Roger W. Babson, educator Anna Morgan, and Clarence Darrow.

Despite earnest talks with Darrow, Jane Addams, and Crane, no spark was generated. Scripps wrote sister Ellen: "Of course, all of them were polite enough to say they considered it a promising idea. However, they didn't overwhelm me with their enthusiasm."

On his sixtieth birthday—June 18—Scripps took time to offer sage fatherly advice to love-smitten Bob. He tried to jar the boy into new thought, writing: "You have determined to live for Bob Scripps. My new institution can only be trusted in the hands of a man or men who will be ever ready to sacrifice themselves for the service of others—those who number themselves by the millions; who are not clever; who are not even possessed of common sense; who are vulgar and base, and wretched."

More to the point, he wrote: "Many lives that might have been otherwise great and useful, have been wrecked—not by some woman or women, but by those men who allowed themselves to be governed by too much passion, sexual or other. All in good time you will have grown and developed into manhood. . . . You can give your wife a home and support her . . . by your own efforts instead of having nothing . . . except what you have received as a gift. . . . The joy of life consists not in reaching summits, but in struggling up to them."

But the message in no way cooled Bob's ardor, or his rebellion.

When the Scripps party finally reached Washington the last week in June, Gilson Gardner, the chief Scripps correspondent in the capital, met them and arranged interviews with dignitaries E. W. wanted to see. Scripps conferred with Secretary of State Bryan, Secretary of the Interior Lane, Louis Brandeis, later to become Associate Justice of the Supreme Court, and several congressmen. "You know how prone I am to damn Jews," Scripps wrote a Jewish banker friend in San Diego. "I tell you that by far the biggest man I have seen since I left San Diego is a

Jew — Louis Brandeis. Last night there were some six or seven congressmen in my room with Brandeis. He was head and shoulders above every one of them; and what is more they all knew it and treated him with the deference that I felt fully his due."

Bryan did not overly impress Scripps, though he considered him "good . . . a man of the people." The publisher turned down the Secretary of State's invitation to lunch, but talked with him two or three times at the hotel. Scripps called on Lane at his office and the two were so captivated with each other that the fifteen-minute appointment stretched into an hour and a half asorbing conversation.

It was not Scripps's purpose to engage in idle gossip; he was trying to "sell" an idea he thought could correct a serious shortcoming of the Wilson Administration. In Scripps's view there still existed some "feeling of distrust of a college president" that had surfaced in the 1912 Presidential campaign. Even Scripps had originally preferred Senator Robert M. LaFollette over Wilson. Now, however, he felt it was bad for the country to be kept in ignorance of "the human and humane side of the President." The Administration was making a mistake in failing to differentiate between the press that was friendly and that which was antagonistic toward the White House. Wilson was, in fact, favoring "those newspapers and those journalistic institutions that were primarily and fundamentally antipathetic to him."

To overcome that, Wilson should add to his cabinet a "Secretary of the People" — a skilled and respected journalist who could serve as a useful information conduit between the President and his cabinet and the press, the friendly as well as the unfriendly.

Both Bryan and Lane liked the scheme. They suggested Scripps propose it directly to the President. Scripps shook his head. They ought to sell it to him. Scripps mentioned Norman Hapgood as a candidate for Secretary of the People. Both Bryan and Lane viewed the *Harper's Weekly* editor as too similar in style to the President, lacking the friendliness and warmth the post would demand. Scripps then volunteered to seek a candidate among his own top news executives.

"I impressed on him [Bryan] the fact that our institutions, newspapers and affiliates, coupled with the United Press, was such an organ as would make it impossible to keep the people in ignorance of any subject that the Administration wanted the people informed about."

Gilson Gardner also urged him to carry the proposal directly to President Wilson. But Scripps, stubborn and irritated, declined.

Despite intermittent squalls, Scripps gallantly hired a chauffeur and a big touring car to take Nackie sightseeing. Gardner, going along, looked askance at the darkening sky and suggested putting up the curtains. Scripps permitted them to be put up on his wife's side, but not on his. Since childhood he had gloried in watching storms.

His decision was a mistake—for a thunderstorm struck them suddenly and savagely. "The rain poured down, the lightning seemed to strike all around us, and the thunder was frightful, and Nackie came as near having hysterics as I ever saw her," he reported to Ellen. Scripps grabbed the spare curtain and he and Gardner held it up against the rain. By the time the car reached the hotel, both men were "drenched to the skin, but Nackie was perfectly dry."

Then the very next morning came the momentus luncheon invitation from the White House—and its surly rejection.

But some wise person at the Executive Mansion made a considered move that would rescue Scripps, and erase his terribly embarrassing faux pas.

After his nasty "no," Scripps for half an hour paced back and forth in his hotel room, unable to "shake off the feeling of uncomfortableness." Then the phone rang again. Tumulty was calling back.

"This time he asked me," Scripps wrote Ellen, "if I would call on the President at eleven-fifteen. As I had an hour to get dressed and compose myself, I replied that I would call."

Not knowing how to get into the White House, he summoned Gilson Gardner to escort him, and entered the President's office precisely at 11:15 A.M.

"I have got another confession to make," Scripps told his sister. "For the first time in my life, I believe, I was stumped and embarrassed, and sat like a ninny for a moment or two until the President started to talk; but we were only a few minutes getting to the subject I knew he wanted to talk about."

Wilson readily conceded his academic background had proven a handicap. "He stated he felt the public's attitude had always been affected by this feeling of distrust of a college president."

The two talked alone fifteen minutes. Scripps had expected to find the Chief Executive "not only stiff in manner, but depleted in health and nerves. On the contrary, he was almost as genial as Secretary Lane himself. Physically he seems to be well set up, and almost stocky. His hand is full and warm, and his hand pressure, if not vigorous, is at least strong enough."

The President confessed he recognized the deficiencies of his Administration. "He regretted that the official pressures had been so great on him that he had not been able to get out amongst the people and talk to them and meet them face to face. He complained that the pressure on his time was so great that he had to 'do his thinking on the run.' "

Wilson was quite enthusiastic about the idea of having a journalistic representative. "We discussed the names of several candidates. He coincided with the view of Bryan and Lane that Norman Hapgood was not the warm-blooded individual that was needed for this position."

They finally left the idea to be discussed further by the Cabinet. Scripps suggested the President send an envoy to his ranch if the White House wanted assistance in trying to find the right man for the job.

"The most I can say," Scripps told the President, "is that this Administration, no matter what its faults are, is so much superior to its probable successor that the people of the United States ought to know about it. They ought to know more about the commonplaceness and the frailties even of the President, in order that they can appreciate him, and perhaps love him."

Getting "somewhat carried away," Scripps volunteered to Wilson that he was "probably the greatest president since Lincoln." Perhaps Lincoln's paramount good fortune had been that "those around him were successful in making him known to the public more as a human being than as a superman."

Wilson's reaction to this praise was "to grin delightedly."

Scripps concluded his report to Ellen: "President Wilson thanked me and the gentlemen of the Scripps concern for our fair treatment of his Presidency and help in the 1912 campaign. When I felt that I had said everything that I had to say, I got up myself, took my hat, shook hands with him and said goodbye."

Later Scripps rehashed the abortive beginning of the episode with Gardner. "Did I really do an awful thing in refusing to take lunch with the President?"

Gardner mulled over the question for a minute or two. "No . . . but I think you made a record. Probably no other man has refused to take lunch with the President when asked."

In a moment Gardner dropped his dubious frown and smiled. "Well, Mr. Scripps, perhaps that's a very good record for you to make."

Scripps had now been on the road almost ten weeks. He felt fagged out, and anxious to go home. He summoned his secretary. "Get our private car ready." Next day the Scripps entourage rolled out of Union Station, westbound. In a matter of a few days, Scripps could expect to once more resume his hermit life on the rattlesnake mesa that afforded such an inspiring and restful view of the limitless reaches of the blue Pacific.

26

The Tomboy Who Tamed Kangaroo Rats

n January 1915, Nackey was poised to go 3,500 miles to Washington, D.C., to enroll in the fashionable Miss Madeira's School. Scripps wanted to send along her saddle horse. "My daughter," he wrote Miss Lucy Madeira, "has been riding since she was four or five. I would like her to devote a few hours riding each day with a lady companion and a groom . . . in the open air." Miss Madeira said no. Riding was dangerous in Washington because of "many accidents" due to automobiles.

That episode was typical of the overly protective "little-girl" restraints Scripps still exercised although his daughter was now sixteen and a half, and emerging rapidly into free-spirited womanhood. To the father she was still only an untamed tomboy, riding at a gallop in rough garb, learning to manage the ranch as the boys had done. Shamelessly, father indulged her whims. He gloried that she loved the outdoors and its creatures—horses, cows, cats, dogs, birds, and chickens. He bragged to friends that she had trained into house pets shy little kangaroo rats and lizard-like horned toads.

Her formal schooling had come chiefly from private tutors at the ranch. Now he was sending her—with great trepidation—to an eastern school to get some of the rough edges knocked off, smooth up her education, and take her away from the muck of the stables for a whiff of pink teas and the drawing room. To his sorrow, life-long misogyny blinded Scripps to quite clear signals that his spoiled daughter was under too tight a rein—troubled and restless, adventuresome, and as willful and headstrong as her despotic father.

Scripps should have been alert to even the slightest hint of revolt for he was still struggling to quell a long and wild rebellion by his eighteen-year-old youngest son. For eight months Bob had been in the throes of a mad passion for Helen McRae. Scripps kept the lovers apart. He vowed to disown his son if he married before age twenty-one. Moreover, he warned he would prosecute anyone who dared help the teenage swain get married. Helen refused to elope, wisely demanding Bob secure parental permission. This romantic furor abated little.

In a quite different way, Nackey, too, was beginning to question her father's autocracy. Her revolt was subtle and secret, slow to congeal, but braver and destined to be more explosive than Bob's. Scripps was convinced his youngsters were so "utterly helpless" it was "necessary for me to think for all of you." He knew he and his "little girl" were not on the same wave length. He begged her to confide in him "everything that you possibly can. I am more interested in knowing what you are thinking than in what you are doing. We have had small chance to talk to each other."

Scripps lived in self-imposed exile on his mesa. He was lonely and moody. "I have become a sort of hitching post," he lamented, "to which is tied everybody else's troubles." He did not again stir off the ranch until there came in early January 1915 another death in the immediate family. It was his brother Will, the irascible printer who back in the early Detroit days had taught the Rushville yokel the case and how to kick a Gordon press, and had been a frequent newspaper partner until their bitter quarrel over brother George's rich estate. Nevertheless, E. W. attended seventy-five-year-old Will's funeral at Pasadena, California.

Only a few days later Nackey started east aboard the *California Limited,* escorted by her mother and brother Bob. They left father wrestling with a fresh child-rearing problem. This time it was arranging a new home for Dolla. Miss Bancroft had recently died. That left her Haddonfield institution no longer ideal for the retarded girl's custody. Dolla, now twenty-five, had just thrown a tantrum, causing her nurse's discharge. Next her companion of eight years, Edith Pollock, resigned, pleading "shattered nerves." Scripps dreaded having to bring Dolla to Miramar. He decided to build a house where she could live alone with her own staff of servants. In San Diego "she would attract too much attention." So he sought a site north of the ranch, toward Los Angeles, to give her, in addition to privacy, access to "theatres and musical entertainments she is so fond of."

Scripps had arranged for Dolla's physician, Dr. Henry J. Berkley of Baltimore, to also look after Nackey. When she enrolled January 11, at Miss Madeira's, Dr. Berkley came over, found her fit, and arranged to check her over at the school once a month. Then the physician accompanied Nackie and Bob on to New Jersey to see Dolla. Her condition was good. Dr. Berkley introduced the Baltimore R.N. he had employed as Dolla's new live-in attendant.

She was Katherine Steelman, thirty-four, a stern spinster and graduate of Johns Hopkins University nursing school. Nackie instantly liked her. Nurse Steelman would attend Dolla but a few months. Then Scripps would hire her as a companion for Nackey. After about a year she would leave Miramar. Then a full decade later Fate would bring her unexpectedly back — by way of Shanghai — into the bosom of the family as a quixotic and controversial figure. The grim-faced nurse was destined to become Nackie's nemesis — and to wield bizarre and incredible influence over Scripps in his final days.

Nackey was unhappy at Miss Madeira's. She was unaccustomed to routine and discipline. Classroom confinement frustrated her. Books tired her eyes. She wearied of trudging up and down to her third-floor room. Few of her sixty-five fellow students seemed to take to the ranch girl. "I have made about six friends," she lamented. Father and daughter exchanged a stream of letters. His were lengthy, thorough, meant to supply helpful counsel. But the dialogue turned quarrelsome. Scripps made an early mistake of criticizing her poor spelling. "I have a headache from using the dictionary," she retorted. Father quickly backed off. "Darling, work the dictionary when you write other people, but let everything go when you write me."

From distant Washington, daughter felt an urge to advise father. "Go riding with mother, or take long walks. You don't take half enough exercise. You always keep it in mind that you are sixty years old and therefore an ancient, but men of seventy have been known to walk. And then I don't believe you apriciate [sic] Miramar or you wouldn't always be talking of going away. . . . If you would take a walk every evening just after the sun had gone down and everything was kind of purple and misty and beautiful, you would see how perfectly lovly [sic] Miramar realy [sic] is. I don't believe you know it at all."

Scripps conceded he should perhaps walk more. He might also go out alone on a gentle horse; but to ride with Nackie made him too nervous. "Your mother holds the reins so slack she could easily make her horse stumble." He commented on the scenery:

> I used to see purple sunsets and was once fairly acquainted with sunrise. There was a time when mountain and sea, foothills and mesa, and green valleys talked to me pleasantly. In those days green trees and shrubs, wild flowers, and all sorts of creeping and climbing and running and flying things were companions.
>
> It is not my sixty-one years that has shut out all these pleasures. Care

and anxiety and lack of sympathetic companionship—and worse still, that of freedom to be alone—have worked to shut out pleasant sounds and sights, and to bar me even from reverie.

Nackey became angry over her father's treatment of the hired companion she had left behind, a Miss Twelker. Scripps found the girl out riding with a groom, and fired her. It was difficult to rebut Nackey's cry that that punishment was cruel and unjust. He tried to explain to his daughter there had always been temptation for ranch men in being unable to tell "the difference between women who are thoroughly bad and those who are thoroughly foolish." Scripps habitually warned new hired hands, including his recent new secretary, Tom Meanley, that employees must not socialize with ranch females. Meanley was young, tall and handsome, and lively. Pointedly, Scripps advised him that the ban on fraternization "absolutely applies to my daughter."

By spring, Nackey was totally disenchanted with her school and begged to come home. Father resisted, and then gave in, assigning his Washington correspondent Gilson Gardner and Mrs. Gardner to bring the girl home via steamship.

Once back at Miramar, Nackey jumped on her horse and raced "all over the ranch, coming in only at meals and at bedtime." Lucy Madeira sharply criticized him for letting the girl quit school. He replied it was "impossible" for Miss Madeira to understand "the torture and isolation" Nackey had felt at being separated from "the dumb animals she loves." But the father fully understood. "I recall," he wrote Miss Madeira, "after my first long six months in the city, I took a long tramp in the country where I found a clump of real wild trees growing as they pleased. I stopped and hugged the trees."

Although in true retirement from business, isolated at his remote ranch, plagued by gritty domestic rebellion, and now suffering mysterious stomach pain, Scripps nonetheless kept close tabs on two of his newspaper babies—the *Chicago Day Book* and the *Philadelphia News-Post.*

The dark angel hovered over the anemic Philly penny paper at the end of the summer of 1914. It already had eaten up $100,000. Scripps sadly observed that no paper could succeed if the editor failed to grow and lead his staff. "Might as well try to make a man out of a few buckets of dirt and water, as to try to make a newspaper out of a printing plant, white paper, a lot of mechanics, and men who write things. The editor is to the newspaper what the vital spark of life is to a human being. When the vital spark of man goes out, you have got a corpse; when the editor of a newspaper does not exist, you have got a junk heap."

Rather viciously, the father struck Jim in a sore spot, saying he was "as well content" in Philadelphia as with his investments "in Fresno and Oakland"—both horrendous debacles. "I can afford to pay my son's tuition bills. I shall not squeal or even complain if you make the tuition bills in Philadelphia much larger than they already have been."

This cutting remark obviously helped bring Jim to a decision. Secretly he got together the coffin and black crepe for the seventh funeral of a Scripps newspaper. Out of the blue, on Monday, September 28, 1914, the *News-Post* business manager opened an official telegram:

CLOSE PLANT IMMEDIATELY PERIOD   ALL EMPLOYEES WHO ARE LEGALLY ENTITLED TO PART OR FULL WEEK'S SALARY ON ACCOUNT OF NON-NOTICE SATURDAY SHOULD BE PAID PERIOD   AVOID ATTACHMENT SUITS FOR WAGES.

Scripps accepted philosophically the demise of the Philadelphia paper after a life span of but twenty-seven months. In Chicago his experimental ad-less staggered on, its cost already $125,000. Scripps still had $40,000 left in the *Day Book* kitty. He was blowing hot and cold on the paper. In April 1914, he found it good reading, bright, humor-filled. "If it proves out," he told Cochran, "the concern would probably concentrate its whole financial force on a scientifically-organized campaign of new ad-less newspapers."

A year later he felt keen disappointment. The paper printed "too much propaganda." He had decided that only 1 percent of the proletariat "wants to think—99 percent want to be entertained." He lamented its low circulation—barely 19,000. His disgust was justified. Compared to other Chicago dailies, *Day Book* circulation was a joke. In the afternoon field the *Chicago Daily News* had 405,375, the *American* 378,941, the *Journal* 124,524, and the *Post* 62,141. The *Tribune,* with 354,250 daily and 558,396 Sunday, was the dominant A.M.

The ad-less philosophy largely had created the bond between Scripps and Charles R. Crane; now they had little direct contact. Mainly they communicated through Crane's aide-de-camp Walter S. Rogers. Helping the liberal *Harper's Weekly* had begun to weary Crane. Scripps's economy experts had drastically trimmed the subsidy it needed to stay alive. Editor Norman Hapgood went to California to confer with Scripps. "The days I spent at Miramar," Hapgood wrote on the train returning to New York, "have been the most stimulating of my life." Even so, *Harper's* continued downhill.

His exposure to magazine publishing, though scant, intrigued

Scripps. He thought this might be a new field for him. He sounded out Ray Long, successful editor of *Redbook* and other Hearst magazines. Long, who would go on to become a giant among magazine editors, had known Scripps as a reporter on the Cincinnati *Post.* Long gave serious thought to starting a new magazine in the fall of 1915 under the Scripps banner. "We could buy *Harper's,*" Long wrote Scripps, May 27, 1915. "Crane is tired of pouring money down a rathole [*sic*]. It's dying of dullness."

Ray Stannard Baker, a top writer at *American Magazine,* asked Scripps and others to back him in starting an ad-less weekly rural magazine. Scripps was not interested. It already had dawned on him that magazines had to "waste" a lot of revenue in soliciting first-time subscribers.

Scripps got involved in Max Eastman's new radical weekly magazine *The Masses.* Lincoln Steffens and Amos Pinchot were soliciting funds to cover the organ's $9,000 annual deficit. Scripps kicked in $1,500 — and also gave Eastman an earful. Studying the magazine's books, Scripps was able to put his finger on a few mistakes. Though Eastman paid nothing for articles from his stable of twenty-two important liberal writers, he did not break even; circulation was stagnant; the weekly's focus was not on the downtrodden, but America's elite. "You haven't got one chance in a thousand to pay your own way," Scripps wrote. "I am not a Socialist, but I consider the end you have in view is, to all practical purposes, the same end I have in view."

Eastman, who initially had been rather stiff toward Scripps, suddenly was impressed. "Your letter," he responded, "is as interesting as any I ever read. It confirms what I have just found out in studying the same figures." Eastman also conceded the thrust of his weekly was out of focus. "*The Masses* falls into an empty hole between the non-Socialist and the Party machinery, appealing to neither." Eastman lost no time taking the train west for a personal conference at Miramar.

Eastman asked E. W. to nominate from his organization a business manager for *The Masses.* Scripps begged off. "It was once said," he told Eastman, "that my papers were 'edited in Heaven and business-managed in Hell.' " Confessing he frequently in the past employed business managers "who only played the game," he could think of none unselfish enough to serve *The Masses.*

"As you know, I am not a Socialist," he repeated. "This is not because I lack sympathy with the Socialist motive. It is because I am convinced, rightly or wrongly, that altruism, which is almost universal, is still almost universally a minor motive in man."

Eastman's best bet, Scripps said quite seriously, would be to find a successful twenty-dollar newsboy or carrier. "Such a youngster would have had to learn what kind of people want a certain kind of paper, and how to get them. Any man who can sell papers can sell advertising, too. A good salesman can sell one thing as well as another."

Scripps investigated the potential for an ad-less daily in Washington. He polled some of his senior men. Everyone thought a paper there would have to be twice as large as the *Day Book,* and thus sell for two cents. It would require "a true genius" as editor, and not the usual fifteen-dollar reporters but several $10,000-a-year writers. The subsidy would have to be about $60,000 a year. "It wouldn't pay for itself in ten years," Scripps wrote Crane.

The biggest drawback, however, was that its focus hardly could be the customary blue-collar crowd. In the nation's capital the dollar-a-day working men were tremendously outnumbered by the resident officials, politicians, bureaucrats, and their ilk. "It would only be a public service sacrifice," Scripps concluded. Crane accepted his reasoning. Scripps thought New York still offered a good field for a non-advertising paper. In late 1915 he was telling Jim they might tackle New York "in the next two or three years." They agreed the next ad-less would have to sell for two cents.

By the spring of 1916 Crane "has had enough of *Harper's,*" Rogers wrote Scripps. "Not only does the paper continue to lose lots of money [$100,000 in the last year] but it fails to gain in influence. . . . Neg Cochran offers to bet that within six months Hapgood and his friends will place the blame on Mr. Crane. . . . I have already seen signs of such a face-saving maneuver." No one wanted to buy the magazine. Crane arranged a merger with the liberal *The Independent.* "When all the bills are paid," Rogers said, "nearly half a million dollars will have vanished in the *Harper's* undertaking."

Crane, however, was philosophical, "hoping that some good comes out of the *Harper's* experience." Writing Scripps on the run aboard the Pennsylvania's Broadway Limited on May 8, 1916, Crane added: "I hope this does not break our personal relationship. I am always interested in the things you and your organization are doing."

For nine months Woodrow Wilson ignored Scripps's suggestion that a "Secretary of the People" be added to the Cabinet to facilitate the shy President's relations with the press. Then abruptly in March 1915, Secretary of the Interior Franklin K. Lane came to Miramar to stir the pot.

"The President would like you to personally assist him in this function," Lane said. Scripps was surprised.

"I was amused and shocked by Lane's suggestion that I myself should go to Washington," Scripps reported later to Bob Paine. "Rumor, working at long distance, had credited me with qualities a thousand times magnified, and some that did not exist. . . . Wilson thinks I am a much greater man than I really am. The only way to not shatter the reputation that others had made for me was to hold my tongue and look wise. But I could not do that."

It was not E. W.'s desire to get his newspapers a journalistic edge inside the White House, nor merely to polish Wilson's public image, but rather to unselfishly create a better link between the people and the Presidency. Scripps had already emphasized this to Lane and the President during his July 1914 trip to Washington. Now to Lane he reiterated his aim. He volunteered to send to the President's side either of the concern's top two editors—Harry Rickey or Negley Cochran. When Rickey declined to go, Scripps had to fall back on Cochran—with some qualms. "Can Neg do any good?" he asked Bob Paine. "I don't know." He added:

> I have no interest in making Wilson's name great in history. At my age . . . there is only one thing worth while for me, and that is to help the right men do the right things. . . . I felt at one time that old Roosevelt had it in him to perform tremendous social service. I even now know that he had that power, although it was offset by a selfish egotism that finally prevailed.
>
> Looking Mr. Wilson in the face, recognizing the tone of complete candor, and even a sort of pained humbleness, as one who is striving mightily to help his own inadequacy, I felt the urge to help.
>
> I know as a matter of course there are rotten weak spots and yellow streaks in Wilson, just as there are the same things in you and me and everybody else; but I think he fights harder against evil tendencies than you or I do—harder than most men I have known.
>
> Would it not be possible, if Neg could get under the President's skin, as it were, and be a real, though unofficial member of his Cabinet, for him to get Wilson to make some . . . very fine strokes?

But the script Scripps was trying to write was destined for some dramatic twists. He summoned Cochran to Miramar to fully explain the "Secretary of the People" concept before sending him on to see the President. Just then—May 7, 1915—a German U-boat torpedoed and sank the British steamship *Lusitania* off Ireland with heavy loss of life, including 128 Americans. The United States reacted angrily. Wilson sent Germany a formal protest, and vowed in a Philadelphia speech, "We are not too proud to fight." But there was dissention in the Administration.

Secretary of State Bryan, perhaps the nation's most ardent pacifist, didn't agree. He talked of resigning.

In the midst of this hubbub over the threat of war, Scripps notified Secretary Lane of his decision to send Cochran. On June 1, Lane responded:

> I am extremely glad to get your letter—and such a hearty, noble-spirited letter. It came this morning, and was so extraordinary in its patriotic spirit that I took it to the White House and left it with the President.
>
> I am sure that great good will come of the effort you are making to gather the people in support of the President. The poor man has been so worried by the great responsibilities put upon him that he has not had time to think or deal with matters of internal concern. I spoke to him this morning of Mr. Cochran and he said that he would see him just as soon as it was possible. He is extremely appreciative of the spirit you have shown.

Next day President Wilson returned the Scripps letter to Lane with a short note:

> Dear Lane:
>
> This is a perfectly fine letter of Mr. Scripps's—as fine as the generous action he is taking. I hope you will let him know how genuinely grateful I am. I am proud to have the support of such a man.

The Interior Secretary bucked that message on out to Miramar June 3, explaining:

> As I told you the other day, I left your letter with the President. This morning he returned the letter inclosing this note which is written by him on his own typewriter.
>
> I had a nice talk with Cochran the other day. He is the right type.

But the capital's continuing conflict over the war threat confounded Cochran. Bryan resigned. On his own, Cochran concluded "in view of the crisis, I am not needed, and would be imposing on the President." He returned to Chicago without calling at the White House.

In isolation out on his mesa, Scripps was racking his brain to clarify his "duty" as a citizen and as an influential publisher. The war threat, of course, worried him. Scripps had campaigned for a bigger navy, favored defense preparedness, but was not trigger-happy to go after the Kaiser. He felt strongly obligated to keep sticking his oar into the political waters, as a soldier for economic and government reform. It occurred to

him that he had never put in writing his personal creed. He began mull-
ing over his beliefs, thinking of precise words that would succinctly
express his own manifesto. He slaved over this for days, and finally
"formulated" a rather high-flown statement, which he titled "The Reform Platform of E. W. Scripps."

> There is one conviction that has become crystalized in my mind, and
> that is this: That it is our business to so alter our political and economic
> government as to make it not only possible but necessary that every man
> who is allowed to live and have freedom from restraint shall be able and
> shall be compelled to win a fair living for himself, his wife, and his family;
> and that every child born and permitted to live shall be adequately nutured,
> trained, and educated, so that, grown, those who shall become men shall be
> competent to perform their duties as citizens and heads of families, and
> those who shall become women shall, by preference, become competent
> wives and mothers.

Scripps must have been inordinately proud of his little creed. He
sent copies to at least a half-dozen personalities—to Wilson, through
Secretary Lane; to Amos Pinchot; to Charles R. Crane, as a document
incorporated in his analysis of the unfavorable prospects for an ad-less
in Washington.

"I have my doubts," he wrote Gilson Gardner May 20, 1915, "as to
whether or not any advance can be made toward the end in view by trust
busting, trust regulating, raising or lowering or abandoning customs
tariffs, taxing incomes and inheritances, confining taxation to lands,
giving votes to women, prohibiting the production and sale of alcohol,
altering the judicial system in any way, adopting the system of public
ownership of public utilities, or carrying out any of the other popular or
unpopular proposed reforms.

"Personally, it seems easy to me to accomplish the one great object
that I have named without any alteration whatever of our ancient national constitution."

As always, Scripps was eager to get the ear of national leaders—on
his own turf, if possible. He jumped when he found in the summer of
1915 that both Theodore Roosevelt and William Jennings Bryan were to
speak at the San Diego Pan-American Exposition. He invited both to
Miramar. Roosevelt declined, but suggested Scripps come to his hotel for
"a private hour." E. W. ignored that. "I don't like appointments," he
explained to Gilson Gardner.

Bryan, however, accepted enthusiastically. Scripps sent his Packard
to fetch Mr. and Mrs. Bryan at the depot at 8 A.M. But a reception
committee waylaid the visitors and they did not reach Miramar until 3 in

the afternoon. "Bryan was all tired out. I told him he was too disgustingly done up to be of any use to me or of any value to himself, and sent him to take a bath and a long rest."

When Bryan emerged about three hours later, Scripps suggested they ride down to the seashore. Mrs. Bryan tagged along. About 7 they had a light supper. Scripps invited Bryan to his room for a chat, suggesting Mrs. Bryan might be tired and want to retire. "She would not hear of it." Mrs. Bryan took a seat between them and for three hours virtually orchestrated their conversation, cueing them, "Now, Will, this . . ." and "Mr. Scripps, that . . .," actually steering which should speak, when, and on what subject.

This performance fascinated and amused Scripps. "Backwards and forward Bryan would swing in his chair, momentarily addressing me face to face, and then swing around facing his wife, as it were, to catch his cue. Her approval or disapproval of suggestions . . . even when not spoken. . . . I could read." Even her tone of voice was a signal for Bryan. There was no discord between host and guest until Scripps bluntly asserted he was "distinctly antagonistic" to Bryan's policy against a big navy and "military preparedness." The former Secretary's face colored and he broke loose with what Scripps termed "a flow."

Mrs. Bryan snapped: "William!" At once Bryan ceased talking. "A broad smile broke out on the face of the great politician; he beamed so kindly on me that I could almost believe by that smile he proposed to subdue a whole nation-wide rising storm of war."

Only for about five minutes to take a phone call did Mrs. Bryan leave her husband's side at Miramar. "Bryan took this occasion to tell me that his wife was a most remarkable woman, and that during his whole career he had never written a speech or a lecture or an editorial or anything else that he had not submitted to her . . . and always made every change that she advised." That gave Scripps an inward chuckle. "It occurred to me that possibly the United States had had, for some two years or more, a lady for Secretary of State."

Scripps sent them back to San Diego in his Packard. As Mrs. Bryan alighted, the car door slammed on her fingers. Her cry of pain flustered Bryan. Two days later his hand-written "thank you" note reached Miramar. Enclosed were two one-dollar bills—a tip for the chauffeur. In the excitement, Bryan explained, "I forgot to thank your man . . . and send this now so he may not think me unappreciative." He also had a kudo for Scripps: "It is a pleasure to find one who is interested in altruistic work."

As danger grew that America might be drawn into the war, President Wilson was too occupied to carry out Scripps's idea. Secretary Lane quit pushing the scheme. Crane's aide Rogers, after several months in Washington, reported to Scripps on November 20, 1915: "There is not much to show. . . . The only word I have had from the President is a letter in which he apologized for not having seen Cochran. . . . From the present outlook there is not much that we can do, but we are going to make one more try . . . about the first of December."

On December 11, Scripps received from Washington a wire signed by Cochran: "Have an appointment with the President for Monday morning. Crane, Rogers and Roy Howard are here. All of us ready to act on any suggestion you may have to offer."

Nothing was ever to come of the "Secretary of the People" scheme. Telling of the White House meeting, Gilson Gardner said Neg Cochran suggested that Wilson "learn the trick of going over the heads of the politicians and getting in touch with the public. My idea all along was that all he needed was to learn to be his own press agent. I pounded that into Colonel House as well as I could. . . . It's up to Wilson now to force publicity on himself."

In Dr. J. Perry Lewis's office on a summer afternoon in 1915, Scripps sat with a glum frown, his whiskered face wreathed in smoke from his ever-present Santa Fe, while the physician studied an X-ray of his stomach.

"The plates were poor and only a cloudy spot indicated something was going on in my stomach," Scripps observed. Dr. Lewis suggested a second X-ray. "I declined. I did not want to know any more. I did not want to think about it. . . . I am sixty-one years old. If something is going to happen, let it happen! It will be time enough to give further consideration to the matter when the torture begins. I will find some way of shortening it."

Scripps dreaded cancer. He was sure that was his trouble. He had watched his brother George suffer and die of it. Scripps did not so much fear death as he did a horrible, lingering demise. His gastric attacks had started that spring. He went to Dr. Lewis when they persisted, and finally, on the urging of Milton McRae, consulted a San Diego internist, Dr. Robert Pollock.

If not truly frightened, Scripps never would have submitted to the harsh regimen imposed by his new doctor. He was put on a bland diet, poached or soft-boiled eggs three times a day, with rusk and Japanese moss at breakfast, a few vegetables and malted milk at other meals, topped off at supper with jelly wine. He was ordered to cut cigars from thirty-six to twelve a day, and avoid whiskey. He had to punish his body with periodic enemas, purgatives, lard-and-turpentine rub-downs "by the Jap boy," and hot packs on a rubber blanket.

Dr. Pollock required a daily "diary" that noted every bite Scripps ate, virtually every thought or action that agitated his emotions, when he played dominoes or read, took a walk or an auto ride, with whom, when he went to bed, how well he slept, and when he awakened. His bowels were, of course, in the spotlight. Scripps had to count his every belch and go to the extreme of measuring and recording his daily "passage" of feces (eight to sixteen ounces) and urine (average thirty-seven ounces in twenty-four hours), bottling specimens daily for the physician's examination.

For ten to twelve months Scripps would remain in this odious medical straight jacket. It is clear Dr. Pollock was trying to soothe his patient's mental tension as much as treat the aches and pains of his digestive tract. Scripps had no malignancy. Both doctors told him so. Yet he was too much a hypochondriac to consider his bowel rumblings, occasional constipation, and actual gas attacks as anything less than life-threatening. Scripps took his medical diary seriously. He stuck rigidly to his diet. "Eggs are beginning to nauseate me," he noted after about two months. He omitted no detail. It required several weeks to cut down to twelve cigars a day. He noted taking about an ounce of whiskey three times a day, and began to sneak an extra shot in the evening. But within a few months he would dispense with liquor altogether, even foregoing his wine jelly.

It is not surprising Scripps's guts were twisted in knots. Tension in the family was frightful, with E. W. at odds with every member except possibly sister Ellen. He was deeply concerned, too, about the European war, and the hard times it was bringing to the newspaper business. Technically and logically, that problem fell on Jim. But the boy-king—now almost thirty—found it difficult to steer through such troubled waters. He was meeting problems that had never arisen before, and making decisions without precedent. "I feel as though I were on an uninhabited island in the sea," he complained to father.

E. W. had posted a "Do Not Disturb" sign. Jim resented that, but admitted, "It is unfair to ask you to still grind further away at hard labor." Even so Jim needed his counsel. "Your time is worth one thousand dollars a day to the family, and I would like to buy some of it," Jim told his father. "I am not joking about this."

Neither was Scripps; he had retired and wouldn't talk business—period. Tension grew between them. Jim wanted to discuss E. W.'s outmoded scheme of granting editors and business managers "working" interests in new papers. Many of these original men were now out to pasture. They still held stock, but made no contribution to advancing their old papers. What to do about that?

Scripps considered Jim too self-centered. He resented the son peeling off increments and steadily building up his own pile while the father's financial interest still carried the main burden of risk. Scripps considered the concern's first order of business should be to pay off his debts to guarantee the validity of his estate. "My life is nearly done," he wrote Jim on May 3, 1915, "and your life of real activity is just beginning. . . . Just when there is the greatest need for loyalty and helpfulness, I am pained to think that any suggestion should come from you that even points to a tendency of segregation on your part."

Jim began to feel uneasy on his throne. Dad could at any moment withdraw his power of attorney. Jim wanted him happy, but found it hard to tell whether the old man was offering "advice" or was issuing "orders." Finally he forced a face-to-face conference with his dad and J. C. Harper, whom he described as "in the old English sense, the family solicitor."

"Jim has become confused by reason of the fact that he knows in a general way what his father is attempting to do and because he can't keep in step with his father's ideas because the business and the family affairs are so interwoven as to resemble a spider-web, and as Jim's father says he cannot go into a detail without going into the whole, this leaves in Jim's mind a number of unanswered questions," reads a memo drafted at the September 24, 1915, conference.

An understanding was reached. "All orders or instructions given orally or signed on the typewriter are to be disregarded by Jim. . . . An order is to be labeled an order; advice shall be labeled advice, and suggestions labeled as such." All three signed the document.

The father kept up a running quarrel with Bob. The poetic son's thwarted romance with Helen McRae wouldn't die. Little Nackey, as usual, was running wild over the ranch. Scripps wanted her to travel and hired Carolyn Macadam, a school teacher, to escort her on an excursion to Alaska.

The outcome of Dolla's return to California surprised and pleased Scripps. He found a piece of high ground with "a spectacular view" overlooking the ocean, the mountains, and the town of Escondido, twenty miles north of Miramar. Nackie built there a twelve-room, $20,000 house, and installed a staff of three servants, with a car and chauffeur.

Though previously it gave Scripps "the horrors" to be around Dolla, now with her house "only a short hour's ride from Miramar, Mrs.

Scripps and I see her frequently," he wrote Dr. Berkley. "I feel a great sense of relief . . . that it is possible that Dolla can live out her life enjoyably without keeping her family in suspense. . . . She is bright, intelligent, and interested, and possesses a remarkable memory. Without any medicine, she functions in a perfectly normal way physically."

Scripps hammered his love-sick son month after month, without mercy. Bob pleaded, and then retaliated with barbs and insults. Rather than run away—deserting a rich inheritance—he tried to stand and slug it out.

In one outburst Bob told his father: "I consider myself a man, and I hold my life in my own hands. . . . You were not unjust, but unkind in refusing my last request. . . . That's what hurt—the seeming brutality in your manner. I asked for bread, and you gave me a stone, to quote the Scriptures."

The old man didn't back down an inch. "You have disobeyed your father and repudiated all obligations to him," he snapped back. "You have declared your manhood before you have reached the age of maturity, and before you have done one single thing to prove that you have the ability to stand up in the world as every man should. I believe you have disqualified yourself for any but a menial position in my affairs."

Later at the ranch, they wrangled face to face. Scripps insisted Bob write a "brief" presenting the father's side of the controversy. The boy produced a thorough, four-page document. It was extremely snide and sarcastic. But Bob did make some confessions. "I have smoked much, and drunk when I should have known better. . . . I have indulged myself sexually and otherwise to my own hurt."

As far as pretty Helen McRae was concerned, Scripps would never give in. Bob absolutely must wait until age twenty-one for permission to marry—anyone. Their romance began to cool down. Helen spent more and more time out of town. By his actions, Bob indicated the affair had become hopeless.

In time he seemed to knuckle under. First he agreed to give up smoking and drinking, and try to get back in tip-top physical shape. Scripps hired a trainer. Bob regularly worked out with him in the Miramar gym. They boxed a lot. Came the day when Bob, with a lucky punch, knocked out his trainer. When he came to, the boxing instructor decided his student knew enough, or too much—and resigned on the spot.

Bob by no means was cowed by his father. He still was full of ginger. It came to him that he really ought to prove himself. With father's blessing, Bob Scripps struck out on his own. He had a small cache of cash and a $100-a-month allowance from dad. So he headed, in the

summer of 1915, to Bakersfield, California, to try to land a job on a
newspaper—of course, not one of his father's.

"You chain my hands with health and propriety," little Nackey wrote her
father from Alaska, "and then command me to run and wave my arms.
What am I to do? I confess that I am very much bewildered."

It was the summer of 1915. Both the youngest Scripps children were
out of the nest trying their wings. Bob, still furiously love-smitten, had
gone into the oil fields at Bakersfield. All he had was youth, zeal, pride,
and $200 or $300 in his pocket. "I did not have to be told," his father
observed to a colleague, "that he was indulging in childish dreams of
striking it rich, and becoming, in a few months, a millionaire, able to
marry whom he pleased and support his wife in style."

Nackey had already experienced an exciting near-shipwreck aboard
the *Mariposa* in a storm off Anchorage. She was now exploring Alaska's
rugged interior with her school-marm companion. Even at the edge of
the Arctic Circle, Nackey still felt the jerk of father's short leash.

"You must remember," she wrote, "that what you would have me do
is very eccentric and different from what others do and that Miss Macadam, of all people in this world, is the most perfectly conventional and
most ready to fall into the footsteps of those going before. She is exactly
the kind of person, as nearly as I can make out, whom you would
approve of as a chaperone and yet you ask me to do perfectly impossible
things with her."

Admittedly Scripps felt uneasy about how his youngest would fare
out in the world. The fear that romance would enter her life too soon
was a constant worry to Scripps, and he was open about it with the
seventeen-year-old. "I have warned you that you and I are going to have
the biggest fight of our lives if you are silly enough to try to become a
woman while you are yet a girl, and silly enough to think that you can
choose a husband before you are a woman." That did not preclude
looking over men—"as types, though, and not as individuals."

He expected her to marry and her choice of a husband would be
life's most important decison.

> Study this creature man! There are whole armies of specimens of the
> onery [*sic*] creature. There are none of them who are not as full of faults as
> yourself; but there are some of them who will have faults that are not so
> irritating as those of other men. Strong men and big men are apt to have
> strong faults and big faults. If you want a nice, ordinary, respectable, lady-
> like sort of chap to carry your parcels, keep your books, and pay your bills,

there are enough of them to be had, and you don't have to be in a hurry to grab the first one you see.

Some day when you choose a man, I am going to object to him; but it strikes me now that I would make less of a row if the man should happen to be one of those found, not where things are being enjoyed, but where things are being done.

"You are out adventuring," Scripps wrote. There was no need to come home on schedule. "Go where you want to go, stay as long as you want to at any place. . . . I have turned you loose on a roving commission which may, if you choose, consume three or four years."

In Bakersfield Bob tried to get a job as a reporter. All he could land was a job as circulation hustler. Rival papers were giving premiums in the battle for customers. One gave a washboard for a month's subscription; the other an iron. Bob got on the washboard paper at $2.50 a day and toted one of the contraptions around while signing up customers.

The work wasn't all that thrilling. After four days, Bob turned in his washboard and looked elsewhere. No other job was to be found. After two fruitless weeks, he moved over into the oil fields at Taft.

"Poor Bob! He is getting experience," Scripps wrote J. C. Harper July 13, 1915. "He characterizes his hotel as no better than a stable; he compared the beefsteak he gets to boot leather; and he says that everybody in the neighborhood is tough. . . . Of course I am anxious for him, and fearful lest his youth and inexperience get him into too dangerous a situation. However Bob is never going to learn by precept from a teacher who is such an old fogie and so stupid as not to know that love does, and should, rule the world."

The lad was still mooning for Helen McRae. He wrote his travelling sister, obviously complaining about his thwarted romance. She, in turn, directly criticized her father for interfering:

> Don't you think you are too hard on Helen? After all she is only a very good example of the modern American girl. . . . Besides she is pretty. . . . The whole business reminds me of the seage [sic] of Troy. Even her name, Helen, fits in. . . . Bob is Paris and she is Agamemnon's wife only there is no Agamemnon and that simplifies matters a great deal. You are Mars, or somebody who got mixed up in the affair.

In Taft, Bob did roughneck work. Finally he became a contractor, building foundations for gas engines and hauling iron pipe. Disaster overtook his new career. One of his workmen broke a leg on the job; the hospital bills wiped out Bob's assets.

Deciding to try his luck in northern California, he took a steamer to the port city of Eureka in Humboldt County. He landed a dollar-a-day reporter job. His beat included the waterfront but one day he hurried with the sheriff to a town forty miles away where a circus got in a brawl with lumberjacks who killed three roustabouts. The editor splashed Bob's story on page one—and promptly chewed him out for going away and failing to gather his regular marine news.

Meanwhile, Dolla had moved into her hill-top house at Escondido. It was beautiful—but no garden of Eden for the Baltimore nurse who had come west with her. They were great friends at first. Then, strangely, Dolla changed. She grew to hate the sight of the slender, dark-haired, saturnine Katherine Steelman. When the retarded girl turned this discord into tantrums, Miss Steelman resigned and departed for Los Angeles where she had friends.

Scripps was angry that Nackey came home with a cold. He upbraided the chaperone; she angrily resigned. Scripps promptly tracked down Katherine Steelman in Los Angeles and asked her to come back to serve as Nackey's governess. Miss Steelman protested that such duty did not justify registered nurse's wages. Scripps argued that his daughter was run-down and needed someone to monitor her health. Miss Steelman came back. Actually she served as a private duty nurse for the whole family, called on to serve the old man frequently in connection with his stomach disorder. One of her unenviable tasks was to bottle specimens to send to Dr. Pollock.

Scripps kept Bob under close surveillance. Perhaps inspired by his own diary for Dr. Pollock, father required son to hand him a daily report on his activities. These show in the main Bob was loafing, dreaming up poems, playing tennis, tinkering with cars, and just passing time. Occasionally he and Nackey drove into San Diego to see an afternoon motion picture show. He palled around some with the secretary Tom Meanley, when he wasn't busy at his typewriter. Bob and Meanley spent hours trying to learn to play the ukulele.

There was an outburst at Miramar around Christmastime. It occurred when Dolla was brought to the ranch house for a costume ball and caught sight of Nurse Steelman. The girl went into a rage. Katherine Steelman was hustled out of the room, and Scripps ordered safeguards to keep their paths from crossing again. The nurse had made a favorable impression on Scripps. In reporting on family matters to Dr. Berkley, he observed: "Miss Steelman and my daughter Nackey seem to greatly enjoy each other's companionship. . . . I consider Miss Steelman a very worthy woman."

In family conferences new plans were worked out for Bob and Nackey. For the time being, she would suspend her travels, and take over actual operation of Fanita under lease from her mother, who owned that ranch. Of a sudden, the blossoming tomboy had developed a great yen to stay home. It is a wonder that the usually alert father did not detect certain signs that would worry him.

Bob wanted to visit Hawaii and Australia, and return by way of China and Japan. Since Helen McRae was in Detroit, the idea of separating the unrequited lovers by not only the width of the United States but also the Pacific Ocean appealed to Scripps. He jumped at the chance to bankroll his son's departure for the Hawaiian islands.

When Nackie undertook to lease Fanita to her daughter as a strict business deal, a legal glitch intervened. Little Nackey could not sign the contract; she was not yet of legal age. The lawyers worked that out, writing a "temporary" lease. On her rapidly approaching eighteenth birthday—which would be May 16, 1916—Nackey would execute a formal contract.

That didn't mean the girl, seventeen years, seven and one-half months old, did not assume full control. She grabbed the ranch with an iron fist. That was not easy.

"Nackey seems to be devoting almost all of her attention to the ranch," Scripps wrote Bob in Hawaii. "I know she is having her troubles. Her foreman recently resigned. However, I am not participating in her anxieties or her labors. So long as her finances are in reasonable shape I am not going to meddle with her."

This letter was doubly ironic. Tom Meanley, the secretary who was taking and typing up that dictation, knew for certain that Nackey was by no means thinking only of Fanita. He must have had trouble looking Scripps in the eye. For despite the father's stern injunction that daughter must not be "silly" enough to think herself a woman and grab the first man to come along, a romance had blossomed. Tom likewise knew he was in blatant violation of Scripps's rule against fraternizing with ranch females. Hence Tom courted Nackey on the sly.

In Honolulu, Bob was vigorously courting the muse—sending his father a steady stream of poetry. Scripps encouraged him. "I agree that the enclosed poem 'Youth' is a strong piece. I think it the best of about one-half dozen of all your productions that I have thought worthwhile." He passed on an observation by Max Eastman that true poets had to constantly keep turning out verse—"to winnow so much chaff in order to recover so little grain."

Tension continued to flicker between Scripps and Jim. The boy-king still found it awkward to run the empire with his authority actually resting on little more than word-of-mouth say-so from E. W. On the least whim, Dad could revoke the power of attorney. Jim again raised this point with his father. "I would like more than anything else to know more definitely about the conditions, whatever they may be, that I will have to work under. I would like to have a contract with you which would have incorporated in it a copy of your will. . . . I would be better able to decide things." Jim got right down to brass tacks: "I would like to go at things harder, or commence to take things a little easier. I don't care very much which it is."

Scripps responded that Jim was "mistaken in thinking I have not arranged affairs so that my death will not bring the least embarrassment to you. . . . On the other hand, you will be the gainer. But for good reasons I have chosen to keep my will entirely secret."

That seemed to satisfy Jim, who was gratified that under his eight-year reign the combined circulation of their newspapers now topped 1,000,000 and that revenue had increased 93.2 percent.

As spring came in 1916 and Nackey's eighteenth birthday approached, Scripps's spirits got lighter. He still looked on her as his little girl. When she blurted out that she some day wanted to adopt seven orphans, he burst out laughing. Others in the family obviously at least had an inkling, but Scripps knew nothing of the serious discussions taking place privately between Nackey and Tom Meanley. Though the secretary was almost nine years her senior, the ranch girl appears to have been the aggressor in their romance.

"On my birthday, I will be of age," she told Meanley. "We can get married — and no one can stop us!"

Tom looked worried. "Well, I don't know."

Nackey, flushing, showed her temper. "Tom, if you don't marry me, I'll leave Miramar! I'll go somewhere — maybe Europe. . . . And you will never see me again!" She rushed out of the room.

On the morning of May 16, 1916, Nackey waited in her auto with a bag packed. Tom slipped out of Scripps's office, leaving behind a typed letter of resignation. They drove into San Diego and were married by a justice of the peace.

Their elopement stunned Scripps. He went white at the news, collapsing into his rocking chair, trembling and twitching. Alternately, he sobbed and raged. Meanley was to blame — the fortune-hungry scoundrel! His little girl would never so callously wound a loving father. She had been led astray. The old man's heart was broken. The most terrible grief of his life descended upon him.

27

Glory and Agony in Washington

I n Sydney, Australia, in mid-September 1916, Bob Scripps ripped open a letter from his father. It was curt and critical. The boy's travels so far had been "a useless expense of time and money." Bob foolishly had visited only "resorts of idlers and men of vicious propensities." Dad would send no more funds. "Before your money runs out," the letter advised, "you should purchase your steamer tickets back to the states."

Bob did, and returned to Miramar at the end of October. Still a dreamy poet, he had no business ambition. His Pacific odyssey did produce — in E. W.'s eyes — one bright spot. In Bob's absence, Helen McRae found a new love interest, a prosperous Michigan seed merchant, and married him. That did not seem to disturb Bob. Back at the ranch, just turned twenty-one, he fell into his old niche of gentleman loafer. He read some of his poems — rejected by magazines — to Aunt Ellen. Impressed, she paid to publish 1,000 copies of a slim volume, "Songs of a Soil Slave."

Scripps, at sixty-two, was struggling hard to break out of his hermit shell. Miramar now evoked too many sad memories and painful emotions. Secretly he plotted to run away — perhaps to Washington, D.C. He thought he would find a welcome there, certainly from President Wilson.

His cancer scare was over. No longer did his stomach trouble him. Impressed by Dr. Robert Pollock, he hit on a medical philanthrophy scheme. Several in the family wanted to erect a $250,000 mausoleum as a memorial to John Paul. Scripps had a different idea. He induced Dr. Pollock, whose annual income was about $5,000, to cut back and "sell" him one-fifth of his working time for $1,000. Scripps's scheme was to

363

open a small hospital exclusively for the blue-collar class in San Diego. No charity cases would be accepted; those would continue to go to the county infirmary; and well-to-do patients would patronize regular hospitals. Room rates at the "John P. Scripps Memorial Hospital For Working Men and Women" would be $1 a day, and doctor fees only $1.

As he did with his cheap newspapers, Scripps mandated a small start-up, wanting slow, solid growth. He put up $35,000, demanding that before the first nail was driven for the one-story *krankhause* [he was taken with the German word for sick house], a giant flagpole must be raised on the site and the American flag flown daily. By February 1917, Dr. Pollock with help from Milton McRae and J. C. Harper had a clinic in operation. Other San Diego physicians, approving the idea, joined the clinic staff.

Scripps was in a generous mood. He purchased a Pierce-Arrow limousine for sister Ellen and provided a chauffeur. E. W. gave Jim all his personal holdings in their newspapers in Los Angeles, Denver, and Dallas. Total value of these three dailies was more than $2,500,000. Dad also handed Jim more of his own stock in the $528,000 *San Francisco News*.

It occurred to E. W. that some of his own writings might be worth publishing. He asked Bob Paine and J. C. Harper to select a "literary executor" to go through his files, which he discovered were "in bad shape." He didn't know just how good his disquisitions were. After dictating one he usually was too exhausted to even check the manuscript for typing errors. "I have as much or more aversion," he told Harper, "to the inspection of the excreta of my brain, as I have to inspecting my physical excrement."

He had invited daughter Nackey to come see him at Miramar so he could give her some general advice about her Fanita Ranch. "Of course, I would expect you to come alone," he wrote. Scripps had no intention of ever accepting or forgiving husband Tom Meanley.

Scripps, with keen interest, watched another girl enter Bob's life. She was a tall, slender brunet with waist-length hair, Margaret "Peggy" Culbertson, daughter of a Pasadena lumberman, and just Bob's age. She came to Miramar, ironically, as a guest of the McRae family, having attended the same eastern school as Edith, John Paul's widow. Peggy Culbertson was serious, intelligent, and kind-hearted. She loved dogs. "I told my parents," she avowed, "that I would never marry a man who won't let me have dogs in the house."

By the beginning of 1917 Scripps believed he had Bob interested in making another stab at journalism. "I am inclined to think," the father wrote Gilson Gardner, "that he can have a very useful and very effective career. . . . Providing he is not an idler and willing to live a fairly clean life, I will not quarrel with him or even meddle at all in his affairs."

Bob's first priority, however, was to get married. He and Peggy announced their engagement, pleasing both families. This was a quiet, serious girl E. W. could like. But all concerned worried about the threat of war. It was surely coming. The *Cleveland Press* on March 16, 1917, sounded the Scripps papers' policy line, jumping the gun with its own declaration of war: "War between the United States and Germany is inevitable and necessary. . . . We are face to face with grim realities. . . . We must fight!"

Romance would not take a back seat to sabre-rattling. Bob and Peggy, in no mood to await the boom of cannon, were married at Pasadena on March 21, 1917. Sixteen days later, while they honeymooned, President Wilson declared war. By mid-April, Bob and his bride were on the train headed east. The old man sent his son off on a special mission with a characteristic mixture of criticism and encouragement:

April 16, 1917

Dear Bob:

I have told you several times that you need waking up. You haven't gone to sleep. You've never been awake.

You are now going on a mission to the East. . . . If you work hard, study hard, think hard . . . without regard to your personal discomfort, your mission may have important results. . . . In a way I am the spirit of the concern. There is no reason why you should not represent the newspaper concern and your father. . . . You know what I think about many subjects and you can with safety and boldness enunciate these opinions of mine.

If possible I would like you to meet President Wilson and convey to him . . . that I am determined to support him during the time of his coming stress.

During this time forget there is such a thing as poetry. . . . Close the book of dreams for the time being; stop philosophizing.

Affectionately,

E. W. Scripps

The time had come, Scripps decided, to kill the *Chicago Day Book*. It had floundered for five years. There was no hope it could ever break even. Scripps instructed Neg Cochran to shut down. But it was not easy to knock the little ad-less in the head. Cochran begged for more time. Scripps felt sympathetic. So he let the little paper struggle on.

He basically blamed Cochran for the failure. Neg could write in simple, strong language. But he was "too highbrow" to get down to the level of the common herd. His plane of thought and morals "are sky-high above the heads of the crowd." Scripps told Cochran he did not recognize the 99 percent brutishness of the public. "The wage slave wants to forget his slavery and misery. . . . That is one reason why he likes to drink . . . go to moving picture shows, to vaudeville, to picnics . . . to fill his mind with something at least less unpleasant." Instead of entertaining his readers, Cochran was trying to stuff them with unpalatable working class propaganda.

The old man couldn't seem to bring himself to wield the death ax. So the *Day Book* tottered on, down to a circulation of 12,000, into the hectic spring of 1917.

Finally Scripps ordered Jim to select the right time and put the *Day Book* out of its misery. He accepted his own share of blame, but wrote Jim March 12, 1917, he still was convinced "the ad-less theory is practicable" and expected to "some day successfully develop it." He reiterated his basic conviction that "the editor makes the newspaper. . . . Scripps was old and didn't care much of a damn for anything, and didn't have to succeed. . . . But Neg had had his fill of glory, had become nigger-rich. He was older. He quit thinking, and was only remembering. He had more time to drink, and he liked to drink. He became sort of a gentleman farmer. Age and conditions robbed both Neg and Scripps of all their virilities. One cannot build a big, successful property as a fad or amusement."

By that time Scripps had dispatched Cochran to Washington as a personal emissary to run various errands. Neg's son Harold was again temporary editor in Chicago.

Out on his remote mesa, Scripps grew fidgety about how President Wilson was running the war. The White House, he thought, could use advice from Miramar—and clearly was obligated to listen. After all, by swinging the pivotal states of Ohio and California with strong support, the Scripps papers were responsible more than any other organization for Wilson's 1916 re-election. Scripps had no doubt his papers "turned the trick."

Early on, the Squire of Miramar urged Wilson to heat up the hunt for German U-boats. He hammered away at the idea of smoking out wealthy American tax dodgers by making public all income tax returns. The White House seemed uncommonly dense on that idea. Scripps sent Harry Rickey to argue personally with the President. After a haggle that spanned months, Wilson concluded it would be illegal to disclose the returns. Undaunted, Scripps wired the President on April 2, 1917:

I strongly urge that we should pay as we go in the war with income and inheritance taxes. All incomes over one hundred thousand dollars should be conscripted. The minimum cash pay for soldiers and sailors should be not less than three dollars a day during the war. Such legislation would cost me more than half my present income.

That was no exaggeration; it actually was too conservative. In 1915 Scripps's personal income was $342,498 and for 1916 would run to $353,024. Scripps was serious about financial sacrifice. He directed the concern to invest $250,000 in war bonds. He offered the military from his Miramar fleet two trucks and five passenger cars. He doubted the government would want his "four or five other cars. . . . They are high-priced new machines, a Pierce-Arrow and Cadillac limousines, etc." He chipped in several thousand dollars with industrialist Henry Timken to test a machine supposed to make newsprint from yucca plants. A stranger came to Miramar claiming to be a Canadian college professor with an invention—a device that could detect submarines. Scripps bought him a train ticket to Washington and asked navy officials to interview him. Both ideas eventually fizzled.

Scripps made the government his ultimate offer—himself! He was vaguely acquainted with Secretary of War Newton D. Baker whose law firm in Cleveland represented his *Press*. On April 5, 1917, he sent Baker a night letter:

I am sixty-three years old. Have had no military experience. I am wealthy and at leisure. Have had very large executive experience and have in this state of California a very large number of capable well-trained business men subject to my order. Can you make any use of my services? If so, I offer them.

Baker sent a polite reply. He appreciated the patriotic gesture, would "take great pleasure in sending the President your telegram." Baker tendered no job but asserted he "would not forget" Scripps's availability.

Suddenly a violent policy dispute erupted inside the concern. Editors split in a quarrel over how blindly they should back Wilson. Bob Paine hotly accused N.E.A. chief Canfield of "crazily roaring . . . and calling all who disagree with him [Wilson] cowards, traitors and sissies." Canfield also had committed the Scripps papers, wrongly to calling for a million United States troops in France by Christmas. Secretary Baker, countered Paine, admitted they couldn't be that rapidly trained for overseas duty.

New conflicts developed with daughter Nackey. Father offered money for her "personal comfort." Nackey correctly interpreted this as an indirect slap at her husband. She rejected the offer. Later she did borrow $3,000 from Scripps to buy beef cattle to fatten for market in the Fanita pastures. But her resentment mounted steadily over the continued ostracism of husband Tom. In a fit of anger, she sent her father a hot letter vowing to never again set foot on Miramar ranch.

That was a fatal blow to their relationship—and to Scripps's remaining in San Diego County. He would be unable to stay on at Miramar, he wrote Nackey, without "casting reflections on you." But he could avoid some "questioning on the part of the community of San Diego by maintaining a residence in another part of the country."

Still worse, Nackey was callously driving a cruel wedge between her mother and father. "That she [Nackie] blames me more than she does you may salve your conscience." But he was deeply wounded because daughter had caused Nackie to come to believe Scripps "was unworthy, perhaps hateful, perhaps even contemptible."

This feud with the free-spirited former tomboy was too much to bear. The gloomy Scripps made a decision. He would leave Miramar—perhaps forever.

The California Limited backed onto the Linda Vista siding on Sunday evening, May 13, 1917, coupled with an iron clang to the private car Columbia, and pulled out for the East. Aboard with Scripps were his wife, her chauffeur and maid, his valet, Joe Naka, as well as a Japanese houseboy and the male stenographer. In the private car also were Dr. Robert Pollock and Jim's executive assistant, Harry L. Schmetzstorff. In Washington H. L. S. was to be E. W.'s aide-de-camp and steady opponent at dominoes.

Reaching Cincinnati, Scripps had the Columbia shunted to a siding for three days while he got Nackie and her servants settled at the West Chester farm for a visit with her mother. Scripps tried to slip into the capital secretly. He took rooms at the new Powhatan Hotel at Eighteenth and H Streets, Northwest, a few blocks from the White House, but declined to register. He didn't want anyone to bother him; but his arrival was hardly a secret because his own Washington staff was self-importantly abuzz with the gossip.

Not only was Scripps fed up with the "discontent" of his old Miramar life, he deliberately was engineering a separation from his wife. He was happy and content in Washington without Nackie. Scripps candidly informed Jim: "I think it would be better for her to stay in West Chester, as long as things are as they are. I do not want her to come here under a sense of duty . . . just because it is the usual thing for a wife to do. . . . It may be better for her to visit me in Washington for a week or two and then return to California to be with Nackey." Their daughter was expecting her first child in the fall. "Your mother should remain there until after a period of a great many months when she can finally make up her mind as to what she wants to do in the long run."

Strangely, Scripps boasted he could easily adjust to living alone. "You have often heard me say that if Fortune threw me onto some desert island for the remainder of my life — providing I had a few books — I could live comfortably." But the same letter disclosed he was scouring the Washington suburbs for a large country estate to rent or buy to have a "costly and comfortable" place for Nackie "on the assumption she will be with me most of the time." He also ordered three new autos — one each for Nackie and himself; the third was to permit Bob and others on his personal staff to whip around town.

Scripps's showing up in Washington at time of crisis set in motion rapid-fire ego-stroking events that overnight hoisted him to an abnormal high. He already was somewhat puffed up about his giant standing as a national opinion-maker. Still he really hoped to stay modestly and quietly on the capital sidelines. His own staffers would not permit that. They flocked around, asking for advice and orders, in the process massaging his growing vanity. "There is a strong indication," he informed Milton McRae, "to consider me as though I am not only the head of the concern, but actively at the head. I can protest until I am black in the face, but it does no good."

The concern already suffered from a leadership tangle, with half a dozen editors in Washington, Cleveland, and California trying vainly to out-shout each other and seize supreme authority. By taking even slight direct action, Scripps only hastened the impending internal explosion. Nor could he escape back-home politics. Linda Vista had just been selected for an army cantonment of 25,000 men. Los Angeles felt cheated out of the camp. Big advertisers in his *Los Angeles Record* sent wires begging him to intercede. Scripps felt unable to favor either San Diego County or Los Angeles, but let Neg Cochran set up an appointment for him with Secretary of War Baker. It was scheduled as a ten-minute meeting.

But Scripps did not emerge from his Sunday morning session with the War Secretary for two hours. Baker was firm on keeping the camp at Linda Vista. Scripps quickly forgot about such an insignificant matter as that. The cabinet officer had insisted on talking truthfully and frankly about the entire war situation, and Scripps came away frightened and alarmed.

"Some of the things that I heard direct, and others that I had heard of, fairly made my blood run cold," Scripps wrote McRae. "This fool censorship has kept the country in ignorance." Scripps complained that his own staffers had been fed false dope for confidential memos to him. As "a responsible chief," government officials were willing to speak more candidly to him than a reporter.

The country was in a bad way on food and fuel. Scripps expected rioting to break out "before next winter is half over." Radicals might trigger a revolt by labor. "The fool Senate," he lamented, "is now whittling down taxes on the rich, adding to public exasperation which is about to burst into flame."

Out on the northwest boundary of the District of Columbia, Scripps found the estate he wanted — Airlie, owned by Samuel Kauffman, publisher of the *Washington Star*. Overlooking pretty Rock Creek Park, it was on Military Road, ten miles from the Capitol. Scripps leased the magnificent layout for $1,200 a month and moved right in, with aides, servants, and Bob and Peggy. He was barely settled when a policy explosion rocked the Scripps organization from coast to coast.

Although every Scripps editor was free to adopt his own policy, since 1915 virtually all had followed the N.E.A.'s national editorial slant. It was largely pro-Wilson: "Stand by the President," in favor of conscripting soldiers, and imposing high war taxes. On May 31, 1917, the *Los Angeles Record* took a contrary view, unleashing a murderous page-one attack on Wilson's policies.

"The plain truth," the *Record* thundered, "is that neither East nor West, North or South, are the people clamoring to go to war. The fact is, as far as public sentiment for this war is concerned, it's a fizzle. It can't be found. It doesn't exist. President Wilson has committed one colossal blunder — first he lulled into silent slumber the military war spirit of America, then he declared war. The people are now responding to his call very coldly.

"President Wilson is asking for more power than was ever entrusted to any English king, any Russian czar, any German emperor. He demands a press gag that can effectively choke to death any honest effort to curtail the abuses of this lordly power. . . . Press censorship . . . murders the truth and puts a premium on lies, buries democracy and makes slaves and serf of free men.

"Keep your eye on the contracts going out of Washington. . . . Never in history was money spent with such a lavish hand. . . . We will be told about it only after our purse is stolen . . . for the grafter and the carpet-bagger. We want to stand back of the President when he is right. When he is wrong, we owe it to ourselves to help him get right. No man is infallible. We will have the courage to think straight and publish the truth, so that our land may be a fit place to live in, and a worthwhile democracy to die for, if need be."

This flagrant flip-flop on concern policy triggered an uproar. Some editors were outraged by the *Record*'s violent tone. The editorial was written and signed by John H. Perry, the Scripps libel lawyer whose astounding success had earned him "Northwest Whirlwind" renown. Jim, apparently wondering what his father thought of it, wired Scripps that the editorial was "an experiment." Around the circuit the cry went up again for someone to be given authority to enunciate a single war policy for all Scripps papers.

Letters and telegrams flew back and forth between Airlie and Jim's office out west. Scripps was not overly excited, asserting "Perry is altogether too nearly right in what he gave the *Record,* but Cochran and I think that utterance was premature, and that something not quite like it should have been formulated for all our papers, the Newspaper Enterprise Association and even Howard's association."

Scripps disclosed that he was being urged by colleagues to seek a personal audience with Wilson to "get his consent and approval for telling the whole people the real situation . . . with regard to war conditions in Europe, submarines . . . food and the necessity of far greater military activity than anyone is now thinking of."

The war situation, Scripps warned Jim, "is far worse than you think it is," and urged him to come to Washington to confer with top men like Canfield, Howard, Martin, Rickey, Thornton, and Cochran.

The old man recognized that his meddling doubtlessly was aggravating the leadership confusion. He tried to at least verbally back off, telling Jim: "I have told all our men, as well as others, that I will not under any condition take away from you any responsibility, or attempt to exercise authority, or even attempt to exercise any personal 'fatherly influence.' "

Scripps was kidding no one.

Newest torment for the Scripps clan was the likelihood that Jim and Bob would be called up for military service. Both registered for the draft. Nackie, with three sons already in the grave, was horrified. She had a typical mother's exaggerated fear of battlefield peril. In tears, she implored Scripps to keep her boys out of uniform. He already was in an awkward dilemma. His papers staunchly advocated conscription—no favoritism, no slackers. Yet he did legitimately need his sons, especially Jim, to run his newspapers, which unquestionably were essential or very helpful to the nation's war effort. Scripps decided to try to get both exempted—but mainly through quiet, behind-the-scenes maneuvers.

Yet both sons seemed determined to go into the army. Jim, playing poker with officers at the new army camp next door to Miramar, was deeply stirred by patriotism and a yen for adventure. Camp Kearney's commanding general advised Jim to seek a lieutenant's commission and become his aide. Both Jim and Bob were indignant that any Scripps should be a slacker. In filling out his draft form, Bob left blank the line for claiming exemption.

E. W. felt certain Jim could not pass the physical examination. Not only overweight, Jim still was bothered by a weak throat from the boyhood tonsil surgery that almost bled him to death. Additionally as a teenager, he had suffered a crippling ankle injury. In a confidential letter, Scripps urged J. C. Harper: "Get Jim to have his foot X-rayed, and examined by someone like Dr. Oatman. . . . This might be a delicate subject for Jim. A man doesn't like to admit to any physical blemish."

Not only was the old man meddling in Jim's affairs, he was hip-deep, anyhow, in sorties on other Washington fronts. Scripps was impressed with Herbert Hoover and feared the dog-tired United States food commissioner was about to work himself to death. He invited Hoover to hide out at Airlie and rest up. They had a talk that alarmed Scripps. E. W. sensed America was on the verge of food riots. He wanted to sound a warning in his papers, but his colleagues convinced him that would be like yelling "Fire!" in a crowded theatre. At his Powhatan suite he met two hours with the British press magnate, Lord Northcliff, wrangling about the need to impose government control on all goods. "Northcliff and I had a hammer-and-tongs sort of interview," he wrote Bob Paine. "I understand he called me 'a belligerent old tiger' after he left."

Finally feeling obligated to pass on to the President his own assessment of public opinion, Scripps asked Interior Secretary Lane to get him an appointment at the White House. "I told him what I wanted to talk to the President about," E. W. reported to Ellen, "and said I knew the interview would be disagreeable and not at all flattering. In fact I said I wanted to talk about the imminence of social revolution . . . because of popular discontent with the great hordes of big business men who have gathered in Washington, and on whom the President was depending too much for counsel."

Lane argued there was no occasion for popular discontent. For nearly an hour he tried to "jolly" Scripps. The old man flared up; Lane didn't have even a 10 percent appreciation of the actual situation. "It would be useless to take up the President's time, and exhaust my energy," Scripps snapped. Lane "paled a little," but insisted on arranging a White House meeting—for 3 P.M., Wednesday, June 27.

Then E. W. began to have second thoughts. How valid were his reasons for pessimism and alarm? Scripps regretted now asking to meet the President. "A great deal of anxiety had oozed out." Still he drove to the White House at the appointed hour and was ushered into the President's office. He described their encounter in a disquisition, "A Short Visit With The President," dated June 29, 1917:

> A storm was about to break outside, and the room was quite dusky. I saw what appeared to me quite a small man crossing the room to greet me. I had seen the President before, and had had the impression that he was quite a tall man and somewhat imposing in appearance. When I saw the President before, he was sleek and groomed to perfection. . . . But this rather small-ish gentleman appeared with his hair somewhat touseled [sic] . . . tanned, if not sun-burned. . . . He seemed not in the least fatigued. His face was anything but careworn; he laughed outright on several occasions.
>
> At times he spoke earnestly; he indulged in a few swear words, especially when he had been making reference to many of the people who had been gathering in Washington for the purpose of making profit off the government's difficulties.

In his thirty-minute visit, Scripps felt he discerned the "why" of the "weak" cabinet. These were "good enough executive clerks" who could be relied on, while Wilson made the decisions. "The President was perhaps as good a man as could be selected for his job." Having come "to talk, not listen," Scripps several times "cut in" to voice his opinions on the war, legislation, public attitudes. He recorded that he bluntly told Wilson "that as he had won the people's confidence, their respect and their affection, on account of his attitude toward the common people, he should . . . continue to more vigorously than ever champion the cause of the unpossessed."

> I told him that while the people had confidence in him personally, I believed they were very suspicious of, and very resentful toward, the great gathering in Washington of capitalists and capitalist representatives, of labor-baiters, and the use he was making of them in the various voluntary committees and commissions. I said that the people were probably, and rightly, becoming alarmed that these people would overwhelm him and, by sheer force of numbers and weightiness of their interest, would wield altogether too much influence over the administration. He told me he was well aware of this attitude on the part of the public, and that he realized the

suspicion aroused was thoroughly justified, and that it would not be long before this cause of suspicion would disappear.

I mentioned three men whose presence and whose activities had become quite prominent: namely Rosenwald, Peabody, and Barney Baruch.

He said, "Referring to the three you have mentioned, I have already determined to eliminate two of them entirely. I recognize their character, their attitude, and what they are here for. But as to the third, Barney Baruch, I intend to use him. I think Baruch has seen the light."

"You think he has ceased to be Saul and has become Paul," I said.

"Yes, I think so," he replied, "but I will find out soon enough, and if not I will send him to join the other two. . . . Barney Baruch knows the inside of all these things probably better than anyone else who is accessible to me. He can give me information and assist me as perhaps no one else can."

I interjected, "Is it your idea to set a thief to catch a thief?"

"Now! Now!" he replied. "I don't want you to regard Mr. Baruch in that light. He's really a nice fellow, and I feel very friendly toward him. I wouldn't like to call him a thief."

"Oh!" I said. "Some of the most genial and agreeable fellows one can ever meet are these men, who in common parlance, are called thieves — I mean such as these captains of industry, etc. etc., for instance like myself, for I am somewhat of a captain of industry also."

He laughed, and said, "Oh, well, if that is what you mean, it's all right; but I think Baruch is going to come out all right, and that he is going to be of great assistance to us. But time and events will show that, and, if he doesn't — well, we can get along without him."

Scripps then took the President to task for blocking the concern's efforts to shame the rich into paying their just taxes by having the government disclose all income tax returns. He commented that the investigation of his own return was so sloppy he could safely have paid only about one-half of his taxes, and felt certain many rich people were cheating. He also urged the President to establish a minimum wage to lessen the people's hatred of the rich. Wilson responded that he was thinking about that.

I had noticed, when I first got a good light on the President's face, that his large nose seemed a trifle red, and there was a suspicion of wateriness about his eyes. One of the windows was open and a brisk breeze was blowing in. The President sneezed once — a mild little sneeze — but I was fearful. I had just concluded one of my perorations on the income tax subject when the President sneezed again, and sneezed violently.

I was pretty sure the President would have been willing to have me stay longer, but I had said all I wanted to say, and there was that sneeze! So, without waiting to be dismissed, I arose and told him I would not further trespass on his time.

The President also arose and accompanied me to the door, and, with a hearty handshake from a firm and warm hand, bade me good-day.

Running the risk of catching a cold — even a Presidential one — was something Scripps would not do.

A day or two later Neg Cochran decided it was time to settle the lingering *Chicago Day Book* crisis. "If I'm to be needed longer in Washington," Cochran telegraphed Jim at San Diego, "we should kill the *Day Book*. The sooner the better." Jim wired right back — go ahead!

Cochran took the train to Chicago, gave his men two weeks pay, found Ohio jobs for his son Harold and two reporters. He did not bother to save for the concern one young *Day Book* reporter who was destined for greatness as America's renowned folk poet and biographer of Abraham Lincoln. "Carl Sandburg," Neg wrote Jim, "can hook on somewhere locally."

Cochran wrote a short and simple obituary: "I got here Friday morning and promptly murdered the *Day Book* that day — Friday. There was no music, no flowers." That particular black Friday was July 6, 1917. The *Day Book* was Scripps paper Number Eight to die. The life span of the odd-ball little ad-less lacked three months of being six years.

Out in his San Diego office, Jim began reading Bob's latest telegram from Washington. His face clouded, turned red in anger; he swore and slammed down the wire. The message announced that E. W. Scripps had just concluded a two-day parley in the capital with Neg Cochran, Earle Martin, Harry Rickey, Roy Howard, and Bob, plus Charles R. Crane's factotum Walter Rogers. "Conclusion: N.E.A., U.P.A. and all papers must take definite stand on war policy. Object wake up country to real fact of serious situation. First step immediate big drive on food problem. . . . Rickey will shift headquarters to Washington, will act as chief on spot, according to election of conference."

Jim exploded. He stormed around his office, flinging things. Despite every avowal that he definitely was not coming out of retirement to again seize the kingship, his father had the unmitigated audacity to virtually elevate Rickey to de facto editor-in-chief without saying boo to Jim! Lord Northcliff was dead right — Dad was a belligerent old tiger! Even worse, a loose cannon on the Scripps ship in Washington!

This action that shoved Rickey up to concern policy czar was merely the trigger that set off between father and son a terrible clash over the empire's scepter. In another overt act, Scripps spiked Jim's intention of appointing Byron Canfield editor-in-chief to fill the void left by John Paul's death. Jim currently had Canfield at his side, running N.E.A. headquarters in Cleveland from the West Coast, while being groomed as the new editorial chief. Scripps said bluntly Canfield wouldn't do, and recommended either Howard or Martin to back up Rickey.

Jim was next startled by E. W. requesting him to order all their papers west of the Mississippi to publish all N.E.A. and U.P. dispatches that might arouse readers to the war dangers. Only hours later came a second telegram. E. W. had arranged for Senator Hiram Johnson to write a special article spelling out the seriousness of the war situation. He asked Jim to order all Scripps papers to play up the piece — in full on page one! Jim gritted his teeth and asked Bob Paine to help him draft such a "must" message and sent it to all editors. For some reason not shown, Johnson never produced the article — a snafu and an embarrassment, of course, to Jim.

Scripps continued on a dictatorial tear. He abruptly fired off a personal letter to every editor in the concern which asserted "because conditions are grave in this country," he was forced to abandon his life-long dedication to granting them local autonomy and felt obligated to switch over to setting up an editorial "czar" in Washington.

> I have come out of retirement temporarily. . . . I have urged . . . that some one man of great ability and experience in our concern should locate himself permanently in Washington during the period of the war, and that he should be empowered to direct the editorial policy of all our institutions and co-ordinate the effort of all in one direct line . . . [for] public service to this country in a period of stress.
>
> I have urged further that this man have both the authority and the responsibility to direct not only what shall *not* be published but particularly what *shall* be published.
>
> You must instantly recognize what a great departure this course is from my lifelong practice of securing absolute local self-government.
>
> There could have been in my mind no such revolution in the policy had I not realized a supreme, unarguable necessity. For the time being, I would like to see every editor and, in fact, every man, no matter how humble his position in the concern, forget circulation, personal ambition, fame and profit, so that every energy may be bent to one end — the country's final victory in the war.
>
> If need were, I would devote every atom of my fortune, every material comfort, and even life itself to this end.

It was impossible now to halt the deadly and rapidly growing rivalry among the more ambitious Scripps subalterns as long as it remained an open question whether Chairman of the Board Jim or Controlling Stockholder Scripps was actually calling the signals and running the show.

Canfield fired off a letter to his N.E.A. lieutenants in Cleveland objecting to an editorial the syndicate had sent out eulogizing Secretaries Baker and Daniel, and calling their critics mud-throwers. Canfield said it obviously had been written by Rickey. "If EWS issues an order it will be implicitly obeyed. Until then . . . you will take orders from me. I am still directing N.E.A. editorial policy, not Rickey."

Boldly, the editor of the *Dallas Dispatch* challenged Scripps, advising that the policy editorials should be tagged only "requested" for use, instead of carrying a mandatory "must" slug. That didn't sit too well. Scripps immediately reiterated to Rickey and Cochran that they should continue to mark important editorial matter "must"—and in so doing tacitly took to himself the mantle of policy czar. On an editorial going out that day from Washington, "What Is America's Duty to Itself and Its Allies?," Scripps promptly stamped "must"—and ordered it published on page one.

Rebellion against the men in Washington kept flaring up on the West Coast. The *Los Angeles Record* came out in late July with another of its own editorials again tearing the hide off President Wilson. Scripps wired Jim a sharp reprimand. The boy-king snapped right back, telling his father "either I have got to boss this job or you have." Rickey ought to be fired, Jim added, revealing that Rickey had wired Canfield to the effect that the *Los Angeles Record* "has the least cause for existence of any paper in the United States." Further, Jim said, Rickey was blatantly "prejudiced against the western and southern papers."

Next the *Record* came out with a series of stories reflecting strong public sentiment in California against conscription. Scripps wired another reprimand, telling Jim "some of your man's statements are false and others unscrupulous." Jim sent back a telegram that he was "puzzled" and argued against carrying out his father's "Washington policy."

E. W.'s next wire asked Jim to "hold up until Roy Howard arrives" to explain affairs.

The old man then wrote Jim that the *Record* articles had practically unhinged the Washington staff. "Neg thinks the government may try to close up some of your papers," the father warned. He volunteered to "get out of the newspaper game" except for continuing to urge Jim to counsel with more men. In the crisis, Scripps revealed, Rickey had worked so hard he was about to break under the strain. "He may have to be sent away to rest."

A day or two later Jim sent another hot telegram to Washington. He once more chastised his father, asserting he had understood policy no longer would be dictated from the capital, yet the *San Diego Sun* had received new "must" copy from Rickey.

It was the father's turn to apologize. He sent a telegram explaining that the latest "must" copy had gone out before Rickey was informed that such authority was now out of his hands. In fact, said the message, Rickey had been "deposed" and there now was no head to the Washington organization. "Neg Cochran will put into effect any orders that I send," Scripps added.

During the height of the father-son clash, E. W. lamented to Nackie: "Ever so often, as you have heard me say, Jim turns up acting like a ten-year-old boy. The spell usually lasts only a few hours or a day or two at most and he comes out again as a hard-thinking and hard-headed 'old man.' "

Apparently Jim had just emerged from such a metamorphosis. He sent his father a "personal and confidential" telegram: "I am not the least offended with anything you have done. I have been slightly provoked, but I think you will admit that even a saint might become provoked during these times. . . . We have worked together long enough to thoroughly understand each other and you can absolutely depend on me to a greater extent in the future than you ever have in the past. This means I will take your advice without question."

"Your telegram is perfectly satisfactory," the old man wired back. "I thank you for it." Still it would be a good idea, Scripps wrote later, for Jim to come to Washington for a face-to-face discussion. Jim declined the invitation, saying he was just then swamped with work out west.

After seven weeks with her mother at West Chester, Nackie got in a sort of stew. Duty, she felt, required her to join her husband. But she couldn't quite decide to leave Ohio. The war kept her nervous and upset. She had terrible nightmares, witnessing the bloody deaths of Jim and Bob on the battlefield. Worse, she clearly saw Nackey die in the agony of childbirth. By mail, she nagged Scripps. Absolutely, he must keep both their boys out of the war! He ought to give up his Washington playthings and take her straightway back to Miramar. Scripps felt a certain sympathy, but he grumbled and growled about her yen to return to Miramar. Nackey would never rest until she got him to "adopt" Tom Meanley!

On impulse, Nackie boarded the train in Cincinnati, wiring at the last minute she would arrive in Washington at 1:30 P.M., with cook and chauffeur. That annoyed Scripps. No train was scheduled to arrive at 1:30, and he didn't even know whether she was on the Pennsylvania or the B. and O. He refused to hang around any noisy depot. He sent Bob with car to wait out her arrival. The train was two hours late.

Their reunion was not totally harmonious. Nackie arrived "in a condition of more or less suppressed hysteria—largely caused by her regarding this draft as a lottery of death," he wrote Ellen. "The thing got on my nerves, too. . . . I can take on a full case of panic just by seeing a scared look in someone's eyes." Nackie kept begging him to go back to Miramar, E. W. moaned to Jim. "Your mother and I have been having some uncomfortable discussions of the subject."

Scripps suffered deep anguish over estrangement from his youngest daughter. He wrote Nackey July 12 that she vexed him but he admired her spirit of independence. "The only way we will ever get together is for outsiders to keep their noses out." He was willing to stake her financially to take a stab at growing wartime food at Fanita. "Next to your mother, you have more of my love than anyone else on earth."

Bob was tagging around with his father's men in Washington. The boy felt called upon to deny to J. C. Harper that he was just on a lark. He avowed that he had finally shelved his ambition to be a poet. "I am honestly trying these days. . . . My work gives pleasure . . . and a sense of adventure." Bob felt he had convinced his old man he was making a hard try at the newspaper game. As to being drafted, he hated the thought of picking up an army rifle and killing someone—but he was perfectly willing to go to the front lines as an ambulance driver.

On July 20, Bob's number came up in the draft at Cincinnati, where he had registered. His father was set to resist the call. E. W. directed Bob to request exemption on the ground he was married and his wife was three months pregnant. The old man instructed his lawyer in Cincinnati to also claim Bob was in an essential industry—newspapers. Anxious just then about Jim's status, Scripps queried J. C. Harper in San Diego by wire. The first draft call didn't reach Jim; he might not even be called in the second. Nackie, more worked up than ever, jumped all over Scripps because he wasn't trying as hard to spare Tom Meanley as he was Bob.

Nackie decided to go back to California. Scripps and Bob accompanied her as far as Cincinnati. While in Ohio, Scripps took Bob to Columbus and introduced him to Governor James A. Cox as "John Paul's successor as editorial head of the Ohio papers." Governor Cox readily agreed to request that Bob be exempted from the draft on occupational grounds. Relating this to Nackie, E. W. changed his tune about needing a "break" from her companionship.

> I needed you awfully: to read to me, to play dominoes with me and to divert my mind. I thought that if you had been here my mind might have been diverted from myself and my troubles in other ways. . . . Harry and I play dominoes some. My books and magazines are too dull to read. . . . I do a good deal of moping around. The one advantage is that I have had time to do a lot of good hard thinking.

Abruptly, a few days later, his mood again changed. He whined to Nackie that the whole family always took all he would give. "Now they should be content to leave me alone unreproached and unblamed for not doing more. . . . I am now in the mood to write some disquisitions that might be of public use if I were free from family anxieties and business worries. But O! pshaw! I have always lived in turmoil. . . . There is no reason to expect to escape any the remainder of my life."

Just then came word from California that Tom Meanley had gone for his draft physical. The medics found him missing two teeth, opposing molars. On medical grounds, Meanley was exempted! Scripps was aghast.

It was not only family and business discord, worry about the draft and the war, nor even a long ordeal with forceps and drill in the dentist's chair that caused Scripps's mood to skitter so wildly from elation to the blues. Once again he was hitting the bottle. He was spending a lot of hours with old drinking pal Neg Cochran. Scripps made no secret of the situation, telling Ellen: "I have consumed more whiskey in five months [the period of time he had been in Washington] than I would at home in fifteen. But so far no bad effects seem to have resulted."

In mid-August Scripps fired off a cryptic telegram to Jim. It was brief, saying only: "The existence of the institution is threatened. E. W. Scripps." Out in San Diego, Jim was unable to make heads or tails of the message. He wrote his father for an explanation. Jim was beset with his own worries about the draft. It now looked like he would be called up. He wired Dad to see someone in Washington about getting him a lieutenant's commission. The X-rays showed Jim no longer suffered from that boyhood ankle injury. He'd been examined by the Camp Kearney physicians and found fit to be an officer—just a little overweight, with slightly flat feet. Milton McRae and J. C. Harper were in a stew about this. They jumped the gun on their own, petitioning the Los Angeles draft appeals board to grant Jim an occupational exemption—even before his number was drawn.

Then came a blow that made Nackie cry out. The Ohio draft appeals board rejected Bob's requests for exemption—both on marriage and occupation. That left open only one final appeal—direct to the adjutant general's office in Washington. The Scripps lawyers got together the necessary papers to make that last appeal.

Meanwhile, out west, Jim was in a tizzy that rapidly grew into near-paranoia. There was too much uncertainty and confusion about his status with his father. He felt events were swirling madly around him, strange and mysterious, actions he hadn't the least handle on. He packed his valise and took the eastbound train. Jim was on his way to Washington to meet the old man face-to-face, in private—and get things straightened out!

On Sunday, September 16, Jim hit Washington spoiling for a fight. "Jim is mad and wants to hit somebody," Scripps reported later to Nackie. "He seemed inclined to rush me and run all over me. . . . His jaw was sticking out about an inch further than usual, and he seemed quite willing to pick a quarrel with anybody and even rather anxious to do so. . . . I have never seen him in any such mood."

Scripps stood his ground. He felt Jim was opposing him just to show he dared. "However, I think it is not only possible, but probable, that a good enough compromise can be made." By now E. W.'s colleagues had explained that his son-king bitterly resented the Washington meddling as undercutting Jim's standing with his own captains and lieutenants. Further, Jim confessed to J. C. Harper he was unable "to hold all the threads in my hand" as his father easily could. Jim needed to tackle one problem at a time. He was angry, in a totally different vein, at some of President Wilson's actions. The babble of mixed signals coming from the old man's Washington satraps frightened, rattled, and angered him.

En route, Jim had paused in Cincinnati long enough to summon Bob there for a huddle. From the outset, the brothers bickered. Now at Airlie the wrangling continued—becoming a three-way set-to. Jim irately told his father not to worry about the future of the concern. Even if he and Bob were killed in the war, the business would virtually run itself for about three years. "Then I could sell it," E. W. reported to Nackie. "He talks about such matters in a way that makes even my blood run cold."

Jim was accompanied by his wife. Josephine startled Scripps by expressing her private wish Jim could move to Washington, taking an estate further east on Chesapeake Bay on the ocean where the whole family could live in a compound similar to Miramar. She felt Jim must get away from San Diego. Hanging around with the officers at Camp Kearney was giving him a "fever" to rush off to war.

Jim was more put out with Wilson than was his father. The President, Jim raged, owed his election to the Scripps papers. Now the White House, as he saw it, was all but ignoring E. W. Scripps. Father tried to cool him down. "It is the country's welfare that's at stake, and at such a time as this it would be treason to resent in any way fancied insults or real insults. We have got the president, and can't get rid of him. The country's welfare depends on support of him." Scripps didn't feel ignored; he had sought little contact with any high official. Despite his resentment, Jim did not want any favor from the White House that would appear payment of a political debt – especially in the matter of draft exemption.

Neg Cochran immediately set up a private lunch for Jim and Bob with Secretary of War Baker at the Powhatan suite. Jim went reluctantly, but came away with high regard for Baker. Present at the lunch also was the *Cleveland Press*'s legal counsel, Tom Sidlo, Baker's law partner. Sidlo was handling exemption requests on occupational grounds for most of the concern's key people, including Bob's case.

Jim was strongly "anti." Scripps explained to Nackie: "He thinks the Administration is going to have a lot of trouble soon enough with the working man and the unwilling conscripts. . . . If the conscripts don't get a fair deal . . . he would rather take their side of the case than the side of the plutocrats, aristocrats and bureaucrats."

For eight days, father and two sons wrangled at Airlie over the future. "There developed," E. W. wrote Nackie, "a surprising lack of harmony between any two of us and between all three of us. That is to say no one of us wants exactly what either of the other wants. This evening I feel as though I had been wrestling with a threshing machine." These stormy sessions gave Scripps a valuable idea – to create a ruling "triumvirate" with his two boys, first audaciously elevating the green and untested Bob to the powerful post of editor-in-chief.

Scripps found a bit of humor in Nackie's failure to comprehend this family squabbling. "I tried to explain that you were like an old hen that had hatched out a lot of duck eggs and who was greatly disturbed because the young ducks did not act like chickens. I have been feeling the last few days some of the surprise and chagrin as much as the old hen herself that my two sons are men and not boys."

By compromising, Scripps worked out a "deal" that settled his strife with Jim. He agreed Jim could pick his own chiefs – even Canfield – as long as he pledged to not allow the papers to publish sensations that would "aggravate the feeling of discontent, riot and revolt." In return Scripps pledged not to act unilaterally; but demanded the sons request and consider his views – thus making his first subtle move toward establishing the triumvirate. From the first Jim assured father he "would do everything that I required of him, both in a business way and a personal way. However, for the first time in his life, his attitude was something of that of a young, strong man who felt it was his duty to take care of a father who was getting old and who was no longer able to fight alone his own battles."

Jim went back to Cincinnati "to think." "Promise not to set off any fireworks—at least for a week, or until you see me again," Scripps urged. Jim agreed, saying he would return to Washington within ten days.

Behind the scenes, Scripps pulled strings trying to keep Jim out of the front lines. He considered his eldest son an experienced "big man" who deserved to serve his country in an important military post. Something interesting sprang up; the government planned to spend $1,000,000 sending pro-American news into Russia. Scripps hurried to see the two men in charge of the project—war news "censor" George Creel, and Walter Lippmann, editor of *The New Republic* magazine, and a confidant of President Wilson. They reacted favorably, suggesting Jim might handle the business side, and Roy Howard manage the Moscow end. Likewise he made overtures to two new wartime friends, Justice Brandeis and Herbert Hoover, to find a place where Jim would fit into the war effort.

Nackie, out at Fanita ranch, sent a letter again begging her husband to quit Washington and come "home." Next day, September 25, 1917, she telegraphed:

> Nackey has beautiful ten-pound baby boy born at two o'clock this afternoon. Mother and child in perfect condition.

Just then Bob was having a fierce struggle with his own conscience. He kept Peggy up most of one night hashing it over. Next morning, Sunday, September 30, he informed his father at breakfast he was withdrawing his personal claim for draft exemption. Scripps was startled. Bob asked him to also drop the claim for business exemption. Scripps refused; he intended to press that. Bob would not be deterred. He typed a letter "volunteering" to go into the army, got an appointment to hand-deliver it to Secretary Baker at 12 noon Monday. Peggy smiled at Scripps, assuring him Bob was doing the right thing.

About 10 Monday Bob left Airlie to keep his noon appointment with Baker. At 11:30 o'clock came a call to Scripps from a Washington "insider"—with startling news. The adjutant general had just granted Bob's personal hardship exemption! It seemed to have come too late; Bob already was on his way to Baker's office. Scripps, flustered, suggested to Peggy they ought to send someone to head off Bob. The bride set her mouth and shook her head. Bob had his mind made up. He could not suffer being called a slacker.

Ironically, a few minutes before noon Bob telephoned Airlie from the Powhatan suite before proceeding to Baker's nearby office. For several minutes Peggy chatted amiably with him—never letting out a peep about the news from the adjutant general.

By next morning, Bob was army-bound. He kissed his wife goodbye and took the train for Cincinnati. Jay Curts, the Scripps lawyer, met him with a new ten-dollar army blanket, a bundle of broken-in towels from his own bathroom—and a 1911 U.S. Army Infantry Drill Manual. Bob had his heart set on making sergeant within a couple of months. Curts fixed him up also with extra sox, his own "lucky" pocket knife, smoking tobacco, and matches. "I never saw Bob more cheerful," Curts wrote Scripps.

Bob hopped the train to Middletown, near West Chester, and was sworn in at 3 in the afternoon with forty-five other recruits from Butler County. Dubbed "temporary sergeant," he was handed the roster and told to herd the recruits onto the train for Chillicothe, Ohio—and Camp Sherman.

In newspaper circles, this event was a hot item of gossip. The baby son of one of the country's wealthiest newspaper potentates was not dodging the draft—he was volunteering for foot soldier! *Editor and Publisher* magazine, the leading national trade publication, handed Bob a nice bouquet—for patriotism and courage.

Peggy intended to follow soldier Bob to Chillicothe. Curts had rented her a ninety-dollar-a-month apartment. Unfortunately, she had already once nearly lost her baby. Her doctor said no travel—certainly not by jolting train. In camp, Bob got lucky. Someone found out he could type. He was grabbed for Headquarters Company of the 322nd Regiment, Field Artillery of the National Army—and stuck behind an Underwood to fill out personnel records. On the third or fourth day, he lined up with other new men for typhoid shots. Disaster struck. Two hundred soldiers fell ill from their inoculations. The camp had few doctors; the only remedy they offered was purgatives. One distraught soldier killed himself. Bob collapsed on his cot, so wretchedly sick he almost wanted to die.

While Bob lay prostrate with chills and fever at Camp Sherman, good news sprang up in Washington. Sidlo, fresh from conferring with his law partner Secretary Baker, called for an appointment with Scripps.

They met in private for dinner at the Powhatan suite. What Sidlo had to impart elated Scripps, and he promptly dispatched a "personal and confidential" letter to Jim: "Baker told Sidlo that this matter of Bob Scripps had been taken up in one of the Cabinet meetings, at the President's insistence, and that several Cabinet members were outspoken in their sentiments that there ought to be no question at all in this matter and that Bob should be released. The President himself spoke in the same strain."

In passing along this confidence, E. W. was trying to make a point. "My idea in telling you this is to impress on you . . . the Administration has shown that it has the highest respect for our institution, and that it values its services, I think, even more highly than you do." He reminded Jim that Wilson had earlier proclaimed publicly that neither he nor the Cabinet would consider any exemption requests. "So it appears they considered this was so remarkably exceptional . . . they made it a special subject for consideration." Scripps's letter warned Jim that no other person, "in the concern or outside of it, should know these details."

Next day Jim showed up in Washington—steaming mad! He was furious about the way the Administration was treating Bob. Scripps at once realized that Jim had left Cincinnati before the confidential message arrived. E. W. explained everything—and Jim cooled down.

Now they could only wait. Somewhere in the military chain of command an order was wending its way to Camp Sherman discharging Bob on occupational grounds. Such communications travel, of course, at what seems a snail's pace. Scripps groaned. Poor Bob might not get out for thirty days, perhaps not for two months.

But father had definitely made up his mind. Bob was to be appointed "assistant chairman of the board" of the whole institution, as well as editor-in-chief, and the man in charge of setting Washington policy. For back-stop and advice, Bob could call on Neg Cochran and Roy Howard—and take counsel from his father and Jim. This proposed appointment worried Jim; he thought Bob too green and unstable to shoulder such an important command. "We need him," Scripps retorted. "We must help him." Bob's new salary would be $500 a month; Scripps already was giving Peggy a monthly household allowance of $500.

Looking ahead, E. W. decided there should be a sort of Scripps "embassy" in Washington, where Bob could meet his staffers as well as entertain dignitaries. By a stroke of luck such a place just then came to his attention—in an unsolicited letter from a real estate agent. It was a four-story mansion formerly occupied by the Belgian minister in what Scripps called the "swell" section of Massachusetts Avenue, N.W.—on the capital's main embassy row. This imposing residence sat on a triangle, had an electric elevator, spacious rooms, and servants quarters. The rent was $8,500 a year. Scripps sent Peggy to inspect the mansion, and then signed a year's lease. He also held onto Airlie and his suite at the Powhatan.

It took the army a full week to order Bob's release, and officially announce it. At the same time, the secret of Wilson's involvment leaked out. The Associated Press spread the story coast to coast, under a Cincinnati dateline:

WILSON EXEMPTS SCRIPPS'S SON

By The A. P. Night Wire
CINCINNATI, Oct. 9—Official notification reached here tonight from President Wilson that he had finally decided to personally exempt Robert Payne [*sic*] Scripps, son of E. W. Scripps, multi-millionaire newspaper syndicate owner, from army duty on the plea of young Scripps that the advocacy of the Scripps newspapers of war and the support of patriotic movements such as the Liberty Loan and the Red Cross had entitled him to exemption from army service.

The application of young Scripps for exemption has attracted wide attention by newspaper editors and newspaper workers owing to its nature.

As young Scripps plea that he was the sole support of a family had failed to move the army conscript authorities, Scripps gave West Chester, O., as his abiding place in his application for freedom from conscription.

Scripps telegraphed Nackie the news. She got confused and thought he had been sent home for some physical defect. She became "too tense to write" but finally on October 16 responded, giving her husband a bit of praise: "I am quite sure that no one but you could have done it. . . . At times it seemed impossible." He replied, offering a little white lie to cover up the White House angle—which was being savagely trumpeted by many newspapers: "I am almost positive that Bob's case did not get to the President direct, or even Secretary of War Baker."

Bob, after ten days in camp, returned to Airlie a physical wreck. He had a heavy cold, with dark circles under his eyes, too hoarse to talk. Even through closed doors his cough echoed through the house. Scripps summoned a physician, who diagnosed severe laryngitis, doubtless triggered by his inoculation which caused mild typhoid fever. The cure was to avoid talking, and get bed rest.

That presented an awkward situation. Jim had come to the capital so the three of them could start up the new triumvirate. Now Jim could only go back to Cincinnati. Without getting their signals set, Bob dragged himself out of bed in a few days and launched his regime as new editorial chief. He and Peggy moved into the "embassy" at 2131 Massachusetts Avenue, N. W. Bob's cozy first-floor den had a fireplace and hot-water radiators. His wife could hear him in there pounding away all day at his typewriter. The new editor-in-chief was busily issuing orders, assigning stories to develop, setting war news policy for all the papers.

With no hesitation, Bob put on the mantle of policy czar. Byron Canfield, now back at N.E.A. headquarters at Cleveland, received sharp orders. Bob did not want to see "any more of a certain line of stuff" that had been going out of Washington. He jumped all over a Rickey editorial supporting censorship, calling that "a rotten idea." He added: "As the war goes on . . . it's going to be a mighty bad thing . . . if the publishers aren't going to be able to speak out freely. . . . What would you think of watching this censorship thing with a hawk's eye. . . . Make a story out of each case that pops up."

In the scattered Scripps newspaper offices, some editors began at once to fret and grumble. They were shocked that such an inexperienced youngster was breaking into the business — at the top! And holding forth from an "embassy" in Washington! Rival newspapers all around the country added to the discord, by heaping scorn on the favoritism that excused Bob from military service. The *San Diego Union* sneered that the appeal to the President "was an absolutely unique example of vicarious patriotism — something quite new under the stars and stripes. A patriot by proxy or a patriot by inheritance is certainly a patriot *sui generis.*" The *Cincinnati Enquirer* asserted Bob "came here to do some little work around the office and beat some of the reporters out of their jobs, and was drafted." The ten-day soldier caught flak in the columns of dozens of newspapers and magazines. E. W. felt called on to send an "explanation" to the editor of his own Cincinnati *Post.* It was rather devious. In part Scripps wrote:

> It is my belief that neither the President nor the Secretary of War intervened . . . [that] all such applications were passed on by military authorities. The insinuation that the President improperly exercised his authority . . . is, I believe, inspired by personal malice as well as political motives. Bob Scripps is a rich man's son, but he has no desire other than to serve with the men and women who do the nation's work. He has been elected to a more difficult and a more dangerous task than that which he preferred to undertake: namely, that of being a common soldier in the ranks of the country's armies.

Surprising even himself, Scripps discovered that his few months' sojourn in Washington had put him in his best health in nine years, was turning him into a conservative, greatly soothed his usually explosive temper, brought him wide-awake, and more eager and skilled in grappling with the uncertain future of newspaper publishing than most of his gray-haired former front-line comrades. He was an ancient emerged from the dead. He felt good enough to jest about it.

> I got out of my self-selected sarcophagus; threw off one cerement, and then another; removed the bandages that held my mouth shut; and brushed off the pennies from my eyelids. I tried one leg and then another, and then an arm, worked my fingers and toes, winked my eye; and there I was— really a live man after all!

That description Scripps forwarded October 27 to Bob Paine upon learning that his first editor and most-trusted confidant was coming east, bringing his family. The old comrades, though their houses were barely twenty miles apart, had let their friendship wither somewhat. Scripps took this occasion to rekindle their old affection with a "personal and confidential" and gossipy letter that ran to about 3,000 words.

Its biggest portion constituted a ringing defense of his elevating Bob to editor-in-chief. He doubted Paine fully believed the affidavit he had filed in behalf of the exemption request which stated Bob was "the second most important element in the concern. . . . Bob is twenty-two. When you and I were twenty-two, we were better men than we have ever been since. When Jim was twenty-two, he was a young giant. . . . Bob has got as good or better stuff in him. . . . I needed Bob and I knew it. Jim needs Bob and he knows it. . . . Bob is not going to disappoint you. . . . Even those who esteem Bob the most only regard him as a boy who had the good (or bad) fortune to have a wealthy, forceful, and a too-affectionate father. . . . I had only one trade to teach my children, and that was the 'king' trade." The "king" trade required steel nerves, and Scripps intended to find out if Bob had them. "Like the old Indian who threw his boy babies into the stream, remarking that if they were good Indians they would swim, and if they weren't good Indians the sooner he found it out the better."

At least one disgrunted Scripps chieftain was certain Master Bob was unworthy of being even tested as a good Indian. Harry Rickey was in a rage. This was the second time the old man had kicked him aside for one of his neophyte sons. Barely three years before Scripps had shoved timid, frightened John Paul down his throat as editorial boss of Ohio. And now Bob—a baby, a stars-in-the-eyes poet, of all things! Green as goose grease, never tested in the hot battle for scoops and readers! (Of course, Rickey was ignoring Bob's experience in the trenches on the late and unlamented *Philadelphia News-Post,* as well as on other papers.)

Rickey barged into Airlie and angrily accused Scripps of being his personal enemy. Rickey wailed that he had spent thirty years in the concern. He had been loyal—but he had never been adequately paid, nor given the top jobs that he really deserved. "I was greatly grieved," Scripps observed, "that Rickey was sorely chagrined and mortified at Bob's appointment, and that he is very, very sore."

Scripps tried to calm him down, readily admitting that the $14,000-a-year Rickey had played a big role in the success of the newspapers. But E. W. reminded Rickey that he had been only "temporary" chief in Washington, and that his reign as "czar" had not entirely pleased Scripps, and definitely drew bitter criticism from Canfield and other editors.

Rickey stormed out of the house. He was still irate. Over his shoulder he flung a threat; he'd resign at once!

Trying to appease Rickey, Bob offered him an important special assignment, going to France to write about what American fighting men could expect. That idea won kudos from older brother. Jim said he backed Bob "all the way" in handling Rickey but cautioned that once Rickey made up his mind "to quit, he will be no good. Better give him six months' salary and let him go."

Out in California, Nackie felt she finally had West Coast family affairs in shape and could return to Airlie. She wrote her husband on November 6: "I am coming to you because I love you and am trusting you and am anxious to be helpful to you . . . the great big man that I have thought you was [sic] in the past."

Unfortunately, Scripps was not at all certain he was ready for her to come back to Washington—not just now, at least. He had to be careful what he wrote her. Nackie at fifty-one was still vibrant and womanly; to have her husband too vigorously reject her offer of tender companionship could easily wound her pride and self-esteem. The old man was just then having other misgivings about family affairs. He wrote Ellen candidly that "Bob drinks too much. . . . But, for that matter, Jim does also."

The sons seemed to trouble him in other ways, too. He lately had sent each a letter about their need to obey the Ten Commandments. "You young men have been altogether remiss in knowing the Bible. I doubt . . . you know all there is in the Ten Commandments." Father gave a hint of his area of concern, telling Ellen: "Matrimony is fraught with many dangers. Something may develop in this department of Bob's life to cause serious results. I rather think that Jim is passing through several crises, some of which cause me considerable uneasiness."

For six months, Jim had been waiting for the other shoe to drop on his military status. He had been drafted in San Diego on June 5, 1917. But E. W. officially asserted his eldest son was indispensible to the management of his newspapers, and authorized the Central Office to appeal. Jim's exemption now was scheduled to be decided November 14, in Los Angeles by the regional board.

To be close to Bob and the old man in Washington, Jim had remained at the Central Office in Cincinnati. He was only overnight from the capital by the B. and O. Railroad. Jim first lived at the run-down West Chester farm; but suddenly rustic life depressed him and his wife. They moved to town, renting an expensive Grandin Road mansion on a bluff overlooking the Ohio River.

Airlie buzzed with excitement—pleasant and otherwise. Bob came in with news that E. W. finally had got his wish on soaking the rich with war taxes. The war was costing billions. "Pay as you go" was impossible—ridiculous. Scripps's eyebrows shot up when he learned the latest law out of Congress would force his concern to pay 1917 taxes of between $400,000 and $600,000. Then came a telegraphers wage increase, hitting United Press hard. "That will cost $36,000 out of my pocket," E. W. moaned.

Scripps was heartened when William Randolph Hearst suddenly ordered his *Los Angeles Evening Herald* to go to bat on Jim's draft deferment. This intervention was something John H. Perry had managed to pull off through newspaper friendships. Although usually the caustic enemy of Scripps's *Los Angeles Record,* the *Evening Herald* ran an editorial headed, "Editor Asks Right to Keep On Aiding Nation In War" which pointed out:

> James G. Scripps, who heads a string of newspapers which are doing their bit for patriotism and freedom all over America, is a general in America's army of patriotic publicity and to remove him from this high position . . . to place him in the ranks carrying only a single musket and capable of aiming at one infinitesimal fraction of the foe's vast forces, would seem a misdirection of endeavor.

The same editorial was published by Hearst's *American* in New York. A similar plea appeared on the editorial page of the normally Scripps-hating *Los Angeles Times.*

Of a sudden on November 12, strange things began happening to Scripps. He picked up a letter, started reading, and his right eye "went blur." Then his mouth felt queer; the muscles on the right corner seemed slack. When he tried to smoke a cigar, he couldn't draw well; his lips didn't fully close on the right. At lunch this "gap" let food and water dribble on his chin. A slight ache, or bearing-down sensation, developed in his right shoulder. E. W. became alarmed, and summoned a doctor.

Dr. William Gerry Morgan, who had been treating Scripps for bowel inflammation, immediately came to Airlie. Scripps described his symptoms. Dr. Morgan examined him briefly, and began muttering. "Mr. Scripps you have been trying to do too much," he said. "If you insist, at your age, doing the work of two men — somewhere, and in some way, you'll pay for it."

There was no doubt about what had happened. Scripps had suffered a slight stroke, resulting in partial facial paralysis on the right side. This clearly was a warning of danger. Dr. Morgan gravely asserted there could be a recurrence, possibly more severe and extensive. Scripps must at once go into virtual isolation — stop all work, see no visitors, cut off mail and the telephone, permit no worry to disturb his mind. For at least six months — complete rest! The first action Dr. Morgan took was to call in a nurse and put his patient to bed.

Bob and Peggy rushed from their "embassy" to the sickbed. Bob sent telegrams to his mother and Jim. Nackie, stunned, packed in a hurry and took the express train east. Jim felt boxed in; he wanted to come running, but feared to do so might alarm his father into wrongly suspecting the doctors were hiding the truth from him — that he actually was on the verge of dying. For a day or two, Jim sat tight in Cincinnati.

By then, the old man was feeling better. Scripps insisted on calling in Dr. Berkley from Baltimore and another neurologist. At his bedside the physicians all agreed — it was a light stroke, and E. W. had gotten off easy. He must remain in bed for a while, and then he ought to get away from hectic Washington. Why not spend the winter down south?

Nackie arrived. The doctors were blunt with her. She must not quarrel or nag. Scripps already was fretting about her presence. Any untoward action on her part might give him a setback. Nackie obediently tiptoed around. Another danger the doctors saw — when Bob, Jim, and the lawyers explained the circumstances — was that rejection of Jim's draft appeal possibly could jolt Scripps into another stroke.

That subject, too, was soft-pedaled in the sick-room. On November 24 the case came up — and Jim lost! One member of the appeals board, Ed Fletcher of San Diego — who ironically had over the years feuded with Scripps over real estate and highway building — was absent on account of illness. However, Fletcher immediately took Jim's side and asked President Wilson to personally overturn the Los Angeles decision.

Nobody bothered Scripps about that. But Jim feared the newspapers might be wrecked if he had to go into the army and leave Bob in command without the old man to help the kid.

Wisely, Scripps agreed he should leave Washington. He had Harry Schmetzstorff order up a private Pullman for a run to Key West, Florida.

Scripps thought he might want to keep the car all winter and live aboard. Once again the old man was about to become a hermit. "The doctors say they are going to order him to keep his whereabouts unknown to everyone," Schmetzstorff reported to Jim. Scripps was making "steady progress" but the physicians conceded he would continue to be agitated— "that thing is bound to be expected, especially until his system overcomes all traces of alcoholic desire, which will not be for many weeks to come."

Getting better, E. W. became bored, restless, and feisty, reverting for excitement to his old imperious ways. Schmetzstorff described one cranky episode in a confidential letter November 26 to Jim:

> Today has been a trying day for your father. He has been extremely nervous and restless today. Everything he wants, he wants right on the instant; and he first makes one plan and then another. For instance, for supper he wanted a quail or a young chicken broiled, and he wanted it right then and there. He wouldn't even wait to have it fixed.
>
> Kenzie [the cook] ran over and got hold of the farmer on the place and grabbed that farmer by the arm and made him go over and get a chicken he said he wouldn't kill for anything.
>
> Kenzie grabbed it off the roost by the neck, yanked the neck hard enough to yank the neck clear off; didn't give the chicken a chance for any dying struggles, but picked off the feathers as he ran for the kitchen; and in twenty minutes he had that chicken at your father's bedside, all fixed for a queen's taste—twenty minutes from roost to table!
>
> Your father had worked himself into quite a stew over wanting that chicken right away. Your mother and Edith nearly died laughing watching Kenzie's lightning speed, as they timed him. But when the chicken came, your father decided he didn't want it after all! But the nurse made him eat it! She told him that that chicken had caused too much trouble for him to pass it up that way, and he ate it, chuckling over the "joke."

Scripps could hardly have found a more tireless, loyal, and efficient major-domo than "Smitty" Schmetzstorff. In a flurry, the secretary got Publisher Kauffman to cancel the Airlie lease without penalty—even buying Scripps's left-over furnace coal, canned goods, extra silver, and bedding. He hurried down and inspected the provisioning of the private car Republic on a siding at Washington's Union Station. Then he tackled a hundred other last-minute chores.

On November 30, "Smitty" helped the nurse and servants carry Scripps aboard, and then began reading to him as the wheels of the Republic started clicking down the rails, leaving behind the grandeur and wartime hubbub of the nation's capital.

28

Call of the Sea and Jinxed Ships

The fifty-foot motor-sailer "Altomary" nosed up to a rickety pier at Marco Island on the lower west coast of Florida in late February 1918. On the eighty-acre island's crest, only forty-eight feet above sea level, stood a rambling weather-beaten house. Scripps limped ashore to inspect the abandoned property on sale for $10,000. Mosquitoes swarmed him. "They look almost as big as a humming bird!" he later wrote Ellen. Nonetheless he decided to buy the old house, and try to turn it into a substitute for Miramar as his "hideaway."

Nackie was with him aboard the "Altomary." His doctors still wanted them to live apart. But having to go into exile bored and frustrated Scripps. His private car had gone straight to Key West, but a clanking nearby dredger caused Scripps to flee to Miami to a sprawling $1,000-a-month concrete mansion that had been occupied but once, by millionaire meatpacker Phillip Armour's son as a honeymoon abode, on the water with its own dock, hidden from neighbors.

By mid-January — about six weeks after his stroke — Scripps felt almost normal. The only reminder of his Washington attack was an occasional twitching of his right eyelid and numbness in his right leg. Harry Schmetzstorff censored his mail. Dr. Morgan from Washington and Dr. Pollock from San Diego came and examined him, and found his condition "satisfactory" but mandated at least six months exile — especially from his wife.

Vaguely Scripps wished Nackie could join him — but tension had grown between them. He noticed his wife, now fifty-one, had somehow lost her choir-girl litheness and good looks. "She has aged tremendously in the last four years," he wrote Ellen. Worse, the flame of their romance was dying down. He lamented to Ellen that rarely were their "relations normal, such as usually exists between husband and wife. Yes, I say that of two years, there has not been all told four weeks when we have been together, living in accord and harmony."

Even so Scripps went secretly to the Western Union office and wired for Nackie—and she came. She was on her good behavior and made the reunion pleasant. Feeling the irresistible call of the sea, Scripps had been going out daily in rented launches from his own dock. But he felt he needed a larger vessel with a lavatory and a berth where he could lie down. He chartered the schooner "The Pueblo"—and kept looking for a better yacht. Going out on a boat, said letters Schmetzstorff sent out, was doing Scripps "a world of good. . . . He likes the roll and the spray and the salt air. . . . A good ocean cruise blows every trace of nervousness away. . . . He likes the open sea, and the rougher it gets, the better it suits him. . . . Boating has done more good for him than any other single thing."

Chartering the "Altomary" which had comfortable owners' staterooms and quarters for his secretary and servants, Scripps and Nackie spent most of February exploring southern Florida. For excitement he ordered his skipper to sail the ninety miles across the straits to Cuba. He found the island much as it was in 1884 when he and Ellen had taken their niece Anna there—"the same noisy streets, the same dirt, and the same everything else that was picturesque and revolting." Scripps sailed back to Florida and tied up at his own dock March 9.

"During the trip," E. W. wrote Ellen, "I had several nervous outbreaks as a result of little differences with Nackie." But he acknowledged he had partially caused them. Yet he vowed to never "endure" more family strife. "I am prepared to spend the remainder of my life entirely alone, as far as my family is concerned."

His family had just grown. A telegram waiting at Miami announced the March 1 birth of his newest grandson—Bob and Peggy's first child, whom they named Robert Paine Junior.

Schmetzstorff came up with a new yacht, the sixty-foot, white-hulled two-masted schooner "Evelyn." Scripps fell in love with the boat. It had powerful engines, twin screws, spacious staterooms. It chartered for $5,000 a month. E. W. didn't find fault with the price, but objected to something else—in his quarters the bathtub was too small!

Although his physicians wanted Scripps to stay in exile, he headed his yacht for Washington. At Jacksonville the schooner ran aground on a sandbar, then smashed into rocks and bashed in the hull. That meant several days in a boat yard for repairs.

In late May the "Evelyn" docked on the Potomac River at Alexandria, Virginia. Nackie was leaving the yacht for a few weeks to visit Jim and his family in Cincinnati. Scripps decided to go ashore. As he stepped on the gangplank, the wake of a passing tug shook his yacht. Scripps stumbled against the rail. He cried out and grabbed his side. Someone summoned a Washington surgeon, who found a fractured rib, applied tape and put Scripps to bed. When the doctor's bill came later, Scripps really howled. The charge for one "boat call" was $550!

After cruising three hundred miles of the shoreline of Chesapeake Bay, Scripps finally found a summer residence, three miles up the Severn River from Annapolis, Maryland, and fifty land miles from Washington, D.C. It was an elegant, roomy $65,000 country estate with ornate fireplaces and a deep-water dock where the "Evelyn" could tie up at his front door. The yacht was the centerpiece of his life; he rarely missed a daily cruise. Only on the water could he shed his cares.

Returning from her Cincinnati visit on his birthday, Nackie was in a strange, ugly mood. Finally she blurted that her doctor there told her she had serious bladder and kidney infection and must return at once to California. Alarmed, Scripps immediately summoned Dr. Berkley from Baltimore, who examined Nackie and found nothing serious. Nackie exploded in a tirade about "ill treatment" from her husband. "The doctor was tactful," say Scripps's "diary notes" for June 19, 1918, "and succeeded in quieting us both."

But when Dr. Berkley next day phoned Nackie the test results on her urine sample, she went into hysterics. Scripps rushed her in his limousine to Baltimore. Dr. Berkley had gone to his farm. Scripps put Nackie in the Belvedere Hotel and chased down the physician. The doctor said Nackie had misinterpreted his call as instructions to go back to Miramar. The Scrippses quarrelled bitterly in the auto on the trip back to Annapolis.

"On the 21st, early in the day," his "diary notes" say, "the old 'debate' started up with us. Mrs. Scripps threatened suicide, and by her violence caused me considerable alarm." Scripps decided to accede to her demands to accompany her back to Miramar, but to stay only two months. Later in the day, calmed down, his wife announced she would not require him to go.

Next day Scripps presented Nackie a one-page typed "program" which granted him freedom to more or less live his own life at Miramar. She flung aside the document, and blew up. Dr. Berkley arrived and told Nackie she had nothing resembling Bright's disease and would get well soon. On June 23, Scripps was on the lawn putting golf balls with Schmetzstorff when Nackie sent Kenzie to summon him. "She smiled in a disagreeable way," he wrote in his diary, and castigated him for "playing an old man's game." Scripps meekly sat down and picked up a book. His diary notes say at this point:

> After a few minutes all was quiet and suddenly she broke in and said, "Ed, I'm going to kill you sometime; I can't help it." I replied, "All right, darling, when you do it, make a clean job of it and do it quick."

Sitting side by side, Scripps continued to read while Nackie knitted. She shot him a few more jibes, but in the afternoon they took an hour's drive together. In the evening she felt pain and asked him to fix her a dose of lithia. His diary then continues:

> On the morning of the 24th, I awakened at about half seven and found that Mrs. Scripps was awake. She came to my room, laid down with me in bed, and began to tell me that she had finally decided that all her troubles had been caused by loving me so much, and that hereafter she was not going to love me anymore; that she would do what I said, however—that she wanted me to understand that she would be obedient—but that she would not love me any more.
>
> I jested with her about this matter a little bit.

The most startling development of the summer was Nackey Meanley's attempt to knuckle under. Through J. C. Harper, Nackey vowed to be a "dutiful daughter" and not force her husband on her father for "any recognition." In a tender July 19 letter to father, she tried to heal their breach. She characterized her elopement as "not defiance . . . but a larger duty to another. I cannot believe there was any wrong in what I did, although I sincerely regret that it had to be done without your approval." Scripps was unbending and ungracious. Replying July 30, he whined he was "old and tired" and still crippled by his stroke. He challenged her for any proof he was "derelict" as a parent, and predicted "discord and misfortune will continue . . . unless the Fifth Commandment is fully observed hereafter." The ex-tomboy of the mesa, it seemed, must do more than disown her husband and kiss her father's boots to acquire his full forgiveness.

A beaming Scripps walked out on a pier in late August at Stamford, Connecticut, for a first look at his new yacht. She was a graceful two-master with gleaming white hull and slender mahogany deckhouse. Eighteen feet wide, she drafted seven feet and was powered by a three-hundred-horsepower six-cylinder gasoline engine. Eight years old, her name was "Kemah" which Scripps later learned was an Indian word for "rain in the face." E. W. led Nackie aboard, and "both instantly fell in love with the yacht," Schmetzstorff noted. Typically, Scripps had let others find the boat — his Cincinnati lawyer Jay Curts and his Florida captain; they looked at a dozen vessels from Cleveland to New York before recommending her. This time he did not charter, but bought the vessel outright for $35,000.

It was August 23 when he had his gear moved off the "Evelyn," bade goodbye to his old crew, and went aboard the "Kemah" and had his captain head south for his Severn River dock. Within an hour and a half, the engine started acting up. They were on Long Island Sound. Near City Island, twenty miles from New York City, the motor gasped, sputtered, and died. It wouldn't start. They had to drop anchor. Scripps's nerves started jangling. He sent Harry ashore in the dinghy to telegraph for help.

Astoundingly, E. W. appealed to a most unlikely rescuer — his rarely-seen Rushville cousin, music impressario Albert Morris Bagby, famous brother of E. W.'s ex-business manager in San Diego and Los Angeles, Hans Bagby. By the time Albert Bagby received the message at the Waldorf-Astoria Hotel, help had already reached the stranded vessel. The muffler had rusted out, choking the motor. During the several days it took to make repairs, Scripps kept in touch with the United Press office in New York. Music maestro Bagby came out by launch for a social call.

The "Kemah," again heading south, couldn't shake its jinx. The engineer had trouble — starting, stopping, moving at less than eight knots. The captain managed to smash the dinghy and lifeboat, and run aground. Scripps, apprehensive, snorted to Harry: "If we get home safely, fire everyone and get a new captain, engineer and crew." Once tied up at their Severn dock, Harry did that.

Schmetzstorff found a plausible explanation for the jinx, writing a Scripps associate: "There is an odd sequence of hoodoos: the boat was purchased on Friday; it was registered from Cincinnati and the license number is 13; Mr. Scripps made his first trip on the boat on Friday; the bill for putting the boat in shape . . . was $1,300; and we are arriving home on Friday!"

There had been little let-up in the quarrel between Scripps and his wife. Jim, responding to a plea from his father while cruising, for help in this "war," brought Bob and three physicians — Morgan and Berkley plus Dr. Taylor of Cincinnati — to evaluate him. They conferred, told him nothing — but talked to Nackie. Scripps told Ellen how he learned the result of their consultation:

Nackie herself told me the next day that the doctors urged her to go away and stay at least three months and that it might be better if she were gone six months.

Nackie told me that she knew, and had learned from Jim, that the whole scheme was mine and I had got the doctors down here to send her away.

On September 28, Scripps saw her off by train from Washington. She paused in Cincinnati to visit her sons and their families. Jim had preemptorily ordered Bob there from Washington to learn the business at his side. Nackie sent a chatty letter sounding like her old self: "I am loving you all the time and hoping that you are feeling better each day. . . . I *do* love you beyond everything and everybody."

The hottest family feud now was between the Scripps sons. Jim was lowering the boom on Bob—and father was painfully aware of it. Others, too, saw the clash. Bob Paine wrote Jim directly: "I am a bit anxious about Bob. That he is to remain in Cincinnati for months would indicate that he had been cut off from his Washington job. He made mistakes, as was natural. He tried to do too much and put his fingers in fires that were bound to burn him. But he had his own ideas. He originated. . . . If he was pulled off, it is my humble opinion that it was premature."

In Jim's view, Bob still was too green to set "must" policy or to appoint editors. Bob didn't mind being *under* Jim, but argued E. W. wanted no one to "stand *between* Jim and myself in any matter of editorial direction," but admitted he didn't know whether his father intended him to be chief editor immediately "or go into training."

In all candor, Jim, too, was "stumped. . . . I don't know what to do." He directed a memo October 7 to Ellen, Bob Paine, and J. C. Harper, seeking their advice: "In my humble opinion it would take my brother several years to learn this business. . . . It would be unsafe or unwise for him to manipulate the levers without knowing all about them."

Jim doubtless knew he was barking up the wrong tree. Bob's destiny would not be decided by the likes of Ellen, Harper, or Uncle Bob Paine. One person only held the answer to the Jim-Bob dilemma—the gray-bearded controlling stockholder. Eventually he would be heard from. But not right now. Scripps had his hands full of new and unexpected trouble at his own front door.

"The 'Kemah' is a lemon!" New engine trouble on his yacht was a major calamity to strike Scripps just as he was ready to sail for Florida. Worse still, Schmetzstorff had to rush to Chicago where his wife was stricken in the Spanish flu epidemic, perhaps mortally. Scripps ordered the engine overhauled, and in anxiety also got a replacement yacht. But it wouldn't do — "not fit for a long voyage," he lamented by wire to his absent secretary. Mrs. Schmertzstorff passed her crisis and began to recover. Scripps started nudging Harry to return. Only weeks earlier Scripps had made another substantial request. In the country's patriotic fervor, E. W. had pointed out, Americans now called sauerkraut "Liberty cabbage" and "German toast" had become "French toast," etc. Harry would do well to adopt the American equivalent of Schmertzstorff — "Smithton." With no hesitation, the loyal Harry had gone into court and made the change legally.

Finally in late October Scripps surrendered his Severn River lease, stepped aboard the overhauled "Kemah" and began his thousand-mile voyage to Florida. The first week was pleasant, but off North Carolina, a cold wind and rough seas buffeted the yacht. In his saloon, Scripps felt cozy; the ship's heating system worked "perfectly." Hardly anything else did. The engine acted up again. "It's old and badly worn," Scripps lamented. Then the small engine which pumped up the starting tanks and powered the electric system broke down. "The batteries are old and shot." Two of the three water closets went on the fritz. A small leak developed and in an hour the saloon was awash with seawater. The power pump wouldn't work. While the sea seeped in, sailors fetched the hand pump. It wouldn't work. Scripps was aghast that it had never been tested. Finally it was repaired, and began clearing out the flood.

At last, November 8, the "Kemah" staggered in to Jacksonville, Florida. The ocean terrors did not leave Scripps a basket case; just the reverse. He advised Jim: "I feel twice as well as I did [at Annapolis]. . . . almost normal."

In side-by-side offices out in Cincinnati, the brothers were drawing concern editors into the debate of whether "hate stuff" should be played up during the "peace drive." Jim gave his views bluntly:

> Nearly everybody has an idea . . . as to peace terms. Any peace terms acceptable to Wilson will be acceptable to me. . . . I am quite sure if someone burnt down my house, and chopped off my little girl's hand, about what peace terms would be acceptable to me, and I would expect my brother and friends, at the very least, to obstruct the doorways to prevent an escape while I administered a pick-handle.
>
> The Washington Bureau should report the facts . . . the people prefer to do the interpreting themselves. Last Saturday night [October 12, 1918]

the *Cincinnati Enquirer* made another prize "bone-head" play in handling the German note which leaked in Washington in some way. The *Enquirer* interpreted the story; that is it handled it in such a way as to cause the people to believe that the Germans had surrendered.

The mayor ordered all the whistles blown and everything that could make a noise in the city was going. Altho the churches are closed on account of the influenza, they were opened and the church bells rang throughout the night. The whole affair would have been a great joke were it not for its serious and pathetic side.

Jim brushed aside Bob's pretensions of editorial czardom and tried to set up a meeting of both brothers and dad aboard his yacht. Scripps's response was lukewarm. Scripps wanted no fight. "You once told me you were rich and powerful enough to tell your Dad to 'Go to hell!' . . . Even if I am on my dying bed, such a course . . . will cause me to retort in kind. . . . I am able to repeat what I said years ago — So long as you run the business at a profit, take care of the working man, and obey the Ten Commandments, there will be no occasion for my intervening."

While America still cheered the end of the war, Scripps leaped into action to try to restore full rights to all citizens. The government should at once pardon protestors who had been silenced by harsh "war juries" and "war judges." He had in mind his friend Socialist editor Max Eastman, who had been indicted for sedition (though not convicted), the jailed labor firebrand Eugene V. Debs, and a host of other big and little conscientious objectors and champions of the underdog. He sent his appeal to the top — to President Wilson.

His letter, dated November 23, 1918, was to become unique and fairly controversial. First, it went by an unorthodox route — through Supreme Court Justice Louis Brandeis. Scripps expected his liberal jurist-friend to personally hand the letter to the President, and to perhaps add his voice to the need for urgent relief. The heavy hand of authority should be lifted in many areas. Censorship of the news should cease. The act no longer was necessary. (Despite almost blind allegiance during the crisis to virtually every White House action, Scripps had been warned a time or two that under the Espionage Act even some of his outspoken personal letters — if published during wartime — would have entitled him to twenty years in prison.)

It is not precisely clear how or when the Scripps letter reached Wilson. White House Secretary Joseph Tumulty briefly acknowledged it on December 11 but indicated the President — rushing off to Europe for the peace conference — had not read it. Weeks later, from Paris, Wilson would respond — but not to Scripps's satisfaction. He drilled his ideas into Bob and pushed him to go to the White House and argue in person.

The day the armistice was formally declared — Monday, November 11 — Scripps was stranded aboard his jinxed yacht in Jacksonville harbor. The town went wild. Scripps cheered with everybody else, but felt his nerves begin jangling. The excitement brought on neurasthenia, but it would last only a day or two. ′

Scripps apparently was not greatly upset by the sensational and ill-timed "scoop" that had gone out over United Press wires the previous Thursday, November 7 — a flash that the armistice had been signed. It was an error that would go down in history as one of the big bloopers in modern journalism. The key figure — and scapegoat — was Roy W. Howard. The feisty little president of United Press Associations was flitting around Europe, helping cover the war. He reached Brest, France, and walked into Allied naval operations headquarters just as an "official" military telegram arrived from Paris announcing that Germany had signed an armistice at 11 o'clock that morning and fighting had stopped at 2 in the afternoon. With the commanding admiral's approval, Howard cabled U.P. in New York: "Urgent. Armistice allied Germans signed 11 smorning hostilities ceased two safternoon." The message crossed the Atlantic Ocean in six minutes, reaching New York shortly after noon. In Brest, the admiral himself had the "armistice" announced in the town square.

All across America, Thursday afternoon newspapers getting the United Press service went extra — the war was over! Factory whistles blew. Church bells rang, people rushed whooping into the streets; there was general pandemonium.

But there was to come a big kick-back — and angry disappointment. The report was not true — not yet! The Associated Press shot out a flat denial. So did Allied headquarters in Paris, although the admiral in Brest tried to explain he had given the report as true to Howard. (It was later suggested that German secret agents may have sent the fake message to Brest as a ploy to create confusion.)

In any event, there were red and perplexed faces throughout the United Press bureaus, at Scripps dailies, and in newspaper offices generally. In San Francisco, the *Bulletin* editor threw the U.P. telegraph operator out of his building. Some embarrassed Scripps editors thought Roy Howard had been too eager, should have verified the report elsewhere. But the old man at Jacksonville seemed to take the hullaballo in stride. E. W. knew that throughout the war the United Press coverage had been first-class, and because of Howard's imagination and leadership, more aggressive and enterprising — and thus more interesting — than the AP in the afternoon field. And no one could question the Scripps organization's allegiance and patriotism. Nor was it the first or only newspaper report that triggered a premature celebration of the "end" of the war. He had only to recall the *Cincinnati Enquirer*'s "bone-head" story in October that set off that wild spree of whistles and bells.

Scripps was still waging his own "war" against the hoodoo that bedeviled the "Kemah." The motor was again overhauled, and when they put out in the Atlantic for Miami, it purred. But not for long. It conked out again, and they limped into port. Scripps was disgusted. "If the war was still going on," he wrote grandson John Paul, "I would send the boat out in the ocean and have a German submarine blow it up!" The jinx kept striking. The yacht had to have new batteries, and barnacles scraped, and her bottom "copper painted." Then dry rot was discovered in the wooden hull. Big sections of planking fore and aft had to be torn out and replaced. Scripps had a box filled with chunks of the rotted wood. "Send that to Jay Curts — with my compliments!" he stormed. Once more he was furious that his lawyer had bought the yacht without close examination. These repairs were not cheap; by now, Harry Smithton estimated, Scripps had $50,000 sunk in the "Kemah," with a new $15,000 engine yet to be bought.

Only twice in three months had Scripps gone ashore — to a dentist to get a cap fixed, and for an hour again to walk about his still vacant Marco Island house. Except for mosquitoes, he thought it would make a good camp. He pictured it to Ellen as "a sort of cave, where as an old, worn-out animal, I could drag myself into . . . and die in."

Tragedy struck on the West Coast — but it was kept from him by a conspiracy of silence. Edith, the widow of his son John Paul and mother of his grandson John Paul, was struck down in the influenza pandemic. She had been working long hours as a Red Cross volunteer in San Diego. She developed pneumonia and died December 2, 1918. The little boy, who had been exchanging chatty letters with grandpa, was left an orphan. Everyone realized the news would shatter Scripps. Harry Smithton alerted Dr. Morgan, and prevented any mail hinting of her demise reaching the old man.

E. W. already was suffering enough because of continued squabbles with Nackie and little Nackey. Daughter wrote another conciliatory letter, but made the mistake of assuring fatherly devotion by asserting, "I love you most of all, next to my husband." That crushed Scripps, and he collapsed in bed for thirty-six hours. Scripps knew well enough how to hate, but every mention of Tom Meanley taught him new ways.

His three months' respite from Nackie was up. They exchanged letters about a reunion. Nackie yearned to join him.

Just then he learned of Edith's death. It was a crushing blow — but also a convenient shield behind which to dodge while declining to permit Nackie to come back.

Bob arrived in Miami with Peggy and little Bob and nurse. Tom Sidlo, the young Cleveland lawyer and partner of Secretary of War Baker, came too, by invitation, bringing his wife. Both couples established themselves in a beach hotel, expecting to cruise occasionally and separately aboard the "Kemah." Scripps intended to feel out Sidlo on becoming his new personal attorney, as well as legal adviser to Bob on editorial matters. Sidlo's first assignment was to devise some sort of living trust that would, after Scripps's death, perpetuate his newspapers to the cause of the 95 percent.

"At the present time, Bob is my 'favorite,' " Scripps informed Ellen. Bob and his family were to remain in Miami "a number of weeks" so father could size him up. "Neither Bob's conversation with me nor his letters irritate me in the least. Were it not for my fear that he drinks too much, I would be in a condition of complete satisfaction with him."

About Jim, however, father was not so sanguine. E. W. was wary of his oldest son, perhaps somewhat afraid. He was startled when Jim in mid-January followed Bob to Miami — to talk. "I dreaded Jim's coming. . . . He's too cocksure . . . almost a bully . . . bigger and more vital and more obstrusive in his personality than ever."

Jim and his father drew up chairs face to face in the saloon and talked intermittently over four or five days. Frequently they would go two hours at a stretch. Sometimes Bob would sit in, and occasionally Sidlo joined them. Between E. W. and Jim sparks frequently flew. Weren't the papers losing their "soul" in Jim's urgent drive to squeeze out profits?

"Dad, I'm in a hurry," Jim retorted, grimly.

Bluntly, Jim discounted Bob's qualifications to become editor-in-chief. His mind was closed. "He fears Bob's radicalism," Scripps wrote Ellen. "You and I know he is justified in having this fear." Scripps had been startled to discover that his poetic youngest son — now only twenty-three — was perhaps more a flaming liberal than even his unorthodox father, leaning strongly toward social revolution, labor reform, and socialism.

Even so, father preferred to gamble on Bob's idealism and unbending dedication to public service than to risk the future on Jim's merciless hammering for dollars. Bob, given free rein, might, Scripps confessed, run down the newspapers' value by several millions; Jim wouldn't. "However," Scripps told Jim, "if Bob is the kind of man I believe he is, if he has full rein the institution in dollars and cents alone, at the end of twenty or thirty years, will be worth from twenty to forty million dollars more than it could be if your policy becomes the policy of the institution."

Scripps reminded Jim that the five Ohio papers were valued at about $10,000,000 and "I brought only ten thousand dollars into the state . . . and that in his thirty-third year Jim found himself with an income of over one hundred thousand dollars a year, and a volume of wealth he himself estimated at over a million dollars, and that this was many times greater than my wealth at his age."

These business discussions ended in a virtual stand-off. Jim was also trying to make peace between his parents. Cold and obstinate, the old man stonewalled. Jim hammered away, and E. W. began to budge. Finally he made several concessions, spelled out in a memo Scripps dictated and signed Saturday, January 25, 1919.

First, he was to remain aboard the "Kemah" until May 1. Then he would go to California where the yacht was to be taken or another chartered so he wouldn't have to permanently reopen Miramar house. Nackie was to spend "two-thirds to three-fourths" of her time with him. The other periods she would spend with her mother or her children.

The block-buster of the "peace treaty" was that Scripps was to get a much larger yacht — a real ocean-going vessel. Jim would either buy or have built a steam or diesel-driven boat 150 to 200 feet in length, with cruising range of 4,000 miles. Not only would Scripps have a world-class "floating" home, his new lust for sailing and adventure could carry him grandly through the salt spray of any ocean on the globe.

Bob basked in the Florida sun while Jim slushed through Cincinnati's snow — and their relationship was equally incompatible. On February 28, 1919, Jim sent his brother a "personal" letter. "Dear Bob: I do not want to offend you. At the same time I think I ought to tell you, and I think you ought to know, how I rate you." In about 2,400 words the older brother told the younger. Age difference was a great part of their conflict. "I had little opportunity to get acquainted with you." They had nothing in common as life goals. Jim was "absolutely astounded" at Bob's willingness to jump in and make a decision knowing less than 5 percent of the factors involved.

"Why, Bob, it takes an average man three years to learn this office alone. . . . It is hard to learn how to learn. . . . If you go on the assumption that [Byron] Canfield and [Earle] Martin don't know anything and you know it all, your face will be turned into a regular floor mop."

While Jim wanted Bob to learn the editor trade at his side or out in the knockdown world of practical newspapering, E. W. thought otherwise. He wrote Jim February 11: "Bob suggested to me yesterday that perhaps he ought to get back to his work. I told him the biggest job he has today, and probably will ever have to do, will be to learn from me all he can of things that I have learned, and that he is more thoroughly on the job while he is with me than he can be anywhere else."

Pointedly, Scripps said it was "impossible" for Jim to estimate the extent of what he himself learned from boyhood as his father's close apprentice. "You absorbed much from me, digested it, the result of this has been mental equipment — virtues and vices and qualities — you would not have possessed had it not been for contact with me . . . and with men from whom I wished you to learn lessons." Bob's chances were less because Scripps was now older and less active, and because the institution had grown and matured. "However, he must have the best chance that I can give him and you can give him."

While Scripps cruised off Florida, a letter — relayed through his Washington office — marked "confidential" came from President Wilson:

> 28 rue de Monceau, Paris
> 5 February, 1919
>
> My Dear Mr. Scripps:
>
> My thoughts have often turned to you since I came over here, because I know your interest in the real truth and how few influences there are in the newspaper world which are attempting to give an impartial view of things. And my thought has several times gone back to the letter which you wrote me and at the time I felt very much embarrassed to answer.
>
> You will remember that you asked me about my attitude toward the third term and also about a general amnesty for the people who had been imprisoned for violation of the Amnesty Act or the Military Service Act; and because I had not formed a satisfactory judgment about the latter question and felt that I had rather let the former alone, I acknowledged your letter without answering it, trusting to your insight to understand.
>
> I shall hope to take up the question of amnesty when I get home. With regard to the other matter, I do not now see why I could not earlier frankly said that my desire is to be released from further service at the end of my present term of office. Moreover the whole service of both terms has been so strenuous, and so cummulatively strenuous, that I doubt whether I could keep the pace up and continue to attempt the active guidance of policy I have attempted during the last six years.
>
> I am sure you will appreciate these feelings, but this letter is merely to send you my greetings and to tell you that things are going as well over here as could have been expected, indeed better than I expected.
>
> Cordially and sincerely yours,
> WOODROW WILSON

Scripps appreciated Wilson's belated response, even though, as he wrote Ellen on February 15, "the President's letter was largely a 'jolly' and more largely still a diplomatic side-step. However, I have felt somewhat complimented by the kind of jollying the President bestowed on me. He felt that I would be flattered or in some way pleased by his recognition of the fact that I had a good reputation for being fair as well as practical in my politics."

Just then Scripps got a new jolt — a letter saying Milton McRae had applied for guardianship of his orphaned six-year-old grandson John Paul Junior, who was, of course, also McRae's grandson. Scripps jumped up, looked wild-eyed, slammed things around, muttering about Mac's "treachery." He fired off a flurry of wires. He demanded McRae hold up, and ordered Nackie and J. C. Harper to see that he did. McRae answered that Edith on her deathbed whispered to her doctor that she wanted her father to be the boy's guardian. However, McRae agreed to delay the matter until Scripps could confer with him.

At once Scripps got a private railroad car and started for California.

The hills were fresh and green. It had rained for a week, leaving the March mornings chilly, though afternoons were sunny. Scripps had his office fireplace lighted at 8 every morning. In his favorite rocker, he reared back and rattled off gravelly dictation. His secretary's pen skittered over the shorthand notebook. This was a disquisition on Bolshevism, running eighty-four typed pages or 30,000 words. Scripps was pretty proud of it. He had a death-lock on the subject. The audacity of his views was sure to raise eyebrows. He hoped so. He felt back in command, aggressive, reckless — again right at home.

Barely a week before, in Florida, he had wallowed in self-pity, lamenting that being dragged back to California would surely kill him. The train trip was miserable, with floods and delays in Louisiana, and choking dust crossing the western desert. But he never complained and was chipper and smiling when he re-entered the portals of his castle on the mesa. His return made Nackie "very happy indeed," but they more or less went their separate ways. Once again Scripps played the hermit. Harry barred the door and censored the mail. E. W. wanted no visitors, nor even the daily paper. He went out once — to visit Ellen.

He plunged into authorship, freeing his mind of ideas generated by hundreds of hours of reading aboard the "Kemah." He tackled a wide range of subjects — economics, sociology, and politics. The first week he turned out one hundred pages of disquisitions. By May 1, his dictation would total 225 pages of disquisitions and thirty-nine of letters, or a total of 73,850 words — enough for an average novel. His neurasthenia flared up. "He knew he had been working too hard," his secretary wrote Dr. Morgan on March 28.

Bob and Peggy and their baby had come west with him. Jim and his family were already back at their house at Miramar. Once again the whole Scripps clan was together. E. W. seemed in no hurry to directly grapple with the problem that had prompted his urgent return — John Paul's guardianship. Two or three times Scripps chatted with McRae, just pleasantries. He was considering how to win his point, by law or by affection. He had Sidlo researching guardianships. He tried to win John Paul's favor, buying him a Smith-Flyer, and bringing him for overnight visits to the ranch. Grandfather was dismayed that the boy preferred hanging around the garage and talking to the chauffeur. Scripps disliked the child's nurse, thought he ought to be more exposed to books, and encouraged to join boys in sports.

E. W. waited ten days before sending his limousine to Fanita to bring Nackey and her little boy to visit him. What easily could have been a tense, acrimonious encounter was not. Father and daughter made their peace — with husband Tom Meanley excluded as though he didn't exist. Nackey was heavily pregnant, expecting her second child in July. Harry Smithton explained to Dr. Morgan:

> Nackey has been accepting each month the money offered by her father, enabling her to not only take life easier, but to enjoy . . . comforts and pleasures . . . her mother felt should be hers. . . . Nackey has been striving to follow her father's plan . . . devoting quite a number of hours to rather deep and heavy books . . . and writing not only reviews and essays thereon, but original thoughts of her own along the same subject.

E. W.'s equanimity could not continue indefinitely. Plumbers began banging pipes in the ranch house. He exploded when he found Nackie had ordered extensive repairs he felt not needed. His stomach pain returned, and he experimented again with a diet of eggs and rusk and Japanese moss, adding a few peas and carrots. At length he and Nackie had a quarrel — that so unnerved him he went to bed for a day and a half. He confessed to Smithton one cause of his irritability was too many cigars — now fifteen a day.

It angered Scripps that President Wilson kept dragging his feet on amnesty. From Miramar in April he sent Wilson a cable urging action; he got only polite acknowledgement. Scripps had Gilson Gardner badger Justice Brandeis for help. In an hour's confidential talk, Brandeis "admits there is great wrong being done in having these people in jail. The sentences, he says, are inexcusably savage. . . . President Wilson, in his opinion, ought to have given heed to your letter last November. . . . The little dribbling leniency indulged in since then is worse than nothing."

One man who might get results, suggested the Justice, was Wilson's confidential adviser, Colonel Edward M. House. Scripps should cable House fully. He did — plus another cable to Wilson on May 15, asserting, "I am more anxious . . . that you should take steps before leaving Europe to grant amnesty and pardon to thousands of Americans who have been cruelly punished for holding and expressing views different from yours and mine. There is real danger threatening because of the existence of discontent, not only on the part of actual sufferers and their friends, but on the part of a vast number of your fellow citizens who respect and love you."

His cable to Colonel House, much longer, described the "desperate urgency." House replied by cable May 22: "The matter has been presented to the President and your suggestion has been warmly supported. He bids me say it will receive his careful consideration. However, I doubt until after peace has been signed he will come to a decision." That didn't stop Scripps. He suggested Brandeis ought to resign in protest, and tried to light a fire under Secretary Baker to also pressure the White House.

Scripps, intent on being a paladin of civil liberties, was turning out something of a Don Quixote. He took refuge and solace in his private writings; there he could let off steam. To a friend he explained: "I found I could enjoy myself more by speaking to no audience than I ever enjoyed myself while talking to the million. This was because I have felt perfectly free to say anything I damn pleased — to write things that might cause me to be tarred and feathered or even hung if what I wrote appeared in the public press. . . . I can look upon my year's seclusion as the most glorious epoch of my life. I was free to be absolutely irresponsible."

Rivalry continued to simmer between the Scripps boys. It preyed on their father's mind. Careful to avoid an immediate confrontation, he secretly worked on a long-range solution. Only he and Sidlo knew anything about it. Jim, by dint of his dad's power of attorney and chairmanship, occupied the throne and held the scepter. Bob wore the purple of a prince and retained his title of Editor-in-Chief. But he could exercise no real authority.

Jim had not forgotten his promise to secure his father a bigger yacht. He got help from the "Northwest Whirlwind," lawyer John H.

Perry. At Orcas Island on Puget Sound, Perry discovered a three-masted schooner, the "Sanwan," one hundred forty feet long, twenty-six wide, drafting fourteen feet. She had ample canvas for crossing the Pacific, an engine with twin screws, nine staterooms below decks. Perry took a six-months lease, with option to buy.

Meanwhile, Scripps made headway with his scheme to devise a living trust that would perpetuate the children of his brain after his death, and would give Bob better opportunity to share actual control of the empire. Of the sons, he felt only Bob was dedicated to preserving the institution's "soul." Tom Sidlo was drafting documents that would create a holding company to bind the controlling stock of E. W. and his sister Ellen, who shared his goal. His will would be rewritten to incorporate the holding company into a living trust, required for one or two generations or longer—to maintain the institution for public service.

The first of May the "Sanwan" reached San Diego. Her skipper was a blustery old salt, a Captain Worth. Repairs were needed, and it wasn't until May 26 that Scripps went aboard with Nackie and several guests. Intending to cruise overnight to Santa Catalina Island, Scripps stood with the skipper on the bridge. Captain Worth ordered the engine started and the anchor hoisted. The heavy chain clanked up a few feet around the windlass—and abruptly stuck. Sailors couldn't budge it. They shut down the engine and took the only course open—dismantling the windlass. That took an hour. Still it wouldn't raise the anchor. For another hour they tinkered with the hoist, and then started the engine. This time, as Smithton wrote later, the winch worked "lovely." But with the anchor "half up and half down," the chain again stuck. Then the engine backfired and stopped cold. It wouldn't start again.

The massive, wood-hulled "Sanwan" was helplessly—and dangerously—adrift in San Diego harbor.

Scripps, by no means amused, suggested dropping the other anchor. Captain Worth gave him a woebegone look. That anchor had been unshipped and moved aft as ballast.

Loose and menacing, the "Sanwan" bore down on the Santa Fe wharf. Onlookers cried out in alarm. The yacht glided past the dock, luckily missing it by a few feet. Just then the current caught her and swung the ship rapidly backward. Now the stern of the "Sanwan" headed straight for a Japanese fishing schooner. This time by only inches was a collision avoided.

"Then we bore down on the cruiser 'Minneapolis' and it looked bad," Smithton related. "All available hands rushed for an oar or a stick or something to ward off the collision. The sailors had been hurried below to get the anchor chain out through the hawsepipe, link by link. I went down and saw them working and didn't envy their job. They had been working on the engine and succeeded in getting that started and clearing the 'Minneapolis.' Then they got the anchor down and brought us to a standstill in the very place from which we had started."

This hair-raising, around-and-around "cruise" of San Diego harbor had lasted from 10 in the morning until 4 in the afternoon. Scripps was disgusted. He led his guests ashore. A few days later Scripps again ventured aboard. This time the "Sanwan" behaved reasonably well. But Scripps was now disenchanted. He directed Smithton to get rid of the schooner. Harry sent the "Sanwan" to San Francisco, fired Captain Worth, and got insurance underwriters to declare the vessel unseaworthy. The Orcas Island owner took the case to federal court where three years later Scripps would be stuck for damages and attorney fees totalling $70,000. The accepted doctrine in marine transactions, it turned out, was "buyer beware."

Seventy thousand dollars for one six-hour boat ride! E. W. snorted that Jim and John Perry had badly let him down. Like Jay Curts, they hadn't adequately checked out the boat. Be that as it may, Scripps washed his hands of the "Sanwan." He hoped to never again sail a jinxed ship.

Knowing he was about to drop a bombshell, Jim stood in his San Diego office and faced his N.E.A. executives. His surprise announcement would be another slap in the face for brother Bob, and a bitter pill for his father. What Jim revealed in this July 9 meeting was that he was promoting Byron Canfield from head of N.E.A. to his own staff as assistant chairman of the concern.

That was, of course, directly counter to Scripps's desire that Bob continue Number Two man in the heirarchy. It was Jim's second callous move in a matter of days that relegated his father to "forgotten man." He had not invited Scripps to sit in his just concluded conference of all the editors. The old man resented that, but had more or less asked for the rebuff by insisting that he must not be at all involved in business. He hadn't even read a Scripps newspaper for nineteen months!

Even E. W.'s valiant efforts to get President Wilson to grant amnesty were rebuffed by the editorial conference. Voting eleven to five, the editors refused to advocate the release of Eugene Debs "and others in prisons for similar offenses." The conference did, however, adopt a "Declaration of Principles" on big issues, outlining fifty-two aims for the Scripps newspapers, including adoption of the eight-hour work day, prohibitively taxing child labor, the principle of collective bargaining, measures for the reduction of the cost of living, the forced development of suburban rapid transit, government ownership of telephones, telegraph, and fuel reserves, opposition to all censorship in time of peace, government erection of low-cost housing for returning soldiers and sailors, and a scientific investigation of the influenza pandemic, among others.

Tension grew between Jim and his father. The son complained to Ellen about his "great difficulty" in getting E. W. to talk to him. Scripps sent a sharp letter admitting the feud was causing him "considerable strain," but asserting he would brook "no more contests" and demanded his right to "maintain a position of unquestioned headship."

Every afternoon Scripps went out alone in his limousine for a long drive, usually sixty or seventy miles. The majesty of the hills and the grandeur of the sea were no longer compelling; he was lost in thought about his sons. Finally his thoughts jelled. As much as he hated it, there was but one solution: He must clip Jim's wings.

The father did it bluntly and boldly. He curtailed the broad power of attorney he had granted Jim, limiting his authority to strictly business matters with the twenty-two newspapers, the N.E.A., and the United Press. He issued a new power of attorney to Bob, granting him authority in all his father's personal affairs—including family trusts, stocks, estates. This meant Bob instead of Jim would have the say in the timing and scope of Jim's future increments, and would represent his father in any business disputes with Jim.

Scripps wanted his motives not to be lost on his eldest boy. In a lengthy and warm letter he reiterated his desire for the concern to devote itself to public service. "I want to increase your confidence in my ability to think straight and teach right. . . . The opportunities that are open to you are simply stupendous." Scripps urged Jim to give command "to the younger men" and take a year or two to travel and read.

Jim hotly resented the change. It was, he fumed, an undeserved insult. From that moment they went pell-mell toward a disastrous rupture—but at this time neither had the least inkling it would be so tragic and fatal.

29

One Tragedy after Another

Each cigar had a white thread tied around its middle. But Scripps, beleaguered and disgruntled, smoked right through this "stop" sign decreed by his doctor, impatiently scattering ashes on vest, desk, and floor. Harry Smithton reported to Dr. Morgan: "I asked Mr. Scripps to let me use rubber bands instead of thread—he wouldn't likely enjoy smoking burning rubber! He almost let me order this!"

This critical and unhappy period—the fall and winter of 1919–20—found Scripps still holed up at the ranch. He was beset by trouble and discord. Jim continued openly defiant. It was a gloomy stand-off; the stubborn father wouldn't budge either. Nackie again began nagging. And suddenly daughter Nackey turned cool. E. W.'s nerves jangled and a lump appeared on his right cheek; it grew rapidly—he feared it was cancer!

In his rocking chair, Scripps on an October morning poured out his disgruntlement to Milton McRae. He expressed shock some in his family considered him, at sixty-six, mentally over the hill. He wondered if his own "natural pugnacity in dealing with others" was triggering his fight with Jim. He asked McRae's opinion but impulsively interjected his own answer which was simply that it was "impossible for me to yield to any sort of opposition." This had him so wrought up that he recorded his emotions in an essay, "A Year of My Life."

"Until I am dead, Mac," Scripps said, "I will be the same sort of man."

"I know it, Ed," McRae replied.

Scripps was hoping McRae would straightway go and have a "heart-to-heart talk with someone"—meaning rebel son Jim.

Mac did. And a few days later Jim bent—a little. He decided Bob could attend the November meetings of the Ohio papers, vote the Scripps stock, and be elected editor-in-chief. Jim would remain king, and control even Bob's editorial policy actions.

The national political scene was so muddled it caught Scripps's eye. He tried to analyze the upcoming 1920 Presidential race. End of the war had failed to trigger the economic and political upheaval E. W. had expected. The lot of the working man was no better. Nor had the income tax proved a panacea.

"I had not fully appreciated the skill and dexterity of the super-men of business," he lamented to lawyer Tom Sidlo. "It appears that the rich have been made richer. . . . There is only one way of keeping the rich man from passing the tax burden on to the other fellow, and that is by killing him."

President Wilson had been paralyzed in October by a stroke. Now he was feeble, and governing badly. Running for a third term was out of the question. Scripps thought his old friend Herbert Hoover Presidential timber, but wanted to know his true beliefs. While Bob was back east getting installed as editor-in-chief, Scripps sent him on to Washington to talk to insiders. No longer a laid-back poet, Bob now swung an iron fist. He gave sharp orders to his men, turned keenly imaginative. He proposed starting a new style two-cent daily called *Today*. It would be four pages, each split in the middle by a black rule. Only news would appear in the three left-hand columns; on the right side would be all the advertising, and it sold by auction. E. W. saw some merit in the scheme, but even so put *Today* on the back burner.

On the train returning to Miramar, Bob wrote a sheaf of memos on politics, concluding the Presidential field was largely has-beens and light-weights except for Hoover and two others, William Randolph Hearst and Henry Ford. Bob Paine almost choked. "I hope," he wrote Bob, "I will not live long enough to see the Scripps concern supporting Hearst for anything more desirable than a term in state's prison." Paine added that pacifist Ford was too open to "public ridicule. . . . Hoover is the most promising."

Scripps, hoping Hoover would be drafted as the 1920 Democratic nominee, had him sounded out in private—and got a shock. "I would not give ten cents for the nomination," Hoover told Gilson Gardner. "Of course, if the people want me, I am willing to do what I can." Scripps got a bigger jolt a few weeks later when Hoover surprised everyone by announcing he was a Republican. Bob directed the Ohio papers to boom him for the G.O.P. nomination.

To escape the turmoil at Miramar, Scripps considered going back to

Florida and spend the winter cruising. He ordered new Winton engines installed on the "Kemah" at Jacksonville. Nackie sniffed, and when she saw he was serious became testy. To get back at her husband, she "fired" Smithton from his assignment as manager of Miramar ranch. Bob hired a new man and told him, "Do whatever Mrs. Scripps orders, even if she says burn the house down!" But Scripps stepped in, and put things back as they were.

Scripps felt he was winning back his daughter. She owed a big bill at Fanita. He let her sell $3,000 worth of cattle he considered his to settle her debt. A few days later she sent a curt note; no longer would she demean her husband by accepting money from dad. E. W., dismayed, couldn't sleep, and his neurasthenia came back. Smithton advised Dr. Morgan it looked like a tactic to pressure Scripps to "recognize" Tom Meanley.

The lump on his right cheek finally drove E. W. to a San Diego dermatologist. Dr. James Jackson excised a small cyst, two pus sacs, and two tiny sebaceous cysts behind Scripps's left ear. All were nonmalignant. Scripps perked up, found his cigars more tasty, his books more interesting, and chirped he felt "just bully — even glorious."

Suddenly the kingship squabble again flared up. Bob issued an order affecting the newspapers, and Jim preemptorially countermanded it. Father exploded. Jim feared an open break was about to come. He wrote Charles Mosher, the Central Office treasurer in Cincinnati: "I guess I might as well quit."

In snowy Cleveland in early January 1920, Tom Sidlo boarded the train for another welcome commute to balmy California. Scripps had summoned his young lawyer for another confab on creating a living trust to maintain the "children of my brain" after his death — earmarking profit sufficent to keep the penny papers battling for the underdog working man.

That posthumous dream was not shared by the whole family. Nackie, influenced by Jim, looked on the newspapers as only money faucets. Milton McRae warned Scripps that Jim talked of refusing to tie up his stock in the living trust. Big money was at stake, said Mac, pointing out the concern's 1919 revenues exceeded $13,000,000. Bob shared his father's dedication to preserving the "soul" of the institution. Nackey Meanley was not a factor; she was to get a $500,000 trust fund, instead of stock in the papers.

If the "soul" was to live on, the torch would have to be carried by Scripps's sons or grandsons. The brood of grandkids had just grown by two — Tom and Nackey Meanley's second son born July 14, 1919, and Bob and Peggy's second, Charles, born January 17, 1920. (Proving the old man's intuitiveness, Charles in 1948 would become chairman of the living trust, and grow into the powerful and durable kingpin of today's gigantic Scripps institution.)

To the outside world, the Squire of Miramar remained pretty much a man of mystery. He did not often go out. He read extensively — mainly books of history, economics, and philosophy, along with scores of magazines, especially articles on science and finance. His aloofness prompted *Pearson's Magazine* in February 1920 to publish a profile — "Scripps: Hermit and Newspaper King." Gilson Gardner observed: "It was amusing because it contained so many inaccuracies." Rumors seeped out about the three-way power struggle between Jim and Bob and their father. The leading trade journal, *Editor and Publisher,* asked pointedly if the concern was suffering a revolt. Assurances were given that only "routine" personnel changes were contemplated.

At length Scripps abandoned the idea of spending the remainder of the winter on his yacht in Florida. Still he wanted to cruise. The "Kemah" now had twin screws, pushing its cost to $75,000. Scripps ordered his captain to head for the Panama Canal and bring his yacht around to San Diego. He wanted to take his grandsons cruising in the Pacific. "The boys are so harum-scarum," he lamented to McRae, "I'll probably have to rope them together so one won't tumble overboard."

Just then came a sad jolt. Nackie's widowed mother, in her seventies, fell ill in West Chester and died in late March 1920. Nackie rushed to Ohio for the funeral, but Scripps did not accompany her; Jim and his wife went. Nackie deeply felt her loss, and made amends of a sort by pledging to pay the $300 annual salary of the preacher at her father's old church where she was once a choir-girl.

Nackie came back to Miramar despondent, ill with flu, and looking daggers at her husband.

In the first week of April 1920, Jim suddenly hit his father with an ultimatum — choose between his sons!

"I have come to a definite conclusion," Jim wrote, "that my brother Bob and myself are not going to be able to get along together in this newspaper business." Jim wanted to quit as chairman, sell part of his stock, "and go out and tackle something entirely outside the publishing game."

How to mollify the rebel son? E. W. suggested Jim retain the chairmanship another year, sort of in name only. "You can sign the papers, I'll take full responsibility for whatever Bob does in editorial affairs." After a year, if Jim still insisted on getting out, they would separate their interests "in an honorable and gentlemanly way."

When Harry Smithton hand-carried such a written proposal next door to Jim's house one evening he hit a buzz saw of objection. "Bob is lazy . . . won't work," Jim stormed, according to Smithton's memo of the incident, which also said: "Jim said, absolutely and positively, he would never let any of his stock go into a holding company. . . . That he'd take 'his own' properties [the West Coast papers] and run them separately if he had to."

While father wrestled with the Jim dilemma, Bob again went east, chiefly to explore Presidential politics. "We do not want to elect the President," Scripps cautioned him. Aim of the Scripps papers should be to stir up national interest, get "people to do a lot of thinking," and derail the back-room machine politicians in both parties, "even if we get an inferior man for President." Scripps saw nothing wrong in deliberately injecting Henry Ford, Hoover, and Hearst into national discussions. "That will stir up talk!"

At the Dearborn tractor plant Bob interviewed Ford for three hours April 6, urging him to join the Presidential scramble — though the Scripps papers would only print what he had to say and might oppose him in the end. Ford was wary. He didn't "give a hang" for office, would not "seek" nomination, but would not refuse to "serve." Bob and Neg Cochran, who was with him, departed feeling the flivver tycoon was "down on machine politics . . . but a good deal of a boob on that subject." They doubted Ford was thinking much about running.

Next day in New York, Bob interviewed Hoover, suggesting the Democrats might try to draft him. Hoover said he wouldn't accept, nor would he join a third party. Bob told Hoover the Scripps papers' main interest was to get two good candidates who would fight and force the American people to think on real rather than camouflage issues. "We want to drag the curtain away from the machinery of politics, party and otherwise, so that the people can see the wheels go round . . . and have an actual President in the White House, not some puppet subject to outside and unknown control."

"Why, damn it," exclaimed Hoover, "that's just about the reason I'm in this thing myself! I'm not a politician. . . . I just don't want to sit by and let the next four years of American political control go by default."

W. W. Hawkins of United Press made an appointment for Bob to have lunch with Hearst at his Manhattan home "to talk politics." Hearst said his papers were against Hoover, and favored Senator Johnson for the G.O.P. nomination, and still undecided on a Democrat.

Out on the ranch, the indecision and tension over command was killing Jim. He called in his stenographer and dictated a strong letter. "Dear Dad: Bob and I are not going to be able to get along together. I know it and Bob knows it. . . . If you and I cannot agree, I should back up to the nearest switch where we can pass each other and each go our own way. . . . There is coming a panic or depression. . . . There is going to be one devil of a mess. . . . Dual management in this business is impossible."

Looking over the typed letter, Jim stole a page from his father's book—and stuck it in his own "Not Sent" file. But holding back the letter in no way dampened the wild rebellion surging inside him.

The gruelling months of anxiety turned into a hellish nightmare for Scripps, too. His private thoughts on the kingship clash are recorded in about 150,000 words of diary entries, memos, and confidential letters. They reveal a troubled mind that gradually descended to dark depths of suspicion and distrust of his sons—not only Jim but also Bob!

This bitter quarrel, his doctors warned, might trigger a fatal stroke. Scripps asked Bob to urge Jim to lay off. Jim refused. Nackie clearly was against him, eavesdropping, scheming with Jim. Maids and chauffeurs gossiped and tattled. Some of Scripps's telegrams "leaked" and his few wire codes were broken. He came to fully trust no one with confidences except Ellen, Smithton, and Tom Sidlo.

To his credit, he felt great sympathy for his rebel son. "Jim never got to live his boyhood," E. W. grumbled. "I put him under the harrow too young. He ought to take off a year or two—get out and have fun, see the world. . . . And then come back to the concern."

He was greatly disturbed about Jim's heavy drinking. Bob's, too. But Jim's boozing was notorious, frequent, almost out of hand. Dad was "very suspicious" of Jim. He was "almost ready to believe that for a number of years" the boy-king had deliberately tried to take selfish advantage "not only of his father, but his sisters, his brother and even his mother."

Nor could he fail to wonder about Bob. Was Bob shrewd and scheming enough to egg Jim on and let him ruin himself? Wouldn't that leave Bob the Number One heir to hog the family millions? Scripps for two or three years had not been certain of Bob's motives, "or whether he had any motives." He'd rather see Bob a "fool" than a schemer. Several times Scripps tried to trap Bob with "shrewd thrusts to discover what was inside him," closely watching the boy's face. Not once did he detect a false flicker, adding:

I would certainly be more unhappy than I am now if I should feel that all along Bob was playing a very shrewd part in allowing developments to take their course without his being implicated.

On April 22, 1920, Jim telephoned for an appointment and rushed over to his father's study with alarming news. Newsprint price increases and the paper shortage were pushing the Ohio papers toward ruin. They supplied 75 percent of concern profit. He brandished a Y-9 form showing for the first quarter the *Cleveland Press* had receipts of $902,410, but after paying war taxes, showed a $64,974 loss. Jim predicted the situation would get worse.

"Do you," Jim said, "hold me responsible for this poor showing?"

"I know no reason why I should not," Scripps responded.

"I don't consider myself responsible — and haven't for several months."

"Why?"

"I can't be responsible," Jim replied, "for accomplishing that which I do not believe in. . . . I have absolutely no faith in dual management."

Scripps was staggered. His knighting of Bob as editor-in-chief seemingly had made Jim virtually throw up his hands. Was his great institution adrift, with no captain in command? He must not permit that! He'd have to break with Jim. The old man moved fast. He wrote Bob, still back east, "If worst comes to worst, I will assume one-man control again myself." Then he prepared an order revoking Jim's power of attorney, and held it ready to issue. He dictated a new codicil to his will, cutting Jim's inheritance in half, adding that portion to Bob's legacy.

On April 28, he sent telegrams to Bob, and Roy Howard. They must immediately come to Miramar on urgent business!

The "Kemah" plowed the blue Pacific May 15, toward Santa Catalina Island. Aboard with Scripps were Bob, and Roy Howard. The old man did most of the talking, strictly business. He outlined terms under which on June 1, they were to take over the concern's editorial and business management. Mainly he spelled out what was expected of the thirty-seven-year-old Howard.

Roy must not relinquish his control of United Press until his successor (they had picked W. W. Hawkins) could do as well as he had. Howard was not locked in; he could quit any time after six months, and should be prepared at the end of five years to either move ahead — or out. In that period, E. W. estimated "R. W. H. would have added to his

wealth from five hundred thousand to one million dollars." A limit of
five years on one job had turned into Scripps's big hobby.

Bob and Roy would get identical "meal ticket" salaries of $18,000 a
year. Their main income was to come from stock and dividends. Scripps
made clear he wanted them to profit handsomely; as for himself he did
not desire to "increase by even one dollar the value of the estate he is
leaving his heirs."

His stenographer wrote up the contract at Avalon Bay. The three
signed it. Next day the "Kemah" sailed back to San Diego. Scripps
wanted to make one more try with Jim. He offered to buy all his stock in
the western papers for $1,000,000, and let him continue as concern
chairman. Jim said no.

All that was left was to break with his son. Scripps put it in writing—a "Memo of Understanding" dated May 29, 1920, for the two of
them to sign. The document granted the son clear title to all his stock,
fully paid for by past services, but none of which could be sold in E. W.'s
lifetime. All stock the father held in papers west of the Rocky Mountains
was to pass to Jim on Scripps's death. Jim would continue as "chairman"
to handle "all business of a general nature" for his father at $36,000 a
year. Jim was to remain at Miramar and be given a clerical staff. E. W.
made clear he retained right of veto over everything.

The memo directed Jim to appoint Bob and Howard as a team to
take command of the other newspapers, as well as the U.P. and N.E.A.

. Typically, Scripps couldn't bring himself to bite the bullet with his
eldest son. Jim stayed out of his way, and the father didn't pursue him.
Days passed—almost four weeks.

Finally on the evening of Friday, June 11, Scripps sent Harry
Smithton with copies of a revised power of attorney and the memo. Jim
was at his Del Mar seaside cottage, twenty miles from the ranch. He
acted drunk, started off kidding Harry, and then turned mean, according
to a memo Smithton made of the encounter.

Jim refused to look at the documents. "Well, you deserted me," he
snapped. "I picked you up when my father fired you. . . . You know a
whole lot you could tell me. . . . You know the old man is all busted up
and no good any more. But you ignore me. . . . You'll get yours!"

At once Jim apologized. "I'm just trying to have some fun out of
you. Read the thing to me. Let's see what it says before we tear it up and
send it over to Dad and tell him to. . . . .(an unprintable remark
deleted)."

Jim noticed the papers included a copy of Bob's new power of
attorney. "The Old Man can try to get me to endorse Bob . . . but he'll
never get me to do it. Why, Bob's a Bolshevik! He's lazy, too. Naw,

naw! . . . The Old Man will try to hold things together, but he can't do anything anymore.

"He didn't keep me as chairman of the board because he wanted to, but because he didn't dare fire me. The minute he fires me I'll bring suit under the increment, and I'll bring suit to prove he's incompetent. . . . He's cut me off his will, hasn't he? Well, that's just it. I don't want him to remember me. . . . I want him to cut me off. . . . His will will be knocked higher than a kite. Why, just today I signed an agreement with mother that neither of us would do anything or sign anything without first getting the consent of the other, in writing, too. . . . I saw mother after she got off the boat today. Yes, you bet we're getting this all fixed up.

"We're ready to begin the battle at the drop of a hat," Jim said. "Mother has lived with the old man for thirty years and she knows how he has changed, and she knows he is 'off.' She says he is not right, and she knows. We've got signed statements from all his doctors — that he's not right and that he's incompetent. We've got the whole story."

"Not all his doctors," said Smithton. "Dr. Morgan has no idea that your father is incompetent."

"Sure thing, he has; and we've got it in writing. He can't go back on his own written statement, and none of the other doctors can, either. . . . Oh, we've got it all fixed up. Mother has a half interest in the estate. Get that? Half! They can never make his Ohio residence stick. So she gets half. I've already got a big chunk. But I get a third of the left-over half. Then there's Nackey."

Jim's face turned dark, and he said, "Just think how cruel the old man has treated my sister. Wouldn't recognize my own sister's husband, but worse than that called him a . . . .! Just think — calling him such a thing! And then for anyone to think he's not bugs. . . . Wouldn't recognize her baby son, just because he hates the baby's father. Well, Nackey gets another third, and she sticks with me and mother. . . . Suppose I smash the old man and take control of everything away from him."

"You wouldn't dare do it," Smithton said. "A pretty picture that would make!"

"Yes, but I won't start it," said Jim. "He's going to try to kick me out. . . . There's going to be a terrible scrap. . . . You wouldn't bet any money on Bob Scripps. . . . And say — Roy Howard will just tie Bob Scripps into all sorts of knots and get him into all sorts of holes, and run away with the whole shebang. The old man has sure rigged up a pretty mess. Of course he's incompetent."

Smithton made another attempt to read the documents to Jim, but he wouldn't listen. Harry departed, and gave E. W. a written report. But Scripps didn't brace Jim with it. He wanted to part peacefully. Yet the son rebuffed his every move. E. W. asked him to notify executives back east that appointment of Bob and Howard reflected "no friction and no disruption . . . no important change in the manner of doing business." Jim wouldn't. Would Jim agree he had been fully paid with stock for his work as personal agent and chairman of the board? No. Nor would he sign the May 29 "Memo of Understanding." Jim called in his own lawyer — Jay Curts, the Central Office counsel, now siding with the western clique.

Thus in the waning days of June 1920, the split finally occurred — by default. There was no angry outburst. Jim merely balked, and his father let him alone. He expected the prodigal to one day return. Tacitly, Scripps let Jim walk off with the seven main western papers — although later he was to say they were stolen. Jim and his loyal lieutenants held 51 percent control of the *Los Angeles Record, Seattle Star, Spokane Press, San Francisco News, Tacoma Times, Sacramento Star,* and the *Portland News.* It was uncertain for weeks whether Jim and his men held enough stock to claim the *San Diego Sun,* the *Denver Express,* and the *Dallas Dispatch.* (Eventually Jim's clique took the latter two.)

While Jim held his empty title, Bob and Roy took over as the dual management team. He was wasting time, Bob concluded, to sit and wait for Jim to clear the air. Bob went east — to roll up his sleeves.

In early October Scripps was aboard a private railroad car heading east to inspect his bob-tailed empire. "I am going through the offices and meeting the men," he explained to Ellen, "more for the purpose of letting them see me and know that I haven't yet become a doddering old idiot, and that I haven't even got one foot in the grave." Scripps was, in fact, in splendid health — despite all the strain.

He had departed Miramar with the Jim problem no better. The "chairman" still refused to function, but collected his $36,000 salary. Father didn't seem to have the heart to give him the axe. Jim established headquarters for his western papers at Oakland, but kept his home at Miramar. He openly boasted to Milton McRae and others he intended to "break" his father's will on grounds he had no legal domicile in Ohio, and was "incompetent." Booze was still his problem. Jim kept whiskey in his San Diego desk, but his secretary told McRae he had "cut down to a pint a day."

Bob launched a hard-hitting N.E.A. campaign favoring the open shop and national labor unions. He shook up the command of his Ohio papers and N.E.A. The top men were stale, he felt, had lost their punch. E. W. agreed. "The future depends on yours and Howard's ability to get *young* men who are also *brilliant* and successful. . . . You are rather loaded up with old men." Scripps grumbled that Jim had in the last few years failed to inject enough new blood, but "on the other hand Roy Howard has been a little cold-blooded in dealing with the old men." Scripps cautioned Bob not to be "unjust or unkind" to his men. "They say sentiment has no place in business — but it has more to do with good business than dollars."

Reaching Cleveland, Scripps had his private car shunted onto a siding in the suburbs to escape the city's noise. He strolled through the *Cleveland Press*'s "back shop" greeting printers who had been on the job thirty years — including two who also were with him back on malodorous Frankfort Street. Bob and Howard had halted the profit plunge. Scripps was told the *Press,* despite first quarter losses, would end the year $100,000 ahead of 1919.

In Cincinnati Scripps was much impressed by his *Post.* It was, he reported to Ellen, his finest property; and he was well-satisfied with all his papers. With Nackie, he drove out to West Chester to look at their "honeymoon farm." He thought it still a beautiful place. Sudden inspiration struck. He called on his old neighbor, bought thirty-five additional acres so he could build a new $100,000 two-story brick home on the highest point of the land. Typically he turned design and construction over to someone else — Bob.

Deliberately Scripps had timed this Cincinnati stop to coincide with the November general election. He showed up at his West Chester precinct, with Bob. Old-timers recognized him; he walked right in and voted. One woman rushed up and greeted him warmly; he recognized her as one of their early maids. E. W. considered this vote-casting a devilishly clever ploy. Now let anyone challenge the legality of his Ohio domicile! Bob, too, though not registered, voted without challenge. "They could see he was with me," Scripps explained to Ellen. Both voted for Cox. Harding's triumph over Cox, 16,152,200 votes to 9,147,353, did not greatly disturb Scripps. Early on he had become bored by the lackluster campaign.

His tour lasted twenty-nine days, and shocked him — no new Scripps paper had been started for twelve years! He had a strong urge to rush out and launch new papers — a lot of them. His concern was earning $2,000,000 a year — so financing was no problem. He wanted to give his employees a chance to share the pie. His annual payroll was nearly $5,000,000; if the workers could save a quarter of their wages, they could funnel a million a year into an investment company that would participate in company expansion, guaranteeing 6 percent return plus dividends. Fifteen years earlier he'd started a similar investment company. Jim, not interested, had let it slide; even so it was worth $120,000.

"So you see," he wrote Ellen, en route home, "I am still dreaming my old dreams."

His return to Miramar gave Scripps a hard jolt. Jim had fallen ill, with something like the flu, and the doctors said his condition was very serious.

It was a dream that wouldn't die. Science did a perfectly miserable job of telling the world its new discoveries. Reports usually were slow, dull, and jargon-stilted. The average man couldn't understand them. Scripps proposed to bridge that gap.

For ten years he had been dreaming of setting up a society of newsmen and professors who could translate stiff-necked research lingo and spark it into man-in-the-street talk. He thought of his creation as a "Science News Service." He volunteered to put up a nest egg of $30,000 a year — and now the newest child of his brain was about to be born.

Bob and other Scripps men would get together with scientists December 26 in Chicago and formalize the new society, which had board members representing the National Research Council, the National Academy of Sciences, and the American Association for the Advancement of Science.

The society would distribute an N.E.A. "human interest" type service of science news and illustrations for a small fee to newspapers, publish popular books, and open a Washington, D.C., information bureau to which reporters could turn for authentic guidance in dealing with new theories and discoveries. Eventually this public service experiment would pay its own way. Until then, Scripps would foot the bill.

This dream was temporarily dampened by Jim's sick spell. His ailment was somewhat mysterious; it started as a cold on a trip to San Francisco. The damage trial over the yacht "Sanwan" fiasco had just started there. J. C. Harper and John Perry, defending E. W., had asked Jim to put in a courtroom appearance for the family. After two days in San Francisco, Jim collapsed and was hurried back to Miramar, where Dr. Lewis put him to bed. It looked very bad for a time. In a few days, however, his cough subsided and he was able to get up.

Relieved, Scripps went aboard the "Kemah." He had not been on a cruise since returning from his eastern trip; and he was up against it for gasoline. There was a post-war shortage. Pleasure boats were rationed. Scripps fumed and fretted. Then inspiration hit. Boats doing scientific research were allowed fuel. Grinning, Scripps took aboard Captain Crandall from the Marine Biological Station — "Bugville" — and promptly got his gas tanks filled at the San Pedro dock — regularly.

Suddenly, in early December, Jim again collapsed. He was too weak to get out of bed. A husky man, he had lost thirty pounds. Dr. Lewis brought in three specialists. They examined him, and emerged with long faces. They diagnosed serious heart and kidney trouble. Jim's blood pressure had spiked to 230. Dr. Lewis told Scripps his son probably would recover, but might be an invalid and never strong again.

Milton McRae, a keen student of medicine, gave a blunt diagnosis to Roy Howard: "Jim is dangerously ill, in my judgment. He has interstitial nephritis, with accompanying heart malfunction. Of course the primary cause of his present disease was alcoholism. Jim really consumed alcohol at a terrific rate for several years and the poor fellow is now paying the penalty. I doubt if he will ever be able to give much attention to business again."

Nackie, with horrifying memories of her vigils at the deathbeds of two other sons, became distraught. Josephine, with a nurse's insight, recognized the grave situation.

But the outside world went on. From the East Bob and Howard wired for permission to start a new paper — in Birmingham, Alabama. That step forward gave the old man a thrill. Though he literally hated doing important business by telegraph, within the hour he sent back his okay. And how times had changed! It would be an eight-page afternoon called the *Post,* selling for three cents, with editor and business manager each drawing $75 a week. The plant would cost $27,000, with monthly running expense of $5,500 — $90,000 the first year. Shades of the ten-thousand-dollar *Cleveland Penny Press!*

To avoid upsetting Jim, Bob suggested postponing the annual meetings scheduled for December 24, where Roy Howard would be elected new chairman. E. W. decided otherwise, saying Jim already knew the change was coming.

All the while Jim kept sinking. On December 22, Scripps wired Bob that "a very critical turn" had occurred. "Perhaps there are two chances to one against his recovering." Next morning Jim was better. But in the afternoon he had another sinking spell. Scripps again wired Bob: Come!

Bob cancelled all plans and started the three-day journey to Miramar. Scripps's secretary instructed Tom Sidlo to take Bob's place at the Chicago meeting which would establish *Science News Service.*

Bob arrived to find desperation and utter despair in the sickroom. Jim, the once brawny "giant," lay shriveled and dazed. Around his bed hovered doctor and nurse, and the family — Josephine, Nackie, sister

Nackey, and Jim's four children: Edward W., eleven, James Junior, nine, Josephine, seven, and Ellen Browning, five. They had never faced such a miserable Christmastime.

Word came from Chicago—Sidlo and Dr. Ritter had succeeded on December 30 in organizing the society. There was a name hitch; somebody had beat them to the one Scripps thought up so they settled on plain *Science Service*. Another child of Scripps's brain had been born.

But the oldest of his loins, only thirty-four, was desperately struggling to stay alive.

New Year's Day came, and passed in sadness. Jim began to flicker in and out of a coma. Then came pneumonia. It looked hopeless. Everyone hovered near, trembling with fear. At 1:30 on the morning of Friday, January 7, 1921, Jim Scripps died.

30

Up against Bared Claws

In the eucalyptus-rimmed family cemetery at Miramar, Josephine Stedam Scripps struggled to mask her surging emotions. Eight business colleagues slowly carried husband Jim's coffin up the hill. She stood erect, a handsome and stylish woman in her mid-forties. (About ten years senior to her late husband, she made a lifelong mystery of her exact age, even to her children.) In the last moments her Teutonic stoicism cracked slightly when the preacher, as the coffin was lowered, recited the beautiful lines Mark Twain had written for his wife's tombstone:

> Warm summer sun, shine brightly here;
> Warm summer wind, blow softly here;
> Green sod above, lie light, lie light —
> Good night, dear heart, good night, good night.

Josephine's thoughts were a sad tangle. She felt confused, uncertain, and fearful of her business future. Moreover, she was furiously — but secretly — angry at her father-in-law. Never once did he visit Jim on his deathbed! That was cruel and unpardonable. (When she threw it up months later, Scripps would explain that he had taken that course to try to avoid agitating his estranged son's wounded feelings.)

This was a time of deep mourning. The mother and the widow wept openly for days, bravely consoling each other and the children. In a vague way, Scripps seemed apart from the grief, and had little to say. The death had confirmed one grim reality — the fate of the institution was again thrust largely into his hands. The green new management team could do first-class with the day-to-day operations. But the big question

426

mark over the future, the imminent threat of the breakaway of Jim's western papers — that was explosive, delicate, and difficult and definitely called for his personal skill and attention, especially if an actual schism was to be averted.

Josephine was being pressured by the western clique's editors and business managers who held minority stock in their papers. They urged her to break away Jim's papers — which they now called the "Josephine S. Scripps Group." The widow had a considerable knowledge of the intricacies of newspapering; Jim had taught her. Scripps conceded she was knowledgeable, to a degree. "She is shrewd," he observed to Bob, "perhaps too shrewd." But being female, she was, in his view, likewise "strongly subject to do foolish things."

Trying to decide which way to jump, Josephine had an earnest talk on January 12 with Scripps. He explained that she had inherited through Jim not quite 5 percent of the entire concern. E.W. held 44½ percent, which with Ellen's 19 percent gave him in excess of 63 percent — and control. Scripps suggested she bring back the outlaw papers. He volunteered to personally train her sons and fit them for future management roles as princes of the publishing empire.

As an alternative he offered to buy the stock she had inherited for $1,000,000, and leave little Eddie and Jim each $1,000,000 in his will.

Josephine was in a quandary. The bitterness of the fight between Jim and his father had left rancor and distrust. She went to Milton McRae and asked point-blank if she could trust Scripps. "Emphatically," Mac responded. On February 21, she came to a decision. "Let me try to run my papers for a year," she told Scripps, "and then I'll decide what to do." That was agreeable to E. W. Josephine forced her clique to accept the year's interlude, and an "outside" chairman — Milton McRae, whose experience E. W. said would help her survive the oncoming business downturn.

Scripps then turned his attention back to his own company. The Birmingham "baby" — the *Post* — was lusty. It was the thirty-fourth Scripps paper (eight of which had died). Launched January 21, 1921, the *Post* by mid-April zoomed to 15,000 circulation and demanded a bigger building and faster press. "I'd take a club to any fool who asked for a $150,000 building," Scripps snapped to Howard. For "show" Howard sent from the Central Office a $50,000 deposit to the *Post*'s bank in Birmingham. That riled Bob.

It was a protocol goof. Howard had signed his order, "agent for E. W. Scripps." That was flat wrong — nobody was Scripps's agent except his son! The management duo acted like roosters in the same barnyard, pecking each other and flashing spurs. That seemed to amuse Scripps. A little hate between editorial and business sides, he chuckled, helped keep alive the "soul" of the concern.

With plenty to do, Bob and Howard skittered about the country. They fixed local problems with a fast hand, plugged profit leaks, dreamed and schemed expansion. They lined up men and machines to launch new papers. Scripps reminded Howard the three of them operated as "a triality" and that would spawn conflict. "I expect you," he wrote Howard, "to be frank and disagreeable in talking to me. Not pigheaded or big-headed. . . . I want to control the stock but I am willing for others to share in the profits. . . . I am spending much time with Bob because he is new in the business; I am letting you run free for several months."

At the ranch, Scripps did not find the domestic environment very pleasant. Nackie excoriated him about Jim's death, wailing that business quarrels caused their son to die of a broken heart.

The specter of the black angel again hovered over Miramar — from far across the ocean. A blind cable arrived saying his sister Jennie had taken ill in Cairo on a cruise. She was taken off the ship and returned to London. Scripps burned up telegraph and cable seeking details. Finally, United Press located her in a London hospital. The red-haired, fun-loving spinster, now sixty-nine, was dying of pernicious anemia. Fortunately two cousins, Hilda Gardner and Floy Kellogg, were travelling with her. In eleven days she was dead. Her ashes were taken back to the family plot at Rushville. Of E. W.'s brothers and sisters, now only two were alive, Ellen, eighty-five, and Fred, seventy-one.

A slow-burning fuse set off the dynamite that blasted apart Scripps's business relationship with Jim's widow. The match was lighted in Seattle. Chief culprit was the dapper little lawyer who had for ten years been an admired business side-kick and trusted friend of E. W. But John H. Perry had turned enemy. The "Northwest Whirlwind" earlier had joined Jim's clique, and now his loyalty was wholly to Josephine. Futhermore, Perry was out to get rich himself. He had concluded, too, that the old man was a sharp operator, capable of deceit, and willing to pull a crooked deal.

The explosion came in late summer 1921 — but Perry had planted the bomb four months earlier, when he became a rival by buying the *Seattle Post-Intelligencer,* the city's only morning daily. It competed with the Scripps's *Seattle Star* which led the afternoon field, and was part of the group seized by the Josephine rebels, one of whom was Perry. Behind Perry was plenty of money. His angel was Charles E. Lilly, millionaire seed tycoon known locally as perhaps the richest man in Seattle — and Perry's father-in-law.

On July 6, Perry triggered the Josephine uproar by firing a thundering telegram to Scripps. "Have report you have called meeting to sell N.E.A. to yourself for consideration two hundred thousand dollars. N.E.A. is worth not less than one million. . . . Your conspiracy to obtain ownership . . . amounts to nothing less than plain thievery. . . . Unless you will not permit this robbery of minority stockholders . . . I will institute action to enjoin this crime and expose the perpetrators."

Scripps, pretending to be away, did not deign to respond. Bob sent a reply next day, telling Perry he was "incorrect" and his statements "altogether unjustified."

In truth, the proposed N.E.A. reorganization was unusual, complicated, unorthodox. If the western papers owning shares in N.E.A. pulled out, the syndicate would be crippled financially. Bob and Howard devised a scheme to "sell" the syndicate for $150,000 to Earle Martin, its new president, and his colleagues. The new N.E.A. would be permitted to sell its output to all comers, with big profits likely.

But N.E.A. also would issue a separate service exclusively to Scripps-McRae to promote their editorial policy favoring the 95 percent. It would provide E. W.'s papers all their present features, illustrations, and comics. The concern would pay $300,000 a year, a saving of $194,400. Scripps would hold the majority stock, but the Martin management would take the biggest share of profit.

Perry did not rush into court, but kept waving aloft the threat of scandal. He actually was putting pressure not on E. W. but Josephine. He wanted to unload his stock in the western papers on her for $650,000. Scripps called that "blackmail," but told her the deal would be a bargain. He offered to lend her the money, to be repaid over ten years. She borrowed it from him. But she blew up at him a short time later when one of E. W.'s private memos fell into her hands. It asserted Jim had violated the "iron clad" policy by not selling back his stock to father. The "insult" infuriated Josephine.

The crisis deepened rapidly. On Sunday, August 7, Josephine called and asked to see him at 9:30 A.M. He was leaving to go out on the "Kemah" but agreed to wait. She was two hours late. When she breezed in, "I spoke harshly telling her she . . . prevented me being able to get my boat in port before nightfall." She offered no apology, but asked ten minutes to read him a letter.

"She started out by saying she had learned from reading some of Jim's letters that he valued N.E.A. at one million dollars and that I proposed to take away [her] share of this property. . . . Unless I immediately blocked this scheme, she would cooperate with other minority stockholders against me and withdraw her papers from our Central Office [severing connection with the institution]."

The next Sunday she again bearded Scripps in his Miramar office. She came to announce the break. And to complain. She reiterated N.E.A. was worth a million. Also E. W. was of no help to her in making business decisions. "I cannot talk to you. . . . You are on the boat or indisposed. . . . Bob Scripps is not inclined to be of assistance. . . . I must make my decisions myself. It is the only way. I do and act as I was tutored by Jim. . . . It is my intention to carry out his wishes. . . . I want you to visit your son's grave and I am sure you will more fully trust me. . . . We want our own Central Office. Also we want to handle our own money. We cannot be efficient without full responsibility."

Then Josephine made her announcement—she would pull the western papers out of the Scripps institution on January 1, 1922.

Aboard the S. S. *Buckeye State* at the San Pedro pier, a dispirited Scripps, grimacing and groaning between spews of cigar smoke, barked last-minute orders to Harry Smithton. It was Sunday afternoon, September 11, 1921, and the old man was once more running away—this time by sea through the Panama Canal to New York and Washington, D.C. Harry was staying behind at Miramar.

No longer could Scripps face the "impossible and intolerable" California turmoil. "I would prefer never to come back to Miramar again, were it not for Ellen. . . . Josephine and her children never even came over to say good-bye. She is going to bring up my grandchildren to avoid me. . . . I haven't been at all satisfied for a year with little Nackey's attitude—total indifference, just tolerating her father. . . . Mrs. Scripps is always rebuking me for something. . . . Josephine doesn't like Bob— Peggy is made the goat. . . . Mrs. Scripps and most of the family have all combined against me. . . . When I die, Harry, there is going to be a nasty mess. Mrs. Scripps and the others are just simply going to tear into everything."

In a conspiratorial whisper, Scripps reminded his aide he had given secret orders to the captain of the "Kemah" to get the yacht "in perfect shape" to be called back to the East Coast for the rest of the winter. "Warn Captain Morse. . . . If anyone gets a hint of this, fire Morse on the spot!"

Mainly he was trying to keep the secret from Nackie. She pestered him to learn his plans. He usually said he didn't know yet. He would have preferred making this trip alone, but, ironically, she was accompanying him—just to be contrary, he grumbled. With a hated cold picked up from Bob's little boys, Scripps remained in his cabin throughout the two-week voyage to New York.

In a five-room Waldorf-Astoria suite, on the backside of the eighth floor away from noise, Scripps holed up like a hermit. But behind the scenes Tom Sidlo and the United Press's Bill Hawkins arranged for a stream of V.I.P.'s to knock on his door. Scripps got a kick out of chatting with these dignitaries—newspaper editors, including Frank Cobb of the *World* who disclosed that Pultizer died not as rich as E. W. had thought; scientists, bankers, economists, politicians. Colonel Edward House chattered away for an hour, titillating Scripps with inside gossip of the palace guard that shielded the stricken President Wilson. Former Secretary of War Newton Baker called, "with more lines in his face than I remembered," and Scripps immediately put him to work with Sidlo in devising the trust that would keep alive "the children of my brain." They talked from 3 to 7, earnestly.

Although personal architect of the scheme to plant Scripps papers in one hundred American cities, Scripps was enormously indifferent to details. The extent of his lackadaisical attitude is reflected in an October 9 letter to Ellen: "I heard the other day that we had started a new paper in Fort Worth." That, indeed, was true. The *Fort Worth Press* was launched October 3, 1921, in the Texas cowtown that already had strong morning and afternoon newspapers selling for five cents.

Now, it seemed Scripps just let Bob and Howard toss the dice. They were audacious gamblers but not as bold as he had been; in one year— 1906—Scripps had started ten papers. Bob and Roy had five cities targeted for 1921. After Birmingham, and before Fort Worth, came the *Norfolk* (Virginia) *Post,* born June 13, 1921, from the start "a wobbler." Final two start-ups of the year were both scheduled for November—in Washington, D.C., *The Daily News* on Tuesday, the eighth; and in Knoxville, Tennessee, the *News* on Monday, the twenty-first—the latter the thirty-eighth brainchild.

Visiting the capital, he did not expect to interview President Harding, nor did he particularly care to again visit ex-President Wilson. He saw both—arranged behind the scenes by his Washington men.

His White House appointment was at 4 in the afternoon. He went reluctantly, feeling he had nothing to say to Harding. The President came across the room to take his hand, beaming and recalling their last meeting four years ago at Airlie. For once Scripps did not feel awed. He began talking—and hardly stopped to let his host get in a word. He sounded Harding on, among other topics, the Anglo-Japan treaty talks, offered tacit criticism of the growing congressional farm bloc, and sharply condemned the "absurd" income tax revision.

E. W. pointed out that although the cost of government had risen only four-fold since 1914, his taxes had jumped sixty-fold. "Of course, my wealth has probably doubled—still that would be a thirty-fold increase!" He told Ellen: "Harding was uninclined or unable to follow me into deep water."

Several times the President coughed. Finally he said, "I've had this cold a week. It doesn't seem to get any better." Scripps blanched, fidgeted a moment, jumped up, and made an abrupt departure. He fled to his dentist "and had myself thoroughly disinfected." Perhaps Harding, knowing Scripps's deathly horror of catching cold, merely used the cough as a ruse, suggests one Scripps authority—to rid himself of a garrulous visitor who had already taken nearly an hour of his time.

Scripps was requested to call at Wilson's residence on a Friday afternoon at 3. He still held a grudge because no pardon was given Eugene V. Debs. Even so, being counted worthy of a chat with an intellectual, a scholar, and a former President flattered him. He was surprised to find Wilson's $250,000 mansion so shabby inside—dark, gloomy, worn. He rode the electric elevator to the second floor. Wilson was seated by the fireplace in a comfortable library, wrapped in robe and shawl. He didn't rise. Scripps leaned over and grasped his hand, and instantly all his resentment evaporated.

"It was a pitiable sight," he wrote in a disquisition for Ellen. "I certainly would not have recognized him had I seen him anywhere else." Wilson's face looked unhealthy, one corner of his mouth sagging, his jaw awry, his skin puffy and bluish. His voice quavered. "He was absolutely a broken man."

Leading the conversation as usual, Scripps threw in a remark about his own stroke, asserting he had taken up sailing "to get away from this damned human race." Wilson, smiling, said, "Well, there is something in that." Somebody had given Wilson a good briefing. He said nice things about Bob, Tom Sidlo, and offered condolences on Jim's death.

"Then he gave me a start," E. W. recounts. Wilson said his brother-in-law, who had greeted Scripps downstairs, was an experienced advertising man. "He would be a good man for you to have," said Wilson. Scripps told Ellen: "I side-stepped that."

When Scripps rose to leave, Wilson clung to his hand, holding him back, thanking him four or five times for coming, and again wishing him success with the Washington paper "and in every endeavor." The visit disturbed Scripps. "If I had ever been as sick as Wilson is now, I would consider it an outrage if my family had permitted anybody to come into my room."

Nackey Scripps Meanley (1898–1981) as a young woman after the elopement with Tom Meanley, one of EWS's secretaries, a marriage that broke the Old Man's heart. (*Tom Meanley Jr.*)

Tom Meanley, an EWS secretary who infuriated Scripps by eloping with his eighteen-year-old daughter. (*Tom Meanley Jr.*)

Tom and Nackey Scripps Meanley, in their sunset years. Despite EWS's censure, they had a steadfast and happy marriage. (*Tom Meanley Jr.*)

[*Left*] A mature Nackey Scripps Meanley standing on one of the hillocks that dominate the old Miramar rattlesnake mesa, in her favorite "Boy Scout" footwear. (*Tom Meanley Jr.*)

433

Negley Cochran, EWS's editor in Toledo, editor of the ad-less *Day Book* in Chicago, and also his trouble-shooter in Washington, D.C., around 1920. (*Neg Cochran*)

Two of Scripps's chief aides, attorney Jacob C. Harper (left) and Harry L. Smithton, probably around 1920. (*Paul K. Scripps*)

EWS began newspapering in the days of hand-spiked type and lived to see his composing room speeded up with the advent of the Linotype. Composing room scene at the Cincinnati *Post* in the 1930s. (*The Cincinnati* Post)

EWS in Florida (1918–19) during his stroke recuperation. He used a cane for a year or two. (*Mrs. H. L. Smithton collection*)

EWS listens to Nackie reading to him aboard one of his leased
yachts in Florida, 1918–19. (*Mrs. H. L. Smithton collection*)

Despite his physicians' warnings that Nackie's nagging might bring
on another stroke, EWS wanted her to rejoin him during his
Florida recuperation (1918–19). Here he shows affection walking
with her to the boathouse. (*Mrs. H. L. Smithton collection*)

EWS steps ashore on a Florida beach while a seaman steadies the dinghy, around 1918–19. (*Mrs. H. L. Smithton collection*)

Nackie Scripps reads to EWS on deck one of their leased yachts in 1918–19, cruising off Florida. (*Mrs. H. L. Smithton collection*)

437

On the ways of the Newport News (Virginia) Shipbuilding and Dry Dock Company, the 172-foot yacht "Ohio" being built for EWS from a Cox and Stevens design is nearing completion in November 1922. The yacht has a beam of 26 feet, drafts 11 feet 6 inches, and can cruise at 12 knots, powered by two 350-horsepower Winton diesels. [*Left*] The comfortable afterdeck of the yacht. (*E. W. Scripps Company files*)

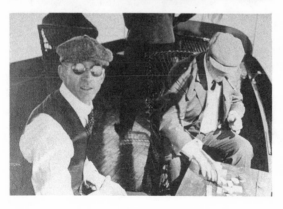

Harry Smithton plays dominoes with EWS aboard the "Ohio," saying the Old Man hated to lose and would cheat if he could get away with it. (*Mrs. H. L. Smithton collection*)

On EWS's Orient cruise aboard the "Ohio," starting from San Diego, March 8, 1923. This is a festive dinner in Hawaii for passengers and ship's officers. Robert P. Scripps is at the right front. (*E. W. Scripps Company files*)

These pen-and-ink portrait studies of E. W. Scripps were done by a Cincinnati *Post* staff artist in 1920, with a reproduction of the Old Man's signature. (*The Cincinnati Post*)

EWS, with his velvet skullcap to ward off feared colds and puffing his cigar, catches up with the news while cruising off Florida on a leased yacht, around 1918–19. (*Mrs. H. L. Smithton collection*)

Caught up on his Washington business, he led Nackie and his little troupe aboard the train for Cincinnati. He wanted to return to West Chester in time to vote in the general election.

Besides, he had a couple of other clever tricks up his sleeve. He was eager to pull them off.

When Bob led his parents to the old farmhouse E. W. blinked in surprise and then gave a resigned shrug. He walked through the rooms, accepting what he saw. Nackie gasped, near tears. She saw not one familiar thing. The interior had been totally remodeled under Bob's direction at a cost of $20,000. Four rooms had new fireplaces, including Scripps's old office. There were two new bathrooms, elaborately tiled. Floors were now level. A new hot water system and modern electric plant had been installed. Only the exterior looked the same; it had not been touched.

The remodelers made one laughable goof. E. W.'s new private bath had four doors. They could be locked only from the outside. Scripps called in a locksmith to fix that.

The remodeling was but one of several unpleasant shocks this return to Ohio gave Nackie. Bob and his father rode over to their Butler County precinct and cast votes. That irritated her, fully understanding the significance of the act. A few days later the governor appointed Bob a trustee of Miami University at Oxford, Ohio, fifty miles north of Cincinnati. Scripps had pulled political strings. To make it palatable to the university, he dangled an offer of immediate money to establish two or three professorial research chairs, to be perpetuated by substantial bequests in his will.

Nackie saw through these clever tricks, and Scripps frankly admitted he was deliberately out to spike the guns she might use after his death to challenge his Ohio residency to break his will and seize a full one-half of his estate under California law.

The romance that blossomed three decades earlier in the quiet moonlight of this very countryside was now dead. Worse, the bubbly wine of their courtship and honeymoon had soured into the vinegar of acrimony and hateful spite. Nackie was openly at war against E. W. — and, as far as business went, against Bob too. "She has no comprehension of what we are trying to do," Scripps complained to Ellen, "but feels it her duty to exert herself to the limit to make our course as difficult as possible."

For six days everyone at the *Birmingham Post* from office boy and printers to reporters and editor got accustomed to a gray-bearded, hulking cigar-smoker peering over their shoulders through little gold-rimmed glasses. Scripps had time to kill; and this was as good a place as any. He stopped off at the fledgling paper November 27, to wait and give his yacht time to sail around from the West Coast. He liked this new brainchild—"but I gave the young men the benefit as well as the discomfort of my criticism."

His interest was keen also in the one-cent *Washington Daily News,* the twelve-page tabloid that started off with 27,000 circulation against established rivals with from 30,000 to 85,000. The *News* did not accept advertising—not yet, but would later when it could boast 50,000 subscribers. Scripps readily conceded this paper was not started to make money, but to influence Congress and other officials.

A couple of copies of the new *Knoxville News* arrived by mail. He was not overly impressed. "Baby papers look like baby humans," he wrote Ellen, "that is they all look alike."

Suddenly Scripps was all pepped up about the South. He suggested the concern launch a new daily in every important southern city. Their leadership and influence could be enormous. He saw, too, the negative side. "Of course, they have long and warm summers, niggers and mosquitoes, but as one enthusiastic Alabaman told me in the hotel, 'We can get rid of the mosquitoes and thank God we are sending a lot of our niggers north.'"

The old "Kemah" jinx again lay in wait for Scripps. He reached Jacksonville December 7, and found her on the ways for hull painting. He moved into the Seminole Hotel. When the painting was finished he went aboard and started a short cruise up the St. John's River. In about thirty minutes a terrible clanking erupted at the stern. The captain raced aft and returned with a woebegone report: "The propellor bearing's busted!" They crept back to the shipyard, got repairs, and a few days later meandered on down toward Key West. Life at sea was again putting a sparkle on Scripps. He felt better, too, when Harry Smithton arrived from Miramar and again took over as major domo.

Then the hoodoo popped up—with a harder jolt. The "Kemah" started from Key West for Havana. About thirty miles out, one engine sputtered and died. For emergency they carried dozens of boxes of spare parts—but not what was now needed; the timing gear had stripped. The sea was rough, pitching and rolling the boat. They turned back to Key West, on one engine.

"I was not exactly frightened," Scripps related to his sister. Still, he got the shakes. His hands trembled, his leg got stiff, his right eyelid twitched, and began to get numb. His vision blurred. He gulped a stiff dose of bromide. Smithton was no help to the boss in this crisis; he was leaning over the rail.

The first week in January 1922, he finally sailed into Havana harbor. Outside the city he found a new two-million-dollar hotel and started to move in for a week or two. Of a sudden he was overcome by the rank smells, the "rattle-bang" of the streets, "those gabbling dagoes." He rushed back aboard the "Kemah." "Cast off," he told the captain, "as fast as you can!"

Mail trickled in—sifted through the Cincinnati Central Office, and passing Harry Smithton's on-board censorship. Near the end of January, while the "Kemah" rode at anchor at Nassau in the Bahamas, an urgent cablegram came from California. Ellen had fallen and broken her hip! Stunned, Scripps ordered his boat immediately to Florida, and instructed Smith to engage a private Pullman to return to Miramar.

Instead of an odyssey of compassion, the trip west disintegrated into a near debacle. En route, Scripps came down with a heavy cold. At Linda Vista he had to be carried off his private car, hurried up to Miramar and put straight to bed, where he was isolated for three weeks, unable to visit his hospitalized sister.

He was back in the very turmoil he had fled. Nackie had her claws out, raising a daily uproar. She accused him of directing a secret vendetta against the outlaw papers. The Miramar atmosphere was heavily poisoned against him. Josephine ignored him, Nackey Meanley remained aloof, his grandchildren were standoffish; only Bob paid homage to his headship of the clan. Even the usually imperturbable Ellen expressed resentment that he had been back four weeks and had yet to enter her hospital room. "I hope that you do not regret having made the trip out here."

By early March Scripps was able to climb into his limousine and daily visit her at the hospital. "I will stay," he assured Ellen, "as long as you have need to talk things over with me." Then he pulled a characteristic blunder. Secretly he sent a crew of mechanics to her home in La Jolla to install gas heaters. Ellen was outraged. E. W. tried to explain he was only thinking of her comfort, knowing she would be confined for months to a wheel chair. That did not mollify her. If she wanted heaters, she would install them; further she insisted on paying for the work. They would squabble over that for weeks, E. W. finally letting her reimburse all but $1,500 of the cost.

His most vigorous antagonist, of course, was Josephine. The rebel daughter-in-law did not come near him, but attacked second-hand through Nackie. Josephine became embroiled in a deadly duel with one defector in her own band of newspaper pirates. Eugene MacLean, whose 20 percent control of the *San Francisco News* could swing control from the outlaws back to Scripps-McRae, decided to do more than "resign" from the West Coast clique. He wanted to sell his stock. It would be "bad faith," MacLean reasoned, to offer his shares to either "Mrs. Jim" or to E. W. He took his dilemma to a close friend, Earle Martin, president of the new N.E.A., offering him the stock for $300,000.

Interested, Martin got together with Central Office Treasurer Charles Mosher and a few other associates in the concern. They couldn't raise that kind of money. They went to Bob. Naturally favoring getting back some control on the West Coast, Bob authorized under his power of attorney a loan from E. W.'s funds to acquire the San Francisco stock—in the name of Martin, Mosher, et al.

If that was a slick trick to cripple Josephine, it was pulled without Scripps's direct knowledge. It transpired either while he was sick or was taking one of his frequent "vacations" from all business discussion. At some later point he heard of the San Francisco deal. He approved. A certain thread of duplicity ran through his nettling habit of often shutting the door on business talk. He easily could satisfy his curiosity about anything going on, because carbon copies of all important—and often trivial—correspondence came to Harry Smithton's files.

Exasperated by turmoil at the ranch, Scripps ordered a private railroad car to take him back to Florida and the quiet isolation of his yacht. There was no let-up in Josephine's war. Angrily, she told Nackie she had been short-changed $1,000 on a special dividend from *Cleveland Press* stock—her own father-in-law was "deliberately cheating" her. Nackie berated her husband as "an Indian-giver!"

Stretched out in his Gloucester hammock on the aft deck on a morning in mid-April 1922, Scripps huddled under two blankets and fretted about having too small a yacht and the threat of hitting unseemly cold weather as the "Kemah" plowed northward off the Carolinas. From the saloon came music from one of his new Victrola records, probably his favorite, "Onward Christian Soldiers." Pondering the future, feeling once again vigorous and healthy now that he was back at sea, he wrote Ellen, "I am quite aware of a sense of gladness that I am four thousand miles away from the absolute certainty of jolts and bumps, pin-pricks and needle-pricks—sword cuts!"

Since his return to the East Coast, he had no reminders of Miramar turmoil; neither his wife nor little Nackey had written him.

Two months shy of sixty-eight, E. W. abruptly vowed to abandon the lamp of learning. "If other people will let me do so," he wrote Ellen, "I am going to drift through the rest of my life, utterly regardless of any obituary-writer who might want to say my mind was clear to the end and to the last I kept up my interest." That was sheer fiction; no way was he about to shut down his volatile mind. In fact, he was en route at the moment to goose up his scientific adventures and launch a bold experiment in population research.

His more immediate interest, however, was in acquiring a larger yacht that could sail 5,000 miles, and safely cross any ocean. Having to give up the "Kemah" depressed him; the little schooner could so easily sail into tranquil coves and along isolated rivers — avoiding the crowds he detested. A two-hundred-foot yacht would have such draft he'd be limited to big, noisy ports. Bob submitted three designs that could be built by the coming November — the most expensive costing $350,000. In his characteristic lazy-boy mode, father left the decision solely up to son.

Scripps easily could afford a new boat; the value of his empire had now climbed to $60,000,000, despite the secession in the West. The concern's 1921 profit was $1,938,262, of which into his personal account went $719,972. As a bonus for that year, Scripps handed Bob and Roy Howard each $47,695.

Posterity — or at least his grandchildren — deserved exposure to his multitudinous essays and other writings, Scripps decided. So he summoned Gilson Gardner from Washington to the "Kemah" and set him to work arranging and editing his piles of disquisitions — starting at the tail end. He considered Gardner not only a sharp writer and editor, but an ideal shipboard companion; he stayed out of sight unless the old man called him for a chat.

Scripps was a decidedly vain author, and Gardner's work in the long run did not please him. Scripps considered his disquisitions often so outrageous he marveled that his stenographer didn't quit. He apologized to Ellen for not submitting every one to her, explaining some were "unnecessarily coarse, cold-blooded, outspoken." (It was not until 1966 that the Scripps disquisitions would be published, in a book underwritten by grandson Charles Scripps, *I Protest,* edited by Oliver Knight, University of Wisconsin Press.)

Gardner also botched revision of Scripps's autobiography. In the end Gardner had the last laugh, writing a lively biography in 1932, *Lusty Scripps* (Vanguard Press, New York). From his long intimate association, Gardner could have sensationalized all the gritty episodes in his patron's life, but his work eschews scandal.

As he now journeyed north, Scripps read with considerable enthusiasm Lytton Strachey's *Queen Victoria,* and Margaret Sangster's works. He dispatched her book on birth control to Nackey Meanley. Already mother of three, she was to bear a total of six children—all boys. On April 1, 1922, his flock of grandchildren had grown to eleven; Bob's Peggy had their third child in Washington, a daughter, who was named Margaret. The old man could not mask his disappointment the baby was a girl.

Scripps was meeting Dr. Ritter from the La Jolla marine research station and would escort him on to Washington, D.C., for a conclave of the new Science Service news association. Also coming aboard at Beaufort, North Carolina, was his new protégé, Dr. Warren S. Thompson, a thirty-five-year-old native of Weeping Water, Nebraska, now teaching sociology at Cornell University. Scripps had Thompson interested in accepting a chair at Miami University at Oxford, Ohio—to delve into all facets of world population. He had put up an $8,000 shoestring endowment. "If he's willing to bet on me," Dr. Thompson wrote Miami's president, Dr. Raymond M. Hughes, "I'll bet on him."

Scripps kept adding to the endowment and Dr. Thompson would go on to gain international stature as an authority on population trends and their influence on world economy. He later helped on the U.S. census, and his study of the Far East would cause him to warn in 1929 that Japan's population explosion would lead the world into war. Following World War II, he was to be one of General MacArthur's key civilian advisers in Japan.

Now the time had arrived for Scripps to plunge back into the newspaper game. He had promised to devote all of May to business. Bob came aboard the "Kemah" April 27, at Norfolk, Virginia, bubbling with ideas and enthusiasm. Scripps took time to visit the offices of the new papers in Norfolk and in Washington, amazed that the latter was nearing 50,000 circulation—running temporarily as an ad-less—only going in the hole $20,000 a month.

He worried about Bob, thinking he should be less of a hands-on chieftain, and suggesting he lease a house up on New York's Hudson River where he could get away from the daily ruckus and carefully think and chart the concern's future.

Just then Roy Howard breezed in to Washington from his tour of the far reaches of the empire—with harsh, wide-ranging criticism. He took several slaps at Bob's editorial direction. Too many old, worn-out editors were still sitting, crippling growth. "It's like a Mexican army,"

Howard scoffed, "all Generals and no privates." Howard shuddered at what lay ahead—he saw the concern at the crossroads—and about to plunge downhill!

Scripps invited his feisty little chairman aboard the "Kemah" and heard him out for two and a half days. Much of the criticism was warranted, "but there is nothing Howard says on the subject that excites me too much," he reported to Ellen. "I take it for granted that in their own interests the present management will bring about the necessary reforms. . . . New men: new methods: new times: new customs."

It was clear to Howard, as he stepped ashore, he and Bob would have to make their own determination at the crossroads, and discover the right path to take. Such agreement might not easily come. Again the editorial and business chieftains were acting like barnyard roosters.

Bob had just fired a stinging personal letter to Roy complaining that business managers were impinging on editors' turf: "If we can't keep these ambitious business managers out of the editorial and composing rooms . . . I am going to order . . . editors to station an armed guard with a sawed-off shotgun at the head of the stairs."

31

Getting Ready to Get Dead

The cry of a night bird echoed over Chesapeake Bay. Scripps jerked awake, sweating and trembling. Lights twinkled far away on the Maryland shore. In a vivid nightmare he had just been wrestling a "reckless" Roy Howard trying to "keep him from jumping the rails . . . over me." The white-hulled "Kemah" lay in a secluded cove. Even asleep, Scripps could not escape what he called "imaginitis" and "people phobia." He thought about running into Baltimore to consult a famous psychoanalyst he'd met and liked at Johns Hopkins, Dr. Rudolph Myers. But his Washington physician, Dr. Morgan, strongly demurred. "Better not try any experiments," he advised. "Just avoid overwork and do not become annoyed or excited or worried."

For four or five weeks the yacht had aimlessly cruised the waters between Washington and Baltimore, avoiding noisy ports and the hubbub of civilization, ducking at nightfall into some remote anchorage. But now, in late May 1922, Scripps was about to be forced to emerge from his hermit shell.

"It is surely a fact," he informed Ellen, "that I have got what I might call 'terraphobia.' For no sooner than I find my foot on shore than I begin to feel conscious of that nasty, nervous sensation that I am so much afflicted with. On the boat, at least when I am sailing, I never think of it. . . . I suppose I ought to blame no one for thinking me eccentric."

Going into Washington for the annual editors' meeting, the Chief seemingly forgot all about people phobia. He limped in with an elastic bandage on his twisted right knee, but blossomed before his rapt audience. The editors were somewhat surprised to find him still a fire-brand, reiterating "my testament."

"You are not only to be the advocates of the plain people, the common people, the 95 percent," he told them, "but you must give the ignorant knowledge, and, at least, mitigate the unwisdom of the unwise. So far as the Ten Commandments are applicable to the profession of journalism, they should be observed."

The Chief led back to the "Kemah" a group of top executives for more serious talk. The climate was right for big ideas. It was agreed to expand U.P. and N.E.A. worldwide, to found dailies in New York, Baltimore, and Philadelphia, as long as the deficit for all new papers did not exceed $1,000,000 a year, with a goal of one hundred papers. The "Kemah" parley ended on such an upbeat note that Roy Howard jumped the gun and immediately bought for $350,000 the *Indiana Times* in Indianapolis, which on May 27, 1922, became Scripps paper Number Forty.

Just then one of the yacht's gasoline tanks sprang a leak and cockroaches finally took over the "Kemah." He was forced ashore while the boat was repaired and fumigated. He was off-stride. Dropping in on a Science Service meeting, he groused and argued, upsetting the dozen top scientists present. They must have thought, he wailed to Ellen, he was just an old fool dilettante squandering money.

From that faux pas he was glad to escape to a serene environment. Bob had leased for the summer the large Milton L'Ecluse estate at Huntington, New York, located on Long Island Sound with nearby anchorage for the "Kemah." Scripps sailed north, reaching Huntington the first week of June. In his wake came the "Kemah's" jinx!

Scripps went ashore long enough to inspect Bob's summer place, but felt more comfortable on the water. Despite mixed weather, he worked out on the aft deck, getting ready to take a stab at something entirely new — writing a novel.

On the morning of June 12, the yacht lay at anchor in Huntington Bay. He elected to work topside. At noon, in barely ten minutes, the mercury shot from sixty to eighty. Old hands along the Sound sensed trouble brewing, but Scripps was preoccupied. In the afternoon the sky darkened and rain came.

At 5 o'clock, a wild storm broke, careening down the length of Long Island Sound flinging gale winds, torrential rain, thunder and lightning. Somehow the hoodoo lost its grip on the "Kemah" and fate totally spared Scripps, as he later reported to Ellen:

> I . . . suffered no real discomfort, although only a few miles up and down the Sound all sorts of boats were upset. I don't think the wind blew

over fifty miles an hour where we were, but in some places they said it blew a hundred.

I was writing you up on deck . . . and when I saw the squall coming, went down into the saloon to finish it, and forgot to mention the storm. It lasted only fifteen minutes. Had I not had my mind on the letter, I might have been on deck and . . . a little scared.

Scripps should have been petrified. Within a dozen miles of the unscathed "Kemah," the fierce storm wrecked two hundred small and big boats, and killed at least fifty people, most of whom were swept out to sea!

An uncanny sixth sense for accurately sizing up men was one of Scripps's many talents. His instincts — and the bald facts — began to startle him about son Robert. It was now clear the boy was destined to become a greater editor and publisher than his father, superior even to his Uncle James whose genius spawned the magnificent *Detroit News,* perhaps even more successful than these two pioneers combined. E. W. bared his soul and his pride frequently on the subject to Ellen.

Bob had learned his trade; he knew what he wanted, and he knew how to get it. His reputation as a young Bolshevik had led E. W. to expect Bob to be a reckless plunger who would have to be sat on by his teammate and partner. It turned out just the opposite. Bob was the thoughtful, steady, cautious custodian of the empire; Roy Howard was the one who shot from the hip. It flabbergasted Scripps to realize that his son, happily married, father of three, and every inch the true commanding general of this sixty-million-dollar publishing empire, still was only twenty-six years old!

"He rather takes my breath away at times," he wrote Ellen. To Nackie, he observed: "Apparently he is in perfect health and full of enthusiasm and joy over his work. He is quite as self-assertive, even with me, as need be."

For fully a year Scripps's main brain strain was devoted to reaching one clear and compelling goal. "You see," he explained to Ellen, "I am getting ready to get dead and make it possible to turn over to Bob the control of a big institution without turning over to him too great a fortune."

One dangerous obstacle lay in his path — the legal battle that, as soon as he died, would erupt to try to discredit his Ohio residency so Nackie could claim half his estate as widow's dower. Though about to turn sixty-eight, his vaunted cognitive power was not dulled. If anything he was even more imaginative and ingenious on estate and inheritance intricacies.

Tom Sidlo was doing what Scripps proclaimed lawyers were supposed to do—not advise you, but show you how to do what you want done. The linchpin, of course, was his living trust. In simple terms it merely assembled in one basket all his business interests and placed them under the exclusive direction of a trustee—Bob—both for the remainder of his life and afterwards. The Edward W. Scripps Trust was to terminate only after the death of the last of Bob's children born before E. W.'s own death—in other words probably close to the year 2000.

In setting up the E. W. Scripps Company, he discovered that his and Bob's holdings would not have to constitute more than 35 percent of the whole to maintain control. By concentrating Scripps interest in voting stock, actual control could be maintained with a surprisingly small *minority*—leaving the lion's share available to be owned by superior lieutenants.

The legal documents were executed June 7, aboard the "Kemah," which rode at anchor in Huntington Bay. With both trust and holding company firmly in place, Scripps then handed over to his heir virtually a blank check of power—far more sweeping than he had ever entrusted to anyone. It was a new power of attorney which authorized Bob "to transact any and all business in or with which I am interested or connected in any way," to sign contracts, vote stock, spend money, appoint agents, to buy or sell or merge newspapers, to take custody of all his father's securities, valuable papers, and personal files, to make loans or gifts to himself, Dolla and Nackey, and the Biological Research Station or Science Service, and to take any action "with reference to my property and my affairs . . . which I could do if personally present or when absent . . . and hereby ratifying and confirming anything and everything he may do under this power of attorney," which, incidentally, was to remain in effect until E. W. chose to revoke it. That right of recision—not at all likely to be invoked unless Bob went unexpectedly haywire—was the only string attached.

In effect, the old king had stepped down completely, and the young prince held the throne.

Bob did not hesitate, but promptly wielded the scepter. He "fired" himself as editorial chieftain, brought back Billy Colver as $30,000-a-year interim "editorial" director, and commissioned himself at $60,000 a year to be instead of a shadow the actual stand-in for E. W. Scripps.

That was exactly what Scripps wanted to happen. Bob should be a "general" and stand back far enough from the front lines to dream and plan. "He must learn to think more abstractly," his father observed, "and less concretely."

Roy Howard, not consulted about this move, was miffed. Everyone knew he had his heart set on taking over the editorial end. In a persnickety pout, Howard demanded a formal "release" from his original assignment before he stepped somewhat aside from the bulldozer onslaught of Robert P. Scripps, now the undisputed Number One man in just about anything he wanted to do in the business.

The old man knew what to do to help mollify Howard—and what he had in mind would serve two ends.

To his dying day, Scripps would never admit he was "getting back" at Milton McRae for what E. W. saw as insulting mistreatment in the guardianship of grandson John Paul, but—

"I am old and disillusioned," he wrote Ellen, "to such an extent that McRae's attitude has not surprised me at all. . . . [He] is just a two-legged human being, just the same kind of ordinary animal that I am myself.

"I decided . . . to gradually change the name of our company from Scripps-McRae to Scripps-Howard. Howard is just another smoke-screen that McRae has always been to me. It has always been a matter of my convenience and comfort that everybody should run to McRae instead of me and McRae knew a hundred prominent citizens over the country to every one I knew. Now I think Howard has something of the same instinct for the limelight as McRae has and I think he will be just as good a smoke-screen for Bob as McRae has been for me, if Bob wants a smoke-screen as I have always wanted one."

At United Press headquarters in New York, W. W. Hawkins kept stewing that Hearst and Pulitzer were acclaimed "heroes" in American journalism while his boss, instead of being rated their equal, was, because he was such a hermit, largely ignored and unsung. That was not fair! Bill Hawkins came up with one means of boosting the E. W. Scripps image. His portrait should be painted and reproductions hung in all U.P. bureaus and Scripps offices. He sounded Roy Howard and Bob. They enthusiastically grabbed his idea, and took it one step further—get the Chief sculpted, too!

Knowing his peculiarities, all doubted Scripps would sit either to be put on canvas or in bronze. True, their suggestion set off several days of grumbling, grousing, and begging off. Then, surprisingly, he acquiesced. They quickly commissioned a young Scot painter, John Young-Hunter, and went after celebrated sculptor Jo Davidson.

Scripps's old-time yen to "bet on a man" and grubstake him was still alive. For several years he had encouraged his nephew, Tom E. Sharp, to find a good town and launch one of the four-page penny papers. Sharp had honed his skills, rising to managing editor of the *Memphis Press.* Finally Tom decided to go into El Paso, Texas. Scripps gave him a $20,000 kitty—of course, retaining 51 percent control—and teamed him up with a young neophyte, Frank Westberg, who had served as a Miramar secretary three or four years. The Sharp-Westberg "baby" was the forty-first Scripps daily—the *El Paso Post,* born August 21, 1922.

Bob had executed the contract for the new yacht. Cox and Stevens expected to deliver her at Newport News, Virginia, by mid-November. Scripps didn't want to hear about it. Every decision was left up to Bob. That is, except one—E. W. insisted on a six-foot tub in his bathroom!

Cruising off New England, the "Kemah" put in at Boston and picked up John Young-Hunter. Lugging easel, paints, and other gear, the portrait painter expected to work leisurely, his subject sitting an hour a day. E. W. didn't take to the artist, an uninteresting, odd sort who objected to people looking at his unfinished work. Scripps decided to hurry him off the boat—and sat seven hours one day and five the next. With the three sittings, Young-Hunter had the portrait far enough along to carry away and finish in his studio.

Bob and others admired the completed portrait, but Scripps was not enthusiastic: "He certainly did make me look like a broken-hearted old man . . . fat and quite aged man . . . and then, too, he has accentuated my nose which I have always known was something of a Jew nose, but I had never recognized the particular Jew-like appearance of its tip."

Jo Davidson had just arrived in Switzerland from America with his family when the cable arrived asking him to do the bust of Scripps. The sculptor was reluctant to turn around and come right back across the Atlantic. At the urging of Bob, Howard, and Hawkins, Lincoln Steffens wrote his friend Davidson:

> You must do a great thing with Scripps. He is a great man and an individual. There is no other like him. Energy, vision, courage, wisdom—he thinks his own thought absolutely. He sees straight. He goes crooked.
> He sees the line he is on and his thinking sticks to that. I regard Scripps as one of the two or three great men of my day. He is on to himself, and the world, plays the game and despises it. He is sincere and not cynical. Really, he should be done, but as a full-length standing figure, so as to show the power of the man—the strength he took care to keep from becoming refined. He avoided other rich men so as to escape being one. He knew the danger his riches carried for himself and his papers.

That sold Davidson. He sailed back to New York and Bob met him at the pier and took him out to Huntington about 10 at night. They stopped in the kitchen for a glass of beer, a luxury in that prohibition era. E. W. thumped down the stairs, the sculptor says in his memoirs. "He had a beautiful head and I was glad I had come. Scripps, however, was not happy about it. After complaining that he didn't want a bust, he requested that I get it over with as quickly as possible."

They agreed to start at 7 next morning. Davidson overslept. He rushed down; Scripps, at the breakfast table, growled: "You're late!" Says Davidson: "While I worked, Scripps never stopped talking; he objected to the making of the bust. He objected to me. He wanted to know why I lived in France. Why did I not live in America. Wasn't it good enough for me? He kept making barbed remarks."

The sculptor's patience wore thin and he finally interrupted to tell Scripps about the Chinese laundryman on New York's East Side whom Davidson and his pals as kids had taunted until the Oriental set the bullies straight by asserting that a white man can't insult a Chinaman.

"From then on, we got on fine. He told me many stories of his life. Every once in a while Scripps would quit talking, yell for his valet who would appear and take the dead cigar out of his mouth, put in a fresh one, light it and go away."

When the bust was finished, Bob was enthusiastic and wanted several copies in bronze for various newspaper offices. E. W. had a reaction that was both mildly vain and a trifle sardonic. "For the life of me," he wrote Ellen, "I don't know if the bust is a likeness of me. . . . Getting a back view . . . I no longer wondered why people always cheered when I got beaten in any game I was playing or why, in all the sensations of others that I had observed, I had never been aware of any real human sympathy. I declared that for the first time in my life, I felt like excusing my wife for the way she had treated me at times."

The cacophony of a murderous anvil chorus assaulted the "Kemah" as she glided up Hampton Roads into the sprawling dry-dock and ship-building complex that dominated Newport News, Virginia. It was Saturday, September 16, 1922. Scripps was arriving to witness the afternoon launching of his new yacht.

Workmen swarmed scaffolds over vessels large and small amid the hiss of steam hoists, clank of banging steel, ruckus of chains and whistles, and riveters' tattoo. On the "Kemah" guests rushed to the rail as they drew abreast an ocean liner that looked as long as three football fields. It was the *Leviathan,* the 907-foot former German *Vaterland* that had been seized in World War I and used to transport doughboys to Europe. Here she was being refurbished to go back as a passenger ship.

The "Kemah" tied up at a Cox and Stevens pier. Bob, with a big grin, pointed across the channel. "There's your new yacht — the 'Ohio.' " His father stared intently at the gleaming white hull with its crisp black bottom. He could see twenty or thirty portholes along the side, six-foot propellors protruding on thick shafts. She was 172 feet long with a twenty-six-foot beam, drafting eleven feet. It was three or four times the size of the "Kemah." Scripps liked what he saw.

The launching went "beautifully." Workers swinging big sledges knocked loose chock blocks; the "Ohio" shuddered and slid with quick grace down the ways. "It was plainly evident," Harry Smithton observed, "that E. W. S. felt a real thrill as his new yacht slid into the water." Spectators cheered. A tug moved in, took her in tow, and moored the unfinished boat at a pier next to the *Leviathan.* The new yacht was so dwarfed that Scripps noted in his diary that the "Ohio" looked like the great ocean liner's dinghy.

That was an unjust comparison; the "Ohio" actually was a miniature $350,000 ocean liner in her own right, strong and heavy enough to breast any sea, with a range of 7,000 to 11,000 miles, its 700 horsepower capable of eleven knots. The yacht was not likely to sink; steel bulkheads separated her into five watertight compartments.

Already Scripps planned an Orient cruise. He wanted to take as his guests Bob and Peggy, Nackie, several grandsons, and newspaper and scientific comrades, including Clarence Darrow.

The stack of typed manuscript that had just come in from the New York secretarial bureau lay on Scripps's table in the "Kemah" saloon. Reading the pages, he often sadly shook his head. It was his first novel — and he didn't like it.

"I am sure," he wrote Ellen, "as bad as my book might have been, the stenographer butchered it."

That might have been a fair assessment, given the conditions under which his creation emerged. He verbalized the story to one of his new secretaries, Alan J. Ewing, who took it in shorthand. Ewing later read his notes into a Dictaphone. Those cylinders were mailed to the Efficiency Typing Bureau in New York City where nameless typists listened and transcribed Ewing's dictation. Their pages Scripps now read.

"I found it easy and very amusing to compose my first story. It poured out in a perfect stream, and I imagine that was partly the trouble with the stenographer. I was thirty hours altogether on the book. . . . Counting the words . . . it would be a four-hundred page novel."

Actually he couldn't decide whether he had turned out a novel or a play. The title was "Theory and Practice." It was heavily autobiographical, and incorporated elements of recent books he had read, including his opinions on eugenics.

His hero was named Francis Wilden, born in the 1880s to a surrogate mother in an upstate New York farmhouse. As a young man he went west to a town named "Wilton," where he became successively newspaperman, hardware dealer, and banker. Somehow he inherited $40,000,000. Then he catapulted himself into Wall Street where he ran his fortune up to $500,000,000.

Love interest was weak, virtually ignored. Francis Wilden was a soldier in World War I and apparently had an incidental affair abroad. In the manuscript, Scripps touched on business evaluation, newspapering, moral values, and boycotts, dual management, eugenics, orphanages, farming, as well as feminine wiles, and often injected French and Italian historical data. At war's end, the hero comes back to the United States.

Scripps concludes his novel with these words:

> The armistice was signed. Francis boarded his yacht and sailed away to the South Pacific and returned to America and the "Golden Bough" ranch three years later. He was then fairly past forty years of age.
>
> But what is Francis Wilton [the name had been Weldon, Wilden, and Wilton elsewhere in the manuscript] to do now? What is he going to do for the remainder of his life? The author does not know and neither does his reader.
>
> THE END

Ellen was curious to read the novel; he sent her the manuscript. This initial failure did not seriously wound his reborn yearning to become a literary figure. He told Ellen he intended to try his hand at three or four other novels — which later he did.

His people phobia was getting bad again. He lamented to Dr. Ritter he dreaded having to sail back to Washington. "All the boat's laundry is there. . . . I almost had rather wear dirty clothes and go without clean napkins, than lie in that harbor the few hours necessary to bring aboard the things."

An unexpected air of mystery suddenly sprang up in early October around the "Ohio." Whispers reached Scripps that shoddy material was being used, and his new boat couldn't perform as specified. Impulsively, Scripps sailed the "Kemah" to Newport News, tied up alongside the "Ohio," and went aboard. He looked around sharply and interrogated workmen. Scripps spotted a dozen flaws. Cruising maximum was only 5,400. Water storage was too scant. Some hardwood looked worm-eaten. Worse, his private bath was fitted with an ordinary tub!

For two days Scripps prowled his unfinished yacht. Convinced Cox and Stevens were "pulling a mean little cheat," he fired them a fierce protest. Just then the Virginia temperature skidded to fifty, too brisk for the Chief. He donned two pairs of long underwear and ordered the "Kemah" to sail for Florida. He left everybody in the shipyard flustered and excited.

Scripps, it turned out, was shooting from the hip, and didn't have all his facts straight. Bob discovered that much of what his father considered "goofs" were misunderstandings. But not on the bathtub! Though the biggest made for yachts, it was too short, measuring six feet outside, six inches less inside. Scripps vowed when he got the boat around to the West Coast he would install his big old-fashioned tub from Miramar, if it came to that.

For protection on the high seas, Bob obtained a one-pound U.S. Navy cannon to be mounted on the forward deck. In the gun locker he put six rifles, eight pistols, and a Thompson submachine gun. "This fires two-hundred-clip cartridges at fifteen per second," he wrote his father. "I fired several hundred rounds with this gun myself and I know what it will do, which is plenty."

His "Ohio" skipper would be Captain Hiram Dixon, fifty-two, with thirty years experience in both Atlantic and Pacific. For a time Dixon had captained Joseph Pulitzer's yacht "Liberty," one of largest ever built, 269 feet long, 35 wide, costing $1,500,000.

That kind of money certainly was not going into Scripps's yacht, but his business was booming. He didn't intend to be caught short of personal funds. He instructed Bob to assemble securities and cash amounting to $500,000 and deposit that in a special—and secret—account in New York's Chemical Bank, subject to withdrawal by no one except E. W.

Nackie rarely let slip a chance to harpoon her husband. In her eyes he had "left her"—three times! Bluntly she told him none of the grandsons would make the Orient cruise with him. The schism with daughter Nackey continued his saddest and most unremitting wrangle. In a long letter to her September 27, he hammered Tom Meanley as a loafer and wastrel. He couldn't manage Fanita Ranch. He ought to be ashamed of taking pocket money from the $750 a month Nackey received from her father.

"Your failure to respect my wishes has had a tendency to make San Diego unpleasant for me. Now that Josephine is running amuck, the case is still worse. . . . Although this, like so many of my other letters, is a scolding letter, it is written with a heart full of love for you."

Fanita Ranch, she responded plaintively October 14, was about to go broke. Tom no longer would get his $75 for personal expenses. They might all leave so he could seek a job elsewhere. "I would like you to write me in plain language about this subject."

Any "plain language" the father sent back would require asbestos paper. He must have been a real spectacle reading her letter — kicking, cussing, throwing one of his fiercer tantrums.

A few days later came a communique from Nackie. She intended to join him in Florida to make the cruise back on the "Ohio." She wanted him to know, however, she could not accompany him to the Orient. She would remain at Fanita. Nackey was again pregnant, expecting her fourth child in the spring of 1923.

This November in Jacksonville was not nearly as sunny as Scripps had expected. Except for that, he was happy. His nerves were unusually calm. He never stepped ashore, passing time loafing and reading "silly" novels. Occasionally the "Kemah" would hoist anchor and go out in the ocean so he could feel sea spray. Ten or twenty pounds lighter, his knees were stronger; he no longer limped. Being in Florida robbed him of a front-row seat at two spectacular events — sea trials for the "Ohio," and the birth of "Scripps-Howard."

Formal announcement of the name change was made Friday, November 5. Emphasis was on the "business romance" — that Roy W. Howard, a once lowly Indianapolis newsboy, had risen at thirty-nine to full partner in one of the country's largest newspaper organizations. Tne *New York World* carried his photo, with slicked-back hair, neat mustache, and trademark bow tie. Founder E. W. Scripps, it was stated, was surrendering his headship of the firm to his son Robert, and Colonel Milton McRae also was out of the company. Thus in the restructuring, the new name actually represented partners Robert P. Scripps and Roy W. Howard.

Neither the *World* nor the *New York Tribune* recounted any of the concern's history, none of E. W.'s struggles, or aims. There were no pictures of the old man, Bob, or McRae. If that offended Scripps, he never let on. E. W. knew McRae would misinterpret the change as a fit of pique stemming from their wrangle over John Paul. "I think Bob and Roy were as kind to Mac as they could be," E. W. wrote Ellen November 15, "nevertheless . . . the pulling down of the old flag in order to hoist a new one is going to make him feel bad."

At precisely 7:30 A.M., Thursday, November 16, the "Ohio" started her engines and pulled out of Newport News for a shakedown cruise to New York. Only Harry Smithton was aboard to represent the owner. Bob waited to greet the yacht in New York. Out on the ocean, the "Ohio" was tested at various speeds and steered to every point of the compass. She behaved beautifully, powerfully—even when the sea turned rough.

"The 'white horses' were running," Smithton noted, "and the waves dashed clear over the bow and sides. Oh, she rides the waves so easily . . . that a rough sea is not only no discomfort but quite a pleasure."

The "Ohio" docked Friday, two hours ahead of schedule. Bob was impressed. He found the crew enthusiastic about her. On Sunday the yacht departed for Jacksonville with Bob and Howard and their wives aboard with four other guests and a crew of twenty. Besides two twelve-by-fourteen staterooms for E. W. and Nackie and six guest staterooms, there were staff quarters for twenty to thirty. On the main deck were the owner's huge dining room, officers' mess, back-to-back living room and library, each with tables, lamps, sofas, and fake fireplaces with glowing electric logs. On the forecastle (top) deck were pilot house, captain's quarters, secretary's office, and wireless room. Swung on davits were a twenty-six-foot owner's launch, a twenty-foot crew launch, a fifteen-foot dinghy, and two eighteen-foot lifeboats, one with a sail.

Bob wrote Ellen: "Dad can be as comfortable on board her as he would be at Miramar or anywhere else. . . . She can stay at sea as safely as a battleship and for as long a period as anything but a sailing ship."

Nackie beat the yacht to Jacksonville, arriving by train November 22. She checked into the Seminole Hotel. E. W. did not go ashore to greet her.

Next morning the gleaming white "Ohio" nosed up the St. John's River and tied up alongside her little sister. Unable to sell at a decent price, Scripps had decided to retain the "Kemah" and let an agent charter her out.

Scripps could give his new yacht little more than cursory inspection. He went aboard and plunged directly into a full day of business discussion with Bob, Roy Howard, and Tom Sidlo. "I had to sign my name to more than two hundred documents," he reported to Ellen. The important papers included finalization of his living trust, incorporation of the

E. W. Scripps Company, and orders that during Bob's absence on the Orient cruise Scripps-Howard would be ruled by a committee of three: Howard, Sidlo, and Bob's editorial chief, Billy Colver.

"I think it is well that our organization should be tested out . . . shaken down so that any weaknesses (and there certainly must be weaknesses) can be revealed. . . . I would prefer Bob spend a whole year travelling . . . away from the temptation to be a detail man . . . to be thinking and planning in a large way for the future."

Howard kept badgering Scripps for detailed instructions. "I had not more than five minutes with him personally. I told him it was his business to do what he should do . . . could do. . . . By sheer force of character and ability, to persuade—to drive—to lead—and to produce results."

Scripps had no intention of granting Howard what he really wanted—full and complete power and authority. "My own scheme of doing things has always been to hold in my hands full authority, and to place in other hands all the responsibility."

By the end of the day, Scripps had acquired a thorough fill-in on all important developments in his empire. Only the day before, November 22, 1922, had been born the newest and forty-second child of his (in a manner of speaking) brain—the *Baltimore Post*. It was, of course, the first newcomer under the Scripps-Howard banner.

With the business huddle ended, and most guests departed, Nackie came aboard and Scripps ordered Captain Dixon to immediately start south for Miami. Now, on a lazy Caribbean cruise, he could concentrate on finding out just what kind of a new yacht he had.

On this initial voyage Scripps had intended to avoid people, noisy harbors, and never go ashore. Nackie changed all that. Surprisingly, she turned out to be an excellent companion. She didn't nag or quarrel. Besides she was a perfect sailor, and "a born loafer." As he told Ellen: "Waiting on Nackie and trying to amuse her—a habit formed by thirty-seven years of association—was too strong."

Together they went ashore for long and enjoyable motorcar explorations in Cuba, Nassau, Watlings Island, St. Kitts, St. Thomas, and elsewhere. They entertained local dignitaries on the yacht and dined ashore with English, American, and native officials as they made a carefree voyage lasting about ten weeks through the Panama Canal to California.

Scripps reached Miramar the first week in February 1923, anxious to firm up plans for departing about March 1 on the Orient cruise. Clarence Darrow finally struck himself off the guest list—"heart-broken and also a little ashamed." The famous lawyer confessed he had been willing "to be seasick, as I always am, all the way." But he was afraid to take six months off from his law practice. "I have seen so many radicals broke in their last years that I always had a foolish and unholy fear of alms and inconvenience."

Even before the Squire could dust off his old rocking chair, the most predatory rooster in the barnyard leaped directly at him, flashing dangerous spurs. Roy Howard, more brash and frenzied than ever before, barged in for a bare-knuckle confrontation. He demanded more power right now, or he would quit!

It was February 18, 1923, when they went eyeball to eyeball. Scripps was not about to blink, and, surprisingly, held his temper.

Howard complained the editorial side was neglected, becoming a shambles. It would get worse, especially if Bob was to be away on the yacht months at a time, and not "on the firing line . . . to furnish detached unhurried judgment of a final authority and supply spot decisions and the direct personal leadership."

Scripps calmly offered to let Howard take over editorial—after two years. Roy didn't want it. Dual management would not work.

The following day Roy delivered a five-page reiteration of his ultimatum: "Without undue egotism, but at the same time with complete candor . . . I would not at this stage of life care to accept a position . . . subordinate to any other than the controlling stockholder. When I can no longer move up, I will cheerfully and uncomplainingly move out—but not down."

From "a purely selfish view," Howard was convinced he should "step aside entirely" if that would make way "for somebody better equipped" to take over as operations czar. "In a word, I am convinced that I would be better off in the long run, and the future strength and development of the concern as a whole would be increased more by my elimination and the appointment of a single executive with freedom to function in both business and editorial under Bob's immediate direction."

This was not the first—nor would it be the last—wrestling match between them. The board chairman's complaint gave Scripps fresh reason to ponder how well his son was performing. Though watching like a distant hawk, he had deliberately avoided talking unnecessary business with his son. "It is wiser for me to wait," he explained to Ellen, "until Bob has got his mind off all business details before I begin to talk generalities with him, and then only philosophically."

His heir, just turned twenty-seven, rather mystified Scripps. "It is hard for me to decide concerning some of Bob's actions, as to whether he is deep or dense. Bob's general attitude is generous and liberal . . . not at all vindictive, or in the least Machiavellian. Time and events, and possibly confidential communication made to me by Bob, will enlighten me."

Bob, the father observed, "is the most taciturn member of our whole family. He very seldom volunteers to say anything to me that could by any possibility touch upon the disagreeable. . . . I have noticed him in our conferences. I can observe him listening intently, evidently thinking but very seldom making any comments. You will recall that George and James had to some extent this same characteristic."

His long afternoons at the Cuyamaca Club poker table had developed Scripps into a much stronger power player than was Roy Howard. The old man couldn't be bluffed; he held all the aces. In no way would he countenance a palace revolt, especially on the eve of leaving for a half year cruising on the far side of the Pacific Ocean.

But he squelched the rebellion in a friendly and calm fashion, a style he could master when occasion demanded. Roy cooled off, and backed down. Still the Chief wanted to show he totally held the upper hand — and all the power. Bob and Roy had asked permission to withdraw part of their bonus to pay income tax.

Nothing doing! Absolutely not! Scripps had given up one-half of his share of increased profits to the new partners, but every last dime of their bonus must be reinvested in concern stock!

"My intention," he said in a February 24 memo, "was not to be generous in my treatment of the two men but be generous in my treatment of the concern. I have been perfectly frank, especially in my talk with Howard, in explaining the object I had in mind in sharing with him my increased profits. I said to him, 'The more stock you get the more certain I am of your having a continued interest in, and being compelled by that interest, to devote a large part of your attention to the concern.' "

Of a sudden, Scripps suspected his new boat had inherited the old "Kemah" hoodoo. His captain abruptly resigned. Prohibition agents swooped down on the "Ohio" at the San Pedro dock and hauled off 168 bottles of wine and whiskey. Scripps let out a howl, but there was nothing he could do. Then, just as he was ready to leave, his new skipper discovered the ship lacked a certain necessary pulley. They had to wait three days for one to be made.

But the most serious, distressful, and humiliating element of his leave-taking was another awful scene with his wife. Both were to blame.

In a remodeling spree the previous winter, Nackie had turned his office topsy-turvy, rearranging his books. She curtained the windows, stained the furniture dark, ripped leather off chairs and sofas and upholstered them in dainty silk. Scripps loathed silk. "I would have preferred," he growled, "that my mother should have spanked me than take me on her lap when she was wearing her usual Sunday-go-to-meeting black silk dress."

Scripps was so distraught he wrote an unusually acerbic 3,000-word disquisition ridiculing the episode, throwing in insults about wills, widow's dower rights, and the general ineptitude of women. He titled it "The Eternal Feminine." He left it lying on the desk, baiting Nackie to read it. She did! Scripps suspected as much. Nackie ignored him for days. The very day he was to start his cruise, he called her in and asked what was the matter. His diary notes:

> She said she had read my disquisition . . . and that in it I made fun of her. . . . I bade her remember that I had always loved her.
> She replied. "I want you always to remember that you killed our son Jim, and now in this disquisition of yours you have killed me."

When the "Ohio" left port, instead of heading west, he turned south—direct to Ensenada, Mexico—where U.S. prohibition laws were meaningless—and stocked his empty rum chest with several cases of whiskey. (That was propitious, he later said in his diary notes, because "for the first two weeks [of the cruise] I drank more whiskey, I think, than I had drank for two years before.")

Then, on March 8, 1923, the "Ohio" turned its prow toward Hawaii with a full load of guests—ready for six months of adventure on the blue Pacific.

32

The Dragon Lady from Shanghai

Gale winds slapped the "Ohio." Decks wildly awash, she pitched and rolled. Nine days out of Honolulu on passage to Japan, they were headed into an even worse storm—a full ninety-mile-an-hour hurricane! Never before had Scripps felt such awe of the sea. The wireless crackled with warnings. Two big steamships nearby, the U.S. *President Lincoln* and the Japanese *Korea Maru,* stopped, put out sea anchors, and were lying-to until the storm blew past. The U.S. battleship *Huron* defied the hurricane, and plowed right into its teeth. On, too, went the doughty little "Ohio"—and at full speed of eleven knots.

From his library window, Scripps watched giant waves shaking the yacht. Nearly all the passengers were seasick. He was not queasy, only frightened in a odd way—"no conscious fear and really no subconscious panic." He summoned the young doctor who had joined them in Hawaii, said he feared going into panic, and asked for chloral. "He advised against this. So I took a spoonful of my usual nerve tonic (bromide)." He got in bed and his valet grabbed sofa cushions and secured him in a makeshift "trough."

He slept peacefully through the night-long hurricane.

About daylight April 8, 1923, the yacht reached Yokohama, one month out of San Diego, having laid over a week in Hawaii. Yokohama port authorities were unfriendly, and forced the "Ohio" to tie up to a mooring buoy. Bob and others visited Tokyo and other points. But Scripps went ashore just once—an auto tour to see the "big Buddha" at Kamakura.

Then emerged the "Ohio's" own jinx—appropriately on Friday, the thirteenth of April. A sudden gale hit the harbor, slammed the yacht 550 feet into a mud bank, dragging both anchors. One anchor broke an underwater phone cable. The harbor master threw a fit, tried to impound the yacht, but Scripps was permitted to depart by posting a $1,000 bond.

Next day the hoodoo brought the "Ohio" within a hair's breadth of disaster. As she passed the Kobe naval station, a destroyer sped out and turned head-on into the yacht's path — and stopped. Frantically the "Ohio" captain reversed engines, turned sharply, and by inches avoided ramming the warship.

"It appeared very much as though an intentional insult was given us," Scripps observed. Later the admiral of the U.S.S. *Huron* confirmed that the Japs had no use for foreigners, especially Americans.

Changing weather and climate gave E. W. a cold. He took aspirin and "drank a good deal of whiskey . . . and as a result have suffered somewhat from my nerves." He was trying to cut down on booze. "I try by reading and playing whist and dominoes to occupy my mind as to give me as little chance as possible to brood. However, I have really nothing pleasant to think about. . . . In a few weeks I will enter my seventieth year and at times I find myself wishing it might be my last. What I am going to do with my time, I do not know."

Facing Scripps in the yacht's cozy library sat a tall, slender, dark-haired fortyish woman with sharp facial features and a no-nonsense air. This was Katherine Steelman, Dolla's former nurse, whom Scripps had not seen since she left Miramar seven years before. The yacht was perched in a Shanghai dry dock, and mechanics were loudly banging in the engine room.

Loathing Shanghai's filth, Scripps had quit his hotel and come back aboard even though his boat's overhaul would take another two or three days. Seeing newspaper reports that the publisher was in port, Nurse Steelman sent her card requesting a visit.

She had an amazing story to tell. In Russia's revolution, she went with an American Red Cross unit to set up a hospital in Siberia. She lived through hell. Her companions, a doctor and a nurse, died of typhus. She barely recovered; and for four years nursed several thousand sick and wounded men, helped only by girl refugees. The Russian government decorated her as a heroine.

She was now a private duty nurse in Shanghai but doled out most of her wages to help refugees streaming out of Russia into China. Scripps whipped out three of his $150 drafts and started to hand them to her when inspiration hit. Miss Steelman should join this cruise, to act as nurse and reader, and get a free ride back to the United States. He made the proposition. She didn't hesitate.

"What pleased me about her," Scripps wrote Ellen, "was her nerve and promptitude of decision. Almost any other woman would have talked and talked and wearied me by her indecision and all sorts of foolish explanations." She accepted on one condition—no pay.

Mainly Scripps counted on her to read to him but found her general vocabulary sparse; yet she could fascinatingly reel off descriptions of gory surgery, and unblushingly described how she treated men for venereal disease, though morally she was a prudish old maid. Also she hated dirt, and irritated Scripps by washing clothes in her cabin. His worst blow: she constantly got seasick!

In bringing aboard his yacht a woman who was quickly and unflatteringly dubbed by some of the crew "the Dragon Lady from Shanghai," Scripps had bought an unexpected bag of turmoil and discord that would haunt him to his dying day.

The old man gradually developed a strong dislike for his captain and had Bob fire him at Hong Hong. "He is a good deal of a roughneck . . . doesn't understand the difference between running a freight boat and a yacht." Bob appointed the first officer, King Galleher, "acting captain—on trial."

Was Katherine Steelman, no beauty but rather a gangling, hatchet-faced, somber, prudish old maid, rekindling some fire in the cold ashes of E. W. Scripps's libido?

That question began to tug at the corners of his own mind. His answer was emphatically no. His interest was only professional and platonic. Yet appearances were bad. Others, he could see, might misinterpret the nature of their relationship. At anchor in Singapore, Scripps called her in for a frank discussion of the "propriety" of her travelling with him.

"The more I see of her the more I like her," E. W. confided June 28 to Ellen, "and the more highly I respect her. I have talked to her. . . . The main difficulty . . . is one of propriety. . . . I have suggested she might get some older woman to go with her . . . and especially someone who would be a guardian of proprieties."

For the autocratic, confirmed misogynist who prided himself on being unconventional to suddenly question the etiquette of having a nurse aboard seems a trifle ludicrous. It could hardly have been necessary to add a chaperone. Already, in the close confines of the yacht, his decorum and behavior were under close surveillance by three sets of feminine eyes. Scripps would not dare create the least aura of scandal that could be detected by daughter-in-law Peggy, whom he prized as "one girl in a million." The two other female guests — Neg Cochran's twentyish daughter Dorothy and Peggy's cousin, also named Peggy Culbertson — hardly could be deceived and would be suspicious of the slightest hint that the old man's closed stateroom door hid illicit sex.

Scripps developed a strong and extraordinary personal interest in the nurse. She reciprocated with attention and loyalty that transcended the role of mere hired servant. Their relationship was by no means smooth. She became at times, in his eyes, "a spitting cat." They had violent quarrels. Yet she gained his full confidence, and exercised tremendous influence over him — and often would preemptorily issue commands in his name on the yacht. She proved an outstanding nurse, well skilled in emergencies. He paid her $12 a day — as much as he paid his captain. Scripps made her agree to nurse him to the end, on promise of leaving her $50,000.

Riding at anchor in the beautiful harbor of Suva in the Fiji Islands the first week in August, Scripps found himself in a sour mood. "It is not pleasant to have a lot of seasick folks for travelling companions," he lamented. "Nor is it pleasant to have a lot of people who have lost interest." He wrote Ellen they had been out too long — nearly six months. Everybody was tired of travel and sight-seeing. Scripps included. Still he dreaded going home.

Worst of all, they were temporarily "marooned," too low on fuel to try to go on. Bob had pushed the boat too hard. Running at eleven knots the twin diesels drank one-fifth more fuel than at nine knots.

The "Ohio" had wirelessed Sydney, Australia, and a tanker was now enroute with enough fuel to get them to Tahiti. From that point they would be okay; a full supply for the yacht prudently had been shipped there in advance from San Francisco.

Despite frequent discontent, he was usually glad to be at sea. "The mere fact that the boat is moving somewhere, I don't care where, is sufficient to keep me from getting restless and bored," he wrote Ellen.

I am reminded of what the captain of Joseph Pulitzer's yacht once told me. He said that from time to time he would go to Mr. Pulitzer and ask him, "Where next?" Pulitzer's only orders were to go east or west or north or south. He said when they got in sight of land he would go and tell Mr. Pulitzer that he couldn't go any further in that direction. Pulitzer would then ask him, "Which way have we been going?" He would tell him, say, east, and Pulitzer would tell him, "Go west." If they were going north and reaching land he would ask him "Where next?" The reply was always "Go south and keep going."

I feel somewhat this way myself. I don't care where I am going, just as long as I am going.

News of President Harding's sudden death came by wireless while the yacht was still waiting for fuel to arrive. Scripps read it in *The Ohioan,* his little shipboard newspaper. It was two typewritten sheets containing news bulletins his radio shack had plucked from passing steamships, prepared overnight by his secretaries. The news startled and saddened Scripps; it also considerably surprised him to learn Harding was so young—fifty-eight.

It was also *The Ohioan* delivered with his breakfast tray in the Fijis that gave the Chief a real jolt. Roy Howard, without saying boo, had purchased the *Pittsburgh Press* for $4,500,000!

"I was greatly surprised and a little put out at the news," he noted. Scripps had no inkling such a deal was even contemplated. When he questioned Bob he learned his son and Howard had discussed it by mail. "I had about made up my mind that our institution was pretty well loaded up with papers and that we ought to go slow for another year before going into any other ventures."

Howard's transaction made the *Pittsburgh Press* the forty-third of Scripps's newspapers, acquired as of July 27, 1923. Down payment was $750,000, with the balance in ten annual installments. Though initially considerably miffed, Scripps in just a few months would boast that the Pittsburgh paper was easily worth $13,000,000.

In her Rolls Royce limousine and carrying a cane, Ellen rode to the San Diego docks September 6, and greeted the arrival of the "Ohio" at noon. Nackie was not present. Ellen, spry for eighty-seven and crippled by a game leg, inspected the ship with bright eyes. Bob and Peggy and other passengers eagerly rushed ashore. Scripps and Ellen sat down for lunch. He didn't intend to go to Miramar, afraid of a domestic buzz saw. However, he rode back to La Jolla with his sister for a two-hour talk about his many problems.

Later in the afternoon he was visited briefly on the yacht by Nackey Meanley who brought along her three oldest sons. Next morning she returned with her baby, four-months-old William Arminger. Their hour-long interview was "a painful experience." Not at all were father and daughter in accord. Nackey insisted Tom should have an important job so they could live in Scripps style. E. W. growled, and wouldn't bend, but assured Nackey he would always provide for her financially. Both barely refrained from harsh words.

"I do not understand little Nackey at all," he noted in his diary of the day. "I am certain that my daughter has never even had a remote idea of what manner of man her father is."

Bob tried to act as peacemaker between his parents. Scripps agreed Nackie could come aboard—with Bob—if she promised not to make a scene. She agreed, came Saturday morning, September 8, and greeted him with a kiss. Bob quickly ducked out, leaving them alone in the library. He knew what was coming.

The Scrippses talked generalities, discussed the family; he mentioned "The Eternal Feminine," and she said it had provoked her, but she was over that now. Then he talked about the Orient voyage and mentioned Katherine Steelman.

"Yes," Nackie said, "I have heard that you have Miss Steelman on board, and I have had to laugh." She spoke with an angry sneer. "You have been so down on everybody connected with Nackey's elopement, and yet it was Miss Steelman who was the principal promoter and assistant of the whole affair."

Scripps reminded Nackie she had promised not to quarrel. She said she didn't care. The only reason she came was to question him about the nurse.

"Then she asked me what room Miss Steelman was sleeping in," his diary notes. He felt Nackie thought the nurse occupied her stateroom.

"You are leaving me ashore," Nackie exploded, "and you are taking another woman on the boat with you!"

"Nackie, don't you know that I am so old and so far degenerated in health that nothing evil possibly could happen, even if my moral character had changed?"

It was a disgrace, his wife stormed, and "a good cause for divorce." She declared she would "make it known."

E. W. hastily summoned Bob, who started to lead her away while she continued to berate the old man. At the door she turned. "No, I won't tell the public and disgrace the family, but I will tell all the family."

When he told Ellen about the clash, she said the situation might give Nackie "grounds for procuring a divorce." Scripps countered: "No two people could be more thoroughly divorced than my wife and I are now."

An equally stormy confrontation followed with the nurse over whether she should continue to travel with him. "Miss Steelman is as stubborn as a mule and as resilient as a rubber ball and as patient as Griselda." In his diary notes, Scripps devotes fully 7,000 words to the dilemma. He wanted her to stay. She was better than a doctor. Finally she agreed to remain aboard.

Though the air was alive with flying personal brickbats, Scripps concentrated on the nitty-gritty of business, calling in Harry Smithton for a review of concern financial affairs that lasted four or five hours. His business was in excellent shape. In 1919, the gross income of all Scripps papers, including Josephine's, was $12,700,000 and profit $2,100,000. Now without the pirated papers, his dailies took in $24,000,000 with profit of over $3,000,000. Total circulation in 1919 was 958,000—now almost 1,300,000. Gross revenue of United Press increased from $1,600,000 in 1919 to $2,600,000 in 1923, with profit rising from $180,000 to $400,000. N.E.A. also was extremely prosperous.

Scripps had decided to sail away on the "Ohio" and "disapear" for several months. His vanishing act required an elaborate scheme. His letters would not give the yacht's location nor date; they would be numbered serially. Only Harry Smithton, in Cincinnati, would know how to reach him. All mail would go through Harry's office. Some letters destined for the yacht, would be routed in triple envelopes through as many as two post offices. Harry set up a wireless code under the name "Lincoln" to cover an emergency, such as the death of Ellen.

While the "Ohio" underwent a week's overhaul at San Pedro, Scripps waited at the St. Catherine Hotel on Santa Catalina Island with his valet, Smithton, and Katherine Steelman.

Now Scripps was ready to get "lost." In Avalon Bay, the morning of Tuesday, September 18, dawned poetically bright and beautiful. At 7:30, the captain reported he was ready to weigh anchor.

"Where to?" he asked.

Scripps momentarily took the Santa Fe out of his mouth.

"Sail south!"

Secretary Edgar Elfstrom ran a tight ship. With Bob no longer on board, Scripps wanted to shuck all responsibility for sailing. He decided to put in charge a "super-cargo," and tapped Elfstrom. With the job went command of everything about the yacht except navigation. Captain King Galleher resented taking orders from a pencil-pusher, especially one not much over twenty.

Scripps's only involvement was to suggest that $10,000 a month ought to cover boat expenses. That didn't include his clothes, books, cigars, nurses, and doctors, all billed to his personal account.

Examining old bills, Elfstrom was astounded. Some were way out of line. Captain Galleher paid $159 for a small boat that on the "Kemah" cost $10. In San Pedro he had gone to merchants who dealt with the ship and collected $1,250. "It looked crooked," Smithton noted. Thus another skipper was headed for the ax.

His first letter to Ellen disclosed only that Scripps was "cruising in the tropics." For once he was totally free of all family gossip and business worries. With Elfstrom in charge, he didn't even know where they were going. He never spoke to the captain. "The only object I have in view is to keep going somewhere and keep out of reach of all news."

Stopping at Acapulco, Mexico, the "Ohio" got involved in a mild episode of cloak-and-dagger intrigue. The American consul was invited to lunch aboard. He asked Scripps for a favor. Hiding in the basement of his consulate was the hunted leader of certain revolutionary forces. If found, he would be shot. Would Scripps take him aboard and spirit him to some haven like Panama?

Why, of course; the adventure appealed to Scripps. He summoned Elfstrom and a plan was worked out.

That night three sailors from the "Ohio" went ashore, visited a number of cantinas, and made a spectacle of themselves by acting drunk, staggering, and singing ribald chanteys. About midnight outside the American consulate, the sailors paused, and one stole into the basement. Under his blouse was concealed a spare "Ohio" sailor suit and cap. The rebel leader quickly donned the crew uniform and joined the other "drunken" seamen.

They all staggered down the middle of the street, singing, toward the pier where their crew launch waited. No one seemed to notice there were now four instead of three intoxicated sailors. They made it safely aboard the yacht. The rebel hid two days in the forecastle. When he came out, they were safe in Panama.

Keeping secrets from Ellen was virtually impossible. Scripps wrote her October 25, revealing his address as Hotel Tivoli, Ancon, Canal Zone. He had been tied up there two weeks trying to get the boat painted again. He fired Captain Galleher, replacing him with First Officer Max Heimbrod who had come aboard in Hong Kong.

Through December, the yacht wandered the Caribbean. He wallowed in self pity. "I have nothing to do. I can't drink — even two or three very small drinks a day upsets me physically. I think if it were possible for me to drink, I would do nothing but drink. . . . What's the good of reading books? I have got a thousand times more knowledge than I can make use of or enjoy."

The advent of the year 1924 found Scripps at sea, en route from Port of Spain, Trinidad, back through the Panama Canal to the Pacific Ocean. The old man was getting homesick! Also no longer did he enjoy sailing the Caribbean. "Especially do I detest niggers. I shall go back to the Pacific and sail north, south or west. I think that by the middle of March I will be at San Diego."

The hermit of the seas began to soften toward his wife. In a January 24, 1924, letter, he told Ellen: "In a way I suppose Nackie ought not to be held to blame. . . . She was unhappy on account of her father and her mother . . . on account of John and her daughter Nackey, and on account of Jim—what he did before he died, and his dying. She has always considered that I was omnipotent and that I could and have done anything that I willed, and hence all that has happened to make her unhappy has been on account of my willful wrongdoing."

Scripps returned to San Diego March 20, 1924, determined to persuade his wife to accompany him on his next voyage. She would, it must be understood, without question or complaint obey his commands. If so, he would show her the romantic vistas she had only heard about—the south of France, Rome, Venice, Naples, Egypt and the Nile, even an overland trek across India. In fact, the whole world.

The "Ohio" would leave in four or five days. Scripps couldn't tarry. He badly needed a long soul-searching session with Ellen. He also was worried about his boy-king. Bob had loaned $25,000 to rescue the beleaguered crusading editor of a small daily in Albuquerque, who was sentenced to jail when his investigation exposed the Teapot Dome oil lease scandal that led to the downfall of Navy Secretary Albert Fall. Bob finally acquired the paper, the *New Mexico State Tribune,* which on September 23, 1923, had become Scripps paper number Forty-four.

Scripps considered that acquisition "wrong in principle." He told Bob: "If you are buying a business, you buy a business solely for business and never for the purpose of prosecuting some editorial plan. As Carl Magee [the editor] proved himself a failure in a business way, he should not have had financial assistance from us." To Ellen, E. W. observed: "Bob . . . is capable of being too much of a Don Quixote."

Bob and Roy Howard had finally killed the struggling *Norfolk Post,* the ninth brainchild to turn up its toes. Scripps was sad but philosophical. "It doesn't pay to keep alive lame ducks," he told Ellen. Bob was sanguine about business; the 1923 profit was the highest ever, $2,300,000. Scripps was proud of another of his son's accomplishments—his fourth child. Peggy had become pregnant on the Orient cruise and on February 24, 1924, bore her second daughter. Bob named her after his sister—Nackey.

Looking ahead, Scripps pulled another of his clever tricks out of his sleeve. That was to submit himself for medical evaluation to a panel of two former family physicians, Drs. J. Perry Lewis and Robert Pollock, and Dr. H. F. Andrews, a leading San Diego psychiatrist. He posed three questions. First, was he physically and mentally competent to do important business? Their answer was yes, but immediate retirement would prolong his good health. What were the probabilities of his life span? The doctors estimated ten to fifteen years. Should he continue to live on the yacht? Yes. Wrote Dr. Lewis:

> We find his mind unimpaired, his mentality keen with no evidence of senile changes. . . . His nervous system is very sensitive . . . [and] he is quickly disturbed by much social or business contact. . . . Any break in his mental placidity . . . renders him uncomfortable . . . and contributes toward a very unhappy state.

Each physician submitted a bill for $500.

For a change, Nackie was not riding her high horse. Apparently Bob was still playing peacemaker between his parents. Nackie agreed to accompany her husband on the upcoming cruise to the Atlantic coast. She and Scripps apparently did not discuss the nurse situation. Katherine Steelman remained aboard. Nackie got the impression from Bob she intended to leave when they reached Baltimore.

When the "Ohio" departed San Diego on March 25, Nackie, repressing her jealousy and suspicion, was on her more-than-good behavior. Likewise "the spitting cat" was trying to purr and not show her claws. Scripps kept the nurse busy, by coming down with a cold that kept him in bed five days.

While the yacht was plowing across the Caribbean in mid-April came the blow-up. Scripps was talking to Nackie and his secretary about taking her to tour the Mediterranean, and discussing cabin arrangements. When he mentioned the stateroom to be occupied by Katherine Steelman, Nackie turned white. She leaped up and stormed out. It was her first inkling the nurse was not quitting at Baltimore.

The ensuing ruckus between husband and wife was terrible. Nackie snapped she was getting off at the first American port—and certainly not going to the Mediterranean. Scripps was staggered by the turn of events. He became angry at Bob, blaming him solely for his mother's false conception. Scripps sent him a wireless in code April 23, via Miami WAX, reading:

RESUDOR KOPFKISSEN HERAUCETLA YFZTOOZBJE XAM-
MOYWFGA YICIPUPCZO ZUXREZOSIH USOHDZUKTH
KOPERKLEUR

The translation: "Robert Scripps. Confidential. Arriving Jacksonville on Friday evening or Saturday A.M. If possible endeavor to meet us there. More trouble. E. W. Scripps."

It seems remarkable that the hot-tempered Scripps would even try to repair this new rupture, much less succeed. Obviously he used what was for him a rare combination of strong-arm threats and stroking tenderness on his disgruntled mate. Nackie already was on edge because the nurse was daily applying an ointment of zinc and tallow to a bad case of exzema that enflamed Scripps's groin.

Somehow he cooled her off. Approaching Jacksonville on passage from Santiago, Cuba, on April 25, she dictated and signed an astounding letter of surrender. She agreed to say no more about the nurse, would not correspond with Josephine or McRae, would try not to cause him unhappiness. Also she would go on the Mediterranean cruise. "In conclusion I promise to do all in my power to make the whole cruise as pleasant as possible."

At Jacksonville Nackie did not get off. But as the ship headed for Baltimore, she recanted on her surrender and resumed the fight. The nurse got mad and threatened to quit. Scripps would make no concessions, fearing "the thin edge of the wedge." He wrote Ellen: "The question has been raised that either she or Nackie must leave the ship. . . . I think I will be more comfortable if both of them go."

He was so frustrated he wanted to tie up his ship and run away, possibly take up residence on an island in the Philippines, the South Seas, or the West Indies "and cut myself off from all communication with anybody and everybody."

The wife-nurse dilemma was still stuck dead-center when they docked in Baltimore. Nackie didn't leave the yacht. Neither did Katherine Steelman. Everyone waited for someone else to make the first move. The weather turned awful—chilly, rainy, and windy. Scripps came down with a cold and went to bed.

In a way, the boat's bad-luck hoodoo helped break the stalemate. Engineers decided the "Ohio" must have a major overhaul. Everyone would have to get off. The boat would be in the repair yard six weeks.

Scripps moved into the Hotel Stafford. Nackie took the train to Indiana to visit her niece. Scripps didn't know if she intended to return to Baltimore, or go back to Miramar. The nurse, no longer threatening to quit, was also quartered at the Stafford, ministering to his chills and fever, and occasionally reading to him.

Bob stepped in and tried to untangle the new snarls in his father's quirky life. He brought over from Washington, D.C., Dr. Morgan who pronounced Scripps physically in good shape but his nervous system near shambles. The physician grilled Katherine Steelman and was startled to learn that one day during his domestic crisis E. W. drank a quart of whiskey. Dr. Morgan warned Scripps that he could kill himself with booze and cigars. "He rather bluntly stated it would be murderous for me to attempt a Mediterranean cruise with Nackie," he reported to Ellen on May 4.

Out of the medical consultation emerged the kind of legalistic protective shield Scripps wanted — "doctor's orders" that kept Nackie off the yacht. She caused stress, Dr. Morgan wrote in barring her, that could bring a "serious breakdown" in Scripps's "nervous and circulatory system." His prescription went further, decreeing he must have a nurse aboard, and delegating Katherine Steelman to the job for two years at $360 a month, with the proviso she was not to quit without Dr. Morgan's permission.

Now that his hope of taking Nackie to the Mediterranean was out, he decided that as soon as he got his yacht out of the yard, he would cruise on the East Coast and the Caribbean, staying close to American hospitals and doctors. Again he would travel incommunicado — with his whereabouts secret from everyone, and Harry Smithton censoring his mail.

Nackie returned to California in mid-May. E. W. got the news from Ellen; his wife did not write. Still trying to be a peacemaker, Bob took the train to San Diego. At Miramar he and his mother had a long talk and he came back to Baltimore carrying a short letter. "It not only surprised but gratified me," Scripps told Ellen. "It was not reproachful, made no mention of our troubles . . . stated that if I ever wanted her she would come and join me." But it would be wiser, he thought, "to continue the separation indefinitely, until the end of my life . . . until her whole attitude toward me has been completely changed."

Recovered from his cold, Scripps finally stirred himself for a visit to his *Baltimore Post,* which had 80,000 circulation but so far had cost $400,000. The plant looked shabby; there was no elevator and he refused to climb to the fourth-floor editorial rooms. "It just looks as if the editor was trying to flim-flam somebody into reading his newspaper — showing off smart. . . . I am afraid that the Scripps institution has fallen almost entirely into the hands of money-makers who haven't sense enough to take full advantage of their opportunities."

Since the start of the *Baltimore Post* in the fall of 1922, William Randolph Hearst had also invaded the field by buying the morning *Baltimore American* and the evening *News.* "Hearst seems to be following me up pretty regularly, although he spends millions where I spend thousands." To Scripps, Hearst was a sort of riddle: "I was never quite bold enough to prophecy the failure of William R. Hearst. The fartherest I ever went was to say that according to all my own principles and ideas, Hearst ought to be a failure. Instead he has been more successful than I have been."

In late June, Scripps got his yacht back from overhaul. He sailed north to meet Bob near his new $130,000 ninety-acre estate at Ridgefield, Connecticut, for a business conference. He found his son and Roy Howard still locked in a feud. Their Scripps-Howard partnership had but ten months remaining of its initial five-year contract. Howard was thinking of striking out on his own.

"Howard asked bluntly whether I didn't think he could do better for nimself if he left the concern," E. W. wrote Ellen. "To this I answered that he had for so long a time been living a symbiotic life — depending upon and being depended upon — that I thought it would be impossible for him to stand alone."

Howard threw up to E. W. that he was "the real purchaser" of the Youngstown and Pittsburgh papers, both of which proved worth vastly more than was paid for them. "I was rich enough at the time of the *Pittsburgh Press* purchase that I could have bought it for myself instead of the concern."

That statement rankled Scripps. "My reply was that I put him in just a position as enabled him to do such a thing because of my high respect for his ability which of course included his intelligence and his morality." He added that Roy's bluster and braggadocio reminded him of the time forty years ago when John Sweeney vowed that unless he personally took command, the *Cleveland Press* would fade and "disappear."

"I wouldn't predict that Roy would make a failure if he were to go into business on his own account. He is an extremely able man and has proved it during the past years when he has been with me. However, as a guesser on such subjects, I would say that Roy's prospects today of becoming worth over ten million dollars are not one-half as great as they would be had he been able to avoid the disease of swelled head."

Now, in August 1924, Scripps found himself at loose ends, and anxious to get out to sea. He had no destination in mind. He called in his captain: "Sail south!"

The yacht put in at Nassau in the 90° Bahamas, and sailed on to St. Thomas, Virgin Islands, to fill the water and fuel tanks for a long voyage.

Scripps wasn't certain where he would go next. He studied the chart of the Atlantic Ocean, running his finger along the upper west coast of

Africa. "I think it will be the Madeira Islands that I will sail for. I can imagine myself as sort of a wandering Jew."

"I am not having a hilarious time by any means."

Far out in the Atlantic, Scripps dictated a letter September 3, telling Ellen he was listless and unhappy. Emulating somewhat the Wandering Jew, the Flying Dutchman, or the man-without-a-country gave him the blues. Both "broken" knees were wobbly again. Rheumatism severely pained his right arm and shoulder. At night he tried to read himself to sleep but "bad memories" often kept him awake. He could feel himself aging.

But he resented anyone else thinking him an old man. He dictated an angry letter blistering Tom Sidlo for demeaning his business judgment. Yet he knew he had been somewhat rattled when they last talked. And he was not anxious to get back where "business cares" would be thrust upon him. So, cooling off, he stuck the letter to Sidlo in his thickening "not sent" file.

The unsent letter reveals E. W. still considered "it is possible that Howard may withdraw from the concern altogether and that Bob may be called upon to replace him with someone of inferior quality." Though still fretful Bob might fail, father thought son's shortcomings were "more than offset by a quality that some might describe as being obstinacy and others might regard as simple firmness."

In the Atlantic, the yacht was buffeted four days by a gale. Finally the weather brightened, but his mood didn't. He ordered his yacht straight ahead into the Mediterranean. He went ashore at Gibraltar, bought some cigars, and quickly departed. At Algiers he got a jolt. It was not the same. At Carthage and Tunis, the French were modernizing—and ruining—the Moorish landscape. Everywhere his old memories were jarred. His letters to Ellen clearly showed it was a mistake to come back to scenes that were so picturesque, romantic, and intriguing forty years earlier.

He was being drawn inexorably toward Rome where in 1878 he had been in the Colosseum at midnight on his twenty-fourth birthday and had dreamed the scheme for his newspaper empire. With the upheavals he already had seen, he began to dread what he might now see back on the banks of the Tiber.

Something went wrong with the yacht engines. She went into a Naples shipyard ten days for repairs. This was Scripps's chance to debark at Civita Vecchia, and motor into Rome to revisit the Appian Way, St. Peter's Cathedral, and the Colosseum. Down with a cold, he spent his first day in Rome in bed at his hotel. He tried to recall his mystical Roman vision, the scheme he clearly saw in his spiraling cigar smoke as he lay in the moonlight on an overturned stone column.

"It was a policy," he reminded Ellen, "I have never since deviated from, at least in a general way of speaking. . . . First, go slow and wait for opportunity. Lay one brick at a time and see it is well-cemented in its place. Fight only when I had to fight, and then fight to a finish. Patience was to be my watchword, and also my persistence."

As a graybeard back again inside the ruined amphitheatre, marveling anew at the great arches and heavy stones, but struggling to mount the steep steps, Scripps fell into new introspection.

Suppose he had never come as a youth to Rome? How would his life have been different? His conclusion was that he was a mere child of Fate—with his destiny more or less preordained. "It is quite probable had I never gone to London or Paris or Rome I would have sooner or later, quite as determinedly, come to the same conclusion. I would also in all probability, have followed the same course."

For quite a while Scripps stood on the upper tier, looking around. Somehow it was not the same. "Ellen, it was not impressive. I was disappointed. . . . This time, I could not get any thrills in Rome."

33

Much Good Pain Wasted

No longer was Scripps just killing time; now he deliberately was making a "world cruise." He had the distances precisely calculated. At Bombay, he would have come 15,813 miles from New York—almost exactly halfway around the globe. From Bombay on to New York, via a swing around Australia, was 15,790 miles.

The "Ohio" had spent six weeks popping in and out of hurly-burly Mediterranean ports. Departing that sea in 90° heat via the Suez Canal, now in mid-November 1924, the yacht was gliding past a thousand miles of the desolate and lonely coastline of northern east Africa. Scripps had never invaded more remote waters—silent, vacant, mysterious, eerie. Off the beaten track, they saw only two other ships. "I have had a queer feeling for the past few days," he wrote Ellen, "of being more away and out of the world than ever before . . . a kind of scary sensation I felt as a child—that of being lost in a wood or left alone in a dark room."

In the four months since leaving the United States, he had been buffeted by radical mood shifts. He snorted that the Middle East was "just one great slum," but strained himself at times as a typical tourist. In Athens he walked the steep hill to the Parthenon. "With the help of my valet . . . at least I was pushed and pulled clear to the top." In Egypt, he "made a fool of myself" riding a donkey to the Sphinx and pyramids. "It took three men to get me on . . . and two or three to get me off."

Time began to hang heavy. At Alexandria the yacht was again overhauled. Scripps lost interest in books. He tired of Mah Jongg. Even his four-handed domino games caused too many squabbles. He fired his valet, and fell out with his new secretary and supercargo, Jerry Clemens. He abandoned his daily half-ounce of whiskey and cut down on cigars.

"I think I am better for both these things," he wrote Ellen.

He just now was morbid. In this mood November 14, he wrote Ellen: "I think if something should happen to end all things for me . . . there could be no more fitting place than somewhere out here in the Indian Ocean." What Scripps meant was that a *big* man deserved a *big* ocean for a grave—since his wish was to be buried at sea.

Shortly before Christmas the boat reached Bombay. It was "one of the dirtiest and least attractive spots on earth." Scripps accompanied the women ashore. Besides Katherine Steelman he had aboard two "readers," a Mrs. Russell, a middle-aged nurse, and Stella McGehee, a thirty-year-old Washington reporter who was his typist. At Colombo, on the southern tip of Sri Lanka, the "Ohio" had again to go into dry dock, to repair a damaged propeller.

The urge to take a new stab at fiction-writing struck just as Scripps entered Australian waters. He plunged into creating an outrageous novel about an implausible heroine named "Anne." Not surprisingly, he reached back in his past for the prototype of his main character. He used his own daughter Nackey as the model for "Anne," a brilliant and dutiful young girl who listened avidly to sage counsel from her wise and loving father. Naturally, the storybook father was cast in the image of the real Scripps.

Events and circumstances in the story forced "Anne" to change from sweet and innocent into an irresponsible, hedonistic adventuress— obviously a Helen McRae type. That was not what the author wanted. He explained to Ellen: "As in my first story I had only a hero and no heroine and no courtship and marriage. I intended to have in 'Anne' a heroine who should make herself be superior to romance and should live single all her life. But I couldn't make my heroine masculine. I had to make her a woman. Well, then I began to mold the story in such a way as to disgust me with her."

His fiction had major shortcomings. He wrote with conviction and clarity. And he knew his subject matter. But his novels largely lacked conflict and drama. His characters were strange and unique, but generally not deeply defined. He was long on dialog and short on action and emotion. Worst of all, when he lost control of his characters, Scripps just threw up his hands and quit.

After writing forty pages, about 11,000 words, of "Anne," Scripps "in a perfect passion of disgust" and snarling out "a few well-chosen epithets and cuss words," shut down his novel in this unorthodox fashion:

* * * STOP! WASHOUT AHEAD! * * *

Thus far I have gone with you, Anne, but no further will I go. Why, Anne, you are worse than dull. You are positively indecent. . . . But I hoped to make something of you, Anne, but being what you are, a damn slut, and incorrigible, I was a fool to hope.

Why, Anne, when I was young and lusty, and chock full of the vigor of life, had I ever met such a woman as you, so far from submitting to her caresses, I should have preferred to have hugged to my naked breast a dead fish, cold and slimy and well on the way to decay.

I will not say I do, Anne. You are going to the devil anyway, and you need no direction from me as to the road you will pursue, yet *go* to the devil, Anne.

Still burning to create, he began another novel. It had a prosaic title, "The Old Man." The plot was quite the reverse, fiercely erotic. Likewise, it was transparently autobiographical. It had a reverse twist, possibly representing Scripps's feeling of sexual repression. He told Ellen:

I have made my hero an old man, that is a sixty years old man, a widower with six grown and married children. . . . In starting this story I had a very well defined plan for it. I organized a perfectly gorgeous mise-en-scène for a sort of satyr. I was going to have the old man who had necessarily become a misogamist amuse himself in his old age by attracting to him a number of fortune-hunting females. Then I began to feel that he was me, and I thought such an old philosopher and great thinker as he was ought to be ashamed of himself to be engaged at his time of life in the Lothario business.

The "Ohio" docked at Freemantle February 6, 1925. Scripps went ashore to talk to newspapermen and tour the back country by auto. He did the same in Melbourne and Sydney. Mrs. Russell had left the yacht at Singapore, and he was looking for another "reader." He hired two. First came Mrs. L. E. Hampshire, fifty, a widow, cultured, a good reader, with a fine vocabulary. The American consul pushed on him stranded Chicago newspaper woman Ethelyn Graham, thirty-four. Both women were anxious to get back to the States. He gave them passage and $4 a day each.

Generally Scripps felt well, but suffered occasional bouts of nerves. He decided whiskey, though he was drinking little, might be harmful. Proudly he informed Ellen he had taken the pledge—total abstinence for the next six months!

Story writing was uppermost in his thoughts. Milton McRae had published his autobiography. A copy of it—*Forty Years In Newspaper-*

dom — had reached him at Bombay. Two or three times he scanned it for an hour or two. Initially he resented the book and grumbled that he must get Tom Sidlo to issue a legal statement correcting the errors, instances of McRae taking personal credit for every success of the concern.

Later reading a few pages one March evening Scripps only chuckled. "I said to myself, 'Oh wad some fey the giftie gi'e us, to see our sel's as ithers see us.' " It would be a waste of time to challenge McRae's recollections. "Every reasonable man I would respect would know that the mere declaration that any book was a biography or an autobiography would be convincing evidence that the book was a fairy story."

Out of boredom, Scripps promptly started a new story. His characters were five young men, two of them friends from his Rushville days. "As the fifth character I have chosen the antithesis of myself in the sense that he is to be everything that I have not been . . . a sort of Freudian psycho-analytical treatment. Naturally he is my best character though his part in the play is only that of a 'walking gentleman.' "

E. W. had been struggling, he told Ellen, to produce a humorous book that would "make old men laugh. . . . But the characters born out of my imagination are none of them humorous. All are more or less didactical and conceited. . . . They all seem to fizzle out. I don't like them."

Once again the sea hermit fell to brooding about saddling his son with the business kingship. It seemed, in a way, unnatural or incongruous for Scripps, one of America's 1,000 wealthiest men, and an opinion-maker rivaled by only two or three hundred, to hide away on the Pacific Ocean, ignoring the "roaring twenties" and the Cal Coolidge "prosperity," the labor government upheaval shaking England, and the ominous Japanese war threat in the Orient.

He started a letter of personal and business advice to Bob, and turned out five pages. Then he abruptly withdrew it, and stuck it in the "not sent" file. "I cannot help feeling there will be a time when he may make some disastrous mistakes, but why may he not just as well make these mistakes now as a few years later?"

Katherine Steelman's old-maid prudishness bothered him. "She would put pantlets on piano legs." Tension on the boat was almost enough to drive a man to drink — but not quite. "I cannot control the wind and the waves, but I can keep the cork in the bottle."

It was not until Monday, May 25, 1925, that the yacht returned to San Diego. Scripps, wary and nervous, plunged into a series of rapid-fire conferences on the boat with Bob. He saw right away business was fine, and he had nothing to worry about. He appointed Curtis Hillyer his personal attorney, charging him with increasing his secret New York bank account by half a million a year through 1927 to provide a cushion for inheritance taxes or meeting some other emergency.

He met briefly with Nackey Meanley — and tried to give her food for thought. "If she will . . . resist the temptation to wait and wait for that which is hopeless, she may well be all the better for her experience. If men build themselves up on their mistakes, why then, not a woman?" He again offered to provide her a chauffeured limousine, and give money to expand her seashore home.

His stop in San Diego proved a cruel blow for Dolla. She suffered a serious nervous attack because of uncertainty whether he would come to see her or invite her to the yacht. When no word came, Dolla stared for hours into space, Ellen reported, and then exploded: "I don't know why my father should expect so much from me. I think I am *wonderful,* considering the lemon that was handed out to me!"

On one visit to Ellen in her La Jolla home, Scripps took along Katherine Steelman and Stella McGehee. He did not take his nurse and reader to see Miramar.

During the three days his boat was tied up in San Diego, Scripps made no attempt to contact his wife. It seems incredulous that E. W. and Nackie had not set eyes on each other for practically a year. They did not write. They exchanged no direct messages; at best they had only second-hand reports about each other.

Sailing away again on May 28, Scripps headed his floating home toward the Caribbean at slow speed, bound for Baltimore and New York. He turned again to fiction, asking Stella McGehee to undertake a book with a new kind of heroine — "a real woman and not the usual conventional simulacrum of femininity. No, I do not want realism, sordid and squalid, and generally disgusting. I would prefer even the soft pedal put on sex."

He had become fond of his amanuensis. "I am sure she has the stuff to make a good writer." He offered to "grubstake" her $250 a month if she would go to a Mississippi farm she had inherited and spend three years writing. But she had already hit burn-out on fiction, and turned down the tempting offer.

On June 20, 1925, the "Ohio" churned eastward across the Caribbean, three hundred miles out of Colon with nine hundred yet to go to St. Lucia. Only two days earlier he had passed his seventieth birthday. He felt unusually depressed. He dictated a letter to Ellen saying he feared he might be destined to live another ten years.

Perhaps, he decided later, his "birthday letter" sounded too pessimistic. He began worrying about that and asked Ethelyn Graham to bring him the letter. The time was almost noon. He looked it over. The letter seemed all right. Suddenly Scripps began coughing. Miss Graham left the library and Scripps stepped into his toilet.

"I coughed still harder. I felt faint. I sat down on the seat. The sweat was pouring off. I felt weak — too weak to move — but I was not faint or even dizzy. I only felt terrible distress. I must get out where I could get more air."

Too weak even to arrange his clothes, Scripps yelled for his valet. Bob was passing the door. He helped Scripps to the couch and ran for the nurse. She came immediately, grabbed cushions, and propped E. W. up into almost a sitting position. "I didn't know I was getting worse. I found it very hard to breathe." Scripps tried to change his position and lie on his side; the nurse wouldn't let him. "I was laboring harder and harder to get my breath. . . . I never did harder physical work in my life . . . than now in sucking air."

Katherine Steelman, scowling, told him to try to go to sleep. "To go to sleep!! I wanted to go to sleep — to end the hard labor. . . . There wasn't any sharp pain. . . . I wanted to go to sleep, and not wake up."

Then he remembered his crack to Ellen about living another ten years. That letter lay in plain sight on his desk. "A funny thing it would be if I were soon to be lying there dead and to have that letter read."

He couldn't seem to get his next breath. For an instant he felt "great fright." He looked at the nurse to see what he could read in her eyes. She was still scowling.

She understood his alarm and tried to soothe him. "It isn't paralysis. It isn't apoplexy."

Such absurd ideas! He tried to rebuke the nurse. Then she said, "You're coming through." Scripps asked how long the attack would last. The nurse said something intended to be encouraging. He called her a liar and told her she looked ugly.

He wanted to divert his mind. "I set up in my mind problems in dominoes. No matter how hard I was striving for breath I kept hard at work on my domino problem . . . arranging in my mind a *grande coup.*"

Scripps dozed, fitfully, awakened two times by the ship's jolt. He found his breath coming a good deal easier. "I asked the time and was told it was a little past three o'clock. I was astonished. . . . I would have thought it had not lasted an hour."

Later Scripps asked the nurse if she remembered seeing fright in his face.

"Yes, I thought it was to be another case."

"You thought I was dying?"

"Yes."

At first she suspected paralysis or apoplexy, but ruled both out when he could move and didn't slur his speech.

"I subsequently found myself thinking what a great pity it was that so much good pain had been wasted and that, but for the interferences of others, I would now have no mind and hence no ability to dread another attack."

On June 22 he called in Miss Graham and dictated a full account as a disquisition, "Much Good Pain Wasted." As soon as he reached Washington, he would consult Dr. Morgan and his story might help the physician. En route, Nurse Steelman refused to let him go ashore.

On July 10 the yacht reached Baltimore. Dr. Morgan came over, examined Scripps, read the disquisition, interviewed Katherine Steelman, and had him X-rayed at Johns Hopkins. He concluded Scripps had suffered dialation of the aorta, and his life had been saved by the expert emergency treatment. In gratitude, Scripps raised her pay to $100 a week, and gave her $5,000 to invest in Scripps-Howard stock. If she remained with him she was to receive $15,600 on June 1, 1928, or $50,000 on June 1, 1930, whether he was alive or dead.

In the picturesque Connecticut countryside around Bob's estate at Ridgefield, Scripps took daily auto rides of two to four hours. He wore his overcoat; though mid-August, it was chilly. The yacht was in New York so the engines could be overhauled. Disgusted with the boat's worn carpets and shabby furniture, he turned Peggy loose to refurbish it. He asked her to hang a bigger framed photo of Nackie.

Scripps found his personal income now ran about $2,000,000 a year. By his estimate, the entire concern was worth at least $80,000,000, and should by his eighty-first birthday (1935) be valued at $300,000,000.

Of a sudden, in late August, Scripps wrote Nackie a nice letter. A stunning coincidence occurred—his letter crossed one from her, also written out of the blue, after a year's silence. He first learned this when a telegram came August 29:

> I had just mailed a letter to you a short time before receiving yours. In it I said I would like to go with you on the boat. Since receiving yours, I am even more desirous of doing so. With love, Nackie.

Scripps was astonished. When handed the envelope addressed in her hand, he began to tremble. He laid it aside, unopened. He still felt her a "traitor" — siding with Nackey and Josephine against him. He told Ellen he might wait two or three months to answer her request — "in the kindest possible spirit. . . . The best I can do will not be very good. . . . I don't fear death, but rather hope for it. But I do fear excessive emotional pain."

The police launch pulled alongside the "Ohio" at anchor in Baltimore the last week in September 1925, and a boyish cub from the *Sun* hopped aboard. Jimmy Young had been sent to interview Scripps. The old man refused to see him. Scripps was extremely busy assembling crew and staff for the upcoming winter cruise.

His "help wanted" ads in New York newspapers brought bushels of mail. Scripps found Harry Smithton trying to sort them, and wagged a finger at the pile. "First throw out all the Jews, then the Catholics — just look for Protestants."

Jimmy Young, waiting to be picked up by the police launch, heard scuttlebutt from deckhands that E. W. wanted a secretary. Just out of college and twenty-two, he had a touch of wanderlust. That night he dispatched a telegram to the yacht offering his services. Scripps admired that kind of push. He discovered that the cub reporter was a native of Rushville and, ironically, distantly related to him. Jimmy was a nephew of *Baltimore Sun* publisher Paul Patterson, himself a second or third cousin of Scripps. He checked out the cub with Patterson. Three days later Jimmy Young was on the "Ohio" payroll as clerk, bound for nobody knew where.

These predeparture days at Baltimore turned into the most hectic week Scripps had encountered in years — a combination of exhausting visitors, more engine trouble, defections and disappointment, and worst of all, another heart attack.

Dr. Ritter came on board. They talked several days. Scripps wanted to found at Ohio's Miami University a chair to carry out "the Ritter idea" — sex hygiene education. Scripps proposed different nomenclature. "I prefer the title of domestic (family) economy — teaching the adolescent what marriage really means and what every young man and young woman ought to know before they undertake the great business of life, that of founding a family, and how it is to be maintained successfully and possibly happily."

The startling new milieu of the "Roaring Twenties" socked Scripps on the chin. He was mystified that his *Baltimore Post,* not yet three years old, grabbed the lead in circulation. He grilled Roy Howard about that. Howard tried to beat around the bush and then admitted it was due to a new serial story, "The Flapper Wife." Howard said the story was not "nice . . . or high-brow. You may think it bad . . . but something is happening in this country. Young men and women, especially the flapper class, have thrown convention and custom, to the winds."

That night Scripps had his nurse read him the last two chapters of the serial. In his diary notes he wrote: "The language was proper enough, nothing very gross or vulgar, but the characters, male and female, were beastly and the scenes depicted were morally squalid." Scripps blamed Bob for letting Howard "and the youngsters" create policy that permitted such features. He moaned about the situation, but kept hands off.

The search for comely females free to travel the seven seas while reading aloud to an eccentric old millionaire unexpectedly boomeranged into one of the most distressing scenes ever played out on the yacht.

Aboard came a woman Scripps had personally selected as one of his new readers. She turned out to be less than stable, and apparently with some misconceptions about the cruise. As he explained to Ellen:

"She was just awful and for a number of hours before they could persuade her to leave the ship she threw all sorts of hysterical fits. I suspect there was something wrong with her brain, if she was not something worse—a potential blackmailer."

Eventually two new readers and a stenographer were hired. Looking somewhat like sisters, they were young, attractive, with flapper bobs and smiles. The readers, Fannie B. Dobie and Lela Brown, were ex-school teachers. The steno was Irene Long of Detroit, whose father had known the James Scripps family.

Bob came to Baltimore for a parting talk. "However, just as he arrived on the boat," E. W. told Ellen, "I felt my heart was going on a rampage again, and I sent him off, telling him to come back later in the day. An idea flitted through my mind that when he came back he might be able to see more of me than I would be able to see of him."

Katherine Steelman again rushed to the rescue. He was fighting for air. She worked over him as before. Gradually his breathing grew easier. The spell lasted almost two hours.

Then he sent for Bob "just so he could see with his own eyes I was still on earth." Father didn't feel like talking. "I bade him goodbye and told him to go on managing affairs just as if I were dead, excepting that it would be safer for him to follow along pretty closely the lines that he would know I would prefer him to take, since like as not I would come back and make it very uncomfortable for him if he got too far off the main track."

On Friday the 13th of November, 1925, the "Ohio" dropped anchor at Las Palmas in the Canary Islands. In the six weeks since leaving Baltimore, Scripps had meandered fitfully around the Caribbean before striking out across the Atlantic. Now the yacht's ice machine was jinxed. From the Virgins they had wirelessed for help.

Tom Sidlo's law partner, former Secretary of War Newton D. Baker, had to jump hurdles. The only factory that made parts was closed by a strike or bankruptcy. Baker had to go into court and temporarily lift an injunction to obtain gears the ice machine needed. He succeeded and these were now en route by steamship to Las Palmas.

That meant laying over in the Canaries about a month. Scripps moved ashore. At the Hotel Metropole, he took seven rooms for his party, arranged for new furniture, and special waiters. Three Hudson touring cars with chauffeurs were hired. The lavish display caused a stir, not only in Las Palmas but abroad. Any yachtsman who lived in such luxury certainly had money to burn. Letters and cables requesting gifts — sometimes ten a day — began coming in, some from people in Spain and Algiers who had only read news dispatches.

Generally, Scripps felt well, but soon had another mild flare-up. It was his sixth, having suffered one at Bob's Connecticut home, then in Baltimore, in San Juan, and in the Virgins. The attacks were not painful and didn't last long; he was losing his fear of them. "I am only an ignorant layman, but I have developed . . . a suspicion . . . the several cases of partial heart failure are nothing more than indigestion, plus touches of the heat."

Ellen agreed with that, urging him to rely heavily on his nurse's help and advice. "Be a cabbage-head, as Doctor (I have forgotten his name) used to tell his patients," she wrote.

Scripps's mind dwelt more and more on death. He wrote a disquisition recalling the saying that a coward dies a thousand deaths, a brave man once. "Well, I am that coward . . . shrinking and shuddering with terror every time some real or imaginary symptom shall be interpreted by myself as a forerunner of death itself." Even so, he found it somewhat humorous that he persistently posed as an atheist. "If I were really an atheist, I would neither fear life nor death. . . . If I believe nothing, it is equally true that I disbelieve in nothing."

In another disquisition three weeks later, Scripps asked: "Why do I fear death when I do not believe in immortality and punishment for disobedience of the commands of God . . . ? All animals struggle their utmost to avoid death. Perhaps man's fear of death has been a carry-over from the time when [he] was not a man, but an animal, into all religions."

Ellen responded by mail to his "divagations" about death by asserting, "I never knew the fear of death. As a child I rather enjoyed the picture of the unique position I should hold at the funeral celebration." She did "love life and living" but held "no thought or imaginings—or even hopes—about the 'after'. . . . So there is no use in wasting effort in conjecture or making 'preparation.' "

For weeks a nightmarish quandry had also haunted Scripps—his wife's desire to join him. He did not actually know how she couched her plea. Her letter came in August, but he never read it. Unopened, it was deposited in the yacht's safe. Her telegram, however, had made clear her desire.

Of everyone, he cared most how Ellen viewed the awkward situation. On October 5, he wrote his sister: "I told you . . . that I shall one day write Nackie a letter, which under circumstances might be of some consolation to her—might be!"

He didn't. By late November he hit on a method of solving the riddle, or easing his conscience, or both. He decided to send no answering letter at all. Instead he called in his secretary and dictated a long rambling disquisition captioned "On Forgiveness." He did not even send that to Nackie. He stuck it, too, in the ship's safe. He explained to Ellen instead of sending a letter the disquisition was to be delivered to Nackie "in case of an emergency," adding: "The gist of all my conclusions is to the effect that no one is to blame for anything that happens; that there is really no occasion for my harboring any resentment."

The disquisition ran about 1,500 words. It fell far short of Scripps's usual bite and clarity. Nackie would be hard put to discover in it a personal message. Most of the essay dealt with mob psychology. He cited two long-ago experiences, having two southern citizens confess to him they helped lynch a Negro, and in Algiers being swept into a bull sacrifice and feeling ecstacy when blood splattered him.

Scripps had ordained a conspiracy of silence aboard the yacht—no word of his illness or death until after his burial at sea, and his days were no more. If that appeared a gesture of utter meanness, he denied it. "I am reasonably certain," he wrote Ellen, "that you and perhaps all other members of the family . . . have thought I am doing what I am doing on account of pique or resentment, or some form of ill nature."

At Las Palmas Scripps finally became bored and restless. He put old memories to use—as the basis for another work of fiction. This time it was a play, which he titled "Up To Date, And Farther Up." The first day he dictated seventeen pages. The story was autobiographical, a thinly veiled account of Nackey's elopement. The play bogged down, both plot and characters eluding him. Frustrated, he threw it aside.

Grumpy and testy, Scripps took to bawling out the help, punctuating a tirade by whacking his gold-headed cane against the nearest chair or sofa. The old grand seigneur expected royal treatment from all hands. Nobody could take that kind of life as a steady diet—not even the unemotional and icy Shanghai dragon lady, an unparalleled model of taciturnity. Since coming aboard in China she had not been out of the sound of the old man's call more than two weeks altogether.

Theirs had developed into an inverted relationship—she the "boss" and he the slave jumping to her command. She dictated the rules of health, set his regimen even to forcing him to drink two quarts of liquid daily. The strain finally chafed—both. They had little chance for levity or a pleasant break. He despised her as a reader. Her domino game was terrible. Her best, and perhaps only, topic for conversation was medicine. She was too picky about dirt. Her old-maid prudishness kept the boss grumbling.

Just after the ice-maker parts arrived and the yacht was ready to sail, she demanded a vacation. She felt the other three women could look after him for two weeks. Scripps bridled. "She wanted me to stay around Las Palmas and let myself be waited on by the other ladies, while she was taking a rest. . . . Anyway, it was sort of a dare. I rather suspected she was only trying me out."

The hermit of the seas would not bow to a mere woman's whim. On December 14, Katherine Steelman stood on the Las Palmas dock and gazed across the sun-dappled harbor as the sleek, white-hulled yacht weighed anchor. Scripps had promised to come back in two weeks and pick her up.

In his library, Scripps heard the engines throb to life. He rang and Jimmy Young came in.

"Go tell the captain, 'Sail south!' "

34

The Ship of Silence

City editors of the Cape Town newspapers began handing out special assignments to their waterfront reporters. Heading toward this port on the southern tip of Africa was perhaps the most eccentric sea-going hermit afloat. E. W. Scripps was bringing in his yacht to get the bottom scraped of barnacles and seaweed. Dispatches from other African ports described the gleaming "Ohio," as not only beautiful, but odd and mysterious. The owner was called "this Diogenes of the sea—a philosopher and student who navigates his yacht in search of health and sunshine . . . his alert face looking out from a massive white beard . . . pulling on a heavy cigar."

Good newspaper copy? Who could doubt it. The Cape Town reporters and photographers got ready to greet him.

It was now 1926. Scripps had returned to Las Palmas to pick up his nurse, and then spent the entire month of January on a desultory cruise south along the west coast of Africa. He was killing time until spring so he could find the weather warm enough for a return to the Mediterranean. One reason for returning to the Mediterranean was to look for a villa in Spain or the south of France.

Books still had little appeal. He tried to take up his play about Nackey's elopement; it wouldn't move at all. He was harried, anyhow. If he tried to dictate or write within two hours of a meal, Katherine Steelman would swoop down and stop him. Must not tax digestive tract and brain at the same time—doctor's orders!

He had lost confidence in both his skipper and chief engineer. Max Heimbrod had been captain for thirty months, but E. W. wrote Smithton that he "is a good navigator, but as an executive he is a cipher." He growled that the chief engineer "tinkered" with the engines and changed factory adjustments. "This whole adventure has been a bungle. . . . The engines are knocking and in a whole lot of trouble." Scripps now thought his valet a "mental defective" and hoped to find a new one in Cape Town.

Not only was the owner on edge, a surge of tension, disenchantment, and carelessness infected the officers and crew. Entries in Jimmy Young's diary reflected conditions. January 5, at Dakar: "Three officers missed the launch at 10 P.M. and slept in a cellar with a lion in a cage and two Spanish stowaways." January 8, off Portuguese Guinea: "EWS made Miss Brown get up at 6 A.M. and play the phonograph for him." January 12: "1st engineer hit 2nd steward this morning at breakfast. Trouble coming." January 17: "Slight fire on top of [Radio Officer] O'Connell's cabin and mine from muffler sparks."

Often Scripps had the blues. "Of course," he reminded Ellen. "I remember that when the devil is sick, the devil a monk would be. While I am feeling well, I can express myself just as I have done, but when I am constantly being frightened as I was for several months with the very disagreeable sensation of not being able to breathe, I know all of my philosophy will fly away from me."

In exasperation, Scripps called in his captain and Jimmy Young and harangued them about the yacht's shortcomings for ninety minutes. Later he sat alone in the library brooding. Then he came to a characteristic decision: Let somebody else do his work and have the worry of it. He called back his young "shirt-tail cousin" from Rushville.

"You are now supercargo," Scripps told Jimmy Young. "Take charge of everything on the yacht — except navigation."

The small scented envelope bearing the La Jolla, California, postmark landed on Harry Smithton's desk at the Central Office in Cincinnati. It was another message from Ellen to E. W. Over the years Harry had become adept at deciphering her broad scrawl, and rapidly typing the full text. Then, with great care, he would edit the letter, censoring all "family" references he knew would upset the boss's placidity.

In this particular letter, dated January 11, 1926, he deleted Ellen's mention that Bob and family were almost freezing in their Ridgefield house, and cut a whole dismal paragraph detailing medical misadventures of various clan members. He retyped the sanitized letter and promptly forwarded it. He saved Ellen's original in a secure file, prudently, in case any question was raised later.

All mail that reached Scripps had to cross Smithton's desk. The Central Office was the yacht's only address. The old man no longer was too secretive, but only Harry could keep accurate tabs on his future ports of call.

Nackie did not write at all. That saved Smithton ticklish decisions, and possibly embarrassment. He knew that E. W. had not yet read Nackie's last letter postmarked San Diego, August 28, 1925. It was still unopened in the "Ohio" safe. Daughter Nackey did not correspond. Neither did Bob. The son-king simply was complying with his father's known wish not to be bothered about business.

Some distressing California news had to go through, regardless. For instance, the *San Diego Sun* clipping about the sudden death in Hawaii at fifty-seven of Dr. J. Perry Lewis, Scripps's personal physician for twenty years. By wireless Scripps had already learned of the death of New York publisher Frank A. Munsey at seventy-one. That, E. W. wrote Ellen, gave him "another jar. . . . Munsey was not in the right sense of the word, either a journalist or even a newspaperman. . . . Sometimes I think my life has been a more important one than . . . such men as [Victor] Lawson, Munsey, Develan Smith, and DeYoung, but then perhaps, that is only because of my vanity."

Carbon copies of all critical correspondence between Bob and Roy Howard and the dukes of the kingdom were bucked to the Central Office marked for EWS's attention. Letters written by Bob received no special handling. Scripps had made it clear he trusted his son and did not need to know what was happening day-to-day—because he did not intend to interfere. Smithton let these business letters stack up. Periodically, he bundled up some and sent them to E. W.'s next upcoming port. Right now he was assembling a package to go to Gibralter around April 1.

Scripps fired Smithton instructions occasionally from various ports, usually to build a fire under the Winton Company about the yacht diesels or to scout for replacements for his ship staff. Despite determination not to meddle in business, Scripps at times succumbed to curiosity. In response to one letter inquiring about Bob and business, Smithton responded:

> RPS has functioned chiefly as the head of the concern and the chief stockholder, rather than as editorial director or as a partner of Roy's. More and more, he is quietly but very firmly taking the dominant position in the concern. His letters deal with much larger and larger affairs. He and his family have been well. Bob has just completed a tour of Mexico.

Harry also would forward to Gibralter a report on business statistics: "Last year was a splendid circulation year; and this year gives promise of being a good profit year, as well as seeing a continuation of circulation growth. This year should see the highwater mark, to date, of profits."

Surprisingly, in view of E. W.'s deep-seated aversion to any kind of publicity, in mid-February the face of a Scripps suddenly stared out from newsracks across the country. It was not the gray-bearded titan, eccentric multimillionaire, moulder of public opinion. It was his serene, sweet-minded, and generous eighty-nine-year-old sister. Ellen had made the cover of *Time* magazine!

The startled Smithton grabbed a copy to send in his Gibralter package. This was one write-up, he felt certain, the Chief would not find objectionable. The cover photo revealed a somewhat regal, white-haired Ellen, in fluffy pale blouse with ruffled lace collar and jabot, seated at her paper-littered desk in her favorite rosewood chair, the folds of her voluminous dark skirt sweeping the carpet. Her expression was a trifle tight and serious, but straightforward and not unpleasant. It was her philanthropy that had made her a "cover" girl.

The magazine's education editor had zeroed in on the creation of a new "Oxford" at Claremont, California, on the outskirts of Los Angeles, a "collection" of colleges. The first had been founded in 1888, Pomona College. *Time* explained how a dream was born for other adjacent colleges to share a common library, laboratories, central administration offices, a metropolis of student villages. Said the magazine:

> So Pomona's first neighbor college was founded — Scripps College For Women. This will open next autumn. Up and down the Pacific coast go praise and thanksgiving for the woman who gave the money, Miss Ellen B. Scripps of La Jolla, Calif., "most beloved woman in southern California."

The *Time* writer was beside himself with Ellen's antiquity. He pointed out that Lord Byron wrote *The Holy Roman Empire* at twenty-six, which was Ben Franklin's age when he wrote *Poor Richard's Almanak*. He cited a dozen other examples, including the fact that William Pitt became Britain's prime minister at twenty-four, Alexander Hamilton a leading authority on government at twenty. Then the 1,800-word article asked:

> But what of a woman who founds a college at the age of 89? What of a woman born under William IV who now discusses the Coolidge Administration — a woman who taught school when Lincoln was a country lawyer, who helped found a newspaper in the year 1873?

Time provided the answer to its own question. She was, quite obviously, a perfect candidate for the cover of a national news weekly.

Emerging from an ocean fog bank into a rain squall and piercing the midnight gloom with its searchlight, the "Ohio" crept into Table Bay at Cape Town and dropped anchor. When dawn broke on this Sunday, February 7, 1926, the sky had cleared. The sleek, white-hulled millionaire's yacht lay still and quiet in the calm water.

A brutal contrast was within a stone's throw—the S.S. *Clan McNair,* a grimy, hard-used cargo carrier with ragged Lascars and coal dust on her deck. Scripps ignored this rusty freighter, but not the weather—it had turned a trifle chilly for him.

Spiffy in officer's whites, Jimmy Young rushed ashore to engage hotel rooms, hire limousines, and get a berth in the graving dock. About 9 o'clock Scripps appeared on the aft deck, anxious to start a motor tour of the South African metropolis he had never before visited. Half a dozen newspaper reporters, and a throng of curious spectators, gathered on the wharf.

Preconditioned to expect oddities, the newsmen exaggerated virtually every aspect of Scripps's arrival. "Such is his hatred of noise," wrote the *London Express* correspondent, "that the decks are heavily padded with canvas and orders are given in dumb show [deaf mute sign language]." Another reporter got a little carried away: "Sailors lowered a launch to take him ashore silently as a crowd of ghosts. Suddenly a block creaked and an officer rushed forward with an oil can to ease it. No other sound broke the stillness, save the lapping of the water, which kings cannot control, as the boat was rowed to the landing."

There was slight fiction here. Scripps, of course, was not rowed ashore, but sped to the dock aboard his handsome twenty-six-foot gasoline launch with its glistening mahogany canopy that protected him from sun and sea spray.

News of his arrival went out by telegraph and transoceanic wireless. It was published in the *New York Times* under a one-column headline:

HERMIT OF THE SEAS LANDS
AT CAPE TOWN
Scripps, Newspaper Publisher,
Arouses Curiosity of South
Africans by Silence

Cape Town was crowded, and busy. No hotel rooms were available, and the yacht couldn't enter dry dock before Friday. More stories appeared in Cape Town newspapers—"Sumptious Yacht in Table Bay" . . ."Farm Boy Who Made Millions" . . ."The Millionaire Who Lives At Sea" . . ."Private Yacht's Cruise" . . ."A Mysterious Millionaire." The reporters were not privy—at the beginning—to the yacht's general personnel housecleaning.

Captain Heimbrod walked the plank. Apparently he was glad to be fired, explaining in an *Argus* interview: "I have no quarrel with the owner, Mr. Scripps. But the ship has to be run as a ship and a home at the same time and I find my duties and those of the nurse, Miss Steelman, who runs the home, overlap." He took the first mail steamer for New York.

The incident inspired a chuckle later in *The South African Review*'s "Rhymed Resume" column

> *Scripps, the millionaire yacht owner,*
> *loses his skipper (Cape Town).*
>
> Captain Heimbold [*sic*] slings his hook,
> Scraps with Scripps and nurse and cook.

Scripps got his yacht out of dry dock at one Saturday afternoon. She bunkered 13,000 gallons of fuel oil, took on food and other stores, and departed north bound Thursday, February 18, under a new captain, T. I. Vatland who had been promoted from first officer. Several new crewman had been replaced and Scripps had a new valet, Marcial Brito.

Four days later the "Ohio" was on passage from a stopover at Luderitz Bay to Swakopmund, the capital of Namibia, when the sky darkened, the wind came up, and the sea turned angry. The yacht was bouncing along the Antarctic current, getting a brisk push, too, from the southeast trades, and with a clean bottom, making two hundred miles a day. They were sailing a lonely stretch of ocean. Since Cape Town they had sighted no other ship—just a wreck piled up on Possession Island. Seeing the derelict gave Scripps pause to consider the awesome power of wind and wave; but he was confident that his yacht's iron skin, powerful engines, and watertight bulkheads guaranteed she would never sink.

Still for all her sturdiness, the one-hundred-seventy-two-foot vessel was a mere speck on the limitless bosom of the ocean. Rapidly the sea grew more violent. A "wet boat," the "Ohio" had a nasty temper of her own in rough water. On this day the Atlantic showed her no respect at all. Giant waves rose up and slapped the boat around like a leaf on a pond. She heeled dangerously, meeting mountainous "rollers" head-on, groaning and shuddering like a trapped animal.

Gray-green sea roared almost continuously across the decks, driving down the yacht's nose. The wind rose to a scream, helping twist the boat. From his library windows, Scripps looked out on the turbulence. Always he had gloried in stormy weather, but these were the worst seas he had tried to penetrate with his yacht since the Orient typhoon. The women were in agony and frightened. "All we could do was hold on tight," Jimmy Young noted in his diary.

It would have helped to steer away from the storm, turn out to sea. But Scripps was no quitter. In the engine room anxious faces hovered over the straining diesels; it would be a disaster to lose power in this crisis. In the pilot house, the captain and the helmsman exchanged nervous looks.

Of a sudden the sea exploded with fresh malice. An armchair skidded across the library, and turned turtle with a bang. Then another. Ashtrays flew off tables. Books started tumbling from the shelves. In the topside office, Jimmy Young's typewriter crashed off its stand, breaking the carriage. "It was a terrible mess," says his diary.

The yacht was about fourteen miles off the coast, facing another hour of this torment before she could reach the harbor at Swakopmund. Puffing on his Santa Fe and looking out on the wild ocean, Scripps fidgeted. Then, abruptly, he surrendered to the sea and ordered the boat to turn out to sea to escape the head-on assault of wind and wave.

Captain Vatland immediately resorted to the best maneuver he knew. He sent sailors scurrying to the rails to tie on lines and drop oil bags over the sides to leak a greasy slick which should somewhat flatten the "rollers" and minimize the boat's wild antics. To find smoother sailing, they went fifty miles off shore and again turned north.

In early March the yacht put in briefly at the tiny Spanish island of Annobon, four hundred miles off the coast of Gabon and 5° below the equator. Scripps was anxious to get up toward the Mediterranean. He set sail for the Cape Verde Islands, 2,130 miles distant, and promptly ran into heavy squalls. Then the "Ohio's" inventive hoodoo began rattling its chains.

The starboard diesel stopped suddenly at 11 o'clock. The engineers leaped into action and quickly found the trouble. The tail shaft generator's belt had broken. In a few minutes they made repairs and started the engine. Thirty minutes later it again konked out. They got it going a second time. At 1 A.M. — it was now Sunday, March 7 — the diesel quit for the third time. The commotion awakened Scripps. He telephoned the engine room, grouchy and loud, demanding repairs be made quickly. They were.

In the morning he bawled out both the captain and his supercargo. Later he eased up a bit on Jimmy Young. "I know you have had a hell of a job on this boat. Young man, I could run forty newspapers easier than anyone can run this yacht!"

On the evening of Tuesday, March 7, Scripps conferred with his nurse and ordered the "Ohio" to change course — instead of going on to the Cape Verde Islands turn east to the coast of Liberia, 150 miles distant.

Shortly before noon on Wednesday, March 10, 1926, the "Ohio" arrived at Monrovia, while the 10,000 residents of the Liberian capital celebrated a national holiday. The weather was hot and humid. The yacht dropped anchor out in the bay, a mile and a half off shore.

Despite the sticky heat, Katherine Steelman urged making a motor tour ashore. Scripps sent Jimmy Young to arrange transportation. He went ashore in the owner's launch and hired the two best touring cars he could find with drivers. They were rattletraps. At 2 o'clock he ferried Scripps, the nurse, the secretary-typist, and the two readers to shore. They set off to see Monrovia, little more than one long street with scattered stores, offices, residences, a seminary, and two-story government building.

Scripps and the ladies were out two hours in the murderous heat, venturing into the suburbs, finding the natives were mainly descendants of freed American slaves. To Jimmy Young, the old man looked flushed when he returned to the ship.

A second trip, Thursday, even more tiring, was all Scripps's idea. He summoned the old rattletraps again and took the ladies up the long dusty road toward the Bong Mountains to visit the million-acre Firestone rubber plantation. Their driver and guide was an American, Conrad T. Bussell of Virginia, acting Monrovia receiver of customs. After the hot ride, Bussell served them tea at the Customs House. As they boarded the launch to return to the yacht, a late afternoon rain shower caught them.

They ducked under the canopy and Katherine Steelman put a red shawl around E. W.'s shoulders. Scripps made a face and said he ought to have a drink of brandy. He grabbed his flask, put it to his mouth, and upended it. The nurse went white. She grabbed the flask to check the measure. Scripps burst out laughing; he had been pretending, not drinking.

During the night, about 1:38 A.M. Friday, Scripps rang for his valet. The regular man, Marcial Brito, was under quarantine. He had come down a week earlier with a runny nose. The nurse said it was coryza, hay fever, and banned him from Scripps's quarters for fear he might carry cold germs. Timmy Ryan, a young Irishman who had come aboard at Cape Town as a steward, was filling in as temporary valet.

When Ryan entered the dark cabin, Scripps was standing in the corner, wearing only pajama tops, running his hands along the wall, seemingly addled. Sweating profusely, he looked sickly and weak, and could hardly stand. Ryan helped him to the toilet and back to bed. At 5 o'clock Scripps rang again and asked Ryan to open all his doors and windows. "Go back to bed and don't worry me," Scripps said. Ryan went and did not mention the incidents to the nurse.

At 7:25 A.M., when Scripps got out of bed, he seemed normal. Ryan helped him dress. Even in warm climes, he wore cotton long johns. He put on a tan tailored suit and vest, and pulled on soft kid rancher-type high boots. He slipped a cord around his neck from which dangled a police whistle, one of his handiest tools. If he blew, someone came running — to help him to the bathroom, or put out a cigar ash fire, etc. At 8 he ate a regular breakfast, porridge, two soft-boiled eggs, a cup of warm milk, melba toast. His appetite was good. He went out on the aft deck and smoked a cigar.

In his office cabin topside, Jimmy Young got dressed and started to go down to breakfast when he remembered he needed to get some pocket gold pieces. He locked the door, drew the curtains, took off his left shoe, and knelt by the safe bolted beneath his bunk. He had written the combination inside the heel of his shoe with a fountain pen.

Opening the safe, he extracted a leather pouch containing at least $5,000 in gold coins. Scripps always carried gold five- or ten-dollar pieces in his vest pocket. There was a fortune in the safe; Scripps needed ready cash on hand, even a multimillionaire had difficulty cashing his check in a foreign port. In the strongbox was $50,000 in U.S. currency, a $250,000 letter of credit, a sheaf of his $150 bank drafts, and the checkbook for his personal account at New York's Chemical Bank.

Jimmy took out half a dozen gold coins and returned the pouch to a slot beside the "Confidential File." Of a sudden, he felt sad and depressed. This mood seized him when he thought of a certain document in the private file — a legal-size white envelope with two globs of red sealing wax on its back. Behind his locked door he frequently checked the safe's contents and thus had memorized the typed instructions on the face of the envelope:

TO BE OPENED IN EVENT OF SERIOUS ILLNESS OR
DEATH OF E. W. SCRIPPS BY HIS SECRETARY,
PHYSICIAN, NURSE OR CAPTAIN OF HIS YACHT.

Private and Confidential Order
Signed by E. W. Scripps

In their many chats, Scripps never mentioned this letter. Nor did he mention the other sealed letter in the safe. Jimmy's reporter training made him curious; it stated clearly on the envelope it was a letter from Mrs. E. W. Scripps that her husband had not yet read.

About 8:30, Scripps called the supercargo to ask about general conditions on the ship. Jimmy Young handed over the fresh gold pieces and said no new problems had arisen. He handed the Chief two newspapers he had picked up ashore from Clifton R. Wharton, the American chargé d'affaires at the U.S. consulate in Monrovia—the *New York Herald-Tribune* and the *Washington Post*. For five minutes they discussed some newspaper business statistics in one of them. Scripps was jovial. Jimmy asked when he planned to leave Monrovia, since the ship's bill of health was about to expire.

Scripps said they would weigh anchor next day, Saturday.

"Sir," said Jimmy, "ships never sail on the thirteenth."

Scripps gave him a look. "Oh, well, it's been done before."

As the supercargo left, E. W. called after him: "Don't get me a car today. It's too hot to go ashore."

Later in the morning, Scripps called in Irene Long and checked a letter he had dictated to Ellen, dated March 10:

Dear Ellen:

I had promised Miss Steelman that I would stop here on my way up. However, I later concluded not to do so and was about to sail by on my way to the Verde Islands, when she informed me that a Baltimore lady, with whose family she was well acquainted, was stationed here as a missionary. As I saw she was quite anxious about the matter, I again reconsidered as Monrovia was only a few miles out of our course.

Instead of very hot weather I expected . . . in the open roadstead, a cool breeze is blowing.

. . . .

The letters I have been writing you lately . . . have been mostly filled with expressions of self-pity and all sorts of matters which cannot be pleasing for you to read. Probably it will be better for me to hereafter write more briefly to you and forebear the matter of complaint.

Affectionately,

E. W. SCRIPPS

A little after noon he had the stenographer put away her pad and read to him. He was currently absorbed in *South Africa* by W. H. Dawson. At 1:30, he ate a "light" lunch—vegetable soup, broiled calves liver, creamed potatoes, steamed squash, vanilla ice cream, baked apple, and thin melba toast. He started with a whiskey glass of Madeira wine.

He smoked a cigar and settled back in a big chair and closed his eyes for his customary siesta.

Late in the afternoon Fannie Dobie read to him. At half-past four he summoned Irene Long and Lena Brown for a three-handed domino game. The boss, Miss Brown observed later, seemed bored and impatient to sail again. He had Irene Long resume reading at 5 o'clock and wouldn't let her quit until she finished the chapter at 6:10. She had to rush to change for dinner.

Changing his clothes, Scripps told Timmy Ryan: "Put away my hat and coat because I won't need them any more."

At 6:20, Jimmy Young was lowering the launch to go to shore and pick up the guests Scripps had invited for dinner — Custom Agent Bussell and his wife. The Swiss chef, Joseph Wipfli, came up frowning. "Mr. Scripps," he said, "looks — well, uncomfortable. I wonder if he didn't enjoy his lunch."

The Bussells came aboard at 6:50 and joined Scripps and the ladies on the quarterdeck. They were called to dinner at 7:30.

Seated at the head of his great oval table, Scripps was flanked by his two guests. Dining with them were his four ladies. The other five chairs were empty. E. W. habitually ate quickly. Wipfli served him a special menu — minced chicken with diced canned mushrooms, plain boiled rice, boiled carrots, steamed cucumber, thin melba toast, canned pears, and vanilla ice cream. As usual, he started with his glass of wine.

He was not talkative and Miss Long decided he was a bit bored. When he finished, and while the others continued eating, Scripps lit a cigar, arose and left the dining room, growling for Bussell to join him later in the library.

By 8:30, the ladies were chatting on the aft deck and Bussell was in the library talking with Scripps, whose mood had brightened. He was leaning forward in his chair talking avidly when Second Steward Leslie Falconer brought in coffee about 8:45. The customs officer was remarking that it would be unlucky for the yacht to sail on the morrow, the thirteenth of March.

Scripps shook his head and chuckled. "It wouldn't be unlucky for me because I'm the thirteenth child of my father."

Making a face, Scripps handed the steward his cigar. "This doesn't taste good. Get me another."

About 9:30, Bussell came out on the aft deck and told Katherine Steelman: "Mr. Scripps doesn't feel well. He wants you."

The nurse found him lying on the library couch, pressing his hands on his abdomen. "Look here, Miss Steelman, I am bloated."

She felt his abdomen. It was somewhat distended but soft. His color was pink and healthy. She took his pulse and found it 84 and regular. His breathing was easy, twenty-two respirations to the minute.

In about five minutes Scripps expelled considerable flatus. He felt more gas coming and asked her to leave and send in Timmy Ryan.

At 9:40, Ryan came out and recalled her. Scripps still lay on the couch. He said he had passed considerably more gas. She put her hand under his clothing and again felt his abdomen, which was now softer and not distended. But his pulse was up to 100, and his respiration faster, twenty-four to the minute. She told him the gas was probably the cause of his distress. She loosened his collar and tie.

"I get scared about myself, don't I?" Scripps said. The nurse told him to lie quiet and not talk. The doors and windows were open but the library was hot. She fanned him.

In deference to the situation, the Bussells went ashore in the launch and Jimmy Young was back in ten minutes.

At 9:50, Scripps grumbled to the nurse: "Smoking too much has made me sick this time." She reassured him; if he overindulged in tobacco he always recovered quickly, she said.

Five minutes later Scripps gagged and tried to vomit, but spit only colorless liquid. Katherine Steelman rang the bell. Timmy Ryan responded and she had him fetch towels and a basin. "Stay — help me," she whispered. She motioned him to get behind her, so his presence would not alarm Scripps. The straining to vomit turned Scripps's face red and he began gasping for breath. The nurse again rang for help. Bedroom Steward Charles Clarke was sent running for her medical kit. Fannie Dobie brought ice bags to put on his head and over his heart. The nurse told her to send Jimmy Young ashore at once to get a doctor and to summon Captain Vatland to the library.

Scripps rolled over on his right side at 10:05, his face turning blue. He was semiconscious, his pulse weak and running. The nurse asked him not to move. He made no response. She seized his shoulders and lifted him to a half-sitting position. It was 10:08 by the library clock. His face turned puffy, and watery foam dribbled from his mouth. Scripps was now unconscious. The nurse feared death was imminent.

Feeling no pulse, she filled a hypodermic with one-thirtieth grain strychnine and injected it in his arm. Then she began raising his arms upward and outward over his head and bringing them down again until the elbows pressed his chest, the Sylvester method of artificial respiration. She clamped the tip of his tongue with a haemostatic forcep to prevent it falling back into his throat.

The men in the room took over the artificial respiration effort in relays. She administered 25 minims Spiritus Frumenti (whiskey and sherry, a depressant) by hypodermic injection.

"At 10:15 P.M. it seemed to me that Mr. Scripps died," Katherine Steelman stated later in her affidavit to consular authorities.

But resuscitation efforts did not cease for another twenty minutes. Men kept pumping his arms, eighteen strokes to the minute. In the library were Captain Vatland, First Officer O. J. Hausken, Timmy Ryan, Steward Clarke, and the nurse. They exchanged looks. She sighed, and motioned them to all sit down. She was steely eyed. Now they could only wait for the physician to come from Monrovia.

He would be too late, of course. Edward W. Scripps was now beyond any earthly help.

Jimmy Young, just back from ferrying the Bussells ashore, was starting to sit down in his cabin when a highly agitated Fannie Dobie burst in. "Miss Steelman says go ashore for a doctor! Mr. Scripps is dying! Be quick!"

He bolted down to the main deck, grabbing the first crewman he encountered, Second Engineer Harold E. Nelson. They lowered the launch and thundered off toward the twinkling lights of the dark waterfront.

A mile from the "Ohio" the launch struck a sand spit and slammed to a dead halt, throwing the two men out of their seats. "Holy Jesus!" Nelson exclaimed. "The damn tide's out!"

It was then 10:10 P.M. — and they were still half a mile from help. Jimmy was frantic. "Maybe we can push off," he shouted. Over the side he clambered into knee-deep water. Suddenly he remembered the .45 revolver he had been wearing since Cape Town. He yanked it from the holster and stuffed it under his hat, which he pulled on tight.

He and Nelson shoved and heaved, but couldn't budge the launch. "Get the light," Jimmy cried. With the electric torch from the launch they began wig-wagging toward the yacht. No one saw them. They kept flashing the light toward the "Ohio" and yelling "Help! Help! . . . Help!"

It was a full hour before the yacht noticed their plight. A lifeboat was launched and six crewmen rowed across toward them. It came in too fast, hit the sandbar, and turned over. The water was shallow enough the sailors were able to right the lifeboat, bail out most of the water, and "walk" the craft across two or three sandbars until they could reach the channel and row to the wharf. It was 1:45 A.M. when Jimmy stepped ashore.

He knew he would need help to locate a physician in a strange country in the middle of the night. He ran along the main road toward the center of town. He knew the house of Wharton, the consulate officer.

He pounded on Wharton's door. Within an hour two Liberian physicians—Drs. R. G. Fuszek and W. O. Wehrle, young blacks—were dressed and ready to accompany him out to the "Ohio."

In the darkness and at low tide, the physicians refused to go across the bay in the lifeboat, a sixteen-foot craft. The crewmen rowed back to the ship and returned with the sturdier thirty-foot longboat. Even that did not satisfy the doctors. Finally they went out in a native surf boat.

It was 4 o'clock in the morning when Jimmy led the physicians and Wharton up the ship's ladder and into the library.

On the great couch lay Edward Willis Scripps, his hands folded across his chest, his eyes forever closed. Katherine Steelman greeted the doctors. She was calm, efficient, professional. "He died about ten-fifteen," she informed them. "I think it was apoplexy." Standing around solemnly were the captain, the chef, and two or three other officers.

The doctors examined the body. They noted purple death spots already appearing on his back. They agreed it appeared a case of apoplexy. Chargé d'affaires Wharton suggested the taking of necessary affidavits to certify the death, from all thirty-six persons on the yacht. Irene Long came with her shorthand pad and Katherine Steelman began giving her statement.

Jimmy Young excused himself. He remembered the sealed letter in the confidential file. He went to his office and removed it from the safe. Instead of breaking the wax seals, he slit the envelope and extracted a single folded sheet on which was typed:

On Board Yacht "Ohio"
At Avalon, California
September 15, 1923

This order is addressed to:
My physician or physicians,
My nurse or nurses,
My Secretaries, and
The captain of my Yacht "Ohio."

In event of serious illness befalling me, no one of my family or associates should be informed until after my death if that should eventuate.

It is also my wish that if death should occur to me while on my yacht, I should be buried at sea.

E. W. SCRIPPS

The instructions were clear: bury the Chief at sea. But in his youth Jimmy felt unsure; he decided he wanted some reinforcement.

He returned to the library and showed the letter. Wharton said burial at sea might require discussion of protocol with Liberian authorities. Jimmy disagreed; the ship was not in port, but in the bay, practically at sea. The doctors suggested that in any event, in the hot weather, burial should be expedited since there were no local embalming facilities.

Jimmy announced he was going ashore to inform the Cincinnati office. It was about mid-morning—Saturday, the thirteenth—when he entered the cable office and sent a brief message that Scripps was dead, adding "Will carry out signed orders of September 15, 1923, immediately unless otherwise notified. The climate and lack of facilities demand immediate burial." The cable operator told him it would be several hours before a reply could come.

The yacht's flags now flew at half-staff. Scripps's body was carried out on the quarterdeck and laid out on a wide board between two chairs. The two physicians returned and made an attempt at embalming, infusing the body with three and a half quarts of 40 percent formalin. Valet Brito dressed the body. The corpse was then wrapped in a rubber blanket and the American flag.

On deck, Jimmy was confronted by Captain Vatland. "You are to get out of the office. I want the contents of the ship's safe—all the money, all the papers!"

Jimmy, open-mouthed, stared at him. "Like hell!" He turned and walked away. The demand puzzled the supercargo. He concluded the nurse was behind the bizarre confrontation, and was working on Vatland's pride, ignorance, and emotion. But for what purpose? Did she think there were papers important to her in the safe?

The possibility had to be considered that the Scripps family might want the body returned to America for burial, despite the Chief's signed order. Jimmy Young had a vague memory of months ago hearing a hint that Mrs. Scripps opposed burial at sea and had consulted a lawyer in California about how a widow might prevent that taking place.

Rather than wait, he decided to prepare now for that alternative. It was possible, he decided, to construct a simple wooden coffin, and if it could be lined with metal and sealed air tight, they might successfully return the corpse to the United States.

He sent crewmen ashore. They came back with lumber, local red gum, and the only metal available—roofing tin. Bill Elbert, an engineer assigned to make the coffin, said he would try to flatten it out. He and an oiler went to work out on the aft deck.

Jimmy went to the radio shack and told his friend wireless-operator Jack O'Connell about his run-in with Vatland. "Until the Central Office instructs otherwise, I'm still supercargo, and I'm not knuckling under to anybody! Will you back me up?"

O'Connell, much taken aback, promised he would. Jimmy handed him a .45 revolver. "Okay. Let's stick close together at all times."

The coffin making went slowly. The work was still underway when Saturday's dusk came. Elbert rigged up a two-hundred-watt light, and went ahead, shaping and soldering the tin lining.

At 8:35 Saturday night a cable arrived from Cincinnati. It said: "Don't carry out instructions until definite word from Smithton and Robert P. Scripps." It was signed "Smithton."

Jimmy and O'Connell went to the aft deck to check on the coffin. Vatland followed them back to Jimmy's office. Again he demanded everything in the safe. Jimmy shook his head. "No way!" He and O'Connell stepped inside, but the captain held the door open. He poked his finger at the supercargo. "You disobey my order—I can put you in irons!"

"Don't try it!" Jimmy exploded. "Anybody tries to come in here uninvited is going to be picking bullets out of his teeth!" He slammed and bolted the door.

At 10 o'clock, the coffin was ready. The corpse was placed inside. Elbert and the oiler began soldering on the tin lid. Just as they finished, the yacht's clock struck eight bells—midnight. Elbert patted the coffin gently and remarked to the oiler: "Well, the Chief will never get out of that."

He snapped off the floodlight. Instantly a loud rattling noise shattered the night stillness. Elbert and his helper jumped, and whirled around, throwing frightened glances at the coffin. Scripps was not responsible for the noise. It seemed to emanate from the bow. They ran forward.

In the dark a German freighter had come up and because of the low tide had let out her chain to anchor near the "Ohio." The engineer and oiler broke out in nervous giggles. Several sailors came on deck to see what had caused the racket and the laughter.

Time seemed to be standing still. It was now Sunday, March 14. Jimmy still felt anxious, but not so tense. Captain Vatland had backed off. At least he was no longer actively pressing Jimmy. At breakfast he treated the supercargo and radio officer with cordial reserve.

What would the Central Office decide? Jimmy racked his brain. He couldn't think of any other contingency to prepare for. The waiting was hard, stressful. In early afternoon, he went ashore. He used his idle time to write his parents in Illinois, timing it at 3 P.M. Sunday:

I am now waiting in a cheap little ice cream parlor in this negro capital city for the cable office to open at 4 o'clock as I am expecting definite instructions as to the disposal of the body.

After three pages of additional news of the event, he scribbled:

P.S. Cables at 4 P.M. say to bury at sea, as per instructions. Doing so tomorrow noon (Monday).

Now that the decision had been made and the waiting was over, Jimmy returned to the yacht. There was a parley on procedure. The consulate official, Jimmy, O'Connell, and Vatland were in accord; the appropriate time for this man's burial would not be at noon, but at sunset—the glorious end of the day, the most beautiful, color-splashed hour.

So it was decided.

At 3:41 P.M., according to the yacht's log, the "Ohio" lifted anchor and departed Monrovia Bay on a west-southwest heading. The coffin was broken open and Scripps's body taken out. The rubber blanket was removed. For precautionary legal purposes, the crew was required to file by and view the remains. Then the corpse was placed in a shroud of double canvas, with twenty-nine pigs of lead, each weighing twelve pounds, placed along the sides and at the feet. An American flag was spread inside. The shroud was sewed up and then lashed with eighteen-thread manila rope. Another American flag was sewed outside. This bundle was then placed alongside the starboard aft quarterdeck rail—the owner's side.

As the "Ohio" cut through the water, Scripps lay in his shroud in his favorite place, under the aft canopy, shaded from the setting sun.

At the rail a sailor cast a sounding line into the ocean. It sank and sank and sank. It went to two hundred fathoms without striking bottom—that was twelve hundred feet, certainly a deep enough vault for the ocean hermit.

At 5:55 P.M., twenty miles out, Captain Vatland stopped the engines. As the yacht lay dead in the water, the crew assembled on the quarterdeck and stood at attention. Present also were Wharton, Bussell, and Dr. Fuszek.

Ropes were slipped under the shroud and four sailors held the ends ready to hoist the corpse over the rail. The location in the limitless ocean was noted in the log—Latitude 6°, 14 minutes, no seconds north; Longitude 11°, 8 minutes, no seconds west.

If anyone deserved a salute from the "Ohio's" cannon, Scripps did. A blank shell was inserted and the lanyard readied.

What words could be said over the corpse of such a giant of the temporal world, who was a master of the contents of the Bible, demanded his family and lieutenants live by the Ten Commandments, and who withal was regarded by many as an atheist, and by most as at least a non-believer?

Jimmy Young had felt obligated to prepare some sort of internment script. He searched the yacht's library for something appropriate. Finally he sat down at his Underwood and pounded out this:

> Whereas, it has pleased the Almighty God to take out of this world our beloved employer, Edward Wyllis Scripps, and in accordance with his oft-expressed wish, we now commit his body unto the deep, with profound faith in the Resurrection of the dead and the life of the world to come through our Lord, Jesus Christ, at whose coming in glorious majesty the sea shall give up her dead and the mortal bodies of those who sleep in Him shall be changed and made into His glorious body by the mighty power through which He is able to bring all things to Himself.
> God gave you.
> God takes you away.
> I cast you into the deep.

The sun was low in the west, about to dip below the far horizon. At 6:03, the cannon boomed for the first time, echoing across the still water. The yacht's company lined the starboard rail, heads bared — except the quartermaster who circled the "Ohio" in a launch, making photographs of the ceremony. (Bob Scripps later sequestered this film so no pictures would appear in any newspaper or magazine.)

Jimmy Young's script was recited.

At 6:08, a second cannon shot was fired. The men holding the ropes over the rail released them. The shroud of the laziest boy in Schuyler County sank beneath the surface at 6:09. Everyone stood in silence for several minutes.

For a third, final salute, the "Ohio's" one-pounder again boomed.

The ladies dropped flowers on the water. The blossoms bobbed on the gentle waves, and finally began to drift away.

Captain Vatland dismissed the company at 6:30. He waited another fifteen minutes and then signaled the engine room. The lame, troublesome diesels coughed and whirred to life. The "Ohio" swung in a wide circle and headed back to Monrovia Bay to await further orders from the Central Office in Cincinnati.

THE END

AFTERWORD

If Scripps somehow could rise today from the ocean depths he would be staggered to discover that his far-flung empire now produces revenues of more than $1,000,000,000 a year—but not at all surprised that sixty-five years after his passing the family still holds control.

He definitely did not want to build up enormous private wealth for his heirs. What he wanted was to preserve and protect the children of his brain. In an uncanny but not surprising way, he achieved that by cleverly locking his controlling stock into a living trust—created in 1922 while he was "getting ready to get dead."

Not everything went according to the Old Man's posthumous strategy. But the solid and unshakable living trust more than held up—even in the face of a high-powered legal challenge by one family renegade. In his trust scheme, as Scripps would say, "I built better than I knew."

Even so, the relentless passage of time and cataclysmic explosion of scientific and commercial manners and mores have struck sledgehammer blows at his cherished dream. That was, of course, for his cheap little newspapers to wage unremitting war for the blue-collar underdog then toiling in factories and shops at low wages. No longer is the working man such a symbol of the downtrodden masses. In fact, to explain to a modern young person just what Scripps had in mind one would have to say: "There has always been a majority lacking the resources to compete on equal terms with a minority which has the advantages of superior wealth, power, and according to EWS, mental capacity."

That EWS dream may shatter completely when the living trust ends. That should occur within a decade or two, early in the twenty-first century.

The trust terminates upon the death of the last of his four chosen and favored grandchildren—all sired by son Robert, and ranging in age (in 1991) from 73 to 67. Then the whole fortune passes into the hands of twenty-eight equally favored great grandchildren, all progeny of Robert.

These great-grandchildren who stand to inherit the majority ownership of the concern—thirteen men and fifteen women, known legally as "remaindermen"—hardly can be blamed if they do not share the Old Man's vision of public service crusading.

E. W. Scripps was born in the Victorian Age and passed from the scene in the roaring twenties. The eldest remainderman was not born until after World War II, and the youngest thirty-nine years after the Old Man's burial at sea. Theirs is a sophisticated and glitzy world vastly different from E. W. Scripps's era of horse and buggy, bustles and bloomers, crank telephone, "staticky" radio, with then no hint of jetliners, astronauts walking the moon, or television.

These favored twenty-eight eventually will become instant millionaires. The size of their fortunes cannot be accurately determined now. Each male great grandchild will receive stock holdings worth from a low estimate of $20,000,000 to a high of $200,000,000.

Such windfalls would gall E. W.; he aimed to provide only middle-class security for his family and descendants, not handed-down fortunes, unearned and thus unappreciated.

Perhaps the most blatant anachronism visible today in his living trust is his provision that female remaindermen inherit only half shares in his estate while all the males will receive full shares. Though some might blithely attribute this provision of Scripps's will to his lifelong misogyny, it doubtless was inspired also by the widely accepted rationale of his time about women. In general, they were not considered competent to vote until 1920, or to handle business or financial affairs. EWS presumably felt women were not naturally endowed with temperament or skills needed to handle money or business. Of course there were exceptions—most markedly his sister Ellen, someone special, wise and patient, and unmarried.

Further, EWS explained to son Robert he wanted his female descendants to have enough income to be independent, and not have to marry for security, and yet not be wealthy enough to attract fortune hunters.

The oncoming dissolution of the E. W. Scripps Trust nudges the company toward a possible soap-opera cliff-hanger. Several heirs may elect to take their money and run. This would not be surprising. Will his institution be broken up and sold to outsiders? Or will somehow enough of his heirs rally, band together, buy out their cousins not interested in newspapering but other business pursuits, and carry on the concern under the Old Man's banner?

One serious flaw in E. W.'s will is pointed up by the exploding feud in the Bingham family in Louisville that triggered sale of their *Courier-Journal* empire to the ravenous Gannett chain. A similar scenario could develop in the Scripps case: Heirs with a valuable stake, and no way to share in operations, or no way to come to agreement as to fair price and cash in, are likely to feel hurt, frustrated, or angry, and that might lead to lawsuits.

Likewise, there is a certain unavoidable inequity in the Scripps will that derives from the fact that the twenty-eight ultimate beneficiaries are of different ages and their life spans cover more fat business years or more lean years than do others. Some remaindermen may not live to enjoy as much income or principal as others. It boils down to a matter of individual longevity.

When Scripps's will was filed for probate in Cincinnati March 31, 1926, it did not immediately precipitate the expected battle to try to break it. The Old Man left widow Nackie $60,000 a year and lifetime use of Miramar, and provided a $200,000 trust and $30,000 annuity for Nackey Meanley, and for her survivors $1,000,000 on termination of his living trust. Son Robert was elevated to actual kingship, not only sole trustee of the living trust but also executor of the estate.

The challenge came two years later from Jim Scripps's widow Josephine. She hired a top lawyer, Charles Evans Hughes, former member of the Supreme Court and former secretary of state. Claiming Jim had an unwritten "partnership" agreement with his father, she sued to recover about $7,000,000 under the old "unearned increment" scheme.

That pitted two legal titans in the courtroom fray. For former Secretary of War Newton D. Baker, who had long been Scripps's attorney, and who had helped draft the language of the trust, represented Bob, who as executor and trustee, was the defendant.

Josephine and Charles Evans Hughes came up empty.

Scripps knew well the story of King Lear, Lawyer Baker argued. E. W. wanted to "educate" his sons, but was unwilling to fall into King Lear's self-dug trap, which was to slice off pieces of his crown and hand them to his sons until he was left with only the hole in the middle. Scripps was taking the entire monetary risk, so there was never a true partnership "contract" with any of his sons, though he rewarded them liberally from the profits created under their administration.

Bob and Baker won. First, ruled the judge, Josephine waited beyond the statute of limitations to bring the suit. Further, it was manifestly clear to the court precisely what E. W. intended his will and trust to accomplish. The ruling, filed July 25, 1928, observed in part:

> The general trend of public thought favors the equal distribution of a parent "per stirpes," among his children and grandchildren, and where one child obviously secures the great bulk of a decendent's estate the natural

impulse of all, including the courts, is to favor a more equal distribution.

But the courts must not be led astray by feelings of sympathy or impulse. It is every man's right to dispose of his property as he may see fit, by will or gift. We cannot read his attitude of mind or heart, nor can we know the disappointments, vexations or motives that prompted the action.

From the documentary evidence we do know that it was his ambition and desire to consolidate his newspaper properties into a lasting monument or memorial to his name. This end at least he has accomplished.

The winds of change were then howling over newspapers and the whole world of communications. Technology that the Old Man might never have dreamed of was about to bring overnight revolution. Radio was growing fast and television was being born. The team of Bob Scripps and Roy Howard moved in the forefront of the tide. E. W.'s trust had committed 30 percent of concern profits to be used in starting more newspapers or allied ventures, and for supporting existing operations, or for rewarding executives who were making significant contributions.

Bob and Roy plunged into New York, buying the *Telegram* in 1927 and four years later acquiring from Joseph Pulitzer's estate the famous *World,* creating a new concern, the flagship *New York World-Telegram.* Next they ventured into radio station operation, and began considering the risk of going into the still-infant television business. (That did not occur until December 17, 1947, when WEWS-TV went on the air in Cleveland.)

Unfortunately, just about the time Bob Scripps and Howard began their ambitious program of expansion, came hard times. In the wake of the 1929 stock market crash began the nation's most serious modern economic depression. Scripps-Howard, like virtually every newspaper company in the country, had to retrench, fire hands, and watch the ledgers hemorrhage red ink.

But an even worse blow came in 1938 — the death of Bob Scripps.

It was an untimely event the Old Man had feared, and tried to warn against. He had counseled his son about whiskey — he certainly could give first-hand testimony about the evils of booze. It was a shame that Bob let the bottle get the best of him; he was a warm, outgoing executive, known and admired for his journalistic éclat, a serious thinker, a disciple of most of his father's philosophy of social fair play.

He, too, loved the sea, and while cruising with newspaper colleagues aboard his ketch "Novia Del Mar" off lower California was struck by a hemorrhage in the lower esophagus. Doctors could not staunch the violent bleeding. His liver, pounded for several years by booze, had come apart. He was only forty-two.

His oldest children were minors: Bob Junior, twenty, and Charles, eighteen—legally too young and professionally too green to take the king mantle. Temporarily, control went to three emergency trustees Bob had designated, Roy Howard, W. W. Hawkins, and George B. "Deac" Parker. They were supported by Newton Baker's law firm, especially Paul Patterson. This leadership encountered serious difficulties, partially from over-expansion in the backwash of the depression, and other factors.

Media historians look critically at this period and conclude that Scripps-Howard stumbled greviously. They cite instances of serious mismanagement, and note a marked retreat by Roy Howard—who vividly feared Communist infiltration of newsrooms through the Guild—from E. W.'s basic belief in the right of labor to organize.

Whatever the true cause, the end result was Scripps-Howard suffered badly. In E. W.'s time the six-day evening newspaper was strong. The morning and Sunday editions then began to win the journalistic wrestling match. Most Scripps papers were PM's, and over the years many became dead weight and were folded or sold. It was a sad list of important dailies—New York, Washington, San Diego, San Francisco, Oklahoma City, Akron, Youngstown, Buffalo, Houston, Baltimore, Fort Worth, Columbus—even the pioneer flagship *Cleveland Press,* which at its peak poured $1,000,000-a-year profit into the Central Office treasury.

The Cleveland paper, often ranked as one of America's ten best dailies, had flown E. W.'s personal banner for 102 years when Scripps-Howard dumped the *Press* in 1980. It was snapped up as a bargain by a Cleveland industrialist, who, possibly looking for a tax write-off, permitted the once-proud publication to rapidly strangle to death.

Two years later came another corporate tragedy—and perhaps an even more stinging embarrassment to the Scripps family. One of the Old Man's greatest claims to fame as a journalistic pioneer and champion of free enterprise had been his creation in 1907 of a wire service to avert an Associated Press monopoly—his United Press Associations. Several years later William Randolph Hearst started his own wire service, which was dubbed International News Service.

Eventually, however, three major wire services could not survive the intolerable rising costs of worldwide coverage. Hearst gave up and dumped his INS into U.P. in a merger from which he reportedly got a very minor interest in the newly created United Press International (UPI).

But UPI, too, began foundering in a sea of red ink. Scripps officials shopped around and tried to find a legitimate buyer targeting, unsuccessfully, Reuters, McGraw-Hill, the Dow Jones Company, and a scattering of lesser known outfits. In the late seventies UPI losses were staggering. Some speculation put the UPI deficit at between $3,500,000 and $10,000,000 a year. No comment on that from Scripps officials; but there was panic evident in the Central Office.

It was felt, for one thing, that some of the remaindermen might look askance at the E. W. Scripps Trust and feel it was imperiling their to-be-inherited wealth. Well and good to hold high the Old Man's banner, and his fame, as creator of the free-enterprise telegraph news organization that kept the monopolistic Associated Press from eating independent American publishers alive. If the UPI hemorrhage could be staunched, wouldn't there be more millions to again undertake expansion? Had UPI already served the purpose EWS envisioned for it? Was there even a glimmer of a silver lining on the depressed wire service horizon? These were questions Scripps lawyers raised.

The Scripps trustees could see the threat of litigation at some point from some disgruntled inheritors. How the Old Man would have hated a family squabble over his legacy, though he had had to cope with a few bitter ones in his lifetime. The trustees felt they had to act; they had to grit their teeth and reckon with United Press International's ever-deepening sea of red ink.

It was impractical for Scripps-Howard to just shut down UPI; the wire service would have to cough up several millions, perhaps ten, in severance pay. To keep UPI going, the company solicited about twenty other publishers to support it financially. Apparently they didn't believe the concern would actually abandon the Old Man's pride and joy. Finally, the Scripps company practically gave away UPI on June 3, 1982, to four small-time publishers and broadcasters. This quartet couldn't make it go either. They, too, managed to unload it. UPI, still teetering on bankruptcy, went into the hands of another set of owners, with no sunshine to lighten its grim outlook. No one seemed able to concoct a magic device that could rescue the wire service from the shadow of the Grim Reaper.

All the while the E. W. Scripps Trust faithfully marches forward under the Old Man's banner, fully aware a Damoclean sword hangs perilously overhead. The trustees are attempting to steer a course that will somehow permit them to accommodate remaindermen who want to jump ship, believing there will continue to be a majority of inheritors who want to keep the institution as a strong, going company.

The two most powerful and dedicated men in the Scripps trust hierarchy are Bob's sons Bob Junior and Charles, who were eight and six, respectively, when their grandfather was consigned to Davey Jones's locker. Bob Junior, now seventy-three (two years older than Charles), has always been a son of the soil in E. W.'s mode, spending most of his life in western Texas, raising cotton, harvesting honey, growing apples and peaches, and running a milling machine as a hobby. He designed and built a steam engine to power a lake boat. For a brief youthful period he tried sitting behind a Central Office desk, but chucked it for the more pleasant life of a farmer. His most successful crop has been children; he has eleven, the largest family—and bevy of remaindermen—in the Scripps clan. Six of his children are girls, who will inherit just half as much as their five brothers. Charles deliberately put himself under the harrow as a young man, starting as a cub reporter in Cleveland, and studying hard to learn his grandfather's trade from the ground up. For him, and for the proud Scripps tradition, that has paid off handsomely. He submitted also to schooling in the intricacies of corporate life from company lawyers and financial experts, and rapidly vaulted from duke of the empire to pretty much its king. By 1948 he was elected chairman of the trust, and has been since 1953—at only thirty-three—chairman of the E. W. Scripps Company, which controls not only the newspapers and syndicates, but also all broadcasting and cable-TV interests—in short, everything. He is intelligent, quiet, and strong-willed—and not one who can be bamboozled about any aspect of the empire.

Both Charles and his older brother are firm believers in their grand-father's concept of "soul" and dedication to public service, not only as an ideal but essential in the long run for corporate survival. These views were fully shared by the third trustee, their younger brother E. W. "Ted" Scripps II, who died at age 57 in 1987. Although living the rustic life, Bob Junior is interested in and knowledgeable about corporate affairs, and invariably supports his chairman brother's ideas and decisions. Now seventy-one, Charles has developed an amazing resemblance to his grandfather in late life, down to his gray, close-cropped beard. (He has never been known, however, to wear the traditional E. W. velvet skullcap.)

Living under the sword of Damocles prompted Scripps executives, led principally by Charles, to consider some method of getting cash on hand sufficient to permit any remaindermen not interested in the publishing business to cash in on their inheritance and go, without wrecking the company.

Finally in 1988 the trustees and management developed a plan to take the company partially public by issuing 8,000,000 shares of non-voting common stock. At an initial price of $16, the offering would bring in perhaps $128,000,000. The issue, though considered comparatively high-priced, appealed particularly to institutional investors looking for long-term prospects. (By mid-1989 the stock was trading around $22.) A similar scheme had been employed in formation of Scripps-Howard Broadcasting Company, 20 percent of whose stock was sold publicly, while 80 percent — much more than control — was retained by the E. W. Scripps Trust.

In no way does the public sale of EWSCO stock endanger the Trust's control of the empire. Retaining a total of 77,780,780 shares of common stock — including all voting shares, the company will still elect seven of the ten members of the board of directors.

Mindful of devices utilized to retain family control of the *New York Times* and Pulitzer organization, the Scripps trust stock offering provided that if and when any remainderman elects to sell his (or her) interest, the stock will be offered first to other family members, secondly to the company, and only then to outsiders. In the latter event provision exists to convert the inherited voting shares to Class A non-voting stock, so traditional family control is not diluted. As Charles Scripps has explained: "This way, nobody's locked in, or locked out."

In going public, the concern was required by federal security regulations to lift the veil of secrecy that has kept the empire's true financial status mysterious and secret since the very beginning.

The figures are impressive. They reveal that in 1990 (the latest available statistics) the concern had operating revenues of $1,296,599,000 with operating income of $162,400,000, and net income of $48,000,000 (which before a national advertising slump in 1989 was $90,000,000). Even a visionary like the Old Man probably would be surprised to discover that the company he estimated as worth about $200,000,000 at his death, now had total assets of $1,521,500,000. And furthermore that it ranked among America's ten largest media conglomerates with 11,500 employees and was rich enough to annually pay its president and CEO $580,000, and shell out for all fourteen corporate executives as a group $2,648,000 in salary plus $757,681 in bonuses.

In step with the modern trend in communications, the Scripps concern has invested heavily in television and cable operations in widely scattered parts of the country. It owns nine TV stations and five radio stations, and also serves about 630,000 cable subscribers in ten states. Even so, newspaper publishing and allied operations, such as being the world's largest distributor of newspaper features and comics (i.e., a roster of writers from Miss Manners to Jack Anderson, and notably "Peanuts" and "Garfield"), and books (topped by the *World Almanac*), provide the bulk of the concern profits. Scripps has nineteen daily newspapers in twelve states and Puerto Rico, with total circulation of about 1,500,000 copies a day.

For the year 1990, publishing accounted for $847,770,000 of revenue, with $235,580,000 from broadcasting, and $199,413,000 from cable television.

It is interesting to note that E. W. deliberately excluded from sharing his estate a total of ten grandchildren: the four of Jim and Josephine, three of whom, two women and a man, are still alive; the five sons of daughter Nackey, the one-time Miramar tomboy (who died in 1981 at 83), and her husband Tom Meanley (who died in 1986 at 98), three of whom survive; and the lone son of John Paul, for whose guardianship he unsuccessfully battled Milton McRae.

By a different route, however, John Paul Scripps Junior was brought back into the fold—though not as an inheritor. He had become a newspaper publisher in his own right, creating a string of small dailies on the West Coast. These were merged into the Scripps-Howard organization in 1986 in a multimillion transaction engineered by his cousin Charles. John Paul Junior then served as an E. W. Scripps Company director until his death at 76 on March 15, 1989.

In creating his living trust, E. W. Scripps was required by existing law to link its termination directly to the lives of only Robert's children who had been born before his demise. Thus only Bob Junior and Charles and their two sisters are involved. The latter are Mrs. Margaret Buzelli, 69, and Mrs. Nackey Scripps Loeb, 67. Mrs. Loeb is publisher of the noted *Union Leader* in Manchester, New Hampshire, inherited from her late husband.

However, Robert sired two additional sons after his father's death, the late Edward W. II, and Sam Holtsinger, 64. Their children also are included as inheritors in the trust liquidation. Thus the remaindermen line up this way: Bob Junior, five sons and six daughters; Charles, two sons and two daughters; Mrs. Buzelli, three sons and three daughters; Mrs. Loeb, two daughters; the late Ted Scripps, two sons and one daughter; Sam, one son and one daughter. The oldest remainderman is 46, the youngest 26.

Nobody can accurately foresee today what struggle may begin when the living trust expires. But whatever the ultimate fate of the concern, nothing can ever obliterate the fact that by dint of his unique and vigorous life and his iron-fisted posthumous ideal, Edward Willis Scripps for more than a full century stamped his personal and distinct imprint on American journalism, and left a monetary inheritance not only to the children of his loins but as well to the children of his brain.

The proud Scripps family has taken steps to make certain that the Old Man's place in history will not be lost. The E. W. Scripps School of Journalism was established in 1983 at Ohio University at Athens through an initial grant of $1,500,000 from the Scripps-Howard Foundation.

A principal aim of the Foundation has been to encourage young people to enter journalism. In addition to providing roughly $340,000 in annual journalism scholarships to nearly 300 college students, the Scripps-Howard Foundation also makes annual cash awards of $43,000 for outstanding newspaper and broadcast achievement by individuals and companies, which honors are beginning to rank alongside the Pulitzer Prizes.

The voluminous personal correspondence of E. W. — perhaps as many as 350,000 pages of his letters, essays, and fiction — were donated in 1988 by Charles Scripps to the special collection archives at Ohio University to be used for historical and graduate program research.

Sadly, one salient memento of E. W.'s life — Miramar — no longer exists. Faced with high taxes on the vacant ranch, the trustees in 1968 sold it for $4,200,000 to a developer who promised to keep it as a museum. But five years later bulldozers rumbled in and today the old rattlesnake mesa is occupied not by a spectacular Morocco-style castle, but instead by a supermarket amid acres of black asphalt for parking, and rows of middle-class houses.

Would the Old Man be horrified? In using native adobe-type bricks he never intended to erect a ranch house that would survive the ages. Today he might only chuckle over Miramar's fate, and say: "I told you so. . . . Move on!"

NOTES

CHAPTER ONE

3 The little barque Minerva: Principal sources of emigration of William Scripps to America, and life of his family here, are in two works: James E. Scripps, *A Genealogical History of the Scripps Family* (Detroit: privately printed, 1903); and Albert Britt, *Ellen Browning Scripps* (Oxford: Oxford University Press, 1960).

3 "I have at last got a help meet": James Mogg Scripps to father, Dec. 7, 1844.

4 "I can remember the days": "E. W. Scripps Autobiography," initially written in 1915, revised and edited in 1922 by Gilson Gardner, unpublished ms., 26.

5 "enormous mortification": Ibid., 31.

5 "My mother had no time": "EWS Autobiography," 26.

5 "She was either teaching me": Ibid., 541–42.

6 "I would have to strike": Ibid., 69.

6 "My favorite diversion": Negley D. Cochran, *E.W. Scripps* (New York: Harcourt, Brace and Co., 1933), 11.

6 "I always liked to work in the dirt": Ibid.

7 "Madam, are you the mother of that?": Carl Sandburg, *Abraham Lincoln,* vol. I. (New York: Dell, 1974), 248.

8 "Plenty of men can join the army": Cyril Arthur Player, "The Story of James Edmund Scripps," unpublished ms., Cranbook Archives, Detroit, 113.

9 Secretly, he copied a list: "EWS Autobiography," 61.

9 "I was only happy": Ibid., 40.

9 "my particular appetite": Ibid., 55.

9 "born poet": Ibid., 84.

9 "the Bible is a true story": Ibid., 42.

9 "I became convinced": Ibid., 56.

10 *The Peter Parley Tales:* E. W. Scripps, "History of the Scripps League," unpublished ms. written at West Chester, Ohio, beginning Dec. 18, 1889, covers details of EWS's

early life but is based mainly on correspondence with JES between 1885 and 1889, 16–18.

10 "Now the idea that": Ibid.
12 "the laziest boy in Schuyler County": Cochran, *E. W. Scripps,* 13.
13 "rough brutes": Ibid., 90.

CHAPTER TWO

15 "as could be trusted": "History of Scripps League," 3.
15 "Come back!" Ibid., 4.
15 "heard the bowbells ringing": Ibid.
16 "Mercy! What a mood": Annie Scripps to EWS, Dec. 8, 1872.
16 "James's resignation": EWS to his father, undated.
17 "I wanted to learn": "EWS Autobiography," 94.
17 "Some druggists are foolish": "History of Scripps League," 10.
17 "Right now": Ibid., 11.
18 "We can make barrels": Ibid., 12.
19 "I never feel homesick": EWS to EBS, Jan. 23, 1873.
19 "Your pa says you do not": Julia Scripps to EWS, March 30, 1873.
19 "You did keep me waiting": Annie Scripps to EWS, Feb. 28 1873.
20 "Remember that *Peter Parley* idea": "History of Scripps League," 20.

CHAPTER THREE

22 "If a Scripps drowns": William Lutz, *The News of Detroit* (Boston: Little, Brown and Co., 1973), 12.
23 "Want to buy the first copy": Player, "James Edward Scripps", 138.
23 "It's a fiasco": Ibid., 144.
24 "The *News* this afternoon": Ibid. 143.
25 "a brilliant crew of pirates": Ibid., 352.
25 "Had I held everything": Ibid., 166.
25 "Have the boys write": "History of Scripps League," 6.
25 "I was nigger rich": "History of Scripps League," 26.
25 "to get into journalism": Ibid., 29.
26 "The best type of boy": Ibid., 32–33.
27 "There's my station": Ibid.
27 "To have a free messenger": Ibid.
27 "Bob, look, I've been here awhile": Ibid., 38
28 "Kid, you can do this": Ibid, 39.
28 "it was not many months before": Ibid, 40.
29 "not the sharp things . . . but the dryest": EWS to Annie Scripps, Feb. 11, 1875.
29 "ready for business": "History of Scripps League," 41.
30 "to escape this continual": "EWS Autobiography," 183.
30 "There is hell to pay out in Lansing": EWS to Fred Scripps, July 1, 1877.
31 "I never smoked before": Cochran, *E.W. Scripps,* 274–75.

CHAPTER FOUR

32 "There were both business and personal": "EWS Autobiography," 198.
32 "Now I know that": EWS to Annie Scripps, Jan. 13, 1878.
33 "I was considering deeply my own case": "EWS Autobiography," 200.
33 "Male and female, old and young": Ibid., 201.
33 "like what the English call": Ibid., 202.
34 "I recognized that I had no choice": Ibid., 205.
34 "Not everybody tips street sweepers": Ibid., 215.
35 "Then he took another tack": Ibid., 218.
35 "Ed began to 'fairly loathe' ": Ibid., 220.
36 "As soon as George came": Ibid., 222.
37 "Everything in and about Rome": Ibid., 223.
37 "I do not remember when": Ibid., 224.
38 "Perhaps my choice was an odd one": Ibid., 225.
39 "I wanted to get back to America": Ibid., 228.

CHAPTER FIVE

40 "Eddie was too green": Gilson Gardner, ed., "History of the Concern," compiled about 1922 from EWS writings and correspondence, unpublished ms, 80.
40 "Besides," Ed cried, "starting": Ibid.
42 "Just wait," he told Ed: "EWS Autobiography," 238.
42 "John, we can't pay ourselves much": Ibid., 239.
43 "Cleveland at that period": Charles E. Kennedy, *Fifty Years of Cleveland* (Cleveland: Weidenthal Co., 1925), 20.
43 "Go north on Bank Street": Francis N. McGehee, "Story of The Cleveland Press," 140-page ms. written in 1931, 41.
44 "What the business men want": Ibid., 18.
45 "Never do anything today": "EWS Autobiography," 238.
45 "I had no time to worry": Ibid.
47 "What are your politics?": McGehee, op. cit., 11.
48 "attempting to appear courageous": *Cleveland Press* (50th anniversary edition), Nov. 1, 1928.
48 "Young man, here is a new": Ibid.
48 "Total November revenue": McGehee, op. cit., 29.
49 "Cowles, glowering and spluttering": Kennedy, *Fifty Years of Cleveland*, 20.
49 "Back to the office": EWS to Annie Scripps, Nov. 23, 1878.
49 "get to hitching, then trouble": EWS to EBS, Nov. 17, 1878.
50 "people are beginning to have": EWS to Annie Scripps, Nov. 23, 1878.
50 "Some way or other": EWS to Annie Scripps, Nov. 23, 1878.
51 "I never cared enough for any woman": Ibid.

CHAPTER SIX

52 "No man shall dress worse": Gardner, "History of Concern," 158.
53 "putting books back in the shelves": Tom Barensfeld to author, April 6, 1983.
54 "When a man is fully": "EWS Autobiography," 266.

54   "chock full of opinions": Ibid.
54   "an almost instinctive hatred": Ibid., 267.
55   "to make an important decision": Gardner, "History of Concern," 130.
56   "He ran with and pokered with": *Cleveland Press* (50th anniversary edition), Nov. 1, 1928.
56   "his whiskers bearing all the hues": McGehee, op. cit., 41.
56   "I will not say that my face": "EWS Autobiography," 260.
57   "I knew I would kill somebody": Ibid., 261.
58   "January 1880 would declare its first dividend": McGehee, op. cit. 29.
58   "There in that case, was demonstrated": "EWS Autobiography," 247.
58   "We had to steam up": Ibid., 248.
58   "I had become used to libel suits": Gardner, "History of Concern," 110.
59   "that unless Perkins was": Ibid.
59   "I told Perkins that": Ibid., 111.
59   "Listen, Mo," Scripps said: Ibid.
60   "Now," he commanded his hackman: Ibid., 112.
61   "With these you can appraise": Ibid., 115.
61   "Naturally I turned to them": Ibid., 116.
61   "Come on, Ed I will go": Ibid., 117.
63   "[Perkins] was sorely tempted": Ibid., 120.
64   "to remind the people of Cleveland": Ibid., 122.
64   "Mr. Chisholm," Ed said: Ibid., 123.
64   "That Mr. Chisholm felt he was a dying man": Ibid.
65   "I may be mistaken": Gardner, "History of Concern," 127.
65   "I still feel constantly impelled": EWS to Annie Scripps, Dec. 29, 1879.

CHAPTER SEVEN

68   "trembling with ambition": EWS to Annie Scripps, May 24, 1880.
69   "In launching his *Post-Dispatch*": W. A. Swanberg, *Pulitzer* (New York: Charles Scribner's Sons, 1967).
69   "Why had I not clung": EWS to EBS, May 20, 1880.
70   "George has ten times": Ibid.
70   "If you think I am big-headed": EWS to GHS, May 23, 1880.
70   "arrogance, visionary bombast": EWS to JES, May 27, 1880.
70   "For the first five minutes": EWS to EBS, May 28, 1880.
70   "I was impatient of delay": EWS to JES, May 27, 1880.
71   "to get angry and write": Ibid.
71   "so we all met": EWS to Annie Scripps, June 4, 1880.
71   "If the paper fails": EWS to Stanley Waterloo, June 8, 1880.
71   "How's 'tail' in St. Louis?": RFP to EWS, Nov. 8, 1880.
72   "No, I advise you to keep": EWS to Annie Scripps, July 18, 1880.
73   "going down, down, down": EWS to EBS, Aug. 18, 1880.
73   "the damned fool": Ibid.
73   "the wherewithal to pay": Ibid.
74   "was a paternalistic chaos": Swanberg, *Pultizer,* 61.
74   "flung a tomato": Ibid., 60.
74   "I understand the ordinary": EWS to EBS, Sept. 9, 1880.
75   "I am to stay here": Ibid.

75   I want characteristic men: Ibid.
75   All my victories: EWS to EBS, Nov. 1, 1880.
75   "a very disagreeable wrangle": EWS to Annie Scripps, Dec.12, 1880.
75   "Out to a card party": EWS to Annie Scripps, Dec. 4, 1880.
76   "I met McIntyre": EWS to Annie Scripps, Jan. 7, 1881.
76   "The terror of my life": EWS to Annie Scripps, Jan. 21, 1881.
76   "bring him down seven pegs": JES diary, Jan. 29, 1881.
77   "I told you when": EWS to EBS, Feb. 4, 1881.
77   "I'll never have another": Ibid.
77   "The worry . . . has unsettled": EWS to EBS, Feb. 17, 1881.
77   "For twenty of the twenty-four hours": EWS to EBS, Feb. 17, 1881.
78   "rain, mud and dust": EWS to Annie Scripps, March 12, 1881.
78   "But we cannot get": Ibid.
78   "My health is broken:" Ibid.

CHAPTER EIGHT

79   "Am I a clap-trap humbug": EWS to Annie Scripps, March 29, 1881.
81   "will avoid paying a big sum": Henry Little to John S. Sweeney, April 18, 1881.
82   "I am in for it again": EWS to EBS, April 17, 1881.
82   "During the trying days": EWS to EBS, April 16, 1881.
82   "The chances are now three": EWS to EBS, April 23, 1881.
82   "Would it not be": EWS to Annie Scripps, May 2, 1881.
82   "The thing idleness is doing": EWS to EBS, May 4, 1881.
83   About dark Ed asked: Bob Paine in *Cleveland Press* (50th anniversary edition), Nov. 1, 1928.
84   "It was very brief": EWS to Annie Scripps, July 7, 1881.
84   "I would like to tear myself": EWS to EBS, June 18, 1881.
85   "would be the cheapest and easiest": EWS to EBS, Aug. 2, 1881.
86   "The *Press* is the only paper": *Cleveland Press,* Oct. 18–19, 1881.
87   "The Libel Suit": Ibid, Oct. 22, 1881.
87   "What about North Africa": "EWS Autobiography," 328.

CHAPTER NINE

89   "I was weary of all": "EWS Autobiography," 342.
89   "a little scandal": EWS to Annie Scripps, June 6, 1883.
90   "you all think I'm such": EWS to JES, June 6, 1883.
93   "dissolute, immoral and thoroughly": "EWS Autobiography," 359.
93   "While it was reckoned": Ibid., 360.
93   "extremely high class": Ibid.
93   "You ought to quit": Ibid., 365–66.
94   "Give me fifteen dollars": Ibid. 363–64.
94   "Now if this were a": Ibid., 370.
94   "You've turned your paper": Ibid., 371.
95   "He never lost": Ibid., 380.
96   "I love you": "EWS Autobiography," 390.
96   "This woman has a story": Ibid., 391.

96 "I think I lost nothing": Ibid., 392.
96 "I will take ordinary": EWS to EBS, Aug. 7, 1883.
109 "As he went down the line": "EWS Autobiography," 395.
110 "and that paper was universally": Ibid., 395.
110 "surprised and shocked": EWS to EBS, Aug. 7, 1883.
111 "I've got to get the *Post*": EWS to Annie Scripps, Aug. 26, 1883.
112 He knew he would have shot: "EWS Autobiography," 260.
113 "I have not left the courtroom": EWS to Annie Scripps, Sept. 30, 1883.
114 "little paper scoring": EWS to Annie Scripps, Sept. 12, 1883.
114 "Oh, I assure you": Ibid.
114 "took possession of my party": EWS to EBS, Sept. 7, 1883.
114 "I one day may be": Stanley Waterloo to EWS, Oct. 7, 1883.
115 "It requires a great deal": EWS to Annie Scripps, Oct. 21, 1883.
115 "Suspicion, slander and treachery": EWS to Annie Scripps, Nov. 12, 1883.
115 "I find myself": EWS to Annie Scripps, Nov. 20, 1883.
116 "Go. Take Corrine with you": Ibid.

CHAPTER TEN

118 "Here I am dragging along": EWS to EBS, Feb. 18, 1884.
121 You can have the money: EWS to Annie Scripps, Jan. 26, 1885.
122 "legitimate or otherwise": EWS to Annie Scripps, May 24, 1885.
122 "she was a very beautiful child": "EWS Autobiography," 403.
122 "She's not a child": Ibid.
122 "Seeing my little girl": Ibid.
123 "I abused myself roundly": Ibid., 404.
123 "I only found myself more": Ibid.
124 I wrote you about: EWS to Annie Scripps, Aug. 31, 1885.
125 "Before I entered": "EWS Autobiography," 405.
125 "I remember that my wife's": Ibid., 407.
126 "If you can eat tortillas": EBS diary, Jan. 30, 1886.
128 "God, man, what do you mean?": Henry Little to EWS, March 14, 1886.
129 Two or three hours had: EWS Disquisition, "Much Good Pain Wasted," June 22, 1925.

CHAPTER ELEVEN

130 "I knew you would": EWS to EBS, May 22, 1886.
131 "Sir, may I help you?": Robert F. Winkler to author, Feb. 24, 1981.
131 "I should be entitled": EWS to EBS, May 22, 1886.
131 "It is not money": Player, "James Edmund Scripps," 460.
132 "for nickname purposes": EWS to EBS, July 30, 1886.
132 "Ed measured our boy": Nackie Scripps to Annie Scripps, Aug. 16, 1886.
133 "Find the weak spots": JES to EWS, Oct. 26, 1886.
136 "George and myself are losing": JES to EWS, Feb. 2, 1887.
136 "on Lizzie's account": JES to EWS, March 11, 1887.
138 "Nackie got mad": EWS to EBS, April 25, 1887.
139 "needs the same attention": EWS to Annie Scripps, June 27, 1887.

139   "surprises were just what": EWS to EBS, July 27, 1887.
139   "uncourageous whims": EWS to EBS, August 5 and 13, 1887.

CHAPTER TWELVE

140   "be good, oh, for ever": EWS to EBS, Sept. 7, 1887.
140   "You're too autocratic": EWS to EBS, Sept. 30, 1887.
141   "That was written": Henry Little to EWS, Dec. 1–2, 1887.
141   "To get good results": JES to EWS, JES to EWS, Oct. 28, 1887.
141   "It was the same old trouble": "History of the Scripps League," 79.
141   "His whole policy": EWS to EBS, Nov. 8, 1887.
142   "Whoop La!": Player, "James Edmund Scripps," 207.
142   "I have been trying to extract": EWS to EBS, Dec. 5, 1887.
142   "Put somebody in charge": "History of the Scripps League," 87.
143   I am glad you have beaten: Nackie Scripps to EWS, Dec. 26, 1887.
143   "You will congratulate me": EWS to EBS, Jan 15, 1888.
143   "Mr. Dee was thunderstruck": "History of the Scripps League," 82.
143   "In the settlement": Ibid., 86.
143   "He is one of those vulgar": EWS to EBS, Jan. 8, 1888.
144   Willis is working 16 hours: EWS to EBS, Jan. 15, 1888.
144   "plain letter": JES to EWS, May 24, 1888.
145   "My great paintings": EWS to EBS, May 17, 1888.
145   Another thing to be considered: EWS to EBS, Feb. 14, 1888.
146   "Where before I thought of": EWS to Annie Scripps, June 26, 1888.
146   "Speaking of themes for sensation": JES to EWS, June 13, 1888.
146   "Nackie felt she had to": EWS to EBS, Aug. 9, 1888.
147   "I took more morphine": Ibid.
147   "a drubbing and a humiliation": EWS to EBS, July 28, 1888.
148   "I hardly dare write": Ibid.
148   "I've thought of John Locke": EWS to EBS, Aug. 16, 1888.
148   "It was painful": EWS to EBS, Sept. 9, 1888.
148   "satisfied with what": Ibid.
149   I am thirty-four: EWS to EBS, Sept. 23, 1888.
149   "Now is my crucial test": Ibid.

CHAPTER THIRTEEN

150   "I am so sorry you were taken": Nackie Scripps to EWS, Oct. 7, 1888.
151   "I feel so strong": EWS to EBS, Oct. 26, 1888.
151   "the machine is running": Ibid.
151   "I hope James": Ibid.
152   "I have quit reading": Ibid.
152   "I kept up my strength": EWS to EBS, Jan. 19, 1889.
152   "like if he didn't own": Ibid.
152   "What in the world": JES to EWS, Jan. 4, 1889.
153   "That's two sets of orders": EWS to GHS, Feb. 8, 1889.
153   "I wrote all I possibly": EWS to EBS, Feb. 8, 1889.
153   "George's short letter": Ibid.

153   "I was a few months ago": JES to EBS, Feb. 17, 1889.
153   "paying out just so-so": EWS to EBS, Feb. 8, 1889.
153   "I am morbid, self-weary": EWS to EBS, March 12, 1889.
154   "Nackie and I were out riding": EWS to EBS, April 21, 1889.
154   "I've had to lay violent": EWS to EBS, Feb. 8, 1889.
154   "We had been in the woods": EWS to EBS, April 21, 1889.
155   "Not a whole lot of money": Player, op. cit., 234.
157   "I am still astonished": EWS to JES, May 27, 1889.
157   "I am afraid you are taxing": JES to EWS, May 8, 1889.
157   "but Great God!": MAM to EWS, April 8, 1889.
158   "Say, Ed, where am I?": EWS to EBS, Aug. 24. 1889.
159   "proved he was a 'good sport' ": "EWS Autobiography," 457.
160   "Those two boys of mine": EWS to EBS, Feb. 21, 1890.
160   "Having a daughter": EWS to EBS, Feb. 24, 1890.
160   "John is a rascal": EWS to EBS, April 22, 1890.
161   "Cincinnati is the gateway": EWS to EBS, July 10, 1890.
161   "While I do not think": MAM to EWS, Aug. 9, 1890.

CHAPTER FOURTEEN

163   "Get me about four hundred acres": "EWS Autobiography," 412.
163   "to starve me into submission": EWS to EBS, Dec. 18, 1890.
164   "a foot long at first sight": EWS to EBS, Feb. 25, 1891.
165   "on which your order can build": EWS to Annie Scripps, Aug. 27, 1891.
165   "The young wife of Bob Paine": detailed in letters RFP to EWS, Feb. 3, 15, 18, 1892.
166   "I tell her all I can": EWS to EBS, Aug. 7, 1890.
166   "Fred has come back": Fanny Blades to EWS, May 14, 1892.
167   "I don't know who gets the money": EWS to EBS, July, 1892.
168   "This I know will be your": EWS to Nackie Scripps, June 16, 1893.
168   "Whether she understood": EWS to Nackie Scripps, June 18, 1893.
168   Remember the story of the old Greek: EWS to EBS, Sept. 14, 1892.
169   "I see it don't make a d---": Willis Osborn to EWS, Feb. 1, 1893.
169   "is now married to a young lady": J.V. Grannum to EWS, Feb. 20, 1893.
169   "I found Paine drinking like a fool": EWS to EBS, May 29, 1893.
170   "Regret to hear you have": MAM to EWS, Nov. 9, 1892.
170   "Let us stop all this": EWS to Annie Scripps, June 21, 1894.
171   "Though not ideal, Mac is": EWS to EBS, Jan. 20, 1891.
172   "made more concessions": EWS to EBS, June 11 and 22, 1895.
172   "was recognized as one of the best": EWS to EBS, July 30, 1894.
172   "I believe," he told: EWS to EBS, Sept. 15, 1895.

CHAPTER FIFTEEN

173   "If you bring them both through": Robert P. Scripps, Jr., to author, Dec. 10, 1985.
173   About three o'clock this morning: EWS to EBS, Oct. 27, 1895.
174   "Nackie seems more beautiful": EWS to EBS, Sept. 1, 1896.
174   "I am frightfully alone": Nackie Scripps to EWS, May 25, 1897.
174   "He also sees no reason": Nackie Scripps to EWS, May 27, 1897.

174 "I regret," McRae wrote: MAM to EWS, July 2, 1897.
175 "Blades gladly accepts": EWS to GHS, Sept. 20, 1895.
175 "a stinking, rotten mess": Willis Osborn to MAM, Aug. 6, 1896.
176 "If you don't either": EWS to MAM, Sept. 17, 1897.
177 "I haven't heard": Willis Osborn to EWS, Oct. 8, 1897.
177 "I nailed one of your sweet-scented": Willis Osborn to EWS, late October, 1897.
178 "I suspect he was full": EWS to MAM, Nov. 19, 1897.
182 "lead natural lives . . . to grow": "EWS Autobiography," 601.
182 "My idea of education": EWS to MAM, May 1, 1898.
183 "The Cincinnati *Post* lawyer was sent": MAM to EWS, Nov. 12, 1896, and Aug. 12, 1897.
183 "Before I knew it, the children": EWS to MAM, March 23, 1898.
183 "It is possible the child": Ibid.

CHAPTER SIXTEEN

185 "It would be folly.": MAM to EWS, Aug. 4, 1898.
187 "I want blind obedience": EWS to E. H. Wells, Nov. 28, 1898.
187 "to see me take almost any": EWS to George Gohen, Jan. 19, 1899.
187 was not low price: Ibid.
188 Ole Hoe press refused: E. H. Wells to H. B. Clark, Feb. 24, 1899.
188 "I wear a full beard": EWS disquisition, "Damned Old Crank," April 5, 1909.
189 "When I have been accused": EWS to MAM, May 1, 1898.
189 "I am one of the few": EWS disquisition, "Damned Old Crank."
190 During these busy years: "EWS Autobiography," 468–69.
191 "ridiculous, like those": Ibid., 469.
191 "An employee is no more": EWS memo, Jan. 16, 1899.
191 Everyone was prohibited from personal use: L. T. Atwood to Cincinnati *Post* staff, April 29, 1899.
192 "The Kansas City *World* was called down": L. T. Atwood to EWS, May 24, 1899.
193 "I am not going to": MAM to EWS, July 27, 1899.
193 "had quit swearing—until": Edwin Chase to H. B. Clark, Feb. 12, 1899.
194 "My blindness makes it a torture": EWS to EBS, May 17, 1899.
195 "Bob is turning out": EWS to EBS, June 8, 1899.
195 "I had to use the club": EWS to EBS, May 17, 1899.
195 "by Mac letting Kellogg": EWS to EBS, June 8, 1899.
195 "by which separation": EWS to L. V. Ashbaugh, June 27, 1899.
196 "I have myself seen": George H. Hazzard memo, "interview with Dr. Edwards," dated April 26, 1899.
196 "is up against it": MAM to EWS, Aug. 17, 1899.

CHAPTER SEVENTEEN

198 "You are clear off your trolley": MAM to EWS, Nov. 11, 1899.
199 "You are not yet an old man": RFP to GHS, Jan. 27, 1900.
199 "happy as a clam": RFP to EWS, April 7, 1900.
200 "Will you have a piece of gum?": Henry Bond Restarick, *Personal Reflections* (San Diego: privately printed), 1938, 272–75.

201 "I cannot eat, sleep": RFP to MAM, April 25, 1900.
202 "It is barely possible": EWS to MAM, July 18, 1900.
202 "Ellen asked me to destroy": EWS to JCH, June 1, 1900.
203 "uses and then throws away": MAM to EWS, Sept. 28, 1900.
203 "No joking, Ed, this": MAM to EWS, Oct. 10, 1900.
203 "You are *personally* on": RFP to EWS, Oct. 16, 1900.
204 "At the hotel, I met Nackie": EWS to EBS, Oct. 27, 1900.
204 As for myself, I can say: EWS to RFP, Jan. 17, 1901.
205 "The main idea": EWS to Cleon Sweeney, April 8, 1901.
206 "tale that I want to leave": Paul Blades to EWS, Nov. 28, 1901.
207 "a giant swearing spell": EWS to EBS, Nov. 21, 1902.
207 "Mr. Scripps is so fixed": Paul Blades to EBS, Nov. 27, 1902.
207 "getting along nicely": Nackie Scripps to EWS, May 14, 1902.
208 "E. W. indicated he was not": JCH to Will Scripps, June 18, 1902.
210 "You can see it will be": RFP to League editors, June 3, 1902.
210 This N.E.A. you fired at me: RFP to EWS, June 13, 1902.
210 "dumped the whole thing": Paul Blades to RFP, June 18, 1902.
210 The latter part of your letter: RFP to E. H. Wells, July 21, 1902.
210 "I want to tell you ": EWS to E. H. Wells, Aug. 22, 1902.
212 "E. W. took his note for $6,000": EWS to W. H. Porterfield, March 11, 1901.
212 This last operation has settled: Nackie Scripps to EWS, Oct. 13, 1902.
212 As for living apart: Nackie Scripps to EWS, Oct. 1902.
213 "I informed Mr. Atwood": notes on conference with Paul Blades in Detroit, Jan. 1, 1903.
213 "Your quandry about getting": JES to Will Scripps, Nov. 14, 1902.
213 "I love you just the same": Nackie Scripps to EWS, Dec. 18, 1902.

CHAPTER EIGHTEEN

215 "your book education must": EWS memo to JGS, July 19, 1903.
215 I don't intend to force: EWS to JGS, July 11, 1904.
216 "She is a good, true, noble": RFP to EWS, Jan. 3, 1903.
217 "Hook yourself tight": EWS to William D. Wasson, Jan. 23, 1904.
217 "This is a grafting town": E. H. Wells to EWS, April 9, 1903.
217 "Be yourself": EWS to William P. Strandborg, May 10, 1903.
217 Make a paper that everybody: Ibid.
218 "work yourself out of a job": EWS to Edwin Chase, May 12, 1903.
218 "Give nobody a title": EWS to E. H. Wells, Nov. 28, 1903.
218 "It was the hardest work": MAM to EWS, June 10, 1903.
219 "Then we took the hat": MAM to EWS, Dec. 12, 1903.
219 "Anyway, I done pretty well": JGS to EWS, Aug. 2, 1904.
220 While I can only applaud: EWS to JGS, Aug. 8, 1904.
220 "I have a great deal of trouble": JGS to EWS, Nov. 25, 1904.
222 "if the whole thing should be": EWS to RFP, Oct., 1904.
223 "the spot where I had my first": EWS to JGS, Dec. 15, 1904.
224 "Dad is going to run": EWS to RFP, April 22, 1905.
224 "The kind of advice": EWS to RFP, March 29, 1905.
225 "Well, boys, that was a great ride": W. E. Ritter memoirs.
225 "the impression that his poise": Ibid.

225 "the only room aboard": H. B. Clark to EWS, Dec. 13, 1904.

226 "Nothing stands out more sharply": W. E. Ritter, *Charles Darwin and The Golden Rule,* ix–xvii; W. E. Ritter, "The Relation of E. W. Scripps to Science," *Science* (March 25, 1926,), 291.

226 "I don't know whether": EWS to EBS, Aug. 4, 1922.

227 "Is there any danger?": EWS to EBS, June 1, 1905.

228 "I believe you have got": EWS to JGS, Aug. 3, 1905.

228 "as though he were a perfect stranger": EWS to L. T. Atwood, Aug. 15, 1905.

228 "Keep your eye on Jim's paper": EWS to RFP, Sept. 4, 1905.

228 "It certainly is the finest-looking": Nackie Scripps to JGS, Sept. 9, 1905.

CHAPTER NINETEEN

230 "When Cox takes snuff": George E. Stevens, "History of The Cincinnati *Post,*" Ph.D. dissertation, University of Minnesota, 1968, 145.

230 "I am not a damn bit holy": EWS to JCH, Sept. 14, 1905.

231 "I am," said Cox: Stevens, op cit., 140.

232 "to drive Scripps-McRae out": William Day to MAM, June 30, 1905.

232 "I am delighted with": EWS to Harry Rickey, July 3, 1905.

232 I can't forget and you must: EWS to Harry Rickey, July 19, 1905.

232 "I hope the editor": William Day to MAM, June 30, 1905.

233 "Perhaps the gang": RFP to Harry Rickey, Aug. 5, 1905.

233 "My personal and private sins": RFP to John Vandercook, Aug. 6, 1905.

233 "not only because it is news": EWS to John Vandercook, Aug. 22, 1905.

233 "as fast as the train": EWS to RFP, Aug. 22, 1905.

234 "It has been said": EWS disquisition, "What of Taft Today?" Feb. 12, 1910.

235 "Secretary W. H. Taft Denounces Cox": Cincinnati *Post,* Oct. 23, 1905.

235 "to assure a fair and honest": EWS to JCH, Sept. 14, 1905.

235 "I am not willing to give": Ibid.

236 "Stir up Pendleton": Ibid.

236 "I would willingly forfeit": EWS to John Vandercook, Sept. 12, 1905.

236 "If you beat Cox": Ibid.

236 "I was tempted to add": EWS to JCH, Nov. 8, 1905.

236 "I have done some big things": EWS to John Vandercook, Nov. 8, 1905.

236 "He kept going through": EWS to JCH, Nov. 8, 1905.

237 One of our Californians: Ibid.

237 The first was Mabley and Carew: Harry Rickey to EWS, Jan. 13, 1906.

237 "We ought to have a bigger man": EWS to RFP, May 8, 1905.

238 "and SHALL be printed": EWS to RFP, Sept. 13, 1905.

238 "Business Manager Hiram Crouse": L. T. Atwood to EWS, Aug. 30, 1905.

238 "I would no more think": EWS to W. W. Thornton, Nov. 7, 1905.

238 "When a man enters my house": MAM to EWS, Nov. 7, 1905.

238 "he hurt the *News-Bee*": W. W. Thornton to MAM, May 12, 1906.

238 "pretty mad at myself": JGS to Jack Hamilton, Dec. 29, 1905.

238 "Take this letter in to Pa": Ibid.

CHAPTER TWENTY

240   "I believe he is insane": EWS to L. T. Atwood, Nov. 15, 1905.

240   "Hell," snarled Ashbaugh: Ibid.

241   "The doctors at Watkins": L. T. Atwood to EWS, Jan. 9, 1906.

241   "adrift from Salt Lake City": E. H. Wells to EWS, Oct. 16, 1905.

241   "He has been drinking": Edwin Chase to EWS, Nov. 15, 1905.

242   "We must take steps": EWS to RFP, Dec. 19, 1905.

243   "the papers in 1905 earned $350,000": EWS to H. B. Clark, Jan. 16, 1906.

243   "But he is not the most robust": EWS to RFP, Dec. 11, 1905.

244   "I have been greatly surprised": EWS to William Wasson and H. B. Clark, Jan. 8, 1906.

245   "either pig-headed or so": EWS to RFP, Jan. 26, 1906.

245   "That gives the News the balls": H. B. Clark to EWS, Aug. 14, 1905.

245   "that makes it sell": EWS to William Wasson, Jan. 22, 1906.

245   I have learned that men: EWS to RFP, Feb. 28, 1906.

246   "Every line of space is worth a gold dollar": EWS to RFP, Feb. 20, 1906.

246   "there is not only a new": EWS to L. T. Atwood, April 14, 1906.

CHAPTER TWENTY-ONE

248   "Find Ham Clark": Hans Bagby to L. T. Atwood, April 23, 1906.

249   "to help clothe": EWS to RFP, May 1, 1906.

250   "mean and selfish": EWS to EBS, May 21, 1906.

250   "perfect right to belly-ache": RFP to EWS, June 4, 1906.

250   "Order him off the place!": EWS to L. T. Atwood, June 5, 1906.

251   "I consider Kellogg dangerous": L. T. Atwood to EWS, June 6, 1906.

251   "It is owned by wealthy men": EWS to John Vandercook, n.d., 1906.

251   "braying . . . thistle-fed ass": RFP to EWS, March 3, 1906.

251   Shale was willing to: John Vandercook to EWS, May 14, 1906.

252   "Give an editor a whole lot": EWS to RFP, May 24, 1906.

254   "Every time I touch": EWS to MAM, Sept. 24, 1906.

255   "I can better afford": EWS to Alfred O. Andersson, Oct. 8, 1906.

255   "feeling like a chump tonight": EWS to MAM, Oct. 10, 1906.

255   "Your refusal . . . will cost": Alfred O. Andersson to EWS, Oct. 17, 1906.

256   At first Dillon: JGS to EWS, Nov. 1, 1906.

256   "I slept in all sorts": EWS to L. T. Atwood, Aug. 21, 1906.

257   I really could not get: Nackie Scripps to EWS, July 16, 1906.

257   "My dear child": Nackie Scripps to EWS, Oct. 20, 1907.

258   "I offer no excuses or": MAM to EWS, Feb. 2, 1907.

259   "Mac feels humiliation": JCH to EWS, April 25, 1907.

259   "looking out for Number One": EWS to JCH, April 13, 1907.

259   "to quiet my nerves": MAM to EWS, April 23, 1907.

261   "Mac decided I was": EWS to RFP, Sept. 18, 1907.

261   "McRae has the shakes": JGS to Nackie Scripps, Oct. 5, 1907.

262   "My partner of twenty-five years": MAM to EWS, Nov. 23, 1907.

262   "Look out, Hamilton": EWS to Jack Hamilton, July 30, 1906.

263   There are too many of these: EWS to Hans Bagby and Byron Canfield, Jan. 7, 1908.

265   "mature as a man of twenty-eight": MAM to EWS, Jan. 13, 1908.

265 "caught on": H. B. Clark to EWS, Jan. 24, 1908.
265 "If I can stand that": EWS to JGS, Jan. or Feb., 1908.
265 "I cannot tell you, Jim": EWS to JGS, Jan. 26, 1908.
265 "If I didn't believe": JGS to EWS, Jan. 1, 1908.
266 "You are the first one": Nackie Scripps to JPS, March, 1908.
267 "Bring your wife, of course": EWS to JGS, March 24, 1908.
267 I have said to you and John: EWS to JGS, March 11, 1908.
267 "I took him into Jim's office": MAM to EWS, Dec. 28, 1907.
268 "You must sell or close": EWS to JGS, April 3, 1908.
268 "My own failures": EWS to JGS, April 3, 1908.
269 "Jim really doesn't know whether": EWS to L. T. Atwood, Feb. 26, 1908.
269 "things are going well": Ibid.
269 "a voice can get": John Vandercook to EWS, Jan. 23, 1908.

CHAPTER TWENTY-TWO

271 Sometimes I feel: JGS to Edwin Chase, April 12, 1909.
272 "I am not going to bother much": EWS to JGS, June 20, 1908.
272 "absolutely unknown": Ibid.
273 "there are enough hard": EWS to JCH, Sept. 24, 1909.
273 "I have also discovered": Ibid.
273 "to drag out a life": EWS to L. T. Atwood, Oct. 30, 1909.
273 "the waters are going deep": Dr. Phillips to EWS, Nov. 12, 1909.
273 "I advised him to get out": John Sweeney to JPS, Jan. 9, 1910.
274 "doing my level best": EWS to W. H. Porterfield, Dec. 28, 1910.
275 "the whole country is going": EWS to Lincoln Steffens, Sept. 6, 1909.
275 "I am still hoping": EWS to W. H. Porterfield, Dec. 28, 1909.
275 "Reactionaryism has": Ibid.
275 "I am more profoundly interested": Ibid.
275 "I must drop out": EWS to Lincoln Steffens, Sept. 6, 1909.
276 "crazy about California": MAM to EWS, June 15, 1909.
277 All the advice I have: EWS to JPS, May 21, 1909.
277 "I got more satisfaction": JPS to EWS, May 29, 1909.
289 "I have just come back": EWS to James Causey, June 18, 1908.
290 "It's on my desk": Dolla Scripps to EWS, Feb. 28, 1910.
290 For a long time I have treaded: EWS to Dr. W. F. Langdon, April 4, 1908.
290 "You might better understand my": EWS to Dr. H. J. Berkley, Jan. 18, 1910.
291 "should be immediately discharged": EWS to R. L. Clingan, July 8, 1909.
292 "getting fat": RPS to EWS, April 2, 1909.
292 "I regard every boy": EWS to RPS, June 14, 1909.
292 "Bob has taken to Claremont": Prof. Charles Stearns to EWS, Sept. 25, 1909.
292 "perhaps the most desirable": EWS to JGS, H. B. Clark, JCH, June 5, 1908.
292 "certain audacity": RWH to EWS, Sept. 29, 1908.
293 "You are a young man": EWS to RWH, Oct. 7, 1908.
293 "Howard should": EWS to H. B. Clark, Nov. 5, 1908.
293 "not so rattle-headed" RFP to EWS, Sept. 16, 1908.
293 "going to pieces": EWS to JGS, et al., March 25, 1909.
294 "I do not believe in the rule": EWS to W. H. Porterfield, Nov. 15, 1909.
294 "I want you to come": EWS to Byron Canfield, Sept. 18, 1908.

294   "the most daring gang": *Portland News,* p-1, Dec. 5, 1908.
294   "Sleeth is a genius": EWS to Byron Canfield, Feb. 21, 1911.
295   "This town is the rottenest": Byron Canfield to JPS, Oct. 7, 1910.
295   "plenty of reasons to distrust": Byron Canfield to JPS, Dec. 13, 1910.
295   "He's the big grafter": Byron Canfield to JPS, Oct. 7, 1910.
295   There is nothing for you: EWS to Edwin Chase, Aug. 26, 1910.
296   "It is up to the *Star*": Byron Canfield to JCH, copy to EWS, Sept. 2, 1910.
297   "The *Times* story is the fiercest": Byron Canfield to JCH, Dec. 17, 1910.
297   "one of the most fortunate things": RFP to W. H. Porterfield, Oct. 13, 1910.
297   "Dad has often said": JGS to W. H. Porterfield, Oct. 13, 1910.

CHAPTER TWENTY-THREE

299   "Steffens can't help but be": EWS to NDC, Nov. 20, 1911.
300   "Big, bulky but not fat": Lincoln Steffens, *Autobiography* (New York: Harcourt,
        Brace and Co., 1931), 666–67.
300   "I can't stand it": Steffens, op. cit., 666.
300   "Darrow wanted to talk": Ibid., 668.
301   The difference between the act: EWS disquisition, "Belligerent Rights In Class War-
        fare," May 1, 1911.
302   "We must condemn": RFP to EWS, May 25, 1911.
302   "I wish we could get": Steffens, *Autobiography,* 668.
303   "We took a vote and it": EWS to NDC, Nov. 20, 1911.
306   "I don't like the name": EWS to NDC, Oct. 2, 1911.
307   "gambling, prostitution, white slavery": NDC to EWS, Oct. 11, 1911.
307   "It set me thinking": NDC to EWS, Nov. 18, 1911.
307   "Why can't you try": Ibid.
308   "So it seems according": EWS to NDC, Feb. 11, 1912.
308   "The sudden and marked effect": EWS to NDC, Feb. 12, 1912.
309   "got the shakes": NDC to EWS, April 9, 1912.
310   "I wrote mother and told her": JPS to EWS, June 1, 1912.
311   "a chip off the old block": HLS to Byron Canfield, Nov. 24, 1911.
311   "Edwards, that's all": *Houston Press* (50th Anniversary edition), May 9, 1961.
313   "We may get nervous": JGS to W. H. Porterfield, Aug. 3, 1911.
314   "You and Sanders": EWS to Byron Canfield, Aug. 28, 1911.
314   "I'd a lot rather": Byron Canfield to JPS, et al., Aug 31, 1911.
316   "Would news of the 95": JCH notes on U. P. meeting, n.d.
318   "steered between Scylla and": RFP to W. H. Porterfield, May 24, 1912.
319   "I will confess": EWS to C. D. Willard, April 4, 1913.

CHAPTER TWENTY-FOUR

321   "I have an oft-recurring": JPS to EWS, Aug. 14, 1912.
321   "Back here," he wrote: EWS to RPS, July 8, 1912.
322   "I won't run after anybody": EWS to K. J. Murdoch, March 14, 1911.
322   On hearing of Roosevelt's: JGS to all editors, Oct. 15, 1912.
323   "varigated and I am doing": RPS to EWS, Aug. 1, 1912.
323   "For thousands and thousands": EWS to RPS, Aug. 3, 1912.

323   "The family moved around": RPS to EWS, Aug. 17, 1912.
323   "I'm going to order": JPS to EWS, Aug. 23, 1912.
323   "I've never been put": JPS to EWS, Sept. 26, 1912.
324   "Neg, this flabby old heart": EWS to NDC, April 28, 1913.
325   " 'We' won, and of course": Dana Sleeth to EWS, May 31, 1913.
326   "really Scripps papers": EWS to Dana Sleeth, Aug. 5, 1913.
326   There is one thing that: Ibid.
326   "Your courage is good": EWS to Marlen Pew, Feb. 6, 1913.
327   "Back East," he wrote: RFP to EWS, March 28, 1913.
328   "But I am getting more onery": JGS to JPS, Nov. 8, 1912.
328   "I have been told": RPS to EWS, Feb. 13, 1913.
328   "serious, perhaps desperate": EWS to MAM, Aug. 15, 1913.
328   "All he did was to": EWS to JCH, Oct. 16, 1913.
329   "being a fool once": MAM to CFM, Nov. 22, 1913.
329   "I really wanted Edith": EWS to MAM, Nov. 8, 1913.
329   "Since white men have lived": EWS to Dolla Scripps, Sept. 18, 1913.
329   "Next day, even to": EWS to Dolla Scripps, Jan. 20, 1914.
329   "I issued orders": Ibid.
331   "a golden reef of opportunities": EWS to Marlen Pew, Feb. 21, 1913.
332   "for a long time past": EWS to JPS, Feb. 2, 1914.
333   "Perhaps you should have": EWS to JGS, Feb. 7, 1914.
333   "This is a very poor time": JGS to EWS, Feb. 10, 1914.
333   "I want to force Bob": Ibid.
334   "John back. It's hopeless": RWH to W. W. Hawkins, March 9, 1914.
334   I am enough of a psychologist: EWS to Ben Lindsey, March 23, 1914.

CHAPTER   TWENTY-FIVE

336   "Sir," said the caller: Entire episode of EWS's interview with President Wilson related in EWS to EBS, July 1, 1914.
337   "is absolutely incapable of": EWS to EBS, May 25, 1914.
338   "drifting apart": Ibid.
338   "It should be comparatively easy": EWS to Lincoln Steffens, March 26, 1914.
339   "who have distinguished themselves": EWS to EBS, May 14–15, 1914.
339   "Of course all of them were polite": Ibid.
339   "You have determined to live": EWS to RPS, June 18, 1914.
339   "You know how prone": EWS to Julius Wagenheim, June 27, 1914.
340   "good . . . a man of the people" EWS to EBS, July 1, 1914.
340   "feeling of distrust": Ibid.
340   "the human and the humane": Ibid.
340   "those newspapers and": Ibid.
340   "I impressed on him": Ibid.
341   "The rain poured down": Ibid.
341   "I have got another confession": Ibid.

CHAPTER TWENTY-SIX

343   "My daughter," he wrote: EWS to Lucy Madeira, Nov. 30, 1914.

344   "utterly helpless": EWS to Nackey Scripps, Feb. 16, 1915.

344   "everything that you possibly can": EWS to Nackey Scripps, Feb. 3, 1915.

344   "I have become sort of": EWS to Nackey Scripps, Feb. 1, 1915.

344   "theatres and musical entertainments": EWS to Nackey Scripps, March 8, 1915.

345   "I have made about six friends": Nackey Scripps to EWS, Jan. 24, 1915.

345   "I have a headache": Nackey Scripps to EWS, Jan. 31, 1915.

345   "Darling, work the dictionary": EWS to Nackey Scripps, Feb. 9, 1915.

345   "Go riding with mother": Nackey Scripps to EWS, Jan. 24, 1915.

345   "Your mother holds the reins": EWS to Nackey Scripps, Feb. 3, 1915.

345   I used to see purple sunsets: Ibid.

346   "the difference between women": EWS to Nackey Scripps, Feb. 16, 1915.

346   "I recall," he wrote: EWS to Lucy Madeira, May 25, 1915.

346   "Might as well try": EWS to JGS, Sept. 15, 1914.

347   "I can afford to pay": Ibid.

347   Close plant immediately: CFM to Leonard Carver, Jr., Sept. 28, 1914.

347   "If it proves out": EWS to NDC, April 2, 1914.

347   "wants to think": EWS to NDC, Feb. 5, 1915.

347   "*Day Book* circulation was a joke": Chicago figures from J. T. Watters to NDC, Oct. 18, 1915.

347   "The days I spent at Miramar": Norman Hapgood to EWS, April 29, 1914.

348   "You haven't got one chance": EWS to Max Eastman, Nov. 24, 1915.

348   "It was once said": EWS to Max Eastman, Nov. 2, 1915.

348   "As you know, I am not": Ibid.

349   "Such a youngster": Ibid.

349   "It wouldn't pay for itself": EWS to Charles R. Crane, Aug. 25, 1915.

349   "has had enough of *Harper's*": Walter S. Rogers to EWS, April 17, 1915.

349   "The President would like you": EWS to RFP, April 2, 1915.

350   "I was amused and shocked": Ibid.

350   "Can Neg do any good": EWS to RFP, April 2, 1915.

350   I have no interest: Ibid.

351   "In view of the crisis": NDC to Walter S. Rogers, June 28, 1915.

352   There is one conviction: EWS memo, May 1, 1915.

352   "I don't like appointments": EWS to GG, July 28, 1915.

353   "Bryan was all tired out": Ibid.

353   "I forgot to thank": William Jennings Bryan to EWS, July, 1915.

354   "learn the trick of going": GG to EWS, March 7, 1916.

354   "The plates were poor": EWS to GG, July 5, 1915.

355   "I feel as though": JGS to EWS, Oct. 7, 1914.

355   "It is unfair to ask": Ibid.

355   "Your time is worth": Ibid.

356   "only a short hour's ride": EWS to Dr. H. J. Berkley, Nov. 25, 1915.

357   "You have declared your": EWS to RPS, Oct. 14,, 1914.

357   "I have smoked much": RPS to EWS, Nov. 5, 1914.

358   "You chain my hands": Nackey Scripps to EWS, Aug. 23, 1915.

358   "I did not have to be told": EWS to JCH, July 13, 1915.

358   "You must remember": Nackey Scripps to EWS, Aug. 23, 1915.

359   Don't you think you: Nackey Scripps to EWS, Aug. 23, 1915.

360 "Miss Steelman and my daughter": EWS to Dr. H. J. Berkley, Dec. 14, 1915.
361 "Nackey seems to be devoting": EWS to RPS, April 14, 1916.
361 "I agree that the enclosed poem": EWS to RPS, April 20, 1916.
362 "I would like more than": JGS to EWS, Nov. 16, 1915.
362 "mistaken in thinking": EWS to JGS, Dec. 27, 1915.
362 "On my birthday I will be": Ed Meanley to author, July 10, 1981.

CHAPTER TWENTY-SEVEN

363 "a useless expense of time": EWS to RPS, Sept. 13, 1916.
364 "I have as much or more": EWS to JCH, Aug. 29, 1916.
364 "Of course, I would expect": EWS to Nackey Meanley, Oct. 6, 1916.
364 "I told my parents": Robert P. Scripps, Jr., to author, Nov. 10, 1985.
364 "I am inclined to think": EWS to GG, Dec. 26, 1916.
366 "are sky-high above the heads": EWS to NDC, Aug. 16, 1916.
366 "turned the trick": EWS to Harry Rickey, Nov. 15, 1916.
367 "four or five other cars": EWS to AAA Club, Los Angeles, April 3, 1917.
367 "take great pleasure in sending": Newton D. Baker to EWS, April 9, 1917.
367 "crazily roaring . . . and calling": RFP to Byron Canfield, April 9, 1917.
368 "casting reflections on you": EWS to Nackey Meanley, June 27, 1917.
369 "I think it would be better": EWS to JGS, June 2, 1917.
369 "Your mother should remain": Ibid.
369 "You have often heard": Ibid.
369 "There is a strong indication": EWS to MAM, June 8, 1917.
370 "Some of the things": Ibid.
370 "The fool Senate": Ibid.
371 "Perry is altogether too": EWS to JGS, June 5, 1917.
371 "get his consent and approval": Ibid.
372 "Get Jim to have his foot": EWS to JCH, Aug. 13, 1917.
372 "Northcliffe and I had": EWS to RFP, June 18, 1917.
375 "Carl Sandburg": NDC to JGS, July 7, 1917.
375 "I got here Friday morning": Ibid.
375 "Conclusion: N.E.A., U.P.A.": RPS to JGS, June 6, 1917.
376 I have come out of retirement: EWS to all editors, June 16, 1917.
377 "If EWS issues an order": Byron Canfield to Sam T. Hughes, July 14, 1917.
377 "some of your man's": EWS to JGS, July 25, 1917.
377 "Neg thinks the government": Ibid.
377 "He may have to be": Ibid.
378 "Neg Cochran will put": EWS to JGS, July 28, 1917.
378 "Ever so often, as you": EWS to Nackie Scripps, Aug. 27, 1917.
378 "I am not the least offended": JGS to EWS, Aug. 19, 1917.
378 "Your telegram is perfectly": EWS to JGS, Aug. 19, 1917.
379 "in a condition of more or": EWS to EBS, Aug. 4, 1917.
379 "Your mother and I": EWS to JGS, June 30, 1917.
379 "I am honestly trying": RPS to JCH, July 18, 1917.
380 I needed you awfully: EWS to Nackie Scripps, Aug. 15, 1917.
380 "Now they should be content": EWS to Nackie Scripps, Aug. 19, 1917.
380 "I have consumed more whiskey": EWS to EBS, Oct. 1, 1917.
381 "Jim is mad and wants to": EWS to Nackie Scripps, Sept. 18, 1917.

381 "He seemed inclined to rush me": EWS to Nackie Scripps, Sept. 23, 1917.
381 "Then I could sell it": EWS to Nackie Scripps, Sept. 18, 1917.
382 "He thinks the Administration": EWS to Nackie Scripps, Sept. 23, 1917.
382 "There developed": Ibid.
382 "I tried to explain that you": Ibid.
382 "aggravate the feeling of": EWS to Nackie Scripps, Sept. 18, 1917
382 "would do everything": EWS to Nackie Scripps, Sept. 23, 1917.
384 "I never saw Bob more": Jay Curts to EWS, Oct. 3, 1917.
385 "Baker told Sidlo that": EWS to JGS, Oct. 3, 1917.
386 "Wilson Exempts Scripp's Son": *Los Angeles Times,* Oct. 10, 1917.
386 "I am almost positive": EWS to Nackie Scripps, Oct. 17, 1917.
387 "any more of a certain line": RPS to Byron Canfield, Oct. 25, 1917.
387 "was an absolutely unique example": *San Diego Union,* Oct., 1917.
387 "came here to do some little": *Cincinnati Enquirer,* Oct. 23, 1917.
387 "It is my belief": EWS to Cincinnati *Post,* Oct. 26, 1917.
388 "the second most important": EWS to RFP, Oct. 12, 1917.
389 "I was greatly grieved": Ibid.
389 "to quit, he will be no good": JGS to RPS, Oct. 30, 1917.
389 "You young men have been": EWS to RPS, Aug. 11, 1917.
389 "Matrimony is fraught with": EWS to EBS, Nov. 6, 1917.
390 "Editor Asks Right to . . .": *Los Angeles Evening Herald,* Nov. 14, 1917.
391 "Mr. Scripps, you have been": EWS to EBS, Nov. 12, 1917.
392 "The doctors say they are": HLS to JGS, Nov. 16, 1917.

CHAPTER TWENTY-EIGHT

393 "They look almost as big as a humming": EWS to EBS, Feb. 26, 1918.
393 "She has aged tremendously": EWS to EBS, Feb. 1, 1918.
394 "a world of good . . . He likes the roll": HLS to Nackie Scripps, Jan. 2, 1918, and HLS to CFM, Jan. 21, 1918.
394 "the same noisy streets": EWS to EBS, March 9, 1918.
394 "During the trip": Ibid.
396 "a dutiful daughter": JCH to HLS, July 31, 1918.
397 "both instantly fell in love": HLD to NDC, Aug. 31, 1918.
397 "There is an odd sequence": HLS to W. E. Scripps, Detroit, Sept. 6, 1918.
398 "I am a bit anxious": RFP to JGS, Sept. 5, 1918.
398 "stand *between* Jim and myself": RPS to JGS, Oct. 3, 1918.
398 "The 'Kemah' is a lemon!": EWS to HLS, Oct. 14, 1918.
399 "It's old and badly worn": EWS to Nackie Scripps, Nov. 10, 1918.
399 "I feel twice as well": EWS to JGS, Nov. 11, 1918.
402 "If the war was still": EWS to JPS, Nov. 27, 1918.
402 "a sort of cave": EWS to EBS, Dec. 12, 1918.
403 "At the present time": EWS to EBS, Jan. 14, 1919.
403 "I dreaded Jim's coming": EWS to EBS, Feb. 1, 1919.
403 "Dad, I'm in a hurry": Ibid.
404 "I brought only ten thousand": Ibid.
407 Nackey has been accepting: HLS to Dr. W. G. Morgan, July 16, 1919.
407 "admits there is great wrong": GG to EWS, May 7, 1919.
409 "Then we bore down on": "The Tale of the Scripps Yacht," *San Francisco Call and Post,* Feb. 18, 1922.

CHAPTER TWENTY-NINE

412 "I asked Mr. Scripps": HLS to Dr. W. G. Morgan, Oct. 3, 1919.

412 "natural pugnacity": EWS disquisition, "A Year of My Life," March 20, 1920.

413 "I had not fully": EWS to Tom Sidlo, Oct. 13, 1919.

413 "I hope": RFP to RPS, Jan. 27, 1920.

414 "Do whatever Mrs. Scripps": HLS to Dr. W. G. Morgan, Oct. 3, 1919.

414 "just bully — even glorious": Ibid., Dec. 13, 1919.

414 "I guess I might as well quit": JGS to CFM, Oct. 14, 1919.

415 "It was amusing": GG to EWS, Feb. 9, 1920.

415 "The boys are so harum-scarum": EWS to MAM, Feb. 23, 1920.

416 "We do not want": EWS to GG, April 1, 1920.

416 "give a hang": RPS to EWS, April 7, 1920.

416 "We want to drag": Ibid.

417 "Jim never got to": EWS diary notes, April 24, 1920.

418 I would certainly be: EWS diary notes, June 26, 1920.

418 "Do you . . . hold me": JGS memo, April 22, 1920.

418 "If worst comes to worst": EWS to RPS, April 25, 1920.

418 "R. W. H. would have added": EWS memo written aboard "Kemah," May 15, 1920.

421 "no friction and no": EWS to JGS, June 24, 1920.

421 "I am going through": EWS to EBS, Oct. 29, 1920.

421 "cut down to a pint": MAM memo, Sept. 8, 1920.

422 "The future depends on": EWS to RPS, Sept. 21, 1920.

422 "They could see": EWS to EBS, Oct. 29, 1920.

423 "So you see": Ibid.

424 "Jim is dangerously ill": MAM to RWH, Dec. 21, 1920.

CHAPTER THIRTY

427 "I'd take a club": EWS to RWH, March 27, 1921.

428 "I expect you": EWS to RWH, Feb. 17, 1921.

429 "I spoke harshly": EWS diary notes, Aug. 14, 1921.

430 "I cannot talk to you": Ibid.

430 "I would prefer never to": HLS notes for private file, Sept. 12, 1921.

432 "Of course, my wealth": EWS to EBS, Nov. 5, 1921.

432 "Perhaps Harding . . . used the cough as a ruse": Oliver Knight, ed., *I Protest* (Madison: University of Wisconsin, 1966), 502, and EWS disquisition, "Two Presidents," Nov. 5, 1921.

441 "She has no comprehension": EWS to EBS, Oct. 27, 1921.

442 "but I gave the young men": EWS to EBS, Nov. 29, 1921.

442 "Baby papers look like": EWS to EBS, Nov. 29, 1921.

442 "Of course, they have": Ibid.

442 "I was not exactly frightened": EWS to EBS, Dec. 23, 1921.

443 "Cast off . . . as fast as": EWS to EBS, Jan. 1, 1922.

443 "I will stay": EWS to EBS, Feb.12, 1922.

444 "I am quite aware": EWS to EBS, April 15, 1922.

445 "If other people": Ibid.

447 "but there is nothing Howard says": EWS to EBS, May 4, 1922.

447 "If we can't keep": RPS to RWH, April 29, 1922.

CHAPTER THIRTY-ONE

448   "keep him from jumping": EWS to RWH, May 26, 1922.
448   "It is surely a fact": EWS to EBS, June 11, 1922.
449   I . . . suffered no real discomfort: EWS to EBS, June 23, 1922.
450   "He rather takes my breath away": EWS to EBS, May 25, 1922.
450   "Apparently he is in perfect": EWS to Nackie Scripps, April 29, 1922.
450   "You see," he explained: EWS diary notes, July 7, 1922.
452   "He must learn to think": EWS to EBS, May 25, 1922.
452   "I am old and disillusioned": EWS to EBS, July 11, 1922.
453   "He certainly did make": EWS to EBS, Aug. 12, 1922.
454   "He had a beautiful head": Jo Davidson, *Between Sittings, An Informal Biography* (New York: Dial Press, 1951).
454   "For the life of me": EWS to EBS, Aug. 29, 1922.
455   "It was plainly evident": HLS to Tom Sharp, Sept. 18, 1922.
455   "I am sure," he wrote: EWS to EBS, Sept. 6, 1922.
457   "This fires two-hundred-clip": RPS to EWS, Oct. 21, 1922.
460   "I think it is well": EWS to EBS, Nov.29, 1922.
460   "Waiting on Nackie": EWS to EBS, Dec. 29, 1922.
460   "heart-broken and also a little": Clarence Darrow to EWS, Feb. 16, 1922.
461   "It is wiser for me to wait": EWS to EBS, Dec. 6, 1922.
463   She said she had read my: EWS diary notes, Sept. 9, 1923.

CHAPTER THIRTY-TWO

464   "no conscious fear": EWS to EBS, April 9, 1923.
464   "He advised against this": Ibid.
465   "It appeared very much": EWS to EBS, April 24, 1923.
465   "drank a good deal of whiskey": EWS to EBS, April 26, 1923.
466   "He is a good deal of a rough-neck": EWS to EBS, June 1, 1923.
467   "It is not pleasant": EWS to EBS, Aug. 4, 1923.
468   "I was greatly surprised": EWS to EBS, Aug. 4, 1923.
470   "Where to?" he asked: HLS diary, Sept. 18, 1923.
471   "It looked crooked": Ibid.
471   "The only object I have": EWS to EBS, Oct. 6, 1923.
471   "That night three sailors" Ed Elfstrom to author, July 8, 1981.
471   "I have nothing to do": EWS to EBS, Dec. 9, 1923.
472   "Especially do I detest niggers": EWS to EBS, Jan. 4, 1924.
472   "If you are buying a business": EWS diary notes, April 5, 1924.
472   "Bob . . . is capable of": EWS to EBS, April 3, 1924.
474   "The question has been raised": EWS to EBS, April 23, 1924.
474   "and cut myself off": Ibid.
475   "Hearst seems to be": EWS to EBS, May 4, 1924.
476   "Howard asked bluntly": EWS to EBS, July 24, 1924.
477   "It is quite probable": EWS to EBS, Oct. 4, 1924.

CHAPTER THIRTY-THREE

480   "As in my first story": EWS to EBS, March 17, 1925.
482   "As the fifth character": EWS to EBS, April 16, 1925.
482   "But the characters born": Ibid.
482   "I cannot help feeling": EWS to EBS, Dec. 18, 1924.
482   "She would put pantlets": EWS to EBS, March 17, 1925.
482   "I cannot control the wind": EWS to EBS, Feb. 8, 1925.
483   "If she will . . . resist": EWS to EBS, May 31, 1925.
484   "I coughed still harder": All details of heart attack from EWS disquisition, "Much Good Pain Wasted," June 22, 1925.
486   "First throw out": Robert F. Winkler to author, Sept. 21, 1981.
486   "I prefer the title": EWS to Dr. Warren Thompson, Dec. 23, 1925.
487   "You may think it bad": EWS disquisition, "Self-Questioning," July 16, 1925.
487   "She was just awful": EWS to EBS, Oct. 21, 1925.
487   "However, just as he": EWS to EBS, Sept. 24, 1925.
488   "Be a cabbage-head": EBS to EWS, Oct. 7, 1925.
488   "Well, I am that coward": EWS disquisition, "The Wisdom of One to Whom Death Appears Imminent," Oct. 7, 1925.
489   "I am reasonably certain": EWS to EBS, Dec. 2, 1925.
490   "She wanted me to stay": EWS to EBS, Dec. 16, 1925.

CHAPTER THIRTY-FOUR

491   "is a good navigator": EWS to HLS, Jan. 27, 1926.
492   "I remember that when": EWS to EBS, Jan. 29, 1926.
493   "another jar . . . Munsey was not": EWS to EBS, Jan. 9, 1926.
494   "So Pomona's first neighbor": *Time* magazine, Feb. 26, 1926.
494   "But what of a woman": Ibid.
496   "I have no quarrel": Max Heimbrod in *Cape Argus,* Feb. 12, 1926.
496   "Scripps, the millionaire yacht owner": *The South African Review,* Feb. 26, 1926.
497   "I know you have had": JRY diary, March 7, 1926.
499   "Go back to bed": Timmy Ryan's affidavit to consular officials at Monrovia, March 17, 1926.
500   "Sir . . . ships never sail": JRY affidavit, March 17, 1926.
501   "Put away my hat and coat": Timmy Ryan affidavit.
501   "It wouldn't be unlucky": Leslie Falconer affidavit, March 17, 1926.
501   "Look here, Miss Steelman": Katherine Steelman affidavit, March 17, 1926.
503   "Holy Jesus! . . . The damn tide's out": all details of trip ashore related by JRY to author, April 23, 1981.
505   "You are to get out": Ibid.
506   "Well, the Chief will never get out": W. H. Elbert to author, March 5, 1981.

INDEX